W9-CCX-148

THE POST CARD
From Socrates to Freud and Beyond

T·H·E
P·O·S·T
C·A·R·D
▪ ▪ From Socrates to ▪ ▪
▪ ▪ Freud and Beyond ▪ ▪

JACQUES
DERRIDA

Translated, with an Introduction and
Additional Notes, by Alan Bass

THE UNIVERSITY OF CHICAGO PRESS
CHICAGO & LONDON

Jacques Derrida is professor at the Ecole des Hautes
Etudes en Sciences Sociales, Paris, and holds visiting
professorships at the University of California, Irvine,
and at Cornell University.

Alan Bass received his Ph.D. from the Johns Hopkins
University and then went on to psychoanalytic training
in New York City, where he is now a practicing analyst. He has published and lectured on both deconstruction and psychoanalytic theory and practice.

The University of Chicago Press, Chicago 60637
The University of Chicago Press, Ltd., London

© 1987 by The University of Chicago
All rights reserved. Published 1987
Printed in the United States of America
96 95 94 93 92 91 90 89 88   5 4 3 2

This book was first published under the title *La carte
postale: De Socrate à Freud et au-delà,* © 1980,
Flammarion, Paris.

Illustrations courtesy of the Bodleian Library, Oxford.
Cover illustration: Plato and Socrates, the frontispiece
of *Prognostica Socratis basilei,* a fortune-telling book.
English, thirteenth century, the work of Matthew
Paris. MS. Ashmole 304, fol. 31v (detail).

Library of Congress Cataloging-in-Publication Data
Derrida, Jacques.
    The post card.

    Translation of: La carte postale.
    Includes bibliographical references.
    1. Philosophy. 2. Poetry. 3. Psychoanalysis and
philosophy. 4. Literature—Philosophy. I. Title.
B2430.D483C3713 1987   190   86-27259
ISBN 0-226-14320-1
ISBN 0-226-14322-8 (pbk.)

CONTENTS

TRANSLATOR'S INTRODUCTION
L BEFORE K

L BEFORE K

. . . and before the epigraphs to this introduction, the acknowledgment. In the course of an analysis of the book you have in your hands, Samuel Weber has very happily spoken of the "owing at the heart of knowing," and of the "peculiar indebtedness at the very core of psychoanalytical thinking." So, to use the vocabulary which I will attempt to introduce here, the translator acknowledges that he owes an unpayable debt to the author for his help (his help? his gift? "his" "time"?) with the translation of "Envois." I thank Jacques Derrida for his generous assistance: I regard this translation as a particularly provisional one, but without Derrida's help it would not have been possible at all.

By placing this acknowledgment before the epigraphs, I am deliberately playing with the usual sequence of the translator's introduction. This too is part of my acknowledgment. One of the major concerns of *The Post Card* is the possible subversion of what is usually taken as a fixed sequence—e.g. Socrates before Plato, the passing of an inheritance from a prior generation to a succeeding one, the death of the old before the young. What if the usual and seemingly fixed sequence were reversible? What if each term of the sequence contained within itself the principle that subverts the usual progression? What could there be between each term and itself that would operate this subversion?

For example, it usually goes without saying that the translator makes his acknowledgments at the *end* of his introduction. My gesture here is to put the acknowledgment *between* the title and epigraphs I have chosen for this introduction. But to position the translator's acknowledgment *between* title and epigraph has a formal analogy with the usual position of the translator's name. Often, the translator's name too comes between title and epigraph on the title page of a translation—e.g. "Sigmund Freud. *The Interpretation of Dreams*. Translated and edited by James Strachey. *Flectere si nequeo superos, Acheronta movebo.*" I am making this "formal" point in order to juxtapose the indebtedness at the core of psychoanalytic thinking with the indebtedness at the core of translation. If the translator and the analyst share an indebtedness, as the etymological sameness of transference and translation, *Übertragung,* indicates, why is this indebtedness usually acknowledged only at "the end"? Is there something at the "core" that the one or the other would prefer not to think about?

This question too, is part of my acknowledgment, for Derrida asks it many times throughout *The Post Card*. Why does a "translator," Freud, for example, often have such difficulty making acknowledgments? Who gave Freud his time, his help, his gift, with the "translation"? Nietzsche? Heidegger? And who relayed the gift? Socrates? Plato? Hopefully, such questions will be more meaningful after you have read *The Post Card: From Socrates to Freud and Beyond.* Nor are such questions without relation to the *place* of the translator's name between title and epigraph, and to the "*location*" of the indebted "core" of psychoanalytic thinking. As Derrida points out elsewhere, the original text is also indebted to the translation for its survival. What we call a text always implies supplementary, unpayable debts. Author and translator name the signers/spenders of an other's debt, the contract for insolvency signed on the title page, underlined by title and epigraphs. Psychoanalysis, as "theory" or "therapy," is a meditation on translation: it also implies such a contract.

The epigraphs, then. From Freud, Heidegger, and Derrida.

> *Dec. 9*—Cheerful, is falling in love with the girl—talkative—a dream with a neologism, general staff map of WLK (Polish word). We must go into this tomorrow . . .
> *Dec. 10*—He told me the whole dream, but understands nothing about it; on the other hand he gave me a few associations to WLK . . . The K corresponds to the "*vielka*" [pronounced as English "vee-el-ka"] = "old." It also reminded him of his anxiety when at school the letter K [i.e. boys whose name began with a K] was being examined, since it meant that his L was getting very near. It would thus correspond to a wish that K should come after L . . .
> —Freud, "Original Record of the 'Rat Man' Case" (Editor's interpolations in brackets), *Standard Edition* 10: 294–95.

In the beginning of Western thinking, Being is thought, but not the "It gives" (*es gibt*) as such. The latter withdraws in favor of the gift which It gives. That gift is thought and conceptualized from then on exclusively as Being with regard to beings.

A giving which gives only its gift, but in the giving holds itself back and withdraws, such a giving we call *sending*. According to the meaning of giving which is to be thought in this way, Being—that which It gives—is what is sent. Each of its transformations remains destined in this manner. What is historical in the history of Being is determined by what is sent forth in destining, not by an indeterminately thought up occurrence.

The history of Being means destiny of Being in whose *sendings* both the sending and the It which sends forth hold back with their self-manifestation. To hold back is, in Greek, *epoche*. Hence we speak of the epochs of the destiny of Being. Epoch does not mean here a span of time in occurrence, but rather the fundamental characteristic of sending, the actual holding-back of itself in favor of the discernibility of the gift, that is, of Being with regard to the grounding of beings. The sequence of epochs in the destiny of Being is not accidental, nor can it be calculated as necessary.

—Heidegger, *On Time and Being,* pp. 8–9; my italics.

. . . by means of a switch point I will send them elsewhere.
—Derrida, "Envois," one of the letters of February 1979.

The citations from Freud's notes on the Rat Man case, like the "Envois," are what remains of a dated series of supposedly private texts that are now public—like a published correspondence, or a series of intercepted post cards. Further, in French, the Rat Man's map is also a card, a *carte*. In a sense, the Rat Man put his return address on the *carte* in his dream. His name was Paul Lorenz, and in the section of the citation that I have elided, Freud says that he associated the *l* of "vielka" to Lorenz. The role of proper names in "private" texts is examined throughout the "Envois." There is another *carte* in the "public" version of the case, the map of the route between a train station and a post office. Derrida refers to this *carte* in one of the letters of 7 September 1977—which is why I chose this epigraph. However, the passage raises many other questions that bear on the "Envois." For example, in the entry of 9 December, Freud does not tell us about the relation between falling in love and the *carte:* you will find much on this topic here. Further, I am intrigued by Freud's deduction that the dream represents a wish that K should come *after* L. Why? Why not L *before* K? In any event, why does Lorenz wish to change the order of the alphabet? To reduce the anxiety of waiting to be called upon to answer the examiner? And if his L comes before K, why the association with "old," with *vielka,* with a *military* (Lorenz was an officer) *carte* (and the military code is particularly important in "To Speculate—on 'Freud'"). What would happen if L came before K on a *carte* (like Plato before Socrates on another *carte*)? What does psychoanalysis have to do with such a question, with the dream language that poses the question in terms of military maps, proper names, and alphabetical order?

An entire reading of this book could be organized around Heidegger's sentence, "A giving which gives only its gift, but in the giving holds itself back and withdraws, such a giving we call *sending*." (See the letters of 5–6 September 1977; note that the Rat Man and *On Time and Being* are discussed on consecutive days in the "Envois," another reason for my choice of epigraphs.) The German translation of "Envois" is in fact called *Sendungen,* which is why I have underlined *sendings* in the citation. Recall that Heidegger is shifting his meditation on the relation between Being and time—or here, time and Being—via a shift of emphasis in the phrase *es gibt Sein:* the emphasis now is on the *es gibt.* In *The Post Card* Derrida radicalizes this shift. The examination of *es gibt*—it gives, there is—in terms of *sending,* and the principles operative in any "sending system" (e.g., the postal system), reveals a certain indeterminacy intrinsic to the concept of *sending.* This indeterminacy leads to questions about destiny—the destiny of "Being"—other than the ones Heidegger asks here. But the surprise, although we should perhaps no longer be surprised, is in the overlap between Heidegger and Freud on the topics of sending and destiny. A question that runs throughout *The Post Card* is, Why this inconceivable union, why the one always in back of the other (like Plato in back of Socrates on the *carte*)? Another paraphrase of Derrida: if Being is sent, then there must be a system that sorts, routes, and delivers it. What if this system necessarily contained a kink, so that despite the absolute authority of its usual sequences (like the absolute authority of alphabetical order), somewhere it contained the subversion and reversal of its own progression (L before K)? What would happen to the thought of *es gibt* as sending? To the destiny of Being?

And to the fate of love? The sending of love letters? The "Envois" are a performance and analysis of the irreducible twists in any sending system, and of the effects of these twists on what is supposedly most private within such a system—e.g. a love letter. The performance of these effects is particularly geared to the "switch points" mentioned in one of the letters dated February

1979. Or, as Derrida puts it in the letter of 9 September 1977, to "the delicate levers that pass between the legs of a word, between a word and itself." The glossary that follows is an attempt to explicate *some* of the levers that operate the switch points of the "Envois." (Note the deliberate reference to routes and to vehicles, to transport, i.e. *Übertragung.*) But this is not a definitive index. I hope that every reader will find omissions and mistakes.

The list itself consists of French words, many of which do not function as switch points or levers in English. Most of those words have been left in French somewhere in the text: thus, it is likely that if you find a French word in the text, you will find an entry on it here. Other words have not necessarily been left in French, but have seemed to require an entry. But no more than it is an index, the list is not a glossary exactly *keyed* to the text. Nor does it provide an exhaustive guide for a pleasant journey. (For example, you will find no entry on *key, la clef:* no secure backup here.) Where can you go, what is your fate, what comes back to you with certainty, if you put your name (e.g. Lorenz) on a *carte,* if you mark the return address, and then L comes before K? I hope you will refer to the list with such questions in mind.

Glossary

a (à) (a-): as the heading indicates, *a* has three major uses, all of them switching each other on and off. *A* as a verb is the third person singular of *avoir,* to have. The preposition *à* means "to" or "in." Note that capitalized vowels may lose their accent marks in French. Thus, the subheading of one of the divisions of "Le facteur de la vérité" is LE TROP D'EVIDENCE OU LE MANQUE A SA PLACE; I refer to *Le facteur* . . . , note 10, for an explanation of the alternation between *a* ("the lack *has* its place") and *à* ("the lack *in* its place"). One of the letters dated 9 September 1977 tells us that *The Post Card* is "dedicated to 'to,' devoted to the dative." The dative, of course, is the case of the indirect object, as in "I write *to* you." A simple rule of French grammar, however, can make the case of a pronoun ambiguous: "I write to you" is *je t'écris.* The pronoun here can be read in either the dative or the accusative: I write *to* you, or I write you. The dative, one might say, is the case of sending, but the possible alternation of dative and accusative asks the question of whether indirection and sending are always operative. (Think of the English phrase "you send me.") *A-* in French and English is also the prefix of negation; thus Derrida's neologisms *ades-*

tination for the structural lack of a certain destination in any postal system, and *athesis* for the lack of a definable thesis in *Beyond the Pleasure Principle,* a book that always takes another step forward no matter what point it reaches. There is also the important word *acheminer,* which does mean to send something on its way, to progress toward a certain destination. Derrida plays on the "*a-*" as a possible negation here, and I have tried to capture this play by translating *acheminer* as "to send something on its *a-way.*" Finally—finally for this entry at least—*a* is one of the sounds of the *fort/da* scene: according to Freud, Ernst actually said "oooo— aaa." The same letter of 9 September 1977 tells us that *The Post Card* is dedicated also to drawling o and long a, especially in the word *dos* (pronounced like English "doe"; see below). Nor will you have forgotten that *a* is the "letter" of *différance.*

accepter means "to accept," with all the resonances of *reception* that are so important throughout. The problem is with *j'accepte* (I accept), which can also be heard as "*Jacques sept*" (Jacques seven). "*J'accepte,*" says one of the narrative voices, "is my signature." This is a complex switch point. First, there is the play on Jacques, Derrida's first name, and on the seven letters of both Jacques and Derrida (see below, *sept*). Next, what is it that *Jacques sept accepte* (accepts)? "*J'accepte,*" he says, *la* and *ta détermination*—determination in general, and *your* determination. On determination, see under *destin* (below).

acquitter means to fulfill an obligation, as in the archaic English sense of "to acquit," whence our expression "to be quits" for a debt that has been paid; it also means to exonerate, as in the modern English sense of "to acquit"; see also "To Speculate—on 'Freud' " (below), part 1, note 7. The legal sense of *acquitter* puts it into relation with *cause* (see below), and with the idea of truth as adequation, of being quits with a thing (*chose;* again see *cause*). If the concept of debt is more problematic than is generally thought, or if there is an irreducible effect of inadequation between "thing" (*cause, chose*) and truth, then one is never quits. Debt and gift supplement each other in the general economy.

adresse: fortunately, "address" has the same double meaning as the French, so I will leave it to you to meditate on the interplay of skillful execution or delivery (address), and delivery of a letter to its destination (address). I note further that in German a similar play exists between *Schick* (skill) and *schicken* (to send, to dispatch).

This is why one of the narrators coins the word "schicanery," with its play on adroit, legalistic argumentation (see *cause*), and the entire problematic of sending (*schicken*). The person most skilled at chicanery is the devil's advocate, a figure analyzed in part I of "To Speculate."

aimer of course is "to love." The difficulty is with *s'aimer*, which is the near homonym of *semer*, "to scatter," to "to plant seeds." The reader familiar with Derrida's work will see here the problematic of dis*sem*ination. Thus, *s'aimer*, to love oneself, can be construed as auto-affection (in the "philosophical" sense) that immediately scatters, the disseminating principle inscribed in self-reference. This principle is at work in every reference of a word to itself, which is why homonyms and homophony—which of course are untranslatable—are so important throughout the "Envois." When a word irreducibly refers to itself, it begins to function as a proper noun (as in *j'accepte;* see above *accepter*); proper nouns too are "untranslatable." And then *aimer* is the homonym of a proper name in French.

aller means "to go," and one of the themes that is analyzed and performed throughout the "Envois" is "going," especially the going that cannot be stopped, that never arrives at a certain destination. But if going cannot be stopped, its pace or speed, *allure*, can vary; *allure* in fact derives from *aller*, and does not have the English sense of "allure." Recall, too, the first lesson of French: "Comment *allez*-vous?" meaning "How are you?" literally means "How are you *going?*" In French, then, one is always *going*, according to one rhythm or another. Certainly the narrator of the "Envois" is always on the go himself, making the entire vocabulary of travel, vehicles, routes, schedules, and running quite important. Note that a round-trip ticket in French is an *aller-retour*, literally "to *go*-return": the relation of the return to going is also a major concern, as in the *fort/da* scene. See also *revenir* (to come back), under *venir*.

ange means "angel," but recall its derivation from the Greek *angelos*, meaning "messenger." See also *courrier, facteur*, and *mais si*.

apocalypse in French and English has the sense of prophetic revelation of imminent cataclysm; see also *ange, mais si*, and *viens* under *venir*. Derrida refers to the "small, library apocalypse" of Matthew Paris's drawing of Plato behind Socrates, the drawing that is contained in the fortune-telling book (again prophecy, revelation by means of the play on numbers, letters, and names, the attempt to forestall disaster). If Plato is behind and Socrates writes, then philosophy's apocalypse has already occurred. The purpose of this entry is to alert you to the theme of foretelling catastrophic fate, whether in the Bible, fortune-telling books, metaphysics, or psychoanalysis.

arriver means both "to arrive" and "to happen." To continue the preceding entry, "apocalypse," the jacket copy tells us that "'a fortune-telling book' watches over and speculates on that-which-must-happen, on what it indeed might mean *to happen, to arrive, to have to happen* or *arrive, to let* or *to make happen* or *arrive, to destine, to address, to send, to legate, to inherit,* etc." Thus, the word *arriver* is a switch point for the deconstruction of the notions of event (to happen) and arrival at destination; see "Le facteur de la vérité," with its demonstration that a letter may always not *arrive* at its destination. A letter that has not arrived may be a so-called "dead letter": there is quite a story about a dead letter in the *Envois. Arriver* derives from the Latin *arripare,* meaning "to come to shore," and there is a constant play on the *rive* (shore) in *arriver.* As always, the question is, Can any shore (*rive*) or border (*bord*) be determined such that mooring to it is certain? For *river* also means "to rivet": does ar-rival imply non-riveting, much as the postal principle (a letter can always not arrive at its destination) implies the athesis, i.e. the sort of concept that cannot be riveted to the spot, that is constantly on the go (see *aller,* above). Implicit here is the critique of the Lacanian concept of the *point de capiton* that "rivets" signified to signifier; see "Le facteur," note 36.

au-delà means "beyond," as in *Au-delà du principe de plaisir, Beyond the Pleasure Principle.* It is also the homonym of *aux deux-là,* "to those two," those two being, for example, Plato and Socrates, or Freud and Heidegger, or any of the "odd couples" to be found throughout the "Envois." Perhaps we might say the the *Envois* are sent *au(x) de(ux)-là du principe de plaisir,* beyond the pleasure principle to those two (who are) of the pleasure principle.

auto- in French and English has the resonances of "self" and "car." As mentioned above in the entry on *aimer,* there is also the reference to the philosophical problem of auto-affection (and time). In the "Envois," the problematic of auto-affection is also "read" as "car love," of loving (oneself?) in cars; thus, the many letters concerned with cars, highways, tolls, trips, vacations. See also *banaliser, doubler,* and *voiture* (under *envoyer*).

banaliser is part of the police vocabulary that runs throughout the "Envois." It means to camouflage a police car by making it "banal" or ordinary—what we call an "unmarked car." I have translated it as " 'banalize' " to indicate this special sense; *banaliser* ordinarily would be translated as "to make banal."

bande, bander: see below, "To Speculate," part 4, notes 3 and 6; and "Du tout," note 4. See also *lier.*

bobine means "spool," as in the *fort/da* scene, but also has the slang sense of "face"—what we might call "mug" or "kisser," especially with the overtones of a gangster movie.

cale, calé, caler, décaler, décalage: a group of words deriving from the Latin *chalare*—to suspend or lower (a sail)—and the Greek *khalan*—to slacken. (Other words with *cal-,* such as *calculer,* "to calculate," and *calendrier,* "calendar," have different derivations.) There is a strong sense of stabilization over a floating medium in all these words. *La cale* can mean the hold of a ship, the inclined plane onto which a ship can be raised for repairs, or a wedge used to keep a car's wheels stationary or to hold open a space. *Calé* as an adjective can mean well situated (i.e. rich), well informed, or difficult. *Caler* as a verb can mean to lower a mast, to sink into the water (with the technical sense of measuring displacement), to retreat, to make something stable (by means of a wedge, for example), or to be immobilized, especially in the sense of stalling a car's motor. *Décaler* means the opposite, with a strong sense of destabilization: to remove what keeps something fixed, to displace, to move forward or backward in relation to the usual position. Thus, a *décalage* is the result of such an action, implying the lack of a usual correspondence or synchrony. For example, the *décalage horaire* is the time difference between various parts of the world. If you forget the *décalage horaire* when you travel, you wind up calling people at odd times: someone always on the go (see above, *aller*), always has to calculate with it. *Calé* as an adjective also has the familiar sense of being particularly good at a certain subject or task; see below, *fort.*

carte can mean card, map, menu. *Carte* and "card" both derive from the Latin *charta,* a piece of paper or papyrus: e.g. what "Socrates" is writing on (in both senses of "on") in the Matthew Paris drawing, that is, the (post) card that Derrida is writing "on" throughout. *Charta* is also the root for the legal document called *charte* in French and "charter" in English, with their implications of contractual engagement. The idea of contracting with oneself, of sending oneself a *c(h)arte* runs throughout. A card in the sense of a post card or a playing card always has a recto and a verso: recall Lacan's analysis of the map game and of Dupin's placing his cards on the table in *The Seminar on "The Purloined Letter,"* discussed below in "Le facteur." Aside from the endless analysis of (or ravings about) the post card, there is also an important vocabulary of card games in the "Envois," particularly poker, with its bidding system, and solitaire, the "self-referential" card game. (There is a French term in the vocabulary of solitaire that has no English equivalent. When one succeeds in setting up a perfect "tray" or row of cards according to the rules of the game, one has a *réussite*—a "success." In one of the letters dated July-August 1978, the narrator wants to photograph his *réussite*.) All words with *carte* are exploited in the "Envois." A *cartable* is a briefcase. *Cartouche* has the senses of frame and cartridge. A *pancarte* is a poster in the sense of billboard or placard, including the posters carried in demonstrations, or on an individual's back as advertising. The *pan-* in *pancarte* does not derive from the Greek *pan-* (all, every), although Derrida plays on this false etymology. *Carte* is also the anagram of *écart* (separation, division) and *trace* (trace).

cause is etymologically linked to *chose* (thing). *Cause* has the senses of both cause and legal case; it is linked to "thing" in the sense of *res,* the particular thing or matter at hand, especially in legal parlance. (See also *acquitter,* above.) The "Envois" often seem to be pleading a case, and thus their (s)chicanery (see *adresse,* above). The "case" (in the grammatical—see above *a*—or legal senses) however, has to do with whether or not a "thing" can be determined, or whether or not "he" can accept "her" determination.

centrale as adjective means "central." It is also both a masculine noun meaning "switchboard," or in general the station from and to which the lines of a network proceed, and a feminine noun meaning generating station. "Central Europe" (Vienna, Prague, for example) thus becomes a kind of letter-generating station (e.g. Freud's, Kafka's) for all of Europe, from Athens to London.

chemin means "way, path, route." *Chemin de fer* is the railway. The verb *cheminer* has the sense of making slow progress on the way somewhere; see under *a* for *acheminer*. *Cheminer* is also the homonym of *cheminée,* "chimney," although the words have different derivations. Recall the letter between the legs of the chimney in "The Purloined Letter."

correspondance: see below, "To Speculate," part 3, note 8.

courrier means both a messenger, a courier, and mail, correspondence. It is etymologically linked to *courir,* to run; the vocabulary of running is important throughout.

dé- is a prefix of negation, like the English "dis-," with a specific sense of separation and *dis*tancing. Derrida often plays on *dé-*words, as he does with *a-* words, for example *dé-caler* (see *cale,* etc.), *dé-marche* (see *marcher*), *dé-railler* (to derail, see *train*). The noun *dé* can mean die (singular of dice) or thimble.

déjà means "already," but like *j'accepte* is also a signature (*de*rrida *ja*cques). What is *already* there is behind one, in back of one: see also *derrière* and *dos.*

derrière means "behind," with the same double sense as in English (adverb, noun). What is behind, or one's behind, are in *back* of one; see also *dos* (back) and *postérieure,* under *poste.* In the endless analysis of the post card, there is much ado about Plato *behind* Socrates and about Socrates' behind. *Derrière,* like *déjà,* is also a signature word: *derri(ère)-da.* The expression *derrière les rideaux*— behind the curtains—is also important throughout.

destin, destinée: le destin has more the sense of fate, while *la destinée*—from the past participle of *destiner,* to destine—has more the sense of destiny. The entire vocabulary of fate is crucial throughout; see *apocalypse, arriver,* and *envoyer* (to send). In German there is an etymological link between destiny, *Schicksal,* and sending, *schicken* (to send, to dispatch). *Destinée* as the past participle of *destiner* can also mean "destined one" (feminine)—is she his *destinée,* his destination? Recall too, that the German *Bestimmung* means both determination and destination: throughout the "Envois" "he" asks over and over whether or not "he" can accept "her" determination; see *accepter.* Fortunately, other words meaning "destiny" are cognates in English, for example *sort* and *lot.* The Jewish holiday *Purim* also means "lots": thus, the extended analysis of the Book of Esther, which recounts the story of *Purim.* The postal principle—that a letter can always not arrive at its *destination*—is related to Lacan's misquotation of the lines from Crébillon that Dupin inscribes in the facsimile of the purloined letter (" 'un *destin* si funeste,' " instead of " 'un *dessein* si funeste' "). See the end of "Le facteur" for Derrida's analysis of this misquotation in relation to Lacan's idea that a letter always arrives at its destination.

dos means back, as in one's back, the back of a card, etc. The sound, sense, and appearance of *dos* (pronounced like "doe") are played on throughout. See under *a* on the sound long o. *Dos* derives from *dorsum*, back; thus to sign a check on its back is to en*dorse* it in English, *endosser* in French. The back of a chair in French is *dossier*: look at the post card, at "Plato" reaching over the *back* of a chair to put his finger in "Socrates'" *back*. Recall the connotations of a hunch*back*: it is supposed to be good luck to touch his hump. Eurydice sees only Orpheus's back; the analys*and* lies on his back with the analyst in back of him. Intercourse from the back is *coitus a tergo*; recall Freud's famous reconstruction in the Wolf Man case of a scene of *coitus a tergo* (see under SP). *Dos* sounds the same as *do*, i.e. the first note of a scale or the pitch C: the "key" of the "Envois," then, is *do*. *Dos* also looks like *dot*, meaning dowry, and *dose*, dose. Both are etymologically related to *donner*, "to give": recall the "dose" given to Socrates, and Freud's theory in *Beyond the Pleasure Principle* that the sense organs sample small doses of the external world. There are also the *do* sounds in *rideau*, curtain, and in Fido, the classic dog's name used as an example in speech act theory (see the letter of 18 August 1979). *Dos* further sounds the same as *d'eau*, meaning "some water." On *dos* in general, see the second letter dated March-April 1979. See also *derrière*, and *revenir* (to come *back*) under *venir*.

doubler can mean to double, to make something double, to pass (as in one car's passing another on the road), and to dub (in the cinematic sense of creating a new sound track for a foreign-language film).

du tout: see below, "Du tout," note 5.

enfant means "child," from the Latin *infans*, meaning "unable to talk." Derrida often plays on the literal and figurative meanings of *ne fais pas l'enfant*, which usually means "don't be childish," but can also (literally) mean "don't make a child." See also *envoyer* for the expression *s'envoyer l'enfant*.

envoi, envoyer: envoyer, to send, is derived from the Latin *inviare*, to send on the way. The root word here is *via*, whence the English via, the French *voie*, and of course the Italian *via*, which all have the sense of "way"; see also *chemin*. The noun *envoi* can mean the action of sending (*envoi de lettres*: the sending of letters), kickoff (as in the start of a football game), something that is sent (espe-

cially in the senses of message, missive, or dispatch), the concluding stanza of a ballad that typically serves as a dedication, the lines
handwritten by the author of a book as part of a dedication, and, in
the legal sense (*envoi en possession*), the right to enter into possession of an inheritance (see *legs*). See under *destin* on *schicken*, to
send, and *Schicksal*, fate, destination. *Envois* in the sense of missives or transmissions are *Sendungen* in German. Every possible
play on *envoi* and *envoyer* is exploited throughout. For example,
the English "invoice," meaning bill of sale, is actually derived from
envoi (and *inviare*), thus linking the senses of sending, message,
and debt. Both "invoice" and *envoi* are homonyms of "in voice"
and *en voix:* the "Envois" are written in many voices. (There are
many references to music for several voices, to madrigals and Monteverdi.) The derivation from *via* leads in the direction of voyage,
with its etymological link to *via*ticum (traveling money). *En-voi*
also beckons toward *voi-ture*, which is in general a means of transport, but is also the usual French word for "car." Note also that
véhicule, vehicle, derives from *vehere*, to carry, which is linked to
the German *Weg*, way, thus bringing us back to *via* and *voie*. (*Weg*
has the Heideggerean resonance of *Holzweg*, literally forest path,
but metaphorically a path or way that twists and turns so as not to
arrive anywhere. *Weg* is also related to the *fort/da* scene in *Beyond
the Pleasure Principle* via the expression *weg!* "go away!") The
reflexive verb *s'envoyer* is particularly important. It can mean to
send oneself, transitively or intransitively (see also under *a* and
carte). In the latter sense, one might say that if one sends oneself,
then one's en-voy (also *en-voi*) or representative has to be one's
double or ghost. This idea speaks to the relations between oneself
and one's heirs, to whom one sends oneself via an inheritance. The
transitive sense of *s'envoyer* has a special slang sense in French.
"To send oneself someone" in this sense means to provide oneself
with someone for sexual purposes. What can or cannot be be sent,
by oneself or to oneself, in all these senses? A child (see *enfant*),
for instance?

est, et, hait are near homonyms in French. They mean respectively
"is," "and," "hates." In the analysis of the post card, then, we have
S et P (S and P), *S est P* (S is P), and *S hait P* (S hates P); see
also *SP*.

été, était are near homonyms. *Eté* is either the past participle of
être, to be, or the noun *été*, summer. *Etait* is the imperfect third
person singular of *être*, i.e. "was."

expédier means "to expedite," but also has the senses of to send, to dispatch.

facteur See below, "Le facteur," note I.

for, fors, fort are homonyms. *Le for* derives from the Latin *forum,* tribunal, and is most often used in the sense of *le for intérieur* (literally "the interior forum"), meaning conscience, the depths of oneself. That *le for* has come to have the sense of inner depths is etymologically paradoxical, since *forum* itself comes from *foris,* meaning outside. A *forum,* of course, was an outdoor place for legal and commercial business. The somewhat archaic French preposition *fors,* from *foris,* means "except," "save": whatever is left out. (*Fors* is the title of Derrida's preface to Torok and Abraham's *Le verbier de l'homme aux loups;* it describes the paradoxical nature of the crypt as something secret and open, inner and outer, perhaps like a crypted letter whose message is as private and public as that on a post card.) *Un fort* is either a fort (where *guards* are *posted;* see *garde* and *poste*) or a strong person. *Fort* as adjective or adverb means strong, but in more ways than in English. For example, to be good at a particular subject, (see *cale*), is to be *fort;* to take one's assurance or confidence from a given precondition is *être fort de.* The French *fort* in all these senses is to be taken in conjunction with the German *fort,* meaning "away" or "gone," as in *fort da.*

garde, garder La garde is the action of guarding, watching over, preserving; *le garde* is the person who performs these actions. *Garder* is to save, to guard, to preserve. In German *Wahrheit,* truth, is related to *Wahren,* to preserve. The problematic of guarding runs throughout the "Envois": to save the letters or to burn them? In the "general economy" there are no reserves: preservation is no guarantee against debt, and all that remains are fragments that have survived the holocaust, the apocalypse that has already occurred. To preserve and to reserve are etymologically the same, from the Latin *reservare,* to keep back, i.e. to "guard" in the French sense. Thus, the contraceptive we call a condom is a *préservatif* in French: it guards against disease and guards semen. For the same reasons we use the word *prophylactic,* derived from the Greek *prophylaktikos* and *prophylassein:* to stand guard before. The Greek *phylakterion,* meaning amulet, has the same derivation, from *phylax,* guard, and has become the English word "phylactery," for the small square leather boxes containing a bit of Scripture that Jewish men strap to the forehead and left arm during morning services. (A meeting of Greek and Jew, of "Socrates" and "Freud"?)

genoux means "knees," but is also the homonym of *je nous*, either "I we" or "I (to) us." The pun is important in terms of the play on *legs*, see below. Recall that many of the "Envois" are written on the narrator's knees while he is on a train or plane; see also the section of part I of "To Speculate" entitled "I Writes Us" ("Je nous écrit").

grattoir means "stylus"—see Socrates' writing implements on the post card—but the English "stylus" loses the play on *gratter*, "to scratch" (e.g. Plato scratching Socrates' back), so I have retained the French word.

legs means "legacy." In current French the "g" is often pronounced, but the original pronunciation was the same as *lais*, from the verb *laisser*, to leave. A legacy is what one leaves, of course; *lais* was both the ancient form of *legs* and the term for a narrative or lyric poem. *Lais* is also the term for the land left bare at low tide. Similarly *laisse*, also from *laisser*, can mean a couplet from a courtly epic, or the lines of high and low tide; its principal meaning, however, is the same as the English "leash." Thus the paradox implicit in *legs:* it leashes, ties up, *binds* (see *lier*) those to whom it is left, while maintaining resonances of tidal, rhythmic return (see *revenir* under *venir*). All these resonances recall the strings of Ernst's spool analyzed in part 2 of "To Speculate," whose title is "Freud's Legacy"; see also notes 1 and 2 of that chapter, and note 20 of "Le facteur." *Legs* branches out in many other directions. The bilingual pun on "legs" is operative throughout: elliptically we might say that Freud's legacy binds his heirs to stay on the go. (Compare the analysis of the limping devil at the end of *Beyond the Pleasure Principle* with the story of the skateboard and the limping narrator in the "Envois.") There is also the reference to *jambes*, legs, and "jambs": the question of what is between the jambs of the chimney in "The Purloined Letter" leads to the question of what is between the "*legs*" in general. Another part of the "legs" is the knees, *genoux* (see above). *Legs de Freud* also sounds like *les deux Freud* (the two Freuds) and *lait de Freud* (Freud's milk). See also *télé*, and "To Speculate," part 2, note 1.

lier means "to bind," see also *bander*. Recall the entire problematic of bound and unbound energy in Freudian theory. *Alliance* means "alliance," derived from *lier*, but can also mean a wedding *band*, the symbol of alliance. Derrida often plays on the homonyms *l'al-liance* and *la liance*. *Liance* is a neologism, joining the group of words in *-ance* (e.g. *différance, restance, revenance*) that name fluctuating concepts suspended between the active and the passive: *la liance* is the *différance* of binding, of being bound by contract or testament to a spouse or legator. On this subject recall the rings (*al-liances*) given by Freud to his "heirs," i.e. the secret "commit-tee" that he himself survived: see below "To Speculate," part 2, note 31.

lit: le lit is "the bed"; *je lis, tu lis, il, elle lit* mean "I read, you read, he, she reads."

lui can mean "him," as in *c'est lui,* "it's him"; or it can mean "to him" and "to her," as in *je lui ai donné,* "I gave him/her." That one does not know the sex of the indirect object, third person singular, without an antecedent, is particularly important for the story of the "dead letter" in the "Envois." The writing of this letter is first men-tioned 30 August 1977. It is returned to sender 8 September 1977. Then, the undated letter just before the letter of 20 April 1978 first speaks of handing over the dead letter to *someone* for safekeeping (see *garder*). The use of pronouns is extremely careful: *lui* as indi-rect object is used only without an antecedent, so that we strictly do not know if the letter has been given to "him" or to "her." How to render this in English? I have chosen the rather inelegant solution of translating this unknown *lui* as "the person," "them," or "to them"; ungrammatical English permits one to say "I gave it to them" in a sense similar to "je *lui* ai donné." To do otherwise, i.e. to translate "him" or "her," would be strictly incorrect, since the antecedents have been withheld—or destroyed. See also *son*.

mandat has all the connotations of "mandate" (delegation, envoy, contract, etc.), but also has the specific sense of money order, espe-cially postal money order.

mais si means "but yes." French grammar requires that *si* replace *oui* in response to a negative question. (E.g. "*Ne revenez-vous pas? Mais si, mais si.*" "Aren't you coming back? But yes, yes I am.") *Mais si* is the homonym of *messie*, which means "messiah," a word with obvious biblical connotations in relation to coming back (*revenir*), the announcement of the Apocalypse, etc. There is no etymological link between *mess*iah and *mess*age, but of course a messiah claims to have been sent by God to deliver his message; see also *ange, facteur.* Further, a messiah's message is often a cryptic one, to be decoded with a key.

marcher means both to walk and to work, to be operative; something that doesn't work *ne marche pas,* literally "doesn't walk." On *démarche,* procedure, see *dé-,* and "To Speculate," part 2, note 2. *Marcher* has obvious ties to *aller,* to *chemin,* and to *legs.*

moi-mois are homonyms, the first meaning "me" or "to me," and the second meaning "month." *Le moi* is the psychoanalytic term "ego"; therefore *mois* is also its plural, "egos."

PP: first, see "To Speculate," part 1, note 18. *PP* is also the abbreviation for "Plato's Pharmacy" (in *Dissemination*), for "private police," for public/private, for primary process, etc.

PR: see "To Speculate," part 1, notes 5 and 18. Recall that the "dead letter," whose story begins on 30 August 1977, was sent poste restante. See *poste.*

pas: see "To Speculate," part 2, note 2.

Platon is the French equivalent of "Plato," or "plato" as he appears on the "card." Derrida often plays on the *plat,* "flat," in *Platon;* see especially his flat hat, as opposed to Socrates' pointed one. "Plato" pronounced with a French accent would be the same as *plateau.*

pli means "fold," from the Latin *plicare,* whence *compliquer,* "to complicate," i.e. "to fold together." The expression *ne pas faire pli* (literally, "not to make a fold") means "to be of no consequence." *Pli* also has the sense of either a folded paper containing a message (an envelope), or the message itself; *envoyer un pli* means "to send a message (in a folded paper)."

poste derives from the Latin *ponere,* to put, to place. It is therefore linked to *position* (also derived from *ponere*), and to the entire topic of the "thesis," the singular position (and the "athesis"; see "To Speculate," part 1). *La poste* is "mail," with all its resonances of postilion and relay; *le poste* is "post" in the sense of position to be held, like a soldier's post (see *courrier*). *Les postes* is the usual expression for the French postal system, the government agency once called the *P.T.T. (Postes, Télégraphes et Téléphones),* and now called the *P. et T. (Postes et Télécommunications).* A post office is a *bureau de poste* or *la poste. Le poste* can also mean a station, as in *poste de police,* police station. Derrida exploits every possible play on "post": *imposteur* (impostor), *imposture* (imposture), "poster," in the English sense, especially with the resonance of "wanted poster" (leading to posse and to bounty, reward). There is also an etymological link between *poser* (to pose, to position) and *pauser* (to pause). *Poser* and *pauser* are homonyms, and the idea of stopping, halting, pausing, is intrinsic to the idea of the thesis, to being set in place at a post which one guards (see *garder*): thus Derrida calls the great philosophers masters of the post, interns of theses that bring things to halt; but this immediately implies post in the sense of sending. The ambiguity inherent in "to post"—to station and to send—is played on throughout. Derrida states several times that the "Envois" are a satire (farce) of the two basic forms of literature, the detective novel and the epistolary novel, which both depend upon *postes.* In "Le facteur," note 6, there is a quote from Littré, who wrote in his dictionary: "Le poste ne diffère de la poste que par le genre," i.e. "post—in the sense of position—differs from post—in the sense of mail—only by gender." Finally, there is the play on *postérieure,* which is the same in French and in English ("posterior"; see above, *derrière*), posterity, etc.

relever is usually "to lift up" or "to relieve," but is also Derrida's translation of the Hegelian term *Aufheben,* meaning to lift up, to negate, and to conserve. For an extended discussion and further references, see *Margins of Philosophy,* "*Différance,*" note 23.

restance, rester: see "To Speculate," part 1, note 5. Recall that an inheritance, a legacy, is what remains of one after one's death; see *legs.*

retro- is a prefix meaning backward or behind. Both French and English have come to use "retro" as an adjective to describe the current copying of old styles; see, for example, the first sentence of the jacket copy: "You were reading a somewhat retro loveletter." In the automobile vocabulary that is so important throughout, a *rétroviseur* is a rearview mirror.

SP: these are the initials of Socrates and Plato, of subject and predicate, of Freud's patient known as Wolf Man (Sergei Pankejev: in German his initials sound like *Wespe,* wasp, *guêpe* in French), of the *secret de Polichinelle,* that is, the secret known to all. See *est, et, hait* for the relations between S and P. Recall also *sp*eculation and *p*sychoanalysis. See also *PP* and *PR,* and the second letter of 9 June 1977.

sept means "seven," and there is a constant play on the number 7. *Sept* is also to be taken homophonically. For example, it can sound the same as *c'est,* "it is," particularly in the expression *c'est écrit,* "it is written" (which as *sept écrit* means either "written seven" or "seven writes": see above *accepter*). On this topic see the letter dated first days of January 1979. *Sept* also sounds the same as English "set," and thus the many references to "set theory." Recall the importance of seven in the Book of the Apocalypse, and the analysis of Plato's Seventh Letter.

somme, sommes: nous sommes means "we are"; *la somme* means both "sum" and "burden," as in *bête de somme,* beast of burden; *le somme* is a nap.

son: le son is "sound"; *son* and *sa* are the possessive adjectives for masculine and feminine nouns third person singular. See *lui* and *ton.*

suis, suivre: je suis means either "I am" (from *être,* to be), or "I follow" (from *suivre,* to follow). *A suivre* means "to be continued." *Faire suivre* is the postal term whose English equivalent is "to forward," as in "to forward a letter."

télé-: first, see "To Speculate," part 2, note 19. *Télé-* is to be understood as homophonically as possible, e.g. *tel est* (such is), *tes legs* (your legacies), *t'es legs* (you're legacy), *tes laits* (your milks), *t'es lait* (you're milk), *tais-les* (silence them, shut them up), etc.

timbre means both "timbre" and "stamp," as in "postage stamp." Both senses of the word are in relation to the Greek *tympanon* with its strong connotation of "striking," as in striking a drum to produce a tone, or in striking a new impression in order to issue new stamps. See also *ton.*

ton, tu: ton is both the possessive adjective for masculine nouns, second person singular, and "tone." *Tu,* of course, is the second person singular, used only when speaking to someone to whom one is close, as opposed to the polite or plural *vous.* This distinction does not exist in English. All the "Envois" use *tu,* are addressed to the singular, familiar you. One of the *tones* of the "Envois" is therefore that of the *apostrophe:* see the remarks on "apostrophe" in the preface to the "Envois." See also *timbre.*

train, en train: train means "train," of course, and is one of the vehicles mentioned most frequently throughout. See also above *auto-. En train de,* used with an infinitive, means to be in the course of doing something, marking present duration; *en train* means "on the train." The implication is that there is always a question of the vehicle, of transport (of *Übertragung*) at work, even in present duration. *Traîner* is "to pull" or "to drag along" (whence, for example the *train* of a dress in English). *Entraîner* variously means "to carry along," "to lead to (consequentially)," "to train" (in the sense of athletic training), etc. *S'entraîner* usually means "to train oneself to do something," but Derrida often plays on the possibility of its meaning "to put oneself on the train"; this play is related to the topics of "sending oneself" (*s'envoyer*) and *auto*-affection. All the words in *train* have to be read in conjunction with the analysis of Ernst's spool as a train, with Freud's train (his followers, his train phobia), and with the trains to Berlin and to the front; on all of this see "To Speculate," part 2.

tranche: see below, "Du tout," note 5.

tri, trier: trier means "to sort," especially in the postal sense of sorting letters for distribution. *Le tri* is the action of sorting. In the first letter of 6 June 1977, which concerns suicide, there is a footnote that plays on *je me tue* ("I kill myself") and *je me trie* ("I sort myself"). *Triage,* in English as well as French, is the action of sorting and selecting: how are the "Envois" sorted, selected? (See the preface on this question.) The false link between sorting and death is contained in the word *meurtrière,* which means both murderess and the vertical slot in a fortress wall through which one can project weapons.

venir, revenir: venir means "to come"; the second person singular imperative is *viens. Viens* is how the prophet or messiah apostrophizes you ("Come to me"), and is often what one of the narrators asks of "her" throughout the "Envois." Saying "*viens*" to *her* is also a citation of Blanchot's *viens* in *La folie du jour;* see Derrida's studies of Blanchot in *Parages* (Paris: Galilée, 1986). Can one say *viens* to oneself? This question is tied to the entire problematic of sending, particularly of *sending oneself* a letter, of writing to oneself, of creating an inheritance, a legacy, and then surviving one's heirs so that the legacy *comes back* to oneself. Elsewhere, (in *Le parergon* in *La verité en peinture*), Derrida writes that the Hegelian spirit, *Geist,* gives itself the order to come, *viens;* there is a similar analysis of Freud's relation to psychoanalysis in "To Speculate—on 'Freud.'" The point involves the complex set of meanings in *revenir,* to come back. First, on *revenir,* see below "To Speculate," part 1, notes 3 and 5. It is worth reemphasizing that a *revenant* (in English as well as French), is a ghost, or *Geist:* it comes back from the "crypt" (see *fors*). *Revenance* is coming back (to oneself): one's texts, that is, one's ghost, *Geist,* spirit, or double, the alter ego implicit in the idea of what remains behind after one's death, are risked outward in order to be told to come back. This is the movement Derrida calls exappropriation; to use Derrida's vocabulary, one might say that exappropriation involves both *revenance* and *restance* (see above) as the *différance* of reappropriation. *Revenir à* also has the senses of "to amount to" and "to fall to," as in an inheritance falling to someone. *La venue* is the "coming," the "arrival" of something; *le* or *la revenue* would mean "he or she who has come back," but *revenu* also has the cognate English sense of revenue, or profit. In the general, or perhaps the exappropriative, economy, one might say that "revenue" consists of the attempt to bring back one's ghostly inheritance, which returns only to leave again, precisely because of the strings that are tied to it (Ernst's spool). Thus the emphasis on *zurückkommen, revenir,* to come *back* (see also *dos*) in Derrida's analysis of the rhetoric of *Beyond the Pleasure Principle,* and in what he calls the "perverformative" of the "Envois." Are the masters of the post (see under *poste*) those with the greatest *return address* (see under *adresse*)?

voler See "Le facteur," note 9.

At the end of the letters of 15 June 1978 and 20 June 1978, you will find some "words" in capital letters. These have been transposed from the original, but they are particularly problematic in the translation. If the "original" text is crypted, as it claims to be, is the translation equally crypted? Is there a possible key to the translation of a crypted text? Does the translation hold out the same promise of decrypting (of translation) as the original? Such are the questions of EGEK . . .

Italics are used in this translation both to render Derrida's own emphasis and for French words that I have left untranslated or have interpolated. *Oblique type,* in "Envois," denotes words, phrases, or proper names that are in English in the original (e.g. *Socrates,* where Derrida uses the English form "Socrates" rather than the French form "Socrate"). Brackets usually signal my interpolations. Derrida occasionally uses brackets himself, but context should make it clear which are his and which mine.

I have attempted to transcribe all formal elements as faithfully

as possible, but there are numerous errors. I have been greatly as-
sisted by three studies of *La carte postale:* Samuel Weber's "The
Debts of Deconstruction and Other, Related Assumptions," in *Taking Chances: Derrida, Psychoanalysis, and Literature,* edited by
Joseph Smith and William Kerrigan (Baltimore: Johns Hopkins
University Press, 1984); Gregory Ulmer's "The Post-Age," *Dia-
critics* 11, no. 3 (1981); and Isabelle Hovald's "'*Viens,*'" in *Les
fins de l'homme: A partir du travail de Jacques Derrida,* edited
by Philippe Lacoue-Labarthe and Jean-Luc Nancy (Paris: Galilée, 1981).

ENVOIS

You might read these *envois* as the preface to a book that I have not written.

It would have treated that which proceeds from the *postes,* *postes* of every genre, to psychoanalysis.

Less in order to attempt a psychoanalysis of the postal effect than to start from a singular event, Freudian psychoanalysis, and to refer to a history and a technology of the *courrier,* to some general theory of the *envoi* and of everything which by means of some tele-communication allegedly *destines* itself.

The three last parts of the present work, "To Speculate—on 'Freud,'" "Le facteur de la vérité," "Du tout" are all different by virtue of their length, their circumstance or pretext, their manner and their dates. But they preserve the memory of this project, occa-sionally even exhibit it.

As for the "Envois" themselves, I do not know if their reading is bearable.

You might consider them, if you really wish to, as the remainders of a recently destroyed correspondence. Destroyed by fire or by that which figuratively takes its place, more certain of leaving nothing out of the reach of what I like to call the tongue of fire, not even the cinders if cinders there are [*s'il y a là cendre*].

Save [*fors*] a chance.

A correspondence: this is still to say too much, or too little. Per-haps it was not one (but more or less) nor very correspondent. This still remains to be decided.

Today, the seventh of September nineteen seventy-nine, there are but *envois,* only *envois* from which whatever was spared or if you prefer "saved" (I already hear murmured "registered," as is said for a kind of receipt) will have been due, yes, due to a very strange principle of selection, and which for my part, even today, I consider questionable, as, moreover, the grate, the filter, and the economy of sorting can be on every occasion, especially if they destine for preservation, not to say for the archive. In a word, I rigorously do not approve of this principle, I denounce it ceaselessly, and in this respect reconciliation is impossible. It will be seen to what extent I insist on this on the way. But it was my *due* to give in to it, and it is up to all of you to tell me why.

Up to you [*toi*] first: I await only one response and it falls to you.

Thus I apostrophize. This too is a genre one can afford oneself, the apostrophe. A genre and a tone. The word—apostrophizes— speaks of the words addressed to the singular one, a live interpellation (the man of discourse or writing interrupts the continuous development of the sequence, abruptly turns toward someone, that is, something, addresses himself to you), but the word also speaks of the address to be detoured.

To filter fire? I have not given up doing so, only justifying or giving a reason for it.

At certain moments, nevertheless, I attempt to explain myself, I call upon a procedure, manipulation, techniques: counterfires, extinctions of voices, fire extinguishers. This was in February 1979 (letters 4, 5, and 6 retain the exposition of several instruments), in March and April 1979 (instructions will be found in the letters of March 9 and 15, somewhat more thought out), finally July 26 and 31 of the same year.

Because I still like him, I can foresee the impatience of the *bad* reader: this is the way I name or accuse the fearful reader, the reader in a hurry to be determined, decided upon deciding (in order to annul, in other words to bring back to oneself, one has to wish to know in advance what to expect, one wishes to expect what has happened, one wishes to expect (oneself)). Now, it is bad, and I know no other definition of the bad, it is bad to predestine one's reading, it is always bad to foretell. It is bad, reader, no longer to like retracing one's steps.

Whatever their original length, the passages that have disappeared are indicated, at the very place of their incineration, by a blank of 52 signs

and a contract insists that this stretch of destroyed surface remain forever indeterminable. In question might be a proper name or a punctuation mark, just the apostrophe that replaces an elided letter, a word, one or several letters, in question might be brief or very long sentences, numerous or scant, that occasionally were themselves originally unterminated. Obviously I am speaking of a continuum composed each time of words or sentences, of signs missing from the interior, if it can be put thus, of a card, of a letter or of a card-letter. For the totally incinerated *envois* could not be indicated by any mark. I had first thought of preserving the figures and the dates, in other words the places of signature, but I gave it up. What would this book have been like? Before all else I wanted, such was one of the destinations of my labor, to make a book—in part for reasons that remain obscure and that always will, I believe, and in part for other reasons that I must silence. A book instead of what? Or of whom?

As for the 52 signs, the 52 mute spaces, in question is a cipher that I had wanted to be symbolic and secret—in a word a clever cryptogram, that is, a very naive one, that had cost me long calculations. If I state now, and this is the truth, I swear, that I have totally forgotten the rule as well as the elements of such a calculation, as if I had thrown them into the fire, I know in advance all the types of reaction that this will not fail to induce all around. I could even do a long dissertation on the subject (for, against, with, and without psychoanalysis), but this is not the place for it. Let us say that this program is in question throughout this work.

Who is writing? To whom? And to send, to destine, to dispatch what? To what address? Without any desire to surprise, and thereby to grab attention by means of obscurity, I owe it to whatever remains of my honesty to say finally that I do not know. Above all I would not have had the slightest interest in this correspondence and this cross-section, I mean in their publication, if some certainty on this matter had satisfied me.

That the signers and the addressees are not always visibly and necessarily identical from one *envoi* to the other, that the signers are not inevitably to be confused with the senders, nor the addressees with the receivers, that is with the readers (*you* for example), etc.—you will have the experience of all of this, and sometimes will feel it quite vividly, although confusedly. This is a disagreeable feeling that I beg every reader, male and female, to forgive me. To tell the truth, it is not only disagreeable, it places you in relation, without discretion, to tragedy. It forbids that you regulate distances, keeping them or losing them. This was somewhat my own situation, and it is my only excuse.

Accustomed as you are to the movement of the posts and to the psychoanalytic movement, to everything that they authorize as concerns falsehoods, fictions, pseudonyms, homonyms, or anonyms, you will not be reassured, nor will anything be the least bit attenu-

ated, softened, familiarized, by the fact that I assume without detour the responsibility for these *envois,* for what remains, or no
longer remains, of them, and that in order to make peace within you
I am signing them here in my proper name, Jacques Derrida.[1]

7 September 1979

1. I regret that you [*tu*] do not very much trust my signature, on the
pretext that we might be several. This is true, but I am not saying so
in order to make myself more important by means of some supplementary authority. And even less in order to disquiet, I know what
this costs. You are right, doubtless we are several, and I am not as
alone as I sometimes say I am when the complaint escapes from
me, or when I still put everything into seducing you.

3 June 1977

Yes, you were right, henceforth, today, now, at every moment, on this point of the *carte,* we are but a minuscule residue "left unclaimed": a residue of what we have said to one another, of what, do not forget, we have made of one another, of what we have written one another. Yes, this "correspondence," you're right, immediately got beyond us, which is why it all should have been burned, all of it, including the cinders of the unconscious—and "they" will never know anything about it. "Left unclaimed," I would rather say of what we have, to one another, uniquely, *destined.* I am ashamed of underlining, of wanting to be intelligible and convincing (as if for others, finally), I am ashamed of saying it in everyday language, of saying it, therefore, of writing, of signifying anything at all in your direction as if

I resemble a messenger from antiquity, a bellboy, a runner, the courier of what we have given one another, barely an inheritor, a lame inheritor, incapable even of receiving, of measuring himself against whatever is his to maintain, and I run, I run to bring them news which must remain secret, and I fall all the time. Enough, drop it. No time today again, only these cards. Never taken, in sum, the time to write you what I would have wanted, it has never been left to me, and if I write you without interruption

I will have sent you only cards. Even if they are letters and if I always put more than one in the same envelope

After the session, the discussions continued on the Balliol lawn. You can guess, above, in the back on the left, the small college apartment in which I slept, above a very narrow stone staircase (what flower is this? comes from there)

Too many beds calling everywhere

I'll call you soon.

3 June 1977

and when I call you my love, my love, is it you I am calling or my love? You, my love, is it you I thereby name, is it to you that I address myself? I don't know if the question is well put, it frightens me. But I am sure that the answer, if it gets to me one day, will have come to me from you. You alone, my love, you alone will have known it.

we have asked each other the impossible, as the impossible, both of us.

"*Ein jeder Engel ist schrecklich,*" beloved.

when I call you my love, is it that I am calling you, yourself, or is it that I am telling my love? and when I tell you my love is it that I am declaring my love to you or indeed that I am telling *you,* yourself, my love, and that you are my love. I want so much to tell you.

3 June 1977
       and you, tell me
             I love all my appellations for you and then we would
have but one lip, one alone to say everything
                             from the Hebrew he trans-
lates "tongue," if you can call it translating, as lip. They wanted to
elevate themselves sublimely, in order to impose their lip, the
unique lip, on the universe. Babel, the father, giving his name of
confusion, multiplied the lips, and this is why we are separated and
that right now I am dying, dying to kiss you with our lip the only
one I want to hear

4 June 1977
       I no longer remember, but I was wrong. Wrong to think that
had not been left to me what at bottom I did not give myself—for
you, to you. To you, what does that mean? Enough, drop it, you
know—no dissertation.
                   Look closely at this card, it's a reproduction.
                                         I confide to
you this solemn and sententious aphorism: did not everything between us begin with a reproduction? Yes, and at the same time
nothing is more simply false, the tragedy is there. I more or less
know by heart what you wrote me the first time: "To choose a post
card is for me a flight which at least will spare you the too abundant
literature to which you would have been subjected if I had dared
speak to you of
       ." We have played the post card against literature, inad-
missible literature.
                   Have you seen this card, the image on the back [*dos*] of
this card? I stumbled across it yesterday, in the Bodleian (the famous Oxford library), I'll tell you about it. I stopped dead, with a
feeling of hallucination (is he crazy or what? he has the names
mixed up!) and of revelation at the same time, an apocalyptic revelation: Socrates writing, writing in front of Plato, I always knew it,
it had remained like the negative of a photograph to be developed
for twenty-five centuries—in me of course. Sufficient to write it in
broad daylight. The revelation is there, unless I can't yet decipher
anything in this picture, which is what is most probable in effect.
Socrates, the one who writes—seated, bent over, a scribe or docile
copyist, Plato's secretary, no? He is in front of Plato, no, Plato is
behind him, smaller (why smaller?), but standing up. With his out-

stretched finger he looks like he is indicating something, designating, showing the way or giving an order—or dictating, authoritarian, masterly, imperious. Almost wicked, don't you think, and voluntarily. I bought a whole supply of them.

Before posting this card I will have called you.

There, I have just hung up in the little red booth, I'm in the street, I hold onto your voice, I don't know where, I am losing myself in it too, *such is* [*telle est*]

4 June 1977

I have continued this back-and-forth. After which I went out to buy stamps, and coming back, going back up the stone stairs, I asked myself what we would have done in order to love each other in 1930 in Berlin when, as they say, you needed wheelbarrows full of marks just to buy a stamp

What impels me to write you all the time? Before I can even turn around to look, from the unique destination, unique you understand me, unnameable and invisible, that bears your name and has no other face than your own, before I can even turn around for a question, at every moment the order to write you is given, no matter what, but to write you, and I love, and this is how I recognize that I love. No, not only in this, also

Your voice just now again (small, red, paned booth in the street, under a tree, a drunk was watching me the whole time and wanted to speak to me; he circled around the glass cage, stopped from time to time, a bit frightening, with a solemn air, as if to pronounce judgment), your voice closer than ever. The chance of the telephone—never lose an opportunity—it gives us back our voice certain evenings, at night especially, even more so when she is alone and the device blinds us to everything (I don't know if I ever told you that, additionally, I often close my eyes while talking to you), when the line is clear and the *timbre* refinds a kind of "filtered" purity (it is a bit in this element that I imagine the return of revenants, by means of the effect or the grace of a subtle and sublime, essential, sorting—of parasites, for there is nothing but parasites, as well you know, and therefore the revenants have no chance, unless there have ever been, from the first "come" ["*viens*"], but revenants. The other day, in the course of a small task, I noticed that the word "parasite" had regularly imposed itself upon me an incalculable number of times, for years, from "chapter" to "chapter." Now, parasites, here it is, can love each other [*s'aimer*]. We

it is this timbre that you address to me then, without any message, any other message that counts, and I drink and I drown myself in what I drink. And yet I get myself back together each time, and from one time to the next. I am, I follow this entire timbre, this series, this consequence of all the times . . . Nevertheless, while I was talking to you with the feeling of hallucinated closeness (but separated and even the separation was good), I was staring at the English drunk, I did not take my eyes off him (he was wearing a kind of uniform), we were both watching each other, sorry, with an attention that my infinite distraction didn't disturb at all. I was sure that he looked like (as I always am, no?) but impossible to know whom, even now. Sorry again (I will have spent my life asking your pardon), I didn't think about the time difference

But I write

you tomorrow, I always say it in the present.

5 June 1977

I would like to write you so simply, so simply, so simply. Without having anything ever catch the eye, excepting yours alone, and what is more while erasing all the traits, even the most inapparent ones, the ones that mark the tone, or the belonging to a genre (the letter for example, or the post card), so that above all the language remains self-evidently secret, as if it were being invented at every step, and as if it were burning immediately, as soon as any third party would set eyes on it (speaking of which, when will you agree that we effectively burn all this ourselves?). It is somewhat in order to "banalize" the cipher of the unique tragedy that I prefer cards, one hundred cards or reproductions in the same envelope, rather than a single "true" letter. While writing "true" letter, I remembered the first (one) coming of (from) you, which said exactly this: "

I would have liked to answer right away; but in speaking of 'true letters,' you forbade me to write any

." I am sending you Socrates and Plato again

my small library apocalypse. Dreamed again of the Englishman staggering around the telephone: he was rubbing a new

pencil against a box of matches and I was trying to stop him. He
was in danger of burning his beard. Then he screamed your name
with a peculiar accent and
                    I have not yet recovered from this revelatory ca-
tastrophe: Plato behind Socrates. Behind he has always been, as it
is thought, but not like that. Me, I always knew it, and they did too,
those two I mean. What a couple. *Socrates* turns his *back* to plato,
who has made him write whatever he wanted while pretending to
receive it from him. This reproduction is sold here as a *post card,*
you have noticed, with *greetings* and *address*. Socrates writing, do
you realize, and on a post card. I know nothing more about what
the caption says about it (it has been taken from a *fortune-telling
book,* an astrological book: prediction, the book of destinies, fate,
sort, encounter, chance, I don't know, I'll have to see, but I like this
idea), I wanted to address it to you right away, like a piece of news,
an adventure, a chance simultaneously anodine, anecdotal, and
overwhelming, the most ancient and the last.
                    a kind of personal message, a
secret between us, the secret of reproduction. They would not
understand a thing about it. No more than about everything that we
have destined each other. And yet it is a post card, two three identical post cards in the same envelope. The essential, if possible,
is that the address be unique. What I like about post cards is that
even if in an envelope, they are made to circulate like an open but
illegible letter
        I write you tomorrow but without a doubt once again I will
arrive before my letter
                    In the opposite case, if I no longer reached you, you
know what always
            I ask you to forget, to preserve in amnesia

5 June 1977
    You give me words, you deliver them, dispensed one by one,
my own, while turning them toward yourself and addressing them
to yourself—and I have never loved them so, the most common
ones become quite rare, nor so loved to lose them either, to destroy
them by forgetting at the very instant when you receive them, and
this instant would precede almost everything, my *envoi,* myself, so
that they take place only once. One single time, you see how crazy
this is for a word? Or for any trait at all?
                    Eros in the age of technical re-

productibility. You know the old story of reproduction, with the dream of a ciphered language

Want to write a grand history, a large ency-
clopedia of the post and of the cipher, but to write it ciphered still in
order to dispatch it to you, taking all the precautions so that forever
you are the only one to be able to decrypt it (to write it, then, and to
sign), to recognize your name, the unique name I have given you,
that you have let me give you, the entire strong-box of love supposing that my death is inscribed in it, or better that my body might be
enclosed in it with your name on my skin, and that in any event my
own or its survival or your own be limited to the life of—you.

And just as
you often give me the word without knowing it, again it is you who
are writing the history, it is you who are dictating while at the same
time I apply myself chewing on my tongue, letter after letter, without ever turning around

what I will never resign myself to is publishing
anything other than post cards, speaking to *them*. Nothing will
ever appear to justify this for me. As an adolescent, when I made
love against the wall, and I said to myself about them—you know, I
told you

What I prefer, about post cards, is that one does not know what is
in front or what is in back, here or there, near or far, the Plato or the
Socrates, recto or verso. Nor what is the most important, the picture or the text, and in the text, the message or the caption, or
the address. Here, in my post card apocalypse, there are proper
names, S. and p., above the picture, and reversibility unleashes itself, goes mad

I told you, the crazy one is you—to bind [*à lier*]. In advance
you corrupt, you detour everything that I say, you understand
nothing, but nothing, nothing at all, or even everything, that you
annihilate immediately, and I can no longer stop talking

Did he get it wrong
or what, this Matthew Paris, get the names as well as the hats
wrong, putting Socrates' hat on Plato's head and vice versa? On
their hat, rather, flat or pointed, like an umbrella this time. On the
proper name as art of the umbrella. There is some gag in this picture. Silent movie, they have exchanged umbrellas, the secretary
has taken the boss's, the bigger one, you have noticed the capital
letter of the one, the small letter of the other, yet surmounted by a
little dot over the *p*. And there follows a very full-length plot. I am
certain that for the moment I understand nothing about this iconog-

raphy, but that does not contradict the inner certainty that I have
always known what it secretly recounts (something like our history,
at least an enormous sequence from which our history can be deduced), what goes on within it and goes without being known. One
day I will look up what has happened to us in this *fortune-telling
book* from the 13th century, and when we are alone, what awaits us

                                                                    You
said to me on the telephone, as if to give me back, and to give me
back what I myself had said to you in that famous gallery

                                                      that I am your
terrorizing "superego" (how asinine, permit me to note) and that
because of that you will always tell me "go away" when I say
"come." Now, now, wouldn't you rather get rid of the superego and
keep me? No, I know that it's more serious and a bit like that for me
too. All this because you didn't want to burn the first letters. That is
where the "superego" has settled in, it has elected domicile in that
little wood chest. I gave it to you very quickly, what a sinister little
gift, with a kind of knowledgeable appeasement but foreseeing the
worst. At that moment we wove a neurosis like a cocoon or a
tangled web, sweet, but harmful. With jealousy. You yourself explained to me that the jealousy begins with the first letter

                                               As I told you on
the telephone just now, useless to write me here, my stay is too
short, not even *poste restante* in London. I'm sending the calendar
separately (do we say "separate cover" for that?).

                                               I had left the door of the
telephone booth open, but he did not come back. On your suggestion I had surnamed him Elijah, you know the secret. I had read in
his glance that he was begging for the impossible

6 June 1977

    I didn't tell you, no time, how it happened, the other day, the
encounter with Socrates and Plato. The day before then, seminar
(at Balliol, around *La différance,* ten years after the lecture I had
given right here, if you only had seen the embarrassed silence, the
injured politesse, and the faces of Ryle, Ayer, and Strawson, okay
+ "philosophy and literature," theme of Alan Montefiore's and
Jonathan Culler's seminar that I told you about, + *Limited inc., and
so on,* I write you the letters of a traveling salesman hoping that you
hear the laughter and the song—the only ones (the only what?) that
cannot be sent, nor the tears. At bottom I am only interested in what

cannot be sent off, cannot be dispatched in any case). In English: more than ever I pretended to speak, or to think what I was saying at the same time . . . Afterward, on the lawn where the discussion continued, wandered along according to switch points as unforeseeable as they are inevitable, a young student (very handsome) thought he could provoke me and, I think, seduce me a bit by asking me why I didn't kill myself. In his eyes this was the only way to "forward" (his word) my "theoretical discourse," the only way to be consequent and to produce an event. Instead of arguing, of sending him back to this or that, I answered with a pirouette, I'll tell you, by sending him back his question, by signifying to him that he must have been savoring, along with me, the interest that he visibly was taking, at this very moment, in this question that I moreover concerned myself with along with others, among them myself. *In private*. And what proves to you, I said to him if I remember correctly, that I do not do so, and more than once. I ask you the same question, by the same courier. Notice that they no longer tell me directly, and the idea (that I should kill myself, and without waiting too long, without making others wait too long) would be rather widespread today, I would dare say in the world, in the newspapers (look at certain headlines), in any event in literature: remember *Lord B.* where the proposition is explicit and

yourself, you would keep me better, and I think with tenderness about all these innocents, these vows of innocence.

Coming back to Plato and Socrates. Yesterday, then, Jonathan and Cynthia guide me through the city. I like them, he is working on a poetics of the apostrophe. While we walk, she tells me about her work projects (18th century correspondence and libertine literature, Sade, a whole plot of writings that I cannot summarize, and then Daniel Deronda, by G. Eliot, a story of circumcision and of double-reading) and we turn into the labyrinth between the colleges. I suspect them of having had a plan. They themselves knew the *carte*. No, not of the city, but the one that I am sending you, this incredible representation of Socrates (if indeed it is him) turning his back to Plato in order to write. They had already seen it, and could easily foresee the impression it would make on me. The program was in place and working. Has all of this been prescribed by the mysterious *fortune-telling book?* Watch closely while Socrates signs his death sentence on the order of his jealous son Plato, then slowly put on *Selva morale* (side 4, remember?), and don't budge again until I arrive within you

I am finishing writing you in the street, I am
posting Plato and Socrates before the pickup, right away I will continue to write you on one of the beds, on the back of the same card,
I write you all the time, that is all I do, interested only in that all the
time that I can't see you or let the song, by itself

they are not sure of it, as
they are of my "suicide"—making my way toward it, you hear, toward you. And *je me trie** [I sort myself]

6 June 1977
out of this atrocious exclusion that we make of all of them—
and of every possible reader. The whole world. The worst of "final
solutions," without limit, this is what we are declaring, you and I,
when we cipher everything, including our clothes, our steps, what
we eat, and not only messages as they say, what we say to each
other, write, "signify," etc. And yet the opposite is not less true. All
those left out have never been so alive, so harassing even, I call
them, like the imperious beggar of the other evening with whom I
communed intensely through the pane at the very moment when I
was turned toward you, following with my hands

Do you think there are
listening devices? That our letters are opened? I don't know if this
hypothesis terrifies me or if I need it

Jonathan and Cynthia were standing
near me next to the glass case, the table rather, where laid out, under
glass, in a transparent coffin, among hundreds of displayed reproductions, this card had to jump out at me. I saw nothing else, but that
did not prevent me from feeling that right near me Jonathan and
Cynthia were observing me obliquely, watching me look. As if they
were spying on me in order to finish the effects of a spectacle they had
staged (they have just married more or less)

I no longer knew what to do
with myself. How to see to the bottom of all those rectangles between *Socrates'* legs, if it is *Socrates?* I still do not know how to see
what there is to see. It gives the impression (look at it from the
other side, turn the card over) that Plato, if it is Plato, does not see
either, perhaps does not even want to know, looking elsewhere and

---

* or "je me tue" [I kill myself], the writing makes it impossible to distinguish
between the two possibilities

further off over the shoulder of the other, what S. is in the middle, *en train,* yes *en train,* of writing or scratching on a last little rectangle, a last little one in the middle of all the others (count them, there are at least 23). This last little one is the most "interior" of all of them, it appears virgin. It is *Socrates'* writing surface, and you can imagine the missive or the rectangular chart, Socrates' post card. To whom do you think he is writing? For me it is always more important to know that than to know what is being written; moreover I think it amounts to the same, to the other finally. And *plato,* distinctly smaller, hitches himself up behind *Socrates,* with one foot in the air as if he wanted to come up to the same height or as if he were running in order to catch a moving train (which is what he did anyhow, no?). Unless he is pushing a baby carriage or wheelchair (*Gängelwagen,* for example, as the great inheritor of the scene will say). Turn it very quickly: *Plato* is pushing himself off on a skateboard (if you can't easily see the scene, put a filter over *Socrates,* multiply the filters, mobilize them, spread them out in every direction, isolate the parts of each personage, put in the film), Plato taking tram fares in a poor country, on the dashboard pushing the young people inside as it gets under way. He is pushing them in the back. *Plato* as the tram conductor, his foot on a pedal or a warning buzzer (he is pretty much a warning himself, don't you think, with his outstretched finger?), and he drives, he drives avoiding derailment. At the top of the staircase, on the last step, he rings for the elevator

you always accuse me of being "delirious," and you know very well, alas, what that means in our code

never have I been so delirious

I am

losing my voice calling you, speak to me, tell me the truth

6 June 1977

also jealous of this Matthew Paris, whom I do not know. Want to wake him up to talk to him about all the sleepless nights between us. The card immediately seemed to me, how to put it, obscene. Obscene, understand, in each of its traits. The trait in itself is indiscreet; whatever it traces or represents, it is indecent (my love, free me from the trait). And to these obscene traits I immediately wanted to erect a monument, or a house of cards, sumptuous and fragile, as barely durable, as light as what I have had to let come occasionally to make you laugh (the best memories of us, of my life perhaps, among the ecstasies, that of which I am stupidly the proudest, as of a grace, the only one, that I really deserved). The spectacle is too upsetting and still remains inaccessible for me. I can neither look nor not look, only speculate, you will call it raving again. Later, others will attempt a scientific and competent reading. It must already exist, asleep in the archives, reserved for the rare survivors, the last guardians of our memory. For the moment, myself, I tell you that I see *Plato* getting an erection in *Socrates'* back and see the insane hubris of his prick, an interminable, disproportionate erection traversing Paris's head like a single idea and then the copyist's chair, before slowly sliding, still warm, under *Socrates'* right leg, in harmony or symphony with the movement of this phallus sheaf, the points, plumes, pens, fingers, nails and *grattoirs,* the very pencil boxes which address themselves in the same direction. The di-rection, the dierection of this couple, these old nuts, these rascals on horseback, this is us, in any event, *a priori* (they arrive on us) we are lying on our backs in the belly of the mare as if in an enormous library, and it gallops, it gallops, from time to time I turn to your side, I lie on you and guessing, reconstituting it by all kinds of chance calculations and conjectures, I set up [*dresse*] within you the *carte* of their displacements, the ones they will have induced with the slightest movement of the pen, barely pulling on the reins. Then, without disengaging myself I resettle [*redresse*] myself again

What is going on under *Socrates'* leg, do you recognize this object? It plunges under the waves made by the veils around the plump buttocks, you see the rounded double, improbable enough, it plunges straight down, rigid, like the nose of a stingray to electrocute the old man and analyze him under narcosis. You know that they were both very interested in this paralyzing animal. Would it make him write by paralyzing him? All of this, that I do not know or do not yet want to see, also comes back from the bottom of the waters of my memory, a bit as if I had drawn or engraved the scene, from the first day that, in an Algiers *lycée* no doubt, I first heard of those two. Do people (I am not speaking of "philosophers" or of those who read Plato) realize to what extent this old couple has invaded our most private domesticity, mixing themselves up in everything, taking their part of everything, and making us attend for centuries their colossal and indefatigable anaparalyses?

The one in the other, the one in front of the other, the one after the other, the one behind the other?

I have always known that we are lost and that from this very initial disaster an infinite distance has opened up this ca-

tastrophe, right near the beginning, this overturning that I still cannot succeed in thinking was the condition for everything, not so?, ours, our very condition, the condition for everything that was given us or that we destined, promised, gave, loaned, I no longer know what, to each other

we lost each other—one another, understand me? (I imagine the computer at the listening device attempting to translate or to classify this sentence. Can always run, and us too: who has lost the other losing himself?

One day, years ago, you wrote me this that I, the amnesiac, know by heart, or almost: "it is curious to see that generally I do not answer your letters, nor you mine

or are we delirious, each alone, for ourselves? Are we waiting for an answer or something else? No, since at bottom we are asking for nothing, no, we are asking no question. The prayer

." Okay, I'll call you right away. You know everything, before me

you will always precede me.

6 June 1977

So you are out of my sight. And you, where do you "see" me when you speak to me, when you have me, as you say, on the telephone? On your left, your right, beside you, opposite you, in front, in back, standing up, sitting down? Me, I look out for the noises in the room around you, I try to surprise what you are looking at or looks at you, as if someone were hanging around, someone who might be me at times, there where you are, and often I stop paying attention to what you are saying so that the timbre alone resonates, as in a language that is all the closer for being foreign, and that I understand nothing (this situation might indeed be the one that keeps me close to you, on your string), and then I am lying on my back, right on the ground as in the grand moments you remember, and I would accept death without a murmur, I would want it to come and I imagine him unable to turn back on *Plato.* He is forbidden to. He is in analysis and must sign, silently, since Plato will have kept the floor; signing what? well, a check, if you will, made out to the other, for he must have paid a lot, or his own death sentence. And first of all, by the same token, the "mandate" to bring back that he himself dispatches to himself at the other's command, his son or disciple, the one he has on his back and who will have played the devil's advocate. For Plato finally says it himself, he sent it to himself, this sign of death, he looked for it, he rushed into it without looking back

                    and in the homosexual phase which would follow Eurydice's death (and that had therefore preceded it, according to me

) Orpheus sings no more, he writes, and he has another one with Plato. Be aware that everything in our bildopedic culture, in our politics of the encyclopedic, in our telecommunications of all genres, in our telematicometaphysical archives, in our library, for example the marvelous Bodleian, everything is constructed on the protocolary charter of an axiom, that could be demonstrated, displayed on a large *carte,* a post card of course, since it is so simple, elementary, a brief, fearful stereotyping (above all say or think nothing that derails, that jams telecom.). The charter is the contract for the following, which quite stupidly one has to believe: Socrates comes *before* Plato, there is between them—and in general—an order of generations, an irreversible sequence of inheritance. Socrates is before, not in front of, but before Plato, therefore behind him, and the charter binds us to this order: this is how to orient one's thought, this is the left and this is the right, march. Socrates, he who does not write, as Nietzsche said (how many times have I repeated to you that I also found him occasionally or even always somewhat *on the border* of being naive; remember that photograph of him with his "good guy" side, at the beginning in any event, before the "evil," before the disaster?). He understood nothing about the initial catastrophe, or at least about this one, since he knew all about the others. Like everyone else he believed that Socrates did not write, that he came before Plato who more or less wrote at his dictation and therefore let him write by himself, as he says somewhere. From this point of view, N. believed Plato and overturned nothing at all. The entire "overturning" remained included in the program of this credulity. This is true *a fortiori,* and with an *a fortiori* different each time and ready to blow up otherwise, from

Freud and from Heidegger.* Now, my post card, this morning when I am raving about it or delivering it [*quand je la délire ou la délivre*] in the state of jealousy that has always terrified me, my post card naively overturns everything. In any event, it allegorizes the catastrophic unknown of the order. Finally one begins no longer to understand what to come [*venir*], to come before, to come after, to foresee [*prévenir*], to come back [*revenir*] all mean—along with the difference of the generations, and then to inherit, to write one's will, to dictate, to speak, to take dictation, etc. One is finally going to be able to love oneself [*s'aimer*]

All of this is not without, it is not to all of you that I will have to teach this, political consequences. They are still difficult to calculate

"One day we will go to Minos."

I am adding several cards, as usual. Why prefer to write on cards? First of all because of the support, doubtless, which is more rigid, the cardboard is firmer, it preserves, it resists manipulations; and then it limits and

---

*I must note it right here, on the morning of 22 August 1979, 10 A.M., while typing this page for the present publication, the telephone rings. The U.S. The American operator asks me if I accept a *"collect call"* from Martin (she says Martine or martini) Heidegger. I heard, as one often does in these situations which are very familiar to me, often having to call "collect" myself, voices that I thought I recognized on the other end of the intercontinental line, listening to me and watching my reaction. What will he do with the ghost or Geist of Martin? I cannot summarize here all the chemistry of the calculation that very quickly made me refuse (*"It's a joke, I do not accept"*) after having had the name of Martini Heidegger repeated several times, hoping that the author of the farce would finally name himself. Who pays, in sum, the addressee or the sender? who is to pay? This is a very difficult question, but this morning I thought that I should not pay, at least not otherwise than by adding this note of thanks. I know that I will be suspected of making it all up, since it is too good to be true. But what can I do? It is true, rigorously, from start to finish, the date, the time, the content, etc. Heidegger's name was already written, after "Freud," in the letter that I am in the course of transcribing on the typewriter. This is true, and moreover demonstrable, if one wishes to take the trouble of inquiring: there are witnesses and a postal archive of the thing. I call upon these witnesses (these waystations between Heidegger and myself) to make themselves known. All of this must not lead you to believe that no telephonic communication links me to Heidegger's ghost, as to more than one other. Quite the contrary, the network of my hookups, you have the proof of it here, is on the burdensome side, and more than one switchboard is necessary in order to digest the overload. It is simply, let me say for the ears of my correspondents of this morning (to whom I regret a bit, nevertheless, that I did not speak), that my private relation with Martin does not go through the same exchange.

justifies, from the outside, by means of the borders, the indigence
of the discourse, the insignificance of the anecdoque [sic]

I have so much
to tell you and it all will have to hold on snapshot post cards—and
immediately be divided among them. Letters in small pieces, torn
in advance, cut out, recut. So much to tell you, but all and nothing,
more than all, less than nothing—to tell you is all, and a post card
supports it well, it is to be but this naked support, to tell it to you,
you only, naked. What my picture

You are going to think that I venerate
this catastrophic scene (my new fetishes, the "hit" of the summer):
Plato, teacher, in erection behind *Socrates,* student, for example,
and in saying "catastrophic," I am thinking, of course, of the overturning and inversion of relations, but also, suddenly, of the apo-
trope and the apostrophic: p. a father smaller than his son or disciple, it happens, p., unless it is S., whom he resembles, devilishly,
shows him (to others) and at the same time shows him the way,
sends him, and at the same time apostrophizes him, which always
amounts to saying "go" or "come," *fort, da. Fort/da* of S. and p.,
this is what it is, this entire post card ontology. What it leaves
strangely unexplained, is that himself he addresses himself to S. or
to others beyond S. But does one ever know

*plato/Socrates,*a o/o a. Look
closely at their mugs [*bobine*], *plato's* hat flat as a plate and the a in
Socrates which mimes within the name above the head the very
form of his hood. All of this seems very prophylactic, very preser-
vative to me, up to the dot on the small p. But who are they? S is p,
my equation with two unknowns. I have always been enchanted by
the passage in *Beyond the Pleasure Principle* when, after so many
laborious hypotheses and useless detours, Freud comes to state in
an apparently embarrassed tone, but within which I have always
perceived some wicked satisfaction: the result to which we have
come finally, is that instead of one unknown, now we have two. As
if he were registering a certain profit at this point. Register, now
there's a word, Socrates is keeping a register (secretly, of what the
other, the gunner, has lifted from him, the funds he has diverted,
the counterfeit money he has had printed with his effigy. Unless this
is the effigy of the two greatest counterfeiters of history, comperes
preparing the emission we are still plugged into while drawing
checks and money orders on it infinitely. In advance they impose
everything, they tax, they obliterate the *timbres,* with their own
effigy, and from you to me

Would like to address myself, in a straight line, directly, without *courrier,* only to you, but I do not arrive, and that is the worst of it. A tragedy, my love, of destination. Everything becomes a post card once more, legible for the other, even if he understands nothing about it. And if he understands nothing, certain for the moment of the contrary, it might always arrive for you, for you too, to understand nothing, and therefore for me, and therefore not to arrive, I mean at its destination. I would like to arrive to you, to arrive right up to you, my unique destiny, and I run I run and I fall all the time, from one stride to the next, for there will have been, so early, well before us

If you had listened to me, you would have burned everything, and nothing would have arrived. I mean on the contrary that something ineffaceable would have arrived, instead of this bottomless misery in which we are dying. But it is unjust to say that you did not listen to me, you listened closely to the other voice (we were already a crowd in that first envelope) which asked you not to burn, to burn in order to save. Nothing has arrived because you wanted to preserve (and therefore to lose), which in effect formed the sense of the order coming from behind my voice, you remember, so many years ago, in my first "true" letter: "burn everything." You had answered me the next day, and this is how your letter ended: "The letter ends on the exigency of this supreme pleasure: the desire to be torn by you" (you are the mistress of the equivocal and I liked it that you left it to me to attribute this desire to the letter, and then you added) "I am burning. I have the stupid impression of being faithful to you. I am nonetheless saving certain simulacra from your sentences [you have shown me them since]. I am waking up. I remember the ashes. What a chance, to burn, yes yes

." Your letter mandated, commanded, made arrive at its destination everything that we feared. And what has betrayed us, is that you wanted generality: which is what I call a child. If we had been able to die already, the one or the other, we would have kept each other better. I recall having said to someone, right at the beginning of our history, however, *"I'm destroying my own life."* I still have to specify: when I first wrote "burn everything," it was neither out of prudence and a taste for the clandestine, nor out of a concern for internal guarding but out of what was necessary (the condition, the given) for the affirmation to be reborn at every instant, without memory. To make anamnesis impossible, symbolically of course, whence the trap. It was within the same impetus that (very

sincerely?) I told you, liked to tell you that I liked to approve of
your desire even if it were not turned toward me. I was completely
crazy, out of my mind, but what a chance! Since then we have re-
neuronecrosed each other, this was good too, but there you are
                                                      Through fi-
delity to the secret demand you wanted to preserve, to preserve, me
too, and here we are deprived of everything. I am still dreaming of
a second holocaust that would not come too late. Know that I am
always ready, this is my fidelity. I am a monster of fidelity, the most
perverse infidel.

        The first catastrophe is the ignoble archive which rots
everything, the descendence into which everything tumbles
                                                      I don't know
when I'm coming back, Monday or Tuesday, I'll call and if you
can't come to wait for me at the station I

8 June 1977

        and I grant you that my "wish" [*"envie"*]—you found the best
word—to immortalize the card might appear quite suspect. First of
all because without a doubt this was on the two impostors' program, the scene that plays itself out between them, the scene of
which Paris made himself the voyeur, or the first *dévoyeur* [corrup-
ter], you could also say *fourvoyeur* [one who leads astray], or *pour-
voyeur* [purveyor], ("purveyor of truth," they chose this translation
for "*Le facteur de la vérité*"), or further the divulger, but he had to
take part in it to do so. The two impostors' program is to have a
child by me, them too. And let it be made in the dorsum.
                                                      The emission of
sense or of seed can be rejected (postmark, stamp, and return to
sender). Imagine the day, as I have already, that we will be able to
send sperm by post card, without going through a check drawn on
some sperm bank, and that it remains living enough for the artificial insemination to yield fecundation, and even desire. But, dear
friend, prove to me that this is not a normal tragedy, old as Me-
thuselah, older than our most upsetting techniques?
                                                      The *impossible* con-
fession (the one we have risked, the one that the other within us has
been able to extort from us by means of this atrocious blackmail by
true love), I imagine that it can be delivered only to children, for
children, the only ones unable to bear it (in us, of course, for "real"
children could also scorn it), and therefore the only ones to deserve

it. One can confess everything to adults, everything and nothing, therefore.

To the devil with the child, the only thing we ever will have discussed, the child, the child, the child. The impossible message between us. A child is what one should not be able to "send" oneself. It never will be, never *should* be a sign, a letter, even a symbol. Writings: stillborn children one sends oneself in order to stop hearing about them—precisely because children [*enfants, infans*] are first of all what one wishes to hear speak by themselves. Or this is what the two old men say

They love (the) address. I have too many, too many addresses, too much address. The disease that is killing me.

Suppose that we had given to one of our innumerable (possible) children an accursed name, a name of malediction, the first name of someone who would be in us like the forever open wound (for example

), how we would have loved it. The wound can have (should only have) just one proper name. I recognize that I love—you—by this: that you leave in me a wound that I do not want to replace.

And they believe that we are two, they want at any price, without knowing how to count, to hang onto this stupidity. Two, neither more nor less. I can see you smile along with me, my sweet love.

I am still sending you the same cards. S. is writing on a medieval scribe's desk as if on a phallus or on a fireplace. Difficult to know if these objects belong to him, but he busies himself on the mount, with both hands. The left, in order to scratch out doubtless, irritates the support, the other dips. Two hands, the mystic writing pad (he destines it, like a post card, to the other bearded old man who wanted to start it all over, anamnesis, twenty-five centuries later, and who, without a warning, nevertheless erases Socrates from the scene of the Symposium [*weg! fort!*]). He is erasing with one hand, scratching, and with the other he is still scratching, writing. Where will all this information have been stocked, everything he will have scratched and scratched, that one? The question deserves a letter to the editor in *le Monde*.

I couldn't answer you on the phone just now, it was too painful. The "decision" you asked me for once again is impossible, you know it. It comes back to you, I send it back to you. Whatever you do I will approve, and I will do so from the day that it was clear that between us never will any contract, any debt, any official custody, any memory even, hold us back—any child even.

Of course this was also the day of the most sacred *liance,* because of it even, but at the moment when the motor started, remember, first gear was passed and we looked at each other through the glass, we said to each other (each to himself aside and each to the other in silence, we said it to each other out loud later, so many times and in so many forms) that the absence of memory and unsworn faith would be the chance, the condition. This was also a vow. Naturally I have never *accepted* it, nor have you, it was not possible, but I still want it, that within me which loves, the only one that can love, I am not speaking of the others, still wants it and adjusts to it. It is killing me of course, but it would be worse otherwise.

I accept [*j'accepte*], this will be my signature henceforth, but don't let it worry you, don't worry about anything. I will never seek you any harm, take this word at its most literal, it is my name, that *j'accepte,* and you will be able to count, to count on it as on the capital clarities, from you *I accept* everything.

8 June 1977

this is the name, like a salvo of post cards, always the same one shooting itself off again, burning its strophes, one after the other in order to try its luck all the way up to you. I had barely posted the preceding one, in order never to miss a pickup when the opportunity presents itself, and here I am again standing up to write you, standing right in the street, so often standing, incapable of waiting—and I do it like an animal, and even against a tree sometimes. But it is also that I like to write you standing up and to accept being surprised doing the thing, exactly the situation I totally reject when it is a question of writing something else, to others and in order to publish it to them. And at the same time, you know that I do not like writing you these miserable scraps, these small dots lost over our immense territory, that let it be seen so little, or even imagined, that occupy it as little as the dot on the I, a single dot on a single I, infinitely small in a book infinitely big. But (I can hardly bear, support this thought in words) on the day that I no longer will be able to do it, when you no longer will let me put the dot on my Is, the sky will fall on my head and the fall will be endless, I will stretch myself out in the other sense of my support. You said it to me one day, I think, I always write *on* the support, right on the support but also on the subject. Expected result, it deforms it, thereby I broach its destruction, all the while showing it, itself, in the course of *being* that which destroys itself, falls into pieces, a bit theatrical, and then incinerates itself beneath your eyes and there is no longer anything but your eyes. You understand that this is the insupportable partition of the support. It is within reason not to support it, and I understand this readily to the extent that I am reasonable, like you and like everyone, but precisely at stake there is reason. Okay.

For example I write *on* post cards, oh well I write on post cards. "I" begins again with a reprosuction (say, I just wrote repro*S*uction: have you noticed that I make more and more strange mistakes, is it fatigue or age, occasionally the spelling goes, phonetic writing comes back in force, as in elementary school where it did not happen to me moreover, only to others whom I confusedly looked down on—plus the *lapsus* or *"slips"* obviously). And by means of a reproduction itself reproduced serially, always the same picture on another support, but an identical support, differing only *numéro*. It dates from when, the post card "properly speaking," do you know? Nineteenth century necessarily, with photography and the stamp, unless . . . Want to write and first to reassemble an enormous library on the *courrier,* the postal institutions, the techniques and mores of telecommunication, the networks and epochs of telecommunication throughout history—but the "library" and the "history" themselves are precisely but "posts," sites of passage or of relay among others, stases, moments or effects of *restance,* and also particular representations, narrower and narrower, shorter and shorter sequences, proportionally, of the Great Telematic Network, the *worldwide connection.* What would our correspondence be,

and its secret, the indecipherable, in this terrifying archive?

The wish to vanquish the postal principle: not in order to approach you finally and to vanquish you, to triumph over distancing, but so that by you might be given to me the distancing which regards me.

Do you think that what went on between S and p regards us? To keep to appearances, but it is only a picture, their eyes are turned elsewhere, they have never had a thought for us.

9 June 1977

Plato wants to emit. Seed, artificially, technically. That devil of a *Socrates* holds the syringe. To sow the entire earth, to send the same fertile card to *everyone*. A *pancarte,* a pan-card, a billboard that we have on our backs and to which we can never really turn round. For example, poor Freud, Plato, via Socrates, via all the addressees who are found on the Western way, the relays, the porters, the readers, the copyists, the archivists, the guardians, the professors, the writers, the *facteurs* right?, Plato sticks him with his *pancarte* and Freud has it on his back, can no longer get rid of it. Result, result, for it is not so simple and as-I-show-in-my-book it is then Plato who is the inheritor, for Freud. Who pulls the same trick, somewhat, on Plato that Plato pulls on Socrates. This is what I call a catastrophe.

9 June 1977

distance myself *in order* to write to you. If now I am still sending you the same card, it is because I would be willing to die, to enclose myself finally in a single place that is a place, and bordered, a single word, a single name. The unique picture then would carry off my immobile, extended body, then slowly

how you will have sent

me away

  you know now on the basis of what catastrophe, what disaster, this mortal desire to wall myself up in the repercussions of a name, to let me beat my head to the song of a name, the only one. And of a picture. The picture and the name are the same. You have given me this but I would like you thereby to get to take me without

The return frightens me and I am even frightened to call. And if you were not there, without having been able to warn me? During trips, at those moments when I am inaccessible, between two "addresses," when no wire or wireless links me to anything, to you, I die of anxiety and then doubtless you give me (and pardon me too) the pleasure which is not far from cresting, as near as possible, without measure finally, beyond everything, that which we, according to the said ecstasy

airplanes [*avions*]—two wings [*deux ailes*], that is what I need

without which, crash, fall from the nest

like a bad card, the losing one,

the underside of which must be shown, not only to the other, but to oneself. When I will know what game I am playing with myself, my love. But when I fly with you why doesn't the anxiety disappear? You yourself are very tranquil, you are turned toward the scenery and you take pleasure in the outside as if you had just been born. I ask myself occasionally quite simply if you exist and if you have the slightest notion of it.

No literature with this, not with you my love. Sometimes I tell myself that you are my love: then it is only my love, I tell myself interpellating myself thus. And then you no longer exist, you are dead, like the dead woman in my game, and my literature becomes possible. But I also know—and for me, moreover, this morning, this is the definition of knowledge, I should publish it—that you are well beyond what I repeat as "my-love," living, living, living, and I want it so, but then I have to renounce everything, I mean that love would come back to me, that turned toward me you let me even hear what I am saying when I say, say to you or say to myself my love

In the beginning, in principle, was the post, and I will never get over it. But in the end I know it, I become aware of it as of our death sentence: it was composed, according to all possible codes and genres and languages, as a declaration of love. In the beginning the post, John will say, or Shaun or Tristan, and it begins with a destination without address, the direction cannot be situated in the end. There is no destination, my sweet destiny

you understand, within every sign already, every mark or every trait, there is distancing, the post, what there has to be so that it is legible for another, another than you or me, and everything is messed up in advance, cards on the table. The condition for it to arrive is that it ends up and even that it begins by not arriving. This is how it is to be read, and written, the *carte* of the adestination. Abject literature is on the way, and it spies on you, crouching within language, and as soon as you open your mouth it strips you of everything without even letting you enjoy getting underway again, completely naked, to the one you love, living, living, living, there, out of reach. The condition for me to renounce nothing and that my love comes back to me, and from me be it understood, is that you are there, over there, quite alive outside of me. Out of reach. And that you send me back

isn't this somewhat what I was just saying? Unless it is the opposite, but you know that with you I never reread

Example: if one morning
Socrates had spoken for Plato, if to Plato his addressee he had addressed some message, it is also that p. would have had to be able
to receive, to await, to desire, in a word to have *called* in a certain
way what S. will have said to him; and therefore what S., taking
dictation, pretends to invent—writes, right? p. has sent himself a
post card (caption + picture), he has sent it back to himself from
himself, or he has even "sent" himself S. And we find ourselves,
my beloved angel, on the itinerary. Incalculable consequences. Go
figure out then if you, at this very moment, in your name
                                                        this is the catas-
trophe: when he writes, when he sends, when he makes his *(a)way,*
S is p, finally is no longer totally other than p (finally I don't think so
at all, S will have been totally other, but if *only* he had been totally
other, truly totally other, nothing would have happened between
them, and we would not be at this pass, sending ourselves their
names and their ghosts like ping-pong balls). pp, pS, Sp, SS,
the predicate speculates in order to send itself the subject
                                                    Real hallucina-
tion just now: you know what it means, you were there. It is 6:10
now, night

10 June 1977. Impossible to write today. Too unwell. You remember: everything had begun with the joyous decision not to write
any more, the only affirmation, the only chance (no more letters,
no more literature), the condition, what one has to give oneself so
that something finally happens. Confess, let us confess: this was
the failure, the triumph of communication, right (we should have
never communicated anything in sum, not even together), the triumph of the negative and worse, semi-failure, mid-mourning, gray,
grayness
    and always this whore of a post and the pick-ups on the sidewalk

10 June 1977
    I arrive now
        Forgot again just now the time difference [*décalage
horaire*], doubtless because I knew that you would not be alone.
You can imagine (I would like us to read it together, losing ourselves
in it) the immense *carte* of the communications called "immediate" (the telephone, etc., call it telepathy) across the distance and

network of "time differences" (all the red points that light up at the same time on our map of Europe). We would have arranged things, this fine morning, first gear passed, in order to speak to each other *all the time,* write to each other, see, touch, eat, drink, send, destine this or that, you or me, permanently, without the slightest interruption, without half-time, simply by counting on relativity, calculating with the universal time difference [*décalage*] (pulling out the stops—*cales*—or multiplying them?). *Moreover this is what does happen.* Between writing with a pen or speaking on the telephone, what a difference. That is the word. How well I know the system of objections, but they do not hold, in sum do not go far enough. You can see clearly that S. is telephoning and behind the other one is whispering

And Freud has plugged his line into the answering machine of the *Philebus* or the *Symposium.* The American operator interrupts and scrambles: Freud is not paying enough, is not putting enough *quarters* into the machine. The great symposium, right, the gag on Europe, Eros in generalized telephonic relation. The demon calls, Socrates picks up, wait here's Freud (what a difference, a very important time difference [*décalage horaire*]) and the demon speaks to Freud, directly, from the beyond, like his ghost which says to him "wait," *hold on,* come back with your spool, don't hang up, here's Heidegger. Myself, I tender Heidegger to the pupil: hold on, take, understand, and me along with it, and me first, you too (wait a minute, on "to tender"—what one does, tenders, when one says "hold on," there is the thought of the "*reichen,*" "to porrect," *porriger* the translators on Heidegger's French switchboard say— and here I take it as "porridge"—on "to tender," therefore, to send, to destine, *schicken, etc. Zeit und Sein,* will have had the power (not Martin Heidegger, not *Zeit,* not *Sein* but something around the *und,* and Heidegger indeed says so), *and* therefore will have had the power of (knowing) (thinking) plugging everything back in, to think plugging everything back in, all the (a)ways of making one's (a)way, every possible and imaginable *Weg,* before the Being and the time that *there is* (*es gibt*) on *what there is to give.* Master stroke and great theater (without representation or mastery, which is even more accomplished), this connection: very great post, right, every (a)way must go through it, pass by it, sooner or later, through this great sorting center, must have itself taxed, stamped, and above all obliterated, after having acquitted itself of the sum due to the memory of the proper name whose effigy you see here, with, in the background, the mountains and forests of

Freiburg. I dream that one day the card S and p will become a stamp, or a sticker on which I will collect royalties, a stamp or sticker with which everyone will have to be quits who . . . who what? I don't know, everything and anything, who think, read, write, telephone, communicate, anything, let them pay at every step finally

a great thinker is always somewhat a great post, but here it is also the (historial, destinal) end of the posts, end of the race, and end of the mail [*fin de course et fin du courrier*], of a great epoch at least, of a great halt of postal technology

power itself (*esti, vermag*) is what there is—and that you give me when you come if you come, but I know that you won't come again—you began by coming back but you won't come back again, neither on your decision (sorry, on your "determination," as you always say!), you won't want to come to rejoin me again, and it's my fault, the impardonable fault of my incorrigible, unbreakable, ineducable innocence. Listen—tenderly I am going to tell you

it doesn't matter if you can't come for me, I'll call you from the airport.

Hold on, ne coupez pas [don't hang up], do you think they mean the same thing?

10 June 1977

what would remain of us thanks to music, not a word, not a letter. Again *en train*—I am writing to you between Oxford and London, near Reading. I am holding you stretched out on my knees. *En train* to write *you* (you? to you?) this thought for Oscar Wilde. What would he have thought of this card? of the inversion of names and places? He knew it perhaps

you have to understand, if I write *on* the card, as I equally would write on you, and I like to, it is in order to destroy, so that nothing is preserved except an illegible support, or even a snapshot, nothing that has deserved, or allegedly deserved, preservation. And if we do not destroy all the traces, we are saved, that is, lost

Think of everything I have been able to destroy in the shape of letters in this short life (how short life will have been!). One day especially (it lasted one entire day, I think we didn't know each other yet), I'll tell you about it, one of the most comic and sinister, most unspeakable, scenes of my existence. It was like an

interminable murder. Technically, materially I could not get to the
end of it, because what with my rush and my absurd fear of being
surprised I chose the worst means. Everything went into it and in
different places, I got there by car (always looking in the rearview
mirror to make sure no one was following me). The most beautiful
letters in the world, more beautiful than all literatures, I began by
tearing them up on the banks of the Seine, but it would have taken
twenty-four hours and the people passing and the fragments that
could have been put back together, all those cops always on my path
as if obsessed about my private life of which they know nothing, all
that. I packed it all back in the car and in a suburb that I did not
know, where I chose to wind up, I burned everything, slowly, at the
side of a road. I told myself that I would never start again

very banal today
the idea that one is killing by burning a letter or a sign, a metro
ticket that the other has held in his hand, a movie ticket, the wrap-
per of a sugar cube. Very banal too the "fantasy," very run down,
but with what force and what necessity it dictates to me, from behind, all my gestures. Murder is everywhere, my unique and immense one. We are the worst criminals in history. And right here I
kill you, save, save, you, save you run away [sauve-toi], the unique,
the living one over there whom I love. Understand me, when I
write, right here, on these innumerable post cards, I annihilate not
only what I am saying but also the unique addressee that I constitute, and therefore every possible addressee, and every destination.
I kill you, I annul you at my fingertips, wrapped around my finger.
To do so it suffices only that I be legible—and I become illegible to
you, you are dead. If say that I write for dead addressees, not dead
in the future but already dead at the moment when I get to the end
of a sentence, it is not in order to play. Genet said that his theater
was addressed to the dead and I take it like that on the train in
which I am going writing you without end. The addressees are
dead, the destination is death: no, not in the sense of S. or p.'s predication, according to which we would be destined to die, no, not in
the sense in which to arrive at our destination, for us mortals, is to
end by dying. No, the very idea of destination includes analytically
the idea of death, like a predicate (p) included in the subject (S)
of destination, the addressee or the addressor. And you are, my
love unique

the proof, the living proof precisely, that a letter can always not
arrive at its destination, and that therefore it never arrives. And this
is really how it is, it is not a misfortune, that's life, living life, beaten

down, tragedy, by the still surviving life. For this, for life I must
lose you, for life, and make myself illegible for you. *J'accepte.*

I have not
yet destroyed anything of yours, your scraps of paper I mean, *you*
perhaps, but nothing of yours. But it would be fatal. (I am still *en
train,* this is getting harder and harder to read no doubt.) It is very
simple, if I always come back to the same card (*plato* making *Socrates* promise, compelling him to sign an engagement: I will leave
nothing behind me, not even counterfeit money with my effigy), finally it is in order to set eyes on it, no matter if they are blind (even
better, for the less I understand the "true" meaning of this iconography, the less my eyes, the color of my eyes, my eyelids, the mark
on one of them and the fluttering of my lashes will be forgettable
for you), it is therefore in order to set eyes on it, I am speaking of
eyes not of sight, the eyes that you sometimes look at upside down
bent over me until we go crazy from seeing nothing other than our
vision reversed in the faces that then become terrifying, if I look at
this card it is in order to set my eyes on it, fix them on a well defined
place, depositing them and then posting the focal point to you, exactly the same where now, right here, now, after having opened the
box and unsealed the envelope, setting your eyes on it in turn like
moistened lips, you cry and it becomes our bed, the bed [*le lit*]—
like an opened letter. You remember the day when we bought that
bed (the complications of credit and of the perforated tag in the department store, and then one of those horrible scenes between us).

vision
and light have to serve to touch the eyes. For this one must see without understanding, without thinking anything about what lets itself
be seen in this excess of evidence.

When I will have interpreted this card (S
and p) appropriately, if it is ever possible, you no longer will be
there
The train *verso Londra,* now, for me, it is always Freud and Adami

10 June 1977

I walked for more than two hours in the same neighborhood
crying, a lost child. I have rather precise memories of this experience, I don't know if I ever told you about it, I was eight or nine, a
fair in El-Biar. I could no longer find my parents and blinded by
tears I had been guided toward my father's car, up behind the
church, by the creatures of the night, guardian spirits. Spirits, why

are spirits always called upon in letter writing? One lets them
come, one compromises them rather, and one writes for them, one
lends them one's hand, but why? You had me read that letter to
Milena where he more or less said that, something like speculating
with spirits, denuding oneself before them; he wrote only (on)
letters that one, one of the last along with Freud finally. This is Europe, *centrale,* the center of Europe, the *carte* between Vienna and
Prague, my own in sum, with an extension of the track or of the
Orient-Express near Athens or Reading, between Oxford and London. And in the same letter he says as always, it seems to me, that
he has a horror of letters, that they are hell, he accuses the post, the
telegram, the telephone. Elsewhere he says that he burns letters and
speaks of epistolary sorcery. Yes, yes—but who will believe it?

Again the
card (S *et* p, this is the proposition made to us and if you get it,
come to the rendez-vous). From the beginning of this trip I have
had the impression—it is taking on a very "compulsive" aspect as
they say (compulsion is a very beautiful word no longer understood, one no longer feels the assembling of the push [you, you are
the push] and repetition compulsion is understood even less)—I
have the impression that everything comes to resemble itself, and
me first of all, in a post card, the post card—that I am, am following [*suis*]. There is but that, this reproduction of a reproduction of
which I am dying and which forbids me, which makes of you, my
living one, an interdiction

they have *intercepted* us.

and I do not believe that one
can properly call "post card" a unique and original image, if some
such thing ever occurs, a painting or drawing destined to someone
in the guise of a post card and abandoned to an anonymous third
party, a neutral machinery that supposedly leads the message to its
destination, or at least that would have its support make its way, for
if the post card is a kind of open letter (like all letters), one can
always, in time of peace and under certain regimes, attempt to
make it indecipherable without compromising its making its way.
Indecipherable, my unique one, even for the addressee. And yet
there are but post cards, it's terrifying.

p. frightens me this evening. Look,
he is the law, is you, is me. And the play of their hands. The hand
that is writing really appears incapable of belonging to S. More like
it has been slipped under his cloak by someone else who is writing
in his place. We played at this in my childhood. One placed oneself

behind the other, under the cloak, and let one's hands stick out front, with all kinds of gestures (scratching the nose, rubbing the hands together, threatening with the finger). We laughed hard, but anxiety was there, and desire: if the hand went a bit lower to describe things, as at Balthazar's feast? These four hands belong to no one, or to a single invisible divinity whose phantom is playing with S and p. Paris wanted to set us astray. Have you ever seen "bonto" players (I don't know how it is spelled)? There are some in the port of Algiers. With stupefying dexterity they move three cards after having you choose one. You are sure that you have been able to follow his movements, and therefore that you can refind the place where he sets it down finally, beside the two others. You are wrong every time, unless by chance you choose one of the two others, which you are sure are not the right ones. They are pulling the "bonto" trick on us—with Plato's works of course. You can always run to find out where they take place, where they are literally posited, where they have been posted, destined to whom. Just so, and first of all will I say, right here, for Matthew Paris's drawing, as for what I am making of it or that affects me here and that you are reading right at this moment.

One day, please, read me no more, and even forget that you have read me

Says he. Look again at their unbelievable hats. In order to pass off their counterfeit money by contraband, not writings under their cloaks as I wrote previously (in the PP) about the two comperes, but counterfeit money under their hats or in their hats, as did, M. tells me, the counterfeiters of the Freud family, from England precisely and to get over the Channel [*la Manche* (the Sleeve)]. Via the *Manche* I think that they passed the *"plates,"* the trays [*plateaux*] or impresses of bills.

I'll see you before you've read this. How nice it would have been if you could have come to the airport. In any event I'll call you from there if I don't see you. Just now it was busy (more than fifty minutes, watch in hand), I died several times, but you see, *"la séance continue."* I am saving some of the lecture money (one day I will talk to you about the problem of money between us and of the absolute prohibition that I've put on it, stupidly, like a horrible Mediterranean macho who spends without counting and never wants to talk about it), I am not changing my pounds and soon we will be able to afford that answering machine.

11 June 1977

it will always be a scandal and no archive will ever take charge of it, no computer will preserve the memory of it. The "photomaton" that I pasted under the *grattoir* on S.'s table comes from Paddington. When I have nothing to do in a public place, I photograph myself and with few exceptions burn myself.

It is true that this reproduction of a reproduction (always a text and a picture, indissociably) has limits, is in principle governed by a law and subject to *copyright.*

you know that he has a kind of genius for unearthing post cards and for playing on them; he sent me one a long time ago with the motto "reproduction prohibited" printed on the border enframed. I never knew what he meant, if he wanted to draw my attention to the "general" paradox of the motto which he knew would interest me, or if he discreetly was asking me to be discreet and to keep for myself what he was saying, or rather barely suggesting in the said card. I have never been sure of what I thought I understood, the content of the information or the denunciation. Terrified, I projected into it the worst of the worst, it even made me delirious.

He had spoken of the *"écart"* [division, interval] and today I perceive—it is even extraordinary that it is only today—that *"écart"* is the anagram of *"carte."* I had played on this inversion of the letters and of the body of words, doubtless too abundantly, for *trace* and *écart,* for *récit* [narrative] and *écrit* [writing]. And you know that if anything I abused the lexicon of the *carte,* the *cadre* [frame], the *quart* [fourth], the *cadran* [gnomon], the *cartouche,* etc. But I had never inverted *carte* into *écart,* into the *écart postal.* A selection had been made and a wire of the computer had been isolated

Imagine a city, a State in which identity cards were post cards. No more possible resistance. There are already checks with photographs. All of this is not so far off. With the progress of the post the State police has always gained ground.

11 June 1977

and then I pillaged the museums, as usual, but I am dispatching again, among others, *plato* and *Socrates,* with a rebus for you above the raised finger. As I am certain that you won't figure it out, I will explain it to you, on my return, only under one condition

plato is ugly
for once, he resembles Socrates whom Paris has avenged, unless he
unintentionally threw out the names by chance, as if they were
coming out of a hat, *Socrates'* hat obviously, or out of a dice cup.
Behind the great man the dwarf with the flat hat, the slave or the
preceptor seeks to hitch himself up. There is a passage of Nietzsche's, will have to refind it, which says about Plato, and perhaps
about Aristotle, that they had the chance to have copyists, whence
the injustice as concerns the predecessors; whence too all the rest of
history, of philosophy and the rest, revolutions, literatures, Marx-
Nietzsche-Freud-Heidegger, and then this minuscule *carte* and ourselves on the *carte* (there, you don't understand any more not
having read the rebus). What Nietzsche, who was right, did not see
or say is that the honorary copyist, the first secretary of the Platonic
party, was comrade Socrates—and that everything had to be reconstructed according to this fabulous genealogy, even if it were worth
only the time of my directed hallucination. One still has to take into
account the interest I might have, myself (myself, that is, a determined historic site, a certain network of telethings), in you, in this
hallucination, in communicating it to you, in taking a certain profit
from it, at your side and at the side of several others, etc. It has
to be reckoned with, with you, which is what I am doing here.

You terrify
me, you are bad for me, when will I cease to be afraid of you, of the
entire picture that you send me back? I don't even know if I desire it.
Perhaps I would no longer love you, and yet I don't love you, not
you, to the extent that I am afraid and to the extent that, as I am
doing here, on the eve of this return from which I fear the worst, I
am writing under your threat. You have your hand raised and if I
continue to enclose myself in the stubborn silence that you know so
well, you are ready to slap me (remember?). In *La folie du jour* (ah
how wise these cards are, even "knowledgeable," like whoever says
"I" in *La folie,* and yet, I no longer know to whom I wrote it recently, literature has always appeared unacceptable to me, a scandal, the moral fault *par excellence,* and like a post card seeking to
pass itself off as something else, as a true letter that would have
to pass through the censor or customs, an imposture in order to get
rid of the duties on everything) "I" (he) "loves" the law, a feminine figure which he frightens, he too, he primarily, and which he
brings to light. She says to him "Ah I see the light," etc.

We have no right,
remember.

"Reproduction prohibited," which can be translated otherwise: no child, inheritance prohibited, filiation interrupted, sterile midwives. Between us, I have always believed (you don't, I know) that the absence of filiation would have been the chance. The bet on an infinite, that is, nul genealogy, the condition for loving each other (*s'aimer*) finally. It happens otherwise, the child remaining, alive or dead, the most beautiful and most living of fantasies, as extravagant as absolute knowledge. As long as you don't know what a child is, you won't know what a fantasy is, nor of course, by the same token, what knowledge is. You know what I am talking about, at least, so adjust yourself however you can, to this economy I mean, from Socrates to Freud and beyond, up to us (included and not included).

One would have to illustrate this picture, or rather illustrate an epic with it, the cover or rather the endpaper.

Plane from Heathrow tonight. I will have tried to call you back again *(collect)* from now till then, if the line is free. If ever I should no longer arrive, you know what will have been my last, my last what in fact? Certainly not will. My last image at the back of my eyes, my last word, the name, all of this together, and I will not have kept my belt buckled, one strophe more, the final orgasm and compulsion, I will swim in your name without turning back, but you will never be your name, you never have been, even when, and especially when you have answered to it. The name is made to do without the life of the bearer, and is therefore always somewhat the name of someone dead. One could not live, be there, except by protesting against one's name, by protesting one's non-identity with one's proper name. When I called you, at the wheel, you were dead. *As soon as* I named you, as soon as I recalled your first name. And you came right out and said so, before the first rendez-vous, timorously invoking, with what lucidity, your "instinct of conservation." By blackmailing your higher feelings ("you say instinct of conservation? don't you find that this lacks a bit of . . . ?") I made you give it up for a time, but according to your criteria, which will never be mine, conservation seems to have gotten the upper hand again. In order to conserve what, the calculation is impossible. I hope to perceive you when I land

25 August 1977

most terrible summer, no, and we have, all the way south, crossed so many beloved cities, lived so many reconciliations, bodies covered with scars that momentarily we no longer see sending us back the image ("we are beautiful, look").

Never, remember, will I have anything to say about your "determination." You decide, both on the moment and the rest. I will understand and approve. *J'accepte.* No, no, this "determination" is unacceptable for me, inadmissible, unjustifiable in me *for life.* And I am indeed saying for life. But there is not only life, have to believe. And despite the life within me, I can see you are right (moreover, I do not see what else I could do if you decide thus, if you finally have the desire and the strength, the preference, for it; I have only to give in to reality—like you, reality as you). I think as you. Alas, have you noticed that the strokes I am pardoned the least are those that have consisted in absenting myself enough in order to agree (for example in *le Facteur de la vérité* a note amounts to agreeing, a note they have not even been able to read it was so unbearable), in a certain way that is mine. Pardon me this too, agreeing with you. My desire is unacceptable, but living.

You know, those interminable, horizonless deliberations, hour after hour, days and nights, on the division of pleasure, on what does not amount to pleasure, on the reckoning and unreckonable of enjoyments, all these implicit evaluations, the ruse and contortion of all these economies, we were sublime in them, unbeatable experts, but it was a bad sign. What was still good was only the necessity, the act of deliberating about it together and as far as the eye could see, the inability to exhaust the subject, the immense preference, clear as day and so much greater than our ratiocinations. Even the trifling quarrels were erotic dispositions. The day that we will no longer have disputes

The only possible "determination" for me—and moreover I obey it every moment without seeming to: burn everything, forget everything, in order to see if the force of starting again without a trace, without an opened path

The symbol? a great holocaustic fire, a burn-everything into which we would throw finally, along with our entire memory, our names, the letters, photos, small objects, keys, fetishes, etc. And if nothing remains

What do you think? I await your response.

28 August 1977. You just called. You asked me if I had heard you call me? Is that a question? I stayed silent. The idea that you might "call" me and that I might not answer overwhelms me. All this telephone between us. I am still looking at our two comperes, S. and p., the unbelievable play of their hands. There is certainly a code to these gestures, I should consult a doctor to find out what all this means finally. For the moment I am cutting and pasting. Admire the economy, I have displaced only *plato's* left hand. Observe the corner of S.'s eye, he was waiting only for that. I still understand nothing about it, for more than two months now, but they are becoming curiously familiar to me, they are my own. I also like them as a souvenir of our vacation. They will have supported so many messages, transported so many complaints and so many confessions (you know, when I say "I love you," it is really a confession—perhaps in the sense of classical tragedy—at the same time as the sublime absolution of every possible crime), they are our mail officials, our personal *facteurs.* In Siena, the copyists (I no longer remember in what painting) had the same instruments, the pen and the *grattoir,* and a similar posture.

29 August 1977

I had brought back, and then ordered, a whole stock of them, I have two piles on the table. This morning they are two faithful dogs, Fido and Fido, two disguised children, two tired rowers. How they will have rowed, these two also. Last night I saw them a bit otherwise. *Socrates,* the grandfather, knows how to write, he has a cigar in his left hand; little *plato,* the grandson, already serious as a pope, turns around him. He demands, commands, sends on errands: somebody has to throw the ball back, somebody has to return something to him, let him write or allow him to speak, perhaps over the top of the podium, the desk, the back of the armchair—or over S.'s robe. Speaking of which, M., who has read the seminar on *Life Death* along with several friends, tells me that I should publish the notes without changing anything. This is impossible, of course, unless I just detach the sessions on Freud, or only the one on Freud's legacy, the story of the *fort/da* with little Ernst. Difficult and abstract without the context of the entire year. Perhaps . . .

They want to *oppose fort* and *da*!!! There and here, there and there the cassette under separate cover: watch out, listen to it alone, don't let the family intercept it, there are several words for you between the movements.

When are you coming back? I will call Sunday at the latest. If you're not there, leave them a message. Leave, for example, so that they won't understand a thing, as in the Resistance, a sentence with "sunflower" to signify that you prefer that I come, without sunflower for the opposite

since I am a true network of resistance, with internal cells, those little groups of three who communicate only on one side (what is it called?), so that nothing can be extorted, so that no one gives way under torture, and finally so that no one *is able* to betray. What one hand does the other does not know (definition of Islamic alms?)

It will end very badly, for a long time I have no longer been able to refind myself, and in fact I betray myself, me, all the time. All those idiots who do not know how to decipher, and who would willingly believe that I lead a very sheltered life, without exposing the body, without obsession and without political earthquakes, without militant risks . . . But it's true, the disdain mounts from year to year, and the disgust, and I defend myself against it in vain (disdain or disgust, no, something else, because there is always mixed with it that kind of sad solidarity, as I told you, a despairing compassion: I will have shared everything memorable (at least that, which is not everything, nor perhaps the essential) with those who have understood nothing. Epoch, that is, halt, and post. Don't even want to take a step outside.

30 August 1977

never in which sense the usage of these round trips. You can't stand the back-and-forth, or the interrupter that I can be. This is the difference between you and me. Or finally between you and you, and me and me. Thank you for the grace period, the decision put off until later, the remission. As long as you want to stay, I am there, and even if you depart without turning back. I still do not know to whom, to what I am destining this fidelity, to a morsel of myself perhaps, to the child that I am carrying and whose features I try to make out. You alone can help me to do so, but at the same time, since the child is to look like you more and more, you dissemble his features, you forbid me to see them, and for as long as I live with you I will understand nothing. Wish to take you out of this "resemblance" finally, to see you appear, you, the other, and not only in the way a "negative" is developed. When I will have seen you, we will leave each other. When we will separate from each other, when I will separate myself, I will see you. I will turn back toward you. But I have never known how to separate myself. I will learn, and then I will take you into me and there will no longer be any distance between us. I already feel in my body, I had pointed this out to you and you had confided the same thing to me, strange mimetisms. Can't stand this calculation between us, these sortings, filterings, selections of signs. You also showed me absolute horror, hatred, injustice, the worst concentration of evil—I was virgin, quite simply, even if I knew everything. Only the song remains, it is reborn each time, nothing can be done against it, and it is only it, within it, that I love. Never will any letter *ever* make it heard. Without the slightest effort it carries itself beyond all calculations, the multiplicity of sites (the crowd of pieces of myself, and of you, differences, "topics," oh! topics! the fidelity to fidelities, perjury as the categorical imperative, phooey . . .

I did not like your sending me that telegram. I thought I felt something other than haste in it, even the opposite, an economical way of not writing to me, of saving your time, of "expediting." You expedite me in a way that I previously would have accepted from no one—but I no longer cry when you depart, I walk, I walk, on my head of course. You forgot perhaps that the first telegram danced (years ago). It came from the neighboring post office, you could have brought it yourself. I understood nothing except that it danced.

and while driving I held it on the steering wheel

our telegraphic style, our post card love, our tele-orgasmization, our sublime stenography

all of it in the most carefree, most shameless "retro" fashion, and turning its back in every possible way

it was near the Italian border, coming back from Florence, customs was not far off, you gave me a very runny cheese to eat while I was driving, and I told you that you transfigured everything, you did not hear me, you made me repeat while turning the radio dial (I still see your finger, the greasy paper of the cheese, and the ring

we are not angels, my angel, I mean messengers of whatever, but more and more angelic.

I had convinced

you, with all kinds of details, on the same road, "galleries" succeeding one another at a great pace (like this summer, in the other direction, at night, I was driving like a madman, you were waiting for me and I was at the end of my strength, I no longer knew when I was in the tunnel or out of it, I called you from every café) that we were living Tristan and Yseult, that is Tancredi and Clorinda in an epoch when telecommunicative technology made all of that untimely, absolutely impossible, anachronistic, outmoded, out of synch, forbidden, grotesque, "old hat." Apparently. For the opposite is also true: we would have been, yes, impossible without a certain progress of telemachination, acceleration in the speed of angels (all angels, all the messengers we have provided ourselves by slipping the coin into the automatic: we could have never gotten away with the manual, supposing that, okay), not a day without a *fort:da* plugged into computers of the nth generation, great-grandsons of *computeurs,* descendants of the pioneers

　　　　　　　　　　　　　　　　　　I have never understood why psychoanalysis is so hung up on such a backward technology of the *fort:da* or of "direct" discourse. But in fact, yes, for it is unfortunately linked to a certain state of the post, and even to monetary exchanges, of the form-money and its emission. Freud had paid for this knowledge. In advance he had paid.

　　　　　　　　　　　　　　　　　for finally the *fort:da* is the post, absolute telematics. And the post is more than it was at the time of the hemerodromes and the foot-runners, as they appear to believe. And moreover, it never simply amounted to that.

　　　　　　　　　　　　　　　　　　　　　　I am still waiting for you to answer the precise, direct question that I asked you, waiting for you to answer it otherwise, in a nondilatory or evasive way. I want no more remissions.

　　　　　　　　　　　Henceforth, the thing cannot suffer any more detours, we owe it to ourselves to suffer no more detours. I have gone as far as I could

　　　　　　　　　　　and these inexhaustible words, these days and nights of explication will not make us change places or exchange places, even though we ceaselessly try to do so, to get to the other side, to swallow the other's place, to move our bodies like the other's body, even to swallow it while drinking its words, mixing the salivas little by little, wearing down the borders

　　　　　　　　　　　　　　　　　　　but there are the others, the others within us I grant you, and we can do nothing about it, that is the limit. There is a crowd, right, such is the truth.

Read the back, what I
write on the *back,* right on the picture, is a single note.

30 August 1977. I repeat that I don't want a remission. When I got
your message (having first admired the harmony between the stamp
and the Madonna) I again called you every possible name. Then
yours came back. In your name you are my destiny, for me you are
destiny. Everything began, you remember, when I pronounced it,
you had your hands on the wheel, and I know that I am writing this,
my destiny, fate, my chance, when on the envelope I *risk,* which is
indeed how I feel the thing, when I risk the first word of the address. I address myself to you, somewhat as if I were sending myself, never certain of seeing it come back, that which is destined for
me. And when I am able to pronounce it, when I softly call myself
by your name, nothing else is there, do you hear, nothing else, no
one else in the world. Even us perhaps and yes our existence is
threatened then. This is why I permit myself everything, in your
name, as long as I can pronounce it to myself aside, preserve myself within it. It absolves me of everything, it leads to, induces, and
governs everything. This did not prevent me from cursing you just
now. We have spoken to each other in every tone, written in every
code, they will never know (I hope and yet will never get over it).
Forgive me the violence just now, in the end I did not call you for
that and we succeeded (true duelists) in listening to each other at
length while avoiding murder, making the blows deviate, without
going back down into hell, without going over the same confession.
No, not yours (yours was sublime and at that date it was the only
letter of yours that I had burned—at your request but I had thought
of it spontaneously—almost in your presence, simply by going into
the bathroom where I saw the box of sleeping pills, and then made
up my mind, no, mine, a single word finally, and "yes" in answer to
your question, an answer that you extorted from me although I had
formulated the question in your place: you ask me if it has been
possible?—yes, yes. I could have added a specification that would
have acquitted me almost, if this is necessary, but absolutely refusing to *speak* of this by putting the dots on the i's, I nevertheless have
just decided to send you a *detailed,* concrete as you say, letter—
poste restante because of all the families. One never knows. Go
pick it up and don't speak to me about it again. Now, to go on to
something else, look at, and keep, what I have put between the S/p
card and the letter paper. Put yourself to sleep by taking it in your

mouth. It is a part of me that I am addressing to you, to your depths. And then watch them move about again: who is driving? Doesn't it really look like a historic vehicle? A gondola? No, even though *plato* is playing gondolier, perched in the back, looking far away in front of him the way one guides the blind. He is showing the direction. Unless the index finger of his right hand is designating S., who is in the course of scratching a name, do you see, for the attention of a third party to whom he is addressing himself with the index finger of his left hand. For there are third parties, in the place where we are.

　　　　　If you do not want to come back right away, will you let me come?

31 August 1977. No, the stamp is not metaphor, on the contrary, metaphor is a stamp: the tax, the duty to be paid on natural language and on the voice. And so on for the metaphoric catastrophe. No more is post a metaphor.

　　　　　We are lost because of the truth, that horrible fantasy, the same as the fantasy of the child finally. Nothing true, as you know, in our "confessions." We are still more foreign, more ignorant, more distant from what "really" happened and that we believed we said to each other, recounted to each other, more deprived of knowledge than ever. And the effects are nevertheless destructive, ineradicable—for you finally, not for me. Me, I can always make up my mind, as you have seen. This is what I explained to you—in "detail"—in the long, somewhat sententious epistle that you must have gotten from the village by now.

1 September 1977. You told me once upon a time that I could ask the impossible of you. You could not bear that elementary madness, for you it has to be near or far.

　　　　　of the opened letter. My taste for (a-b-s-o-l-u-t-e) secrecy: I can take pleasure only on that condition, from that condition. BUT, secret pleasure deprives me of the essential. I would like everyone (no, not everyone, the best telescopic soul of the universe, call it God if you wish) to know, to testify, to attend. And this is not a contradiction, it is for this, with sights set on this that I write when I can. I play the secret against the weak witnesses, the particular witnesses, even if there is a crowd of them, because there is a crowd. This is the condition for witnessing—or for voy-

eurism—in principle universal, for the absolute nonsecret, the end
of the private life that finally I detest and reject; but while waiting,
the private (eye) has to be thrown in. Implacably, and the secret and
the crypt and the reserve. I do not refuse the absolute publicity of
testifying, I reject the witnesses, certain witnesses. One after another, this is true *up to the present,* and almost all of them. Myself
occasionally, which is why I write a bit without believing in anything, neither in literature, nor in philosophy, nor in schools, the
university, the academy, the *lycée,* the college, nor in journalism.
Up to the present. This is why I am somewhat hung up on post
cards: so modest, anonymous, offered, stereotyped, "retro"—and
absolutely indecipherable, the interior safe itself that the mailmen,
the readers, the collectors, the professors finally pass from hand to
hand with their eyes, yes, bound.

the discord, the drama between us: not to
know whether we are to continue living together (think of the innumerable times of our separation, of each auto-da-fé), whether we
can live *with* or *without* the other, which has always passed outside
our decision, but at what distance, according to what mode of distancing. And there-

1 September 1977.
        S. is P., Socrates is Plato, his father and his son, there-
fore the father of his father, his own grandfather and his own grandson. That the stroller overturns after having "bumped" against the
threshold is the first true event in *La folie du jour,* after which the
day "hastens to its end." Already a kind of primal, and repeated,
scene. Divine, who can guess what is going to happen to us. Whatever happens, I can do no more about it. I await everything from an
event that I am incapable of anticipating. No matter how far my
knowledge goes and however interminable my calculations, I see
no way out that is not catastrophic. The deal is implacable, we are
losers at every turn. We must have been looking for it. Tempted, for
the first time in my life, to consult a clairvoyant. *I can't tell.* I like
that expression, because of the sonority, and all the meanings that
resonate together in it: to count, to recount, to guess, to say, to discern. For us, for our future, *nobody can tell.* One day I will go to
Oxford to see Plato and Socrates and to consult their *"Fortune-
telling book."* When he says one day in a lecture that the "divine
Plato" had been the "victim of Socratism," Nietzsche alludes to
"fortune-tellers." I want to transcribe the translation for you—and

I like that he speaks of a scar of Plato's, "he who for the love of Socratism trampled on his profoundly artistic nature, reveals in the bitterness of these judgments that the deep wound of his being has not yet been scarred over. If he speaks ironically of the true creative faculty of the poet and if he places it on the level of the talents of the seer and the fortune-teller, it is because the poetic gift does not consist in a clear knowledge of the essence of things (. . .) what is proper to the Platonic dialogue is the absence of form and of style engendered by the mixture of all forms and of all styles . . ." He goes a bit too far, I think, and what if the opposite is true? Mixture is the letter, the epistle, which is not a genre but all genres, literature itself. In any event, Paris, whom I would really like to know, executes a masterstroke by making both of them figure at the opening of a *fortune-telling book.*

Will you like my latest decoupage, with the musical note on the card? The card is the score [*partition*] the *partition* (the unbearable partition of the letter), and *plato* the music master, orchestra leader, *conductor.* Who conducts? *Socrates* is writing or transcribing the *partition.* Who is playing? One hears nothing from this card, but the cadence is very clearly marked.

Again
afraid to die before finishing my sentence.

You have still not gotten the letter that I sent to the village P.R.? I await you. Have we ever seen each other?

1 September 1977. We see them, but in fact they doubtless never exchanged a glance, I mean a real one, lying one on top of the other, and if possible upside down. Neither seen nor heard, no relation between S. and P. Only dialogues, the dialogue of P., that the one, or the other, writes taking dictation—from the other, who remains absolutely invisible, inaccessible, untouchable for him. No relation. It is too obvious, to use your words as always, that S. does not see P. who sees S., but (and here is the truth of philosophy) only *from the back.* There is only the *back,* seen from the back, in what is written, such is the final word. Everything is played out in *retro* and *a tergo* And moreover nothing will ever prove, from looking at this card, that S. ever wrote a single word. At the very most, dipping his pen, or more sensuously one of his fingers, into that which has the office of inkwell (attached, I have cut out for you the calamus and the orifice of the said inkwell so that you can see clearly what I spend my time doing when you are not there), he prepares himself to write, he dreams of writing, what he is going to write if the other lets him or indeed gives him the order to do so; perhaps he has just written, and still remembers it. But it is certain that he is not writing presently, presently he is scratching. Up to the present: he does not write. You will say that "to write" is indeed to scratch, no, he is scratching in order to erase, perhaps the name of Plato (who has succeeded, moreover, by inventing Socrates for his own glory, in permitting himself to be somewhat eclipsed by his character), perhaps a dialogue of Plato's. Perhaps he is only correcting it, and the other, behind him, furious, is calling him back to order. Perhaps he is playing with the blank spaces, the indentations, the simulacra of punctuation in the other's text, in order to tease him, to make him mad with grief or with impotent desire. It is still the absolute enigma, those two. If it is not some clumsiness and coarseness of line, or rather of the point, Plato's eye indeed bespeaks anger.

I am writing again because just now, at 6 P.M. precisely I called as agreed, you were not there, or finally that is what I believed I felt.

2 *September 1977.* I am really very, very surprised that you did not find my letter sent P.R. I do not believe your explanation or your hypothesis, not at all. That postal employee would be risking too much, even if she is there only for the vacation. And even if she is motivated by the childhood rivalry that you mention, she will put the letter back into circulation once she has read it. Moreover, I guarantee you that she would understand nothing. Nor would you perhaps. In any event I will never rewrite it, this little "detail" cost me too much, when all is said and done. Perhaps it is better that it remains illegible for you. On the telephone you screamed again, just now. But no, I did not "drive you crazy," not so crazy. Or yes, I did, and if I did, it is because you knew, without ever being able to be sure, that I was addressing myself only to you. To you uniquely, you, you, and you cannot stand it, you are afraid, you grow agitated, you flee, you seek to distract yourself, or to make me wrong, as if I were turned, myself, elsewhere. This second I think: and if, in order not to have to acquit me, you were feigning that you never received the P.R. letter? Just as I do not want to have to rewrite it for the reasons I told you, nor to reread it, for the same reasons, I was not going to keep a typed carbon and send you the original regis-

tered with notification of receipt! Will we ever be finished with this
law and this secret police between us?

2 *September 1977.* You just called. "I would be able to forget you,
if you asked me to." I don't doubt it, you have already begun, you
began right away, this second, from the first second that

                                          sorry, erase that
right away, I want to laugh with you, and this is by far my best desire. Unbelievable, the story they are telling you about the route between the station and the post office. It will have to be searched,
officially. There is a center in France which assembles all lost
letters, all the letters sent P.R. that are not picked up by their addressee after a certain date (the time limit is shorter than you would
think), the letters whose addressees and senders cannot be found. I
don't know how long they keep them, before destroying them I suppose. It is in Bordeaux, I would very much like to know why. A
very, very long time ago, I had to deal with this machinery. On a
trip, I had sent to myself, Poste Restante, a packet of letters that
I did not want to keep on myself. I thought that I had a very
wide interval at my disposal for picking them up, after my return.
Mistake: when I presented myself at the post office, they were
unfindable. Personnel confused: they had doubtless been sent to
Bordeaux (since this was a time that I hadn't put my address on
the back; which was precisely what I wanted to avoid in this case).
And in Bordeaux it is always difficult to refind anything. In any
event, everything is opened and read in order to divine, with the
best intentions in the world, the name of a sender or of an addressee. When I came back into possession of these letters two
months later, they had in effect been opened. Once more become
the post cards that at bottom they already were. I have destroyed
them since, and quite sincerely I no longer recall which letters were
in question.

    I am spending my time rereading you. Yes, "words are delayed
for us and like them [do you mean words or S. and p.?] we have
only a single sex." In effect, it is a "curious cuisine, our destiny."
Almost 6 o'clock, I am coming.

                      You were there, in the sun.

                                The departure for Yale
is set for the 27th, we will have to act quickly. When does the se-
mester start again? Finally you will be there, no more letters during
these few days before my departure. We should no longer write—

3 September 1977.
I swear that I sent it, and even with address of sender on the back. Therefore they will have to be able to return it to me, and the case will be proven. In the meantime, have you asked for the official search? Of course I felt, at the second that I was writing, that this letter, like all the others, was intercepted even before any hands could be put on it, any accidental interception—for example by the woman postal clerk, the rival of your childhood. All the precautions in the world are taken in vain, you can register your *envois* with a return receipt, crypt them, seal them, multiply coverings and envelopes, at the limit not even send your letter, still, in advance it is intercepted. It falls into anyone's hands, a poor post card, it ends up in the display case of a provincial bookseller who classifies his merchandise by name of city (I confess that I have often dug around in them, but only for you, searching for memories of our cities that would have transited into other memories, other histories, preferentially from before we were born, in the *belle époque*). Once intercepted—a second suffices—the message no longer has any chance of reaching any determinable person, in any (*determinable*) place whatever. This has to be accepted, and *j'accepte*. But I recognize that such a certainty is unbearable, for anyone. One can only deny this self-evidence, and, by their very function, those who deny it most energetically are the people charged with the carrying of the mail, the guardians of the letter, the archivists, the professors as well as the journalists, today the psychoanalysts. The philosophers, of course, who are all of that at once, and the literature people.
In effect I believe that the idea imposes itself, this is indeed the word, in any event imposes itself upon me and I want it (want it horribly, flight, no, to enclose myself in a book project, to deploy all possible ruses and a maximum of consciousness, intelligence, vigilance, etc., while remaining, in order to remain (as you said to me one day) enclosed in this puerile (and masculine) enclosure of naïveté, like a little boy in his playpen, with his construction toys. That I spend the clearest part of my time taking them to pieces and throwing them overboard changes nothing essential in the matter. I would still like to be admired and loved, to be sent back a good image of my facility for destruction and for throwing far away from me these rattles and pieces of tinkertoy), finally you will tell me why I still want this, and in a certain way for you, in order to prepare in your absence what I will give you on your return, at the end of time. What is it? to make of the false preface to the Freud a long

(counterfeit) description of the painting, or rather of its reproduction, of the post card itself, as if my Freud were a *fortune-telling book*. S and p would be put on the cover. I see, I don't see but I feel, all kinds of strings to pull. Doubtless the book will be called *Legs de Freud:* because of the march and the legs, Freud's *pas* which never advances in *Beyond,* all of whose *démarche,* deambulation, interminable preambulation I follow, the legs, *jambes* which make their (a)way as much as the jambs of the letter or of the fireplace in Poe, and you know that I always play with anglish words; legacy also of the "movement," inheritance and filiation, Freud's grandsons and the institution, and the cause, and the daughters and the rings and the son-in-law, etc., in order to make a detour—very necessarily, you know how I work—toward *lait de Freud* and *les deux Freud;* and in order to parody also, by taking it elsewhere, a beloved expression ("*legs de Freud*") of Lacan and of Granoff. Now, this scene of inheritance, repeated in another way in *Plato's Pharmacy* (right after chapter 7 of the PP, "The Inheritance of the Pharmakon: The Family Scene"), *interests* Plato and Socrates in the very position in which you see them posted on this card. The presumptive heir, Plato, of whom it is said that he writes, has never written, he receives the inheritance but as the legitimate addressee he has dictated it, has had it written and has sent it to himself. *Fort:da,* violent seizure, in one stroke, in a second, just as Freud sent himself his will in order to survive his heirs, but just as Ernst, Heinele and several others dictated it to him in turn, etc. This is the demonstration that I would like to perform, in this book I am (following) Plato, Ernst, Heinele, etc., as seriously as possible. This is the inversion that interests me (narcissistically, but we both have experienced sufficiently that narcissism is one of those post card concepts, one of those double-bind or double-faced logics, like the logic of introjection and several others, *me,* ego, for example: the more there is, the less there is), the inversion that Paris's design, such as I am hallucinating it for you, seems to me to emblematize.

Plato's dream: to make Socrates write, and to make him write what he wants, his last command, *his will. To make* him write what he wants by letting (*lassen*) him write what he wants. Thereby becoming Socrates and his father, therefore his own grandfather (PP), *and killing him.* He teaches him to write. *Socrates ist Thot* (demonstration of the PP). He teaches him to live. This is their contract. Socrates signs a contract or diplomatic document, the archive of diabolical duplicity. But equally constitutes Plato, who has already composed it, as secretary or minister, he the magister. And the one to the other they show themselves in public, they analyze each other uninterruptedly, *séance tenante,* in front of everyone, with tape recorder or secretary. What happens when there is a third party in front of the couch? Or another analyst who is providing himself a *tranche?* Obliquely, the book would also deal with Freud's correspondence (or Kafka's, since this is what you want), and with the last great correspondences (still hidden, forbidden), and it would also inscribe *Le facteur de la vérité* as an appendix, with the great reference to *Beyond* . . . , to the *Symposium,* and then above all to the *Philebus* on pleasure, which Freud never cites, it seems to me, although in a way he translates or transfers its entire program. As if via so many relays Socrates had sent him a post card, already a reproduction, a stereotype, an ensemble of logical constraints that Freud in turn comes to reproduce, ineluctably, without being too aware of it, in an incredible discourse on reproduction and on the repetition compulsion.

As soon as, in a second, the first stroke of a letter divides itself, and must indeed support partition in order to identify itself, there are nothing but post cards, anonymous morsels without fixed domicile, without legitimate addressee, letters open, but like crypts. Our entire library, our entire encyclopedia, our words, our pictures, our figures, our secrets, all an immense house of post cards. A game of post cards (I recall at the moment that the French translation of *Beyond* . . . makes Freud's pen put a house of cards in the place where he literally says, I think, that his edifice of "speculative" hypotheses could crumble in an instant, at any moment). There it is, to speculate on post cards, on shares embossed with crowned heads. What do post card collectors do? Have to observe them.

What can this ciphered letter signify, my very sweet destiny, my immense, my very near unknown one? Perhaps this: even if it is still more mysterious, I owe it to you to have discovered homosexuality, and ours is indestructible. I owe you everything and I owe you nothing at all. We are of the same sex, and this is as true as two and two are four or that S is P. Q.E.D.

4 September 1977.
Every day you give yourself one more day, and I really have the impression that you no longer want to come back. Still no news on the "search"? Let me know

What a couple! I think that yesterday I wrote you something like "two and two are four." I announce that this is true. The paradigmatic scene of the *fort:da* in *Beyond* is a scene of four, *fort:da* between the generations, postal and telecommunicative: four corners, a charter between Grandpa (*Pépé*) Sigmund, Sophie, Ernst and, and the other, the fourth to whom it is perhaps signified (but by whom?) "go away," return to sender. This is the son-in-law, the husband, the father. The widower, who is "inconsolable," says Freud, after the passage of seven years. And he is also a specialist in reproduction, the photographer Halberstadt. Marika, with whom I had lunch at the Rostand, suggests: the phO-tOgrApher HAlberstAdt, O O A A A.

He envowels himself [*il s'envoyelle*] his father, does the little one, and he sends him back too (go away!) by inventing the post and the railway.

Of course, if I am following the word *post*, as you say, if I am reciting it to myself and sucking it all the time, if I always have it in my mouth, to the point of fusing and confusing myself with it, it is that it is hermaphroditic or androgynous, *mannweibliche*, the neuter or third or first sex (initially taken up by Freud from the mouth of Aristophanes after Plato, he dares to say, had "let him develop it." *La poste, le poste*, the two love each other [*s'aiment*] and send back to themselves the other (what a couple!), this is the law of the genre/gender as was said in the note of the *Facteur* that they evidently have not read at all, the note that discreetly *installs* the entire program, note 6 precisely: "*Le poste* differs from *la poste* only by the gender" (*Littré*). This entire vocabulary, this entire postal code, if you prefer to play, would work very well, at a great essential depth, with that which imposes itself upon me in the reading of *Beyond* . . . , to wit the typology of postages, postures, impostures, of the *position* above all (*Setzung, thesis*), the thesis, the athesis and the hypothesis. And it is the *postal*, the Postal Principle as differantial relay, that regularly prevents, delays, endispatches the depositing of the thesis, forbidding rest and ceaselessly causing to run, deposing or deporting the movement of speculation. And this is why his daughter remaining mute, my sweet philately who patiently bends over my post card dissertation while keeping an eye on your watch (you have just come out of the water, the mailman has just come and soon it will be noon, you will watch the sun while myself, at that very second . . .

the day that you will no longer come to this rendezvous, my

course stops and I am dead of a death that is no longer my own, ours), this is why the old man always starts off again, from hypothesis to hypothesis, from thesis to contra-thesis. He runs after the post, after the beyond of the PP, from one *pas* to the other he speculates interminably, it speculates in his back, it pushes him, he wants to inherit from himself, he never sits down, or very little, and always behind. On the topic, try to decipher what I scribbled under *SOcrAtes'* plate, right on the elephant's trunk, it is for you.

I have just hung up, it is still as difficult as ever. Agreed, at 6 o'clock Sunday evening, I dance in the water with you (Astor Piazzola, Libertango, Meditango, Undertango, Adios Nonino, Violentango, Novitango, Amelitango, Tristango) and I will stop only at the point of exhaustion, dead of fatigue.

From now till then I will have called you at least three times, don't let the parents or children answer before you. But I would prefer that you really come, if you see what I mean, you

there, right here where I am and where I will reach you.

4 September 1977.

if you knew, but it's killing me with my mouth wide open, and you don't have to be afraid to send me walking: *weg!* One day it is you who will tell me, as I pretended to threaten you occasionally, "so long!" Go away! and to the war indeed, the worst one, we will march off again, the war of all against all, once the telephonic wire is cut: for if we deliver, yes, deliver ourselves to a war without mercy, the worst of all, if it lasts at least and still holds us together, it is that we are peace, you will not forget, at peace as never anyone, and for eternity.

Hanging up just now (as always, "hang up," —"No, you hang up,"—"No, you,"—Hang up, you," "Hang up, you," "I'm hanging up," etc.), I was in seventh heaven, I was laughing softly over the sage conversation (we are completely crazy!) concerning the word "philately." Sage, finally, is saying a lot. For in the end, Diotima, they are somewhat lacking a dictionary in your country house. No, philately does not mean love of distance, of the term, of the *telos* or of the tele-, nor the love of letters, no, my very near one full of sun, it is a very recent word, it is only as old as stamps, that is of the State monopoly, and it treats of *ateleia* (the *facteur,* not the truth). *Ateleia* is franking, the exemption from

taxes, whence the stamp. It is true that it maintains therefore a relation with one of the senses of *telos:* acquittal, exemption, payment,
cost, expenditure, fee. From acquittal one could go to gift, offering, and even, in Sophocles, marriage ceremony! Phila-tely then
is love *without,* with/without marriage, and the collection of all
stamps, the love of the stamp with or without stamped love. But
along with all the other senses of *telos* (particularly that of power,
of absolute jurisdiction or of full power, that of the pleasure principle, the PP that I talk about all the time in the *Legs*), you can see
all that one might do. I will leave the thing to be done all by itself,
I always prefer. But I would really like to call the book *philately*
in order to commemorate secretly our somewhat nutty phone call.
                                                                      We are
monstrous angels, all this bad economics, this expended energy,
this time that we will have spent analyzing the tax that we pay
in order to remain together, the price that it costs, the impossible
calculations, the qualitative registers yes my dear of evaluation,
the more or less sublime profits of sublimation, the secret debts,
the charges on the suffering of the others within us, these step-by-
step discussions, these interminable analyses, all our ratiocinations
would have been ignoble, the opposite of love and the gift, if they
had not been made in order to give us again the time to touch each
other with words. What counts and is counted then, is what we do
while speaking, what we do to each other, how we again touch each
other by mixing our voices. Not that (no kidding) the infinite sub-
tleties of the *do ut des* would have the upper hand on us, nor its
ungraspable ruse, but so that you are there, and your voice again—
proximity loves me, this is what I say to myself, she still loves me
since she is speaking to me. She is not here but there, she is speaking to me, she brings me near to myself who am so far from everything. She touches me, she takes me in her voice, while accusing
me she cradles me again, she makes me swim, she engulfs me,
you becloud me like a fish, I let myself be loved in the water.
                                                          What counts
then is that it is still up to us to exhaust language, and reason
swerves (and we forget everything that we say, an archive bigger
than the world would be necessary for it, no place would be capable
of it, no imagination which still would stop itself at Himalayas of
books, of dossiers, of cassettes, or of electro-encephalograms, but
in the front rank I recall the position of the bodies, the movement
of the legs which are bent or that always otherwise unbend themselves, the sketched out steps of a false-departure, and that fixed-

ness of the gaze, that way of getting drunk by together fixing upon, for hours and hours and hours, the same picture on the wall, a bit above the secretary, and without seeing it, without even looking at each other, only the ferocious duel, the badgering about which I have never been able to decide which body offered itself to it first, which let itself be butchered, the body of words or yours or mine and this is doubtless a bad question, this irrepressible quibbling, the apparatus of this court of justice permanently in session (we never should have, you see, it never should have happened to us), with eloquent asperities, an amorous rhetoric that recoiled before no genre because it believed itself saved by love—and it was, but all the same—and this attorney general's poetics, this courtroom Orphism which refined the argument to the point of the most delirious overbidding, the most comic transfiguration—and then ecstasy. Overkill, my sweet love, is what drove us crazy, the aphrodisiac overkill of discourse, not ours but the arsenals of reasons, the logistics with which we were armed. For us, ourselves we were naked and without arms. And it is indeed to someone else that we address *ourselves,* and in order to tell him something else, in the close game that we will have played; and that will be played with us for we have lost it, don't you think, and both of us I hope. The others too. We have never been right, nor vanquished anything. It is so sad, to be right I mean. And then I believe that in the end we have never been able to lie to each other. *Mais si, mais si,* listen to me, listen to us

4 September 1977.
        Hound them at the post office. Does the search go through them?
        No, I will never rewrite it, that letter.
                        You have spoken to me again of your "determination," what does that mean? "Determination" is the limit—and first of all of pleasure (from the *Philebus* to the *Beyond* . . .), that which binds energy; it identifies, it decides, it defines, it marks the contours, and then it is the destination (*Bestimmung,* if one wishes to be named that way), and the law and the wasp (Sp) when it is not mad, when it wants to know who and what: and me, then, what do I become in this affair, it would still have to be returned to me somewhat, the letter would still have to come back to its destination, etc.

First stamp, or frank, then obliterate, or punch.

And when I say that I address myself, I address myself one point that's all. Not in order to say this or that, a message or whatever, not even a message that I address to myself, I try to stretch myself a bit, I address myself in the way one arches oneself. And I do not believe that this is my individual lot. Under these conditions how to be sure that one arrives at whatever or whoever at all? The stars decide without which nothing happens.

You who guess everything, guess what I stumbled upon this morning! You are not going to believe me because you have never admitted that I could be so amnesic and so faithful at the same time. *Mais si, mais si,* they are somewhat the same thing. Thus, I had forgotten a passage of Plato's Letter II, that I had cited at length nonetheless at the end of the PP, and that I have refound this instant. I had wanted to reread these Letters, thinking that perhaps I will describe *Socrates and Plato* as an introduction to the *Legs de Freud.* So, here it is, I am copying for you (directly from the translation, too bad): "Consider these facts and take care lest you sometime come to repent of having now unwisely published your views. It is a very great safeguard to learn by heart instead of writing [how many times have I told you!]. It is impossible for what is written not to be disclosed. That is the reason why I have never written anything about these things, and why there is not and will not be any written work of Plato's own. What are now called his are the work of a Socrates in the flower of his youth. Farewell and believe. Read this letter now at once many times and burn it. Enough on this matter . . ."

Good, there, enough on this matter, I am stopping, this is enough, let us go on to something else (*Tauta men tautē*), all the orders that one already pretended to give *oneself,* and more easily by writing letters, more lightly than in another situation, I don't know, in a bed or in a book. Plato already did so, with the carefree familiarity that gives the tone to so many letters. How this brings him near. Okay, I change subject, I come back to my subject so that I do not bore you, but in fact the order that I then feign receiving from you is a permission that I give to myself—and I give them *all* to myself—, the first being to choose my subject, to change subject, to stay with the same one while I am caressing another one with *the same hand,* and while I am irritating a third with my pen or my *grattoir. Tauta men tautē.* I "paralyze" myself.

The order
given to D. by Letter II is indeed the most amorous, most crazy
order, which I had also given to you, my angel (I have never called
you my angel, only written it) and that you did not hear. This order
was not an order, despite the imperative, as they believe (I have just
read another wise book on linguistics and speech acts: "Come"
[*Viens*] would be an order since it is the grammar of an imperative.
One would think that they had never asked themselves what an
order is, that it does not interest them, nor does knowing what
"order" they are "obeying" then, nor how grammar or language can
command, promise, leave to be desired, etc., and the rule of apparent quotation marks, etc. Okay, let's drop it.) My order was the most
abandoned prayer and the most inconceivable simulacrum—for myself first of all. How could I ask you to burn, which is as much as to
say not to read, what I was writing to you? I immediately placed
you in an impossible situation: do not read me, this statement organizes its transgression at the very instant when, by means of the
single event of an understood language (nothing such would occur
for whoever has not been instructed in our language), it assumes
command. It compels the violation of its own law, whatever one
does, and it violates it itself. This is what he destines himself to, at
the very instant. He is destined to violate himself, and this is his
entire beauty, the sadness of his strength, the hopeless weakness of
his all-powerfulness.

But I will arrive, I will arrive at the point where you
will no longer read me. Not only by becoming more illegible than
ever for you (it's beginning, it's beginning), but by doing things such
that you no longer even recall that I am writing for you, that you no
longer even encounter, as if by chance, the "do not read me." That
you do not read me, this is all, so long, ciao, neither seen nor heard,
I am totally elsewhere. I will arrive there, you try too.

4 September 1977. Another pickup, I am coming back.
But in fact, yes,
you had understood my order or my prayer, the demand of the first
letter: "burn everything," understood it so well that you told me
you copied over ("I am burning, stupid impression of being faithful,
nevertheless kept several simulacra, etc.," isn't that it?), in your
writing, and in pencil, the words of that first letter (not the others).
Another way of saying that you had reread it, no?, which is *what*

one begins by doing when one reads, even for the first time. Repetition, memory, etc. I love you by heart, there, between parentheses or quotation marks, such is the origin of the post card. And of all our cheap lithos. P. asks D. to reread before burning, so be it, in order to incorporate the letter (like a member of the resistance under torture) and to take it in him by heart. Keep what you burn, such is the demand. Mourn what I send to you, myself, in order to have me under your skin. No longer *before* you, like someone from whose gaze you could turn away, rejecting his advances, your object, but within you, speaking to you and kissing you without interruption even before you have the chance to breathe and to turn around. To have the other within oneself, right up close but stronger than oneself, and his tongue in your ear before being able to say a word while looking at yourself in the depths of the rearview mirror, in an automobile that passes [*double*] all the others, this is the most mysterious thing, the most worthy of being thought, the least thinkable, my idea of you, the infinite anamnesis of that (which) I saw (the) day

over dessert, almost without transition, she told me that she could only come with someone else. I didn't understand the syntax of her sentence right away.—But of course, it has to be someone else! And she burst out laughing, understanding that I did not understand. Then she explained to me that she experienced as a kind of delicious pathology of which she was not sure she could be, or in truth wanted to be, cured: everything was staged, from the beginning, so that at the last moment she thinks, imagines, invokes, how to put it?, makes present for herself another than the other who was to be found at that instant coming in her. She did now know if she did it on purpose, but she lived as a fatality the necessity of destining her pleasure to the absent one, who moreover was not always the same, the other of the other always possibly being an other. This is naturally, and here I have to quote her, a "surplus" of always available pleasure, and a "fatal deprivation." After a silence: the day that I love someone, man or woman, I am certain, or I believe that it will stop, in any event this is how I will recognize love. I have loved a lot, however, without ever sufficiently abandoning myself to those I loved, presently I mean. And up to the present. Another silence (I had already asked for the bill) and without anything provocative or vulgar, with a kind of confidence which I still like to think of: I have the feeling that with you [*vous*] it would be different.

What has struck me most this morning is that p. writes in a letter (destined to be burned at his request) that it is S. who has written everything. Does he or does he not want this to be known? Now what he puts onstage in his letter to D., is indeed our "frontispiece." *Plato* shows *Socrates* (shows to *Socrates* and shows to someone else that he is showing to *Socrates*, perhaps), he indicates, with his finger, Socrates in the course of writing. And young, as is said in the Letter, younger than *Plato*, and handsomer, and bigger, his big son, his grandfather or his big grandson, his *grandson*. And since Plato writes, without writing, without wanting that a trace be preserved, since he writes, without writing, that Socrates, who passes for someone who has never written, in truth will have written, whether this is known (or not) and will have written just that which he will have written (but who, he?), you can try to forward the inheritance. It is true that Plato specifies: he speaks of the corpus of composed works (*sungramma*). Thereby he would be able to have excluded the letters, *this* Letter of course. Although the question of the criterion for distinguishing between books and letters remains open. I do not believe in the rigor of such a criterion. Everything happens as if our 13th century *Fortune-telling book* (*Prognostica Socratis basilei*) had without seeing or without knowing it, but who knows (could Paris have read this Letter?), illustrated this incredible chicanery of filiation and authority, this family scene without a child in which the more or less adoptive, legitimate, bastard or natural son dictates to the father the testamentary writing which should have fallen to him. And not a daughter in the landscape, apparently, not a word about her in any event. *Fort:da.* Don't they look serious, the two of them, and down to work on their accounting. Look at them closely. Having uncoiffed *Socrates* I have necessarily had to replace the S by an s.

I have put off my departure for a week, for very superstitious reasons that I cannot tell you. In any event it gives us more time.

5 September 1977.

Soon everyone will be there, and me, I will have to leave. The virgin vine has now covered the entire pane [*vitre*], the entire life [*vie*], the room is in darkness, one might say algae, a twilight, I have the impression of floating in a glass coffer, between two waters, long after we

I think that these are, you understand, the last
letters that we are writing each other. We are writing the last letters,
"retro" letters, love letters on a bellépoque poster, but also simply
the last letters. We are taking the last *correspondance*. Soon there
will be no more of them. Eschatology, apocalypse, and teleology of
epistles themselves.

For the same reason there will be no more money, I
mean bills or coins, and no more stamps. Of course the technology
which is replacing all that had already begun to do so for a very
long time. It remains that Plato, who wrote to Dionysos in order to
tell him that the young Socrates had written everything, and to
Freud, whose correspondence is part of his corpus, even including
his "cause," along with everything that still stands in its theoretical
and practical institution (and especially the secret correspondence
on which I am writing at this moment), from Plato to Freud there is
some letter. It is the same world, the same epoch, and the history of
philosophy, like literature, while rejecting the letter into its margins, all the while occasionally affecting to consider it a secondary
genre, was counting with it, essentially. The guardians of tradition,
the professors, academics, and librarians, the doctors and authors
of theses are terribly curious about correspondences (what else can
one be curious about at bottom?), about p.c., private or public correspondences (a distinction without pertinence in this case, whence
the post card, p.c., half-private half-public, neither the one nor the
other, and which does not await the post card *stricto sensu* in order
to define the law of the genre, of all genres), curious about texts
addressed, destined, dedicated by a determinable signer to a particular receiver. These guardians belong, like that which they believe they guard, to the same great epoch, to a great halt, the same,
which forms a set with itself in its postal representation, in its belief in the possibility of this type of correspondence, with all its
technological conditions. By hiding this condition from itself, by
living it as a quasi-natural given, this epoch guards itself, it circulates within itself, it automobilizes itself and looks at itself, up
close to itself, in the image that it sends back to itself—by the post
precisely. Plato and Freud, the same drama, they live under the
same roof or almost. The trajectory of the *fort:da,* in any event,
remains very short (at least in the *representation* that they have of
it, and which rests on the postal tradition, for outside this familiar
and familial representation, they are without relation, moreover
like S. and P. between them, at an infinite distance that no epistle

will ever be able to traverse), let us say the post office down the
street, a mailman on bicycle with clips on his pants deposits the *Philebus* at Berggasse 19 like a pneumatique, and there you are
                                                                        I am teaching
you pleasure, I am telling you the limit and the paradoxes of the
apeiron, and everything begins, like the post card, with reproduction. Sophie and her followers, Ernst, Heinele, myself and company dictate to Freud who dictates to Plato, who dictates to Socrates
who himself, reading the last one (for it is he who reads me, you see
him here, you see what is written on his card in the place where he
is scratching, it is for him that is written the very thing that he is
soon going to sign) again will have forwarded. Postmark on the
stamp, obliteration, no one is any longer heard distinctly, all rights
reserved, law is the rule, but you can always run after the addressee
as well as after the sender. Run in circles, but I promise you that
you will have to run faster and faster, at a speed out of proportion to
the speed of these old networks, or in any event to their images.
Finished, the post, or finally this one, this epoch of the destinal and
of the *envoi* (of the *Geschick* the other old man would say: everything is played out in this, once more, and we will not get around
Freiburg, let it be said in passing. *Geschick* is destiny, of course,
and therefore everything that touches on the destination as well as
on destiny, and even on "sort"—it means "sort," as you know, and
there we are close to the *fortune-telling book*. I also like that this
word *Geschick,* which everything ends up passing through, even
the thinking of the history of Being as dispensation, and even the
gift of the "*es gibt Sein*" or "*es gibt Zeit,*" I like that this word also
says address, not the address of the addressee, but the skill of whoever's turn it is, in order to pull off this or that, chance too somewhat, one dictionary says the "*chic*"—I'm not making it up! And
schicken is to send, *envoyer,* to "expedite," to cause to leave or to
arrive, etc. When Being is thought *on the basis of* the gift of the *es
gibt* (sorry for the simplifying stenography, this is only a letter), the
gift itself is given *on the basis of* "something," which is nothing,
which is not something; it would be, hmmmm, like an "*envoi,*"
destination, the destinality, sorry, of an *envoi* which, of course,
does not send this or that, which sends nothing that is, nothing that
is a "being," a "present." Nor to whoever, to any addressee as an
identifiable and self-present subject. The post is an epoch of the
post, this is not very clear, and how can I write you this in a letter,
and in a love letter, for this is a love letter, you have no doubt, and I

say to you "come," come back quick, and if you understand it it
burns up the road, all the relays, it should not suffer any halt, if you
are there—

P.S. I have again overloaded them with colors, look, I made
up our couple, do you like it? Doubtless you will not be able to
decipher the tatoo on *plato's* prosthesis, the wooden third leg, the
phantom-member that he is warming up under *Socrates'* ass.

6 September 1977. I can't go on, I would like never to miss a
pickup, and at least describe to you my impatience so that you
hurry up a bit.

Okay, I've calmed down, and I will profit from it by clearing
up, a bit, the story of the address, finally of the *Geschick.* This is
very difficult, but everything is played out there. If what is called
the post in the usual sense, in the strict sense if you wish, what
everyone believes they understand under this heading (a same type
of service, a technology which goes from the *courrier* of Greek or
Oriental antiquity, along with the messenger who runs from one
place to another, etc., up to the State monopoly, the airplane, the
telex, the telegram, the different kinds of mailmen and delivery,
etc.), if this post is only an epoch of the *envoi* in general—and
along with its *tekhnē* it also implies a million things, for example
identity, the possible identification of the emitters and the receivers,
of the subjects of the post and of the poles of the message—, then
to speak of post for *Geschick,* to say that every *envoi* is postal, *that
the destinal posts itself,* is perhaps a "metaphoric" abuse, a restriction to its strict sense of a sense which does not permit itself to be
narrowed into this sense. Doubtless this is what Martin would object. Although . . . For finally, one would have to be quite confident
of the notion of "metaphor" and of its entire regime (more than he
himself was, but there we would have to see . . . there is also what-
I-call, citation, "the metaphoric catastrophe") in order to treat the
figure of the post this way. The thing is very serious, it seems to me,
for if there is first, so to speak, the *envoi,* the *Schicken* reassembling itself into *Geschick,* if the *envoi* derives from nothing, then
the possibility of posts is always already there, in its very retreat
[*retrait*]. As soon as *there is,* as soon as it gives (*es gibt*), it destines, it tends (hold on, when I say "come" to you, I tend to you, I
tender nothing, I tender you, yourself, I tend myself toward you, I
await [*attends*] you, I say to you "hold," keep what I would like to

give you, I don't know what, more than me doubtless, keep, come, halt, reassemble, hold us together, us and more than you or me, we are awaited [*attendus*] by this very thing, I know neither who nor what, and so much the better, this is the condition, by that very thing which destines us, drop it), as soon as there is, then, it destines and it tends (I will show this in the preface, if I write it one day, by rereading the play of *Geben, Schicken,* and *Reichen* in *Zeit und Sein*). If I take my "departure" from the destination and the destiny or destining of Being (*Das Schicken im Geshick des Seins*), no one can dream of then *forbidding me to speak* of the "post," except on the condition of making of this word the element of an image, of a figure, of a trope, a post card of Being in some way. But to do it, I mean to accuse me, to forbid me, etc., one would have to be naively certain of knowing what a post card or the post is. If, on the contrary (but this is not simply the contrary), I think the postal and the post card on the basis of the destinal of Being, as I think the house (of Being) on the basis of Being, of language, and not the inverse, etc., then the post is no longer a simple metaphor, and is even, as the site of all transferences and all correspondences, the "proper" possibility of every possible rhetoric. Would this satisfy Martin? Yes and no. No, because he doubtless would see in the postal determination a premature (?) imposition of *tekhnē* and therefore of metaphysics (he would accuse me, you can see it from here, of constructing a metaphysics of the posts or of postality); and above all an imposition of the *position* precisely, of determining the *envoi* of Being as position, posture, thesis or theme (*Setzung, thesis,* etc.), a gesture that he alleges *to situate,* as well as technology, within the history of metaphysics and within which would be given to think a dissimulation and a retreat [*retrait*] of Being in its *envoi.* This is where things are the most difficult: because the very idea of the retreat (proper to destination), the idea of the halt, and the idea of the epoch in which Being holds itself back, suspends, withdraws, etc., all these ideas are immediately homogenous with postal discourse. To post is to send by "counting" with a halt, a relay, or a suspensive delay, the place of a mailman, the possibility of going astray and of forgetting (not of repression, which is a moment of keeping, but of forgetting). The *epokhē* and the *Ansichhalten* which essentially scan or set the beat of the "destiny" of Being, or its "appropriation" (*Ereignis*), is the place of the postal, this is where it comes to be and that it takes place (I would say *ereignet*), that it gives place and also lets come to be. This is serious because it upsets perhaps Heidegger's still "derivative" schema (perhaps), upsets by giving one to think that technology, the position, let us say even metaphysics do not overtake, do not come *to determine* and to dissimulate an "*envoi*" of Being (which would not yet be postal), but would belong to the "first" *envoi*— which obviously is never "first" in any order whatsoever, for example a chronological or logical order, nor even the order of *logos* (this is why one cannot replace, except for laughs, the formula "in the beginning was the logos" by "in the beginning was the post"). If the post (technology, position, "metaphysics") is announced at the "first" *envoi,* then there is no longer A metaphysics, etc. (I will try to say this one more time and otherwise), nor even AN *envoi,* but *envois* without destination. For to coordinate the different epochs, halts, determinations, in a word the entire history of Being with a destination of Being is perhaps the most outlandish postal lure. There is not even the post or the *envoi,* there are *posts* and *envois.* And this movement (which seems to me simultaneously very far from and very near to Heidegger's, but no matter) avoids submerging all the differences, mutations, scansions, structures of postal regimes into one and the same great central post office. In a word (this is what I would like to articulate more rigorously if I write it one day in another form), as soon as there is, there is *différance* (and this does not await language, especially human language, and the language of Being, only the mark and the divisible trait), and there is postal maneuvering, relays, delay, anticipation, destination, telecommunicating network, the possibility, and therefore the fatal necessity of going astray, etc. There is strophe (there is strophe in every sense, apostrophe and catastrophe, address in turning the address [always toward you, my love], and my post card is strophes). But this specification gives one the possibility of assimilating none of the differences, the (technical, eco-political, phantasmatic etc.) differentiation of the telecommunicative powers. By no longer treating the posts as a metaphor of the *envoi* of Being, one can account for what essentially and decisively occurs, everywhere, and including language, thought, science, and everything that conditions them, when the postal structure shifts, *Satz* if you will, and posits or posts itself otherwise. This is why this history of the posts, which I would like to write and to dedicate to you, cannot be a history of the posts: primarily because it concerns the very possibility of history, of all the concepts, too, of history, of tradition, of the transmision or interruptions, goings astray, etc. And then because such a "history of the posts" would be but a minuscule *envoi* in the network that it allegedly would analyze (there is no metapostal), only a card lost in a bag, that a strike, or even a sorting accident, can always delay indefinitely, lose without return. This is why I will not write it, but I dedicate to you what remains of this impossible project. The (eschatological, apocalyptic) desire for this history of the posts worldwide is perhaps only a way, a very infantile way, of crying over the coming end of our "correspondence"—and of sending you one more tear. And this does not happen one day in the world, this is the world, the becoming-world of the world, etc. The *Geviert* too, the loveliest post card that Martin has sent us from Freiburg, but he already was forwarding it moreover: the simplicity (for a post card is never but a piece of a letter, a letter that puts itself, at the very second of the pickup, *into pieces*, and every piece *appears* simple, simpleminded, ingenuous and above all indivisible, unanalyzable) the simplicity of the fourfold: the sky and the earth, the gods and the mortals.

How nice it is that you called me back immediately. I caressed your voice, and do so again now. The sense of urgency has been somewhat relaxed, *but please, come.* Leave them, they don't need you, those ones, not you really, you see. Me, I wait.

7 September 1977.

of course it is to Socrates that I am addressing myself at this very moment, you are all a crowd, my sweet love, and you see him reading me at this very instant, already in the course of answering me. I would do anything for him, he is the only one who listens to me.

I clearly see that you were shocked by what I had to tell you that really went on with her (nothing in fact, but I tell you everything). She used the finest words on earth in order to describe what she was missing. And that she visibly wanted to give me or expect from me;

that you are "my wife" was not obvious at the outset, and it was necessary to multiply marriages and alliances, but this is less and less doubtful in my eyes, if destiny (sort, lot, chance) means in the end the end of a life. And yet—

No literature, yes, but still.

Our delinquency, my love, we are the worst criminals and the first victims. I would like not to kill anyone, and everything that I send you goes through *meurtrières* [vertical slots in the wall of a fortification for project-

ing weapons; murderesses]. As for the children, the last ones I might touch, the holocaust has already begun.
We have never yet seen each other. Only written.

7 September 1977.

yes, I was speaking to you of the *Rat Man*. Nothing about it has been understood yet, or so I feel. There are other way-stations, doubtless, and here I am not referring to the itineraries between the post office and the station (F.'s little drawing), nor to the stories tied up with it. The dependence of "Freudism" as concerns the postal or monetary moment is not limited to "external" technology. Between the so-called "external" technology and the most apparently pure conceptual theorization (the "speculation" on the agencies, on the relation between the "principles" of pleasure and reality, between the primary and the secondary) as well as the concepts of practice, the modes of writing, Freud's "autography" and "autobiography," between the so-called "external" organization of relays and everything I have just enumerated pell-mell, the passage is essential, constitutive, irreducible. Not a step of Freud's which does not come back to it.

I don't know if I'll send you this letter since you are here in so few days. I will give it to you. But I cannot stop myself, nor miss the chance of a pickup, I have to write to you all the time when you are not here—and even when you are here and I am still alone (the old impossible dream of exhaustive and instantaneous registration—for I hold to words above all, words whose rarefaction is unbearable for me in writing—, the old dream of the complete electro-cardio-encephalo-LOGO-icono-cinemato-bio-gram. And flat—I mean first of all without the slightest literature, the slightest superimposed fiction, without pause, without selection either of the code or of the tone, without the slightest secret, nothing at all, only everything—and flat in the end because if such a card were possible, even if for only a very brief lapse of time (afterwards they would need centuries of university to decipher it), I could finally die content. Unless it sent me directly to hell, for there is nothing I fear more than this exposition without envelope [*pli*]. And for me to go away content it would still be necessary that I be able to send it to you registered, this final total card (my absolute *pancarte*), that you be able to read it, hold it in your hands, on your knees, under your eyes, in you, that you inherit it and guard it, reproduce my pictures and my caption—and above all that in my absence you again be seduced in my confession to the point of dying for love. In the last analysis I do nothing that does not have some interest in seducing you, in setting you astray from yourself in order to set you on the way toward me, uniquely—nevertheless you do not know who you are nor to whom precisely I am addressing myself. But there is only you in the world.

7 September 1977. So I telegraphed again to announce that I had to delay my arrival. They will wind up by getting angry at me or by no longer wanting to have anything to do with me. Before you I was irreproachably punctual, I never kept anyone waiting.

Fine, to distract you, know that in the moments when I stop writing to you I am working, or rather the posts continue to work on me, posts of every genre and sex. In "encyclopedia" style (and the encyclopedia is an immense poste restante), here are some extracts from Voltaire, that I count on using for my preface. They are from the article *Post,* and you will be amused to note, as I have underlined, that everything is *done* [*fait*] there, or *to be done* [*à faire*], the post office is the site of the great affair, truly; for me the post office is a church in which secret rendez-vous are given, Notre-Dame on Sunday afternoon in the crowd, at the time of the organ concerts, or a Great Synagogue in all its brouhaha, at the end of Yom Kippur. Everything is possible there. When I enter the post office of a great city I tremble as if in a sacred place, full of refused, promised, threatening pleasures. It is true that inversely I often have a tendency to consider the great temples as noisy sorting centers, with very agitated crowds before the distribution begins, like the auctioning of an enormous *courrier.* Occasionally the preacher opens the epistles and reads them aloud. This is always the truth. Okay, here are the selections from Voltaire that I typed out for myself (sorry, I am keeping the copy): ". . . if one of your friends needs to have access [*faire toucher*] to money in Petersburg and the other in Smyrna, the post is just what you need [*fait votre affaire*] [except of course if you want to be paid by hand, and not be taxed, and run the risk of counterfeit money, without a bank, without a post office, without a stamp, without a guarantee, neither seen nor heard, another affair] . . . should she be in Bordeaux, and you before Prague with your regiment, she regularly assures you of her tender feelings; through her you get all the news of the city, excepting the infidelities she commits [*fait*]. Finally the post office is the place of all *affairs,* all negotiations; through it the absent become present; it is the consolation of life." I could cite this masterpiece in the *Legs* (at the end of *Beyond* . . . in a passage that detains me at length, Freud speaks curiously of "consolation" and cites a citation from Scripture). Why Bordeaux and Prague I ask myself. (Speaking of Bordeaux, do you have any news about my letter and your demand?) I like to copy over long texts for you, for you only, otherwise it's a drag. I am your old secretary, you burden me with everything, even with *my* letters (that's hypercrypted and if one day these crosswords fall into their hands, they can always run around in order to catch up with a meaning in them.

Our amorous bureaucracy, our erotic secretariat, we will have confided too much to them not to lose the control and memory of it. They now have the autonomy which is killing revolutions (getting fat and the police). The real enigma, the absolute stenography— one has to be right in the room in order to know how to decipher, along with the other. But I would like to be your secretary. While you were out I would transcribe your manuscripts of the night before or the tapes on which you would have improvised, I would make several discreet interventions that you alone would recognize, I would watch the children that you would have given me (this is indeed your dream, no?, yours too), I would even breast-feed them, and almost permanently would hear the next one breathing in my belly. We would keep all of them. You always would be in me or behind me, I would be accessible, at bottom, only to your tongue, your tongue alone.

On stenography, old Voltaire again: "To circumvent the crush of the curious, it was first imagined to write a part of the dispatches in ciphers; but the portion of ordinary characters sometimes served to lead to the discovery of the others. This inconvenience led to the perfecting of the art of ciphers, called *stenography.* Opposed to these enigmas was the art of deciphering them; but this art was very faulty and very vain. One succeeded only in making [*faire*] the unknowledgeable believe that their letters had been deciphered, and one had but the pleasure of causing them to worry. Such is the law of probability that in a well made [*fait*] cipher it is two hundred, three hundred, four hundred to one that for each numeral you will not guess the syllable it represents. The number of chances increases with the combination of these numerals; and the deciphering becomes almost totally impossible when the cipher is made [*fait*] with any art at all. Those who boast of deciphering a letter without having knowledge of the *affairs* [again!] treated in it, and without having some preliminary assistance, are greater charlatans than those who boast of understanding a language that they have never learned." A king and his police, with all its lieutenants, is what haunts Voltaire's discourse. Each time that it is a question of *courrier,* in one guise or another, there is police, royal police—and a basilica, a royal house, an edifice or edification of the law, the place in which justice is rendered (with merchants near the lower porticos) or a temple, a religious metropolis. All of it, if possible, in the service of the king who disposes of the *courrier,* the seals, of the emissaries as well as of the addressees, his subjects. Finally he would consent, see *The Purloined Letter,* and the queen too, and Dupin too, and the psychoanalyst too—but there you are, there is the post card which supports partition and which always opens on the side of literature, if you are willing to call this adestination. At this point it no longer comes back circularly. No rigorous theory of "reception," however necessary it might be, will get to the end of that literature. There, basta for tonight, my *Prognostica Socratis basilei* . . .

7 September 1977.
        the one that I call Esther. You know, I confided to you one day, why I love her. Her or her name, go figure it out, and each letter of her name, of her syngram or her anagram. The quest for the syngram Esther, my whole life. One day I will divulge, I do not yet accept them enough to tell them. Only this, for you, today. Estér is the queen, the second one, the one who replaces Vashti for Ahasheuros. What she saves her people from, a holocaust without fire or flame, you will understand nothing about without the circulation of money and missives, without the itinerary of the royal *courrier,* of the one who runs: to transmit orders, and to ensure order. The king gives money to Haman, he gives him at first the royal seal in order to put his project into execution. And Haman, who then wields the king's signature, gives the order of extermination. To secretaries, to "actuaries." One imagines them seated, perhaps, while the bearded old man dictates the horror to them. I copy Chouraqui's translation, I don't know what it's worth: "The actuaries of the king are convoked / the first lunar cycle, the thirteenth day. / It is written all that Haman has ordered / to the king's satraps, to the pashas of towns and towns, / to the ministers of peoples and peoples, / town and town according to his writing, /

people and people according to his tongue, / written in the name
of the king Ahasheuros, and sealed with the seal of the king. /
The acts are sent in the hands of runners / to all the towns of the
king / to exterminate, to kill and to betray / all the Yehudim, from
the youth to the old man, children and women, in a single day, the
thirteenth of the twelfth lunar cycle, / itself, the cycle of Adar, /
and their spoils to be pillaged. / A copy of the writing is given as
law to every town and town, / as evidence to all peoples to be ready
on that day. / The runners go out in haste with the king's word. /
The law is given in Shushan, the capital. / The king and Haman sit
down to drink." Then Mordecai informs Estér: about the money
given to Haman, about the law whose "copy" he has had transmitted to her. What Estér then succeeds in doing, therefore is suspending death—"the death sentence" (*"l'arrêt de mort"*)—(this is
the subtitle chosen by Chouraqui—I suppose that this is his choice,
and in his preface he says that "Estér is to be recited in the syn-
agogues 'as one reads a letter.'") Estér suspends the carnage by de-
touring a letter, when all is said and done. She arrests, she intercepts (although it was essential that she *be found there,* that she be
on the itinerary). And she substitutes another one for it—for the
counter-order, the one which is "written to revoke the acts of the
plan of Haman ben Hamdata, the Agaqui, / that he wrote in order
to betray the Yehudim / who are in all the towns of the king," this
counter-order of revocation gives rise to the same scene of writing:
the royal seal, the acts, the "runners mounted on royal coursers"
"dispatched and hurried with the word of the king." Etc. I am going
to tell you now what intrigues and interests me the most at the moment: it is what links these *arrêts de mort,* these letters which give
and suspend death, what links them to *fate,* to good and bad fate, to
the writing of chance, of destiny, of accident, of prediction in that it
throws out a fate (*prognostica* and *fortune-telling,* if you prefer).
For the feast of Estér (Purim) is a feast of fate. Haman, in his "ma-
levolent plan," "had thrown the *Pur*—lot—in order to destroy
them and betray them." "For which reason they have called these
days Purim / according to the name of the Pur, / for which reason,
for all the words of this missive / and for what they had seen on this
matter / and for what had happened to them, / the Yehudim fulfill
and accept / for themselves and for their seed / and for all those
who come to join them, / and this will never end, / to be to make
these two days / according to their writing and their time / in every
year and year. / These days are commemorated and celebrated /
from age to age, from town to town, from city to city. / These days

of Purim will never end among the Yehudim, / their memory will not be finished for their seed. / Estér, the queen, daughter of Avihayil, / written with Mordecai, the Yehudi, with all authority / in order to fulfill this Purim missive, the second. / He sends these acts to all the Yehudim, / to the one hundred twenty-seven towns [. . .] The pronouncement of Estér finishes these words of Purim: / it is written in the volume." 127, does that remind you of anything? divine. And the thirteenth of the twelfth lunar cycle? One day I will write a long narrative for you, not a detail will be missing, not a candle light, not a flavor, not an orange, a long narrative about what the Purim cakes were in El-Biar, when I was ten years old and already understood nothing.

I am still waiting for you.

7 September 1977. Just hung up. Your question was wounding. I repeat, my love: *for you.* I write for you and speak only to you. You are perhaps the only one to know it, but you do know it, and in any case better than anyone; and you have no reason to doubt it, no more than this card that you are reading now, that you are holding in your hands or on your knees. Even if you did not believe what I am writing on it, you see that I am writing it to you, you are touching it, you are touching the card, my signature, the body of my name, me—and it is indeed you who, now, right here . . .—do you love me?

7 September 1977.
        And if instead of Judith I called you Esther? I would surprise the entire globe by saying that for me you resemble her. This would make it necessary to expose so many invisible trajectories (certain ones still are invisible for me). In any case, what is most singular for me is that she had two names, apparently, somewhat like you, but Esther was not, contrary to what I believed, her Hebrew name. It was her name as a Persian queen, the wife of Xerxes or of Assueros, as you will, her public name, her official name. While for me—finally for what (of myself, without me) I have recently been led to presume about my attachment to the literality of this sublime name, Esther is a Hebrew and hidden name, remaining such today even though I know nevertheless, from reading *The Interpreter's Dictionary of the Bible* (a gift from the one who gave me this name of Esther), that this was the name of

the queen and not the name of the maiden. We all have so many
first names. But you also will like her name as a young orphan, I
would like to make you wait before telling you it and leaving you
with it, withdrawing while leaving you with it, it lacks nothing:
Hadassah.

Mordecai "is the guardian of Hadassah, herself, Esther, / the
daughter of his uncle. / No, she has neither father nor mother." The
only one I could marry. At the moment of marrying, in order to
marry, if by chance it were possible one day, there no longer would
be either father or mother (I'm telling you, or this is what I tell myself occasionally). And guess what Hadassah means. Try, it's something that you gave me one day, and that you followed, some time
after, with an explicative letter, miming the science, no, not astrology, try to divine (to help you along: the science of plants and the
science of religions).

Between us, the truth is that I am not at all sure of
being attached to the name of Esther, despite the spectacularly
probable and well-supported character of the hypothesis according
to which it should be the most precious name for me, the name of
names on the basis of which I make everything, how to put it, descend, yes, descend. I would descend all of them starting from Esther. The commentators on this book have often been struck by its
abandon, if not its irreligiousness. Everything aiming at the feast of
Purim (fate, then) and not a reference to God. I am copying for you
(this typescript of which I am keeping the copy is with sights set on
my preface and on what will follow from it, it will be my first book
of Esther), here it is, without translation: "*The book of Esther itself, however, seems deliberately to avoid specific references to
God or to religious practice. God is not mentioned in the book,
even when the sense seems to demand it, as when Mordecai suggests that deliverance for the Jews may arise 'from another quarter'
if not from Esther herself (4:14). Prayer does not accompany fast-
ing in Esther's preparation for putting her request before the king
(4:16). Victory seems to depend, not so much on loyalty to Juda-
ism (cf. the book of Daniel), as on the use of political maneuver and appeal to self-interest. It is going too far to say that Esther 'has no religious content and can arouse no pious thoughts'
(Schauss . . .) but certainly piety in its usual sense receives little
emphasis in this book.*"

Further on, "*Pur, that is the lot.*"

Everything in this book
remains "*difficult to tell,*" they say, this is what is important for me

doubtless, but in order to hide what? *"Whether the author invented a wholly fictional account together with the festival of Purim which it purports to explain, whether he was putting in Jewish form a Babylonian festival which originated in mythical adventures of the divine cousins Marduk and Ishtar, or whether he based his romance on some incidents involving the historical Xerxes and Marduka [. . .] is difficult to tell. In any case, it seems probable that the book of Esther is primarily romance, not history."* Here you are set. *"Xerxes' queen was neither Vashti nor Esther, but Amestris."*

By all appearances Esther, if not Hadassah, does something entirely different, even the opposite, if you compare her to the queen of *The Purloined Letter*. Here it is the king who pays, who pays a minister, it is true, and not a private police, and then the king again who takes back his (public) missive in order to substitute another one for it, following the order or the desire of the second queen. But these are the appearances and why compare? Finally she sets things up further to have Haman, the minister, hanged, yes hanged (*pendre*), after having had him replaced by another minister who is her uncle, or her adoptive father—whose "dream" she thus fulfills (in the Additions to the volume translated from the Greek, everything begins with "Mordecai's dream")—who then is substituted for Haman, he whom we "called our father. He occupied the second place after the royal throne."

Tomorrow, if I want to write this preface, I will set myself to running down all the paleo- and neo-testamentary *courriers*. And why not, while I'm at it, all the death sentences [*arrêts de mort*] and all the police regulations [*arrêtés de police*] on the pretext that they are sent or signify! and that everything that is sent willy-nilly is law . . . Also turns the law, plays on it, but that's the law.

I am terrified at the idea of this return and yet the impatience

7 September 1977.

when you cease frightening me and making me watch out for signs. I am always ready for everything, for the worst sentence, from one instant to the next. It's true, you were not aware of it, that you have made the disaster irreversible by telling me with the cruelest vulgarity "the day it happens, I will not even send you a telegram." At this second, when I wish that you no longer existed, that you had never even seen daylight for me, that you were nothing but a proxy, I let this phrase be heard, and I see again the very place, the situation in which you dared to drive it into me. You were behind me, glued to me, I felt your breath on my neck—I came close to screaming but I held back the malediction, once again. As so often with you, I was sure that my head had ceased belonging to me.

8 September 1977. At this moment the mailman gives me back, "into the proper hands," the letter that I had sent you P.R. I had mistaken the postal code and there are several villages with the same name in your department. Luckily, as I always advise you, although you never listen to me, I had my address on the back of the letter. This story is unbelievable. The mailman explains to me that if it is a little hamlet and they suspect an error because they know everyone there, they return to sender, at least when possible. Strange story, you again will suspect me of not having sent it. I do not dare open it to reread it. Moreover these are "details," as you said to me one day, only details which I thought would make me look innocent in your eyes. I am no longer sure, I no longer recall very clearly what I wrote (I mean the detail) and this is why I no longer dare open it. I will show you the envelope when you have returned, so that you believe me. But I will not send it to you a second time—in any case I believe that I will never reread it. When you will have seen the still sealed envelope, I will destroy the whole thing, doubtless. Taking my point of departure from the sacred principle that you must believe me (declare me innocent or pardon me, acquit me or forget, as you will, but believe me without proof, without narrative, without detail). In any event what has happened here remains infinitely foreign to you, does not touch you, and is not to touch you in any way; infinite distance. It doesn't touch me, doesn't concern me *myself,* I who wrote to you, who you know and who loves you.

8 September 1977.
       You just hung up (the intermittent hissing that always follows: it drives me crazy enough to kill). Don't insist, please. I wrote to you yesterday (you will receive the note today or tomorrow doubtless) and say it to you again at this second: I believe that I will not go back on my decision not even to reopen the letter and especially not to send it to you a second time. You have to believe me

and my reasons are the best in the world, my intentions too. My decision grows firmer since yesterday, moreover, and from hour to hour. We shall have never to speak of it again, the letter and what it contains. As for what it contains, I am myself already beginning, I must say, to transform, to deform it, or rather to becloud it, to make it flare out, I don't know. I no longer see its borders distinctly. Amnesia, what a force. It is necessary to forget, to know how to forget, to know how to forget without knowing. To forget, you understand, not to confound. Naturally, I don't believe it at all. Nor you—

9 September 1977. I am not well this morning. There will never be any possible consolation, the disaster is ineffaceable. And yet, at this very moment when the ineffaceable appears to me as the self-evident itself, the opposite conviction is just as strong. The entire misfortune, the unlivable suffering that you know always will be capable of dissipating itself at this second, was in sum due only to a bad chance, a stroke of fate, an instant that we are no longer even sure had the slightest consistency, the slightest thickness of life. Disaster—we have dreamed of it, no? One day will suffice that—

I knew you would fall into the trap. No, Hadassah is myrtle. I think I was wrong the other day: in fact it was I who brought some to you (in a pot, with something red planted in the leaves), and it was you who, as if in return, had addressed to me that sage letter about the rites, symbolic meanings, etc., of this plant sacred to Aphrodite. I will have to refind what you explained to me so eruditely. Today, I read that "the name of this plant" "serves to designate either the clitoris or the woman's genital"! A fine distinction, don't you think? In turn, since you are called Hadassah, I will explain to you all the stories about Myrrhina and about Myrrha, the "seducer of her father," and all the "perfume" of Adonis is not far off, which is connected by some to the name of *hēdonē.* You recognize my sources. I have always suspected perfume of being at the very principle of pleasure, and (but) this is just why I have always been a bit afraid of it: as if perfume were immoral and vulgar, associated with venal sexuality, and at the same time a sign of impotence or of fear (they need it in order to desire or to make themselves desired, they are so anxious!). Why am I thinking now of that eau de cologne that they pour over the dead by liters, at home, before the body is placed in the bier? Of my father, precisely?

.

9 September 1977.

and I write to you that I love the delicate levers which pass between the legs of a word, between a word and itself to the point of making entire civilizations seesaw. Suppose that at the end of reading something, one of the voices of the book murmurs to you something like: every time I said *"arrive,"* I was thinking of you, not in the sense of the accident that happens [*arrive*], of the event that happens [*arrive*], of the letter that arrives, or not, but of you. Not of what I expect *from you,* as if your coming were still an accident of yours, but of you, uniquely, you who arrive, who are what arrives, you who are for me what arrives, what comes to me from a single venue. The text then sees itself transfigured by this, they would have to reread everything, and the other texts from the beginning of time, or at least, which is not so bad, from the dawns of the French language. And if another voice in the same book says: everything is connoted in *do,* there are only the *dos* that count, look back over the entire scansion (not the *das* as in *fort/da* or derrida, but also the most trailing, drawling *dos,* like *derrière les rideaux* [behind the curtains]), then it would be necessary to go through everything once more, which is one more book. And if another voice comes to add that everything was calculated, more or less, in order to accentuate, in other words to sing the play of the *pours* [fors] and the (long) *às* [tos], and that the entire book is *pour toi* [for you], but for this very reason dedicated to "to" ["à"], devoted to the dative, by chance then they can always run. And everything would be done so that they might run: never oblige them to stop, except to catch their breath, for one desire is to leave them their breath, and life. And simultaneously, this is what leaves reliefs in the text, always more than you think.

No matter which way you turn, you see again the back of a post card or of a hunchback. You always have something to caress, it brings happiness.

9 September 1977. I will come to wait for you. This will be my last letter, I mean before you are there. Do I write to you in order to bring you near or in order to distance you, to find the best distance—but then with whom? The question is posed when you are in the next room, or even when in the same room, barely turning my back to you, I write to you again, when I leave a note under your pillow or in the letter box upon leaving, the essential not being that you are absent or present at the moment when I write to you but

that I am not there myself, when you are reading, that is, still there, myself, preventing you from breathing, from breathing without me, otherwise than through me. You can't stand it any more, no?
                                                            If you came
back alone we could once again abuse the photomaton in the station. As always we would not succeed in looking at each other, turned symmetrically the one toward the other hoping that the machine's eye finally will surprise, in order to fix it, the point of intersection, the unique one, of the two glances. The one then will look at the other who will look elsewhere, and it will remain like that in a wallet. When I photograph myself alone in stations or airports, I throw it away or tear the thing into little pieces that I let fly out the window if it is a train, leave them in an ashtray or in a magazine if it's an airplane.

My letters are too knowing (stuffed epistles) but this is in order to "banalize" them, to cipher them somewhat better. And then in any event, I no longer know whom I wrote this to one day, letters are always post cards: neither legible nor illegible, open and radically unintelligible (unless one has faith in "linguistic," that is grammatical, criteria: for example to reach the conclusion from the fact that I say "it's nice that you are back [*revenue*]" that I am certainly writing to a woman; this would be as daring, in your case, as using it to infer the color of your hair), offered to all the transfers of collectors—and it takes right away because of the stereotypes behind which one imagines fabulous stories of voyages, one speculates on unbelievable or too believable family romances, with police stories, commercial trafficking, intrigues from which all the cards might be recomposed, and then they are all dead, and then because of the clichés the letter is immediately dispersed or multiplied, a divided echo of itself (finally it consists only of its "proper" support, or almost, and this support is already a reproduction, which moreover, like every support, is something less than ideal, and therefore can be destroyed without remaining), it is lost for the addressee at the very second when it is inscribed, its destination is immediately multiple, anonymous, and the sender, as they say, and the addressee, yourself, my beloved angel; and yet how I miss you, you, you alone now, I cry over you and smile at you, here, now, right here. And since we have already spoken, much better, much more abundantly about all that, along with my tears these are memories that I am sending to you, the essential remaining that I send to you, that I touch you by sending you whatever, even if it is nothing, even if it is without the slightest interest.

As concerns the "knowing" letters, you know, you alone, that I have always known how to use knowledge in order to distance the curious and in order to make me loved by you by giving free rein to my jealousy, in order to try to make the most untranslatable, most untransportable, least supportable messages, unbearably idiomatic messages reach you—by the post, by all the public *facteurs*. But this is impossible, in any case it can only await your grace, if you are willing to give me what I write to you, you my immense, you my unique destiny. I do not use the language of everyone, the language of knowledge, in order to bedeck myself or to establish my mastery, only in order to erase all the traits, neutralize all the codes and you know, I believe that I could manipulate all the codes, all the keyboards, all the genres (this disgusts me), speak in every tone—and this anguishes me, and at every instant the comedy seems ready to take over every word, then I silence myself, I send you voluble, interminable letters, which are but poor post cards, this is my shame. We are experts in shame, thus we leave to the obscene its chances. In your second letter you already had played on this word, "obscene," in order to say what you desired for us, and I see myself again, walking without looking around me (sudden state of weightlessness) after having unsealed the letter (

                              had crossed my path and put a hand on my arm). What I have not yet accepted must indeed be called divulging. The part of divulging in the slightest, most reserved, most neutral publication I still find inadmissible, unjustifiable—and above all r-i-d-i-c-u-l-o-u-s, comical a priori. Not condemnable but a priori deriving from the comic genre. There is someone in me who kills with a burst of laughter whoever appears to find it necessary, opportune, important to say what he thinks, feels, lives, or anything you like. Of course I do not escape the slaughter. In the name of what, in the name of whom publish, divulge—and first of all write, since it amounts to the same? I have published a lot, but there is someone in me, I still can't quite identify him, who still hopes never to have done it. And he believes that in everything that I have let pass, depart, a very effective mechanism comes to annihilate the exposition. I write while concealing every possible divulging of the very thing which appears to be published. For tell me what is the imperative, in the end? With sights set on whom, for whom accept to divulge?

Let everything become a post card again, they will have only post cards from me, never the true letter, which is reserved uniquely for you, not for your name (moreover you have too many of them, now, names, and they are on all lips), for you. For you the living one.

You will tell me that this apparently disdainful detestation (it's not that) contradicts both my cult of post cards and what I state about the impossiblity that a unique addressee ever be identified, or a destination either, therefore. Nor therefore an answer or a responsibility. And that this is not in tune with the fact that a letter, at the very instant when it takes place (and I am not only speaking of consciousness), divides itself, puts itself into pieces, falls into a post card. Well yes, this is our tragic lot, my sweet love, the atrocious lottery, but I begin to love you on the basis of this impossibility; the impasse devoted to fate cannot leave us to await anything from a chance to see it open itself one day. We know that this is unthinkable, and that God himself could not provide for the aleatory in this form (yes, God would be impotent to make possible today what you know remains forbidden to us, God himself, which should give you the measure of the thing), but the chance of the impasse devoted to fate can be the impasse itself, and what comes to pass in it for being unable to pass. This chance (affirmation without exit) can only come to us from you, understand? Do you understand me? Do I have to invent another name for you so that you give us the chance? or that the other finally awakens, another of your secret names?

           I am rereading (and indeed for the first time since I have been writing to you) because you overtook me while writing at the moment when you called from the café. No, I repeat what I have just told you: there was nothing "decisive" in my PR letter—moreover I have not reopened it—, only details which perhaps, perhaps would have made you understand and approve, if you wanted, if you could. Okay, let's drop it. I am rereading myself, thus, and at the word "lottery" I am thinking of this, three things: of my mother who was playing poker (already, always! while—no, she hardly plays at all any more, and I regret it, although I previously used to resent it) at my birth, at the moment of the first pains which overtook her with cards in hand; of our bridge games, even before our beginning (you kept score on scraps of paper that you still have); finally, very soon after the birth, ours, that singular evening at the casino (you remember what came after, the period, the mad return, the two drunk sailors, those red-bearded Englishmen who wanted to enter the hotel with us, and we had closed the door). Yes, a lot, the atrocious lottery, we will be able neither to keep nor to lose ourselves, and this is what loves us, what holds us "by heart." This bottomless misfortune, the disaster of this chance, I understand that others do not succeed in bearing it, it is unbearable and myself I do not seek to bear it. One can only lose one's breath winning out over it [*à en avoir raison*] (whence reason, which is nothing other, but with reason we do not love each other)

I mean when Plato, for example, sends that recommendation, and not to just anyone, to the tyrannical power himself, to Dionysos (you remember, we had spoken of jumping over toward Sicily that summer, we were right near it, you were against it when misfortune would have it that, on the coast south of Rome, that accursed phone call broke out over us, truly a blow— and the worst is that nothing had obliged me to call that night myself), when he writes that he has written none of all that, that there is no work, no "syngram" of P., only of S., doubtless without thinking a word of it but who knows, he speaks of the best "safeguard," of the best "guard": not to write but to learn by heart. The word *guard* [*garde*]: at this second I love it, I tell it that I love it, I also like to say it to myself, make it sing, let the *a* drag on for a long time, stretch it out at length, it is the voice, my vowel, the most *marked* letter, everything begins with it. In Greek it is also a superb word, *phulakē: la* garde but also *le* garde, the sentinel (want to relate this word to what is said in *Beyond* . . . about the *Lebenswachter,* the guardians of life who are also the satellites of death (*Trabanten des Todes*). *Phulakē* also says the *place* of guarding, the prison for example, and then surveillance, defense, protection, etc. The law and the police are not far off. And "phylactery" comes from that. You know what this represents for us, for us Jews finally. But you will understand why I started just now reading this definition in my dictionary: "*phulakterion* . . . place for guarding, *post,* guard corps . . . prophylactic . . . talisman, amulet . . . for the Jẹws, a *pancarte* worn suspended from the neck and on which were inscribed lines of Mosaic law . . ."

La garde,
guarding, keeping, such is the truth. I do not say it primarily because it is the same word, and not only in German as the other grandfather reminds us, who himself is prudent enough, precisely, the slippery one, to demonstrate also that the truth is the non-truth.

The truth,
it is in its cursed name that we have lost each other, in its name only, not for the truth itself, if there were any, but for the desire for truth which has extorted the most terrifying "confessions" from us, after

which we were more distant from ourselves than ever, without getting near to any truth at all by even one step. Moreover, it is in order to take this lesson into account (which moreover has taught me nothing new) that I have more or less decided not to send you back my letter (the one that came back to me from the PR): in certain details it is more true than everything that I have told you, and of a truth which absolutely absolves me of every perjury, but these are details that have no chance of finding grace in your eyes unless you love me; or if you love me, my chance, you should have no need to receive these specifications, these details, these minuscule analyses which could satisfy only a perverse desire to see or to show (I believe you quite capable of this, which is madness). All these secrets are false secrets, they merit only forgetting, and not at all confession. Nothing of all this concerns us. After those miserable confessions that we have extorted from each other (extorted in appearance, but they could be only on the basis of a certain grasp offered by the one to the other, the compulsive urgency to confess under torture. After which there remains only the instruments of torture—what we had to wish to keep, and the interminable test, the galleys in perpetuity, row, row, write in order to purge the pain, never again stand upright, no longer love to dance. With, on the sex—and on the back—these *pancartes* of truth, nothing more was possible. We send back each other

I have gotten back to work, no, not only to the "big" work, as I sometimes say (on us, on me, and all these mournings, right here), but to my little secretariat. Thus I am rereading the Letters of Plato and all those admirable discussions around their "authenticity," of their belonging, the one says, to the *corpus platonicum* such as it has been constituted from the time of Thrasyllus. An enormous library of exegeses: for can one in truth be certain that these letters (for example the one that says in the name of Plato that Plato has written nothing, no work, but that everything has been scratched out by Socrates at the time of the flower of his youth), can one demonstrate that they bear Plato's seal? And if they were "apocryphal" (bastard, as is most often said in Greek)? The debate is prodigious, and I would be tempted to speak about it at length in the preface to the *Legs,* if I write it one day (if you leave me the strength), all the while trafficking with things a bit and with the other hand describing, by throwing in shadows and blanks, the Oxford scene (S and p). I could recount all this to you but it is difficult in a letter. It would be as long as the seventh, the longest and most famous one. Funny that it fell out on the seventh (you know all these fascinations, mine in particular, and my fascination with Freud's fascination with this figure). The accusation of "plagiarism" was often thrown around. A multiplicity of authors has been suspected, more precisely that each letter or all the letters had several authors at once, several masked signers under a single name. Or rather—so as not to confuse signer and sender, receiver or correspondent and addressee—more than one destination. For they know, all of them, what to destine means! This is the unity of the epoch, from Socrates to Freud and a bit beyond, the great metaphysical *pancarte*. Concerning the 7th, one of them says, paraphrasing the other: "impression of a collection of pat phrases borrowed from the dialogues and whose style unfortunately is ruined by oversights and gross errors . . . ," etc. What I cannot succeed in understanding, in holding together, is this cohabitation, the admirable patience of these archivists busying themselves around the finest testaments, the noble and subtle competence of these guardians (what do we not owe them . . .) associated with that fundamental, ineducable imbecility, and that vulgarity, that vulgarity in their imperturbable assurance: they know, they wish to know and to divulge their index cards, they have a properly mathematical—and therefore teachable—certainty of what an authentic destination is (and none of our old men escapes this, not even the one from Freiburg, I fear, even if in this respect he remains the most prudent one), they know what apocrypha and bastards are! And their taste! Oh their taste, they will kill us with their taste. They want to authenticate. As if one could not pretend to write fictive letters with multiple authors and addressees! and even oneself to write to oneself! While saying that one has never written anything oneself.

and I who am the purest of the bastards leaving bastards of every kind almost everywhere

suppose now that I wanted to recount fragments— tiny, insignificant ones, but all the more pregnant for their reserve—of you, to recount you, you, the most beautiful unique story of my life, so that our great-grandnephews, those who will no longer even carry our names, sniff out something, almost nothing but that turns their souls, suppose that they guess through all the secret ciphers, all the relays and postal codes, that they inherit a desire to have lived this beauty (not the beautiful things that will die with us, but their beauty) in our stead, a jealousy they then would conceive—and in my case, the jealousy of the most jealous man who has ever existed (it is true that it was only jealousy of you, my "natural" state, you can laugh, not knowing any jealousy, and this too is one of your poisoned gifts, my jealousy is you) then, then, I would write, I would write to myself for them the most fictive, most unbelievable letters possible, they will no longer know with what aim I feign telling the truth by feigning to feign. As far as the eye can see (I think I say that, "as far as the eye can see" [*à perte de vue*], in *Le facteur de la vérité* and elsewhere; am I the real and unique author of this letter, and the same as the author of the *Facteur . . .* who himself . . . ? *Prove it*), and they will get lost in it just as we lost sight of each other, one fine day, both of us. They will no longer be able to untangle themselves from this inheritance and they will be part of "our own": all our children, and all our dead children, since already, as I told you one day, we are surviving them. And yet (and this is why) I love them, I wish them no harm, on the contrary. It's true, it's true [*mais si, mais si*]

                                                                            I also
want to betray them, and have them know nothing about us, have them be unable to keep anything, or divulge anything, no inheritance, let them be unable even to pretend to it, I would blow up the entire world for that. And for the opposite. You see then, you no longer see me but you see . . . And they, my hope, will they see the color of my soul, the color that tints one, at least one of my voices, when one unhappy evening I spun out this within it

                                                                with you as
destination.

copyist's humor, a real monk. I am alone, alone, deathly alone. I weep soundlessly, you hear me. Want to condemn myself to death, everything is my fault, you know why and you have more than a little to do with it. What is one doing when one says "I am alone"? Since it is neither true nor false, it is primarily a question, but this is true of all phrases, of producing an effect on someone, of saying "come."

These letters of "Plato," that Socrates, of course, would have neither read nor written, I now find them greater than the works. I would like to call you to read you out loud several extracts from the "stands" they have mandated, commanded, programmed for centuries (as I would like to use them for my *legs,* I am typing them, or rather one day you will return this letter to me). You'll see, these people are imperturbable, especially the great profs of the 19th century. And if I read out loud, we would laugh till we burst as we do sometimes (the best moments of our life, the most irreplaceable ones, don't you think, and especially when we were eating after making love, and were imitating all kinds of couples or people cruising in restaurants, *pieds-noirs* preferentially—you always imitate better than I). Listen, this is the Englishman, John Burnet, he is willing for the letters to be false or bastard, but on one condition: that the counterfeiter be a great irreproachable expert, and a contemporary of Plato's, because 50 years later, impossible to master the idiom to that extent. And what's more he is not sure that he is wrong, but listen to him finally, imagine him for example behind his podium at the University let us say of Manchester: "I believe that all the letters of some importance [*sic*] are Plato's, and consequently I will make use of them." He will make use of them! And then the Germans discourse endlessly "über die Echtheit der platon. Briefe." One pronounces himself in favor of a given letter (Zeller, pushing things to the extreme, declares them all apocryphal, I believe), and another the partisan of such and such a letter. Notice that today there are many great intellectuals taking part—still camping on positions for or against—the ones for Sexuality, the others against (it has done much harm, police, tortures, the gulag—which is not even false but all the same . . .), for or against War (it has done much harm, throughout history, etc.), for or against Judeo-Christianity, or one-half only (it would have done much good or much harm), for or against Discourse, Power, The Media, Psychoanalysis, Philosophy, The USSR, China, or Literature, etc. Who would have predicted twenty years ago that we would come back to this, who would have predicted it centuries of "culture" ago?

Here is the summary given by the Frenchman of the German works on the subject: "Ritter, after a rather profound study of the linguistic criteria, admits the authenticity of III, VII (at least substantially [*sic*!!!]) and VIII. Or at least, he asserts prudently, if these epistles are not by Plato himself, their author composed them according to the philosopher's notes. For a long time U. von Wilamowitz-Moellendorf had appeared skeptical, and made an exception only for the 6th Letter . . ." [reread it as if I had written it myself, starting from the "philosopher's notes," especially the end which more or less says this—but the whole thing would have to be retranslated: "This letter, all three must be read together as much as possible, if not two at the same time and as often as you are able. Look at it as a way to take an oath and as a convention having the force of law, on which it is legitimate to swear with a seriousness mixed with grace and with the badinage that is brother of the serious [in fact, it is *paidia*, "sister" of *spoudē,* they always translate sister as brother on grammatical pretexts]. Take as a witness the god chief of all things present and future, and the all-powerful father of the chief and of the cause, whom we will all know, if we philosophize truly, with all the clarity possible for men enjoying beatitude." It has to be read in Greek, my very sweet one, and as if I were writing it to you myself.) So then I pick up my citation again, of the Frenchman speaking of the German, Nietzsche's brother-enemy ". . . von Wilamowitz-Moellendorf had appeared skeptical and made an exception only for the 6th Letter, against which he confessed [!] that he had no serious objection. As for the 7th and the 8th, he rejected them resolutely [!!! certainly, it is the Frenchman who is speaking but the other in effect had begun by rejecting resolutely], for the reason that Plato was not in the habit of exposing himself thus in public [!]. But he makes honorable amends [!] in his work on Plato and declares himself henceforth in favor [!] of VI, VII and VIII. Such also is Howald's recent opinion (*Die Briefe Platons, 1923*).

It is very late, you should sleep, I want to come: 7 hours in the car with the old film of the accident to resolve everything, I can hear them from here, "we'll never know if it was on purpose that he threw himself against the tree and sent himself flying in the air" (it really means what, precisely, to send oneself flying in the air?) etc. "We know, don't we what a car accident means, it never happens by accident, to just anyone at just any moment. You think so too? moreover I was certain, and then it was pouring all around him," *and so on* . . . I think that I made this film for myself even before I knew how to drive. If I were not afraid of waking everyone I would come, in any case I would telephone. When will we be able to call without ringing? There would be a warning light or one could even carry it on oneself, near the heart or in the pocket, for certain coded calls, some signal.   you will have received nothing, understood nothing, you neither. Okay, let's drop it, I will continue to scratch, to read while writing my knowing letter, rather than taking notes on those little white pieces of cardboard that you always don't give a damn about. France now, the French university. You accuse me of being pitiless, and above all unjust with it (scores to be settled perhaps: did they not expel me from school when I was 11, no German having set foot in Algeria? The only school official whose name I remember today: he has me come into his office: "you are going to go home, my little friend, your parents will get a note." At the moment I understood nothing, but since? Would they not start all over, if they could, prohibiting me from school? Is it not for this reason that I have for ever ensconced myself in it in order to provoke them to it and to give them the most urgent wish, always at the limit, to expel me again? No, I do not at all, but not at all, believe these hypotheses, they are seductive or amusing, manipulable, but without value, they are clichés. And then you know that I am not for the destruction of the universitas or the disappearance of the guardians, but precisely one has to make a certain war against them when obscurantism, vulgarity above all, becomes ensconced, as is inevitable. So I come back to it, to France and Plato's Letters. "In France," the same one says, "the question has been very little studied. With reason the preference has been to utilize the certain documents for knowledge of Platonic philosophy." Do you hear? Laugh to tears? no, mustn't. Saisset: "From whatever point of view one considers them, these letters, without even excepting the seventh [okay, let's go], are totally unworthy of Plato." Cousin, Chaignet, Huit (one would have to reproduce the scenario, make them appear together on a stage, make big posters of them for the hall—and, of course, take into account the era, the state of the tradition, and of the university mail at the time, all these extenuating circumstances, but all the same) Cousin, Chaignet, Huit throw all the letters into the garbage. Fouillée: "very reserved" (quite right, me too). The summit, not far from us, Croiset (1921), on immortal heights: "Among the *Letters*, two only have some value: the third and the seventh, which appear to have been edited based on a rather precise document, and which are useful sources for Plato's biography. As for the others, they are either insignificant or ridiculous. In sum, the entire collection is certainly apocryphal; even in the third and in the seventh letter, one finds absolutely nothing which recalls the manner of Plato." Thus, he knew THE manner of Plato, that one. What would he have thought of his manners, maneuvers, and other manipulations when he traffics with all his hands (more than two doubtless) in *Socrates'* back? Plato's ghost must be jubilant over the busyness of these guardians. This is indeed what he sought by letting-himself-be-made-to-write by S. Can you imagine your letters (I am sure that you are dreaming at this moment) in Croiset's hands? You will read, if you wish, the study that follows, on the epistolary genre in literature (my thesis: it does not exist, rigorously speaking, I mean that it would be literature itself if there were any, but *stricto sensu* I no more believe this either—stop—letter follows—stop), it is in the same tone as his on-the-whole-interesting-remarks on the decline of

Hellenism and the proliferation of letters in this "dying rhetoric," on the "Sophists who were fond of this procedure" (because they were "incapable of producing the great works of art of the preceding ages"). This "permitted them to develop their personal, political, and other ideas while covering them with the authority of a great name." And the Frenchman adds calmly: "These epistles have often created confusion, and criticism has occasionally had difficulty undoing the subterfuge." You don't say. They not only allege that they know how to distinguish between the authentic and the simulacrum, they do not even want to do the work, the simulacrum should point itself out, and say to them: "here I am, look out, I am not authentic!". They also want the authentic to be thoroughly authentic, the apocryphal and the bastard also. They would like the counterfeiters to have themselves preceded by a *pancarte:* we are the counterfeiters, this is false currency. As if there were true currency, truly true or truly false currency; what above all throws them off the track in their hunt is that the epistolary simulacrum cannot be stabilized, installed in a certain place, and especially that it is not necessarily, and completely, intentional. If the imposture were perfectly organized, there would always be some hope, a principle, a point of "departure," a partition would be possible. There would be a chance to follow the thread. But there it is, one never knows, the part of the unconscious is itself never properly determinable, and this is due to the postcarded structure of the letter. The same one has just spoken of the letters of Phalaris, of Solon, of Themistocles, and even Socrates (if I wish to speak of this seriously, but I think that I never will, it's already starting to bore me, and I wish to run off toward other things, if I want to be competent on Socrates the writer, of letters or of other things, I would have to read the dissertation of Guilelmus Obens, *Qua aetate Socratis et Socraticorum epistulae quae dicuntur scriptae sint,* 1912), and he adds, read following my finger (I am citing, but as always rearranging a little. Guess the number of false citations in my publications . . .): "the Sophists supposed the correspondences of the men of state, of famous writers, of orators, and publicized them or had them circulated among restricted circles of initiates. Once again, all was not voluntary and deliberate subterfuge: several of these productions were only pure school exercises; and their authors would have been highly surprised if they could have foreseen their success. In the mass of documents that has come down to us, it is nevertheless not easy to make a distinction [he insists upon it, the distinction] for sorting the deliberately false ones from the simple rhetorical exercises." Above, he already was accusing: "whether through cupidity, or through love of art [?] and as an exercise." This, you see, this interests me, the "deliberately false" which indeed betrays something, everything cannot be transformed into the false, in every aspect, even if only the desire for the false, about which it never will be possible to say if it is true or false, with all the consequences. For here it is, and I am (following) our Sophists here, what you can no longer tax as deliberately false, can you call it authentic (as concerns what?) or true? It's very, very late, I hope you are sleeping, I am watching you sleep, trying to get under your eyelids (where there is something like a film), in order to watch your eyes upside down, bent over you but behind you, trying to govern your dreams, to protect you the way one guides a beloved sleepwalker, a queen (my mother was one as a girl, and my grandfather followed her in the street when he did not attach her to her bed—I will always be sorry that you never knew my maternal grandfather, a kind of a sage with a little Vandyke, I don't know if I ever loved him, he was the man (and moreover the generation) in the family most interested in books, he had some—books in French for the most part—on Jewish morals and religion, and he had a mania for dedicating them, to his son and grandsons, I think). Are you sleeping? And if I called? And if I placed this record near the receiver, without saying anything? Which record? Divine, divine.

Still scratching, I would like to write with both hands, and the one, as we did one day, would draw between your eyes and on your stomach, by pasting those little stars you had bought God knows where and that you had kept on without washing for several days. Always our secretariat erotomania—we had constituted between you a kind of astrology, and you in turn

"the epis-
tlers or their addressees in general represent public personages, and their letters take the form either of short notes in which an often insignificant moral thought is expressed with a certain amount of effort, or of veritable opuscules which are on the discursive, or even novelistic, side. The author takes his theme from history and lets his imagination run free [. . .] the epistolary composers equally seek out the subjects of their embroideries in ancient traditions: this is a characteristic that they will attempt to display in more or less imaginary narratives, a doctrine that they develop in the manner of the supposed personage, an event that they envelop with more or less verisimilitude with all the charms of legend. In order to verify these affirmations it will suffice to go through the *Epistolographi*

graeci and to read, among others, the Socratic letters in which are grouped the anecdotes concerning the life, method, and even the death of the Athenian philosopher . . . ."

And further: ". . . the name of the three addressees [what luck, they can count, of course this is about Epicurus] . . . must not, in effect, abuse us. This is but the symbol of the adopted literary genre, but in reality Epicurus is addressing himself to the circle of his disciples and, in the epistolary form, is summarizing for their benefit the substantial points of his doctrine." This is what never could happen to us, don't you think, my unique one, my only, lonely one, and not only because I have no doctrine to transmit, no disciple to seduce, but because my law, the law that undividedly reigns over my heart, is never to borrow your name, never to use it, not even in order to speak to yourself, only in order to call you, call you, call you, from afar, without a phrase, without a consequence, without end, without saying anything, not even "come," now, not even "come back."

He obviously already had some difficulty distinguishing between private and public letters: ". . . even earlier, Isocrates had edited a certain number of letters, several of which are veritable little moral and political treatises. Obviously the pieces of this collection are not all *private* letters, some of them revealing the existence of an already well defined and rather widespread genre from the fourth century before Christ. They are rather 'open letters,' destined in part to the expressly designated personage, but above all to the great public. These missives were not to remain secret; they were written to be published. To be convinced of this it suffices to notice the coquettishness with which the author polishes his thought and embellishes his style, the care that he takes not to transgress the rules of his art." And here is the example that he gives of this art: "I still would have many things to say, given the nature of my subject, but I am stopping myself. In effect I think that you all easily will be able, you and your most distinguished friends, to add all that you please to my words. Moreover I fear abusing, for already, little by little, without noticing, I have gone beyond the limits of a letter and have reached the proportions of a discourse."

10 September 1977.

and I am well despite the lack of sleep, because you are going to arrive very quickly now, doubtless. Remind me to tell

you the dream of Josephine Baker which seems to have occupied
the brief moments of my sleep last night (I jotted down several
words on the night table without even putting on the light). I am
picking up again the play of citations interrupted barely several
hours ago (still the same book, and I am incapable of writing anything else). A bit further on then (citation of another letter by Isocrates): ". . . Do not go off believing that this letter has any other
aim than answering to your friendship and that I wish to make a
display of eloquence [*epideixin,* ostentation, exhibition]. I have not
yet reached that degree of madness of being unaware that henceforth I might be incapable of writing things better than the ones I
previously published, when I am already so far from the age of
vigor, and that by producing some work more mediocre I might acquire a reputation quite inferior to the one I now enjoy among you."
[. . .] If one joins to all these editorial artifices the numerous allusions to the literary and political role of the Greek orator, this
affectation of simplicity which covers the writer's rhetoric, all appear to me the very clear indices of Isocrates' aim in some of his
letters; he does not content himself with reaching a unique reader,
but wants to be acknowledged by the ordinary lovers of fine language. One part of Isocrates' correspondence belongs to literature
under the same rubric as overblown oration. Henceforth would we
be able to reject Plato's letters *a priori,* on the pretext that a mass of
apocrypha was composed and published at a later date? [. . .] Will
it be said that it is unbelievable that "Plato himself had kept copies
of his letters in his personal library" or that his correspondents had
conserved "his communications, such that fifty or one hundred
years later it was possible for those who inherited them to agree in
order to respond to a presumed call from the first editors in Athens
or Alexandria?" (Huit, *La vie et l'œuvre de Platon*). You, can you
imagine Plato's library? How do you think this Huit represented it
to himself in 1893? Together we should bring to light a history
(genesis and structure) of the libraries of the great thinkers and
great writers: how they kept, arranged, classified, annotated, "in-
dexed," archived what they really read, what they pretended to have
read, or, more interesting, not to have read, etc. "Fifty or one hundred years later," this was a lot for him. But really, on the whole a
short sequence, an imperceptible sequence in the short subject.
Title: X. lets himself be dictated by telex, by his inheritors precisely, the legacy that he destines to them without even being able
to identify them. They enclose him, glue him to his secretary and

address him orders by telex, in his tongue or in theirs. He comes and signs. The essential is not what he gives, but that one keeps his signature along with his name, even if he has not by himself thought a single word of what they desire to make him sign. When will they know that Socrates will have written under my dictation the will that institutes him as my universal legatee among others, and that behind me, my immense one, you whispered all this in my ear (for example while I was driving on an Italian highway and was reading your tongue in the rearview mirror)? And yet I have not yet seen you, despite the eternities that we have spent drowning in each others' eyes, with the certainty that the gods had come, coupled, and that henceforth eternity overtook us in thought. Yet the disaster is there, now, you have never seen yourself in me, you no longer know quite well, right here, who you are, nor do I know who I am.

The Oxford card is looking at me, I am rereading Plato's letters, have the impression of discovering them all alive, close, animated, I am living with them, on the sea, between Greece and Sicily (this is another of your hidden first names, this country that I really fear we will never get to), am thinking more and more of making this epistolary iconography into a beveled preface to the reading of *Beyond the PP* and Freud's correspondence. For a thousand reasons, many too many reasons. The athesis and the postal pause or pose (what is "to pose," to posit? etc.), and first of all this story of principles, the relation of postal *différance* between the Pleasure Principle (PP) and the Reality Principle [*Principe de Réalité*] (PR), with the very "political" figures granted this relation by Freud (*Herrschaft*, mastery, authority). The necessity of "intersecting" this politico-postal motif with, for example, Letter II to Dionysos, the one which alludes to a prophylactic guarding of the letter incorporated in the "by heart." Here, there is the theme of the secret, of the esoteric doctrine (no, not yet, not as in the *Prognostica Socratis basilei*) which is to be exposed only in ciphered letters. In this letter "enigmatic" writing precisely concerns the "nature of the principle," of the "first," of the "king" of all things (thus, "you allege, as concerns what he relates [nothing is ever presented live in his works, he always reports, feigns reporting, as if he were reading, as if he were receiving what he is giving you to read from a reflecting surface, for example what S. in his turn comes to read or to write], that the nature of the First has not been sufficiently revealed to you. Thus I must speak to you of it, but through enigmas, so that if some accident overtakes this later on land or sea, reading it will be impossible to understand. Here is how the matter stands: all Beings gravitate around the King of the Universe (*pantôn basilea*); he is the end of all things, and the cause of all beauty; around the "Second" are found the second things, and around the "Third," the third things. The human soul aspires to know their qualities, for it considers whatever is in kinship to it, without anything ever satisfying it. But when in question are the King and the realities of which I have spoken, there is no such thing. Then it is up to the soul to ask: this nature, which one is it then? It is this question, oh son of Denys and Doris, that is the cause of all misfortune or rather it is the painful effort of childbirth that it provokes in the soul, and so long as it is not delivered, it will never succeed in reaching the truth. You tell me that in your gardens, under your laurels, you yourself had reflected on this and that it was your own discovery. I answer you that if this were really so, you would spare me many discourses."

It remains that the royal truth passes through so many literal pathways, so many correspondences, so many relays, so many postes restantes, so many *facteurs*. At the beginning of the same letter, he had already proposed to Denys to write him the truth, if the other asked it of him. And as always, in question was a truth *in response* to an accusation, within a trial, the effect of a *cause* ("I have learnt from Archidemos that, according to you, it was not myself alone who was to have kept silent about you, but that my friends themselves indeed were to have kept themselves from doing or saying anything at all disagreeable about you [. . .] I am telling you this because Cratistolus and Polyxenes have told you nothing reasonable. One of the two alleged he had heard on Olympus a great number of those who were with me in denigrating you: perhaps his hearing is better than mine. In any case, I myself have heard nothing. There is only one thing to do in my opinion, if a similar accusation is renewed against one of us: interrogate me by letter: I will tell you the truth without hesitation or false shame.") And to link this truth, their "liaison" says the translator I am following in order to go quickly, their *sunousia,* to the essential truth, the one found by going back to the First or to principles: "Here then is our reciprocal situation: we are unknown, I would say, for no one in Greece, and our liaison is not a secret. No more should you overlook that even in the future it will not be passed under silence, however numerous are those who have received the tradition of it, as of a friendship which was neither weak nor hidden. What do I mean by this? I will explain it to you by going back to the principle. Wisdom and power naturally tend to unite. [. . .] All this to show you that after our death, our renown will not be silenced: and also that we must watch over it [. . .] the dead have some sentiment of the things here on earth [. . .] I have come to Sicily with the reputation of surpassing by far the other philosophers and I arrived in Syracuse to receive testimony of this from you, so that, in my person, philosophy received the homages of the crowd itself. But I have not succeeded. The cause? I do not want to repeat the one that many others will invoke, but you appeared no longer to have any great confidence in me, you looked as if you wanted to send me away and to call upon others: you seemed to be seeking out what my designs could be, through distrust of me, apparently."

Now, for all these messages between philosophy and power, between the dynasty of the philosopher and the dynasty of the tyrant, for all this transmissive dynamics *facteurs* are necessary, and they are little spoken of. For example, faithful Baccheios, *o ten epistolen pheron,* how I would like to know him: he transports the viaticum, at once the money and the letter (as in the book of Esther, but contrary to what apparently goes on in *The Purloined Letter* in which the money and the letter circulate in the opposite sense: the letter is exchanged, in principle, against the money, the queen pays Dupin who puts the letter on its return route). The scene of the fetishes is superb, try to transpose it into a Cartoucherie pushing political sophistication rather far. In order to recall that as absolute master (*autocrator*) he had first been charged with the "safekeeping of your city" before having been shamefully "sent away," Plato in the first Letter employs a word from the same family as that of the prophylactic guard of which I spoke to you the other day. He then confides both the letter and the money to this Baccheios, who one morning must have set out with the money order, both the sum and the note registered. This entire itinerary right up to us. Supposing that nothing is apocryphal and that some Dupin or, more wickedly still, some narrator skilled in making him talk . . . The whole thing would have to be retranslated: "Henceforth I will reflect upon choosing the kind of life that distances me more from humans, and you, tyrant that you are, you will live in isolation. Baccheios, the bearer of this letter, will return to you the very brilliant sum that you had given me for the departure: it was simultaneously insufficient for the expenses of the voyage and without utility elsewhere. It would bring, to you the donor, only the worst dishonor and hardly less to me, if I accepted it [. . .] Farewell. Acknowledge your great wrongs to me, so that you will treat others better." He is never wrong.

The absolute dissymmetry that he institutes. No matter what he says, I am not sure that he finally gives it to himself by virtue of his position as philosopher, knowledge speaking to power. Simply, he is writing, it is he who destines (he thinks), and the other is placed on stage by a letter the rest of which is supposed to bear witness. The other does not answer, is not published. This dissymmetry of "authority" reaches the height of arrogance in the second Letter: "In a word deference from you to me is an ornament (*cosmos*) for both of us; from me to you a shame as much for the one as the other. Enough on this matter." So you see—

I have never written you such a long letter, overburdened like a felucca with small pieces of knowledge. Forgive me, it is in order to chase away the anxiety (you did not call as promised), to get rid of delirious images. You know them better than I, which is what always will prevent me from being delivered of them, you were there before me. This has separated us, infinitely separated us, but in order "to live" (if you can call it living) this separation and in order to love a secret based on it, based on what holds us together without relation, the one addressed to the other, the one backed by the other, yes both. And I scratch, I scratch in order to make things last, because tomorrow, on your return, the expiration perhaps, the "decision," fate for me. I await you as in that story you had told me (Russian roulette on the quay . . .)

And then I am not writing falsely knowledgeable letters in order to keep me from the delirium which possesses me, I am writing delirious letters, knowledge walls them up in their crypt and one must know crypts, delirious letters on the knowing letters that I make into cards. I summon them to appear, that's all. I shuffle and let them unshuffle. So, to continue turning round in the Encyclopedia, here for my archives is the end of the Voltaire, which fits me, they will say, like a glove. "As for those who familiarly send you by the post a tragedy on large paper and in heavy print, with white sheets for your observations, or who regale you with a first tome of metaphysics while awaiting the second, one can tell them that they do not have the requisite discretion, and that there are even countries in which they would risk making known to the minister that they are bad poets and bad metaphysicians." That's me, I can hear it said by so and so who by chance falls upon this letter and has quite an in-

terest in saying so. All of this is so programmed, that I send to the
devil, I mean to the end of the preceding article, on possession. It
suits me too, just my size, I have never felt myself so possessed,
played upon, telepathically, phantomatically. No, not by you, by
the specters who dictate war to you and address us the one against
the other at the best moment.

No, I am not the devil, nor are you, but we
have him, and devilishly all year long we persecute each other with
unbelievable contract stories or, like F.'s painter, double contracts
. . . Here is Voltaire (a pretty name finally, don't you find?), on Possession, which I would place between the *Prognostica Socratis
basilei, a fortune-telling book,* and all the devils of which Freud
thinks he can call himself "the advocate" in *Beyond* . . . in the
middle of all these cards to be played: ". . . in the forest of Fon-
tainebleau. [. . .] Each village had its sorcerer or sorceress; each
prince had his astrologer; all the ladies had their fortune told; the
possessed ran through the fields; playing at who had seen the devil,
or would see him: all of this was the subject of inexhaustible conversation, which kept spirits in suspense. At present we insipidly
play cards, and we have lost something by becoming disabused."

You also
want it, and as soon as we received that order, we were at once
saved and lost: we could no longer be either faithful or unfaithful to
this anonymous law, nor to ourselves. No more sworn oath that
holds.

P.S. I am going to slip one of the Oxford cards into this letter again,
so that you sniff something out, divine. Perhaps because of the insomnia, I also feel them both diabolical, and threatening. Not (a
step) in the air like that, in the course of announcing the worst news
to me or of making charges against me, indicting me for my unnameable treachery. An incomplete pair of terrible grandfathers.
Bearded and forked. Look at the feet, I am cutting them at neck
level, and am pasting them here, one would say a single forked
foot, each time. And the three eyes like fixed points. They frighten
and they are frightened. They are terrified by their own conjuration. Afraid of us, of each other. The devil is them, him, the couple
Plato/Socrates, divisible and indivisible, their interminable partition, the contract which binds them to us until the end of time. You
are there, look at the scene, take their place, S. signing the contract
that p. dictates to him after a sleepless night, make of which what
you will, he is selling him or renting him his demon and the other in
exchange engages himself through his books, his letters, *and so on,*

to be forwarded. And thus, without the slightest knowledge they predict the future, like kings. No, they do not predict it, they preform it, and this is a pictorial, a pictorial magazine that you will be able to buy at every kiosk, in all the station bookstores for as long as there are trains and newspapers. Will always be new episodes. A pictorial performative which never ends. I always will be stupefied by this couple of plotters, the one who scratches and pretends to write in the place of the other who writes and pretends to scratch. By investing an enormous capital of counterfeit money, they make the plans for a gigantic highway network, with relays for the airbus or *auto-couchette* trains (sleeping cars above all, ah yes, sleeping cars, everywhere you read them while sleeping, you read "Cook's Tours" from Oxford to Athens and return, via this chamber, that other sleeping car in which Ernst is playing with the spool and Sigmund is dreaming of trains), a totally informatized system of telecommunications, stewardesses in uniform everywhere. Whatever course is borrowed (nothing is given), and as soon as you open your mouth, and even if you close it, you have to pass through them, stop at the toll booth or pay a tax. You have always to acquit yourself of an income tax. They are dead, those two dogs, and yet they step up to the cashier, they reinvest, they extend their empire with an arrogance they will never be pardoned for. Not them, themselves, they are dead, but their phantom comes back at night to do the accounts, in their name. It is the name which comes back ("names are revenants"), and of course you will never know, when I pronounce or write their names, of these two dogs, if I am speaking of them or of their names. This is the problem of " 'Fido'-Fido" (you know, Ryle, Russell, etc., and the question of knowing whether I am calling my dog or if I am mentioning the name of which he is the bearer, if I am utilizing or if I am naming his name. I adore these theorizations, often Oxonian moreover, their extraordinary and necessary subtlety as much as their imperturbable ingenuity, *psychoanalytically speaking;* they will always be confident in the law of quotation marks. The misfortune, or the chance, is that Fido, Fido, either you do not write it, and it's all over, or you do write it, and again it's all over, you can always run in order to know which you will catch first. And it can always bite, even the celestial constellation, or bark. And in the center of a very good book, you stumble, it must be said, over these examples which appear to pose no problem (at least in their exemplary content) in this context (I am not putting the quotation marks too close in order not to confuse every-

thing, but so what?). Here are two sentences cited as two types of different functioning (and in effect are, apparently): "
> Socrate did not write
> 'Socrate' has seven letters "

and the "test of substitutivity": "
> 'Socrate' = the name of Plato's master (true)
> 'Socrate' has seven letters   (true)

the name of Plato's master has seven letters (true) "

Yeah, okay, nothing to be said against the *laws* which govern this problematic, if not to ask the question of the law, and of the law of the proper name as concerns those pairs called quotation marks. I say (to them and to you, my beloved) this is my body, at work, love me, analyze the corpus that I tender to you, that I extend here on this bed of paper, sort out the quotation marks from the hairs, from head to toe, and if you love me enough you will send me some news. Then you will bury me in order to sleep peacefully. You will forget me, me and my name.

The author of the book of which I am speaking, himself, not his name (therefore he would pardon me for not naming him) is himself reserved as concerns the very interesting "position of Quine" ("a word-between-quotation-marks is the proper name of the word which figures between the quotation marks, simultaneously an occurrence of the word which is between the quotation marks and an occurrence of the word-between-the-quotation-marks, the latter including the former as a part"—and it is true that this logic of inclusion perhaps is not very satisfying in order to account for the "simultaneously," but small matter here), and making an allusion to a "forgetting," his word, a forgetting "evidently facilitated by the resemblance that there is between a word and the name of this word formed by its being placed between quotation marks," he concludes, I quote, "But one must not let oneself be abused by this resemblance, and confuse the two names, no more at least than one confuses *vert* and *verre*." *Say* it, re*say* it. *Ver* is *vers*. No more at least, says he. No more at least than . . . No more at least, uh oh, it never arrives? Well, better not. "One must not." Okay, promised, we won't any more. Not on purpose anyway. Unless we forget, but we will not forget on purpose, it's just that they resemble each other so much.—Who?—Socrates, I'm saying hi.) They are dead and they travel through us in order to step up to the cashier, not them, their name, at every instant. At this very moment. How they re-

semble each other. Never forget that they have existed outside their
names, truly.—How is that, you say.—Well, like you and me.—
Not possible?—*Mais si, mais si.* And then every word must be
franked in order to be addressed to whomever. Au-to-ma-tic-al-ly.
Whatever I say, whatever I do, I must paste on myself a stamp with
the effigy of this diabolical couple, these unforgettable comperes,
these two patient impostors. A little engraving with this royal, ba-
silical couple, sterile but infinite in its ideal progeniture. Cynically,
without a cent, they have issued a universal stamp. A postal and
fiscal stamp, by making themselves appear to advance funds. And
on the stamp both are to be seen in the course, the one in front of
the other, in the course, *en train,* of drawing a stamp and of signing
the original. And they plaster themselves on the walls. An immense
poster. This is a stamp. They have signed *our* I.O.U. and we can no
longer not acknowledge it. Any more than our own children. This is
what tradition is, the heritage that drives you crazy. People have not
the slightest idea of this, they have no need to know that they are
paying (automatic withdrawal) nor whom they are paying (the name
or the thing: name is the thing) when they do anything whatsoever,
make war or love, speculate on the energy crisis, construct so-
cialism, write novels, open concentration camps for poets or homo-
sexuals, buy bread or hijack a plane, have themselves elected by
secret ballot, bury their own, criticize the media without rhyme or
reason, say absolutely anything about chador or the ayatollah,
dream of a great safari, found reviews, teach, or piss against a tree.
They can even never have heard the name of p. and of S. (hey, I see
them as very chirpy, suddenly). Via all kinds of cultural, that is
postal, relays they pay their tax, and no need for that to be taxed
with "platonism," and even if you have overturned platonism (look
at them, turn the card, when they write upside down in the plane).
Of course the tax goes only to the names, that is to no one (for the
"living," notice, this is not absolutely, rigorously different), since
the two pilots are no longer there, only subject, submitted, under-
lying their names, in effigy, their heads topped by their names. No
more than Hegel, Freud or Heidegger, who themselves had to put
themselves into the position of legatees, from the front or the back.
Standing or lying, not a movement, not a step without them. I even
would like to believe that those who liberate themselves better and
more quickly, those at least who desire to pay the least and to "acquit" themselves most properly, are those who attempt to deal directly with them, as if this were possible, the patient philosophers,
historians, archivists who are relentless over the issuing of the

stamp, who always want to know more on this subject, dream of the original imprint. Me, for example. But naturally, the busier one gets liberating oneself, the more one pays. And the less one pays, the more one pays, such is the trap of this speculation. You will not be able to account for this currency. Impossible to return it, you pay everything and you pay nothing with this Visa or Mastercharge card. It is neither true nor false. The issuing of the stamp is simultaneously immense, it imposes and is imposed everywhere, conditions every other type, *timbre*, or tympan in general; and yet, you can barely see it, it is minuscule, infinitely divisible, composes itself with billions of other obliterating positions, impositions, or superimpositions. And we, my angel, we love each other posted on this network, at the toll booth one weekend return (fortunately we can love each other [*on peut s'aimer*], in a car), crushed by taxes, in permanent insurrection against the "past," full of acknowledgements however, and virgin from debt, as at the first morning of the world. This story, the trap of who signs an I.O.U. for the other such that the other finds himself engaged before having known a thing about it, even before having opened his eyes, this children's story is a love story and is ours—if you still want it. From the very first light of dawn

Now make the image move, with lateral movements, pass yourself the film. Himself, he wants to issue seed (he talks about it all the time, right?), he wants to sow the entire world, and the best lever at hand, look, is S., the sterile midwife. So he sends him to himself, he sends himself a child via him, an *ekgonon*, an offspring or an interest. You can see the pickup of the multiplied levers, the big and little syringes. All this happens in less than two seconds, in the other's back who looks as if he notices nothing. And with reason, it falls by the side, has to, it writes itself like that and no longer ceases to proliferate, this old couple of bearded grandfathers, these inveterate counterfeiters who come to haunt our nights with their discourse on truth, on phantasmata and logoi, and pleasure and the beyond of pleasure, and politics, and tyranny, and the first and the second, and then Eros. They have never believed in it. And they make neither one nor two. Now here we are at their command and on the program. And I who always insist on paying more than anyone, my higher bid, believe me.

It is broad daylight now. You arrive soon and I have liked waiting for you without sleeping, or so little. You are coming back with your "decision," your "determination," and I prepare myself for it without knowing, like a condemned man in his cell. One is never sure if he is hoping for a "grace" or if he is not dreaming of being able to refuse it at daybreak, so that it finally stops, his death. Thus I am going to close this letter (I have not reopened the other one and I don't yet know what I will do with it, doubtless it will depend on you), I have told you the essential, that you could have known for years moreover, long years: we have lived everything and said everything an incalculable number of times, in every form, more or less, in words and without words, and every letter, the smallest mark, once fixed, becomes a very dry speck of salt in the sun, on the skin, and you can hear yourself saying, here it is, here's the Mediterranean, keep it, it's nothing but it has no price, keep it like a ring, a vulgar aquamarine, it's nothing, above all no preciosity, it is priceless if you will, we have swum in it, and it forgets us at every instant. If you don't understand any more, no one can accuse you, by definition, especially not me. Up to you "to determine." *There are* rings, that one never gives, neither keeps nor returns. One can give oneself over to them [*s'y adonner*], that is all, abandon [*abandonner*]. As I do not want you to receive this letter via the post after god knows what scene, I am putting it into an envelope and will give it to you at the station.

      When I am creating correspondence (which is not the case here), I mean when I write several letters consecutively, I am terrified at the moment of putting the thing under seal. And if I were to make a mistake about the addressee, invert the addresses, or put several letters into the same envelope? This happens to me, and it is rare that I do not reopen certain letters, after having failed to identify them by holding them up to the light at the moment of throwing them into the box. My sorting [*tri*] and my postal traffic is this scene. It precedes and follows the obsession of the pickup, the other one, the next one or the one that I missed. The obsessional moment occasionally lasts beyond the imaginable. Once the letter or the lot of letters is gone (I have finally unclenched my hand), I can remain planted in front of the box as if before an irreparable crime, tempted to await the following pickup in order to seduce the *facteur* and to take everything back, in order to verify at least one last time the adequation of addresses (I did this once, but it was somewhat different, in order to intercept my own mail which was going to be "forwarded" to a place that I did not want it to go, and where it would have arrived before me) and that there is indeed only one letter, the right one, per envelope. The situation is that of a confession without a crime (as if this were possible; *mais si, mais si!*), of an exhibit which becomes the cause of a crime. In any event, this confession before the mailbox does not await that one write, I mean "missives" in the impoverished sense, but already when one speaks, when one touches, when one comes. Not only is there always some post card, but even if you leave it virgin and without address, there are several at once, and in the same envelope.

like the difference between the *Cedex* (*Courrier d'Entreprise* [Business Mail]) and the *Cidex*. The *Cidex* (*courrier individuel à distribution exceptionnelle* [individual mail distributed in exceptional fashion]) is the country: a battery of mailboxes in a given place (e.g. a small mountain village), is installed by the Post, the *facteur* passes by car or by motorcycle, and the addressees, the "users" come to withdraw their mail. It is set up so that the users can maneuver a signal if they wish the "carrier" to come to them the next time. One calls the *facteur* without a word, with a luminous signal. And he comes, to give or to take.

The Postal Prospect is henceforth the site of the psych. and po problematic (the question of women, of psychoanalysis, and of politics, it brings them all together); the question of Power, as they still say, is first of all that of the post and telecommunications, as is well known. Then one must know: that the volume of mail is going to increase by 3% per year approximately, "spread unequally," says a principal Inspector of the P. and T., "over diverse objects of correspondence, with a higher percentage for the 'economic' mail and a levelling off for 'household' mail. This increase will be congruent with the development of informational systems which, in the years to come, will overwhelm not only the highly industrialized countries, but also the rest of the world." Suppose that I write a book, let us say "Plato and telecom.," it necessarily falls into the hands of Monsieur Brégou, principal Inspector of the Posts and Telecommunications, and he decides (because I quote him) to put it on sale, as they do sometimes, in all the post offices, the proceeds for the mailmen's benefit funds. The book is displayed in every branch, it wouldn't do badly. And then the translations. What's more, while increasing the sales (the price of one or two booklets of stamps) it would make Plato penetrate the hamlets. To increase the sales, on the publisher's advice I would criticize the publishing apparatuses and the media (which are also a postal agency) and would have a band placed around the book: the only writer to refuse such and such a show. I would be invited to be on it immediately, and at the last moment, to the surprise of everyone obviously, and I would accept on the condition of being permitted to improvise freely on the postal agency in the Iranian uprising (the revolutionary role of dis-tancing, the distancing of God or of the ayatollah telekommeiny giving interviews from the Parisian suburbs) provided that I nuance it a bit the next day in one of the dailies or weeklies. A very trivial remark, the relations between posts, police and media are called upon to transform themselves profoundly, as is the amorous message (which is more and more watched over, even if it has always been), by virtue of informatization, so be it. And therefore all the networks of the p.p. (psych. and pol). But will the relations between the police, the psychoanalytic institution, and letters be essentially affected? Inevitably, and it is beginning. Could Poe adapt *The Purloined Letter* to this? Is it capable of this adaptation? Here I would bet yes, but it would be very difficult. The end of a postal epoch is doubtless also the end of literature. What seems more probable to me is that in its actual state psychoanalysis, itself, cannot read *The Purloined Letter,* can only have itself or let itself be read by it, which is also very important for the progress of this institution. In any case, the past and present of the said institution are unthinkable outside a certain postal technology, as are the public or private, that is secret, correspondences which have marked its stages and crises, supposing a very determined type of postal rationality, of relations between the State monopoly and the secret of private messages, as of their unconscious effects. That the part of "private" mail tends toward zero does not only diminish the chances of the great correspondences (the last ones, those of Freud, of Kafka), it also transforms the entire field of analytic exertion—and in both the long and the short term, with all the imaginable and unimaginable consequences for the "analytic situation," the "session," and the forms of transference. The procedures of "routing" and of distribution, the paths of transmission, concern the very support of the messages sufficiently not to be without effect on the content, and I am not only speaking of the signified content. The "letter" disappears, others must be found, but this will be simultaneously the unlimited empire of a postcardization that begins with the trait itself, before what they call writing (even before mail as *sticks-messages* and as *quippos*), *and* the decadence of the post card in the "narrow" sense, the decadence which for barely more than a century, but as one of the last phenomena, a sign of acceleration toward the end, is part of the "classic" postal system, of the "posta," of the *station* in the mail's making its (a)way, of the "document" to be transmitted, support and message. In everyday language the post, in the strict

sense, is distinguished from every other telecommunication (tele-
graph or telephone, for example, telematics in general) by this
characteristic: the transport of the "document," of its material support. A rather confused idea, but rather useful for constructing a
consensus around the banal notion of post—and we do need one.
But it suffices to analyze this notion of "document" or of material
support a bit for the difficulties to accumulate. (You have just called
from the station, you are settling down in the train, I feel so calm
suddenly. Several hours more and I am coming to get you.) Now, a
certain form of support is in the course of disappearing, and the
unconscious will have to get used to this, and this is already in
progress. I was speaking to you just now of the progressive disappearance of private mail and of my terror before the "collective"
envelope. I had not read Monsieur Brégou at that moment. I have
just done so. Imagine our entire history, and the most recent history, imagine it in Monsieur Brégou's "prospect": "The development of informational systems, as much for the post as for the
users, certainly will permit the installation of new modalities for
the transmission of information. In the years to come, exception
made for the mail of private individuals ["exception made," which
one, until when?], it can be thought that it will no longer be writing
that will be transported, but the perforated card, microfilm, or
magnetic tape. The day will come that, thanks to the 'telepost,' the
fundamentals will be transmitted by wire starting from the user's
computer going to the receiving organs of the computer of the post
office nearest [all the same] the residence of the addressee, who
will be charged with the impression of the order or the bill [his distinction between the mail of individuals and the other supposes a bit
quickly that the individuals, ourselves, we send on their way something entirely other than orders and bills: in fact these great tech-
nologues always really have a metaphysician's naïveté, it's part of
the same thing]. It will remain for the postal employee only to place
the envelope into distribution, which moreover will be able to en-
compass several correspondences emanating from different senders. The traditional process thereby will find itself upset for a major
portion of the mail." Yes and no: for as long as it is not proven that
into each of our so secret, so hermetically sealed letters several
senders, that is several addressees have not already infiltrated themselves, the upset will not have been demonstrated. If our letters are
upsetting, in return, perhaps it is that already we are several on the
line, a crowd, right here, at least a consortium of senders and addressees, a real shareholders' company with limited responsibility,

all of literature, and yet it is true, my unique one, that Monsieur Brégou is describing my terror itself, Terror itself. He insists, with all the satisfaction of a factory boss demonstrating the new machines he has just received. And he is waiting for others which will increase the returns, for the good of all, producers and consumers, workers and bosses: "At a time when rural civilization is giving way to an ever increasing urban concentration, the post will have to adapt itself to the needs of its clientele: a painful mutation, for example when the postal traffic of certain rural areas no longer justifies the maintenance of an office, while the lack of personnel makes itself felt painfully in the large agglomerations. To get to this point, perhaps it will be necessary to upset certain habits. Why not envisage an extension of the capacities of the post [here you are going to believe that I am inventing the words for the needs of my demonstration] which, *omnipresent* by means of its offices or its '*facteurs*' [I like the way he went at it with these quotation marks], could *treat all* [my emphasis] the operations placing the population in contact with the administration?" Hey! and even the contact between THE Population and THE Administration! Why not envisage omnipresence, says he. Of the offices and the "*facteurs.*" I can't decide what is most striking here: the monstrosity of this future that the principal Inspector envisages, with a beatific and quite forward-looking insouciance (while he calmly converses with us about the worst of State and trans-State police, of generalized perforization: for example S. inanalysis with P. will be able to, and even will have to, because of the traffic jams, at the time of his session, send his tape or his cards of associations—free associations of course—to the said P., passing through Monsieur Brégou's omnipresent one. And in order to insure the autonomy of the psychoanalytic institution as concerns the State, the latter would name, at the proposal of the corps of certified analysts united in a General Assembly, and no matter what group they belong to, a Commission of wise men—they could be seven, for example—which would watch over all the transferences passing through the omnipresent one, so that confidentiality will be well maintained, out of the reach of all the police, even the secret police. Naturally, so that all this remains in conformity with the psychoanalytic vocation (how is it to be called otherwise?), with the spirit and the letter of Freud, six members of the Commission of the rights of psychoanalysis would be inanalysis, at least for a time, with the seventh, who in some fashion elected by general suffrage (it is a democracy that I am describing) would have to figure things out all by himself with the omnipresent one or with one of his *facteurs,* for example Monsieur Brégou) I don't know what terrifies me the most, the monstrousness of this prospective or on the contrary its ancestral antiquity, the very normality of the thing. In its essence, of course, in its *eidos* it is more than twenty-five centuries old. Okay, enough on this subject. I am going to wait for you, to await all of you on the platform, I am finishing this little note quickly (in which I have said nothing in comparison to what you know in advance that I would have wanted to say to you

for it has not escaped you that the other omnipresent one, my immense one, is you. And I want it thus. That none of my most secret thoughts can ever be taken away from you. No, not the same omnipresent one, the other one, you.

Please, don't persecute me any more with the "details," and don't ask me any more to send you back the letter that came back to me.

It's too late now. I am leaving, or anyhow, I am coming. When you get off the train, I still will wait for us to be alone—and I will begin to love you (I am bringing you this letter).

22 September 1977.

between us song was anachronistic, and ecstasy itself. One day I was talking to you about it—as I do too often—and you pronounced across the parasites (for we were telephoning each other) "god of the time difference." I am still keeping the two watches on my arm, on the left I am six hours ahead of everything that I appear to live at Trumbull. I simulate everything, that you are simultaneous for me, my love, and that at the moment when I call you, by your name, light and the rhythms of bodies, sun and sleep, no longer make a screen. And it's not so illusory. I woke up at about the same time as you this morning (but it's only the first day, yes) and very soon you are going to "ring," I am going to count the times. Yesterday at Kennedy, same scenario as the preceding years, I had the impression it was yesterday: Paul and Hillis waiting for me, come down from Yale (how is an appointment possible, despite all the intervals and transcontinental differences, and the fidelity on which I live, and this miracle before which I will always remain a child?). After saying hello, I made them wait (again), as always, in order to call you from the public booth, the only one that I know here along with the one in Grand Central or Penn Station, the only one from which one is not obliged to call *"collect"* at the expense of the addressee. In a second I had you in the night, you were going to bed with me in the big bed, and I came out of the airport crushed by the sun (the New York heat in August which never goes away), serene and desperate, amiable with my friends and incapable of re-membering myself. I less and less know where my body is—and all these phantoms, here or there, and at what time. Keep me, keep us, give me time.

Like him (M.B.), I like the word "disaster," to name thus the bottomless misfortune to which the first morning, the first sleepless night had destined us. Despite the time that will forbid us to reach [*joindre*] (what a word, don't you think?) each other—(you have just called, you have just entered into the room), disaster brings us together. I love all the words, all the letters, in the word disaster [*désastre*], its entire teeming constellation, all the fates cast in it, and even that it sublimates us a bit.

The time difference [*décalage horaire*] is in me, it is me. It blocks, inhibits, dissociates, arrests—but it also releases, makes me fly, I never forbid myself anything, you know, finally not me, and it is toward you, it is to you that I fly. Uniquely. At this very second.

23 September 1977.

What would we have done (love at a distance, for example, and our entire teleorgasmization) at the time of Rome (the other one), at the time of the *cursus publicus* (170 miles, a day and a night, not bad for the times but all the same for us)?

Listen, I am (following) you all the time. And you you are all the time for me you give yourself all the time to me especially when you are not there you are omnipresent here and I cry for you I cry over you in you pulling your hair toward me in handfuls it is never long enough you are above me and never again will I let you go even if you won't see me any more, even if you look elsewhere one day to seek out

I feel so much smaller than you, I am so afraid of distracting you from life, from everything that awaits you, from everything that the others desire from you (I feel them all fascinated by you, begging for a word or a look, and that you write them, to all males, everything that (to all females too) you write to me. I went by the department, there was still nothing from you, but that's normal. The intra-university mail is slower, at Yale itself. If I had an address in town (like last year at Bethany) I would gain several days. When I receive nothing from you I am like a dying tortoise, still alive, on its back. You can see it erect [*bander*] its impotence toward the sky, and never by itself will it be able . . .

That which, when we are out of arguments, at the end of our rope, we between us call "the past," I defy the languages of the world, all of them, to translate one day. When we speak of it ourselves, as of the most pitiless destiny that would strike the gods themselves with impotence, we do not understand very well what we are saying. This is one of the things that I tried to explain to you in the letter that came back to me from the PR (I have brought it here but I am afraid to open it, and little by little I am forgetting it, forgetting the "details," but there were only details, and they were not apt to clear me unless you were willing to receive them in a certain way. What is important is that I told you them, and an empty envelope would have done the trick just as well. Therefore, you must believe me, must not need them if you love me. It is also for this reason that I will not send it to you a second time)

I am continuing on one of the cards—I brought a lot of them with me. Turn it over and look at it horizontally, Plato on his back. He is a pain at moments, that one. He did not want to die.

24 September 1977.

and I think about those great cynics: they abuse their public credit in order to pass off, by the route of the press, on a publishing circuit, "personal messages." The radio transmits, people buy, no one understands anything, but finally it's interesting, there is always the investment of something. And this is not the exception, from Socrates to Freud, they have all done it. And the collectors of post cards open libraries, write theses, found universities, research institutes, departments of philosophy or of comparative literature.

this, my love, me: the last photomaton.

I will have written to you, written also in every code, loved according to every genre. All colors, all tones are ours.

Have still received nothing from you, it is long, I miss you. Yesterday already I invested the place, as I do everywhere that I arrive. Translation: I am preparing the maximum of pickups for myself, counting them, very attentive especially to such and such a one, that I must not miss, for example Saturday afternoon or Sunday. This is the first appeasement, when I am without you, and in order really to feel what I am talking about, I mean about my body, you must recall what an American mailbox standing in the street is like, how one opens it, how the pickups are indicated, and the form and the weight of that oblique cover that you pull toward yourself at the last moment. And then I go over to the other end of the mall, the large, all-white post office, to buy series of rare or recent stamps and how well you know that this becomes a rite, a slow ceremony for every letter. I choose, I calculate, I write to you on the envelope with all these *stamps* (every autumn I again find the lady who sells the stamps by bulk or for philatelists, she is enormous and has difficulty moving around in the glass booth where she is enclosed; she is very bossy and very lively nevertheless, I think she really understands me, she would like to take part in a great scene that she does not see, she treats me a bit like a son who comes to make obscene confidences to her). It's new, the love of stamps, in me, it's not a collector's love but only a sender's love. And I want you to look at the envelope for a long time before you open me. Here I am not speaking of the word "*timbre*," with which I have a very old liaison (along with the types, the tympans, qual quelle, etc.), but of the little rectangular sticker charged with captions and pictures. It is an allegory of all of history, our history, that I would like to recount to you interminably in the letter every time, as if I were boasting by lodging it there entirely. For example, suppose that one day a stamp of S. and p. is made. Well then, in advance those two would comprehend us. Using a certain art of classic composition, and of recomposition, one could tell everything, tell us everything, tell everything about us with the traits of this scene. I bet that nothing is missing and that we are there. It suffices to manipulate—as they themselves do moreover (tricks, sleight of hand, maneuvers)—, to cut, to paste, to put in motion or to parcel, with displacements of filters and a great tropic agility. It would even be possible, I bet, to make out of it a transcendental false-stamp into which every other possible stamp could be translated, kings, queens, wars, victories, inventions, flowers, religious or state institutions, communism and democracy (say, for example the one that I am pasting on the envelope, with a bird's feather in an inkwell and the caption, "*The ability to write, a root of democracy*"). To finish up with the daily card of my itineraries at Yale, there are long stations in those stores that never interest me in France: *Cards 'n' Things*. I spend hours in them choosing reproductions, and especially those unspeakable, unpresentable cheap lithos that I am going to inundate you with for weeks, and then all the *stationery* material (letter paper with inscriptions, envelopes of every size, aerograms—but I'm not going to buy any more of them, I can't stand those letters without envelope—). Okay, I'm stopping.

Do you believe that ecstasy, what they call orgasm, and the synchronic if you please, releases [*lève les cales*] the time difference [*décalage horaire*]? Myself, I do not. Among all the follies of Alcibiades, one of the most sublime, at the end of *Funeral Rites* I think, a sober and inflamed eulogy, a reasoned mysticism, as I like it, of anachronistic coming: to give the other time, to give it to him to come alone (ah, in front of you, of course, but what does this mean? in front of you and thanks to you), would be the purest gift of love, the only, the untimely one, when you remain alone on the other shore. The synchronic, the contemporaneous is the attraction of all vulgarities, don't you think? Still it is necessary, while the other appears occupied elsewhere, look, sex in hand, but whose, to know this, that you will be able to keep quiet as our absolute secret:

and after the telephone call, I will turn my back to you to sleep, as usual, and you will paste yourself against me, giving me your hand, you will envelop me.

25 September 1977.

I am coming back from the department, only one letter from you, how long it is, the one you had sent before my departure. This discrepancy is killing me, and it also is making me live, it is enjoyment itself.

Yes, you really did sniff it out, guessed finally, rather than identified. It was that patchouli from the Trône fair (how you had mistreated me!), I had come across it in the bathroom. But contrary to what you seem to believe, it wasn't only in Socrates' beard, but there was some elsewhere, too, look again, if any remains. And you're right, the "correct," expert interpretation of S. and p. will change nothing. The icon is there, much more vast than science, the support of all our fantasies. In the beginning was their own fantasy, that was to engender everything, up to the work of Paris. According to *Plato* it was first *Socrates* who *will have written,* having made or let him write. There is there a *souffrance de la destination* (no, not a fate neurosis, although . . .) in which I have every right to recognize myself. I am suffering (but like everyone, no? me, I know it) from a real pathology of destination: I am always addressing myself to someone else (no, to someone else still!), but to whom? I absolve myself by remarking that this is due, before me, to the power, of no matter what sign, the "first" trait, the "first" mark, to be remarked, precisely, to be repeated, and therefore divided, turned away from whatever singular destination, and this by virtue of its very possibility, its very address. It is its address that makes it into a post card that multiplies, to the point of a crowd, my addressee, female. And by the same token, of course, my addressee, male. A normal pathology, of course, but for me this is the only *meurtrière:* one kills someone by addressing a letter to him that is not destined to him, and thereby declaring one's love or even one's hatred. And I kill you at every moment, but I love you. And you can no longer doubt it, even if I destroy everything with the most amorous patience (as do you, moreover), beginning with myself. *I'm destroying my own life,* I had said to him [*lui*] in English in the car. If I address myself, as it is said, always to someone else, and otherwise (right here, again), I can no longer address myself by myself. Only to myself, you will say, finally sending me all those cards, sending me *Socrates* and *Plato* just as they send themselves to each other. No, not even, no return, it does not come back to me. I even lose the identity of the, as they say, sender, the emitter. And yet no one better than I will have known how, or rather will have loved to destine, uniquely. This is the disaster on the basis of which I love you, uniquely. You, toward whom at this very moment, even forgetting your name I address myself.

                    A bientot, à toujours,

                         I'm going out to post this letter at the corner, slipping in Dupont and Dupond again (the second bloodhound totologizes, goes further, like the disciple in the dialogues, raising his finger: "I will say even more"). Don't go off believing that they are two. If you pay the necessary attention, like us they secretly resemble each other, they "send" themselves each other—a bit more than a picture, I will say even more than a fantasy, the madness of this constant increase that we experience to the point of exhausting our strength.

                         I am going to call you from the *phonebooth* on *Elm Street* after having given this to the big glutton who will restore it to you a long time afterwards. I am going to call you *"collect"* on behalf of Monsieur Brégou, you will hear my voice and I will hear you refuse, saying that the woman who answers to your name is not there. It will not have cost us ten cents. Well yes, here I am in *"connect, I cut,"* as the little one said from the empty fortress.

26 September 1977.

after the first classes, I got back to work. I am thinking occasionally, once more, of the preface to the *Legs* which would announce the book of the *postes* (as one says book of the dead), all the while caressing, with other hands, among other things and other words, our enclosed friend, I mean "Fido" and Fido. And of course, there is not only the *facteur de la vérité, du tout,* there is not only the family scenes, the scene of inheritance, and the questioning of the "cause" of the analytic movement, etc., there is also, as you pointed out to me right away, the chance that must not be abused: the Reality Principle [*Principe de Réalité*] (and who knows this better than us?) is the poste restante [PR] of the Postal Principle, I mean of the Pleasure Principle (PP). And this is demonstrable, with death at both ends. If I had the time I also would write on the necessity and the abuses of these false formalizations, playing on the initials. And why this is being developed today (I have several hypotheses). But you know that I never write *on* anything, not even on the post card or on telethisthat. Even if I feign writing about it, and no matter what I say, before all else I am seeking to produce effects, (*sur toi, on you.* What do they do here in order to avoid the plural? Their grammar is very bizarre. I would not have been able to love you in English, you are untranslatable. Or I would have had recourse, more than ever, to anachronistic procedures, even more retro, I would have made you theatrical, divine. Do you think it would have changed something, you, *toi,* this singular in disuse?). And also "liaison" (amorous or postal), this is the word that very legitimately knots together the propositions of the preface with the entire problematic of bound energy, of *Bindung* in *Beyond.* Basta, as Fido says, enough on this subject. Did I tell you that we are the infant twins (heterozygous but homosexual) of those two Double-doubles [*Sosie-sosie*]?

Got nothing from you this morning. I am without strength for anything, even for writing you, although I want to do it without any interruption. And, moreover, even when you are there. Even when you are there you haunt me, I want to recall you to my aid, perhaps so that you leave me absolutely, and so that finally I no longer lack anything. Don't believe a word of it, there it is you who are speaking in me. You recognize your discourse. You love me only when I am there. But there is a word that we have never been able to translate for ourselves, the one to the other. Nor is to, *à* (to you, *à toi,* I give, I am, I follow, I address myself, I dedicate, I obey). The day that you know what it means, call me up without delay

Far from you I let myself fall all the time. This is why I have to hang on to you, hold you by the hand or by the hair while writing without interruption. For I do write you, you didn't know, without interruption—even if I don't send everything. If I then lose my life, it is that along with the correct destination (since you are not there), the tone [*le ton*], is also refused to me. *Ton,* this for me is the name of God, my God [*mon Dieu*], the one that I do not find. All of them, do you understand, I know all of them, and they are all virtually possible for me, I am so old, and all the genres. I can't stand any of them, right away I recognize in them a genre clause. At the limit, I would like to erase all the traits of language, coming back to the most simple (you know, like when I breathe into the phone without saying anything and then you laugh and the Atlantic recedes), no not in order "to-create-my-love-a-new-language" (I am not going to play that trick on you again, although I still believe in it, in that old postal code), but in order to send you "words" that are "true" enough for me not to recognize them. Then I would be absolved, no genre could be identified, suspected, no more than if I copied for you, now, in the most irresponsible fashion, a Persian dictionary (and yet you might believe that this was calculated, Persian, like all those cheap lithos, calculated because of Esther or Cyrus, the great "conceptor" of the postal empire, the great master of order, others would suspect taking a more provincial position than ever, a tourist's declaration on the Iranian uprising: you know what I think of it). How to proceed, how to continue to walk? I fall all the time (in one way or another). You alone can lift me up in silence, if you say "come" to me again, right here.

I have told you what I expect you to say to me, but don't be afraid.

27 September 1977. I'm writing to you in the train that's taking me back from New York. I'm not feeling well, too much memory, too many memories which overlap and exclude each other without mercy.

Tell me, my love, give me the truth, let me finish with it, choose the dose (a terrible word, we know it well in all the folds of its history, one night, I asked the same thing of you and you told me that truth cannot be dosed or cannot be given, I no longer remember which. I've had enough of being frightening. Of whom am I afraid? who is he afraid of, this child, and who uses him in order to send terrifying signs everywhere, in order to get pleasure from it and to be absolved of it at the same time, in order to write? I miss you. When will we pardon each other my love? Oh, if you had only been able to read the letter that came back to me, if it had been done in one single time, without complication and without any back-and-forth. Now you will never read it, I refuse, and you will never pardon. You could have, however, without my even having a word to justify myself. You could have forbidden me the gesture which consists in explaining oneself, in describing—and taking a stand. Did I not do so? Yes, comparison is not possible and dissymmetry remains infinite, but precisely, precisely.

27 September 1977.
        "Disastrologies"—would be the title, do you like it? I think it suits us well.
        One day you were walking in front of me without knowing me, without looking at me. I fell on you.

28 September 1977.
        As you come to me from the only place in which I do not feel myself loved, I also have the feeling that you are alone in loving me, alone in being able not to love me. And this starting from that place on the board, you know, the chance of the very first encounter—so improbable and so fatal. As we often ask ourselves: what would have happened if such and such a detail, at such and such a time (and it is always a question of cars and trains, and of course of letters)

2 October 1977.
        For the day that there will be a reading of the Oxford card, the one and true reading, will be the end of history. Or the becoming-prose of our love.

3 October 1977.

A whole packet of letters, finally, here they never arrive one after the other. I am reborn, I was afraid. Everything you say to me is so good.

It's true, let's talk about it again a bit, that I am neglecting somewhat the schema of fraternal rivalry between S and p. And you are right to remind me that I nevertheless have paid for this knowledge, in my family, pharmacist's side, and the name of the eldest is written here in its entirety. They can only send each other children and put them to death, *while writing each other.*

5 October 1977.

I am rereading one of the letters received yesterday. Understand that these "details" are of no interest to you, however true they might be, that there is no reason for them to become to such an extent a life-and-death question for you, or for the right to abandon you, as you say, to your love. In any event, it is a question of things that I, myself, have lived alone, and which never, no matter how little, could have contaminated our life. I myself have never understood or admitted the "secret," not even that it might be possible (that one might think something and that one might, already physically, keep it to oneself, that it is not read instantaneously on a giant screen, bigger than the forehead, is a monstrosity that will always remain unthinkable for me, but unthinkable like the slightest failure of the Omnipresent One, like your absence, and that however close, you are not there at this moment when I am writing to you while from another table in this restaurant a couple of students has just ordered the waitress to send me a beer *"because they enjoyed your lecture"* (the lecture *in English* on Searle—this does not mean that they "took pleasure" [*joui"*] from it but all the same, since it happened to me more often than usual that I no longer understood what I was saying, in this text translated by Sam, I find here a rather fine allegory of pleasure, *jouissance*). Therefore I will not send back that Letter that chance or mischance returned to me and that I would succeed in forgetting without you. Do as I do, and learn faith. I don't even recall if, commenting on the "confession," if it can be put thus, that you had extorted from me—and this, yes, can be put thus—I had indeed specified that I said "it's not impossible," and not, as you constantly repeat, "it's possible."

6 October 1977.

and when I say *"je suis,"* with you, I am playing poker, I am (following) you the way one follows a raise, and taking the step, betting on your faith, I come back—and I wait for you to come back, yourself, on your "determination" (I hate that word, which your mouth is full of, say "Bestimmung" while you're at it or "destination"! and what's more, you change it, without warning, as if this were customary, as if you were standing at the gaming table, and if I sent you back my small pro domo plea from September, you would really be capable of continuing to play with me).

7 October 1977.

how I loved all that you said to me just now, your voice was intact. What strength you give me

and I got myself back together, back to work too, and to running. It's true, never has there been such a beautiful couple.

inseparable. Everything comes back to the child. Look at the discourse they address each other on the immortality of the soul. In truth they had nothing to say on immortality. By writing to each other they have made immortality the way we made love. This is our interminable symposium, our council or our conclave.

You are very interested in their beard, I see, me too; have you noticed that every time we leave each other I get the idea of letting mine grow? I did it once, at Easter (your "determination" was more definitive than ever), I had stayed alone on vacation and I had kept it for seven days (at the demand, it is true, of the two boys). The "seven days," at home, are the first week of mourning, above all the men are not supposed to shave. One says "he has done the seven days." No meals are taken outside the home. When we got back together, I think that it had not displeased you.

You who know, tell me the truth, tell me your secret. In truth, what does to destine mean? I am rereading before sealing (which I have a horror of, and almost never do, it is as if I wanted to control, hold back, or filter what I tell you, to give in a bit to accursed literature), and I recall that already in the car, one day, you had said to me, or I had said, yes, the only couple in the world. Keep us, I am drawing us, here, there, and I call you by your name.

7 October 1977.
        I have been loaned a radio and a tape recorder. You will get
the cassette that I just sent you in three or four days. To calculate it
"widely," call next Sunday (at midnight for you) at the moment
when you start to listen to me (well, it's mostly music, the song of
another voice, but you will accept it as me, and then I have added
several words, very little, that I could not bear to hear again, you
know my allergy). It will be 6 o'clock here. I will be on the floor,
lying on my back
        Don't leave this tape around.

7 October 1977.
        No, the truth, that's the dose.

7 October 1977.
        two brothers, one of whom is dead and the others jealous,
beyond the pleasure principle (II).
        When we fell upon each other, I knew
right away, you can verify this in the very old letters, that everything was played out in advance, written into the disaster, an
ordered set of parts "like music paper."

7 October 1977.
        This couple drives them crazy, you understand. One must
not help them to erase or to appropriate the thing, to enframe it in
their vulgar little space. I want you to remain noble, you are no-
bility itself and I love only you, this crazy alliance which is now
making you afraid. Do not let them poison our love. Let the dose
remain between us. You must not leave to them the measure of life
and death. This letter, I am quoting you, is interminable because it
asks of you the impossible.

7 October 1977.
        At least help me so that death comes to us only from us.
Do not give in to generality.
        It's true, I will have—the word in which you
complain is doubtless once again the most correct one—"intercepted" my own letter. But I confirm that it will be irreversible.

Moreover, this is the law, which no letter ever escapes. It can never be enclosed, and an intercepted letter, this is what I would like you to understand, is without value, it is as if it were at everyone's disposition, another post card. You are not going to decide about your life, about ours, on a post card? And about theirs. Then you have to believe in us. And it is because I believe in us that I regret even having written that narrative, having sent it, and that now I forget it. Or almost, finally, but already I am confusing the details a bit and no longer know very well of whom or of what I wanted to talk to you.

7 October 1977.

One can say, in effect, that he is writing on a mirror, or on a rearview mirror, and that only the color is missing. Not the music: *Plato,* you recall, as orchestra leader *(conductor)* and *Socrates* instrumentalist. But the color, yes, I had not thought of it. One day you will forget all the messages in lipstick on the little mirror in the bathroom. Sometimes you were gone at the moment when I shaped this kind of rebus, always somewhat the same, at other times I came because you were looking at yourself in the mirror, I was behind you, I took the red stick and passing my arm under yours I drew, while you watched me, continuing with your makeup.

8 October 1977.

is it to silence a name, or rather to sing it? Myself, I sing it while multiplying it to infinity, while dissimulating it under all the other names that I give to your name. The danger is mortal but the Thing too, and the name, yours, resonates only at this price, at this monstrous risk that I have made you run from the very first second. In your name, *par* the detour of your name, *via* your name which is not you, not even a part of you, I can always lose you en route, because of the homonyms, all the names of things that I substitute for it while singing, because of your tricky resemblance to all your names. Then the call can be arrested en route, come to a halt through the vocable *(par, per* the very echo of the call), through my voice itself I begin to lose you, I lose you if you do not answer. Which you can always do; this is what I explained to you in the September letter. But I plead, I plead, and I no longer want to have to defend a cause to you.

9 October 1977.

and after, when you called me back, that word hurt me, I did not dare say it. For me it wasn't any "playback," no part of my body or of my soul let itself be distracted.

none of that "bad" playback please, the other one is fatal and we would not say anything to each other otherwise.

The disaster, I used to say the carnage, is this cursed part of *par* in every word. For as long as I call you by, *par,* your name, if you do not have faith in me, if you do not yet help me to say me, and you must start over every day, at every instant, right here, playback will come to hover between us. Between my lips, it passes via, *par,* your name which I deliver to you, to the chance that you would give it. This *per* between us is the very site of the disaster, it can always miss the chance. If then you do not come toward me with a simple step, *pas,* in a single trait, you let the call be detoured, perhaps this has always happened, and you abandon me to the perversion of playback, to all perfidies, the worst ones, to all perjuries, you set all my letters on the wrong path, you permit infidelity right at this second. *Per* is the post, the halt, *souffrance.* This law, sweet lord, is in your hands. Play well.

10 October 1977.

Just a few more days and you will no longer have this six-hour advance on me, I will catch you, will catch up with you, you will turn around and I will be there.

These cables between us, and soon satellites, all these satellites. The image rather pleases me, and you too, on the little photo, with the word "gravitation" behind. If you depart (but yes, whenever you wish, whenever you're "determined" enough), well then depart, you can't do anything about it, about gravitation.

11 October 1977.

and I got myself back to work. Translate, you have the code, I work (myself) and it is always a question of my mourning, of you, and the infernal division which turns me away from everything. To myself, since you, I can no longer address myself. The part of me that you keep is bigger than me and the slightest doubt is terrifying. Even before abandoning me you lose me at every in-

stant. Even if you do not depart, if you never leave me, the forgetting of me in you becomes devastating. For I must love it. For example, I see proof of the fact that for me you are forgetting, I would
even say the proper name of forgetting, one of its synonyms in any
case, in my September letter (it came back to me on the 14th, I'm
pretty sure): if I progressively forget its contents, not only the "general" sense, but the minute descriptions—terribly honest, I must
say, and from me you can believe it in advance—, it is not by virtue
of some "psychological" failure of what they call memory. It's
much more serious—and beautiful. It's you. Turned toward you, I,
the obsessional "passist," the great fetishist of memory, I let the
most sacred part of my history annihilate itself. And it's not even I
who have the initiative for this, it's you, it's you who are losing my
memory. If you have a good understanding of what I am saying, you
will rejoice over the slip concerning the postal code—and that
since I refuse to send you back this letter, this archive which interests no one when all is said and done, neither you nor me nor anyone. Depart if you wish, as you have done, but remember what I
have just told you.

Thus, I was saying, I am working. I'm taking notes for
the preface. In it I would have (practically, effectively, perfor-
matively) to make, but for you, my sweet love, my immense one,
the demonstration that a letter can always—and therefore must—
never arrive at its destination. And that this is not negative, it's
good, and is the condition (the tragic condition, certainly, and we
know something about that) that something does arrive—and that I
love you. Who would I have loved, otherwise? My family, perhaps,
starting with my father. As for the two robed transvestites, what is
doubtless most important is that each *is carrying* the name of the
other above his head. The one supports the name of the other. Confusion of names, they only have a single one ("Fido"-Fido). You
can see the one who is losing and is swearing by the name of the
other. The carrying of the name, the carriage of the head. And all
those doses of perfume around them. They stink (on this topic, yes,
the *pharmakon* can be a perfume, Plato did not like perfumers, I
think—to be specified). They make us say everything, confess
everything (this couple of crazies, this brochette of two, look at the
double play of hooks and crooks between *Socrates'* legs, this duo
forms a single matrix, a reserve of types, a treasure of discourse).
They stand guard and satellize every one of our phrases (one day, I
will be dead, if you reread the post cards I sent you, by the thou-
sands not so, even before I fell upon *S.* and *p.*, you will notice per-

haps (if you pay the necessary price) that everything I write is legendary, a more or less elliptical, redundant, or translatable legend, caption, *of the picture*. Of the icon which is found on the back of the text and watches over it, or, in a somewhat more perverse way, precedes or follows the *envoi*. Never have I said anything to you, only transferred what I saw or believed to see—what in truth you let me see. And first of all, it's true, there were the hours spent in all those stores or museums choosing what had to be seen to show to you.

Sorry for the beginning of this somewhat dolorous letter. It's always the same thing that comes back, the same wound, it speaks in my place as soon as I open the lips, my own, however.

Promise me that one day there will be a world. And a body.

12 October 1977. You just called a moment ago. I confirm: Roissy, Saturday, 7 o'clock (French time). If I can take an earlier plane, I'll call from New York or when I arrive. After four days without anything (an absolute fast, and I somewhat suspect the Department secretary of being too interested in us—no, she's very nice, but I never see the *mailman* here, all the *courrier* goes through the University), several letters from you, very long. I am lying down and rereading (I had first done it on the course between Harkness Hall and Trumbull). This is always how I imagine the effects of a blood transfusion in the last extremity: the warmth comes back, it invades everything, simultaneously very slowly and all at once, one no longer knows, but from the inside, never from the place of transfusion. You speak to me and send me my blood from the depths of me. Despite everything, never have I been so happy as at this very instant. Of course these letters are six days old, but you knew in advance, didn't you, even if now I am alone with your words and you are in the course of exchanging others with God knows who (I am looking at your schedule: yes, I see). Forgive me this morbid joke that I cannot get away from suddenly: one must never mistake the blood group (A, B, AB, O, + or − Rhesus factor, etc.), or it's death that one sends with a stroke of the syringe. One of your letters, one day, a telegram.

You're right, I am not making you say it, psychoanalysis ended. We breathe this end as the air of our history. It will not have lasted too long finally. What is also opened up, and for the same teleo-eschatological reason, I mean along with the interminable end of this reason, is perhaps a new era, post-psychoanalytic and post-postal. But we will still love each other, we have only just begun. First it is necessary that psychoanalysis and the post arrive, that they arrive, if this is possible, at their ends.

13 October 1977. Don't get too wrapped up in Esther. I don't believe too much in it, perhaps it's only a fine psychoanalytic solution (elegant, economical, as is said of a mathematical demonstration, a formalization of great style). She would open up the passage for me, she would liberate fruitful paths, but she can also remain the most sterile (most paralyzing) of hypotheses. Sterility must be accepted, always.

Yes, yes, I approve completely, literature must remain "insupportable." Which I also understand as: without the slightest support.
I will arrive before, my love, what I am writing to you here, that I love you, and that you knew already. But if ever "something happened to me," as my father would have said, keep us and believe in my last thought.

P.S. I forgot, you are completely right: one of the paradoxes of destination, is that if you wanted *to demonstrate,* for someone, that something never arrives at its destination, it's all over. The demonstration, once it had reached its end, would have proved what it was not supposed to demonstrate. But this is why, dear friend, I always say "a letter *can* always *not* arrive at its destination, etc." This is a chance.*

You know that I never say that I'm right and never demonstrate anything. They support this very badly, consequently they would like nothing to have happened, everything wiped off the map. Wait for me.

*P.S. Finally a chance, if you will, if you yourself can, and if you have it, the chance (*tukhē,* fortune, this is what I mean, good fortune, good fate: us). The mischance (the mis-address) of this chance is that in order *to be able* not to arrive, it must bear within itself a force and a structure, a straying of the destination, such that it *must* also not arrive in any way. Even in arriving (always to some "subject"), the letter takes itself away *from the arrival at arrival.* It arrives elsewhere, always several times. You can no longer take hold of it. It is the structure of the letter (as post card, in other words the fatal partition that it must support) which demands this, I have said it elsewhere, delivered to a *facteur* subject to the same law. The letter demands this, right here, and you too, you demand it.

14 October 1977. I depart in several hours, or finally I am coming. Train to New York (Paul is accompanying me to the station), then Kennedy again. At the moment of the valises (the final arrangement, the sorting of papers, etc.), I do not know what to do with my September letter that I have been dragging around with me, for more than a month, like a strange, mute, eloquent, thing, with its moments of sleep, talkative sequences, imagine an inexhaustible corpse—and then sometimes, all of a sudden, nothing more. Incapable of making a decision (I go and come from one to the other without interruption), at this second I'm making up my mind to bring it back, to keep it on me for some time still.

In the notes that I have taken here, always my little pieces of white cardboard (on the post in the Anglo-Saxon countries, I should send them all to you, all by itself it would make an immense epic, the history of the posts is very lovely), I refind this which I transcribe for you. In sum it is a question of the service corresponding to the one which at home, in Bordeaux, stocks, before destruction doubtless, lost letters. They call this "dead letters," and for *envois* without assignable addresses, they can also end up in an auction (*auction* was also the word for the sale of slaves, I saw an inscription barely erased on a wall in Virginia, in Charlottesville); "*Dead Letter Office.—Letters or parcels which cannot be delivered, from defect of address or other cause, are sent to the Division of dead letters and dead parcels post. They are carefully examined on both front and back for the name and address of the sender; if these are found, they are returned to the sender. If the sender's address is lacking, they are kept for a period, after which dead letters are destroyed, while dead parcels are sold at auction.*" "*a period . . . after which . . .*" how do they count with time? I will never understand. Either they do not count, or they have no calculating "principle," and this amounts to the same thing. "Division of dead letters" is a stroke of genius. Myself, I say "division of living letters," and this is what more or less amounts to the same. Everything is played out, remains, wins-and-loses, on the basis of my "divisibility," I mean on the basis of what

I call thus (the partition of the letter which works upon the ideality of the signifier like a Principle of Ruin, shall we say). I ask myself, and truly speaking they could never give me a satisfactory answer on this question, how they distinguish a *letter and a parcel, a dead letter and a dead parcel,* and why they did not sell a *so-called* dead letter at auction. The one that I have in my pocket, for example, if instead of coming back to me it had gone to Bordeaux, or rather if you had been American, why not, and then a *Zip Code* affair, etc. I am affixing myself to put an end to my letter: another photomaton of myself, pitiless no? I am sending it to you to ask you to rip it up and to throw it in little pieces out of the window of your car, going fast, this is always how I disperse things. When you do it, I will have come back.

November or December 1977.
You are still sleeping as I depart. What I have wanted to tell you since my return—and that I can only write to you—is that, although understanding, justifying, accepting all your "reasons," I do not know what is decisive, determining, if you will, in your sad "determination," for me this remains an unintelligible secret. A feeling that another decides for you, destines you to this "determination" without your really knowing yourself what is going on. There is an other in you, who from behind dictates the terrible thing to you, and she is not my ally, I have certainly never had anything to do with her, we (yes, we) do not know her. Without her, not one of all your good "reasons," which, once more, I understand perfectly, would hold for a second. It would suffice that we look at each other, that you turn toward me, and pff . . . we would be alone together, no force in the world could unjoin us. Truly speaking, for me what remains sealed, hermetically, what leaves me enclosed in myself, on my side, irremediably, is not the possibility of your "determination" (I have been thinking it and preparing for it from the first day, I love you on the basis of this thought itself), it is the date. Yes, the "moment" that you choose and which seems to have no relation with anything significant (the argument of the September letter has no value and I will never take it into account). Why not years ago or in years? Why this time? How are you counting it? I sometimes have the impression that the other is drawing lots (drawing me at lots—and this is an arm) within you. And

with what kindness, with what diabolical solicitude you announce
to me the "result of the lottery," how you handle the dose. Sorry for
this word, I erase and keep the entire malediction for myself.

17 November 1977. I again liked the rendez-vous, always the same,
intact, virgin, as if nothing had happened. You wanted it thus, my
destiny, and from you *j'accepte* everything. Once again we said almost nothing to each other (the tea, the lemon pie, one thing and
another, what we then said to each other, as so many other times, is
greater than everything, more inexhaustible than everything that
was ever said, even between us, greater than the very thing that includes it—oh, not me—) and despite everything, all the rest, above
all I admired you: how well you know where you are going! how
well you appear to know where you have to go, and to go to choose,
and to go to sacrifice in order to save what you choose. You are
loved, my beloved love, admired by a monster.

And yet it is you who are
the violent one, my sweet, you who are hacking around in your life,
and are forcing fate. You are so grand, from you *j'accepte* everything. I receive everything, even what you do not know, what you
know less and less.

November or December 1977. You are right nearby, you are reading
in the big bedroom, and I am writing to you my back on the wall,
on the small bed (I brought back the datebook that you left on the
night table and without "digging around," I swear, without reading
or deciphering anything in it, I have torn out this page, at the date
you can see, only in order to write you, and to do so with the pencil
that you had left between the pages). Despite the "determination"
(the word slays me, more than the thing perhaps), you are very
close, since the return from Yale. Moreover this is always what you
say, in those moments, lacking the ability to say anything better to
me: you know, I am right near you. What's more, I believe that it's
true, you are of an absolute sincerity. But you no longer know very
well what you mean. Outside the moments of "determination,"
when we are together for the time of a "remission," (useless to
specify, you know very well what I myself mean by that), you do
not need to throw me this "proximity" as a sop. I myself am in
mourning. For you, by you, smeared with death, and paralyzed.

Paralyzed: paralysis does not mean that one can no longer move or walk, but, in Greek if you please, that there is no more tie, that every bind, every liaison has been unknotted (in other words, of course, analyzed) and that because of this, because one is "exempt," "acquitted" of everything, nothing goes any more, nothing holds together any more, nothing advances any more. The bind and the knot are necessary in order to take a step.

I no longer know what to do with the *"dead letter"* that you again spoke to me about, as if it could make me hope for a new "remission" (no, not of the pain, but of an illness that I will not get out of alive, I know it now without the slightest possible doubt, the premises of the thing are fatal, written above our heads, they surpass our forces, and yourself, my God, you could do nothing about it, this is why I am so passive at bottom). No, I do not know what to do with it. I do not wish thereby to give you the slightest hope of reading it one day (I've told you and retold you why), no more than you would engage yourself to promise whatever in exchange, in any case to promise it to me in a way that is clear and that binds you irreversibly. I don't know what to do with it, which means only: I don't know where to put it. I wish neither to leave it in the house, nor to hide it somewhere, nor to keep it on me. All the same I am not going to rent a safe deposit box in a bank (although I did get information, it's very complicated and doesn't suit my project in any way).

More and more I ask myself if we respond to each other, if I respond to you, if you have ever responded to what I expected from you, for what you are for me.

I am going out to walk for a bit, I'll be back right away, probably I won't go far.

November or December 1977. I will die without knowing how it arrived for you, in your depths. Even how I arrived at you living, if I did at least, and what you could have felt once the film had gone through, at the very moment

You have chosen generality and you are betraying us, both of us. The only chance was monstrousness, as I had announced to you (like good news) from the very first day. This is nothing other than the children, the family, and everything that follows, another way of knowing them finally. And to let oneself be known by madness (it knows me), to leave the door open to it as to

Elijah, for a visit whose hour and day it would decide. The non-family is still the family, the same network, the same destiny of filiation. There are better things to do and we had only one life.
                                                                I am waiting
for the "remission," I no longer believe in it. It is as if there were a *meurtrière* between us and we look at each other through it. It depends upon you, finally, it does not depend upon me for this to cease. But for as long as we talk to each other, even if to tear each other apart, to curse, to damn each other, the disaster is supended, you are there. Unless I am already speaking all alone and playing like a smart monkey on a typewriter.
                                                I am coming back very, very late, this
session will be longer than the others. You can not wait for me. Don't forget the little tune and the record left on the turntable.

9 December 1977.
            I liked it that you cried at that moment, when we re-found each other on the floor and I cried too. In an instant there was no longer anything, anything between us, no one. Or rather (pardon this rhetoric, I no longer know, I know less than ever in what mode to write and writing horrifies me, more than at any other moment in the past) everything remaining *between us,* there was no longer anything between us. When we could no longer wait, after a simple glance, a divine decision (divine because we no longer know who says yes to the other, who suddenly acquiesces, and there is nothing more to suffer, no longer any delay), we fell on each other, we have forgotten the very idea of nudity. I forgot you yourself, never had I been as happy, I even forgot that there had been other times, so many other times, even a first time. And this entire history, our past already, which watched over us, I forgot it along with you. Your specter (the other one, the bad one, that maternizing milliner who dictates sententious "determinations" to you) had disappeared as if by magic, finally alone, the one addressed to the other on the floor (very hard, huh, the floor, never have I so loved the ground, death is the bed, it's so good).
                                                An hour later ("the same ones, an
hour later," you had said in analogous circumstances, on a little street in Athens. You were walking on my arm bursting with laughter, we had left hell, with all its maledictions, only two or three clock hours behind us and already we were looking for another restaurant), one hour later we ate a lot (fish, fish) and yet I knew, you

barely hid it from me, that we were entering into the phase of another "remission." The duration alone remained indeterminate and for the first time I had the idea of a fortune teller. No, not in order to have a date finally, a certainty, a foreknowledge, but in order to know what a fortune teller was, how she analyzed all that. And who really was your specter, or that twin sister that you do not have. I am your twin sister, how do you want us to get out of it? And when you "determine" yourself, what you determine is no longer you. I am stopping (you have just called, I like it that you profit by the "intervals" this way).

December 1977 (between the 9th and the 22d). You are there, right nearby, and I still need to write to you. You were right to call me back the other night, me too, at the moment of the worst absences, I tell you "I am here" and it appears derisive to you even if you receive it smiling. The remission is good (the *"renvoi,"* right, until later, while waiting for what? but to be sent off again finally, to oneself or to the other). I am here, several meters away from you, I can hear you moving around. I've never been so strong.

Got back to our friends. Fido and Fido appears very gay suddenly, for a week now. A complete turnabout (like you, thanks, thanks for no longer talking to me about the *"dead letter"* even if I know that you have not forgotten it and still desire it). S. is visibly the double of p. Twice his size, look, and yet the same. And yet S. is a part (an instrumental part, metonomy or synechdoche of instrument), the pen of p. S. is smaller than p., once seated, and he is offering himself a *tranche*. It has always been believed that they were two and it is not certain that this is wrong. Nevertheless, p., the double of S., you can feel that he has a hard-on [*il bande*] in his back. Look at the oblique kolossos, at how he is shoving it in between the other's loins, beneath the robe. Like the movement of his arm, he defies all the laws of geometry, of optics, of topics, he defies verisimilitude, such was his purpose, and every classical representation of sets, of the relation between the whole and the part, one and two, the couple and the pair. Once again, profiting by the remission, I want to reread the entire *corpus platonicum* and to settle into it as if into a very refined brothel, with confessionals and peepholes everywhere, mysteries without the slightest vulgarity. No one would ever encounter anyone, I would finally be alone with you, my *noblesse* itself (I shape this word like *diablesse*), the gold of my birth. In the *corpus* it is still the *Letters* that excite me the most, after the Parmenides, and the ones whose authenticity is most suspect. For it is in what is most apocryphal that I recognize my Plato. I'm in letter VIII. For example: "God for wise men, this is the law, for the mad (*aphrosin*) it is pleasure (*edone*)." In the preceding sentence he had said: "Measure is submission to God (dependence, subjection, *douleia*) unmeasure (if it is addressed, says the translator) to men." God, the law beyond the pleasure principle. Now, listen to the instruction of the translator-establisher of the text, a certain Souilhé, in a note: "The logic of these last two propositions is more in Plato's thought than in the formulation he gives of it [???]. To take the two sentences materially [???], one could make them express exactly the opposite of what the author intended, for if it is just to submit oneself to God, since, for some God is the law, for the others pleasure, the ones and the others will act 'according to measure' in obeying their divinity. This is evidently not what Plato thinks [!]. Therefore, one must suppose an intermediary idea, etc."! "Evidently," it is too evident. I will not decide. But look at it, the pleasure they are taking, in making laws, in binding themselves, in coupling their names, the one more divine than the other, I can see us between their legs, we are the law for eternity. In the extent to which we age together, we have centuries behind us, the enjoyment of you becomes more and more sublime, further and further beyond pleasure. I have never loved you so, I have never been so sure of our descendance for I am calling you, like the other, beyond your name, beyond all names.

December 1977 (between the 9th and the 22d).

                              Worked well, I am leaving this note (the money is on the fridge) before leaving. I'll telephone you from there (all things considered, a name, not so? can only telephone itself). Play again with the initials in the sand or the snow: S/p is liaison. Now liaison is the relation secondary/primary under the law of the pleasure principle, the law and the god of liaison, of the *Binden,* of the *Desmos* also. *S et p (hait p),* this is the primary liaison, the liaison of the primary process (the *pp,* not to be confused with the PP, the Pleasure Principle) by the *ps* (secondary process [*processus secondaire*], a linking of madness enough to make one mad. Nothing stands any more, it is the ruin of everything when one sets oneself to playing with initials like this. Our favorite game, you excel at it, big fireworks and the serious people return home somber, suspicious, speculating in the night with the feeling that their investments have been replaced with counterfeit money, that their money already was nothing but a card game to be played out. There remains but a great burst of laughter between us, when we finally run off alone down a very dark little street and you become crazier than I am

December 1977 (between the 9th and the 22d).
here is the spectacle that is given to me, today, men and women, all the psychoanalysts, lying on their backs, you can see them clearly, *supplicating* the old couple ("S/p please") to come to let themselves be taken into analysis. With them oh yes, today! And the blessed old couple doesn't want to hear a word, always running, going on about this and that. Between two strides it sends back the invitation: if contrarily, yes contrarily, you want to come talk a bit with us, the couches are all set up, we'll do it as simply as possible, there will be friends passing through all night, we talk all the time, we hardly ever go to bed.

December 1977 (between the 9th and the 22d).
We have always been preoccupied with dates. Too much so in my opinion, a very bad sign (ages, periods, the birthday superstition, all these arithmetics of fate). But don't worry about anything, only good things can happen to us now.

You are beginning to get caught up in the play of my little speculations on Sp. I speculate, I speculate, but I am also the object of the speculation of Sp. For 25 centuries, and as the other old man says upon the death of his daughter, "*la séance continue*"! Despite his uncle the counterfeiter, who took a good deal of initiative in this domain, and we have not finished paying for this knowledge, the grandfather of Psychoanalysis was himself, inversely, speculated by Sp. On the program of their double and interminable reciprocal self-analysis, the definition of the blessed couple. Combine, play with the *tranches:* S. in analysis with p.: which makes him write or permits him to write. S. analyzes p.: he listens looking elsewhere and without the other's seeing he takes notes (out of which, moreover, he will write no book, no work or "syngram"). In the intervals, since they are both members, legitimate, certified by the SPP thing, they each have *tranches* with the other, transference against transference. And they publish everything.

S. is part of p. who is but a piece in S., a big piece, certainly, and not badly placed, but a piece, that the other, the master, tries to treat from under the leg. They are each a part of the other but not of the whole [*du tout*]. This is our lot, my love, nothing is to be hoped at all [*du tout*]. The children don't settle anything. In S. and p. the limit between introjection and incorporation is unfindable, this is what Matthew Paris meant in the 13th century, I decree it: p + S does not make any whole [*du tout*], is not all, makes perhaps a couple or an ego, or two, but not a whole at all [*pas du tout*]. It only tranches. This is why they love each other [*ils s'aiment*], almost as much as we do (truthfully they were the only ones before us) but they despise each other. Question of limits: they no longer know where the one begins and the other ends. And they send each other cards that they never receive, like children (corruptions, plagiarisms in the strict sense, and from the first *envoi* abortions—they were both against, but correctly, and it can occur even after birth). I venture this enormity: they will have had no progeniture (nothing, zero, absolute misunderstanding, error over the names, not the slightest socratico-platonic heritage that really holds) although they have had all the descendants in the world. This is what is trailing us, not so bad. Our holocaust is to come, very close even, I feel it.

December 1977 (between the 9th and the 22d).

If they had had a child together, I mean a real one, a little Greek from the 5th century, what would they have called it? I note what you told me this morning in order to make use of it in my coming publications (you know that I am still thinking about the preface to the *legs?*): it is not Socrates but his demon who is having a *tranche* with young Plato. The latter than starts to hear voices, as it happens to me to hear your specter dictate your sinister "determinations" to you: he does not know, or does not want, that you love, and especially that you are my sun, the beloved of my life. I say "he" but I'm convinced that it's "she," your specter.

December 1977 (between the 9th and the 22d).   *Socrates* is having his period, this is why.

December 1977 (between the 9th and the 22d).   This   reproduction   makes
me sick to my stomach now. Look at them. I don't want *to know*
anything more about it. Afraid that the stroke of genius will get lost
in generalities (remember what I reproached you for one day: for
having chosen over us generality, in other words, the law, the children, etc.). Let them live, that is without us, these two little ones
who are teaching each other to read and to write. We have better
things to do and they have everything to gain.

                                                              and p. says to his mama (he
has a family, nieces and all that, I'll tell you one day): "you know, I
think I have a crypt." No, not a grippe, that's all over, the vaccine is
commercialized: a crypt. I ask myself what we can do about that. I
feel myself vaguely guilty; actually I never feel guilty, indeed I believe that this *has never absolutely happened* [*arrivé*] *to me,* but
accused yes, and within myself, this is the worst, by I don't know
who, always by children, a child who resembles me.

22 December 1977. I am leaving you this note on your secretary so
that you can reflect upon it in my absence.

                                          It now appears played out to me,
more than probable. To think that this too derives from the slip.
Yours, of course, you didn't want to know any more about it, but for
myself an immense tenderness ordered me no longer to put you on
your guard. Your desire has always been mine, and each of its faux-
pas. Since the last "remission" I have been feeling this obscure met-
amorphosis of you, and as always I have been accompanying it in
my body, the mists of a new serenity above the worst anxiety: the
irreversible this time. I knew all this in advance, it had to happen
[*arriver*]—in order not to happen [*arriver*]. Since this is how it is, I
beg you, don't let me make the decision all by myself (this would be
the first time, you are so attached to your autonomy). Whatever you
decide will be fine, I will approve and will take it on myself, will
burden myself with it as if with my own life, as much as possible.

                                                                     In   any
event you have to depart, now, the formalities are over, after the

vacation you will still be mistress of the decision. There again, and more than ever it is the case to say so, I am (following) you, I am still living in you and for you. Christmas (the most propitious period) will give you the time up there to ripen the thing. Even if the worst happens, never will I have been so happy (with the tragic twist to which I bend this word, an entire criminal style, a visitation card). During the vacation I am speculating on Titus's small rectangular *coffins*. This, as I will show, again occurs between S and p, our immense and impossible paradigm (he will have had the foreseeing of everything, we are inscribed in it as on a fortune teller's table. Sp knows everything, even the worst and the best of what will have to happen to us, as soon as you return. He knows everything and say it to themselves. And between the two, there never will have been any other choice for "me," any other place than the back-and-forth without interruption, without interrupter, between two forms of death. From one death to the other I am like the courier who bears the news, good news, bad news. He warns of the other death, seeing the one or the other come. Too lucid and almost blind, he goes from one wall to the other, recognizes the situation of the *meurtrière* in the stones and the cement of the fortification. The missive has been deposited in it. Thus he hastens to the other fortress: another *meurtrière*, without meeting anyone he deposits in it the message come from the other. He must not and cannot decipher it en route, he is only a *facteur*. He attempts to divine but what a job. He would have to be able to stop running.

This transparent phrase: you know what the children are for me.

9 January 1978.

I would have preferred that you not go with me to the clinic, but there was no other choice. When you left again, the night before, I was furious with you. You let me make the decision all by myself. And if I died in this clinic, alone, without anyone having been warned? When I awoke (the nurse was holding my hand, everything was white), I was however, I don't understand why, reconciled with you. You felt it, I hope, when you came back to see me. I couldn't say anything. I cannot bear your solitude, that is all. It makes me dizzy, it calls to me like a child.

I have never so desired what I could not desire—this cry between us.

me, it only happens to me.   All this had to happen [*arriver*] to

Undated (probably between 9 January and Easter 1978).
                                          I came back very
quickly (I had forgotten the keys—and my checkbook is still in
your pocketbook). To follow up our little dialogue from last night
(genre, aporetic): just as for us, the problem of the child posed itself for them only in a second, at the very second when they accepted their homosexuality, not at all before this second of truth.
                                                         But yes,
my dear-bid, almost all my slips are calculated, you will not catch
me.

Undated (probably the same period).
                                  One does not *count* with children
(neither contract, nor exchange, nor calculation, nothing). If there
are any, they do not make a sign. Nor a symbol. Nor a *mandat* (if
there are any, one must sacrifice the poste, *autodafé*), one demands
no more, commands no more. I am speaking first of all of the child
in itself.
   Once again this "remission" is indeed the last one, and I believe in
it. You are distancing yourself again, I do not cry, I only become
more and more grave, I walk more heavily, more seriously, I like
myself less and less. You are not only sending me, myself, away,
you are sending back to me, myself, as one emits a poison that
reaches the heart without waiting, an "image" of myself that I will
have a hard time pardoning you for. I try to remain light, to resemble the person you believed to love, I force laughter. I no longer
have anything to say in my name. I only draw our symbol, these
interlaced lines of life, there, I put into it all the slowness and all the
application in the world
                       The day that I no longer will be able to write to
you, I will still send them to you on the back of a post card, you will
know what I want to say to you, and that I am right nearby. Now
let's chat a bit, my friend. We, in general, we sign with this symbol,
at the end of our epistle. In order to "stuff" ["*farcir*"] the latter
(understand on the subject of the stuffed epistle, that stuffed epistles are generally satiric strophes: they were sung on the occasion of

the feasts of the Donkey, of the Mad, etc. They mime, in the burlesque mode, the sacred epistles, the ones read at mass), understand then that he, if indeed it is he, *"Plato,"* inscribed his symbol
at the beginning of his epistole in order to guarantee its authenticity.
But since he says so in a letter whose authenticity is not absolutely
certain, the Thirteenth, you can always hang on: "Arkhē soi tes
epistoles esto kai ama sumbolon oti par emou estin." Here is the
master of the perverformative, he writes to you: it is indeed me,
here is my signature, you will be able to recognize it, it is authentic, and in order to be more certain, it comes in the first place,
above left, I the undersigned, and below right: let the beginning of
this letter be for you simultaneously the symbol that it is indeed
from me. Wait, it's even more vicious, and visibly destined to Searle
and company, with their entire axiomatoque of the serious/not serious. Further on in the same letter, Plato in effect specifies: "On
the subject of the symbol that distinguishes from the others those of
my letters that I write seriously, spoudē, you recall, I think [oimai
men se memnesthai, if he were sure of it, he would not remind you
of it, and a counterfacteur would not proceed otherwise] which one
it is. Think about it however, and pay close attention. They are, in
effect, numerous, those who ask me to write to them, and it is difficult to refuse them openly. My serious letters therefore begin with
'God,' theos, and those that are less so with 'the gods,' theoi." He
does not say, the devil, "not serious," he says "that are less so,"
etton. You can always run after the proof: as if I were saying to
you, here it is, it is I who am speaking, and I am speaking to you,
uniquely, each time that I write "you," it is that I am addressing
myself authentically to you, with full and true speech, presently.
When I say "all of you" [*"vous"*], when I pluralize, it is that I am
addressing myself less seriously to you, that my letter is not really
destined to you, that it is not destined to arrive at its destination, for
you are, yourself, my unique, my only destination. When I have the
appearance of overflowing you and of speaking to the others somewhat as I do to you, it is that I am overflowing myself. You know to
what point I am solicited, I cannot not answer a bit.
        In the same epistole he
talks a lot about money, of what he is sending for the children, of
the myrtles that he had "set aside" [*"mises en garde"*], says the
translator, and that had rotted, of the dowry that he owes to those of
his nieces who will marry during his lifetime, and of the price that
tomb of his mother would cost him if she came to die: "not more

than ten mines." So much for the farce. On all these subjects also see Letter III (315, 316). I leave you, but do not abandon you, go.

Undated (probably the same period).
                                   but it only depends on you that it is you. And then this note belongs to you, I signed it, to whom else do you want me to say this, this very thing, right here? That you have put an end to the "remission" by once again remembering the *"dead letter,"* the "past" and all the rest does not astonish me. That you did it last night, at a given hour, leaves me stupefied. Can you explain to me, in some more satisfactory fashion finally than what you invoke by speaking of "work," of time for work, of "high and low," etc.? If I understood, I could withdraw more easily. But I still have the impression that the final blow is coming to me from your double, the old-fashioned demon, a small maternal specter, an elegant woman of 1930 coiffed with a little hat and calculating to the last penny (modest prices, monoprix and green stamps). I don't have a damn thing to do with it, I'm not there yet. As for the *"dead letter,"* I had forgotten to tell you (this was at a time when we were stingy with discourse) to whom finally, not knowing where to guard it, I had confided it
                                   and naturally we can be sure of that person's [*sa*] discretion. No question, it goes without saying, on the contents of the thing. One indeed had to suppose that it was rather serious, even vital, but in any event I would have said nothing, not even about the destination since I have enclosed everything in a virgin envelope. I had first signed on the borders, on the V, you know, where the two parts stick to each other, the lips, the one on the other, such that the letter could not be opened without deforming my signature on the line where it rejoins itself, from one border to the other. Then I judged this gesture inelegant, that is, insulting, in contradiction with the very confidence that I was intending to testify to thereby. Therefore I put back the whole thing into the most banal of self-sealing envelopes and I gave them [*lui*] the virgin thing, from hand to hand. I greatly admired, with something a bit more than gratitude, their very attentive discretion. Perhaps a bit too solemn, but after all why not? What I gave them to guard could justify it. We must see each other again.

20 April 1978.
     From the airport I made my inquiries about a hotel close
enough to the University so that I would not have to walk too much.
I got there by taxi without too much difficulty. At the hotel, stupidly, I asked for a room one flight up, as if I did not know of the
existence of elevators and the economy one can anticipate from
them. Result, infernal noise, a sleepless night. The cast and the two
canes made my appearance before these students who had never
seen me theatrical, and I must confess that I play on this provisional
infirmity more and more. I am enjoying it all over (you have nothing to learn from me on this subject. Even so it is remarkable that
the fall took place precisely at that date, you told me so yourself:
new period of "remission," eve of the departure for vacation, the
son's skateboard, the unfortunate exhibition watched by the father-
in-law, all these texts and dreams of walking, of steps [*pas*], of
ankles, of shoes that have been dancing around me for so long, but
in more literal fashion, if it can be put thus, for two or three years.
Bah, we know everything that can be ventured on this subject, all
the words that crowd in (*scapegoat* comes back to me often), but
even so there must be something more idiomatic and that remains
secret for me: tell me the truth, you.
                         Did you know that the biggest postal
museum is to be found here in Geneva? As soon as I can walk I will
get myself there (I am continuing my investigations, more or less
continuously). In the "modern" period of postal becoming (in my
language I intend by that the period that follows the epoch of the
"imperial" territory and of the politico-military investment—Persian or Roman empires, Cyrus and Ceasar—then the epoch that I
really would like to name the "university" period, because in the
13th century in France, during the long process of remonopoliza-
tion, of the renationalization of a dispersed network, the University
of Paris had seen itself granted a privilege, I'll tell you about it, in
the circulation of the mail. Louis XI puts an end to it, little by little
reproduces centralization—of the Roman type, with his own censorship and his own "black cabinet"—and the process, fatal to the
University's privilege, winds up, in our day, with the monopolistic
regime, in 1681 I believe), yes, in the "modern" period the country
of the Reformation has played a rather important role, it seems to
me, in postal reform—and I believe the fact significant. The Universal Postal Union was born in Berne (1874–78), and is now an
institution under the jurisdiction of the U.N. No, I don't have any
big hypothesis about the conjoint development of capitalism, Prot-

estantism, and postal rationalism, but all the same, things are necessarily linked. The post is a banking agency. Don't forget that in the great reformation of the "modern" period another great country of the Reformation played a spectacular role: in 1837 Rowland Hill publishes his book, *Post-Office Reform: Its Importance and Practicability*. He is an educator; and a reformer of the fiscal system. What was he proposing? but the stamp, my love, what would we have done without it? The sticking stamp, that is, the uniformization of payment, the general equivalent of the tax, and above all the bill before the letter, the payment in *advance (the uniform rate and a system of prepayment,* which were adopted in 1840 after great popular agitation, the famous battle of the pp, *"popular agitation for the 'penny post'"*). And under the proviso of *further investigations*, I believe that the post card comes to us from there too, very recently (from Australia, 1869, to England, 1870, but the private *picture postcard* was authorized only in 1894). And now I am taking my plaster leg, my canes (I never know where to put them, these prostheses, particularly when I'm at the podium), and I leave you, but read closely, turning slowly, the four corners, around the 4 times 4 rectangles, perhaps it does not form a single sentence but this is my life and I dedicate it to you.

4 May 1978.
        I had forgotten to tell you that the famous museum is called the Palace of the Post. As soon as I stop limping ("Scripture tells us it is no sin to limp," these are the final words of *Beyond . . .* , the fall, or the *envoi*) my first visit will be to the Geneva PP.
                                                            Before taking the plane I telephoned the person, I prefer to tell you. Not the slightest question about the confided letter. We never talk about it any more, I only feel that everything we say remains magnetized by this mute message the guarding of which I have confided to them. On their side I indeed feel that *volens nolens* a work of reconstitution and of appropriation is in progress. Inevitably. But what to do? I could not keep the letter on me. Be calm, I am doing nothing to favor their "approach," if it can be put thus, to the inside of the dead letter. Perhaps I was wrong, it is true, to tell them the truth, to wit that I had mostly *forgotten,* as concerns the answer and the details, the content of this little missive. Answer: "forgotten" certainly not, buried, "repressed." No, no, above all not that, forgotten, you heard correctly. And I set off on a long discourse about this forget-

ting that overflows the economy of "repression." Without saying that it was you, but I don't have many illusions about this secret. In any event what I told the person about my "forgetting" appeared on the one hand to give them pleasure, on the other to worry them, like someone who already was concerned by what I was saying there. But always with a marvelous discretion, a capacity for attention which nevertheless knows how to exercise itself in its very retreat. This is so rare. We must call each other back, but this time I will refuse myself the slightest allusion concerning us or touching on the September letter. Don't worry about anything, *in any case.*
I am in the same *Hotel de la Plaine,* this time on the top floor. The cast is bothering me. I deck myself out with these canes, this limping, and especially the skateboard (you can imagine the small supplement of seduction), but I'm fed up, especially with these trips and these courses (I took up *"La vie la mort"* and *"La chose"* again, it's going all right). I have *imparted* [*je me suis* fait part] something to myself with this fall, but what, who? (To impart to oneself, to make it part, *se faire part, ce faire part,* immediately one thinks of marriage, death, mourning). Of whom did I impart to myself, did I make myself part [*de qui me suis-je fait part, la part*] (no, not the pair, that's exactly the problem, the part). All right already. I'm going to put myself to bed.

18 May 1978.
        Already the third trip to Geneva. This continual envoyage is exhausting and yet . . . Everything would be easier, you think, and I think as you do, if you could come with me. But you do not leave me for an instant, I take you around everywhere (or finally as much as a single leg permits . . .), I speak to you all the time, tell you stories and describe (to) you, infinitely. I will have to talk to you about the Hotel, about the colleagues and students who stop by (sometimes to live there, and we visit each other after dinner, to "have a little chat," as you say—I can't stand this expression, and the thing too, finally, but don't worry about anything), about all my friends at the Bagdad, about their ingenious host.
                                When I am not set off the track by courses and work meetings, I still find the time to work at the hotel. I am rereading *Beyond* . . . with one hand (everything in it is marvelously *hermetic,* which is to say postal and *trailing,* [*traînant*],—a subterranean railway, but also lame, trailing the leg behind: he tells us NOTHING, does not make a step that he does

not take back at the next step. You will say that Hermes did not limp, that he had wings on his feet, yes, yes, but this is not contradictory, limping does not prevent him from running and flying, the old man. Nothing works [*Rien ne marche*], but everything goes very fast, absolutely fast, in this paralysis, which I know something about. Very struck, this morning, by what he says, or rather by what he does not say about "fate" neuroses (*Schicksal,* always the destination, the *envoi, schicken,* etc.) in Chapter III. In the story from Tasso's *Gerusalemme Liberata* he is absolutely not interested in the confusion of the sexes for its own sake. This trait of the story seems to him completely secondary. We mistook the sexes, you are Tancredi and you have taken me for a man. Because of the armor. In the forest (divine which, I leave it to you to put a name to it), you cut me in two, the blood spurted from the tree, and since then you hear only my voice, Clorinda bewails the pain that her beloved, once again . . . Do you know that I am really crying, right here, look. This inversion of the places always scandalizes you, you yourself are mistaken, false, think about it a bit, *mais si, mais si* . . . I myself am not suffering from a fate neurosis, but from The neurosis of The destination. And you, my immense one, from a psychosis of "determination." I am leaving, I have to leave now, I love you, remain me.

A day in May 1978. I am writing to you from the *Ecole* where I will work all afternoon. I had put in my pocket, without reading it right away, the note that you had left in the car. I know very well that you "would like to write a book of the unique, and of the absolutely unequivocal. Madness itself, don't you think? I even ask myself what this means." Me too, but you are mad and I love madly that which makes you write this, and nothing else. It is still true that you are "as forgettable as the law of gravitation." Just that—but it's true. This is why I give you my benediction and *"bless"* you all the time, even without knowing it and that *"tu m' "*
                                      no my love that's my wake.
The other day, while speaking to you about all these pp (private *picture postcard* and *penny post*), I was first of all struck by this: prepayment institutes a general equivalent which regulates the tax according to the size and weight of the *support* and not the number, tenor, or quality of the "marks," even less on what they call the meaning. This is unjust and stupid, barbarous, even, but of an immense import. Whether you put one word or one hundred in a let-

ter, a word of one hundred letters or one hundred words of seven letters, the price is the same, this is incomprehensible, but this principle has the capacity to account for everything. Let's drop it. In writing *penny post* I had also foretold in my memory that *Jean le facteur* (Shaun, John *the postman*) was not very far off. Another fraternal couple in pp making war on itself, *the penman and the postman.* The writer, Shem, is the heir of H.C.E., *Here Comes Everybody,* which I translate in my idiom as "Here comes whoever will have in body loved me" [*"Ici vient quiconque m'aura en corps aimé"*]. So I looked for the *penny post* for two hours, and here it is, at least here is one that one day you might bind to an all-powerful *"he war"* (YHWH declaring war by decreeing *la dichemination,* by deconstructing the tower, by saying to those who wished both to make a name for themselves, the Chemites, and to impose their particular language as the universal language, by saying "Babel" to them, I call myself and I impose my name as father, a name that you confusedly understand as "Confusion," try, I beg you, to translate but indeed I hope that you will not be able to, this is my *double bind*) while passing through *"his penisolate war"* and the *"sosie sesthers"* of the first page. Here then, from page 307 of *Finnegan's Wake:* "Visit to Guinness' Brewery, Clubs, Advantages of the Penny Post, When is a Pun not a Pun?" Facing this, in the margin in italics, the names, you know. Here: "Noah, Plato. Horace. Isaac. Tiresias." On the preceding page, I'm sampling only this, for later: "A Place for Everything and Everything in its Place, Is the Pen mightier than the Sword?" which pulls the following string for example (p. 211): "a sunless map of the month, including the sword and stamps, for Shemus O'Shaun the Post . . ." Reread what follows in the vicinities of "Elle-trouve-tout" and of "Where-is-he?; whatever you like . . ." etc. Look at them, Sword/Pen.

I just called you, it was impossible, you understood clearly, one has to be naked on the telephone. But at the same time it suffices that you undress for me to see myself naked. Our story is also a twin progeniture, a procession of Sosie/sosie, Atreus/Thyestes, Shem/Shaun, S/p, p/p *(penman/postman)* and more and more I metempsychose myself from you, I am with the others as you are with me (for the better, but also, I see clearly, for the worse, I do the same things to them). Never have I imitated anyone so irresistibly. I am trying to shake myself for if I love you infinitely I do not love everything about you I mean those inhabitants of you with their little hats

the uniquely each time
that I love: beyond everything that is, you are the one—and therefore the other.

A day in May 1978.

Of course everything suggests that since this date,
these two dates, these three dates (count carefully) nothing goes
any more. But it suffices to distance oneself a bit so that immediately   As
soon as "come" ("*viens*") did give itself to be heard, in response
we walked the one over the other, with the most final force. All the
cruelty in the world.

Holocaust of the children
God himself had only the choice be-
tween two crematory ovens: with whom to begin? When? And the
always imminent catastrophe
From myself I depart, I depart myself, how
do you want me to write, I am an out-of-tune instrument, an instrument in two. I write folded in two with a double, bifid, perfidious,
perjuring instrument. I scratch and I erase everything with the other
hand. Therefore you must not read me. In order to hear the song
one must know my suffering, love it, absolve it. It is innocent and
infinite.

One does not send oneself a child, nor does one keep it. One loses
desire in order to keep it. One does not confide a child to guarding,
perhaps one confides guarding to it, which for me would amount to
learning you by heart.

I truly believe that I am singing someone who is
dead and that I did not know. I am not singing for the dead (this is
the truth according to Genet), I am singing a death, *for* a dead man
or woman already [*déjà*]. Although since the gender and number
remain inaccessible for me I can always play on the plural. And
multiply the examples or working hypotheses, the hypotheses of
mourning.

Thus I have lost my life writing in order to give this song a
chance, unless it were in order to let it silence itself, by itself. You
understand that whoever writes must indeed ask himself what it is
asked of him to write, and then he writes under the dictation of
some addressee, this is trivial. But "some addressee," I always leave

the gender or number indeterminate, must indeed be the object of a choice of object, and chosen and seduced. "Some addressee" winds up then, to the extent that the approach, the approximation, the appropriation, the "introjection," all progress, no longer able to ask anything that has not already been whispered [*soufflé*] by me. Thereby everything is corrupted, there is only the mirror, no more image, they no longer see each other, no longer destine each other, nothing more. Do you think that this exhaustion is happening to us? We would have loved each other too much. But it is you I still love, the living one. Beyond everything, beyond your name, your name beyond your name.

PS. So as not to forget: the little key to the drawer is now hidden in the other book (I leave it to you to divine the page).

1st June 1978.

    I am the *privé* [the private, the deprived one], more than anyone else henceforth. And I can hear you: the private detective (no, I have renounced literature, everything in it is a post and police affair, finally, a police station affair); so then the *privé* of everything, and of all women, the *privé* of these ladies? No I was speaking of the desire to pose or to post myself in a kind of absolute privatization (but in this case there must no longer be any position that holds). The secret without measure: it does not exclude publication, it measures publication against itself. For whoever takes this measure and can keep to the scale, at how many thousands of readers does the family circle end, and the private correspondence?

                             Let us come back to what you said to me at the airport, about suffering [*souffrance*], about ours (what suffering): I do not for an instant believe in the neurosis of destination, as I said the other day. On the day that they can tell me what they are thinking under the headings "fate," "destiny," or "destination" especially, then we will talk about all this again (to say nothing of "neurosis"). You understand, I suspect them of thinking nothing, nothing but the trivial, the dogmatic, and the benumbed under all these words. And then the historical teleology to which it leads directly, that letter that always arrives at its destination. They deny it in vain, the "course of history" is not far off, several stations or stases in the unconscious, several supplementary topical complications and there we are, we have never departed from it, from speculative idealism. As soon as it arrives at its destination, history will have had a course, and a circular one if you please, in its "proper" course.

doom, always to prefer the child. The child in itself, in oneself.

the worlds apart.

and never to rest on anything, on anyone, not even on oneself, absolute insomnia. Satellites everywhere, those of which we are thinking when we write, those of which we are not thinking and which dictate the essential, those which watch over, censure, decide (*tranchent*) and trans- all that you like, even when we write without writing, how do you wish to confuse and to clear these trails? By mixing genres? By exploding the tone from tone to tone? By passing very quickly from one tone to another (for the tone is the final index, the identity of some addressee who, lacking anything else, still dictates diction. And this confuses itself and explodes all by itself, nothing to be done, unity of tone does not exist.)

But who is persecuting you then?

Says he. Here are my two hypotheses. 1. We are Hermaphrodite himself. (Someone has just called me on the telephone imitating a female student who and that—it's nasty. Too bad for you, I was *en train,* in the course, of writing you.) Hermaphrodite, not hermaphrodites despite our bisexualities now unleashed in the absolute *tête-à-tête,* Hermaphrodite in person and properly named. Hermes + Aphrodite (the post, the cipher, theft, ruse, voyage and *envoi,* commerce + love, all loves). I have ceased being interested in my old Thot-Hermes story, etc. What fascinates me now, concerning the son of Hermes and Aphrodite, is the repetition and redoubling of the story: once united with Salmacis he forms with her, anew, a double-natured body. Then he obtains that whoever bathes in Lake Salmacis (of which she was the nymph) will lose his virility. As for Hermes, he attracts me even more these days by virtue of the entire network of little bands (*bandelettes*) that his history is wrapped up in (his legendary skill at undoing "bonds" [*liens*], at making lyres, musical strings, out of them: for example with the intestine itself, the most intestinal of sacrificed animals; he knew how to stretch [*tendre*], to relax [*détendre*], to bind, to unbind, to analyze, to paralyze, to tighten, to band—more or less strictly. And now here, Salmacis, is my second hypothesis of the morning at the Hôtel de la Plaine: if *Plato* resented *Socrates* to death (this is certain, this is my premise, even if he loved him he could only resent him to death), it is that the latter, one day, one night, one morning, for example after some discussion following a banquet, must have inflicted an impardonable affront upon him. I don't know, a slap, one of those ineffaceable jests, a mockery that hit home, at the very spot that was not to be touched. My hypothesis doubtless goes against even the common sense of the chronology but it does try to explain what happens, what arrives to us from this couple with common sense. Their liaison was embodied at that very moment (it always begins with a wound, and young *Plato* was virgin at the time, no one would have dared and he would have permitted no one), but very badly, which is to say that it came to an end at its birth (a kind of abortion destined to reproduce itself until the end of time). Now, once upon a time, *Plato,* despite his love for *Socrates,* and even along with this love, has never again ceased to avenge himself, all the while defending himself against this (very sincerely moreover). He avenged himself for the age of *Socrates* first of all (he was there before him, question of generation, he had lived a great deal, he was far from being a virgin, etc.). And then he allegedly demanded excuses. Written ones, look at him. The other plays at docility, lowers his forehead, but he knows that one confides nothing to writing, neither excuses, nor promises, nor oaths. He excuses himself with one hand, he scratches with the other. So then *Plato* makes the big play: he deploys the entire *corpus platonicum* and affixes to it, for eternity, *Socrates'* signature: it is he who wrote or inspired my entire output, and "at the time of the flower of his youth"! Naturally he does not believe a word of it, neither a word of his attribution nor a word of his corpus. And since *Socrates* was already no longer there and moreover never was asked for his opinion, you can see what we have been working on for twenty-five centuries! When one reads everything that is still written today, and so seriously, in such a businesslike way (*spoudaios!*) on the subject of this great telephonic farce . . . In compromising Socrates Plato was seeking to kill him, to eliminate him, to neutralize the debt while looking as if he were taking on the entire burden. In *Beyond* . . . , precisely on the subject of Aristophanes' discourse, Freud starts it all over, he forgets Socrates, erases the scene and indebts up to Plato (this-is-what-I-show-in-my-next-book). Nietzsche, to whom Freud does the same thing, more or less, had come to suspect some rather murky story. But he was not always vulgar enough, awakened enough to measure the entire vulgarity of the scene (you are going to accuse me again of not staying close enough to the truth, and you are right, but I only wanted to make a scene for you, make myself a bit interesting, to force your attention with those two: for they have succeeded, by means of this monumental altercation, to fill it up, to convene the whole world, to the point that everyone, I no longer know to whom I recently made the remark, declares himself ready to pay the *heavy* [*fort*] price for taking them today, right here, into analysis).

I call you, I will have arrived, and doubtless one more time will have left again before my letter (the boxes here are red—and rather rare, but the pickups are sufficient).

15 June 1978.
and if I had to live like this (as I am living), I would not live, I would not make it. Not at all [*du tout*], not a single instant. Therefore there must be something else.

From the airport I also telephoned that other doctor (rheumatologist this time—but also, as if by chance, more or less in analytic training, and who reads me, L. tells me, L. who sends me to him recommending me warmly: he prefers that I see him before going to the kinesotherapist. I told you so. In fact everyone tells me that the clinic doctor should have prescribed re-education sessions after the removal of the cast in order to avoid the swelling of the ankle in particular. The thing now appears interminable to me. Do you think that one day I again will be able to walk, if not to run?

There was no room at the Hôtel de la Plaine, I am writing to you from another hotel—that friends recommended to me, a bit further from the University.

You are my only double, I suppose, I speculate, I postulate,

in sum everything that sets me on the march today, the entire postulate of my practical reason, all my heart, and I speculate on you, you are now the name, yourself, or the title of everything that I do not understand. That I never will be able to know, the other side of myself, eternally inaccessible, not unthinkable, at all [*du tout*], but unknowable, unknown—and so lovable. As for you, my love, I can only postulate (for who else, with whom would I have dreamed this?) the immortality of the soul, liberty, the union of virtue and happiness, and that one day you might love me.

I am going to post
this note and then take the tram which goes down toward the University (Plainpalais Place).

(I hope that you won't have had a problem with
the key, on leaving I had left it in the place that you know, but dissimulating it a bit on the side.)

EGEK HUM XSR STR

20 June 1978.
I had not come back to Zurich since spring 1972.
You accompany
me everywhere. Hillis, who was waiting for me at the airport (the de Mans arrive only this afternoon) drove me to the cemetery, near to Joyce's tomb, I should say funerary monument. I didn't know that he was here. Above the tomb, in a museum of the most costly horrors, a life-size Joyce, in other words colossal in this place, seated, with his cane, a cigarette in hand it seems to me, and a book in the other hand. He has read all of us—and plundered us, that one. I imagined him looking at himself posed there—by his zealous descendants I suppose. We continued to walk around in the cemetery speaking, I believe, about Poe and Yale, all that. At the end of an alley, the tomb of the inventor of something like the telescripter: Egon Zoller, *Erfinder des Telephonographen*. This inscription is engraved in stone between two globes, one of which bears the Alpha and the Omega, and the other meridians and a kind of telephonic device spitting out a band of paper. After the raucous burst of laughter we spent a long time musing in front of this phallus of modernity. I like that he is called Zoller and with his name beckons toward the toll, customs, debt, taxes. We also looked for Szondi's tomb without finding it. It is there, once out of the water his body had been brought back from Berlin.

If you believe it, that is, that it has already happened because one writes to the dead, so then, living one, hail, once again you have understood nothing, hail and be well, as we say to each other with that desperate compassion each time that we know that one instant later we are going to die for one another, each on his own behalf, hail!

To those two [*aux deux-là*] I continue to speak as if to an *odd couple* (*odd* is the password for all these cards, it holds for p/S, for Poe, for Dupin and the narrator, it holds for so many others and it pleases me that it inverts the *ddo,* because it

enters into composition with such other necessary idioms in this
place as *to be at odds with each other, to play at odds, what are the
odds,* etc. To those two [*aux deux-là*] I continue to attribute much
but they remain camouflaged in the picture, mute as carps, like all
the *odd couples,* but what acrobatics beneath the robes, and it
works unprotestingly, and it runs on orders, what a deformatics,
what a catastropics
                    logroperatergo, this is the subversion that I had told you
about. And *do ut des* which I translate in my language: the gift as
throw of the dice, *le don comme coup de dés*
                                             this is still ciphered, and I
who curse nothing so much as the secret, I contort myself cultivat-
ing it like a madman in order better to guard the non-secret. You
know this better than anyone, you told me one day that I had the
secret, supreme address in pulling off the *tour de force,* but it will
wind up badly.
       on this subject I find you a bit unjust and severe, in sum
prejudiced. One must leave [*laisser*] things to be done (one *must*
not even, *it leaves* [*ça laisse*], in any event), and the scene to be
unfolded by itself; it's very ancient but it also has only just begun,
this is what I try to resign myself to. And then it is the only proof of
love, if there is any.
       When *Socrates,* for example (pronounce it English
style, as at Oxford, Socrateze or *Ulysses:* Socrate has seven letters,
well the name of Socrate has seven letters and the name of *Socrates*—who is the same, himself—which? himself—has eight
letters, or seven like Ulysses moreover, who is making a return
here), when Socrateze, then, or Socratesse sends a message, he
does not address something to someone, or not only, he "sends himself" ["*s'envoie*"] something or first of all someone (always divisible, not so?). But the *s'* of the *s'envoyer (Socrates's)* is not there
right *up to the present* to receive it, neither before nor during nor
after the emission or the reception if some such thing ever *presented itself;* and it always remains to be continued, to be forwarded
[*à suivre*]
       whence this infinitely subtle text, reserving all blows (and the fu-
ture), which interminably debates itself between several plans, several loves, with a candor of the soul that does not exclude immense
resources of bad faith. Intelligence itself, there it is—and, question
of taste, I will always prefer
                              on the subject of "to send oneself" ["*s'envo-
yer*"] (who or what), this is an expression that I found the most

"apt" in the thank-you letter that I sent her for the great truths she had just proclaimed. By correcting, or by co-erecting as I always say, by restoring what fell to [*revenait*] the ones and the others, she was not arresting (which is fine) the question, which therefore remains to be continued, to be forwarded [*à suivre*], of knowing whatever (who and what) *she* (or he in her or she in him or she in her or him in him, have I forgotten any?) was sending herself (flirting in the wings), as for what concerns me, the *facteur* has legibly (?) marked this fatality for "incorrigible indirection": "in order to make another step to the side." That what "she" sends herself this way (and us as well), and who, and if it comes back or does not come back, how can you know? Moreover never does it regard anyone. Regard S. and p.: they give the impression of never regarding each other and of regarding no one. Above all they cannot see each other.   What I admired most, what I got the most pleasure from in her *tour de force,* is not everything that she does well to leave aside (the essential question, *"an extremely complex one with which we cannot hope to deal adequately here,"* a wise precaution followed by a note which does not conclude circuitously, had to get there: *"Is it not equally possible to regard what Lacan calls 'full speech' as being full of precisely what Derrida calls writing?"* Unbeatable, I tell you: nothing to say against this plenitude, however gross it may be, since she was full *only* of all of you, *already,* and everything that all of you would have to say against it. This is what I call in English the logic of *pregnancy* and in French the foreclosure of the name of the mother. In other words, you are all born, don't forget, and you can write only against your mother who bore within her, along with you, what she has borne you to write against her, your writing with which she would be large. And full, you will never get out of it. Ah! but against whom had I written?—I would like it to have been your mother. And she above all.—Who?), what I admired the most, then, is rather the overturning, or say rather the final *reversement,* for it might indeed be a question of that, and the English word *(reversed)* puts us on the track of the French *reverser* better, even if it primarily means overturned or inverted, permuted. So then, patience, look closely at S and p on the one hand (everything is there, all possible "positions") and on the other illustrate them with this caption: *"If it at first seemed possible to say that Derrida was opposing the unsystematizable to the systematized, 'chance' to psychoanalytical 'determinism'* [did I really do that? is Derrida or 's "Derrida" in question?] *or the 'undecidable' to the 'destination,'*

ENVOIS 151

the positions seem now to be reversed: Lacan's apparently unequivocal ending says only its own dissemination, while 'dissemination'
has erected itself into a kind of 'last word.'" This passage is immortal and every word deserves a book, the "positions," the "seem
now to be," and let's not talk about "reversed." And for everything
to be in order, "my" "dissemination" has to erect itself by itself,
has already to have done so, so that the last word can be the last
word. I have nothing against erection, but as concerns this word—
and so many others—if I had insisted even more in sayng that there
was no master word or last word or first word, if I had insisted more
(was it possible?) in saying that "dissemination" was one of those
words, among so many others, that is to pull beyond every "last
word," I would have been reproached, precisely by virtue of my
insistence, for reconstituting a master word, no matter which. What
to do? I am loved but they cannot stand me, they cannot stand that I
might say anything that they might not be able to "reverse" in advance each time that the situation demands it (naturally, my "position," my "place," my places, answers or non-answers, etc., are a
part, only a part of the aforenamed situation and of "what is at
stake here"—I forgot to add that the correction is always ready to
be corrected itself, and the process of restitution always remains
open, to be continued: "But these oppositions are themselves mis-
readings of the dynamic functioning of what is at stake here." In
effect. What is at stake I cannot tell. You have clearly seen the
carte: even while saying in "apparently unequivocal" fashion that
"what the 'purloined letter,' that is the letter 'en souffrance,' means
is that a letter always arrives at its destination," Lacan in truth
meant to say what I said, what I will have said, under the heading of
dissemination. What next! As for me, all the while apparently
speaking of dissemination, I would have reconstituted this word
into a last word and therefore into a destination. In other words, if it
can be put thus, Lacan already meant what I said, and myself I am
only doing what he says he is doing. And there you are, the trick
has been played, destination is back in my hand and dissemination
is "reversed" into Lacan's account. This is what I had described to
you one day, three-card monte, the agility of those expert hands to
which one would yield oneself bound hand and foot. With a bit of
that chance which is found on the program, it is admirably translating dissemination (the word or the title mattering little). Suffices to
give oneself the time to read. I had brought all this literature with
me for the trip and to browse through the rest of the issue a bit (very
spotty). I fall over it and do not yet accuse myself of inventing this

typo, I'll show it to you: *". . . Lacan has seen in the castration complex the crucial point of divergence between Freud and Plato: 'Castration is the altogether new motive force that Freud has introduced into desire, giving to the lack in desire the meaning that remains enigmatic in the dialectic of Socartes* [sic, I swear] *although conserved in the account of the Symposium"* (*Du Trieb de Freud,* p. 853). I don't have the French text at hand, but this "although conserved" enchants me. As for the translator, he knows everything about Platonic idealism, *he knows everything as to "what love is merely" und so weiter: "In the scheme of Platonic idealism, love is merely the path* [quite simply, for he also knows what a *"path,"* a *"way,"* a passage, a road, a step, is, and even what it is to quicken one's step, to hurry . . .] *along which the philosopher presses his way towards the vision of fullness, and the journey* [he also knows what a journey is] *itself* [and the journey itself!] *gets under way with the* Aufhebung *of the maternal."* And if *fullness* were full of something else, and if Socrates and Descartes and Hegel had spoken only of castration, try to follow.

      I am quite tired, my sweet love, I am going to accompany these amiable phantoms to their car and I am coming back to sleep with you (too bad that you can never come with me here), I am going to dream.

                (promise? you will tell me when I come back?). I draw,

          EGEK HUM RSXVI STR, if I am not mistaken.

22 June 1978. I am writing to you now from Basel (you recall the itinerary of these two days: plane Geneva-Basel—where I have just arrived and had myself taken by taxi near the bridge, on the right bank—, soon, at 6 o'clock, train for Strasbourg; three quarters of an hour later I will be there, just the time to write you to tell you all about it; this evening, doubtless after dinner in rue Charles-Grad, Philippe's Antigone, which I am rereading out loud in the plane without anyone noticing; tomorrow morning, early, plane for Paris where I am having lunch with the Laportes: have the impression that I'll never see you again, all these eternities that we will have waited [*attendu—attendues*]?)

      I am seated on the platform, wiped out. I have multiplied the trajectories, it is as if I were writing under hypnosis.

29 June 1978.

retreat [*retrait*] of metaphor. I have made a story of voyages (and not a narration of a voyage) and of the very very divided trait (*Riss*) out of it, in commemoration of us. What I said remained, as always, as you well know, unnoticed. Last trip to Geneva, to which you never will have accompanied me finally.

This part apart from me that you know better than I do, I don't know if it is keeping me under hypnosis or if it is I (or you) who is putting it to sleep, a sleep of writing. I don't know whether hypnosis is when I leave or when I come (reassure me, it can't be both at the same time?), and what I call sleep of writing, whether it is when I write or when I don't write, when I write to you or not to you.

let it be said telegraphically, I am terrified at the thought of that other "summer" ["*été*"]—and that it is still before us.

But since you have promised me to come to Orly this time, I will arrive before my telegram and I even will have forgotten it, like the rest.

You know everything, guard us.

July-August 1978.

Look, he is out for a walk, in the summer, on the streets of Athens, caressing Socrates' poster(ior). The other one continues to write tranquilly, hypnosis I tell you, he dreams and prepares, prepares himself for the suicide (last wishes, makeup, "banalization," the great parade, he knows that he will not make it and that someone will have to lend him a hand, the dose has to come to him from elsewhere. And from where he will have never known. He "combats unconsciousness." "The unconsciousness more vast than Socrates' un-knowledge," isn't this the birth of tragedy? Do you remember? If you come back before me, know that in reality I never leave you.

July-August 1978.

and soon we will be back together. We have not yet left each other, and already there is anxiety, we are beginning to make our (a)way. You have never been so near (with something peaceful or resigned, something suddenly mute, which hurts me), I am watching you write from the window, I want to run toward you. You are up now, you have gotten up. Want to photograph this *réussite* (I thought you were writing).

July-August 1978.
          I am going out for a while to make reservations. This specification all the same, so as not to leave the final word to your chicaneries and ratiocinations of breakfast time: 1. I had hoped that, like me, you would succeed in forgetting the *"dead letter,"* not only its contents, which moreover you don't know and of which you have, I assure you, no need (it does not concern you, not at all), but even its existence. Moreover it would be difficult for me to claim it now. 2. In terms of good Oxonian scholasticism, a promise can only promise. One never promises to succeed [*arriver*], to succeed in keeping one's promise, only to do everything to succeed in keeping it if possible. One does not promise to arrive, one promises to have the intention to arrive and to neglect no aspect of all that is in one's power to do in order to arrive. If I do not succeed [*arrive*] in arriving because it is not in my power, because of this or that, this one or that one, in me or out of me, will have kept me from it, then I am not breaking my promise. I still want to arrive, but I do not succeed [*arrive*] in arriving. I have not ceased to be faithful to my engagement. You will say that all this is not serious, that they are not serious at Oxford, that this "in me or out of me" is terribly equivocal or hypocritical, that the notion of the possible or of intention makes you laugh, that I am taking my argument from a discourse of which I do not believe a word (*mais si, mais si*—and it is in the name of the serious that the Oxford people speak, you know that they have *Plato* and *Socrates* in their library). And then a promise, a sworn oath, does it derive from the serious, is it serious, tell me? It's much more grave and dangerous, much lighter too, more numerous: but not serious.

July-August 1978.
          and wouldn't we be happier—and even more in love—if we did not know anything, anything about each other? Never, at the end of the road, having heard of each other? I am waiting for you, soon I am coming to pick you up to go with you in the car, I don't want you to go alone, no one there knows you.

July-August 1978. You are still sleeping, I want to stroll in the forest with you (the ankle is much better). Right at this moment, do you know what is happening: as if I had never known, the radiant certainty of loving only you, who have only one body, you alone, but so alone. Your solitude frightens me, fortunately you are still sleeping, I would like to rock you to put you to sleep all the time.

24 September 1978.
very lovely summer [*été*], very peaceful finally. However, it had started badly, with your questions on the eve of the voyage. I told you the truth and we did what you wanted, we went where you wanted to go.
Here, the same scenario, you know. I have not yet gone out of Trumbull, and I woke up very early, because of the time difference, and you see, I am writing to you barely out of bed. Yesterday, as usual, Paul and Hillis at Kennedy (they know that I leave them right away to go telephone—I got you right away, I made night in myself, your night, the one in which you were preceding me by six hours). Right away I will start over investing the places, going over the same itineraries, checking the pickups, buying the first cards in the drugstores open on Sunday. I begin tomorrow.

25 September 1978.
of course, it is to hell that we have destined each other—we have preferred it, it was indeed necessary to prefer it, and to be able to afford it, to offer oneself, my sweet love, the techno-teleothingamajig. How to succeed in taking pleasure from t.e.l.e.? (This is the pretext of all our scenes, the program.) In letting you write, and writing it in every way (I count at least seven), turning in all tongues, my foreign one. Myself, I have no tongue, no genre (I also mean no sex) and on this basis, I love you. Inaudible sequence (as is said of tape-recorders).
and swore never to inhabit what is called cohabitation.
you help me, we help each other to die, not so, you will be there

26 September 1978.
very worried, going from one doctor to another (I had forgotten to talk to you about the letter and the telephone call on the

eve of my departure—which appeared to make them very anxious. I was as reassuring as possible (I believe moreover that it is fundamentally, I do not like this word, "hysterical," this is not the first time that these things are happening to them). At the proposition (this was the pretext) of returning the *"dead letter"* to me ("one never knows what might happen"), I forced myself to laugh as one does in front of old people or invalids when they speak of their death ("you can't be thinking of it," "don't be silly"). And I said "out of the question," of course.

I have gone back to my "legacy." I don't know if I will bring it to a conclusion. I like the time that I have here. But I miss you too much. How I will have missed you.

Obviously, Socrates is writing, and in order to say: Socrates is not a musician. You remember our friend's "posthumous fragment," ("the monstrous lack of artistic and mystic talent," "the enigmatic advice always repeated by the apparition in the dream: 'Socrates, make music'" . . .). So then, he is writing, and taking dictation, this is what he represents.

I would like to write you something so unheard of that you finally stop hating me. Know that I have no secrets from you. But I know that I will always make myself detested (by you, by you first of all) because I have no other (veritable) addressee than you, but because you do not succeed in being sure of it. How could I write to you, what could I say to you to reassure you? Obviously even to touch you would not suffice. You have to believe me. Even if this fatality of faith drives you crazy, even if you no longer clearly know who you are. Nor I. I cannot get away from the *souffrance* of this madness any more than you, at least this you are certain of. Our cipher is unique, here it is:

26 September 1978. I have just called from the street, the line was never free. You always act as if you did not know of the permanent possibility of suicide, for me (sorry, we swore to each other never to threaten to kill ourselves: I only wanted to tell you that I was very impatient in the booth, that I lightly thought of killing myself, not for an instant but all the same, and that I never will accept that you have any telephonic equipment, I mean that works, finally, when I am not calling: that you see people perhaps makes me suffer less—or finally this is what I thought in the street). Fortunately there was the letter that you had sent before my departure. It was waiting for me here. The dream that you tell me about is terrible. That anonymous voice warning you that a forbidden tomb bore your name, are you suggesting that this was me? Forbidden for whom precisely? Yourself? Let's change tone, please, this is too sad. Speaking of cemeteries, I announce to you that I have begun to run with Jim (after the very obsessional purchase of equipment, he chose everything, like a layette) and we run in the big cemetery. Talking all the time, as is correct, and from time to time I stop, panting, next to a tomb (lots of Yale professors in these alleys, I mean dead ones too), Jim takes my pulse (he's marvelous, I'll tell you about Jim, he's a little crazy with his jogging, I don't know what he is settling with it, but in everything and for everything he is a master, I think he knows everything).

As last year I am sending you a cassette, along with several hairs, I recorded a fragment of Monteverdi on it—the *Combattimento* again, I am reading it in every language, Tancredi che Clorinda un uomo stima Vuol nel'armi provarla al paragone . . . Er eilt stürmisch nach, und schon von weitem verrät ihn das Geklirr seiner Waffen. Sie bleibt stehen und ruft (it is he, the narrator, who is speaking, and now Clorinda) *What are you bringing me? Why are you in such haste?* TESTO (the general narrator) Rispone: TANCREDI—E guerra, e morte. CLORINDA—Krieg und Tod sollst du haben. *NARRATOR—Says she:* CLORINDA—was du suchst, will ich dir gerne geben:—ich erwarte dich . . . zögernd, langsam gehen sie aufeinander zu, wie zwei Stiere, von Eifersucht (you remember, I had already underlined this word in German in the first book that I gave you) und Zorn entbrannt. *O night* (still the narrator), *thou that obscured in darkness this memorable deed—a deed worthy of the sun's brilliance, of a theatre full of spectators— let me atone for thy remiss, and bring it to light, for posterity . . .* Sie weichen sich nicht aus, achten nicht auf Deckung oder Geschicklichkeit, ziehen sich nicht zurück . . . *so blind are they . . .* Der Fuss rückt sich nicht aus der Spur . . . l'onta irrita lo sdegno a la vendetta, e la vendetta por l'onta rinova . . . I have recorded what follows, with something else for you, up to the end when I die alone, saying "S'apre il ciel; io vado in pace." Afterward you'll call me?

PS. You see, Tancredi, in French it's not possible. Can one kill oneself loving in this language? That's just my luck, it's always like that, and it only happens to me, I had to fall upon this language and had to have only one, and had to hang on to it like a drowning man,

I who am not even French (*mais si, mais si*). How can you find the tone, with this whore of a language? How can you espouse it? and make it sing? I bless you, I do not send you my blessing, I bless you, there, my hand on your eyes.

27 September 1978.
Behind Socrates he is as stiff as justice.

Justice, law (*nomos, nemein,* take it as you wish, and the more you give and the more you are rich) is distribution, this is indeed what it means: always mail [*du courrier*], of course, what else could one distribute, and share, give, receive shared out? The new secretary of the Department is putting, I am certain, a kind of ill will into it, not to suspect her of the worst. She does not give out the letters as they arrive. And I also have the feeling that I am tiring the fat lady of the rare stamps. Nothing going well, you know? I really know that things are happening elsewhere, than where I think that there is no more post, but all the same. I am trying anew to work on my legacy and on this accursed preface. It's only going very irregularly. What you tell me does not help me a lot, you let the milliner get the upper hand, I see, as soon as I have my back turned, and let your "determination" regather strength. But what is this part of you that is stronger than us? I am sending you back *Socrates* by himself, I have cut him from his partner, an adroit stroke of the scissors. Behind, I draw poorly the little (unisex) hat from 1930, this is your demon, someone from your family, an uncle from middle Europe, or an aunt you did not even know. "The demon is the unconscious," says about Socrates our friend, whom I am reading in the translation of our friends. And what is more, this: "Whoever has perceived, in Plato's writings, even just a breath of that divine naïveté and of that certainty in the Socratic conduct of life, also will feel that the prodigious motor of Socratism in a way is turning *behind* Socrates [not my underlining] and that it has to be looked at through Socrates as though through a shadow." Reread the whole thing (p. 100), it's wonderful: "Socrates did not think for a moment that tragedy could 'state the truth' . . . in exchange for which the young tragic poet Plato began by burning his poems in order to be able to become Socrates' disciple." (Here I think that what Plato did is even more twisted.) Look also at what he says on p. 133 about higher education and journalism, and elsewhere about the invention of the novel by Plato, and elsewhere about Aristophanes, for whom Socrates was the greatest Sophist. That Freud, in *Beyond* . . . , retains only his discourse already says a lot about the relation of psychoanalysis to all of this. What does it mean "to have behind oneself"? This is the question that I asked on the subject of the grandson who, as seriously as possible, instead of dragging [*traîner*] the train behind him (which the grandfather would have preferred) invented the postal principle, and even the post without support (in the usual and strict sense), the post without post, without "document," and even without wires, without cables (in "closed circuit" or "open circuit," as is said in the technology of telecommands: in the "open circuit" the operator's order has the form of all-or-nothing, and one awaits the results; in the "closed circuit" a two-way liaison tells you if the order has been received and executed, if for example the lock has been closed—what interests me the most in the technology of telecommanding is the theory of the breakdowns, the ones which occasionally multiply contradictory orders without causing a stoppage, and produce what they call a "jam." Often, in order to avoid mistakes, the message is repeated.)

You tell me that you too are writing someone dead whom you do not know (I am quite persuaded of this, more and more) and whom I represent. Therefore you kill me in advance (it is true that often I await your signs like death sentences), but you also bring back to life. Do you think that we are dealing with very singular revenants or rather that this is the destiny of every correspondence? Are we busying ourselves around *one* tomb or indeed, like everyone . . . Both, doubtless, the one doesn't go without the other.

my terror of forgetting telephone numbers (there is only one that I am sure I will never lose, it is older than I am, the first one, my parents' number in El-Biar, 730 47—I know someone, a Platonic love of my youth, who still dreams of it—) and when I called you just now without warning, after having written it down in order to read it figure by figure in English, I drew a blank, I could no longer remember for what precise reason, and there was one, I had decided to telephone you.

What we are doing with these *air mail* cassettes is marvelous but, you are right, somewhat frightening too. Suppose that I should die before you have received the last one . . . There is one thing that I will never do, you see, the worst sin if it is one, incomparable to any other: to plug in a tape recorder at the moment when the other is burning up the post by telling you his love or another secret of the same genre. And even if it is done with the best intentions in the world, the most pious ones.

and my familiarity, my familiarities terrify them, literally, I see them faint suddenly.

What to tell her? that liking her (well enough, a lot, I no longer know) I could only hope this: that what she had "expedited" this way (myself, in sum) should get to her, come back to her intact, the same, and that she can do with it whatever she wishes, and about which I don't know a thing. But I have nothing to do with it any more—and everything that she says I could have said. And moreover haven't I said it, if one is willing to pay attention? She remains as enigmatic for me as the future.

I have run again today, my wind is coming back, I no longer feel my ankle.

I am already counting down the time.

28 September 1978.

Socrates, says he, the ideal "snoop," an expression to be taken with all requisite delicacy. I now see him as our abortionist [*faiseur d'anges*]. He writes under hypnosis. Me too. Says you. Which is just what I mean. You speak and I write to you as in a dream everything that you are willing to let me say. You will have resoundingly stifled all my words.

Moreover Plato too makes himself out to be an angel. His trickiest imposture, and therefore, as always, his most naive one: *eidos,* ideality, for example the ideality of the letter or of the signifier. What would they have done without me, if I had not, on the way, intercepted the card that they were writing to each other through Freud and his entire limited liability company? It's true that in this teleguided speculation it just had to be that I am to be found in their wake, and however aleatory it might appear, my place too was prescribed on the *carte.*

In order to check the interception, in order to pass between all the schicaneries, to scatter [*semer*] the ones and the others, this entire transposition, the rhetoric of the banal camouflaging to which one will have had to yield! Incalculable, I can count up all these calculations. It is always a question of setting (something) on its way/voice [*voix*], and alley oop, by pressing on a well-placed lever, to compel unplugging, derailing, hanging up, playing with the switch points and sending off elsewhere, setting it off route (go to see elsewhere if I am there: and someone is always found there, to carry on, to take up the thread of the story, you follow).

For it to work, you will say, there have to be supports (ah yes, but the "substance" of the support is my entire problem, it is enormous and it concerns all posts and telecommunications, their strict, literal, figurative meanings, and the tropic post which turns them one into another, etc.), there has to be some support and, for a time, copyists, seated copyists. And there again, one has the feeling that everything is given over to the aleatory, to the chance of having a copyist or a secretary. Our friend says that Aristotle and Plato did not miss having this chance (this is in *Die Philosophie im tragischen* . . . : they were not lacking "copyists," *Abschreiber,* and there is here a "providence," *Vorsehung,* for the books, a *fatum libellorum* that was so unfair (which remains to be seen) for Heraclitus, Empedocles, Democritus, etc. At the limit, the survival of a book is in the hands of the scribe, whose fingers might tire (or concern themselves, I will add, with something else), but also equally depends upon insects or the rain). In other words, before getting to the point of reading any given *Fortune-telling book* of the 13th century, the bearer of the pictures of S and p, never forget that there is something to say, to recount, to discern, *something to tell, to be told,* on the subject of the *"fortune" of the book,* of the chances that it was able to have to get to us intact, for example to fall into my hands one fine day in 1977, the remainder remaining to follow [*à suivre*] (and in the night where you are, it is 2 o'clock in the morning, you have nothing to do with it, which is the least one might say, but they will never know). What would he have said about that portrait of Socrates, that fine Socrates which perhaps resembles Alcibiades, who himself, in that other painting which Monique and Denis talk to me about, is represented as a woman? Nietzsche always insists on his ugliness, the flat nose, the thick lips (if you look at Paris's picture, it is somewhat your lips that he has drawn, at the moment when I distance myself, no one knows them), the protruding eyes of the "censor," of the great persecutor, prophet, and priest who speaks "for posterity." In a posthumous fragment translated by our friends (one must also speak of Nietzsche's chance), after again having insisted on the Socratic origins of the novel, he "turns himself back" again toward Socrates, "who meanwhile has unquestionably transformed himself into a monster: 'He already looks like a hippopotamus, with fiery eyes and terrifying jaws.' Of what species is the genius for engendering from which

Socratism does not cease to grow [. . .] *time* imposes itself upon me as little as upon the geologist my contemporary [. . .] to dispose of millennia courageously, as if of something perfectly unreal, for the birth of *one single* great work of art." One single one, without which there are none, and I will add: that each one be single, by itself, all and all alone, without which there are none.

1st October 1978.
　　　　as soon as I got Paris (one second really, I had just picked up), I hung up, I thought that it really wasn't worth it.
　　　　　　　　　　　　　　　　　　　I have seen them again this morning. Without a doubt it is the croup that induces the scene, the word croup on which everything is mounted this time. And there it is, you have our casino, and the boss of the joint watching over operations (it is he who accumulates all the profits, in the evening, the rackets, the downtown prostitution, etc.) and for the moment he is standing behind the croupier who manipulates the cards and distributes, redistributes the bets, skillfully plays the rake, obeys without appearing to the instructions of the godfather.
　　　　It's going well [*ça marche bien*].
　　　　　　　　　　　　　　　　　　　I adore her, but like the others she thinks she knows what the post, in the usual, literal, or strict sense, "means"; she is sure that the exchange around the purloined letter does not concern *"the efficiency of the postal service."* Mais si, *mais si*—it is not sure that the sense of the p.s. *(postal service)* is itself assured of arriving at its destination, nor is the word to post [*poster*].
　　　　Are you sure, my love, of really understanding what this *poster* means? It doubles, passes, you all the time (I can't write the word *"doubler"* without thinking of us, of us in two cars I mean, and in particular of that day when having passed me in a traffic jam without noticing—or rather I had stopped for gas, I have forgotten—you no longer knew that I was following you, you thought I was ahead of you and you accelerated, accelerated, I did not succeed in catching up with you. We both had our feet to the floor. We were leaving everyone behind us but never was an accident more probable.
　　　　　　　　　　　　　　　　　　　And as I explained to him (he had just asked me why I wrote so much—"you don't take the time to live," and I would have called him a jerk too, which he is not, if I had not heard between the lines: "it is to

me that you should write," "it is with me that you should live"), I
was risking accidents in the car when I write on the wheel or on the
seat next to me, except, as you well know, when you accompany
me. And I added that in fact I never write, and that what I note in
the car or even while running are neither "ideas," of which I have
none, nor sentences, but just words that come, a bit luckier, little
precipitates of language.
          I have brought along with me, go figure out why, a
very old letter of yours.
          you never sign
          is it an order, a demand, a recommendation,
a prayer? Or an affirmation, the deposition of a conclusion?
    What is suspect in all this, when I tell you my love, is that I tell
you my love and you are no longer able to analyze, you no longer
know what I call you—and if it is me, and if it is you or the other.
Our double auto analysis [*notre double auto analyse*].

3 October 1978.
    The countdown is accelerating, don't you think? Afraid of
an accident, afraid that in the end you decide not to come back to
me. An accident for me (it is like a car or plane accident) is what I
call your "determination." It is always possible "at the last moment," it is the last moment: I am never coming again. You are my
Destiny, my Destined One, and one day perhaps you will not have
happened to me, not have gotten to me. And I would not even have
known what to call you, nor, above all, and this is what is most
serious for me, what you call yourself in secret.
          for a love of post cards
(made perfectly ordinary so as to set their police, all of them, off
the track): once that Hermaphrodite is separated from himself,
"apart from himself," and separated from Salmacis, it only remains
for them to write: and always open generalities, selected by our
censor with the flat nose, legal platitudes.
          But myself, don't be childish,
you know very well that I refuse myself nothing—through all the
chicaneries I authorize myself everything, I send myself everything—on the condition that you let me do it. You are my only
judge—says he.
    At the other end of the world, in the shaded area of my
life, this is where I am already, there, in the west, and I await you,
there where we are not yet, neither the one nor the other.

Day after tomor-
row, New York, appointments on arrival—at lunch time (at the
Modern Art) and the lecture at night at Columbia. I'll call you from
there, from the station one is not obliged to telephone *"collect"*
(this calculation is completely ridiculous in our case, as if one
could know who pays for the communication, and who decides it.)

4 October 1978.
the X-rays are in fact not reassuring, to believe them (but
why keep me up to date in this way of the slightest visits to the
doctors? I answer regularly, in as appeasing a way as possible). Your
hypothesis, according to which this illness would be the price to be
paid for their indiscretion ("doubtless one can only fall ill after
having read the *'dead letter'*"), seems to me as clever as it is unbelievable. And it above all betrays your aggressiveness: you hide it
more and more poorly. Please, forget all that.

It is a veritable "possession"
(*kathexis* which guards, retains, intercepts also, wields, captures,
arrests, attaches itself, etc.). This is Alcibiades' word (I am rereading the wonderful eulogy, a work of genius from word to word, I am
very touched at the moment by what he says about our tears). Plato
could not listen to Socrates, he was afraid, and he *made* him write,
he has recounted that he wrote (his own texts), he got him down to
cases. I often cry thinking of them. What sadness this morning. I
would like to be there with you, I know that I am going to die soon
(help me) and you are immortal, my love, my survival, you are too
beautiful, I found you too beautiful on the telephone last night.

5 October 1978.
train for *Penn Station* in an hour. Two appointments at the
Modern Art on arrival.
Very early this morning, even before you rang
while leaving, I worked or dreamed, I never know (always the fort/
da and the tekhnē of telecom. in the age of psychoanalytic repro-
ducibility, the *Symposium,* the *Philebus*). That vicious Plato: did
you know that he inscribed in the *Symposium* a line of poetry, a
single one, about which it is not known whether or not it is by him
parodying Agathon? And what does this line say? the properly
erotic desire to make for oneself (no, not children) a name, and a
renown for the eternity of all time. Well played. He has installed his

name by holding a discourse on installation (question of letters again, of correspondence and of epistole, of stele and of epistole, the Greek lexicon is marvelous in this area: *epistello,* I send, is also "I mandate, order, arrest"—a decision, an order but the idea of arrest or of installation, the *stellen* if you will, the idea of pause or of post, of halt, works upon the entire family; what I prefer: *epistolen luein,* to open a letter, *to unbind* the strings of a letter, even before alleging to analyze. One did not unglue, one did not cut, one did not tear.)

the desire "to make for oneself a name" I was telling you. Plato's desire, yes, but think first of all about this desire for someone or for those who would bear as their proper name the common noun "name" or "renown," Shem. The sons of Shem said, at the moment of building the tower of Bavel, "Let us make for ourselves a name." Aside from the essentially insoluble problem of translation (the proper name does and does not belong to language), the essential issue in this story is often neglected, the battle for the proper name between YHWH and the sons of Shem. Themselves, they want to impose their name (of name) and their particular language (their lip, Chouraqui precisely translates, and this is Safah, the name of my mother or of my maternal grandfather that I had played on in *Dissemination*), and himself, he deconstructs their tower ("Let's go! Down! Let us here confuse their lips, man will no longer understand the lip of his neighbor"), he discheminates them by imposing his proper name ("he proclaims his name: Bavel, Confusion": remarks the dilemma of the translator, compelled to play on two names, the one proper and the other common, and to add the second one, to add a capital letter to it, to translate confusedly, QED, an ambiguous proper name which meant "confusion" only by means of a confused association within language). YHWH simultaneously demands and forbids, in his deconstructive gesture, that one understand his proper name within language, he mandates and crosses out the translation, he dooms us to impossible and necessary translation. And if this *double bind* is firstly that of YHWH, if each time that there is this *double bind* in the structure of the proper name, there is "God," the name of God, well then, I let you follow [*suivre*], you can forward it [*faire suivre*], the writing of the proper name, that of the *penman* Shem, sees itself interminably given over to the detours and wanderings of Shaun the *postman,* his brother.

One day you wrote to me "you can ask the impossible of me." I have obeyed faithfully, I await you.

6 October 1978.
    I am writing you in a taxi. I avoid the subway, here too,
precisely because I like it. And because I get lost in the *correspon-
dances,* although the system is much simpler than in Paris. It's like
an express fact. Last night, after the lecture, I crossed the entire
city in a taxi, all the way to Washington Square, this was after the
reception (it was already very late, it was nice, I was drunk, I loved,
I went home almost immediately after).
                    Tomorrow, return to Yale, day after
tomorrow excursion in Hillis's sailboat.

7 October 1978.
    they would take me for a madman and would not believe
that I could write you all the time. But you can bear witness. The
train travels along beside small ports all the way up an irregular
coast, I am starting to know my itineraries well.
                    but don't let that prevent
you, my very sweet one, from coming up behind me, you would
read more or less the same thing as I do (always a bit more slowly,
but little by little I have accustomed myself to your rhythm or rather
I go back over what I have already read), and I would feel your
breath between my neck and my ear.
                    I was in the course [*en train*] of ad-
miring the *Philebus.* My pleasure is to read that *with you* for example. It is visibly (everything is in it) a small piece of Plato's post
card that Freud has translated into *Beyond* . . . , a small piece,
there on top, after having kept it in a drawer for ages. Although this
in no way limits the genius of *Beyond* . . . (it too is a unique "work
of art," and the only one), everything is dispensed within it right at
the outset [*coup d'envoi*] by the *Philebus,* arrange this as you will
(the discourse on the limit, the tendency to hegemony, rhythm and
intervals, etc., to say nothing of the difficulty of stopping at the
sixth generation and of Orpheus's prescription). One more citation,
for you, and I'll stop reading, I am slowly turning around toward
you, you are smiling
                    "and we, we say, like children, that a thing rightly
given cannot be taken back." This is said in the *Philebus,* you see.
Rightly, *orthōs,* what is this? Directly, straight, adroitly, with the
address which consists in not getting the address wrong, without
any mal-address? Mal-address is what I follow everywhere, myself, I track it down, and it persecutes me without end. Happily you

are there. Safe. You alone. But this thing which cannot be taken back, is it what the child says or is it what says the child, the desire of the child? *You couldn't tell.*

I have almost gotten there, arrived, this time. At this instant a completely crazy idea comes to me (from Thot, doubtless, another old friend whom I have refound at the beginning of the *Philebus:* to write only to you, to you alone, to the exclusion of every other possible addressee, I will explain to you. I must stop now, they have all gotten out of the train, I am alone. I miss you.

9 October 1978.

and to "recount" it has always appeared impossible to me and infinitely desirable. Of us there will never be a narrative.

what I read in my date book for the next two days, I invent nothing: *travelers,* photocop. (how easy and inexpensive it is here), send package, paper, barber, bank, post. Sinister, no? But if you reflect on it closely, without these itineraries you cannot engender any of the (epistolary or not) romanesquerie of the literary posterity of the Socratic novel. If you challenge me to it, I will demonstrate this to you, insisting especially on the traveler's checks because of the double signature (signature/countersignature), which for me is a veritable muse. They don't know how many times, very legitimately, you have signed in my place.

last week in the East. Thursday, New York again, this time I'll be at the Hotel Barbizon. Departure for Cornell the next morning very early.

from the very first *envoi:* no gift, gift step [*pas de don*], without a b s o l u t e forgetting (which also absolves you of the gift, *don,* and of the dose), forgetting of what you give, to whom, why and how, of what you remember about it or hope. A gift, if there is one, does not destine itself.

13 October 1978.

therefore I went to bed as late as possible. You know the program (lecture on Nietzsche, after which I wanted to walk on the border of Central Park, I went into one of those discos, you know

I hadn't noticed that it was a Friday the 13th. Here is the somewhat crazy project I spoke to you about in the train that was taking me back to Yale: it's like a vow, the sublime idea of a fast, I will speak to you, in my letters, of nothing that is not you and legible by you alone, if this is possible. In any event I engage myself to do everything that is within my power or the power of language for this. Above all I will no longer write to you, as I do too often, and in a necessarily insupportable way, circling around our (hand) writings [*écritures*], our mail [*courrier*], our *envois,* our back-and-forths, the post, what we write otherwise, from Socrates to Freud, while passing through all these waystations. In sum, I am going to cease recounting to you that we are spending our life and our love writing to each other, by asking myself how this is possible, where it comes from and where it is taking us, where it is passing through and how it comes to pass, and whom and what it does without, so many things that I can leave to others or write to others (which, moreover, I support less and less, whether it is a question of readers, which at bottom I do not like, not yet, or of that triumphant jubilation, that mania which bursts out in all writing, even the most desperate: manic phase of mourning, he will say, but he is not rigorous on this question and I have more than one objection to make to him, more than one question to ask him). Therefore, henceforth (starting tomorrow—and until you put an end to your "determination") I write nothing else to you, I write (to) you only, yourself, to yourself.

It's six o'clock in the morning, noon for you, I have just called you, you were not expecting it, visibly. I'll never forget that burst of laughter in your voice. You come back to me very quickly now. In two hours, flight to Cornell, day after tomorrow California. But now, the more I go west, the closer you get. I will never push you away.

First days of January 1979.
        as if you had wanted to unbind me from my vow, and that by once more writing to you as before through some detour I cease to address myself to you. As if the unleashed violence of this fast, the orgy of this uninterrupted prayer which made all my words rise in you (and I have never written to you so much as during these two months) in order to reserve you, for you alone, all alone, knowing that they were being burned alive, as if the song had suddenly made you afraid.

        This "remission" will have been the last, you seem more certain of it than I do, I who will never accept believing in it—and moreover will act such that, I swear to you again, it never happens. I remain fascinated by the apparently totally chance character of the event (of the accident: only an accident, and this time the worst one, can happen, *arrive*, not so, happen to happen, arrive to arrive), as if you had let the date impose itself arbitrarily: *let us say* the last or next to last day of a given year, toward midnight. Is it only apparently that this chance (one could easily once more find a 7 in it: I have a small sheet on my table, I am accumulating figures on it and several very simple operations. Without any artificial manipulation, I can see the figure 7 reign, I can see it radiate over our anniversaries, our great events, the great encounters. A written 7 [*7 écrit*], as in the Apocalypse. Finally more or less, of course. I still remain fascinated by the suddenness, the apparent unforeseeability of that which suddenly takes on such a fatal dimension (two hours before you were not even thinking about it, you were living in another world: this I believe despite your denegations), thunderstruck especially by the significant vulgarity of the pretexts and the places that you have chosen in order to let your 1930 milliner come back, your "determination," which I had finally believed to be discouraged: those stories about bad music (on this subject I maintain everything that I have said: I had nothing against it, but it was bad, and after a while we had better things to do), this carrying on about television, and then that language on the telephone (there I had the milliner right on the line: "we are not weather vanes," "in what spirit are you calling me?" as if you were negotiating key money with a real estate agency, or as if I were bargaining over an end of series (the "series" for us, is the mystery, the law of series, the manner in which the blows of fate that "only happen to us" group themselves). I am just a few steps away from you, I hear you, you seem so foreign now, I love you and I would even like to love this milliner, if I could. It is surely a widow you are putting up there, she has remarried badly, she's not making the best of it and is jealous of us. She loves me more than you, that is the catastrophe—and neither the one nor the other of you confesses it to herself or to each other.

January 1979.

I arrive from the hospital and you are not yet back. I prefer to write to you than to speak to you on this subject. The experience is very painful and awakens I don't know what or who within me. They are increasing the tests (apparently negative, or in any event that's what they are saying to the family), the X-rays, the biopsies, the lumbar punctures. Although the analyses "show" nothing, the signs of weakness are multiplying and the family is worried, which I am beginning to understand. Don't be mad at me if I go there so often. I feel that my presence is good, and there is a demand there which I do not feel I have the right to evade. Finally, I especially wanted to tell you (confess to you) that I have not been able to speak to them about the letter, as you had suggested to me before the vacation. To tell the truth I have thought it necessary not to do so, the violence and indiscretion of such a gesture is something I do not feel capable of. What is more, my confidence is without reserve, it is as if I had given the letter to my father or my mother. Later I'll see.

Strange that this is happening to me at the same time as the glasses— the problem with close reading has accelerated suddenly. And those two gold tombs at the back of my mouth.

January 1979.

Of yourself, of you alone are you jealous. Your only right.

What I have (put) inside you (in me) and that I will never take back, for I will never take myself back, you are now going to drag around everywhere: I think of the bounty hunter who attaches the body of the *"wanted"* man behind his horse in order to finish him off, and then brings the cadaver back to the sheriff's office stopping off at all the saloons. That's what the West is for us.

I had been told of her death, I entered into the house, Josephine Baker was stretched out at the back of the room. Everything was gathered around her mouth, apparently a cancer that swelled her lips and paralyzed her in a kind of frightful muteness. Then, as soon as I arrived, after my first steps toward her, everything changed, she began speaking. I no longer know if it was only on awakening that the desire of her legs, a kind of admiration equally, covered up everything. I have a thousand hypotheses, I'll tell you.

I am not leaving this note on the secretary in order to convince you or in order to plead my case, only to tell you that without accepting anything, I accept [*j'accepte*] your "determination." You must know that it still remains secret for me, governed by a secret (one day you will have the courage to write it to me and this will be the last blow, I won't learn anything about it but everything will be revealed concerning what we have lived as a negative), and it especially remains anonymous for me. It is not you who "determines" yourself in this way. You become someone by determining yourself but what determines you or whoever is determined it is not you. Yourself, we love each other, and this self-evidence dazzles you. Even today: for me too this is too evident. But I accept [*j'accepte*].

Our only chance for *survival*, now, but in what sense, would be to burn everything, in order to come back to our initial desire. Whatever "survival" it might be a question of, this is our only chance, I mean common chance. I want to start over. Shall we burn everything? that's this morning's idea, when you come back I'll talk to you about it—as technically as possible.

January 1979. Just returned from the hospital. The whole family was there. Apparently I was not the only one to regret it, I don't know what's going on, the doctors aren't saying anything. They are waiting for the new analyses, but I had the impression that the nurse knew or foresaw something that she couldn't say. As if they all knew what must happen. Sinister, I would like not to go back again, I am leaving all my strength there.

Sublime nothingness, you know that it preserves everything. The "correspondence" will be destroyed better if we pretend to save several laughable fragments of it, several snapshots good enough to put into everyone's hands. Forgetting—our only chance, don't you think?—will forget us better, it will let us start over. Perhaps one day I will meet you anew. I hear you open the door.

January 1979.
"Go to the war."

You must now, via a destination without end, turn away infinite hatred from yourself. And the disaster, the sacrifice of the eldest, guilt without limit, simultaneously divine and diabolical (because it is double and contradictory, the god himself cannot absolve himself, it is older than he is).

I was going to tell you two things last night, right before the little car crash: 1. *Plato* is *Socrates'* modest widow who speaks in his inner *for* ("oh! all these widows who will not leave me alone, is it because I love them that they are widows, because I marry all of them and immediately make them wear, in my presence, mid-mourning? is it that I love them surviving, permitting them to survive me (themselves)? is it that I accuse them of surviving me in my presence? On the contrary, what I need is that widowed you will keep me alive, I only love life," etc.). I had not told you upon my return from Cotonou, at Christmas, what had happened to me there. It was in Abomey, in the palace-museum of the ancient kingdom: the guide leads me to a kind of crypt of beaten earth. Forty women, among all the widows of a given king (I have forgotten who is in question), had themselves buried alive upon his death. Too beautiful to be true. I thought very hard about them, without knowing clearly which side I was on, which death. All too beautiful. And the guide adds that in fact for this grand suicide, the most beautiful ones had been chosen. And that they had been helped to die with "hemlock" (his word, I swear). Is it to you that one day I had announced Socrates' simulated or organized suicide? He is *also,* on his part, Plato's widow. Don't laugh, there are only widows, *mais si . . .* 2. The second thing, is, I couldn't talk to you about it last night, the end of the story, of history. Of ours, this is too obvious, of the delirium or nightmare from which you believe that you have to awaken. This is too obvious. But also the end of my delirium around S and p. Prose begins here, starting with the expertise of the doctor who comes to teach me how to read the card. I had called him in for a consultation and here is his answer (he is writing to J.C., you recall that he had offered to take on this mission to the *Kunstgeschichte* specialist): "Dear Sir, your question can be answered quite simply. One has but to read the miniature verbally. Socrates is in the course of writing. Plato is beside him, but is not dictating. He is showing, with his index finger pointed toward Socrates: Here is the great man. With the left index finger he is drawing the attention of the spectators, who must be imagined more to the right toward the philosopher who is writing. Therefore he is rather subordinate, of lesser size and with a more modest headpiece. Please accept my kindest regards." He has to be believed, he is right. "Read verbally" must mean "literally." I am persuaded that he is literally right, and the entire context that one might imagine (and of which he himself has knowledge), the code which governs the gestures and positions in all this iconography, all of this, I have never doubted it, makes him right, and me too. It is I who should have read somewhat "verbally" and thereby unleashed literality. He reminds me a bit of Schapiro in his diagnosis. That being said, if I were given the time, I could demonstrate that nothing in my delirium is literally incompatible with his "very simple" answer, all that I'm doing is developing it a bit, and this is our history, and our difference. Moreover, the expert can be objective only in the extent (what an extent) to which his place is designated, assigned on the card, in the picture, and not facing it: a moment of the desire for objectivity, a tremor of the epistēmē whose origin regards you here in two persons. They are setting you, literally, and with a shake of the wand, on the way: know clearly, know clearly that, it must indeed be known, here is the truth of the picture, hold it close, the answer is very simple. Useless to lift up so many robes, it tears out the eyes.

Last night I felt that the worst vengeance was on its course, and that it was avenging someone else, neither you nor me. Your desire has set in place, and on its way [*en voie*], everything that you feared, and which has wound up finding you. In you, apart from you. I would like to be *sure* that it is you, uniquely you, alone and directly, who finally have accepted (without deliberating for a second) the idea of this great fire, call it "burning": that there literally will remain nothing of what we have sent each other, this entire eternity, that one day or another we will become younger than ever and that after the burning of the letters by chance I will encounter you. I will wait for a birth, I bet. And I know myself to fall in love with you at every instant. With what a love without a past you forget yourself within me, with what strength: I forget everything in order to love you, I forget you, yourself, in the second that I am going to throw myself toward you, fall on you, and now you would not like to come again, only that I preserve you, and remain "close to myself," etc., or nothing. All of this means nothing, the milliner herself does not believe it.

The feather on *Plato's* "modest headpiece," there, that's kind of like the thirties. We are living in the seventies! you are on the verge of forgetting it.

The becoming-prose of our Socratic novel, I am giving it a symbolic birthplace: *Zentralinstitut für Kunstgeschichte*. And since I have never renounced knowing, I intend to go back to Oxford, to take the investigation to its end. Upon my return, this summer, the great act of faith, the great burning of us—

February 1979.

once the sending off [*renvoi*] is signified, I believe that I prefer to write to you (even if you are facing me, or as at this moment at your secretary, just next to me), you push me away less. Or even, despite all the suffering that attaches me to this device, to telephone you. I am hanging up now on the telephone, by myself (as if I were still keeping some autonomy, the freedom to regulate the distance at the other end of the wire, or as if I were only sent off "until-later," with the illusion of being able to reappropriate for myself our entire history, of holding it in my hand the way one holds a "combined set"—the receiver and the emitter in the same sex held close to the ear, the S/p framework). You are the messenger of my proper death, you no longer make any sign in my direction that does not signify it, but I have always loved you within this self-evidence. You are my fortune teller, the seer and indicator of my death.

you told me just now, in order to justify your preference for your "determination": "I don't know, and neither do you doubtless, whom you are addressing yourself to." This is true, and I don't take it as an accusation. Can one ever know? Not that I am overlooking the matter (and everything depends upon you, it is only up to you that your answer destines my love to you), but it can never be the object of knowledge. Between to know and to destine, the abyss. I do not want to abuse this kind of remark, nor even to draw an argument from it, but it seemed to me, shall we say symbolic, that you said this to me while looking elsewhere. I could always tax you with the same "distraction," for there is only one kind, it's the same "*volant.*" Even when you say my name in my mouth, when you call me by posing my name on my tongue, we are still taking pleasure from distraction.

You are my daughter and I have no daughter.

February 1979.

I just went to Locatel (everything is arranged, automatic payment, etc., they didn't have anything in color left). I am taking your car [*voiture*] (the word is more and more abstract for me, *voiture,* that which makes a *voie* into a *voie,* your *Weglichkeit* (?) etc. Will we ever amuse ourselves again by passing [*doubler*] each other on the road while pasting messages on the windshield?) I am stopping off at the *Ecole* and then time to come. You're very sweet at the moment, like a surgeon of expert hand, very sure of what he is going to do, you are managing, managing, managing. I'm pretending to be asleep, I no longer recall myself to you (but I still call myself, be sure to know it, you, yourself).

February 1979.
and no one has passed beside me in this way.
I spoke to him again about that ignoble show [*émisson*] on sexual pathology, about the word "intromission." He seemed skeptical when I spoke to him about the telephone, especially when I stated, in order to shock him a bit, that it was *always* telephonic.
His friend had told me one day (or wasn't it you?) that a given, apparently rigorously theoretical text was written such that it gave him an erection whenever he read it.
A bit of respite since yesterday, want to get back to the preface. On this subject I am conceiving a rather perverse project, which is really not perverse at all but which I fear that you yourself will judge monstrous. But you know, I am monstrous, in my innocence and in my very fidelity. I'll talk to you about it tonight when you return. I always speak to you in the present, no matter what happens.

February 1979.
"Should have come, you aren't very far away." — "I was on my way back but I couldn't."
I would still like to convince you. By publishing that which, concerning the post card, looks like a "post card" (let's say the brief sequence of a secret correspondence between Socrates and Freud conversing with each other at the bottom of the post card, about the support, the message, the inheritance, telecommunications, the *envoi,* etc.), we will finish off destruction. Of the holocaust there would remain only the most anonymous support without support, that which in any event never will have belonged to us, does not regard us. This would be like a purification of purification by fire. Not a single trace, an absolute camouflaging by means of too much evidence: cards on the table, they won't see anything else. They will throw themselves onto unintelligible remainders, come from who knows where in order to preface a book about Freud, about the Platonic inheritance, the era of the posts, the structure of the letter and other common goods or places. The se-

cret of what we will have destroyed will be even more thoroughly destroyed or, amounting to the same thing, by all the evidence, with all its self-evidence more thoroughly preserved. Don't you think? Never will I have loved so much. And by means of the demonstration that only *is* [*est*] the post card, beyond everything that is, we will remain to be reborn. We will begin to love each other. I also like the cruelty of this scene, it still resembles, it resembles you. And then I would operate such that it would become absolutely i l l e g i b l e for you. You will recognize nothing yourself, you will feel nothing, and when you read even I will pass unnoticed. After this final murder we will be more alone than ever, I will continue to love you, living, beyond you.

February 1979.

I only wanted to say that all women would be you (but I only know one of them), when they are beautiful for having said "yes"—and you are a man. Strange *"dispositif"* no? And I have used this —*"dispositif"*—in order to mark that everything within it is always "posted."

as for our Socratic novel, our infernal post card history, that I found it "comic" does not disaccord with the sublime. It is the sacred, for me, today still, but as such it also makes me laugh, it does leave us laughter, thank God. There, nothing is ever forbidden us.

I am reflecting upon a rather rigorous principle of destruction. What will we burn, what will we keep (in order to broil it better still)? The selection [*tri*], if it is possible, will in truth be postal: I would cut out, in order to deliver it, everything that derives from the Postal Principle, in some way, in the narrow or wide sense (this is the difficulty, of course), everything that might preface, propose itself for a treatise on the posts (from Socrates to Freud and beyond, a *p*sychoanalysis *of* the *p*ost, a *p*hilosophy *of* the *p*ost, the *of* signifying belonging or provenance, psychoanalysis or philosophy operating *since, on the basis of* the posts, I would almost say: on the basis of the nearest post office, etc.). And we burn the rest. Everything that from near or far touches on the post card (this one, in which one sees Socrates reading us, or writing all the others, and every post card in general), all of this we would keep, or finally would doom to loss by publishing it, we would hand it over to the antiques dealer or the auctioneer. The rest, if there is any that remains, is us, is for us, who do not belong to the card. We are the card, if you will, and as such, accountable, but they will seek in vain, they will never find us in it. In several places I will leave all kinds of references, names of persons and of places, authentifiable dates, identifiable events, they will rush in with eyes closed, finally believing to be there and to find us there when by means of a switch point I will send them elsewhere to see if we are there, with a stroke of the pen or the *grattoir* I will make everything derail, not at every instant, that would be too convenient, but occasionally and according to a rule that I will not ever give, even were I to know it one day. I would not work too hard composing the thing, it is a scrap copy of scrapped paths that I will leave in their hands. Certain people will take it into their mouths, in order to recognize the taste, occasionally in order to reject it immediately with a grimace, or in order to bite, or to swallow, in order to conceive, even, I mean a child. You yourself will do all that, simultaneously or successively. I would have you, yourself: *semée.* And myself if you can console yourself for this. The truth is that of this I wish to make a deposition: we have lost each other. So that, of course, as soon as we are lost from each other's sight, I know that you will never grant to agree without reserve to this innocent monstrosity: it's that you will no longer support anything from me, neither to refind yourself nor not to refind yourself in the book. Not even, perhaps (but here you would be wrong), the signs of the infinite respect that I owe you, that we owe each other and that I preserve as the best part of my life.

In any event, rest assured, it would be a sequence (or, if you prefer, a very brief session) of our life, barely a film, a snapshot, a Polaroid, from Oxford to Oxford, two years more or less, almost nothing out of our immense literature. Plato and Socrates, and Freud, it's very short, it's already the end of a history, only that. Out of these two years, I would deliver to them only fragments circled with white and they would all bear upon the post card, from Socrates to Freud, upon telecommunications, upon *Beyond the Pleasure Principle* and other trivialities good enough for the marketplace: in a word, everything that concerns the *voie,* viability, crossroads, walking, feet and legs, back-and-forth, the *fort/da,* proximity and distancing. Of course it will be difficult to decide, to sort out, to separate on the one hand and the other: when is it a question of all this directly, or "literally"? And when by means of a detour, a figure or presupposition? Have confidence in me for once.

I will get around all these difficulties. In all of this the issue is to turn around and to detour, a letter and first of all attention. Lots of tropes will be necessary. There will be several books in this book, I count four, we will read it as our Tropics.

Before all else it is a question of turning one's back [*dos*]. Of turning my back to them by pretending to address myself to them and to make them bear witness. This conforms to my taste and to what I can support from them today. Of turning the back of the post card (what is *Socrates'* back when he turns his back to *Plato*—a very amorous position, don't forget—? this is also the back of the post card: as we remarked one day, it is equally legitimate to name it recto or verso). Our great tropics: to turn the "*dos*" in every sense, to all sides. The word "*dos*" and all the families that swarm behind it, beginning with behind. There (*da*) is behind, behind the curtain or the skirts of the crib, or behind oneself. *Dorsum* and *la séance continue* for Orpheus, he sings, they will believe, accompanying himself with the lyre that the other tendered in the way you know, while ripping out the sex. To turn one's back is the analytic position, no? I am behind (*dorsum*) or rather I have my back turned, and it is denied in vain, hypnosis, or narcosis, remain on the scene. Socrates knew something about this. Sleep [*dors*], I am drowsy, somnolent, sleep still, I summon [*somme*] you to sleep, dream, speak, turn your back to me, remain on your back, I am only *somme, nous sommes, le somme, les sommes,* no more counting.

And I am putting all of this on Socrates' back, I am reading the check that he is in the course of signing, I am slipping it back to them without endorsing it and I am not involved. Neither seen nor heard, I am founding an entire institution on counterfeit money by demonstrating that there is no other kind.

There is only one good institution, my love, it is us.

They are listening, eh! Who? Who is listening? Be reassured, no one.

La séance continue, how do you analyze that? I'm talking grammar, as always, is it a verb or an adjective? These are the right questions. For example (I am saying this in order to reassure you: they will believe that we are two, that it's you and me, that we are legally and sexually identifiable, unless they wake up one day) in our languages, I, Fido, lack(s) a sex. Now all possible accidents might happen in the interval that separates the subject (who says I) and his attribute. By saying *I* only, I do not unveil my sex, I am a subject without a sexual predicate, this is what had to be demonstrated about "S is p," this is the performance.

In sum a pedagogic short subject, a documentary about our great precursors, the grandfathers of philosophy, of the posts, and of psychoanalysis. On the subject of film (for this additionally would be our small private cinema) shall we also burn our rolls (*pellicules*), the films and the photos? Myself, I would be for. We would keep only the word film (the membranes, the sensitive pellicles, the veils, the coverings, and by means of this word alone we would cover everything with a light cloud: I only would have filmed. No?)

Beginning of March 1979.
and if you have the time to look up the etymologies of *chemin* for me (*cheminer, être en chemin* or *acheminer,* everything that goes in the direction of the step, but also of the chimney, *cheminée:* you can see what I am looking for, in the direction of the hearth in which things are burning and in the direction of the legs or the jambs, nel mezzo del cammin de nostra vita). Only if you have the time, thanks
on the Greph side, I reserved the seats just now, I'm leaving for Besançon on Friday with Graciet. Four hours in the train, I'll be back Saturday.

9 March 1979.
Didn't go badly, you know my taste for this genre.

In the train, without telling him the essential, I recounted a bit of the project for a "fiction": a kind of false preface, once again, which, while parodying epistolary or detective literature (from the Philosophical Letters to the Portuguese nun, from the *liaisons dangereuses* to Milena) would also obliquely introduce my speculations on Freudian speculation. The entire book, accordion astrologies of post cards, would initiate into speculation via the reading of Sp. Finally that is all there would be, everything could come back and amount to the patient, interminable, serious and playful, direct or detoured, literal or figurative description of the Oxford card. It would hold for itself and for all the others. The other day you protested again: but after all aren't they "my" letters? To whom do letters belong?

Actual legality has no jurisprudence here, and even if you don't want to give them back to me I could reinvent them. In any event I will retain only whatever might be *combined* as a preface to the three other texts (*Legs de Freud, Le facteur de la vérité, Du tout*). The ensemble will even be a combine, an emitting-receiving device: nothing will be seen in it, only calls, or wires, in every sense will be heard, that which reads the post card and which first will have been read by it. Socrates reading Socrates, if you will, and suddenly not understanding a thing, and just on the verge of waking up. It's cold in this hotel, I miss you, you can be sure that if your schedule permitted I would have asked you to accompany me.

So I re-counted all this to him, in outline, while asking him not to talk about it. I have a very superstitious relation to this text, and you know why. He seemed to approve but I think he is prejudiced. And he correctly pointed out to me that the "informationist" aspect (communication, language, form of exchange, theory of the message, emission/reception, etc.) risked being top-heavy and unbalancing it the way a thesis would, even if this is what I have been putting into question for centuries. One must take into account, he says to me, the fact that they do not read. And yet I am breaking my back, yes, in repeating to them that all of this (in a word, postal *différance*) does not *relève* anything, does not derive from anything, neither from the logic of communication, of language, or of information, whether or not they are structured like an unconscious, nor from the logic of production (which at bottom is the same, despite the apparent opposition), nor from negative dialectics.

When I told you yesterday from the station, on the telephone, that we will not be able to replace each other, I was very sincerely talking about forgetting. And about the eternity of my love. You substitute yourself for yourself all the time, I forget you in order to fall in love, with you, from the very next second. This is my condition, on the condition that one loves.

I felt it right away, I was uplifted, a kind of levitation, and as soon as you called me, the first time, I forgot you, I lost consciousness. I am going to sleep now. You should not have le(f)t me. You should not have let me depart alone. One day, when one of us will no longer be able to say "I love you," it will suffice that the other still have wind of it, nothing will have changed. You should not have let me write, you should not have kept the letters.

14 March 1979.
You couldn't accompany me to the Gare du Nord, but I
hoped that at the last minute, as if you had gone crazy (this happens
to you less and less), you would appear, as the last second, in the
compartment. And then I resigned myself, thinking that this time
you no longer would take a single step, because of what I had just
told you, somewhat brutally, about the *"dead letter"* (nevertheless
you should understand that I cannot now demand of the family that
they return it to me, supposing, supposing that the said letter supposedly is to be found, that it is put away, classified, or hidden
somewhere. It could have been destroyed as a precaution without
my knowledge (which would be just like them, as much because of
the discretion as because of the violent indiscretion of such an initiative). And further, to claim it at such a moment not only would
be indecent, it would be to induce them to look for, perhaps even to
find and to read—don't forget that the envelope is virgin, and therefore easily replaceable—what it is doubtless in our interest to leave
forever lost in a corner. All the more that, I tell you again for the
last time and I would like us not to talk about it any more, I have all
the more easily forgotten the "details" of this letter now that they
were forgotten as if by themselves, and it is of this above all that I
wished to speak to you. These "details" have never belonged to
memory, they have never had access to it. I even believe that in this
letter, at bottom, I was talking to you only about yourself, in essence). In the train, even before the departure, at the second preceding it, a real hallucination, as at the beginning when I saw you
all the time in the street. You appeared at the other end of the cor-
ridor, a gift in hand, a little box. It went away so fast, I would have
liked to kiss you for a long time standing between the cars. How can
a hallucination lift one so joyfully? One second suffices, and I ask
for nothing else. There is no illusion in this, no facility, I very
quickly knew that I was leaving *alone,* so alone, for Brussels, on a
given day, 14 March at 2 PM, but life had been given back to me.
                                                              Your ab-
sence is reality for me, I don't know any other. This is when I know
that you are not there, that you are away from me, have gone away
from me, are going to go away from me. This is my reality principle, the most external necessity, all my impotence. You mark for
me both reality and death; absent or present moreover (you are always there, over there, in the course of going back and forth), all
this amounts to the same, you mark *me,* you signify reality as death
for me, you name them or show them with your finger. And I be-

lieve in you, I remain attached to you. An other, whom I know well, would unbind himself immediately in order to run off in the other direction. I bet that he would fall over you again, I have happily fallen into it, so I remain.

15 March 1979.
This torment, *tourment,* I am calling it *tourment* because that's the word, the words for it (if at least one wishes to send oneself language), this torment has just relayed the other one. Now it's the project of "partial publication" that has become insupportable for me, not so much because of the publication—they will only be blinded by it—, as because of the minute cross-section to which all of this should, for my part, give rise. I see him as a perverse copyist, seated for days in front of a correspondence, two years of voluble correspondence, busy transcribing a given passage, scratching out a given other one in order to prepare it for the fire, and he spends hours of knowledgeable philology sorting out what derives from this or that, in order to deliver nothing to publicity, absolutely nothing that might be proper (private, secret), in order to profane nothing, if this is still possible. The activity of this copyist all of a sudden appears ignoble to me—and in advance doomed to failure. I shouldn't have spoken to you about it. I now feel myself bound to you by the fact that, despite all the reserves that you formulated at first, and that I understand very well, you now seem to hold to this fiction. But I don't know any more. Now it's of this (the relaying of torment) that I feel infinitely guilty. Henceforth there is nothing that does not wound me, and it's always you; and even my innocence, which I hold to be virgin, is guilty of feeling innocent. I no longer understand anything about you, you have lived everything from another side, on the other hand, where I have never gone and where I'll never see you again. I no longer know to whom I am writing, how could I consult you about the innocent perversity of my project? I know it less and less, in this compartment I have the impression that I am writing to my most foreign homonym.
                    I have over you, not having known how to address myself to you, I mean uprightly, directly, no right. And I wouldn't have had any if I had been able to arrive right up to you. I have an infinite respect for you, without any common proportion to myself. Even though my terrifying jealousy is not unrelated to this respect, I believe that I have never been

jealous of you yourself, but rather of me, and of a bad coupling that profaned us.
You can't do anything about it, from you I will continue to receive everything, in advance I have accepted everything. This is our infernal and divine higher bid. No one will ever know who, you or me, will have been the strongest, the furthest. Neither you nor I will ever know it. Who will have thrown himself the furthest, the strongest, always so that in the end the other comes back. We have taken all the risks of interruption.
The train is approaching Anvers. We are barely three-quarters of an hour from Brussels, and I had intended, even before the lecture, to come here alone for several hours. Want cities unknown to you, to which you could have accompanied me, and I no longer know whether I am taking them in order to give them to you or to take them away from you. I had told you that I would come to Anvers, this morning, and why, in this city about which I know only the name and a few clichés. If you were crazy you would have come to wait for me like someone hallucinating, I would have run toward you on the platform, right next to the track, I would have done everything so as not to fall

15 March 1979.
I wanted to write to you, otherwise, but always with the same foreign language (they don't know how much a language is foreign). I'm in a restaurant for an hour before getting back on the train. In the rain, I jumped from taxi to taxi, from museum to museum (always my barbarity), and then I stayed in the Plantin house for a long time, as if in my church. I'm bringing back scores of cards for you. I just sent one to Paul de Man, this is his city.
                                                                    and when I
write you you continue, you transfigure everything (the transformation comes from behind the words, it operates in silence, simultaneously subtle and incalculable, you substitute yourself for me and right up to my tongue you "send" it to yourself and then I remember those moments when you called me without warning, you came at night at the bottom of my throat, you came to touch my name with the tip of your tongue. Beneath the surface, it took place beneath the surface of the tongue, softly, slowly, an unheard-of trembling, and I was sure that at that second that it was not coming back, a convulsion of the entire body in the two tongues at once,

the foreign one and the other one. On the surface, nothing, a patient, applied pleasure leaving everything in place, forcing no movement of the tongue: and then the tongue is all you hear, and we are
alone I believe in receiving its silence. It never says a thing. Because we know how to love it, after our passage, without anything
having changed in its appearence, it accepts no longer knowing who
it is. It no longer recognizes its own, proper traits, it is no longer
the law in its own house, it even has no more words. But for it to
consent to this madness, it must be left alone with itself at the moment you enter (you recall that one day on the telephone I had said
to you, I think we were talking about Celan, leave me that word
alone, and you had said yes; what I still wanted to do with it by
letting myself be taken or penetrated I can't tell you (

                                           I certainly under-
stand them but it's not *strong* [*fort*] enough, it doesn't go far enough,
nothing much happens, *in the last account,* when one throws oneself onto language like a feverish virgin ("wait till you see what I'll
do to her") who still believes that the tongue can be taken on, that
things can be done to her, that she can be made to cry out or can be
put into pieces, penetrated, that one can inscribe one's claws in her
as quickly as possible before the premature ejaculation and above
all before her own pleasure (it is always her pleasure I prefer

                                         (they will no-
tice it, if this hasn't already happened, one day, after all the free-
doms that they believed they have taken with her, after all the epi-
dermic violence and bulletins of revolutionary victory, the old lady
has remained impenetrable, virgin, impassive, somewhat amused,
all-powerful, she walks the streets in vain it's me she loves (

                                         one day I heard
her quietly, without a word, mock their infantile compulsion: to believe that they violated everything by breaking the toy in order to
throw the pieces far away, and then to yell loud [*fort*], very loud

                                         (no, to let
the other love you completely dressed, to surprise the thing fast
asleep, as if you were governing a dream, barely, and upon awakening no one any longer recognizes a thing, no one gets back the disposition of the smallest piece of tongue, no one can any longer
write a letter, even less sign one

                                    (for all this one has to be my age and one
has to know that one does not play with the tongue with impunity, it
can't be improvised, unless one accepts never being the best at this
game)

and myself, who in the event appear to be in a better position than all these expert bloodhounds on our heels, I am losing the track, I no longer know to whom I am speaking, nor about what. The difficulty I would have in sorting out this *courrier* with the aim of publication is due, among other perils, to this one: you know that I do not believe in propriety, property, and above all not in the form that it takes according to the opposition public/private (p/p, so be it).

This opposition doesn't work, neither for psychoanalysis (especially with the tranche-ferential sectoring that is being lowered onto the capitals like a net that they themselves can no longer master: this is the fatality of the parallel police forces), nor for the post (the post card is neither private nor public), nor even for the police (they leave us, whatever the regime, only the choice between several police forces, and when a pp (public police) doesn't accost you in the street, another pp (private parallel police) plugs its microphones into your bed, seizes your mail, makes you spit it out in full ecstasy—and the secret circulates with full freedom, as secret you promise I swear, this is what I call a post card.

but the worst mistake of our expert bloodhounds will consist in naming you, something I never would have dared to do. If I name me, myself, it's only in order to add to the confusion. You can understand that yesterday, 14 March, in my first class compartment (a compartmented train, this is what I'm talking about, and about classes: did you know that the *post card,* in the United States, is part of the *first class* mail? It goes as quickly as our letters; at home it's the opposite, it is supposed that the reading of a post card can wait and this is a good calculation), yesterday, then, all alone in my compartment, doubtless because I was so alone, I decided to blow up all the (private and public) police stations [*postes*] and even all the post offices, in the city and in the country, one after another, and in fact to do it all alone. I'll do it right under their beards, beneath their beards, by caressing the beards of *Plato* and *Socrates,* by lifting, as I am doing here, words without final destination, the only ones that escape the pps, by multiplying anonymous letters. And they won't ever find me, they will look in every kind of direction, will imagine all kinds of motives, including the most pathetic ones. They will not know that it is you, and that it is you I love, because this is the most evident thing.

You yourself were getting lost by naming yourself, this is the mistake that you made by choosing or decreeing your "determination," under the law of the milliner. You believed that you could deter-

mine, my poor one, and better yet, determine "yourself." Your innocence is disarming. Never have you been so obedient as at the
moment when you believed that you were taking yourself back in
hand, and your autonomy. I saw you then, you believed you could
stop everything, stop everyone (I am speaking of arrests), stop time
itself, and make it sign a contract with itself, you burst into the saloon, armed to the teeth: no one moves, everyone in his place, state
your identities one after another, not all at once. Above all you were
afraid that someone would change place or occupy several at once.
You wanted to keep everything under your glance, to know who was
who, who was allied with whom, and first of all, my all-determined
one, with you whom I love. And now, because I love you better
still, I leave you: more undetermined than ever. And over your determination I cry. In the depths of unhappiness I tremble for joy, a
very singular joy. We are a crowd, you and I, and this is good, an
immense dispersed collection. We would have run the risk, if I had
bent myself to your determination, and already one could see this
coming, of forming a society, or worse, a State within the State, an
empire. We would have closed all the borders on our secret. Our
secret, I like it that henceforth it reigns without limit. And without
law.   It's
good that you didn't come to the station.

March-April 1979.
        I've started to reread, to sort, to dig around in the box
(my first *gift*, suddenly it no longer sufficed). It overflows everywhere, never will I be able.
                    You will never get to know, nor will they,
whether, when I use a name it is in order to say *Socrates* is me or
"Socrates" has seven letters. This is why one never will be able to
translate.

March-April 1979.
        the mothers? but it is they who read letters. Ask any
adolescent, and it's due to jealousy that they open drawers.
                                                    what a couple
we have here!
        I've decided to reproduce only the words, no iconography,
save the Oxford card. Otherwise what would we have done with all
the others, the films, the cassettes, the piece of skin with the draw-

ing? So that only insupportable supports remain, post cards, I am
burning all the supports and am keeping only several purely verbal
sequences.
       The royal couple we have it here between the father and the son.
                                                            I spent
an hour taking stock of all the English meanings of the word *"post,"*
"poster." I should have written the same book in several languages,
just to see. I have done so a bit, but with my habitual negligence and
without insisting, too bad, I'll never bring anything to a conclusion
                                                            and to
unplug [*débrancher*] everything, right up to the telephone, from
every familial branch.
       I'll never resign myself to it, for *to leave to* one's
heirs, is not to leave them, not to leave them to be or to live. I will
abandon nothing to them, there are only poisoned inheritances, and
I am already too poisoned myself. The better they forget me, and
you, the better they'll know that I love only them. Thus they disappear before me.
       Wechsel der Töne, this book would be of a polymorphous
perversity. Fine arts in order to commemorate the assassination of
an infanta, our only daughter, perhaps. Not a word that would not
be dictated upside down, programmed on the back [*au dos*], in the
back of the post card. Everything will consist in describing Socrates with Plato making him a child in his back, and I will retain
only the lexicon required for every line [*trait*] in the drawing. In a
word there will only be back (*du dos*), and even the word "*dos*," if
you are willing to pay faithful attention to it and keep the memory.

March-April 1979.
              the heading of the accusation or the receipt for the letter
(*le chef d'accusation ou l'accusé de reception*). No longer to hope
to have knowledge of it one day.
                     so that they can no longer read, read with-
out going crazy, beyond the pleasure principle.
                                   my voice carries beyond
the pleasure principle.
              useless to wait for me, sit down to eat without me, I
don't know when I'll arrive.

March-April 1979.
   so many strings [*fils*], and not only my own, but I am
the last to pull on them, to allegedly hold them in hand. I am rather
the marionette, I try to follow the movement.
                         I'll call from the office to tell
you at what time you'll be able to reach me (doubtless it will be
very late, it always drags on with the questions). If you're not there,
leave a message on the answering machine. In any event, I'm leaving you the car and the papers.

March-April 1979. No, if I die, it's because there are *two* injuries.
A single one never broaches anything. Two injuries and a single
wound, the hell in which I now believe for having let myself be sent
into it—the two form an inseparable couple

9 May 1979.
   Sam came to pick me up at the station, and then we went for a
long walk in the forest (a man came up to greet us thinking that he
recognized me, and then excused himself at the last moment—he
must be suffering, as I am, more and more, from prosopagnosia, a
diabolical impulsion to find resemblances in faces, to recognize, no
longer to recognize). I said a few words about my post cards, asking him to keep it as secret as possible. This morning, in Freibourg,
to which he accompanied me by car, I understood that he had immediately spoken of it to Kittler, my host here, and perhaps to his
wife (psychoanalyst). The secret of the post cards burns—the hands
and the tongues—it cannot be kept, q.e.d. It remains secret, what it
is, but must immediately circulate, like the most hermetic and most
fascinating of anonymous—and open—letters. I don't cease to verify this.
   S. was to summarize and translate my lecture (at the *studium generale*). I stopped at the places that he *himself* had chosen and
checked off in my text (still on *"La folie du jour,"* the title this
time), and he took this as a pretext to speak longer than I did, if not,
I couldn't judge, to divert the public's attention, or even the sense or
letter of my discourse. We laughed over it together and between us
laughter is a mysterious thing, that we share more innocently than
the rest (somewhat complicated by the strategies), like a disarming
explosion and like a field of study, a corpus of Jewish stories. On

the subject of Jewish stories: you can imagine the extent to which I
am haunted by Heidegger's ghost in this city. I came for him. I am
trying to reconstitute all his paths, the places where he spoke (this
studium generale for example), to interrogate him, as if he were
there, about the history of the posts, to appropriate his city for myself, to sniff out, to imagine, etc. To respond to his objections, to
explain to him what he does not yet understand (this morning I
walked with him for two hours, and then I went into a bookstore, I
bought several cards and reproductions, as you can see (I'm also
bringing you back an album, *Freiburg in alten Ansichtskarten*), and
I fell upon two books of photographs that cost me a great deal, one
on Freud, very rich, the other on Heidegger, *at home,* with Ma-
dame and the journalists from the Spiegel in 1968). So that there it
is, back at the Hotel Victoria (that's where I called you from), I laid
down to flip through the albums and I burst out laughing when
I found that Martin has the face of an old Jew from Algiers. I'll
show you.

9 May 1979.
          I am writing you in the train that's taking me back from Stras-
bourg (I almost missed it, once that S. was accompanying me: he
always arrives late, always the last—when he arrives—there I was,
waiting for him in Rue Charles-Grad where I had stopped over as I
did on the way. We spoke about the Athaeneum—and about more
than one symposium on the horizon: for we have to do it over, and
several times in the year to come).
                    if you don't do it, I won't die, I don't
want to charge you with this. Choose your moment therefore.
                                                      Just now,
when we almost missed the train, I remembered the only time when
that happened to us, late at night, guess where.
                              I don't yet know if you will
have been able to come wait for me.
                         I'm flipping through my albums. For
all the time that I've been talking about her, and that she has been
obsessing me like your double, I had never seen Sophie. Here she
is, with her father, I'm trying to describe her in the way that I see
her (through Freud's eyes, of course).
                          what a couple! inseparable. More-
over they are reunited in the same photograph, he full face, looking
out toward the world, she, a bit lower, in profile, turned toward him

(tender and protected). Always the same scenario, there is also a photograph of Heidegger (young, in military uniform, one can see the epaulettes) *"H. & his fiancée, Elfriede Petri 1916."* He is looking straight in front of him and she, in profile, very beautiful, her eyes lowered, in love, in truth presses her face against Martin's, as if she were seeking refuge in him, as if she were sheltering herself, taking shelter in him. These photos of couples are terrifying, with the master who is looking at you and she nestled up against him, no longer seeing anything else. We have another politics of photography, not so?, not that you are always a good master and that you give me the right to look elsewhere, but all the same. In the end I suspect these instant pictures of being more difficult to decipher, I watch out for all the impostures beneath these photographic poses "for eternity." The photographer Halberstadt must have seen some things in them, for example between his father-in-law and his wife or, if you prefer, his daughter. All the portraits that he will have dedicated, the old man, all the gifts that he affected to distribute, that he promised, had awaited, granted with conditions, his Mistinguett side or, closer to us, you know who I'm talking about
Opposite
this photograph, an extract from Freud's letter to Max Halberstadt after the death of his daughter or, if you prefer, of his wife: he says to him that he knows his pain as he knows his own (I'm not inventing anything), that he will not seek to console him, just as "you cannot do anything for us" (*ich mache Keinen Versuch, Dich zu trösten, wie Du nichts für uns tun kannst*). "But then why am I writing to you?" (*Wozu schreibe ich Dir also?*) Etc. All of this falls under the heading of what else is there to write? And yet, with the other hand he wrote the letter that I cite in the *Legs* (*la séance continue,* after seven years of happiness, the son-in-law has nothing to complain about, etc.). Moreover in this letter that I'm reading at the moment in the train (I have the album, it is heavy and thick, on my knees, this paper posed on Freud's head which covers the entire page), he tells him that one must not "complain," one cannot, nor dig too deep. One must bow one's head under "destiny's" blow and *"mit den höheren Gewalten spielen"*! Several pages later you can see him with Heinz on his knees (his *je/nous*) and Ernst standing, and in truth pressing up against him. Then Heinele by himself, naked, younger: Norbert, my dead younger brother. Seven letters again, twice.

It's the end of an epoch. The end of a race also or of a banquet that is dragging on until the small hours of morning (I no longer

know to whom I was saying that "epoch"—and this is why I am
interrogating myself on this subject—remains, because of the halt,
a postal idea, contaminated in advance by *postal différance*, and
therefore by the station, the thesis, the position, finally by the *Setzen* (by the *Gesetzheit des Sichsetzens* that he talks about in *Zeit
und Sein*). The postal principle *does not happen to différance*, and
even less to "Being," it destines them to itself from the very "first"
envoi. Now there are also differences, there is only that, in postal
différance; one can still, by means of a figure folded back over onto
itself, name them "epochs" or sub-epochs. In the great epoch
(whose technology is marked by paper, pen, the envelope, the individual subject addressee, etc.) and which goes shall we say from
Socrates to Freud and Heidegger, there are sub-epochs, for example the process of state monopolization, and then within this the
invention of the postage stamp and the Berne convention, to use
only such insufficient indices. Each epoch has its literature (which
in *general* I hold to be essentially detective or epistolary literature,
even if within it the detective or epistolary genre more or less
strictly folds it back onto itself).

Here Freud and Heidegger, I conjoin
them within me like the two great ghosts of the "great epoch." The
two surviving grandfathers. They did not know each other, but according to me they form a couple, and in fact just because of that,
this singular anachrony. They are bound to each other without reading each other and without corresponding. I have often spoken to
you about this situation, and it is this picture that I would like to
describe in *Le legs:* two thinkers whose glances never crossed and
who, without ever receiving a word from one another, say the same.
They are turned to the same side.

The master-thinkers are also masters of
the post. Knowing well how to play with the *poste restante.* Knowing how not to be there and how to be strong for not being there
right away. Knowing how not to deliver on command, how to wait
and to make wait, for as long as what there is that is strongest
within one demands—and to the point of dying without mastering
anything of the final destination. The post is always *en reste,* and
always *restante.* It awaits the addressee who might always, *by
chance,* not arrive.

And the postal principle is no longer a principle, nor a
transcendental category; that which announces itself or sends itself
under this heading (among other possible names, like you) no longer
sufficiently belongs to the epoch of Being to submit itself to some

transcendentalism, "beyond every genre." The post is but a little message, fold (*pli*), or just as well. A relay in order to mark that there is never anything but relays.

Nancy, do you remember Nancy?

In a word, this is what I am trying to explain to him. *Tekhnē* (and doubtless he would have considered the postal structure and everything that it governs as a *determination* (yes, precisely, your word), a metaphysical and technical determination of the *envoi* or of the destinality (*Geschick,* etc.) of Being; and he would have considered my entire insistence on the posts as a metaphysics corresponding to the technical era that I am describing, the end of a certain post, the dawn of another, etc.); now *tekhnē*, this is the entire—infinitesimal and decisive—*différance, does not arrive.* No more than metaphysics, therefore, and than positionality; always, already it parasites that to which he says it happens, arrives, or that it succeeds in happening to [*arrive à arriver*]. This infinitesimal nuance chances everything in the relation between metaphysics and its doubles or its others.

Tekhnē does not happen to language or to the poem, to *Dichtung* or to the song, understand me: this can mean simultaneously that it does not succeed in touching them, getting into them, it leaves them virgin, not happening to arrive up to them [*n' arrivant pas à arriver jusqu' à eux*], and yet it has to happen to them like an accident or an event because it inhabits them and occasions them.

In Strasbourg, I had wanted to tell her that I love her all the while being afraid of her seer's lucidity, which is frightening because she sees true (*juste*), but she is mistaken because she is just, like the law. I did not dare say it to her, and moreover we have never been alone together.

The entire history of postal *tekhnē* tends to rivet the destination to identity. To arrive, to happen would be to a subject, to happen to "me." Now a mark, whatever it may be, is coded in order to make an imprint, even if it is a perfume. Henceforth it divides itself, *it is valid several times in one time:* no more unique addressee. This is why, by virtue of this divisibility (the origin of reason, the mad origin of reason and of the principle of identity), *tekhnē* does not happen to language—which is why and what I sing to you.

If only you respond to me, my response, my *responsa,* my *promise,* my promised one, you, it will be you. But for this it does not suffice to respond once, with words, but always anew, without reserve, we have to be followed everywhere. If you knew how I love you, my love, you would do it, you would not resist any more. Who are you, my love? you are so numerous, so divided, all compartmented, even when you are there, entirely present and I speak to you. Your sinister "determination" has cut us in two, our glorious body has been divided, it has become normal again, it has preferred to oppose itself to itself and we have fallen, we have let ourselves fall on both our parts. Our former body, the first one, I knew it to be monstrous, but I have not known a more beautiful one, I am still waiting for it.

You have not known how to play with time, and when I am in the train, I take all the measurements again. The meter in the train is no longer quite the same as the same which remains on the platform. We should have lived in the train, I mean much faster than we have done. Often I think of the example of the pregnant woman who, traveling in space at a given speed, after nine months of the time of her child, comes back to bring him to daylight on earth, and everyone has aged twenty years, all the conditions have changed. I also think about the "black holes" of the universe in which we have loved each other, I think about all the letters that I never will have sent you, about the entire correspondence that we have dreamed together, I think that I no longer know where I am going, I think about all the blows of fate, I think about you

if you were here, I would drag you off somewhere and without waiting we would make each other a child, and then we would come back to sit down in this compartment as if nothing had happened.

May 1979.
I found the list and I'm going out shopping. Look at this clipping that I received this morning: it's straightforward, and I must have done everything to deserve it, at bottom I should rejoice, but when I see them mounted against I don't know who (against me, the most vulgar and stupid ones say) I always ask myself why *they* do not ask themselves what they are thus mounting guard before, these dogs, with all their concern and solidarity for public morals.

I "worked" this morning but you know now what I mean by that: mourning— for me, for us in me.

(no) more revenants, it would be a spectral book . . .

to give the police just enough to divert it, and along with it all the posts [*tous et toutes les postes*], the institutions, the computers,the powers, the dupins and their bi-spoolarity (*fort/da*), the States, this is what I am assessing, or computing, what I am sorting out in order to defy all sorting out [*tris*].

May 1979. I have thought a lot about your briefcase dream, so then

May 1979. What cannot be said above all must not be silenced, but written. Myself, I am a man of speech, I have never had anything to write. When I have something to say I say it or say it to myself, basta. You are the only one to understand why it really was necessary that I write exactly the opposite, as concerns axiomatics, of what I desire, what I know my desire to be, in other words you: living speech, presence itself, proximity, the proper, the guard, etc. I have necessarily written upside down—and in order to surrender to Necessity.

and *"fort"* de toi.

　　　　I must write you this (and at the typewriter, since that's where I am, sorry: sometimes I imagine an analysis, tomorrow, with a patient who would be writing on his knee and even, why not, typing; she, the psychoanalyst, would be behind and would raise her finger in silence in order to mark the beginning or the end of the session, punctuation, indentations) in order to answer one last time a question that has henceforth expired (it always had, in fact): the only thing that I regret having lost is the envelope. For the milliner the postmark would have legitimized it.

　　　　　　　　There would only be *"facteurs,"* and therefore no vérité. Only "media," take this into account in every war against the media. The immediate will never be substituted for them, only other frameworks and other forces.

　　　　　　　　The Wolfman died 7 May. A little bit of me is gone. Had I told you that I am also Ernst, Heinele, Sigmund, Sophie and HAlberstAdt (the latter, the reproducing son-in-law, the genitor of Ernst, was, don't forget a phOtOgrApher)? This is the story that I write myself, *fort:da* and 4 + 1 (*à suivre*). The four corners and blind man's bluff simultaneously. This book will be your *De fato,* your *Destinies,* your *Fortune-telling book, Moira,* your *Dit,* a Fatum, the lot that has fallen to me by distribution, *ich kenne Dein Los . . .*

question concerning the Wolfman: does an "incorporated" letter arrive at its destination? And can one give to someone other than oneself, if to give, *the* giving must also be introjected? Have we ever given ourselves to each other? If we have given ourselves *something* we have given ourselves nothing. This is why more and more I believe in the necessity of burning everything, of keeping nothing of what has *passed* (been given) between us: our only chance.

no longer spermit. And when I appear to want to assure myself of a power or of a possession, especially in relation to you, if I can say, when you are in question, it is that I am wounded, wounded to death.

The letter "interiorized" in whatever mode (sucked, drunk, swallowed, bitten, digested, breathed, inhaled, sniffed, seen, heard, idealized, taken by heart and recalled to whoever, or on the way to being so, *en voie de l' être*), the "letter," when you take it on to yourself and do not content yourself with "incorporating" it by leaving it closed in a place of your body, the letter that you address yourself presently, and even voiced [*en voix*] and even exposed to the quick, the letter then can not arrive at its destination, and less than ever: it does not succeed in having itself arrive to the other [*elle n'arrive pas à s'arriver à l'autre*]. This is the tragedy of myself, of the ego, in "introjection": one must love oneself in order to love oneself, or finally, if you prefer, my love, in order to love.

A date, for example when sending a message [*à l'envoi d'un pli*], is never perceivable, one never sees it, it never comes to me, in any event to consciousness, there where it strictly takes place, whence one dates, signs, "expedites." There, there is only twilight and mid-mourning. Everything comes to pass in *retraits*.

I must leave now. We'll meet after the session. It will be the last one, I no longer dare to say the last one of the year, all appointments pain me from now on. Our time is no longer the same (it never has been, I know, but previously this was the chance). You uttered the word "irreversible" on the telephone with a lightheartedness that left me breathless (is she crazy? is she dead then? but this is death itself and she doesn't even have the slightest idea of it, the idiot. Does she even know what she is saying? Has she ever known? The word "irreversible" even appeared somewhat dumb, to hide nothing from you, also sprach your milliner.) But I have decided to be gay tonight, you'll see.

31 May 1979.
     small dress rehearsal *before* the Etats Generaux. Even though
it didn't go badly, I understood that we could expect the worst, I can
see the outline rather clearly. Yet another of our ingenious "concep-
tions": to flee like the plague but doubtless it had to happen and I
rushed into it, like everyone, once again. You'll see, they'll all be at
the appointment.
     It's too late to continue to write you. The Jolys invited
friends to dinner, I'll tell you about it. Tomorrow morning, very
early, they're accompanying me to the airport.
                                         I'd like to die. In the moun-
tains, a lake, long before you. This is what I dream of, and this
postal sorting nauseates me. Before my death I would give orders.
If you aren't there, my body is to be pulled out of the lake and
burned, my ashes are to be sent to you, the urn well protected
("fragile") but not registered, in order to tempt fate. This would be
an *envoi* of/from me *un envoi de moi* which no longer would come
from me (or an *envoi* come from me, who would have ordered it,
but no longer an *envoi* of/from me, as you like). And then you
would enjoy mixing my ashes with what you eat (morning coffee,
brioche, tea at 5 o'clock, etc.). After a certain dose, you would
start to go numb, to fall in love with yourself, I would watch you
slowly advance toward death, you would approach me within you
with a serenity that we have no idea of, absolute reconciliation.
And you would give orders . . . While waiting for you I'm going to
sleep, you're always there, my sweet love.

23 June 1979.
     you had left me, I was following the dream in a docile way, I
was steering with a very light hand. Someone, it wasn't completely
you, but all the same, was leading me into a flowered labyrinth, an
entire town that was opening up beneath my steps once through the
vestibule of a Parisian house. This followed the symposium devoted, in the afternoon, to Peter Szondi. Celan was much spoken
of. His wife was there. She bears a strange name. I didn't know her,
and we greeted each other almost without saying anything. He was
between us. Haven't finished vindicating myself to these two suicides (two drownings also, you know what I'm talking about) and to
these two friendships (between them and between us). They form a
couple, for me now, for me and with me. What happened behind
our rare and mute encounters, remains unthinkable for me, others

speak to me of it now insistently, in France and in Germany, as if they knew about it for having read it. My voice trembling I ventured several words when it was my turn to speak, I pronounced Celan's name all the while refusing it. Similarly, by means of an ellipsis I mentioned my reservations about a given opposition (I no longer know where it came from, from Benjamin I think, another rojudeosuicide) between the literature of the "newsstand" and of the "treasure chest": there is never a choice between what is to be read in an open book (as visible as the nose in the middle of one's "face"!) and the most hermetic crypt. It's the same—insupportable support. I didn't dare say "like a post card," the atmosphere was too pious. On the way out, diverse presentations. "With you, one can no longer present oneself," a young American (I think) woman says to me. She gives me to understand that she has read (before me, therefore, she was just coming from the U.S.) *"Moi, la psychanalyse"* in which I let play, in English, the so-difficult-to-translate vocabulary of presentation, of presentations, of *"introductions,"* etc. As I was insisting on getting her name (insisting is too strong), she said "Metaphysics," and refused to add a single word. I found this little game rather clever and I felt, through the insignificant frivolity of the exchange, that she had gone rather far (I was told afterward that she was a "Germanist").

I understood that it was you. You have always been "my" metaphysics, the metaphysics of my life, the "verso" of everything I write (my desire, speech, presence, proximity, law, my heart and soul, everything that I love and that you know before me)
to set
all the bounty hunters off the track, leave them a photomaton, a post card in the style of a composite portrait, a placard or poster (*"wanted"*): let them desire to have his skin but without being able to do anything about it. This is literature without literature, in order to demonstrate that an entire epoch of so-called literature, if not all of it, cannot survive a certain technological regime of telecommunications (in this respect the political regime is secondary). Neither can philosophy, or psychoanalysis. Or love letters. The ones that you write me I reread running in the street and I scream with pain like a madman, they are the most beautiful that I've ever read, the first that have ever been written but also, I must tell you, the last. You were not only predestined for me, you were predestined to write the last love letters. Afterward, they no longer will be able to, nor will I, and thus conceive a bit of pain for you. Not only because your love takes on a somewhat eschatological and twilight tinge

from this, but because, no longer knowing how to write "love-
letters," they will never read you.

> "*Wachs, / Ungeschriebnes zu siegeln, /
das deinen Namen / erriet, / das deinen Namen / verschlüsselt.*",
this is Celan, *Mit Brief und Uhr,* in *Sprachgitter* which he had
given me in 1968.

End of June 1979.

and I say ardently that I, let me, die. Or ardently that
this book is, let this book be, behind me. "Life is a positive but
finite goods, whose term is called death. The term of the positive is
not the negative, it is zero." This is signed by the one who you
wanted to appear to cite one day in order to tell me (without telling
me) the worst (an extract from the *Confessions,* I think). Now I
have fallen from my flying trapeze. Is it because all of a sudden the
net is promised to me? Or the opposite?

By sending you only post cards, in
sum, even if as an uninterrupted flow of interminable letters, I have
wanted lightheartedness, insouciance, for you, never to weigh on
you.   I
have already fallen but this was the beginning of a "countdown" (I
can never use this expression without thinking of this book, of our
grammar of perfumes, and of the other *Symposium,* Dante's, that
Dragonetti is having me read: "The simplest quantity, which is the
one, is more odorous in the odd number than in the even.") At the
end of the affair, first chance or first term [*échéance*], the great
burning of this summer. You'll be there, say it, at the last moment,
one match each to start. I propose that we do it in September just
before my departure (not only because of the 7, because of my father's agony, and everything decisive that was played out for us
every year on this date, from the beginning to the end, remember,
but also because I need all this time to work on it, to prepare myself
for it, all this time for mourning and for celebration. We will touch
upon the fire on a day of great pardon, perhaps, it will be at least
the third time that I play with fire on that day, and each time for the
most serious departure. You will not know a better profaner, a more
faithful perjurer—and the worst thing, my God, is that the trapeze
artist of the tale is in vain considered to be a virtuoso, for which
they have a hard time forgiving him moreover, he is not amusing
himself. He has no choice, and he risks his life, at least his own, at
every instant.

End of June 1979.

I can't go on, I'm going to run. Spent hours rereading. I'm trying to sort [*trier*], it's impossible, I can't even reread any more, I'm drowning myself, in you, in our tears, in memory without bottom.

Afraid of dying, yes, but that is nothing next to the other terror, I know no worse: to survive, to survive my love, to survive you, those whom I love and who know it, to be the last to preserve what I wanted to pass on to you, my love.

Imagine the old man who remains with his will, which has just come back to him, in his hands (Freud said that the most monstrous thing is to see one's own children die, this is the thing of his that I have best understood—and you, of mine, the least well perhaps, unless it is the opposite—and this is why I found it monstrous that after his daughter's death he could have said "*la séance continue*"), the old man who remains the last to read himself, late at night.

I ran for half an hour (always after you, you know, speaking to you continuously as I always do). I also thought that upon reading this sorted mail [*courrier trié*] they could think that I alone am sending these letters to myself: as soon as they are sent off they get to me (I remain the first and last to read them) by means of the trajectory of a "combined" emitter-receiver. By means of this banal setup I would be the earpiece of what I tell myself. And, if you are following closely, *a priori* this gets to its destination, with all the sought-after effects. Or further, which amounts to the same, I find the best means to find myself *a priori,* in the course of awaiting or reaching myself, everywhere that it arrives, always here and there simultaneously, *fort und da.* So then it always arrives at its destination. Hey! this is a good definition of "ego" and of fantasy, at bottom. But there it is, I am speaking of something else, of you and of Necessity.

End of June 1979.

you believe me when it's convenient for you and you will be sure of being in the right.

Dream from just now: obsequious, around the word obsequious. I was being pressed, I no longer know by whom, obsequiously, to publish, to let be read, to divulge. But the word "obsequious" was centerstage. I'm trying to understand, to follow in the direction of that which remains to be seen [*reste à suivre*], of

all requisite obsequence, of the surviving mother who follows the
"dead letter."
      I am rereading, sometimes sinking into our immense mem-
ory, sometimes with the meticulous attention of the philologist.
Even in the years and years which preceded the Oxford sequence
(by the way, I've decided to go back there after the Strasbourg symposium, around 15 July, I'll go alone), the "postal" lexicon is already overabundant, for example the play on the word *timbre*, and
even before the obsession that dates from Yale. At the moment I am
thinking that every "production," as they say, of a concept or a system which is never without a name and an effigy, is also the emission of a postage stamp, which itself is a post card (picture, text,
reproduction, and most often in rectangular shape).
                                              Timbre: type: *Prä-
gung des Seins.*
      The anxiety of influence is born then in that in order to take
a given course, in order to transmit or transfer a given message,
you must in advance pay for the stamp, have it punched or obliterated, have yourself taxed for this or that, for Platonism, for example. The payment due does not fall only to the dead who are
dead but to their name (this is why only mortals are nameable and
one dies of the name itself), and nothing *simultaneously* happens to
a name and its bearer. A master thinker emits postage stamps or
post cards, he constructs highways with tolls: but contrary to appearances, no one perceives or receives a thing.
                                              There is also the word
"voiture"—to think that we have spent our life *en voiture*, and several *voitures* that meet, are immobilized in front of each other at the
first rendez-vous, and steering wheels held with 4 hands, and pur-
suits and crossings and I pass you and you pass me [*je te double et
tu me doubles*] and the routes that are lost in the night, the gates
that slam and you walk over me and *je t'envoiture* again, and the
breakdowns and waking up on the side of the road, you had stopped
me in the middle of trucks
                        This secret between us is not ours.
                                              I have more and
more difficulty writing you. I now know what these letters are
doomed to, but I've always known.

4 July 1979.
      I just called you from the restaurant and then got back to the

Cité. Yes, but what a calming down after hell. Pardon me, I feel too unwell.

This does not prevent me from "living" or from appearing. Strange symposium, the most amicable, if one can put it thus, even the most "familial" (Martine is occupying the room next to mine, and she looks rather gay). They're all here

Metaphysics too, whom I had spoken to you about.

And you are here, right nearby, you do not leave me (despite all the "determination" in which you believe so much, I am guarding you, I am guarding us jealously.

Under the pretext of the "law of the genre" and of "*la folie du jour,*" I will speak of you, they won't know, and of the I/we of my only daughter, of this mad ally who is my law and that my "yes" terrifies. Guard yourself

(I'm coming back by plane on Monday, but from now till then I will have called you).

8 July 1979.

and I have thought a lot about Bettina. Oh, she is not you but the situation is terrifying and it must be spoken of without gynemagogy. The most innocent and most pained victim places you in the worst *double bind:* whatever initiative "he" might take with her and her writing he was *a priori* guilty.

Ah! if only between the two, to write and not to write, salvation came to us from the post card, and innocence! Alas.

yes, but I ask myself who has guessed that this "law of the genre" was a coded telegram, and you had received it even before I "deliver" it here, and you were already dead ten times.

To be really logical, "the law of the genre" should have figured, under the heading of open correspondence, in our "dossier" on the date of May-June 1979. You can see where this logic becomes maddening. The word "dossier" came, doubtless, because of the secretarial work with which I am going to bandage my wounds this summer; and doubtless induces from behind, from the *dos,* that of the post card, that of *Socrates* and everything that I should have leaned on myself. Notice this: the back (*dossier*) of the armchair figures the only wall between S and p. It is, mutatis mutandis, the skirted curtain over which the spool goes *fort:da* (all the yoyos brought back from Yale). *The dossier that could suitably be placed here, between them, is a contract, is the hymen, my love.*

Happily, that letter of Hölderlin's on the subject of the *Wechsel der Töne* (my principal, I do not say unique, preoccupation) has been in question.

8 July 1979.
during all the time that I spent cutting out these two little flowers for you.
follow the line of my drawing, my life line, my line of conduct.

8 July 1979.
from the same drawing I answer your question, for not just anyone who wants to does so: not just anyone buggers Socrates.

8 July 1979.
and even if I had wanted to, I would not yet have confided this secret to you, it is the place of the dead being for whom I write (I say the *dead being,* or more than living, it is not yet born despite its immemorial advent, because I know nothing of its sex), it is this being who separates me from everything, from all men and women, from myself no less than from you, and which gives to everything I write that look of *Geist eines Briefes* (do you recall where we had seen it together?). And yet this secret that I cannot confide to you is nothing, or rather is nothing outside of you, it is closer to you than to me, it resembles you. If you could look at yourself as in a dream that I have of you looking at yourself one evening you would tell me the truth
try to translate "*nous nous verrons mourir*" ("we will see ourselves/each other die"). Yesterday, during the symposium, a Canadian friend tells me that in Montreal, during a very well attended lecture, Serge Doubrovsky had wanted to get a certain effect from some news that he believed he could bring to the knowledge of his audience: I was supposed to be in analysis! A swollen head, don't you think? One day or another I am going to talk to him about it, particularly as concerns the itinerary. This friend, whom I have no reason to doubt, tells me that the context was more or less the fol-

lowing: do you know that J.D. is in analysis, as I myself (S.D.) have been, this is why I have written what I have written, let's see what's going to happen with him!! I tell you. The big deal here, what truly fascinates me in this story is not the stupefying assurance with which they invent and drag out the sham, it's above all that they do not resist the desire to gain an advantageous effect from it (revelation, denunciation, triumph, enclosing, I don't know, in any event something that suddenly gets bigger from the fact that the other is "inanalysis": what is *true* in any event is that this would really please S.D.). Remark, I'm not so surprised. Once that upon the appearance of the *Verbier* and of *Fors* Lacan let himself go at it right in his seminar (while running the risk of then retracting the faux-pas under ellipsis in *Ornicar*—I'd really like to know what made him feel constrained to do so, but I have several hypotheses), the rumor in a way became legitimate. Why does one wish that someone be inanalysis? Of whom does one say in this case: if it's not true it has to be invented? And by the same token it becomes "true": true that *for* Lacan and Doubrovsky, for example, it is *necessary* that I be inanalysis. One must start from there and analyze the phenomenon: who am I and what have I done so that this might be the truth of their desire? that one of the greats of psychoanalysis does not resist the desire to invent in this domain (at least such a "hypothesis," which was his word apparently, and the hypothesis became certainty in Quebec), that publicly he throws the thing out to be digested like a piece of interesting news, and according to what I was told about the scene, destined to reassure via derision (the people in the seminar laughed, apparently, to hear that someone was inanalysis), this is what we have not finished meditating on, and is what by far goes beyond my own case. I would not say as does another that this is *the* question, a symptom of *the* question, but in the end it is true, I am told, that they are very numerous, those who do not believe and therefore do not support that I have never been inanalysis. And this must signify something not negligible in the air of their times and in the state of their relation to what they read, write, do, say, live, etc. Especially if they are incapable of the slightest control at the moment of this compulsive invention. If at least they were to show themselves more nimble, if they said prudently, "setting aside all the facts," that I must indeed pursue a kind of analysis outside every "analytic situation" of the institutional type, that I pursue my analytic work here, for example, while writing, or with all the readers that I come to privilege transferentially, with Socrates, with my posthumous analyst or with you for example, okay, this is even what I say all the time. But this is true of everyone, the "news" would lose all interest, and this isn't what they're saying, those two. In fact, I'm acquainted with several people who know, support, explain to themselves that I'm not inanalysis (you know who I'm talking about), they can measure the amplitude of this question and I believe them more lucid about the history and actual state of the analytic institution. And about whatever concerns, on the other hand and keeping things in proportion, my "state" and my "work." Do you agree? To be continued, in any event, I'm sure that it won't remain there.

Refound here the American student with whom we had coffee last Saturday, the one who was looking for a thesis subject (comparative literature), I suggested to her something on the telephone in the literature of the 20th *century* (and beyond), starting with, for example, the telephone lady in Proust or the figure of the American operator, and then asking the question of the effects of the most advanced telematics on whatever would still remain of literature. I spoke to her about microprocessors and computer terminals, she seemed somewhat disgusted. She told me that she still loved literature (me too, I answered her, *mais si, mais si*). Curious to know what she understood by this.

Between 9 and 19 July 1979. Fool that I am, and *j'accepte!*

For we are also an "equation with two unknowns," as he says in *Beyond* . . . I do not refind you any more, my love, you camouflage everything with a vengeance. But what do you have to dissimulate that is so serious, and from yourself doubtless.

yes, I'm sure that this was the only possible decision: for in the end, between us, who could have inherited these letters? I believe in effect that it is better to erase all the pictures, all the other cards, the photos, the initials, the drawings, etc. The Oxford card is sufficient for everything. It has the iconographic power that one can expect in order to read or to have read the whole history, between us, this punctuated sequence of two years, from Oxford to Oxford, via two centuries or two millennia (are you sensitive to the fact that each moment of us is greater than our entire life, and our memory so much vaster than the entire history of the world? Today we are floating in it like idiots. We are swimming from one "black hole" to another. At a given moment I had thought of adding (I'm coming back to the pictures) a single card, the one that Bernard Graciet sent me some time ago, but I have decided not to, ours is to remain alone. The interest of the other is that it would figure as the inversion of the Sp, its back if you like. It's a photograph by Erich Salomon, it's entitled *Professor W. Khal's Course:* seated at his table (or rather a slightly oblique desk), a bearded professor raises his finger (remonstrance, threat, authoritarian explanation?) while looking toward the back of the class that one does not see. But he appears not to see the student turned in the direction of the blackboard whose head is to be seen in the foreground. One cannot say that they are facing each other even though they are not turning their backs to each other. The student has his head bent, one sees his profile and the nape of his neck like a big white spot at the level of the magisterial desk, just below it. The master is seated in an armchair (rounded arms, textured designs, floral motifs?). On the back of this card, a note from Graciet: "—" "says he, alone, at the lectern, barricaded behind the overelevated magisterial desk, strangely near, terrible, pointing his right index finger toward I know not what final knell of the question, what final Salomonic law.—The inhabitant of the other shore—shadowy, curving his frail and juvenile glabrous nape under the invisible yoke of the test, noted with application snatches of the discourse, fragments of the initiating distance, at the risk of the height of ignorance, consenting to the worst, to be passed over in silence."

I am sure that a decidable divulgation would appease them. These simulacra will drive them crazy. To the extent that I love them, I wish it and am afraid of it at the same time. What else to give them? Sometimes I wish that everything remain illegible for them—and also for you. To become absolutely unknowable for them. For me the absolute mystery is you, I don't know if you will enjoy recognizing via the cross-section and mounting of the phantomaton.

Between 9 and 19 July 1979. "I am true to you everywhere," says he. And you, tell me. You can say it but not write it, without mistake I mean.

What I expect from you? but absolution, nothing less, and from your hands extreme unction.

Between 9 and 19 July 1979. Look, my melancholy resembles you, don't you think?

Between 9 and 19 July 1979. I got up very early. Sudden wish to take a small census of pointed fingers in painting, there are so many, genre Virgin of the Rocks, other da Vincis, etc. Don't wait for me to go out. (Reflected on what you were saying last night: why not, take a stand, riposte, form a kind of union—because it's a real management that you are dealing with).

Between 9 and 19 July 1979. Read this. It's falling into place (in the end, I would have preferred to avoid this synchrony): if it appears, it will be at the moment when the so-called "telematic revolution" of the French posts will make it spoken of (*Videotex* and *Télétel*).

Between 9 and 19 July 1979. Again you were stronger than I last night. Always you go further. But I will never accept anyone's interposing themselves or playing their game between us, I believe in no disinterestedness and I ask you to make them understand this to-day—discreetly but without equivocation. Don't leave them any hope. I'm coming back right away. (Really insist, please, as if I had charged you with this message: what I support the least are the insinuations. And theirs were of a vulgarity—the impardonable itself).

Between 9 and 19 July 1979.
          It is while looking at Socrates as he does (in the same direction, but from the back) that Plato must have said to himself: it always arrives, it had to arrive at its destination since it has arrived, happened, I come after him. But I can only say it, this is the right word, *a posteriori*. I aposteriorize, this is how to handle all impossible situations, all impasses.

Between 9 and 19 July 1979.
          no more brioche. It will not replace anything, but if you have the time look at what I am leaving on your secretary. They all come from the bookstore in the Rue Gay-Lussac where I

am spending hours at the moment. It is specialized. All those incredible reviews! Just what are they collecting? The difference between a collector of post cards and another (I am thinking of all of Freud's collections and of the collector that he already must have been miming, reproducing in himself), is that he can communicate with the other collectors with the help of post cards, which enriches and singularly complicates the exchange. In the bookstore I felt that between them they formed, from State to State, from nation to nation, a very powerful secret society in the open air. The collectors of rocks cannot communicate with each other by sending each other the rock. Even the collectors of postage stamps cannot. They cannot write to each other right on the thing, right on the support, they cannot accumulate by writing to each other on the subject of accumulation. This is why they only make collections. While that—and this is the whole story, this is the entire adestination of *envois*—when one sends oneself post cards (or the dialogues of Plato) in order to communicate on the subject of post cards, the collection becomes impossible, one can no longer totalize, one no longer encircles.

This suits the necessarily "untimely" aspect of the MPs, the Master-Thinkers [*Maîtres-Penseurs*] or Masters of the Post, they love anachrony, they would die for it. But the quality of the enjoyment, the one that brings the water to the mouth of their name, the essence of this pleasure that is so much to come that no one will be there for it, the savor of this pleasure beyond pleasure, they know it, doubtless, but it is indescribable, it is their secret. They know how to die with it.

What pain they cause me, what pity: not that they deprive themselves of everything, in the time of their existence, not at all, but the others believe so and avenge themselves for it, they make them, presently, pay for it, up to the present.

Between 9 and 19 July 1979.

you will have imposed upon me, says she, your revenants. Today again, perhaps you are imposing me on your revenants. And even on the secret of your milliner.

You didn't believe what I told you just now on the telephone about the flight to Oxford and the plane accident. I truly think it—but it is true that I have never felt myself so alive. Precisely.

Whence, as reasonable as it is (and I can only understand it), the regrettable weakness, I would even say the essential imbecility of the "determination" to which you hold.

19 July 1979.
I feel very sick, this time it's the end, I feel it coming.
                                                              Even before taking a step in the town, I prefer to write you. Look at them, both of them, all the twos in the world, they are waiting for me under shelter. I am in the station and I am going to take a taxi to Balliol where I see Alan again. From the airport I took a bus, and the ticket "read," as one can only say in English, read itself "to Reading Station → Oxford." From the Reading station I called Montefiore. You are with me but I would like you to be with me, up to the last moment.

19 July 1979.
taking all my recommendations I went right over, in the morning, one hour after my arrival, to the Bodleian. The librarian seemed to know me (I didn't understand very well, she alluded to the difficulty that my book seems to have given her), but this did not get me out of the oath. She asked me to *read* it (it is a question of engaging oneself to respect the rules of the library, the treasures to be protected are priceless). Therefore I read it and handed her back the cardboard covered with transparent paper that she had tendered me. At this point she starts to insist, I had not understood: no, you have to read it out loud. I did so, with the accent you make fun of all the time, you can see the scene. We were alone in her office. I understood better the marriage ceremony and the profound presuppositions of Oxonian performativism. What would an oath that you did not say out loud be worth, an oath that you would only read, or that while writing you would only read? or that you would telephone? or whose tape you would send? I leave you to follow up. All that being said, she must have assured herself, while chatting, that I knew enough English to understand the text. Enough? She didn't notice that my mind was so elsewhere that I did not seek to translate for myself all the "details."
                                                              and all of a sudden, I am abridging, the small volume was there, on the table, I didn't dare touch it. I think

that this lasted a rather long time, to the point of intriguing my neighbor. I felt myself watched just at the moment when I would have liked to be alone, as I can be alone with you. The only part of me that remained was Superstition, you know, the all-powerful, omnipresent one. The preparations were too lengthy, and for a long time I believed that I would not be given the thing, that I would be forever separated from it. Doubtless it was in order to obey the neighbor that I wound up spreading the pages while holding the bound cover in both hands. I didn't know where to start reading, looking, opening. After quite some time, anxious or reassured I no longer know, I had not found anything, not the slightest picture. I remembered Martine's father, you know, the time in the Saint-Eugène cemetery in Algiers when he could no longer refind his father's tomb, in 1971, or rather he was confusing it with another one whose stone was split—he had come back for it and was beginning to suspect the worst damages—when I showed it to him beneath his feet. I was going to protest: this isn't the book that I desired, for which I came by plane having asked you long ago to prepare it, to prepare yourselves to let me see it, etc. The card said "frontispiece" and there isn't any frontispiece in this book (I was very anxious all of a sudden: just what does "frontispiece" mean?). There were indeed two other drawings near the beginning and two-thirds of the way through the volume, and in the same style, but not the one I was looking for. In truth it is you who I called upon for help when all of a sudden I saw them, but very quickly, while running the edge of the pages under my thumb, as one sometimes does in a card game or with a big roll of bills in a bank. They disappeared immediately, truly like thieves in a noise of leaves, or like squirrels. I hadn't dreamed! I set myself back to digging around patiently, but truly, I exaggerate nothing, as if in a forest, as if they were thieves, squirrels, or mushrooms. Finally I've got them, everything stands still, I hold the book open with both hands. If you only knew my love how beautiful they are. Very small, smaller than in the reproduction (I was going to say life-size). What a couple! They could see me cry, I told them everything. The revelation, enough to make your heart pound like life and truth, is the color. This I could not have foreseen, neither the presence of the colors, nor that they would be such and such. The names are red, *plato* and *Socrates* red, like crests above their heads. Not a drop of red elsewhere. The colors seem to be added, with a schoolboy's application, over and above the lines of brown ink, between maroon and black. Then, everywhere that you see gray shadow on your card, green, on the two vertical supports of the frame, on the band where the little flowers are planted, that kind of base beneath *Socrates,* on the back of the chair and beneath the seat, on the border of the small rectangular surface above which *Socrates* is holding his *grattoir.* And if *plato's* is without color, I mean brown like the lines of the pen, *Socrates* is wearing a blue beard. Here too the tint has been applied, almost sloppily, above the brown hair. Blue, the same blue, are also the 4 darkened corners of the frame. It was too much. I was stupefied, speechless. You know how in such moments I have to leave everything in place and go out. One has to give back the book, never leave it on the table. Certain that it was being put on reserve for me and that it would be given back to me on my return, I took several steps in the street. I tried to call you but it was busy, then no answer, you must have gone out.

with the help of all these guides I was beginning to understand. After lunch (in the College, with Alan and Catherine) I returned, and I spent the whole afternoon with them. They were given back to me without difficulty. At five o'clock I went out again, but I didn't dare to call you, afraid that you might not be alone. And just moments ago you appeared so far, so distant. This is such suffering now that I ask myself if I myself am living it. If I had to suffer what I am suffering, I would not support it, I could not live it myself. You reassure me in vain ("I am right nearby"), there is a glass in the center of you that I have not succeeded in melting down. I can only see my death in it. You send me back myself all the time, and occasionally I have the feeling that you push me to busy myself with these pictures in order to distance me, you push me to write like a child to play by himself while the mother, freer in her movements, etc. (But watch out, I am playing with cards, and the polymorph deprives himself of nothing). It would be good if I died tonight, in the college, after having seen the thing at the end of the race.

19 July 1979.

I went back out to call you, you were surprised and that joyous laughter, so near, so abandoned to my voice, at the "yes" that I said to you almost with lowered voice, I brought it back here, as promised, this is what I was begging for and that you always give me even before the first word, I slept with it, it was you. Immediately afterward I slept a bit, I'm wide awake now, it's 2 o'clock in the morning

So then
I have to explain to you. The *Fortune-telling book* is in three parts. Three systems, if I have understood correctly, three types of predictions in the same volume, a small volume that no longer has all its pages. Each section carries a frontispiece. Each time, men of knowledge, of a mathematical, cosmological, astronomic science. The first is Euclid and I no longer know who, with a telescope between his hands. I think that he is looking at the sky, I will verify tomorrow, I've forgotten somewhat. The third, Pythagoras, is by himself, facing out, his legs open beneath his robe, somewhat faunlike and ready for anything. Above him his name (Pitagoras) between the opened curtains or spread draperies of a theater. Everything seems open, offered, prepared for who knows what obscene dispensation of occult knowledge. Spread apart also, this is what is most remarkable, and remarkable in their span, the right hand even overflowing the frame, are his two arms. Bent just enough to write, for he is writing, the fine devil (pointed beard and hat, the right tip touches the curtain). Like Socrates he is writing with both hands, if it can be put thus. The right hand is moistening the pen in an inkwell drawn right on the frame, the left hand is applying the *grattoir* on a kind of chart or rectangular papyrus. This support of writing is itself supported by a stand curiously held up by two columns with capitals. The tip of his right foot is leaning on the lower border of the frame and surpasses it a bit. It is very hard and pointed, it too. Differing from all the others, he permits one to guess at a greedy or cruel smile on his lips, I don't know. The direction of his glance is very clearly marked: toward the tip of the *grattoir* (of the knife or scalpel, says a German catalogue, *Messer*).

and I am no longer lacking life, it is exultant, if you could come right away, I'm sure that we would start over.

The second, then, let's be patient, the second illustration in the center of the volume is our duo. On the left-hand page and beneath them, the explanation or the way to use the book: how to question it in order to decipher one's *sort*. It's rather complicated, and it's difficult for me to read this writing. I have to get some help. I'm going back tomorrow. Did I tell you, the oath that I had to swear out loud (and without which I would never have been permit-

ᚨH erit bonu ire grātiā domū vel ꝉ—ſon.	ᚨH erit bonū ire ad poteſtat em. vel non.	ᚨH Eger poterit euade re. vel non.	ᚨH reſ amiſſa poterit re cuparī. vl̃ n̄o.
ᚨH poterit eſſe quod aueꝛ riſ. An Hor꜀	ᚨH erit bonū ducere uxorē vel Hor꜀	ᚨH erit bonū ire negociatum vel ꝍor꜀	ᚨH cogitatꝰ tuuſ poᵗ ad impleri. vl̃ n̄o.
A		**G**	
ᚨH Amicuſ noſter diligat nos: uel Hon	ᚨH er bonū ire ſuper inimicū tuum. vl non	ᚨH captꝰ po terit euadere. vel ꝉ—or꜀	ᚨH ho qui eſt ī labore poᵗ euade vl̃ n̄o
ᚨH erit bonū contrahere ſo cietatē. vl̃ Hon	ᚨH er bonū rē ſuā alicui com endare. vl̃ ꝉ—n̄o	ᚨH mulier grā uida pariat fili um uel filiaā	ᚨH ho q eſt erit domū re dibit. vel non
B		**D**	
ᚨH erit bonum ire extra domū vel ꝉ—or꜀.	ᚨH eger poᵗ erit euadere. vel ꝉ—on.	ᚨH erit bonum ire ad poteſtatē vel ꝉ—or꜀	ᚨH reſ amiſ ſa poᵗ recu parī vel n̄.
ᚨH amicuſ tuꝰ diligat te vel ꝉ— o——H	ᚨH captꝰ po terit euadere vel ꝉ—or꜀	ᚨH homo qui eſt ī labore poᵗ ire euadere. vl̃ n̄.	ᚨH er bonū ire ſuꝑ inimi icum. vl̃ n̄o.
e		**z**	
ᚨH erit bonū ducere uxorem vel ꝉ—or꜀	ᚨH cogitatꝰ tu uſ poᵗ adim pleri. vl̃ n̄o.	ᚨH poterit ē quod queris vel ꝉ—or꜀	ᚨH erit bonū ire negociat um. vel n̄o.
ᚨH homo qui eſt extra domū poᵗ redire. vl̃ n̄o.	ᚨH erit bonū contrahere ſocie tatem. vl̃ non	ᚨH ajulier grā uida pariat fi lium ul̃ filiam	ᚨH er bonū rē ſuā alie co mendare. vl̃ n̄.
	o		**r**

AE	AZ	AT	AO	CE	CZ	CO	CT
Aquila auis	constā tinopoł	Ristar ella. a.	co. uestia	erus alē. cī	orbel luf. aoł	Ras ciuit.	nisei ḣar. ṡpe
Alcol ciuitā	uultur auis	Acem i. fctus	eritui ciuitas	pan uer̄. a.	cyrus ciuitā	Gime ra. Aui	ems ꝛꝛ. a
Falconi ꝛ auiu	et. i. Speae	erebe zus. ci.	ftux auis	Abar ra. ci	oma gnatā fuec	Unnā uestia	pu pa. a.
Ficus fructꝰ	ipzū ciuitā	car auis	osa flos.	omū ci nū	Brolo mā. ci	Ru na. fe	esar ca. ci.
rilalo el. spēr	ebast en.fru	ares flos	Abilo nia. a.	oned ula. A	copaꝛ ꝛ. bus uestia	iola flos	Ha piter a
dina ciuitā	Auo Auis.	Aodi ca. ci.	mb̄ Sperē	oyre ciuit	Veet auis	ami cut. cī	imp hea. flos
ntep sice. fci	oma ciuitā	erin flos	ꝑeꝰ Auis	epus uestia	ała macia na. f.	berin flos.	Ixa fruct
orbel auis	uron fruct.	Argat ciuitā	Ixa Grossa fonte	Apho ra. spē	cearo ciuit	Rus auis.	ma ciuitā
Elmei sa. cū	Abac uestia	Allia muscāt spees	Ripo luf. ci.	ic. up ick. oziol	elon el. fc.	Alem ra. cū	ulpi uestia

ted to enter) stipulated, among other things, that I introduce neither
fire nor flame into the premises: *"I hereby undertake . . . not to
bring into the Library or kindle therein any fire or flame . . . and
I promise to obey all rules of the Library."* I am going to sleep
with you.

20 July 1979. I am seated at this table, I have marked it with a cross
on the card. The Duke Humphrey Room, in the *Old Library,* is the
sanctuary of the most precious manuscripts. I am attaching a layout
of it to my letter. I arrived at opening time, just now, still dragging
along with me this dream: all around someone sick and visibly in
danger of death, several doctors. The patient, a man whose traits
I do not see (only the sheets, movements of a white sheet) is
stretched out, passive, immobile. The doctors, this is very clear,
are waiting for the diagnosis or response of an eminent "chief" who
is bigger than they are and silent, even closed in on himself and
barely attentive to his disciples. He seems preoccupied and hardly
disposed to reassure anyone at all. He is bending over the patient's
chest, he has a lamp on his forehead (like the E.N.T. man who ter-
rorized me every time I head an ear infection during my childhood). Atmosphere: anatomy lesson. The death sentence [*arrêt de
mort*] won't be long now, everyone appears to be waiting for it. The
disease is visibly at chest level (my father), on which is fixed, in
order to investigate, to cause pain and to burn, the cyclop's ray of
light. Something in the sheet is raising itself up, like a theater curtain, but barely at all and discreetly, and there is a woman's leg,
beautiful enough to drive me crazy.

          Once again I am holding the book open
in its middle and I am trying to understand, it's not easy. On the
right hand page, facing *Socrates,* as close as possible to that table
on which he is "scratching," a chart: 32 compartments, twice 16.
In each compartment, in each box, a question. The 16 questions of
the upper quadrant are simply reproduced in the lower quadrant.
The two quadrants are separated by a thick braid. Each group of 4
questions (4×4 above, 4×4 below) carries, in its center, a letter (A
B C D E, etc.). Then: if you follow the more or less legible explanation under the feet of *Socrates* and *plato,* you begin by choosing
your question. You want to know for example (!), this is the first
question in the upper left, *An erit bonum ire extra domum vel non*
(are there any others?), you notice that this question belongs to
group A above and is to be found reproduced in group E below.

Thus, AE. What do you do then? If at least you want to know what your *sors* or your *fors,* your fortune, is, whether it is good to go out of the house, for this is indeed our question, not so? you turn the page. It is missing in the book (if I publish this, they are going to believe that I am making it up, but they could verify it). Now, this is the page of the aleatory decision. But, if one follows the explanation, one understands that it showed a circle with numbers. Without hesitating, thinking about your question, you choose a number in the circle, which was to have 12 of them, you choose at random and "sodenly" *("ever first take your noumber in the Cerkelle sodenly thynkying on the question."* The catalogue confirms, I see: *"It would seem hence that a leaf or schedule containing the inceptive circle has been lost").* Your choice of number in the "inceptive" circle determines all the rest of the itinerary: it is there, in the place of this missing page, that you determine yourself as if by chance, *randomly.* Everything that follows is on the track, you're going to see, there is no longer the slightest chance element. Suppose that you have chosen 4. On the next page a double entry chart, a small *computer,* if you will *(Tabula inscripta "Computentur capita epigrammatum"),* gives you, in AE 4, *Spera fructuum,* referring you thereby to one of a series of circles, each divided into 12 sections and 12 names. The circles are six, it seems to me (Spera specierum, Sp. florum, Sp. bestiarum, Sp. volatilium, Sp. civitatum, *Sp. fructuum* finally, in which you have just fallen, in AE 4, then, and in the section [*tranche*] "ficus".) Are you following? You take yourself off then to the circle of fruits, you look for the slice [*tranche*] "fig," as on a menu or a pie [*sur une carte ou sur une tarte*], and you read, under the heading "Ficus," our question, *An erit bonum ire extra domum vel non.* This is indeed the question, not so? Underneath, you are again referred elsewhere. To whom? But to the King, my love, and the king of Spain, *Ite ad Regem Hispanie.* There are, it seems to me, 16 kings, and each one proposes 4 answers, 4 sentences, 4 *"verses or Judgements."* Since your figure is 4, your sentence is the fourth one. Guess what it says

One day I will be dead, you will come all by yourself into the Duke Humphrey Room, you will look for the answer in this book. And you will find a sign that I am leaving in it now (after others, for there has been no lack of barbarians, nor of perjurers, before me).

The principle is at least analogous in the other tables, even if the "contents" differ and if one operates with, for example, the 12 sons of Jacob, birds, judges, prophets. So that our tableau might be complete, know that in Pythagoras's prognostications one question says "Si puer vivet." You are referred to the birds, for example to the dove which gives you a judge's answer (each one has 12). The play of the 4, as you might guess, is rather fascinating, notably in the case of the kings. In *le Facteur de la vérité* I also say that they go by fours, the kings, etc. I am still dreaming over our couple, I could spend my life admiring them. Even if I trust J.C.L.'s expert, I do have the right to say that, showing S. with his finger ("here is the great man"), *plato* is naming *Socrates:* here is Socrates, he is Socrates, this individual is Socrates. Fine. Is he naming "Socrates"? or Socrates? For do not forget, above all do not forget, Fido: that this is an effigy surmounted with a name and not Socrates "himself" (well yes, Fido has been conceived at Oxford, by Ryle I believe, whom I met more than ten years ago and who is dead now, there remains nothing but his name). He says that the other is Socrates, but he is not calling Socrates (according to the expert). He is saying or indicating his name, but is not calling him. *Why not? Prove it.* And if I, myself, were to say (but I'm very tired and I would prefer to walk in the street with you, holding you very tight by the waist, and my hand would seek to wrap itself over your hipbone, following your movement at every step), that *plato* is calling *Socrates,* gives him an order (jussic performative one says at Oxford, of the type "send a card to Freud," there, right away, it's done). And if I, myself, were to say that by showing the aforenamed *Socrates, plato* is saying to *us* (for, the expert tells us, he is addressing himself to us): you all transfer everything, and everyone, onto *Socrates.* You do not know if this is an order or an affirmation. Nor if the amorous transference takes place *because* Socrates is writing or precisely because he is *not* writing, since armed with the pen and the *grattoir,* presently he is doing both while doing neither the one nor the other. And if he is not writing, you do not know why he is not writing presently, because he has suspended his *pen for a second* or because he is erasing by scratching out, or because he cannot write or because he can not write, because he does not know how or knows how not, etc., or quite simply because he is—*reading* and that it is always on some reading, you know something about this, that I transfer. And Socrates himself, look at him, pursues his analysis; with his back turned he transfers (only one *tranche,* with each of his disciples), and simultaneously he translates or transcribes everything, all of the other's interpretations. He is taking notes having in mind a project of publication in modern times. He is pretending to write but he has a small pocket tape recorder under his mantle, or rather above his head, under his pointed hat: the arm of the mike is stretched above the head of *plato,* who, dazzled, doesn't see a thing. All of this will be published by (guess) in the (guess) collection under the title *The Dialogues of Plato.*

and me I call you my love, I miss you. When I called you the first time, you were at the wheel, you woke up while receiving the name that I was giving you (I have it from you, this you did tell me much later). I have not named you while showing you to others, I have never shown you to others with the name they know you by and that I consider only the homonym of the one that I give you, no, I have called you, yourself. And thereby I have taken your name. *Mais si,* and somewhat in the way, as they say in their system, that a woman takes the name of her husband. Every time we start again, in our innumerable secret marriages, I have become your wife. I have never ceased to await children from you. Si puer vivet . . . Beautiful children, no, a beauty of children.

Going to return the book and leave the library. Date with Montefiore and Catherine, I'm taking them to dinner in one of the numerous Indian restaurants in the city.

21 July 1979.

this Stephen Saint-Léger, of the predestined name, is a former student of Montefiore's. I had put him on the trail and he had communicated some certain information to me about Matthew Paris (about whom I have decided, fifteen or twenty years hence, after having thoroughly prepared myself, to write my thesis). This summary and preliminary information had been transmitted to him by one of his friends whose name he has silenced. Probably someone who can approach the thing with the requisite competence. He sent to Stephen Saint-Léger, along with a letter that the latter gave me a fragment of, a post card or Spanish reproduction (*letrart*) that I also have at hand. Recto or verso, I no longer know which, a Fragmento of *El jardín de las Delicias,* by El Bosco, which is found in the Prado. On the other side, typed, the information, a kind of initial installment on Matthew Paris: "lived in the priory of St. Alban and at Oxford, *composed chronicle Historia Major (1259) and its (longer) abridgment Historia minor. manuscripts of former in Corpus Christi, Cambridge (aaaargh) and of latter in Arundel manu-*

script in BM. Also (in Cambridge and London) a history of the EL-EPHANT (with drawings), an illustrated itinerary from London to Jerusalem, and several natural philosophical discussions of the four elements and the winds. meanwhile, in Ashmole MS 304, there is (see xerox) a vellum book in M.P' hand on fortune telling. Philosophically ? influenced by the Platonist revival of ca. 1180 (see Abelard): hence brilliant and bizarre references in history writing to the state, nature, the world-soul, the Mongols as devils unleashed from hell, etc. There are certainly connexions with the Tartar Khan's Englishman (see recent book by G. Ronay), who was a monk at St Albans who defected, became the writer of Magna Carta, John's ambassador to the Arabs (offer that England would convert to Islam), finally the ambassador of the Mongols to the Pope: connected to Matthew through St Albans . . . eh." Here the card is torn, doubtless intentionally by Stephen Saint-Léger who seems to have lifted out a piece, more personal I imagine, just as he cut out, at the upper left this time, another piece, symmetrically, for the same reason.

After which, having sent this *Jonah and the Whale* to Marika (that Hebrew Bible must be superb), my decision made, I bought a map of the region. I found several lakes or ponds on it.

she had just—you told me—arrived to see you at the moment I rang, and I understood in vain that you could not speak to me, that you had to affect a kind of vaguely playful indifference, nothing penetrated. My resolution was very calm, never had it frightened me so. I followed the instructions that you had the time to give me. I walked for more than an hour, I entered Somerville College on my last legs, I believed in virginity, I wrote you at length (by now you must have received all those mauve envelopes, a chance, that I found right near the College: everywhere I felt myself followed by a girl and from end to end, along the entire itinerary, I was dying to turn around). I love my sadness like a child from you.

21 July 1979.

it's right near Heathrow, I came by subway from London. The hotel is sinister, impossible to do otherwise (the plane leaves very early tomorrow morning and I'm exhausted). I went back over all the itineraries, again spent a long time looking at all the Turners. From the National Gallery I wanted to send you these Pontormos and then thought that you would find the gesture laughable. I called you from the basement and the anxiety that agitated our laughter then gave me to think: once that the machine, out of order, no longer demanded another coin in order to continue functioning over such a great distance, we couldn't decently make the decision to hang up, neither the one nor the other, and to put an end to such a bargain. There was no longer any external motive to "hang up," you had plenty of time, me too (as always) and we should have waited for the museum closing (5 hours later!) to separate from one another. Neither you nor I could assume the responsibility at the end of a good forty minutes ("enough now, we have said everything to each other for the moment, etc."). And we slowly negotiated, not neglecting a single stage, with all the trickery and sweetness of which we are capable, the most beautiful, the most elegant of conclusions. We will never know who hung up first).

I'm going to read *L'enfant au chien-assis* by Jos, alias *L'été rouge*. What I have seen of it frightens me a bit, it speaks to me in another language but from so near—

26 July 1979.

and just before the departure of the train, already in the station parking lot, you again had become

We were already dead, the certainty of it was unshakable, but so was the virginity of what was said, very quickly, like the first time. I believe that I love only the first and the last time, you have given them to me

and then I must again prepare the promised great burning, and hunch over the letters, less like a copyist or a scribe, but scalpel in hand like a circumciser (circumscribe, cut out, lift off, limit the *souffrance,* equalize, legitimate, publish, etc. Do you know that in certain rites—in Algeria, I think, but not at home—I read that the mother sometimes ate the morsel after the ceremony, the PrePuce?). I already feel myself impotent to give fire its due, I will explain to you very precisely why. Happily the arbitrariness or aleatoriness of the short subject (Oxford 1977–1979) serves me as a guardrail. We are really in agreement to burn everything that precedes, aren't we? Happily too, there is the fiction of the preface; and the strict injunctions come from the S/p corpus as from the three essays to introduce, I am awaiting a *laser* effect which in return would come to cut out the surface of the letters, and in truth of our body. *In principle* it could justify every one of my choices, govern the movements of the electric typewriter (I can transcribe this, keep that, put this in the fire, skip, omit, punctuate—everything comes back to the punctuation and to the tone that it imprints). But in principle only, and if fire's due is impossible to delimit, by virtue of the lexicon and the "themes," it is not for the usual reason (give fire its due, light counter-fires in order to stop the progression of a blaze, avoid a holocaust). On the contrary, the necessity of everything [*du tout*] announces itself terribly, the fatality of saving everything from destruction: what is there, rigorously, in our letters that does not derive from the *fort:da*, from the vocabulary of going-coming, of the step, of the way or the a-way, of the near and the far, of all the frameworks in *tele-*, of the adestination, of the address and the maladdress, of everything that is passed and comes to pass between Socrates and Plato, Freud and Heidegger, of the "truth," of the *facteur*, "*du tout*," of the transference, of the inheritance and of the genealogy, of the paradoxes of nomination, of the king, of the queen and of their ministers, of the magister and of the ministries, of the private or public detectives? Is there a word, a letter, an atom of a message that rigorously speaking *should* not be withdrawn from the burning with the aim of publication? To take an example, the most trivial and innocent example, when I write to you "*je vais mal,*" the phrase already derives from the thematics and the lexicon, in any event from the rhetoric of *going,* the *aller,* or the step, which form the subject of the three essays just as it belongs to the corpus of S/p. If I circumcise, and I will, it will have to bleed around the edges, and we will put in their hands, under their eyes, shards of our body, of what is most secret in our soul

Very intrigued, at Oxford, by the arrival of the kings and of the answers by 4. They intersect with the *Facteur,* its title and its theme. On the last page of the volume of the Letters to Milena, which I wouldn't have reread without you, on the last page of *L'échec de Milena,* Blanchot cites Kafka: "I who on the great chessboard am not yet even the pawn of a pawn (I am quite far from it), now, against all the rules and at the risk of confusing the game, I would also like to occupy the place of the queen—I, the pawn of the pawn, and consequently a piece that does not exist and therefore cannot participate in the game—and then at the same time I perhaps also would like to occupy the place of the king or even of the whole chessboard, to the extent that, if I really wanted it so, it would have to occur by means which no longer would be human.

30 July 1979.
       this round-trip will have been so brief. I have never been so
alone. During these three days, continuing to filter, to sort out, to
torture (it is a question of our heart, literally, and this surgery hor-
rifies me. Do you think that I am giving in to it out of love or rather
is an unlimited resentment coming to purify itself by itself right
next to the fire in order still to bear witness, to give in to the judgment, to organize its trial and choose its witnesses?), I hesitated:
what to do with the proper names? Concerning all those that I leave
in or that are easy to identify, to verify, I am afraid that the readers
will exclude them too quickly, will conclude precipitously: these
are third parties, they cannot be the secret addressee of these letters. This would be a bit airy on their part. Take the example of the
first name, one of my father's first names, the most visible one, will
they have guessed that he was well loved? Will they have guessed
my mother's secret first name that I am even less ready to divulge?
       Perhaps
they are going to find this writing too adroit, virtuosic in the art of
turning away, perhaps perverse in that it can be approached from
everywhere and nowhere, certainly abandoned to the other, but
given over to itself, offered up to its own blows, up to the end re-
serving everything for itself. Why, they ask themselves, incessantly
let the destination divide itself? You too, perhaps, my love, you too
question yourself, but this perversion, first of all, I treat. It is not
my own, it belongs to this writing that you, you alone, know me to
be sick of. But the song of innocence, if you love me, you will let it
come to you, it will arrive for you.
       Whoever you are, my love, and even if
you tremble because you know nothing about it yourself, doubt no
longer: I have never loved anyone but you. It's already a long time
now that you can no longer say "I love you" to me. Myself, I can do
so and this suffices, your love is safe.
       How could you be there, hundreds of
kilometers away, where I know you are now, and also be waiting for
me, in ten minutes, at the Gare d'Austerlitz?

31 July 1979.
       while listening to Monteverdi that of the word "madrigal" I
was not sure of. It is a song with 4, 5, 6, 7 voices. Without musical
accompaniment (around the 16th century). The word would have
a relation to the "herds," to the song of the herd, but some also

juxtapose it with a form in Lower Latin (matriale, read "matri-monial").

You have to know that even in the Grande Chartreuse they now have the telephone.

This proximity was unbearable for us, we loved each other too much and the sweetness was mortal, I will always prefer this end.

This ignoble secretarial work distracts me from the suffering, the one that does not *pass* and that never will cross over a word (I do not believe that joy is unsayable or that it resists song, but I do believe it of my suffering, it is the unsayable itself (impossible for any card, the insupportable itself) and if I say that it still comes to me from you, if it takes refuge in your name and carries itself there, if it still attempts to summarize itself in your name, I will have said nothing). The ignoble secretarial work happily turns me away from that which is occupying me, you. While transcribing the cuttings (I am talking about the "publishable" cuttings, they are small news items, newspaper cuttings), I cauterize on the line of blood. On the scar of what I am taking away from the fire still quite alive I am applying another fire, the same nevertheless. I would like to give nothing except to the first one. I promise to the fire what I love and I keep the rest, and a piece of us remains, it is still breathing, at each beat I see the blood arrive for me, I lick and then cauterize. I must not let anything pass, not an index, not the slightest lapse, the slightest betrayal. But where is one to pass this blade, or apply the tip, even, of this *grattoir?* For example do I have to yield all the words which, directly or not, and this is the whole torture, refer to the *envoi,* to the mission, to *tranche-mission,* to emission (of stamps, or of tele-programs), to "remission" (which nevertheless was a word sanctified by us), to commission, to the *commis-voyageur* [traveling salesman], without forgetting omission? This on the pretext that the book and its preface treat the *envoi* in all its forms? Should I also cauterize around the "destinal" prepositions, "to," "toward," "for," around the adverbs of place "here," "there," "far," "near," etc? around the verbs "to arrive" in all its senses, and "to pass," "to call," "to come," "to get to" " 'to expedite,' " to all the composites of *voie,* voyage, *voiture,* viability? It's endless, and I will never get there, the contamination is everywhere and we would never light the fire. Language poisons for us the most secret of our secrets, one can no longer even burn at home, in peace, trace the circle of a hearth, one must even sacrifice one's own sacrifice to it. Your suicide itself, it parasites it from you. But you'll see, they will get nothing from us, you yourself will recognize nothing, I will mix up everything. I will irreversibly repress the parasites, I will triumph over all whatever it costs me—and I will remain alone with you for the great fire, even if at the last moment you tell me that you no longer can come. It now resembles a rebroadcast, a sinister *play-back* (but give ear closely, come near to my lips), and while writing you I henceforth know what I am sending to the fire, what I am letting appear and that you give me back even before receiving it. *Back* could have orchestrated all of this starting from the title: the *back* of Socrates and of the card, all the *dossiers* that I have bound, the *feed-back*, the *play-back*, the returns to sender, etc., our tape-recorders, our phantom-cassettes. And even the scene in the subway before your departure, atrocious: we could not stop catching up with each other at the last moment, and then going away in opposite directions while turning around unceasingly, coming back on our steps, going away again in the labyrinth of the station. And then your "determination" carried the day again, and you pretended to believe in the automatic barriers. Even before descending via the escalator, you again gave me your arm, I asked myself why Valerio had abandoned that project for an Orpheus in the subway when I was already in the course [*en train*] of preparing the text.

Rereading the *Legacy,* it's urgent now, I fall upon a letter from Neil Hertz that I was thinking of citing. He himself cites, in English, a citation from *Civilization and Its Discontents* on which he has just fallen. It's about the "*cheap pleasures*" of technology: "If there were no railway to make light of distances my child would never have left home and I should not need the telephone to hear his voice."

1st August 1979.
> it will be our Beyond the pleasure principle.
> > and I will be safe
save for you my last card.
> > never will I lay them all on the table, you know
that it will be only one book, afterward I pass onto other things, after the fire if you accept, if you come back.

1st August 1979.
> all the times that, after the worst, I made the leap (no

more memory and no more debt). And then you wanted, forgetting
even this forgetting, to reconstitute *your* memory and my trial, a
whole dossier.

it's good that you called me back just now, that you did not
hesitate to do it. I looked again, I saw ("will you let me look?"—
Who? Me, my love.—By whom? What?) that it is indeed a sword
that little p is sticking, what rhythm, in Socrates' loins. A medieval
sword. Do you remember the "little pawn" on the chessboard of the
letters to Milena? Here is what you now give me to read (It's without title in K.'s Journal, and I am transcribing extracts of the translation): ". . . my friends fell back in manifest alarm. 'What's that
behind your head?' they cried. Since my awakening I had felt something preventing me from bending back my head, and I now groped
for it with my hand. My friends, who had grown somewhat calmer,
had just shouted, 'Be careful, don't hurt yourself!' when my hand
closed behind my head on the hilt of a sword. My friends came
closer, examined me, led me back to the mirror in my room and
stripped me to the waist. A large, ancient knight's sword with a
cross-shaped handle was buried to the hilt in my back, but the blade
had been driven in with such incredible precision between my skin
and flesh that it had caused no injury. Nor was there a wound at the
spot on my neck where the sword had penetrated; my friends assured me that there was an opening large enough to admit the blade,
but dry and showing no trace of blood. And when my friends now
stood on chairs and slowly, inch by inch, drew out the sword I did
not bleed, and the opening on my neck closed until no mark was
left save a scarcely discernible slit. 'Here is your sword,' laughed
my friends, and gave it to me. I hefted it in my two hands; it was a
splendid weapon, Crusaders might have used it. Who tolerates this
gadding about of ancient knights in dreams, irresponsibly brandish-
ing their swords, stabbing innocent sleepers who are saved from serious injury only because the weapons in all likelihood glance off
living bodies, and also because there are faithful friends knocking
at the door, prepared to come to their assistance?"

1st August 1979.

and then I slept for the whole afternoon (the television
was on). I feel a bit drunk, I am getting back to the typewriter looking at Socrates from the corner of my eye. I can see him carpeted in
the image, he is looking out, he is pretending to write. We will
never know what he is truly in the course of plotting, if he is read-

ing or if he is writing, if he is or is not behind the words, you can die from it. Contrary to what I had indicated to you, I think, he did not commit suicide (one never commits suicide, one has oneself killed, and there is no reason why he should have succeeded at this better than anyone else. Nonetheless, after his death there was an epidemic of suicides in the city, all the widowers, all the widows. And the more suicides there were the more there were, for the spectacle of suicides becoming unbearable, it induced others. Everyone felt himself betrayed, not only abandoned. Platonism came to check the disaster.

1st August 1979.

"Now Socrates was precisely that *second spectator* who did not understand ancient tragedy and therefore did not respect it. Certain of his alliance, Euripides dared to proclaim himself the herald of a new art. And if tragedy perished from this, the principle murderer is to be sought in aesthetic Socratism. Nonetheless, in the extent to which this combat was directed against the Dionysiac element of the ancient art, we recognize in Socrates himself Dionysus's adversary, the new Orpheus who arises against Dionysus and who, although destined to be torn apart by the Maenads of the Athenian tribunal, nevertheless compels the all-powerful god to flee—and the latter, as in former times when he sought to escape King Lycurgus, in Aedonides, had to take refuge in the depths of the sea, I mean in the mystic Ocean of a secret cult which little by little invades the entire world."

2 August 1979. You will follow me everywhere. And I will never know if I am suffering in you or in me. This is my suffering.

I just heard you and of course I think as you, I understood you clearly. But I repeat: who do you want it to be, to whom else do you think that I could speak as I do? I can say yes only to you, and moreover it depends upon you that it be you. You have only to renounce your "determination." You determine yourself only by cutting me off, the forfeiture is your accursed "determination."

Me, but I say everything. And I have never spoken *of* you, never to any third party whomsoever, I couldn't.

To whom else do you want me to say it? There is only one

body, you are right, and it is yours. You know my attention to and respect for irresistible multiplicities (myriads I said to you just now, not maenads), but my conviction is all the more firm and I don't think it contradictory despite appearances: there is only one body and it's you.

I remarked just now that following certain typos, certain types, "*devil*" closely resembles "*deuil*" [mourning].

You are my hallucinogen. Ecstasy: to relive the first time better than the first time, and first of all to anticipate this in the void of the first of the first times, *and so on.* Socrates knew this.

And if you now asked me to burn the book (I am not only saying the letters, this is decided), I would do it in a second. Nothing is easier, whatever you might think. This would be a fine gift, but a small chain would risk being hidden in it still. In the end, what's the use, everything that I say, you know it and already have said it to yourself, you have said it to me, I hear you saying it to me. Always I think as you.

2 August 1979.

"a day at the races," all the humor (New York Jewish) is lost in the doubling or the subtitling, only the idiom holds.

even if they see blood, they will not know whose, what group, and if at the last moment transfused

I have a hard time resigning myself to burning the photographs. How to sacrifice the ones that we took during the last trip to the island, that whole series for which I had put on a hat, that low-cut dress, and you overloaded me with makeup? What to do with that piece of skin? and with the eyelash pasted right on our initials? What I had traced on my skin remains illegible for me. I am resolving myself to it precisely by setting aside the idea of sacrifice. And should I also keep the dream of Josephine Baker because of the legs (step, legacy, jambs of the fireplace in *le Facteur,* etc.? but it is *the* legs that I love, this is atrocious, there are only two of them, not another one in the world, all the same I am not going to give them that!) Our mother language sucks everything, the dirty vampire, I'll get her back for it.

In the final reckoning, it will only be a great phantomatonic symptom that can run through the streets by itself, without you or me. But you, you know that I wrote you something entirely other, you are this itself (for me this is your only *good* determination): the one who knows that I am not there, that I have written you *something entirely other.*

3 August 1979.
I am putting these crosses on the passages to be kept, I mean to be thrown *outside* the fire, I am checking them off before transcribing, again going through the alleys of the cemetery in order to pick out epitaphs. Several days ago, on the radio, I heard about a tragicomic error by the Funeral Services: the family in Corsica receives a coffin awaited in Caen, and vice versa. I wondered how the exchange had been verified.

I no longer know what I am doing, and how I am "scratching," if I am erasing or writing what I am "saving." I no longer know which complicity to count on. In "determining" yourself, you have taken back your name. You have taken mine and I no longer know who I am. Your wife, of course, but what does that mean now?

You just called, I didn't dare say it to you, on the subject of that bad dive: but when one swears so lightly on the heads of children, one should not be surprised that so many accidents happen to them ("they happen to him all the time," you said to me, worried; and it was indeed a question of his head, and what I am saying is in no way obscurantist, it suffices to follow: the unconscious itineraries). Inversely, the children drink, the parents get drunk.

and you had asked me: is it true that men can have children until their death?

4 August 1979.
imagine a book reduced to testamentary sentences (strophes, vignettes, cartouches), the last words of a whole collection of guys before their suicide, the time to eclipse themselves
and I distinctly read "decidedly these people bore me," and then, further on, "an autobiographical literature is not this or that, it is a remainder which no longer lets itself be cut off from a crypted referent" (???). I know who will not like this book. Perhaps they will believe, not without

reason, that they are not without being, for one *part,* and this is what is unbearable, its "true" addressees. They will not support the partition. The post card would be full of secret dedications, collective murders, embezzlings of funds, tight transactions with poker face, impasse or blank check, and I make flowers and I *"self-address,"* as they say, optical money orders, and I call myself so that it answers busy and afterward have the communication gratis, with which I offer myself bargain alliances, poisoned strokes of the syringe, the most respectful homages, all of this in the heart of the underworld, at the center of police intrigues ("I don't know in what sense, you are intriguing all the time"), of liaisons, all the liaisons one could wish, amorous liaisons, railway liaisons, dangerous liaisons, telephonic liaisons, the liaisons of energy, the liaisons between words, innocent liaisons, eternal alliances, the *carte* will be full of inaudible murmurs, of deformed names, displaced events, real catastrophes, with passers in every sense, mad exchangers, abortions right in the confessional, a breathless informatization, absolutely forbidden sufferings, and the virgin who traverses everything with a love song, our oldest game

never was my step so young. You are there now, very close, we are alone, they will believe that we are two

and you can hear the old game; you laugh at the old theme: because it wants to be fictive through and through, it is of a blinding truth: "it's them indeed, this couple of criminals, truer than life." Okay, okay, ourselves, we would not have believed, eh

"decidedly these people bore me." You can see them with their finger stretched toward the truth: they believe in the ideas that we give them, they compose dialogues with that, they interrogate our slaves, they banish the plagiarists, they follow all leads, in the hypothetico-deductive mode, up to the principle of that which is in truth: it is us my love, but we are there for no one, we are the good in itself and they won't find us again.

5 August 1979.

by virtue of you, I intrigue. Sending nothing to anyone, nor anyone, I am fomenting a resurrection. Had you finally encountered him, Elijah? You were right nearby, you were burning. I had put you on the track and if because I love them too much I am not publishing *your* letters (which by all rights belong to me), I will be accused of erasing you, of stifling you, of keeping you silent. If I do publish them, they will accuse me of appropriating for myself, of stealing, of violating, of keeping the initiative, of exploiting the body of the woman, always the pimp, right? Ah Bettina, my love

and it will be even worse if I publish your letters under my name, signing in your place. Listen Bettina, do what you want, I will restore everything to you, *j'accepte* everything, from you I will receive my last breath. I have no right to the history that we have told each other

receive everything that you give, *there is* only that, there is only to receive (this is why a theory of reception is as necessary as it is impossible). And the less I speak of him, the more the grandfather is present. This is why S hates p [*S hait p*], the very omnipresence of the grandson, of the grandfather remaining a grandson and driving the wagon.

in sum, four sequences of unequal length, among them this one, the stamped, timbred card, the card as timbre in order to frank the card and let the transference float

next to us it will be nothing, a minuscule, infinitely small phrase on all mouths, just enough to mark the scale, the infinite disporportion—and we will be elsewhere. I even contend that elsewhere we will find ourselves better than ever.

and each time I blessed you on the step of the door while kissing you on the forehead

and then you would not have supported, not that my soul so regularly distances itself as part of you; but contrary to what you say, that we fascinated each other from too close the one in the other and in the place of the other. You would not have supported the dementia praecox of our narcissism. With a short-circuit we would have blown up all the resistances. We were dead and we could no longer die the one for the other, it would have been unbearable for us. "This is why your separation was organized in advance, you have begun by living the inheritance of a fatal divorce, you were living on a will, the capital and interest of goods to come, on a death that was decreed." Just as one can arrive before the letter, one is destined to survive the legatees, one's own children, the descendance that one destines oneself—and who, if you are really following me, necessarily do not exist.

5 August 1979. I ask myself what I am contravening by lending myself to this strange occupation. To whom, to what oath, and in order to seduce who, who would no longer be you. The question is absurd, all questions.

Trrrrr goes the machine on which I am preparing in sum the critical apparatus of our loveletter in order to take them away in advance from every center of, as they say, genetic criticism. Not a sketch will remain to uncover the traces. Trrrrr, *je trame,* I weave, *je trie,* I sort, I treat, I traffic, I transfer, I intricate, I control, *je filtre,* I filter—and as I have done so often on leaving, I am leaving the note in the box.

Am I cheating with this fire wall, tell me, you who know.

What Plato could not pardon himself for, Socrates has pardoned him for. In advance, because he loved him too, and for the other this permitted him to write and to leave us his dialogues on our backs.

and you well know, better than anyone else, that the first card, the very first one, the absolutely first one, was the effigy of a Greek philosopher.

When I put you on your guard against dangers, I always think of the others, neither of you nor of me (nothing could ever happen to us), but of the others within us.

"That cannot belong to the same history"—*mais si, mais si.*

Who, again? But divine, it's you. You the one alone, so alone.

In order to reassure themselves they say: deconstruction does not destroy. No kidding, my own, my immense, my immortal one, is indeed worse, it tampers with the indestructible. And it has the timbre of my death, with a single coming you sign.

6 August 1979.

and soon I'll have to leave again, nearly two months without you.

In history, this is my hypothesis, epistolary fictions multiply when there arrives a new crisis of destination

and in 1923, while telling her that she is killing herself by analyzing so much, while sending her money, while giving her advice about the devaluation of the mark, while asking her not to divulge anything to the world at large: "Little Ernst is unfortunately not a real replacement for Heinele for any of us." They give me a pain those two little ones, the one more than the other. This will be (attached) the last photomaton, doubtless.

6 August 1979.
the poverty of the pub. in general.

I repeat to you, it was dangerous to keep these letters, and yet I had cravenly dreamed that they would be stolen from us: now they have to be destroyed, the countdown has started, less than a month, you will be there.

Who pays the rent? said the father, lacking authority. And the analyst's office? (Question of the *Facteur*).

I made the connection at Juvisy: a *pancarte* on the platform made reference to "*télépancartage.*" You can see what this is—I'm not inventing anything—, the destinations and the schedules composed at a distance.

Above all one must *not* have (or let be) circulated (in circulation), above their heads, permanently, the charter of a law, a satellized pocket superego.

I have just hung up, I am still lying on the floor, nude: of no interest, this suicide, if you don't first pass them the film.

I no longer know to whom, imprudently, irrepressibly, I wrote this: that Socrates' back is the back of the post card (a curved and beautiful, beautiful surface, I am always tempted to walk with him, to stroll around while slipping my hand into his revolver-pocket) and when he arrives at his depths, having probed them with his tongue, he is afraid, he invents platonism, he gives him a child in the back.

when you speak to me, my 'orseros, of your expedients, do you believe that I believe you? You only want to help me to die.

dos, do, *dot,* dose, Fido.

the poster of Socrates would make a fine placard (speak about it to the Flammarion Press Service).

8 August 1979.
      useless to send these back to me, I am selecting in advance.
                                                                  plato,
pickpocket, he is cleaning them out, he wins the return hand and
then the last one too (the last one is the end of the *Facteur*). Like
Freud's grandson, he causes to be written, he "lets" be written *for
him,* he dictates and persecutes Socrates. Remains to be seen [*à
suivre*].
      that I did not let myself be loved, that I do not support being loved,
as you said to me, is not completely true. This is only an image that
you send me back. It depends upon you, or rather upon a given
other within me. The secret of that which does not let itself be loved
remains hidden for me—and for the moment, up to the present, by
virtue of some telemachic disorder.
                  I've just received an invitation from
Rome: a symposium, to commemorate I don't know which birthday
of Einstein's, on the relations between relativity and artistic cre-
ation. A fine subject, countersubject. The imprudent ones have put
everyone on the notice, they will have no one, except (guess). I
leave you, I'm going to run (you know that they *do not support* that
I run), and I cannot do it except by telling myself that you are at the
end of the line and that I am making my way toward you, you can
see me coming from afar.
                  Who *will prove* that the sender is the same man,
or woman? And the male or female addressee? Or that they are *not*
identical? To themselves, male or female, first of all? That they do
or do not form a couple? Or several couples? Or a crowd? Where
would the principle of identification be? In the name? No, and then
whoever wants to make a proof becomes a participant in our corpus. They would not prevent us from loving each other. And they
would love us as one loves counterfeiters, imposters, *contrefac-
teurs* (this word has been looking for me for years): while believing
that they are still dreaming of truth, authenticity, sincerity, and that
out of what they burn they are paying homage to what they burn.
One can only love that, the truth (ask Freud's uncle). Do you believe
that one can love that, truly?
                  and you, you would have made me give birth
to the truth? Stretched out on my back, you know the scene well, I
would have asked you, every night, "tell me the truth." And you,
"but I have nothing to say to you myself." I wind up believing it.

While waiting I talk and you listen, you understand more or less
nothing, but this has not the slightest kind of importance
                                                      for this reason
Plato loved Socrates and his vengeance will last until the end
of time.
  but when the syngram has been published, he no longer will have
anything to do with it, or with anyone—completely elsewhere—,
the literary post will forward it by itself, q.e.d. This has given me
the wish, *envie* (this is indeed the word), to publish under my name
things that are inconceivable, and above all unlivable, for *me,* thus
abusing the "editorial" credit that I have been laboriously accumulating for years, with this sole aim in mind. Will anyone let himself
be fooled by such an intensely political demonstration? They are
going to tell me again that I would not sign just anything: *prove it*
                                                                what I
publish I set aside and raise.

9 August 1979.
              she is a new one. Black, very beautiful, she comes regu-
larly and earlier. As she is only a replacement, I'm always worried,
I give her money each time (a telegram, a certified letter, etc.). She
rings every time. To myself I call her Nemesis and not only because
of the "distribution": she has *all* the traits of it. And she looks as if
she knew what I await from you
                          yes, my athesis will be the apost. And this
will be marked right on the bill, *facture,* as it must be, and on the
contrefacture for every letter. I would entitle the preface *envois,* in
the plural, but I will regret *invoice,* because of the voice that can be
heard in it, if one wishes, and that can be transcribed *en-voie.* And
especially, of course, because in English the *envoi* named *invoice* is
reserved for bills, *factures.* Now, in order to take myself with you
beyond the payment principle (this is the only step that I like, the
only one that interests me), I must speak to you interminably about
debts, money, sacrifice, ingratitude (mine is out of all proportion as
concerns you), about guilt and "acquittal," about sublime vengeance and accounts to be settled. I must speak to you about them.
I must speak to you about them. I will always be asking for something with you. Our alliance was also this domestic economy. We
burn what carries us beyond, and I leave them a wad of bills, of
devalued notes, of false laundry tickets.

10 August 1979.

a speculation *without term,* ratiocinating and animated, even heated, a discourse as unquenchable as it is contradictory, on the origin, benefits, and end of their love, or more precisely of Love in them, for they did not get over this visitation, they spoke of it somewhat as of a third party come to haunt them, a stranger, a phantom, or a myth, almost an intruder who would not be far from upsetting their intimacy, the ageless complicity, the common forfeiture that had bound them from all time. Eros had surprised them after the crime

they are not a couple but a double blow [*coup double*] and Plato must have hated Socrates (or Bettina), hated him as one can hate whoever teaches you hatred, injustice, jealousy, resentment, bad conscience. As one can hate more than anyone else. Whence the vengeful plot that is called Platonism, and that insatiable mob. Reconciliation is impossible. Until the end of time, the ignoble descendance will know how to get effects from everything while washing their hands of it. To know how still *to get an effect* from suffering or from love is the very essence of the ignoble: not to know how to burn

let me tell you this dream (you interrupted it by calling so early this morning, Nemesis had not yet come by: on this topic, you were asking me what "before the letter" means in my little postal code: well, it is an unthinkable time, I would say for example that you had arrived for me before the letter, or that from me before the letter you had departed: fortuitous significations always. While I'm at it, I'll answer the other question: "to cable one's own burial" imposed upon me rather, and bizarrely, the image of the ropes with whose help the coffin is lowered to the bottom of the hole. I see four men, it is feared that the bonds might break, I watch over the operations, I am lying on my back and I give orders, they can't get to the end), yes that dream: I no longer remember the beginning

she took it, tore a page out of it, put it on one of her knees (one only, this was an insistent detail) and undertook to unfold it. She set to it with a great deal of application, a marvelous patience. As soon as a small fold, a slight rustling appeared, she erased it with her finger. The leaf unfolded, I read on it (or pronounced rather) the word "*thym*" [thyme] or "*tain*" [the surface of a mirror] or "*teint*" [*tint;* all homonyms], and then the folds reformed themselves. At the end of a very long moment, after she had unfolded the thing as never before,

in an absolutely capricious way, apparently, she throws it behind her
(a beach or an empty lot, I no longer know).
                        What you told me about
Socrates' vulture (on the Vinci-Freud side) appears very necessary
to me, I'm going to look. I like to make rapprochements.
                                              How short life
will have been, my love, I mean ours. We have not had the time to
turn around and now I will spend the rest of my days trying to
understand how I have spent it, how *you* arrived for me, how you
lived, yourself, the life that you gave me: this is the last thing that
today I pretend to know.
            I would like to convince you: the fact that you will
recognize almost nothing in this short subject, that you will not like
its tone, its pace, its very affectation, and the film of ice which distances us from every image, this fact liberates you, and me therefore. It is not about us, us was something else. And elsewise interminable
so, they'll think what they like. All the same, I wasn't going to sit
them down around your letters, so much longer, more numerous,
too beautiful. I will be the only one to know. With a finite knowledge, I also know the infinite evil that I have committed, this is my
crypt under the open sky.

11 August 1979.
            among all the names of sacred places, only one in my
memory bears the name of "way" ["*chemin*"] (divine).
                                    The other day, on
the telephone, I went crazy, "farewell" ["*adieu*"] is such a foreign
word for me (I recognize no language in it, its tone is unbearable
for me, it dresses up its absolute insignificance with a soutane before which I would make signs of conjuration rather . . .). Doubtless I wanted to find an arm and I picked one up anywhere I could.
You had just said something even worse, you forbade me even the
fire, the holocaust of us.
                    The test of strength has not ceased but at some
moments your absence becomes sweeter.
                                I don't know how to describe the
narrow, strict, dim, stormy passage (the Channel at night) from
which I perceive the shores, the cliffs of what I am writing presently
(what am I doing with these letters, tell me). The passage is open

and closed, I see poorly without any daylight coming from the outside, it's brief and intermittent, it can't last much longer now, short
words are necessary (*Gang, über,* lapse, glob). What counts in all
of it is the pace, the step
you will be, like me, the last one to be able to
read. I am writing this, this very thing which must remain illegible
for us. And first of all insupportable. Like me, I exclude you absolutely from the marketplace. You are the excluded one, the kept
one, the absolute non-addressee of whatever would still remain
legible. Since it is to you my love that I say I love you and that I
love you cannot be posted. Nor read with lowered voice, like the
Oxford oath.

Obviously when beneath my public signature they read these
words they will have won out (over just what?) but they will be
right: it's not at all like that that it comes to pass, you know well, at
this moment my intonation is entirely other
I can always say "it's not me."

11 August 1979.
he is knocking himself out, with his tongue, too hard a
tongue, underneath the plump buttocks. The other doesn't flinch, he
pretends to read or to write, but he doesn't miss a single one.
James (the
two, the three), Jacques, Giacomo Joyce—your *contrefacture* is a
marvel, the counterpart to the *invoice: "Envoy: love me love my
umbrella."*

They will never know if I do or do not love the post card, if I am
for or against. Today they all chew up the work for the computer,
they punch themselves in by themselves in order to step up to the
cashier from one month to the next. (When I went to Freiburg, it
was explained to me that today Germany holds this record, the
record for records precisely: for every subject the greatest quantity
of information stocked on the State computer. The great central
switchboard spits it all out for you in a second, the civil, medical,
scholastic, judicial und so weiter dossiers). For this one has to submit oneself to bi-spoolarity, oppose here to there, there and there,
be for or against. You have surely noticed, among other subtle categories, that since last year some are camping on the position of
"optimism," others are making a career in "pessimism," the ones
are religious, the others not. And they take out their index cards,
produce references, in the end other post cards on which they can

no longer read anything except the perforation (B A, B A , O A, OA, R I, R I). What fatigue.

I forgot, Giacomo also has seven letters. Love my *ombre, elle*—not me. "Do you love me?" And you, tell me.

12 August 1979.
there, it is to the heritage of the unknown one that I would have liked to devote an institution, a temple, a poem, and that they can no longer detach their thought from Matthew Paris, from his image, from his hand tracing the names of *plato* and *Socrates,* in this place and not in any other. I wanted to give pleasure to this monk, this brother, who I imagine to be a bit crazy, and to everything *that he represents for me.* For he represents for me and this illustration was destined to me, via this fact. It was really myself who fell over it, no? Plato and *Socrates* I hardly give a damn about, I am not saying the names of *plato* and *Socrates* drawn above their heads. Above their hands, which nevertheless play so well with me, I place the hand of Matthew Paris, or finally what his name represents today for me of that hand that was

it can only be yours. I would like you to have only one, as in those rare moments when jealousy is silenced
they will indeed have to understand that our "real" correspondence, burned to a white heat, will have been entirely other.

To plant seeds by "dispersing" without the slightest hope left of arriving at one's ends.

We
will no longer be able to write each other, will we, already it becomes impossible for us. For them too.

12 August 1979.
between the preface and the three others, the phone calls will buzz like wasps in full transference.

No, you heard incorrectly, I wanted to present him over and above [*en sus*], p. There is a little p. cut off from its cutting edge in *Glas.* Here, in *espe,* it is unleashed suspicion and speculation. I have only these letters in my mouth, I bootlick both of them

such will have been the fate [*destin*] of these letters. The word "*destin*" is quite hard in the mouth, one does does not

suck it like destination, or let it float like destiny. But in any event
the hardness of stone is at the center, the arrest, the stasis, the stop
and one does not need an etymological confirmation to feel it
                                                         just as for
the *dead letter,* whether it or the rest are in question, it arrived, happened, that's all. What was not to have arrived, what should not
have arrived has arrived, arrived for us, happened to us. Therefore
this very thing was to arrive, always, later, you will be able to tell
yourself, I think as you, my heart.

13 August 1979. You are right in part, it would have to have been
made into, precisely, a post-face, this is indeed the word, in particular because it's unintelligible if you do not begin with what follows—if not by the end, and as they never reread . . . Too bad. You
are also right about Joyce, one time is enough. It's so strong that in
the end nothing resists it, whence the feeling of facility, however
deceptive it might be. One asks oneself what he wound up doing,
that one, and what made him run. After him, no more starting over,
draw the veil and let everything come to pass behind the curtains of
language at the end of its rope. A coincidence nonetheless, for that
seminar on translation I followed all the Babelian indications in
Finnegans Wake and yesterday I wanted to take the plane to Zurich
and read out loud sitting on his knees, starting with the beginning
(Babel, the fall, and the Finno-Phoenician motif, *"the fall (bababa-
dalgh) [. . .]. The great fall of the offwall entailed at such short
notice the pftjschute of Finnegan [. . .] Phall if you but will, rise
you must: and none so soon either shall the pharce for the nunce
come to a setdown secular phoenish . . .")* up to the passage on
Gigglotte's Hill and the Babbyl Malket toward the end, passing
through *"The babblers with their thangas vain have been (con-
fusium hold them!) [. . .] Who ails tongue coddeau, aspace of
dumbillsilly? And they fell upong one another: and themselves they
have fallen . . ."* and through *"This battering babel allower the
door and sideposts . . ."* and the entire page up to *"Filons, filoosh!
Cherchons la flamme! Fammfamm! Fammfamm!"* through that
passage that you know better than anyone (p. 164) and in which I
all of a sudden discover *"the babbling pumpt of platinism,"* through
that other one around the *"turrace of Babbel,"* the entire passage
about Anna Livia Plurabelle, translated in part, in which you will
find things that are absolutely unheard of; and that everything that

comes around *"A and aa ab ad abu abiad. A babbel men dub gulch of tears."* or around *"And shall not Babel be with Lebab? And he war. And he shall open his mouth and answer: I hear, O Ismael . . . and he deed . . ."* up to *"O Loud . . . Loud . . . Ha he hi ho hu. Mummum."* I draw out the text, as one says of actors, at least up to *"Usque! Usque! Usque! Lignum in . . . Is the strays world moving mound of what static babel is this, tell us?"*

17 August 1979.
He was sure that his death would arrive in 1907. And of course I enlighten as always, through a simple reverberation, the entire secret correspondence within the Committee of the seven rings.

You document yourself, you are making a dossier of the words in *do*, they are all on call, not one is missing.

To survive one's own, to survive one's children, to bury one's heirs, nothing worse, is there? Imagine Socrates dying after Plato. And who would swear that this does not happen? And always, even. On the subject of the seven rings, again the desire to survive the heirs, and even psychoanalysis, a plaintive and horrified desire, certainly, but an essential desire that eats away at the entire scene of inheritance. He writes to Ferenczi in 1924, as always with poetic citations: "I am not trying to move you by this complaint to take any step to retain the lost Committee. I know: gone is gone, and lost is lost [*"Hin ist hin, verloren ist verloren,"* Bürger]. I have survived the Committee that was to have been my successor. Perhaps I shall survive the International Association [but this is certain, old man, you can sleep peacefully]. It is to be hoped [no kidding] that psychoanalysis will survive me. But it all gives a somber end to one's life." Not at all, not at all. And you know the story about Rank, about the six photographs of the members of the Committee and the six or seven wolves on the Wolfman's walnut tree. He had been furious about this hypothesis and he had asked of the patient, *by letter*, a kind of attestation concerning the dates of his dream. Against Rank! about whose therapy he wrote: "it has not accomplished more than would be done if the men of a fire brigade, summoned to deal with a fire from an upset oil lamp, contented themselves with merely removing the lamp from the room in which the conflagration had broken out. Much less time would certainly be spent in so doing than in extinguishing the whole fire." At this time he didn't give a damn about Rank who also believed in short analyses. On the subject of fire, did you know that Freud had destroyed his correspondence in April 1908, one year after his "death" in sum. He awaited it in 1907. Jones associates: "enlarged his apartment and destroyed his correspondence," as if they were related. It was an interesting year (first international congress, etc.), and I ask myself what he destroyed thereby, doubtless notes from Nietzsche, among others, from Socrates surely.

I will never know what has become of my own letters and since I do not retain any copies . . .

Of course, each time that I keep the word "*voiture,*" it will be a thought for Ernst, for the *Wagen* that his grandfather would have wanted to see him pull along behind him. I think that I never told you, in the course of my long dissertations on the *Geschick* (that which is destined, the *envoi,* and the address) that Freud was speaking precisely about the *Geschick,* about the skillfullness with which his grandson sent the thing off and made it come back.

No, they are opposing the *there* to the *there,* they are giving to the two *theres* (*fort* and *da*) not only a different but a contradictory fate.

What I had not told you also is that *Socrate* is now the name of a *logiciel.* You don't know what this is? One calls *logiciel* the corpus of programs, procedures, or rules that assure the smooth functioning of a system in the treatment of information. The storage banks depend upon a *logiciel.* Each firm gives a name to its *logiciel.* CII has chosen *Socrate.* Me too, as if by chance, from the very first day, *just to drop a postcard* and please forward, do you follow?

17 August 1979.

to stop becomes impossible. That way you have of taking yourself back—and of taking me back. A listening post would have cried over it. Fortunately for you you do not hear yourself.

They will believe that you are alone, and it's not sure that they are mistaken (it will all be on the post card's back). One must learn to let, to leave.

It's true, everyone says so, on the telephone Pierre now has the same voice, he is often taken for me. You are unjust in saying that we form a royal

couple and that this distracts me from you. But it is true that these
few days of solitude with him, although we hardly saw each other,
are watching over our letters, imprinting on them a slight deviation
                                                                    he
rarely leaves his room (guitar, records, his typewriter noisier and
more regular than mine, I'm downstairs), yesterday it was to show
me this passage from *Thomas the Obscure* (I'll tell you how he fell
upon it) that I had totally forgotten, although two or three years ago
I had commented on it at length: ". . . I was even the only possible
dead man, I was the only man who did not give the impression of
dying by chance. All my strength, the feeling that I had of being,
while taking the hemlock, not Socrates dying, but Socrates aug-
menting himself with Plato, that certainty of not being able to disappear possessed only by those who are struck with a fatal illness,
that serenity before the scaffold which gives to the condemned their
true grace, made of each instant of my life the instant when I was
going to quit life." I now have the book on my table, I am rereading
chapter II, which begins with "He nevertheless decided upon turning his back to the sea . . ."

18 August 1979.
          others will believe that we are four, and they might indeed
be right. But whatever the number decided upon, it is you whom I
love uniquely, to you that, without even deciding upon it, I always
will be faithful. *Because* you are crazy, you alone, and not *in order*
to drive you crazy by saying the impossible to you. If you are crazy,
it is you whom I love, uniquely. And I am monstrously faithful. You
too. Fido, Fido, that's us.
          (I had wanted to wish them "stout heart," they
were all reunited, they had called each other in for a consultation,
coming from all the countries, a kind of consortium of the International Society of Psychoanalysis (dissidents included and reinte-
grated at their own request) and diverse affiliates of the societies of
analytic philosophy; they had reached an agreement to form a great
cartel and together to hunch over, conjugating their resources, for
example, a given statement
          Ah yes, Fido, I am faithful to you as a dog.
Why did "Ryle" choose this name, Fido? Because one says of a
dog that he *answers* to his name, to the name of Fido, for example?
Because a dog is the figure of fidelity and that better than anyone

else answers to his name, especially if it is Fido? Because he answers to his name without needing to answer, and because thereby one is even more certain of his answer? Fido answers without answering, because he is a dog, he recognizes his name but he never says anything about it. What do you say about it? If he is there, Fido, he cannot make the reference lie, without saying anything he answers to his name. Neither a stone nor a speaking being, in the sense of the philosophers of all times and the psycho-linguists of today, would answer without answering to the name of Fido. Neither a stone nor you my love would answer so adequately to the requisite demonstration (" 'Fido'—Fido" in Ryle's *Theory of Meaning*). Why did Ryle choose a dog's name, Fido? I have just spoken at length about this with Pierre, who whispers to me: "so that the example will be obedient."

Despite everything that opposes them, it's always the same thing that they do not support, it's around the same thing that they mount the guard. Of course, I always want to put to Freud, in Socratic style, the "epistemological" questions that are put to him across the Channel and across the Atlantic. Of course the inverse also appears necessary to me. But there always comes a moment when I see their anger mount on a common front; their resistance is unanimous: "and quotations marks—they are not to go to the dogs! and theory, and meaning, and reference, and language!" *Mais si, mais si*

18 August 1979. Is it true that you call me only when I'm not there?

One day you told me that I was a torch

"come" which is not valid without the tone, without the timbre, without the voice of mine that you know. So much for the fire.

They had put everything on a picture (of the one, of the other, of the couple), and then they remained attached to the betting, and they are still speculating but they are no longer there. Each of them to the other: you were in league to have me destroyed, you conspired, you have covered all the trails, get out of it yourself.

And this short philosophical dialogue for your distraction: "—What is it, a destination?—There where it arrives.—So then everywhere that it arrives there was destination?—Yes.—But not before?—

No.—That's convenient, since if it arrives there, it is that it was destined to arrive there. But then one can only say so after the fact?—When it has arrived, it is indeed the proof that it had to arrive, and arrive there, at its destination.—But before arriving, it is not destined, for example it neither desires nor demands any address? There is everything that arrives where it had to arrive, but no destination before the arrival?—Yes, but I meant to say something else.—Of course, that's what I was saying.—There you are."

As I gave her to understand, I don't know if she was right to write *what* she wrote, and this is quite secondary, but in any event she was right to write it. Right *a priori*. I know nothing about how it happens, how it arrives for her, and it won't be soon either, it's only just beginning, but she cannot have been wrong to send herself that.

If you want to understand what an "anatomy" of the post card might be, think of the *Anatomy of Melancholy* (this is a genre that is not unrelated to Menippean satire: Frye recalls the influence of the Last Supper and of the Symposium on this genre, interminable banquets, encyclopedic farrago, the satiric critique of the *philosophus gloriosus,* etc.).

Be stoic, it will be our expyrosus, the end of the world by fire.

19 August 1979.

it's only a poker play (you know the auspices under which I saw day) and in speculating on this card, defying the accomplice cheater who sees S/p over my shoulder (I can feel him in my back making lots of signs), I raise to death, I make the bidding mount

and when you will no longer come back, after the fire, I will still send you virgin and mute cards, you will no longer recognize even the memoirs of our travels and our common places, but you will know that I am faithful to you. I will exhaust all the modes and all the genres of fidelity for you.

21 August 1979.

overlook nothing in order to come close (to oneself, each other) at every blow, spare oneself nothing, turn the blows back against oneself

I had an appointment at Flammarion.

It is what is called a canonic composition.

I remember especially that I liked to hear her speak German on the telephone (had I told you that Metaphysics speaks Hebrew? I even think that it's her native language, but she speaks German, English, French just as well).

"I love you," "Come," *given a certain context of course,* would be the only X's to run through the post. On the condition that each time it takes place only one time. You should have believed in me, and have in-de-fi-nite-ly given it to me, carte blanche as concerns the unique time.

I have just fallen asleep, as I do every day, watching *Mysteries of the West* and *Charley's Angels* (four female private detectives, very beautiful, one is smart, their orders arrive on the telephone, from a boss who seems to be "sending himself" a fifth by speaking to them) and in passing I caught this: only the dead don't talk. That's what you think! They are the most talkative, especially if they remain alone. It's rather a question of getting them to shut up.

21 August 1979.

You're right, I love you is not to be published, I should not shout it from the rooftops.

But I tell you again, I am keeping only a very brief sequence of our film, and only of the film, a copy, a copy of a copy, the thin black roll, hardly a veil.

It's true that before Oxford our letters said all this otherwise, whence the arbitrariness of the cross-section and this unjustifiable rhetoric. Let's say that I have demonstrated it.

I wanted to make the demonstration of you, yours, and prove that I will never be able to take myself back, it's not like you.

I am only a memory, I love only memory and reminding myself of you.

21 August 1979.

it's all the same to me, the months/mes that you send to the devil, months/mes, everything unforeseen that might happen, arrive, every encounter and me, I run, I am going to encounter you without hoping for anything that is not chance precisely—and fortuitously encountered (but when I say that I run, I'm not talking about jogging, although . . . but even though they cannot bear that I run, or that I write, they infinitely prefer that I practice *jogging* or writing for publication: it never goes very far, it comes back in a closed circuit, it plays like a child in its playpen. What they cannot bear is what you know: that *jogging* and writing for publication are for me only a training with you in mind, in order to seduce you, to have some wind, for some is necessary, the strength to live what I risk with you). Toward this fortuitously encountered encounter, I make my (a)way backward, *à rebours* (too bad that this family is not played with like the other one, I mean with the economy of the words in way, *chemin*, as with that of the words in *Weg*). You have closed my eyes, and my eyes closed I go to encounter you, to the encounter of you. Who, me? you always ask while accusing me. Don't accuse anyone, I manipulate nothing, and if I no longer knew very well myself, whose fault would it be? And if I knew very well, I would not come to encounter you, this is all that I know in myself, but also that I will never catch up, that never will you get to me, arrive at me: it is this, you see, that already has happened to me and that I can only lose my breath taking into account. You have passed [*tu es passée*], you are not a passerby (*une passante*), but the passed one [*la passée*], the past, whom I will always wait for

(*la passée*, I borrow this word from E.L.)

and now to say you are right (as opposed to me) becomes my only appeasement. And knowing that I have understood nothing, that I will die without have understood anything.

Another short philosophical dialogue of my own composition (to be read while taking your sun bath): "—Hey, Socrates!—What?—Nothing." I just missed calling you a short while ago to ask you what you thought of this brief exchange (divine, you the divine), what you thought came to pass between them. This was a pure pretext for calling you, and then I was afraid of upsetting the family and that you might not be alone next to the phone to speak to me.

I am rereading your note from yesterday: what counts in post cards, and moreover in everything, is the tempo, say you. Okay, in the end more or less, precisely, as my "poor father" said (and that too is one of his expressions to speak his own; and when in a heated discussion he

248 ENVOIS

was out of arguments, he planted you there with an apparently con-
ciliatory proposition that always left him the last word, of the type,
for example: "fictive, okay, but in the end more or less, all the
same." Sometimes I was furious with him, sometimes I burst out
laughing. What naïveté! what antisocratic sapience, also, in the
end more or less, an entire knowledge of living. And you also talk
to me, my beloved, about forgetting him, of forgetting the forgetting; and you ask: is repression to go to the dogs? And to forget,
beyond repression, what does that mean? But precisely, there I answer you, it is to finish with it. I hear myself: to recall oneself to
finitude. It cannot repress everything, keep everything inscribed
elsewhere. I know only God to be capable of repression without a
border of forgetting (remark, perhaps this is what Freud meant
without wanting to: oh my God how you repress), after all. But infinite memory does not repress at all, only a finite memory re-
presses, and the bottomless bottom is still forgetting. For in the
end, it dies, no? there you are. Death arrives, no? Not at its destination, okay, but it arrives, no? Oh really, it doesn't arrive? it arrives
for no one therefore it doesn't arrive? Oh really, it's possible in
effect, I'll tell him. In the end, when I'm dead you'll really see
(light, light, more light!), you will have closed my eyes.

22 August 1979. Again! But don't be childish. It is to you that I
speak, uniquely, you are my—puzzle it out, my little puzzle.
Above all, never be afraid, we cannot be mistaken or unfaithful to
each other.
    Soon ten months already.

22 August 1979.
    The countdown is accelerating, I am terrifyingly calm.
Never, nonetheless, have I cried so much. On the telephone you
understand nothing, I smile at you, I let you tell me stories, always
stories about children and about parents, vacation, in other words. I
no longer dare to bother you, "I'm not bothering you?," to ask you
if you have the slightest idea of me, of what is coming to pass on
this side of the wire.
    I'm rereading my *Legacy,* what a tangle. And the little
one's spool is a firing squad. When someone gives the order to fire,
and to give the order is already to fire, everyone goes to it.

Because   I'm
sure that you are there eternally, the most unbearable suffering (that
makes death into a game) I am suffering from finding it slight, as if
from one instant to the next, the time to blow on it . . . is that what
you call a "fantasy"?
and you tell me

22 August 1979.
you would not have liked it if I had collected your letters.
Suppose that one day I had said to you "your hundredth letter . . ."
We would have separated from each other, as if it had been proven
(but I don't believe it at all) that the *liance* was not gold.
I saw her as a sub-
urban Amazon, dragging behind her, into all the neighborhood
bars, the beloved's body. I thought it aside to myself, but I didn't let
it show. She does not know what she is dragging. For him, said
she, her (own) body was but a category, one of the charges in the
accusation.
I am writing to you now on the typewriter, it can be felt. You
remember the day that, trying out *your* machine, the electric, I had
written: this is a *machine veuve* [*neuve*, new, *veuve*, widow]?
We had to
eliminate all the bothersome witnesses, all the intermediaries and
bearers of messages, one after another. Those that remain will not
know how to read, they would go crazy, I would begin to like them.
Never doubt: what is not said here (so many white signs) will never
get there. By the same double token, what is black will remain
black. To you yourself they will say nothing, you will remain "unconscious" of it. Differing from a letter, a post card is a letter to the
extent that nothing of it remains that is, or that holds. It destines the
letter to its ruin.
Hanging up just now, I said to myself that perhaps you no
longer understood anything, that I would never be sure and that
to be faithful I had to continue to say to myself what I say to you.
The naive will believe that henceforth I know to whom I am speaking, the shore is certain, it suffices to analyze. That's what you
think. And those who proffer this discourse, before even ratiocinating about a destination, have only to be seen in order to burst out
laughing.

Now they will think about us, without letup, but without knowing
about whom, they will listen to us without our having an appointment with them, not even taking the pain to turn toward them. At
risk of penalties, permanent session. We all will be lying on our
backs, the voices will come from the screen, one no longer will
know who interprets what.

23 August 1979.
                    doubtless you're right, I don't know how to love. Or yes,
the children, only the children, but that's a lot of people.
                                                    I'm still laughing
(you are the only one, for this too, to know that I always laugh)
thinking about your exclamation just now, when I spoke to you
about Socratic intrigues: "that guy is crazy." Don't be childish and
follow me: in order to intrigue, they wanted to hide themselves in
common places, in places of shame, in places of knowledge ("Platonism," the "determination," *and so on*). When they got lost in
them, when they saw that they could no longer see each other, they
drew out their knives, their scalpels, their syringes, and they hacked
out of each other what they had given each other. Triumph of the
accursed witch, it was all her idea. Under her hat (which she had
whipped up with her own little hands), she had conceived dialectics, as one creates prose.
                    I'll see you again very quickly now, your re-
turn frightens me. Not that I'm thinking about the fire, it has become almost a very airy picture, strangely peaceful, almost useless.
As if it had already taken place, as if the work were done. In the
meantime
        no, it happens that without you I lack nothing, but as soon as you
are there I cry over you, I miss you to death, it's easier to bear your
departure.

23 August 1979.
                    I've just received the slide in color. Be very careful with
it, I'll need it for the reproduction. I have never found them so resigned to their beauty. What a couple.
                                    The back [*dossier*] of the chair be-
tween the two bodies, I know what I mean, is a marriage contract. I

always think about those contracts that are only signed by one—they are far from being without value, on the contrary. And even when both sign, it's twice by a single one.

these three letters that I keep on my green postage meter. I have never been able to answer them and I will always have difficulty forgiving myself for it. All three died differently. One of the three I saw alive again after I had received his letter (it was my father, he was in the hospital, he spoke to me about analyses and punctures, and with his bedridden writing he had concluded: "this is the first letter that I have written in two weeks," "I think I'm leaving the hospital tomorrow perhaps," and my mother added a word in the same letter: "his hands are trembling and he could not write well, another time . . ."). Another, Gabriel Bounoure, I never saw again, but I was to go to him in the weeks following his letter, in Lesconil (a long and marvelous letter, in it he spoke in his way about a bookseller "worked over by the demon of procrastination," with that card of the fishermen for Pierre). The third one committed suicide shortly after (that Norwegian whom I had spoken to you about: a few typed words, excuses for the delay, "due to difficult circumstances in my situation," of a presentation on ideology, and then I saw his wife again and his parents come from Norway, their relations were strange, I tried to understand).

Right at the moment of slipping this into the envelope: don't forget that all of this took off from the wish to make this picture the cover of a book, all of it pushed back into its margins, the title, my name, the name of the publisher, and miniaturized (I mean in red) on *Socrates'* phallus.

24 August 1979.

I again tried to decipher the piece of skin. In any event it's a failure: I will have succeeded only in transcribing a part of what is printed or printed over on the subject of the support, but the support itself, which I wanted to deliver naked, we will also burn. I ask myself what might be made of that which remains. Some will think, rightly or wrongly, that there is not one true word, that I am writing this novel to kill time in your absence (and is that untrue?), to spend another moment with you, yesterday, today or tomorrow, that is, to beg yet another bit of your attention, a tear or a smile (and is that untrue?).

In the meantime, we will have put the viaticum onto the block, and we will begin to make the bidding rise. The richest, most generous—or most eccentric—buyer will carry it off as vacation reading, a book of traveler's checks, or a last insurance, a last sacrament that one administers to oneself hastily in airports (you know, at the moment of embarkation one hastily calculates what sum would fall to one's own in case of accident. I have never done it, but purely out of superstition.)

I truly understood the word "viaticum," you can translate "loved," only at the moment when she told me that a given text

would be for him, for the entire summer, a viaticum.

24 August 1979.

you know the end of the detective story: Socrates knocks off all of them, or makes them kill themselves among themselves, he remains alone, the gangbusters take over the locale, he sprays gas everywhere, it's all ablaze in a second, and behind the cops the crowd presses forward somewhat disappointed that they didn't get him alive or that he didn't get out of it, which amounts to the same.

25 August 1979. I also wanted to say a word to you, the *kolophon.* I think, but I'm not sure, that the Jews have come to designate with this name the metal finger, the index finger pointed toward the text of the Torah when it is held up at arm's length. So then, *plato's* kolophon? The word signifies the highest point, the pinnacle, the summit, the head or the crowning (for example of a discourse), sometimes also the maximum (you have reached the maximum of your fine engagements, says he in Letter III). And then in the

Theatetus there is a certain coronation (*ton kolophona*) that I would like to give you, it's a gold chain (*ten krusen seiran*). Too bad, I transcribe the translation: "*Socrates.*—Well, need I say more? I could go on about absence of wind, still water and all that kind of thing—about how states of inactivity rot things and destroy them, whereas states of activity [the others, *ta d'etera*] preserve them [literally save, assure salvation, *sozei*]? And on top of that, I might cap everything by producing Homer's golden chain. I could suggest that he means nothing but the sun; and that what he's indicating is that, as long as the heavenly cycle and the sun are in motion, everything is and is preserved, in the realms of both gods and men; whereas if that motion were tied down, so to speak, everything would be destroyed, and, as they say, the whole world would be turned upside down (*ano kato panta*)."

26 August 1979. I am stupefied, but marvel all the same, that I have never thought about it over these last months. She is truly the only one that even indirectly by means of one trick or another I have not named. I never thought of doing so, didn't think of her, and doubtless never would have recalled her by myself.

It's rather impressive, I was a bit more than four years old, my parents were down in the garden, I was alone with her in what we used to call the veranda. She was sleeping in her cradle, I remember only the celluloid baby doll that was aflame in two seconds, nothing else (neither having lit it myself, nor the slightest emotion today, only my parents running up). That I burned the baby doll *instead of* taking it out on her—if I publish this people are going to believe that I am inventing to suit my compositional needs. I notice that in speaking of readers with you, I have always called them people, what do you think of this?

and that she is the only being, this sister, the only one in the world with whom I have no memory of even the slightest beginning of dissension, not the least virtual reproach. It's true that I don't know her, that I only know her somewhat, as Martine's mother. Nor will they believe me if I say that the word valise for me will always be the piece of something I shouted out at her birth, a child's joke famous in the family: "Put her back in her valise." (At this moment I am saying to myself that "put back" says no less than "valise"). My mother's father had just introduced me into the bedroom after the delivery, they had come up with nothing better: to leave me believing that the valise (in my memory an enormous trunk that doubtless contained all the necessities for delivery at that time; it had been in the room for weeks), that this valise (say, A, I) was preparing her birth, perhaps even contained her like a belly. They tell me further that my grandfather laughed at it more than anyone else. Doubtless this was the first desired holocaust (as one says a desired child, a desired girl).

27 August 1979. You just called. Ah no, above all not Phoenix (which for me, moreover, is first of all, in my fundamental language, the brand of a kosher anisette in Algeria.

I am thinking again about Ophelia the complaisant one, this is indeed who she is. This one did not go crazy, she married so young, I could almost say at the age of 7. On the topic (on the topic of my theory of sets and of the family romance, of the entire *set theory* that governs our paradoxes and enlarges us, each one aside from himself, beyond everything. We are beyond everything, and myself in your pocket, smaller than ever)

and on the card's itinerary, short pause, you encounter Aristoteles: the male who begins to have sperm at twice 7 years, the gestation of fish that corresponds to a period divisible by 7, the death of newborns before the 7th day and this is why they receive their name on the 7th, and the foetus that lives if it is expulsed at 7 months, and not at 8 months, etc., so only circumcision was missing from this history of animals. The first telephone number in El-Biar, the unforgettable one I had told you, 730 47: in the beginning was a seven, and at the end, and in the middle 3 + 4, and it turns around zero, the central.

28 August 1979. I just got up, Nemesis had rung. Your letter still succeeds in making me laugh. That we laughed again is the real miracle, and I owe it to you.

No, not the apostles, the epistles, that's my novel. I follow the order: Paul in the first place (the little brother dead before me, a year before I think, and they have never wanted to know or to say of what: "He fell badly," I heard once, yes, yes, I swear. He was only a few months old.) Then Jacques, of course, then Pierre and Jean. And never was anything done on purpose.

Here is
another S.P., agreed (I mean a *secret de Polichinelle*), but I would
put my hand into the fire, it's really the only one. For the rest, they
will understand nothing about my clinamen, even if they are sure of
everything, especially in that case, the worst one. Especially there
where I speak truly they will see only fire. On this subject, you
know that Freud's Sophie was cremated.

29 August 1979.
                7, my god
                        "A ministering angel shall my sister be, when thou liest
howling."
    and libido, said Christiane Hegel's brother, never comes to dis-
turb the peace between brother and sister, for this is a relation
"without desire"
                You can see it coming, no, tell me.
                        Don't forget, Paris's *Socrates*
had a blue beard. It doesn't work/walk [*ça ne marche pas*] but Paris
paints him shod like a nobleman, and *in front of,* before the little
slave with naked feet, little *plato,* his pupil, his pupil who sees him
without being seen, who shows him and *presents* him. But each
other, they *represent themselves,* and this is the aporia, this is
where we have gotten to.

30 August 1979.
                the return. You are right nearby now. The proof seems to
be made? No, precisely, and moreover for whom? This is the only
question that counts. Everything is possible.
                        Look at them always, they are
inseparable. They are still intriguing, they are making plans, they
want to come back. I want you to love them.
                        Reread the little one's letters,
they are of an outraged bitterness, of an unpardonable vulgarity.
But pretend to believe the professors, they are almost all apocryphal; a fictive correspondence, you said to me one day, innocent
of everything. I would be willing to believe it.
                        I know that you are "very
close" but the unavowed end of this final letter (semi-fictive, se-
melfactive) is—

you should be able to guess, to say it in my place, for we have said everything to each other.

I would have liked, yes, to give you everything that I did not give you, and this does not amount to the same. At least this is what you think, and doubtless you are right, there is in this Necessity.

I will ask myself what *to turn around* has signified from my birth on or thereabouts. I will speak to you again, and of you, you will not leave me but I will become very young and the distance incalculable.

Tomorrow I will write you again, in our foreign language. I won't retain a word of it and in September, without my even having seen you again, you will burn

you will burn it, you, it has to be you.

TO SPECULATE—ON "FREUD"

1
NOTICES (WARNINGS)

THE ATHESIS

As if it had an *incipit*, I am, then, opening this book. It was our agreement that I begin it at the moment of the third ring.[1] Perhaps you remember. If not, perhaps you have verified the consequences during the course of these ten sessions: from the first one on I had pulled in, and I do not say justified, the title of this seminar, *life death* [*la vie la mort*].

To verify even the consequences of that which one does not remember, perhaps this is where the stakes go.

Pulling in this title, I had then advanced the proposition of another logic. Or so the malignant might say or translate it, it being no longer a question of "logic," and even less of a "proposition" here, for the reasons I will give. The issue rather is *to rebind* [*relier*], but precisely by means of the analysis of the notions of binding, *nexum, desmos* or stricture,[2] the question of *life death* to the question of the *position* (*Setzung*), the question of positionality in general, of positional (oppositional or juxtapositional) logic, of the theme or the thesis. To posit, we asked: what does this amount to,

1. The text on whose borders this discourse would be attempting to maintain itself is Freud's *Beyond the Pleasure Principle* [in volume 18 of the Standard Edition; all references in the text by page number]. In effect, I am extracting this material from a seminar which followed the itinerary of the three rings. Proceeding each time from an explication with a given text of Nietzsche's, the seminar was first concerned with a "modern" problematic of biology, genetics, epistemology, or the history of the life sciences (readings of Jacob, Canguilhem, etc.). Second ring: return to Nietzsche, and then an explication with the Heideggerian reading of Nietzsche. Then, here, the third and last ring.

2. These three words refer to the most obsessive motif of *Glas*. Let us say that here I am adding or relating a supplementary "judas" from *Glas*. An incision tattooed, for example, between pages 270/272, left column.

come back to [*à quoi cela revient-il*]?[3] And to whom? For whom? Let us stop. The "position" thus suspended, one has a glimpse of the consequences, or rather the descendants. We are to speak, here, of everything that the "position's" fall would drag along with it—the discredit, ruin, and bankruptcies it could not fail to cause. I am leading you in the direction of the register of accounts, of the financial, the fiduciary, or the speculative: today I will speak of speculation. At least I am betting that I will.

In a word, from the first session on, it had been stated that a "logic" of the *beyond*, or rather of the *step beyond* [*pas au-delà*], would come to overflow the logic of the position: without substituting itself for this logic, and above all without being opposed to it, opening another relation, a relation without relation, or without a basis of comparison, a relation with what it crosses over via its step or with what it frees itself from at a stroke. But neither the stroke nor the step have any indivisible characteristic here.

I will attempt the beginning of this book then, will attempt to draw it toward me for the third ring. But is it a ring? and not rather more or less tightly drawn collars with laces that do not close at the moment of coming back [*revenir*] to their beginnings? They cannot close, but in this incapacity [*impouvoir*] they enclose each other. Imagine *Indra* and *Varuna*[4] deciding to interlace their names

3. Translator's note (hereafter abbreviated as TN). The multiple meanings of *revenir* are played upon throughout this essay. Among many other things, *revenir* can mean to come back, to amount to, to fall to (as in an inheritance). In French as well as in English a ghost is a *revenant*. Derrida's "topic" in general in this essay is *revenance*, which we might call the mode of return of the ghostly inheritance. I will indicate the play on *revenir* in brackets throughout (cf. below, note 5).

4. "Varuna is the 'Binder': whoever respects *satyam* and *çraddhā*, that is, the diverse forms of exactitude, is protected by Mitra, but whoever sins against *satyam* and *çraddhā* is immediately bound, in the most material sense of the word, by Varuna. (. . .) this is the story of Manu, the slave of *çraddhā*, preparing himself to sacrifice his wife on the demand of the demonic priests; the mechanism is released, blind and fatal; if Manu does not go to the end, if he has a shudder of humanity, he sins against the law of sacrifice and falls into the bonds of Varuna. Thus, he does not hesitate: he will go to the end. At this point a god suddenly enters, a pitying god who, taking the initiative and responsibility for resolving the terrible dilemma, decides that the sacrifice will not take place and that Manu, nevertheless, will have the profit of it. This god is Indra." Georges Dumézil, *Mitra-Varuna*, chap. 6 "Nexum et Mutuum, IV," Indra contre les liens de Varuna, pp. 113, 125. Compelled to sacrifice, bound by his law if he wishes to avoid being bound by Varuna, Manu is absolved from the *double bind* without losing the "profit" of it. But will he have the strength to unbind himself (but thinking of what profit?) from Indra's grace? Before the miraculous chance of this gift, will he be able to inhibit acknowledgment within

in order to sign, at the bottom of a contract, the engagement henceforth to interlace their names each time they will have to sign, by
virtue of which they sign from then on.

Beyond the Pleasure Principle: I will propose a selective, filtrating, discriminating reading. Not without once more going down,
according to a pedagogy to which one must not become blindly attached, some too well trodden paths. I would like to make legible the
non-positional structure of Beyond. . . , its a-thetic functioning in
the final judgment, which is as much to say that which exempts it
from the quest after a final judgment, that is of any judgment at all.
Elsewhere I distinguish restance⁵ from judgment [instance].
How to gain access to the restance of Beyond. . . ? How is this text
to work, to walk, and with what step above all, if some day we are
to become sensitive, today, as opposed to so many readings that are
as partial as they are canonic, i.e. academic, to the essential impossibility of holding onto any thesis within it, any posited conclusion
of the scientific or philosophical type, of the theoretical type in
general? Let one refer to any of the aforementioned judgments—
the impossibility of a resting point pulls the textual performance
along into a singular drifting.

I have abused this word, it hardly satisfies me. Drifting designates too continuous a movement: or rather too undifferentiated,
too homogenous a movement that appears to travel away without
saccade from a supposed origin, from a shore, a border, a coast
with an indivisible outline. Now the shore is divided in its very outline, and there are effects of anchoring, collapses of the coastline,
strategies of approach and overflow, strictures of attachment or of
mooring, places of reversion, strangulation, or double bind. These
are constitutive of the very process of the athesis, and must be accounted for, if at least there is here something in such an event to be
read and to be reckoned with.

I will not rush to call this textual process, which cannot be dominated by any judgment as such, (especially not a theoretical judg-

---

himself, to "acquit" himself [cf. below note 7] not only of the debt, but of the very
movement of gratitude? In sum, will he avoid no longer loving anyone but Indra?

5. TN. Restance is the noun derived from the present participle of rester, to remain. (See also, for example, différance, revenance: these gerunds are all in the
middle voice, between active and passive.) For Derrida textuality is a question of
restance, of that which remains because it cannot be judged, the undecidable excess. Restance will be retained as a neologism throughout. To continue note 3,
above, this essay explores the relations of restance, revenance, and différance in
Freud's thought.

ment of the scientific or philosophical type), "fictional" or even less "literary." Rather, I would like to pursue the analysis of *restance* in order to attempt to recognize, using this example, the conditions for the fictional, and for that type of fiction called, confusedly sometimes, literature. And to recognize its conditions "today," that is, since we inhabit psychoanalysis, living with it, in it, around it, or beside it. And more strictly—and this is why this example is exemplary of not being absolutely replaceable—since *Beyond the Pleasure Principle*. The athesis of *Beyond* . . . will come forward. As such, before and beyond any judgment. It will come forward in its (unbound, absolved, if this is possible) relation to the theoretical thesis in general, as well as to the laws of its decidability.

It is not fortuitous that the athesis is indefinitely suspended as concerns *life death*. It is not fortuitous that it speaks of the enigmatic death drive which appears disappears, appears to disappear, appears in order to disappear in *Beyond* . . . I call it *enigmatic* because it appears disappears while telling many stories and making many scenes, causing or permitting them to be told. Occasionally these are called fables or myths.

And in question also is what sets off an entire descendance that is fabulous or mythical.

Will we reach these shores in three or four sessions? Certainly not. In order to gain time, and to make my calculations more accessible, I must, along with you, capitalize upon several previously published essays.[6] Another preliminary: since the course of these laced rings is to lead us back each time to a point of departure in Nietzsche, there is no longer any ease here. Therefore I will be brief. To take the shortest route I will recall, for example, what was said of childhood, of play, and of the without-debt. Of what was said about them on the basis of Nietzsche. How does the so-called child indebt himself, and what is his debt, in a so-called play without-debt? On what without-debt does play speculate in secret? And where is the place of such a secret to be situated, according to what topics?

6. An allusion to "Freud and the Scene of Writing" (1966) (in *Writing and Difference*), *Glas* (1974, in particular as concerns fetishism, the *double bind—le, la les double(s) bande(s)(ent)*—and the economic problem of masochism), *Le facteur de la vérité* (in *Poétique* 21, reprinted below). To these I add here *Pas* (in *Gramma* 3/4, 1976), *Spurs/Eperons* (1972–78), *Fors*, the preface to *Le Verbier de l'homme aux loups* by N. Abraham and M. Torok (also in *The Georgia Review*), *La vérité en peinture*, 1978.

NOTICES (WARNINGS) 263

And, once more, I will recall the scene made by Freud in Nietzsche's memory. He never misses him within the grasping movement of a denegation. The avoidance never avoids the inevitable in whose grasp it already is. Freud is so at ease in such an embarrassing situation, he declines the debt with such a hurried assurance, such an imperturbable light-heartedness, that one asks oneself: is this his own debt? Or the debt of another? And if debt were always another's? How to feel and not to feel simultaneously, in advance, "acquitted"[7] and guilty for the debt of another when the latter, lodged within oneself by means of the effect of a singular topic, comes back to, amounts to [*revient à*] oneself according to a filiation about which everything remains to be thought? How to speculate on the debt of another coming back to, amounting to [*à soi revenant*] oneself?

I have cited it elsewhere, but once more I reread the declaration of avoidance which performs the inevitable. It is in the *Selbstdarstellung:* "Nietzsche, another philosopher whose guesses and intuitions often agree in the most astonishing way with the painfully laborious [*mühsamen*] findings of psychoanalysis, was for a long time avoided (*gemieden*) by me on that very account; I was less concerned with the question of priority than with keeping my mind unembarrassed" (XX, 60; tr. sl. mod).

What is most painful and least bearable (brief sigh), is that that which has been paid for with so much pain (what is most painful), to wit, the laborious findings of psychoanalysis, is given to the philosopher without pain, gratuitously, graciously, as if by playing, for nothing. What is most painful is that the painful is not painful for others, thereby risking the loss of its value: counterfeit coins, in sum, produced by this unworthy ancestor of psychoanalysis. As if it had cost him nothing.

As for the notion of "avoidance," it had already appeared just above. There, it was philosophy in general that had to be "avoided." What is closest *must* be avoided, by virtue of its very proximity. It must be kept at a distance, it must be warned. It must be turned away from, diverted, *warned*. In truth *must one* deflect it from these warnings?[8] It isn't even necessary: the closest is avoided in the inevitable itself. The structure of its proximity distances it, and pre-

7. TN. *S'acquitter* in French means both to acquit oneself in the familiar English sense, and to liquidate a debt, to be quits. I will use "to acquit" (in quotation marks) to indicate that both senses are intended.
8. TN. "Warnings" are *avertissements*, which also has the sense of "notices," as in short book prefaces. The title of this chapter in French is actually *Avertissements,*

scribes that the *da* be *fort* even before a judgment of denegation comes to affix to it the specificity of its seal. The avoidance of philosophy, already in place like a counterfeiter, soon will introduce us more directly into *Beyond* . . .

Although this is the passage I have most often cited,[9] it is not the only one of its type, nor even the first one in the fabulous genealogy of psychoanalysis. There is the appendix to the *Traumdeutung:* Rank is not content with simply seeing Nietzsche as "the direct precursor of psychoanalysis," as concerns the relations between the dream and waking life. He acknowledges another merit of Nietzsche's: to have awakened us to responsibility for the very things we believe ourselves not responsible for. One can be guilty of that which one believes oneself to be essentially innocent, in debt for that which one always feels oneself in advance "acquitted." [10] Nietzsche dared to link responsibility, debt, and guilt to the unconscious. For example, in *Dawn.* That which can no longer be assumed in consciousness henceforth becomes insolvent: the debt of another comes back, in dreams or elsewhere, to torment you, or to be annulled in

---

which is why I have given it as "Notices (Warnings)" in relation to Derrida's analysis of Freud's "avoidance" of philosophy.

9. For example in *Qual Quelle* (in *Margins of Philosophy,* p. 306).

10. The existential analytic of *Dasein* situates the structure of originary *Schuldigsein* (Being-responsible, Being-forewarned, or the capacity-to-be-responsible, the possibility of having to answer-for before any debt, any fault, and even any determined law at all) on this side of any subjectivity, any relation to the object, any knowledge, and above all any consciousness. Cf. Heidegger, *Being and Time,* sec. 58. For the same reasons, Heidegger here does not speak of the unconscious, a notion which, according to him, would belong to the conceptual system and philosophical epoch to this side of which the analytic of *Dasein* must come back [*revenir*], *Dasein* no more being man than it is the subject, no more consciousness than the unconscious.

Schuld (simultaneously fault and debt, the obligation in general) is precisely the object of *The Genealogy of Morals,* and singularly of its *Second Dissertation* (sec. 4 and *passim*). We know that this genealogy and analysis of debt propose a theory of "repression" (sec. 21). It is to the "author" of this theory of debt that Freud wished to owe nothing, and it is about him that Freud wished to know nothing.

Defense, avoidance, misconstruing: this *turning away* of Nietzsche or *before* Nietzsche henceforth belongs to Freud's legacy. After him, occasionally, it even takes on a form that he never gave it, that of the snicker or the grimace. For example in this text, which specifically turns around the question of "symbolic debt" and justifies itself thus: "I am not reviving here the shoddy Nietzschean notion of the lie of life . . ." (Lacan, "The Freudian Thing," in *Ecrits: A Selection,* trans. Alan Sheridan, New York: Norton, 1977, p. 118).

As concerns referring *Being and Time* to *The Genealogy of Morals* on the question of *Schuldigsein*—I will attempt it elsewhere.

denegation. You are willing to be responsible for everything, cries Nietzsche, except for your dreams, and the name of Oedipus soon will be sounded, since this apostrophe is first of all destined for him. But this is also the Nietzsche that the *Selbstdarstellung* nonetheless declares to have "avoided." Just like, several lines earlier, philosophy in general. Which supposes that Nietzsche was still a philosopher. Now, did he not dare to think that which philosophy as such could never do anything but deny? But does one think or not think what one *posits* in the form of denegation? What is called thinking?

The avoidance of philosophy is more active than ever, more deliberate too, more circumspect in "speculation." Speculation: what Freud names in this way reassembles the entire difficulty that interests me here. What does philosophy *not have to do* with psychoanalytic "speculation"? And why would the latter cause one to write in the mode of the athesis, for example in *Beyond. . .*? Who will have speculated? On what? On whom? What will have been engaged? What will have permitted itself to become engaged in such a speculation?

Did Freud *give* himself over, *abandon* himself to speculation? Did he want to? Did he want to want to? And why was his relation in this respect always double, apparently divided? In the *Selbstdarstellung,* interpreting his latest so-called "speculative" works, those of the period of *Beyond . . .* (before and after 1920), Freud defends himself against having abandoned himself to speculation:

> The attempt [the metapsychology] remained no more than a torso; after writing two or three papers—"Instincts and their Vicissitudes," "Repression," "The Unconscious," "Mourning and Melancholia," etc.—I broke off, wisely perhaps, since the time for theoretical predications of this kind had not yet come. In my latest speculative works I have set about the task of dissecting our mental apparatus on the basis of the analytic view of pathological facts and have divided it into an *ego,* an *id,* and a *super-ego.* The super-ego is the heir of the Oedipus complex and represents the ethical standards of mankind.
>
> I should not like to create an impression that during this last period of my work I have turned my back upon patient observation and have *abandoned* myself entirely to *speculation.* I have on the contrary always remained in the closest touch with the analytic material and have never ceased working at detailed points of clinical or technical importance. Even when I have moved away from observation, I have carefully *avoided any contact with philosophy proper.* This avoidance has been greatly facilitated by constitutional incapacity. I was always open to the ideas of G. T. Fechner, and have followed that thinker upon

many important points. The large extent to which psychoanalysis coincides with the philosophy of Schopenhauer—not only did he assert
the dominance of the emotions and the supreme importance of sexuality but he was even aware of the mechanism of repression—is not to
be traced to my acquaintance with his teaching. I read Schopenhauer
very late in my life. Nietzsche . . . (XX, 59; my emphasis).

Three brief remarks.

1. No more than to Nietzsche, nothing is *due* to Schopenhauer.
As such, psychoanalytic theory *owes* him *nothing*. It has no more
inherited from him than one can inherit conceptual simulacra, in
other words counterfeit money, bills issued without any guarantee
of value. Schopenhauer's and Nietzsche's words and "notions" resemble psychoanalytic discourse to the point of being mistaken for
it. But they are lacking the equivalent of a content proper to psychoanalysis, which alone can guarantee value, usage, and exchange.
Above all, one must not inherit such assignats, that is, such a
manufacture of bills, a machine that issues, more or less fraudu-
lently, and with the most uncontrollable facility, such "shares." And
because of the resemblance, because of all the too natural imputa-
tion of inheritance, this affiliation must at all cost be avoided. One
must break with it at the moment when the identification threatens
at closest quarters. One must not assume the debt: not only because
it is the debt of another, but because the other has indebted himself
in an insolvent (unpardonable) way by issuing simulacra of concepts.
This is like another story of collective responsibility: whether he
analyzes it or not, Freud submits to an imperative which prescribes
that he interrupt the chain and refuse the inheritance. And that he
thereby found another genealogy. I am alleging that what he writes
as concerns (philosophical or non-philosophical) speculation has
something to do with this scene of intolerable inheritance. Something to do, in other words not to do. What he writes, or again, in
other words, *the fact that* he has something to write.

As goes without saying, the discursive rationalization of this
scene supposes a naive self-assurance concerning the concept of
counterfeit money, and concerning the relation between a word and
a conceptual value.

No more than to Nietzsche, then, no more than to philosophy in
general, which he defends himself against by *avoiding it,* Freud intends to owe nothing to Schopenhauer. The acknowledgment of the
debt is annulled or, if you will, denied, confirmed, at the center of
Beyond . . . This occurs at the moment when certain discriminating propositions (I do not say theses) are advanced, at the moment

when the power to make the decision is conferred upon them, at least for a stage of the argument. In question is the recognition of the dualism of instinctual life. Freud invokes Hering's theory, the two groups of processes in "contrary directions" (*entgegengesetzter Richtung*) which continuously unfold in all living substance: the assimilatory (*assimilatorisch*) process and the dis-similatory (*dissimilatorisch*) process; the first is constructive (*aufbauend*), the second de-structive (*abbauend*). *Abbauen:* the word that certain French Heideggerians recently have translated as "to deconstruct," as if all were in all, and always ahead of the caravan. It is true that this translation is not simply illegitimate once it has been envisaged (rather recently). Unless one manipulates an aftereffect [*l'aprèscoup*] precisely in order to assimilate, and in order to reconstruct that which is difficult to assimilate. It is true too, that in this area the competition becomes all the more bitter in that one can always pass off the already-there of a word as the anteriority of a concept, with which one then allegedly indebts, i.e. fecundates, everyone. One puts one's hands on a mark, and reapplies everywhere. Thus, from the other side, so to speak, one can see the word "deconstruction" fall from the sky into the text of Marx. Until now, "*aufgelöst*" has been faithfully translated as "resolved" or "dissolved." A recent translation of *The German Ideology* gives "can be deconstructed" for "*aufgelöst werden können*" without any other procedure, and without the slightest explanation. I would not linger over the theoretical ingenuousness or the tactical ruse of such an operation if it did not tend to confuse the reader. Because once the amalgamation is accomplished, the appropriation incorporated, it is implied that "deconstruction" is destined to remain limited to the "intellectual critique" of superstructures. And this is put as if Marx had already said it. Here is this new translation, which we hope will become historic in the annals of Franco-German relations: ". . . it [the new materialist conception of history] does not explain praxis according to ideas, it explains the formation of ideas according to material praxis, and consequently arrives at the result that it is not by an intellectual critique, by a reduction to 'self-consciousness,' or by a transformation into 'revenants,' or 'phantoms,' or 'obsessions,' etc., that all the forms and productions of consciousness can be deconstructed [*aufgelöst werden können*], but only by the practical subversion [these last words, substituted for the classical translation of '*praktischen Umsturz*' as 'practical overturning,' economize the thorny problem of overturning, while flirting with a 'subversion' that fits better; and—too tricky a trick, and therefore a bit crude—we are led to believe that 'deconstruction' is essentially 'theoretical,' that is, theoreticist, which thereby permits another economization, that of reading] of real social relations, from which all this idealist folderol has emerged." And without blinking, a footnote refers to the *Editions Sociales,* without even specifying, as the Academy would have it, "tr. sl. mod."

We will briefly remark, since this is the essential destination of this apparently philological citation for me, that Marx makes little of the "phantoms" and "revenants." This is our problem.

If one now were to translate *abbauen* as "to deconstruct" in *Beyond* . . . , perhaps one would get a glimpse of a necessary place of articulation between what is involved in the form of an athetic writing and what has interested me up to now under the heading of deconstruction.

Our homage rendered to all militant zealousness, I come back to the two "contrary" processes. Freud sees a relation of opposition (*Entgegensetzung*), at least in Hering's doctrine, between the process of constructive assimilation and the process of deconstructive dissimilation. This is what would impose a limit on the translation, if one agreed to consider that deconstruction does not simply oppose itself, but works otherwise (and *without* working, if work is determined as opposition). I leave this question to operate in silence, it awaits us elsewhere.

Freud then asks himself if we may venture to recognize "our two instinctual impulses," the "life instincts" and the "death instincts," in these two processes. And he adds: "There is something else, at any rate, that we cannot remain blind to . . ." Thus, there is something, something *other,* that we would be tempted to hide from ourselves, something, other, that we would have preferred to avoid, or not to recognize. What? "We have unwittingly steered our course into the harbour of Schopenhauer's philosophy. For him death is the '*eigentliche* Resultat' [the true, proper result, the appropriate, properly named result—this is a citation] and to that extent the purpose of life,' while the sexual instinct is the embodiment (*Verkörperung*) of the will to live" (49–50).

New paragraph: "Let us make a bold attempt at another step forward (*einen Schritt weiter zu gehen*)."

On the trail we will follow all the steps, step by step and step without step, that lead *Beyond* . . . down the singular path of speculation. Such a path does not exist before the pathbreaking of athetic writing, but it does not construct itself by itself like the method of Hegelian speculation; and however concerned with revenants it may be, it does not come back over itself [*ne revient pas sur lui-même*], it has the form neither of the dialectical circle nor of the hermeneutic circle. Perhaps it makes them visible, but it has nothing to do with them [*Il les donne peut-être à voir mais il n'a rien à voir avec eux*]. It constructs-deconstructs itself according to an interminable detour (*Umweg*): that it describes "itself," writes and unwrites. But what is it that impels this writing-(un)step [*pas d'écriture*]? Death, the "proper result" and therefore the end of life, the end without end, the strategy without finality of the living—all this is not solely a statement of Schopenhauer's. It also coincides almost literally with several Nietzschean propositions that we had attempted to interpret: on life as a very rare genre of that which is dead (*Gay Science*), a "particular case" and "means in view of something else" (*Will to Power*), this something else necessarily participating in death; and finally on the absence, in the last analysis, of anything like an instinct of conservation. The unconscious port of registry, at the distance of this generality, also will have been Nietzschean. Which it is one's due to avoid, just as it is one's due to avoid what is due; one must dare to detach oneself from it, or absolve oneself for it. Nietzsche very rigorously describes this scene in the *Second Essay* of *The Genealogy of Morals,* to which I refer you.

2. The expression "perpetual recurrence of the same thing" appears, between quotation marks, in the third chapter. Nietzsche's name is not mentioned, but small matter. The passage concerns the existence in psychic life of an irresistible tendency to reproduction: this takes the form of a repetition no longer taking into account the pleasure principle, and even placing itself above the pleasure principle. In the fate neuroses this repetition has the characteristics of the demonic. The phantom of the demonic, and even of the diabolical, reappears measuredly in *Beyond* . . . Coming back (*revenant*)—subject to a rhythm—this phantom deserves an analysis of the passages and the procedure, of everything that both makes him come back and conjures him up cadentially. The very procedure of the text itself is diabolical. It mimes walking, does not cease walking without advancing, regularly sketching out one step more without gaining an inch of ground. A limping devil, like everything that transgresses the pleasure principle without ever permitting the conclusion of a last step. Limping is the devil, but also absolved of who knows what debt by the one who at a given moment calls himself the "*advocatus diaboli*" of the death drive, and concludes with a citation in which each word can be remarked with Scripture—and

with literature: "Scripture says that it is no sin to limp," in the "words of the poet."

The figure of the diabolical simultaneously looks in the direction of *Beyond* . . . and in the direction of *Das Unheimliche.* Elsewhere I have described the systematic and kinship ties between these two essays. In them, the devil comes back [*revient*] in a mode which is neither that of an imaginary representation (of an imaginary double), nor that of an apparition in person. His way of coming back [*revenance*] defies such a distinction or opposition. Everything occurs and proceeds as if the devil "in person" came back [*revenait*] in order to double his double. So, as a doubling doubling his double, the devil overflows his double at the moment when he is nothing but his double, the double of his double that produces the "*unheimlich*" effect.

Now, the simple opposition that distinguishes between the original "in person" and its mask, its simulacrum, its double, this simple oppositional dissociation, on the contrary, tends to allay uneasiness. Everything concurs in order to produce and guarantee it—and oppositional logic, whether dialectical or not, here places itself in the service of such a calm, in order to acquit itself, so to speak, of the double.

A small footnote in the *Letter to d'Alembert* invokes the devil "in person," so to speak, and his apparition under the guise of the phantom of his double: on a stage, the stage on which he was simply represented, as was conventionally believed. As an actor or as a character, the thing is unclear. An apparition, then, of the devil "himself," over and above his representation; an apparition or presentation of the "original" over and above the representative that is supposed to supplement him; an apparition, in the sense of a visitation, of the "thing in itself" as the supplement of its "own" supplement. Such an apparition doubtless upsets the appeasing order of representation. However, it does so not by reducing double-effects but, on the contrary, by expanding them, by expanding the effect of duplicity without an original, which perhaps is what the diabolical consists of, its very inconsistency.

This brings fright to its climax, says Rousseau. *Unheimlichkeit,* Freud would say. Here is one of the two logics of repetition that are at work, it seems to me, and interlaced in *Beyond* . . . I will explain this interlacing elsewhere. Here is the footnote to the *Letter to d'Alembert.* I take it as the exergue to my discourse. The note is appended to the word "devil"; "I read, when I was young, a tragedy, which was part of the Escalade, in which the Devil was actu-

NOTICES (WARNINGS)   271

ally one of the actors. I have been told that when this play was once performed, this character, as he came on stage, appeared double, as if the original had been jealous that they had had the audacity to imitate him, and instantly everybody, seized by fright, took flight, thus ending the performance. This tale is burlesque and will appear much more so in Paris than in Geneva; however, whatever suppositions we may indulge in, in this double apparition will be found a theatrical effect and a really terrifying one. I can imagine only one sight simpler and more terrible yet, that is the hand emerging from the wall and writing unknown words at the feast of Balthazar. The very idea makes one shudder. It seems to me that our lyric poets are far from these sublime inventions; to no avail they make a great fuss with scenery for the purpose of horrifying. Even on the stage, not everything should be said to the eyes, but the imagination must also be excited." [11]

Which is Freud's devil? The one that he counterfeits, or that he represents as the devil's "advocate," doubtless in order to *defend* [12] him judiciously, taking up his cause, the cause in the "something else" ["*autre chose*"] that "we cannot remain blind to," but also, perhaps, so that in this defense which de(for)fends him it is forfended [*défendu*] that he come back [*revenir*] in person, that he come back otherwise than by means of the representation of his advocate. In this trial the double is de(for)fended [*défendu*]. But what *trial* could this be? Who is accusing whom? Which is the devil that impels Freud to write? What the devil by impelling him to write in sum writes in his place without ever writing anything himself? Is this to be analyzed beyond Freud's self-analysis? And what are Freud's "unknown words" which are written with another hand, also his own, at this strange feast? Which is the revenant? To whom, to what, and from whence will he come back [*revenir*]? It is in the future that the question will be asked.

3. The *Selbstdarstellung* wants to present, to stage, if possible, an avoidance: of Schopenhauer, of Nietzsche, and of philosophy in general, which apparently means many things and many people.

11. TN. Rousseau, *Politics and the Arts: Letter to M. D'Alembert*, trans. Allan Bloom (Glencoe, Ill.: Free Press of Glencoe, 1960), p. 121.

12. TN. Derrida plays on the double sense of *défendre*—to defend and to forbid—throughout this paragraph. I have used a combination of "defend" and the archaic "forfend"—thus "de(for)fend"—to indicate this play. The " 'something else that we cannot remain blind to' " refers to the citation above in which Freud speaks of having "unwittingly steered . . . into the harbour of Schopenhauer's philosophy." In French the "something else" is *autre chose,* and Derrida is also playing on the common derivation (from the Latin *causa*) of *chose* and *cause,* thing and cause.

Apparently. But let us not interpret too fast. If avoidance there is, if something is avoided with so much insistence, there has to be a tendency, a temptation, envy. Freud acknowledges this. As they say, he is the first to do so, and with reason. A bit earlier [13] he noted that in the works of his later years (among them *Beyond* . . .), he has "given free rein to the inclincation, which I kept down for so long, to speculation" (XX, 57). He seems to retain an ambiguous kind of regret for this. If he is to be believed, then one has to admit: 1. A "constitutional incapacity" (XX, 59) to philosophize. This is an occult, i.e., obscurantist, language: what, in psychoanalytic terms, is a "constitutional incapacity" to philophosize? 2. a "tendency"—nevertheless—to speculation. 3. a deliberate avoidance of philosophy, a rejection of the philosophical debt, genealogy, or descendance. 4. a non-avoidance of what Freud calls "speculation," which then, *stricto sensu,* must not be either philosophy or scientific or clinical experimentation in their traditional modes. Thus, we must ask ourselves whether, beyond this avoiding or denegating behavior motivated by whatever reasons, something that goes by the name of "speculation" does not reach what I hesitate to call, for reasons that we will see, the "theoretical" ("theoretical" speculation as it is usually understood). This could not be reduced either to a philosophical or to a scientific logic, whether this logic be pure, *a priori,* or empirical.

Here I break off these preliminary remarks. For reasons of principle I have placed them facing the *Selbstdarstellung:* in order to open onto that which *holds together* the new position of the question of death in psychoanalysis, Freud's apparently autobiographical point of view, and the history of the analytic movement. That which *holds together* does not maintain in the form of a system. No (logical, scientific, philosophical) concept of system, perhaps, could be authorized to do so, or could in fact be capable of such an assemblage. A concept itself is but an effect thereof.

Now, this is what counts for us here. And counts for us beyond what Freud himself could state about it. For example, when he relates the works of the second period of his life (*Beyond* . . . among others) to the rhythm of his own "biography," and particularly to the fact that "it seemed as though my life would soon be brought to an end by the recurrence of a malignant disease" (XX, 71) (he writes this in 1925, but the disease mentioned had declared itself a

13. TN. That is, earlier than the passage on Freud's late acquaintance with Schopenhauer (XX, 59) cited above.

few years earlier), the connection appears to be an externally empirical one, and for that reason does not get us far. If we wish, in another style, with other questions, to interlace the networks of a so-called "internal" reading of the writings on life death with those of the autobiography, the autography, the autothanatography, and those of the "analytic movement," to the extent that they are all inseparable, then we must begin, at least, by pointing out in the hastily named "internal" reading the places that are *structurally* open to intersecting with the other networks. What appeared elsewhere concerning the parergonal supplement [14] implies not only the possibility, but also the necessity of such an intersecting, along with all the paradoxes with which the motifs of the frame, the border, the title, and the signature then become engaged.

This concerns *bios* in its autobiographical import. From one instant to another it indeed could veer off in the direction of the heterothanatographical, if there escaped from our hands what we still believe we grasp under the heading of writing. As for *bios* in its biological or biologistic register, the one we followed in reading Nietzsche or Heidegger, Canguilhem or Jacob, we will quickly see it reconstitute itself in *Beyond. . .* , and will see it cross with the other register, cross itself with it. I leave the word "crossing" to all its genetic or genealogical chances. A certain writing will make its bed in them.

I WRITES US

Thus, *Beyond the Pleasure Principle*. Which I open to the first page, without any other precaution, as naively as possible. Without having it, I am giving myself the right to jump over all the methodological or juridical protocols which, with all the legitimacy in the world, could slow me down to the point of paralysis here. So be it.

Nevertheless, the first page of the first chapter already contains:
I. a certain reminder: of the present state and acquisitions of analytic theory. Psychoanalytic theory exists. The performance of the first words implies this fact in any event: "In the theory of psychoanalysis we have no hesitation in assuming . . ." Etc. One is not obliged to believe that it exists, one does not have to consider it valid, yet one must nevertheless rest assured—as is implied by the reception of this *speech act*—that Freud means to say that it exists, and that things are happening in it. His statement is not *stricto*

14. Cf. *Le Parergon* in *La Vérité en peinture* (Paris: Flammarion, 1978).

sensu a performative, he is allegedly declaring and attesting. But he is attesting to an act whose producing agent and first subject the speaker knows himself to be, wishes himself to be, or alleges himself to be. Which he will have been; and those whom he has associated, or who have associated themselves with the movement of this production have all accepted, in principle and consciously, the contract which institutes him as producer. Whence the singularity of this performance. When Freud advances a statement implying that psychoanalytic theory exists, he in no way is in the situation of a theoretician in the field of another science, nor is he any more in the position of an epistemologist or of a historian of the sciences. He is attesting to an act whose contract implies that the act come back [*revienne*] to him, and that he answer for it. In a certain way he seems to have contracted only with himself. *He would have written himself.* To himself, as if someone were sending himself a message informing himself by certified letter, on an official document, of the attested existence of a theoretical history to which he himself— such is the content of the message—gave the send-off [*coup d'envoi*].

2. the taking of a position as concerns philosophy. This is also the taking of a non-position, the placarded neutrality of a declaration of indifference which, if not indifferent in itself, must take its determination from elsewhere. In any event, Freud insists: the question of knowing whether the establishment of the pleasure principle is or is not close to a given philosophical system is "of no concern."

3. a concept of reflection which, under the heading "speculative," henceforth derives neither from metaphysical philosophy, nor from experimental science, even if linked to psychoanalytic experience as such.

The first two sentences are already very enigmatic: "In the theory of psychoanalysis we have no hesitation in assuming . . ." In question, then, is the theory, the unique and singular theory, such as it is supposed to exist, constituted more than twenty years ago, with indubitable results and a contractual institution permitting one to say "we," I-we, Freud's signature engaging and representing all the partisans of *the* theory, of *the* cause, which thus could not be divisible. It articulates itself, it sets off, and sets one off like this [*ça marche et fait marcher comme ça*].

"In the theory of psychoanalysis we *unbedenklich* [without hesitating, without scruples, without reflecting] have no hesitation in assuming that the course taken by mental events is automatically [*automatisch:* omitted in the French translation] regulated by the *Lustprinzip.*" The translation of the latter word by "pleasure principle" is not without pertinence, but let us not forget that *Lust* also designates erotic enjoyment [*jouissance*] and desire ("concupiscent desire," says Laplanche in *Life and Death in Psychoanalysis*). Freud continues: "We believe, that is to say, that the course of those events is invariably set in motion by an unpleasurable tension (*unlustvolle Spannung*), and that it takes a direction such that its final outcome coincides with a lowering of that tension—that is, with an avoidance (*Vermeidung*) of unpleasure (*Unlust*) or a production of pleasure (*Erzeugung von Lust*)" (7).

One can already follow the avoidance literally traced (*Vermeidung*); Freud indeed will have avoided a painful tension at the very moment of stating the law of this avoidance, and he has "avoided" it by cutting off any given "philosophical" ascendent. "Philosophical" is his word, each time. But what could this genealogical unpleasure have been?

"In the theory of psychoanalysis we have no hesitation in assuming . . ." The reminder escapes any alternative. It is not yet either a confirmation, or a putting into question of the well established. But it will *never* become—such is my hypothesis—either a proof or a disproof. Nevertheless, for the moment, let us attest to the following: Freud presents this state of the theory as the possibility of an assumption which might be imprudent: "we have no hesitation, *unbedenklich,* in assuming," we assume, and without raising an eyebrow, as if it went without saying, the authority of the pleasure principle. Thus, too self-assured, too authoritarian, if not too authorized an assumption concerning the dominating authority of this pleasure principle and the belief ("We believe . . .") in the consistency of such a principle. When Freud says "regulated by the pleasure principle," he adds, "We believe, that is to say": this belief might be the effect of credulity, and this suspicion immediately suspends belief. But what remains suspended at this point is not only the state of this regulatory law, this relation or relation of relations between quantities. Suspended also, as we shall see, is the qualitative essence of pleasure. And therefore of unpleasure, and therefore of the law of avoidance. The search for pleasure, the preference of which pleasure is the almost tautological, analytical object, the substitution of pleasure for unpleasure, pleasure linked to a decrease in tension—all this supposes that one know, at least implicitly, what pleasure is, that one pre-comprehend the meaning of the word ("pleasure"). But all of this tells us nothing about it, to the extent that it is all supposed. Nothing is said of the qualitative experience of pleasure itself. What is it? What does it consist of? It is on this question that soon, with all the requisite irony, an interrogation of the philosopher will be feigned.

The definition of the pleasure principle is mute about pleasure, about its essence and quality. Guided by the economic point of view, this definition concerns only quantitative relations. When it associates topographical and dynamic considerations with the economic ones, metapsychology is "at present" the "most complete description" (*Darstellung*, representation) "we can conceive" (*uns vorstellen*, represent for ourselves). (7)

But what about the relation of this "presentation" or "representation" to philosophy? Amiable indifference, well-meaning independence—so states Freud. It is of no concern to us, he says, that we might confirm any given, historically determined philosophical system. Rapprochement or annexation do not bother us. We aim for neither priority nor originality. We are only formulating "speculative assumptions" in order to explain and to describe the facts that we observe daily. And Freud adds: "we" (psychoanalysts) would be very grateful to philosophy if the latter were willing to tell us the meaning (*Bedeutung*) of the sensations of pleasure or unpleasure which act so "imperatively" or "imperiously" on us.

The "speculative assumptions," therefore, would not be of a philosophical order. The speculative—here—is not the philosophical. The speculative assumptions are not formed *a priori*, neither in a formal nor a material *apriori*, whether they are inferred or offered for immediate description. Here is a speculation which would have nothing to expect from philosophy.

In pretending that he will not haggle over his gratitude should the philosopher tell him what pleasure is, Freud ironically gives us to understand that even when he is speaking of pleasure—and what philosopher will not have?—the philosopher does not know and does not say what he is talking about. He presupposes the common experience of it, certainly, and common sense, but this presupposition is as dogmatic, as "*unbedenklich*," as it is in psychoanalytic theory *at present*.

Later, a root of this common dogmatism will be unearthed: there is a pleasure which is given to common experience, to commonly determined experience, to consciousness or to perception, *as* unpleasure. In general, nothing appears more irreducibly *phenomenal* in its very structure than pleasure. Now, the phenomenon of unpleasure can, shall we say, translate pleasure, another, non-phenomenal experience of pleasure. The demonstration or translation of this translation will come later, without "showing" anything in the phenomenal sense of the experience.

Speculation, *this* speculation thus would be foreign to philosophy or metaphysics. More precisely, speculation would represent the very thing which philosophy or metaphysics guard themselves from, which philosophy or metaphysics consist in guarding themselves from, maintaining with it a relation without relation, a relation of exclusion which signifies simultaneously the necessity and the aporia of translation. And it is within the "same" word—speculation—that the translation is to find its place, between the philosophical concept of speculation in its dominant, apparently legitimate determination, the determination granted to the elementary consensus of the philosophical tradition, and the concept that is announced here. This latter has been able to be the other's other by inhabiting it, by letting itself be excluded without ceasing to work upon it in the most domestic fashion. Whence, again, the necessity (which calls upon the possibility) and the aporia of this translation. It cannot be said that Freud operates this translation in a thematic and always coherent way, for example in his usage of the "word." But a certain reading of his text, the one I am attempting here, cannot fail to come across its work. The speculation which is in question in this text cannot purely and simply refer to the speculative of the Hegelian type, at least in its dominant determination. No more than it can refer, beyond the empirical description, to the knowledge of laws extracted by more or less self-assured induction: this knowledge has never been called speculative. And nevertheless Freud does not, under the name of speculation, call upon a pure and *a priori* theory that simply precedes the so-called empirical contents.

What to do with this inconceivable concept? How to speculate with this speculation? Why does it fascinate Freud, in a fashion doubtless ambiguous, but irresistible? What is it that fascinates under this heading? And why does it impose itself at the moment when it is a question of life death, of pleasure-unpleasure, and of repetition? To keep to the classical criteria of philosophical or scientific discourse, to the canons of genre, one cannot say that Freud *elaborates* this inconceivable concept for itself, that he makes a theme of it, or works in order to *present* its properly theoretical originality. It is perhaps that its originality is not of the theoretical order, is not purely or essentially theoretical: a non-theoretical speculation. What is ungraspable about it (a stronghold all the more strong in being inscribed in no recognized place: the supreme ruse of a mirage in an unassignable topology) serves a strategy whose finality cannot be clear, cannot be *itself*. No more for Freud than for anyone else. This speculation renders services of which one does not wish to speak or to hear spoken of. Perhaps he who carries the name of Freud can neither appropriate for himself the speculative of this singular speculation, nor identify himself with the speculator of this speculation without precedent or ascendant, nor even exclude him, detach himself from him, renounce the one or the other.

Here, I am asking questions in the dark. Or in a penumbra, rather, the penumbra in which we keep ourselves when Freud's un-analyzed reaches out its phosphorescent antennae. Reaches them out across the unexpected structure of this text, of the movements within it which, it seems to me, do not correspond to any genre, to any philosophical or scientific model. Nor to any literary, poetic, or mythological model. These genres, models, codes are certainly present within the text, together or in turn, exploited, maneuvered, interpreted like pieces. But thereby overflowed. Such is the *hypothesis* or the athesis of the athesis.

We are attempting to approach the first chapter. It resembles a simple introduction. It is very short. Its conclusion curiously confirms belief in the authority of the pleasure principle. Uneasiness had been expressed, certainly, and the formulation of a series of objections had been permitted. And yet, despite this confirmation, and although the so-called objections have shaken nothing, Freud comes to prescribe that one "raise fresh questions" (*neue Fragestellungen*), formulate a new problematic. He does so, therefore, without the slightest demonstrative necessity. Having efficaciously rejected the objections and confirmed the authority of the pleasure principle, he could have stopped there. But not only does he call upon new contents, but also on new problematics, other modalities of questioning.

I am going right to the end of this first chapter, toward the site of this first pause where, despite the return to the immobility of the point of departure, despite the paralysis, despite the *pas de marche* in that the pleasure principle is unshaken (the pleasure principle in person, or in its modified form as the reality principle, for the same chapter will have shown that the latter only modalizes, modifies, modulates, or represents the former), Freud finally concludes: "This does not seem to necessitate any far-reaching limitation of the pleasure principle. Nevertheless the investigation of the mental reaction to external danger is precisely in a position to produce new material and raise fresh *Fragestellungen* bearing upon our present problem" (11). What is it that gives the impetus to go further? Why does the confirmation of a hypothesis, after the rejection of the objections, remain unsatisfying? What is it that here provokes new questions? Who imposes them? The first chapter will have been contorted in its very brevity. From the first moment on, Freud has acknowledged that the sensation of pleasure-unpleasure remains mysterious, strangely inaccessible. In sum, no one has yet said anything about it, neither the psychological scientist, nor the philosopher, nor even the psychoanalyst. And nevertheless we cannot "avoid" touching upon it. Once more, we cannot "avoid" (*vermeiden*). It is "impossible." Hence, it is best to try the most open, least rigid, "loosest" (*lockerste*) hypothesis. Which hypothesis is this? Here, it seems to me, we must pay the greatest attention to Freud's rhetoric. And by the the same token, to the scene, the gestures, the movements, the filtrating strategy, the busy selectivity. The procedure here is no longer governed by a reassuring model of science or philosophy. For example, Freud admits here that he is completely unarmed concerning the question of knowing what pleasure-unpleasure *is*, admits that he has to choose the "loosest" hypothesis, and he continues: "We have decided . . ." *Wir haben uns entschlossen . . .*

Decided what? To privilege the economic point of view, and to establish, *from this point of view*, a first relation. A relation, thus, between two quantities, and not between two essences. The law is one of a relation between the quantity of something whose essence is unknown to us, (and even, which makes the operation even more unexpected, something whose qualitative appearance or experience is uncertain, as soon as pleasures, we will come to this, can be experienced as unpleasures), and a quantity of energy (unbound energy—*und nicht irgendwie gebundenen*—Freud specifies between dashes) whose presence in psychic life is presumed. We know that this appeal to the notion of (bound or unbound) energy loses none of its difficulty in that it is so trivially manipulated in Freudian doxography. In chapter IV Freud refers to the distinction established by Breuer between quiescent (bound) cathectic energy and freely mobile energy. But, he specifies immediately, it is better to leave these relations as "indeterminate" as possible at first. The source common to Breuer and to Freud is the distinction proposed by

Helmholtz between the two energies, taking into account the principles of Carnot-Clausius and of the degradation of energy.[15] Constant internal energy would correspond to the sum of free energy and bound energy, the first tending to diminish to the extent that the other increases. Laplanche suggests that Freud has very freely interpreted, with an "exasperated irreverence," the statements that he borrows, notably by displacing the "free" of "freely utilizable" into "freely mobile."

Let us arbitrarily leave aside all the problems posed by the borrowing of this energetic "model," if borrowing there is, and if clarity concerning what "borrowing" means here is supposed. Once the borrowing is operated, and within this very hypothesis, it nonetheless has to be recognized that the introduction of the energetic term in the relation proposed by Freud does not proceed without an internal and essential complication. What then does the principle of this relation consist of? Unpleasure would correspond to an increase and pleasure to a diminution of the quantity of (free) energy. But this relation is neither a simple correlation (*einfaches Verhältnis*) between two forces, that of the sensations and that of the modifications of energy, nor a directly proportional ratio (*direkte Proportionalität*). This *non-simplicity* and *indirectness* promise, on the threshold of the "loosest" hypothesis, an inexhaustible reserve for speculation. This reserve does not consist of substantial riches, but rather of additional turns, supplementary angles, differential ruses as far as the eye can see. Time must be of the party. Time is not a general form, the homogenous element of this differentiality—rather, it must be thought in return on the basis of this differential heterogeneity—but it has to be reckoned with. It is probable, remarks Freud, that the "decisive" factor here is the amount of increase or diminution in time, "in a given period of time."

Before the names of Schopenhauer and of Nietzsche, the *Selbstdarstellung* had cited Fechner: this time there is homage, an acknowledgment of the debt without a declaration of avoidance, the

---

15. " 'It seems certain to me that we must distinguish, within chemical processes as well, between that portion of the forces of affinity capable of being freely transformed into other kinds of work, and that portion that can only become manifest in the form of heat. To abbreviate, I shall call these two portions of energy: free energy and bound energy.' " Helmholtz, 1882, "Über die Thermodynamik chemischer Vorgänge," cited by Jean Laplanche in *Life and Death in Psychoanalysis* (trans. Jeffrey Mehlman, Baltimore: The Johns Hopkins University Press, 1976, p. 119) in a chapter which I presume to be read here.

inheritance accepted. Fechner, the "investigator of such penetration," arrives here in order to guarantee the hypothesis. In 1873, he had already posited as a psychophysical law that every motion is accompanied by pleasure when it approaches complete stability, by unpleasure when it tends toward complete instability. In the long citation of Fechner, Freud drops, forever it seems to me, the allusion to a " 'certain margin of aesthetic indifference' " between the two limits. Is this not like a free zone, a place of free exchange for the comings and goings of speculation? An agency that I will call "duty-free" providing, with a general equivalence, the means with which to pass, as authorized contraband, an always ideal border, and in both directions? More or less ideal.

In any event, immediately afterward stating that the psychic apparatus represents a "special case" of Fechner's principle, Freud concludes that the pleasure principle can be deduced from the principle of constancy that itself has been revealed circularly by the facts which imposed upon us belief in the pleasure principle: the psychic apparatus seeks to maintain the quantity of excitation present in it at as low a level, or at least as constant a level, as possible.

Here, then, the pleasure principle is indeed confirmed in its authority, in its sovereign domination (*Herrschaft,* Freud already says, and we will take this into account).

First objection. Is it feigned or seriously accepted by Freud? Only the ultimate finality of a demonstration or of a thesis could, in the last analysis, decide the logico-rhetorical value of such an objection. If such a finality were lacking in the end, or even if it were not assignable according to the given criteria available in advance, then the distinction between the feigned and the serious would escape us totally, just as it would escape the "author" in the extent to which he would find himself in the same situation as we are.

Here is the objection, it is simple: If the pleasure principle were absolutely dominant, if it were the absolute master without any possible contradiction, whence would come the unpleasure to which experience bears witness in so incontestable a way?

We suffer, says this experience.

But what is its authority in this regard? What is experience? Is it so certain that we suffer? What does this mean? And if it were pleasurable, here or elsewhere?

These questions are not asked by Freud, not here, and not in these terms. He takes the objection into account: there is unpleasure, and this seems to create an objection to the absolute authority of the pleasure principle. The first response to this objection is well known, but here I must ceaselessly call upon the grounds of the "well known" in order to attempt to march to another beat. First response then: the pleasure principle, as its name indicates, is a principle, it governs a general tendency which, tendentially then, organizes everything, but can encounter, as Fechner also recognized, external obstacles. These obstacles do sometimes prevent it from coming to its conclusion or from triumphing, but do not put it into question *as* a principial *tendency* to pleasure, but on the contrary confirm it as soon as they are considered as obstacles.

The inhibiting obstacle, the one familiar to us, familiarly known in its regularity, we situate in the "external world." When the simple, direct, and imprudent affirmation of the pleasure principle puts the organism into danger, then the "ego's instincts of self-preservation" force the principle into retreat, not into disappearing by *simply* yielding its place, but into *leaving* the reality principle in its place as a delegate, its courier, its lieutenant, or its slave, its domestic in that it belongs to the same economy, the same house. One could also say its disciple, the disciplined disciple who, as always, finds himself in a situation to inform, to teach, to instruct a master who is sometimes hard to educate. "Hard to educate," for example, are the sexual drives which conform only to the pleasure principle.

The reality principle imposes no definitive inhibition, no renunciation of pleasure, only a detour in order to defer enjoyment, the waystation of a *différance* (*Aufschub*). On this "long indirect road" (*auf dem langen Umwege zur Lust*) the pleasure principle submits itself, provisionally and to a certain extent, to its own lieutenant. The latter, as representative, slave, or informed disciple, the disciplined one who disciplines also plays the role of the preceptor in the master's service. As if the latter produced a *socius*,[16] put in "motion" an institution by signing a contract with "discipline," with the assistant master or foreman who nevertheless does nothing but represent him. A false contract, a pure speculation, the simulacrum of an engagement which binds the lord only to himself, to his own modification, to himself modified. The master addresses to himself the text or the corpus of this simulated engagement via the detour of an institutional telecommunication. He *writes himself, sends himself* [*s'envoie*]: but if the length of the detour can no longer be mastered, and rather than its length its structure, then the return to (one)self is never certain, and without return to sender the engage-

---

16. TN. That is, a companion or ally.

ment is forgotten to the very extent that it becomes undeniable, unshakable.

As soon as an authoritarian agency submits itself to the work of a secondary or dependent agency (master/slave, master/disciple) which finds itself in contact with "reality"—the latter being defined by means of the very possibility of this speculative transaction—there is no longer any *opposition,* as is sometimes believed, between the pleasure principle and the reality principle. It is the same *différant,* in *différance* with itself. But the structure of *différance* then can open onto an alterity that is even more irreducible than the alterity attributed to opposition. Because the pleasure principle—right from this preliminary moment when Freud grants it an uncontested mastery—enters into a contract only with itself, reckons and speculates only with itself or with its own metastasis, because it sends itself [*s'envoie*] everything it wants, and in sum encounters no opposition, it *unleashes* in itself the *absolute* other.

ONE TWO THREE—SPECULATION WITHOUT TERM

In sum, Freud could have stopped there (and in a certain way he does, I think that everything is played out in these first pages, in other words that everything will only repeat his arrest, his *pas de marche,* but it is repetition, precisely, that is in question here): the speculative possibility of the totally-other (*than* the pleasure principle) is in advance inscribed within it, in the letter of engagement that it believes it sends to itself circularly, specularly, inscribed as that which is not inscribed within it, the opener of a scription of the other that *overlaps* [*à même*] the principle. The very surface of the "overlap" no longer belongs to itself, is no longer what it is as such. Writing affects the very surface of its support. And this non-belonging unleashes speculation.

You must already find that I myself am corrupting the "properly Freudian" usage of "speculation," of the notion or the concept, and of the word. Where Freud seems to make of it a mode of research, a theoretical attitude, I am also considering it as the object of his discourse. I am acting *as if* Freud were not only preparing himself to speak *speculatively* of this or that (for example of a beyond of the pleasure principle), but were already speaking *of* speculation. As if he did not content himself to move *within speculation,* but insisted upon treating of it also, on the bias. And it is the bias of this procedure which interests me. I am acting as if the very thing he appears to analyze, for example the relation between the two principles, were already an element of speculative structure in general: simultaneously in the senses of specular reflection (the pleasure principle can recognize itself, or no longer at all recognize itself, in the reality principle); of the production of surplus value, of calculations and bets on the Exchange, that is, the emission of more or less fictive shares; and finally in the sense of that which overflows the (given) presence of the present, the given of the gift. I am doing all this, and I am alleging that this must be done in order to gain access to that which is played out here beyond the "given," to that which is rejected, withheld, taken back, beyond the principle of what Freud presently *says,* if such a thing were possible, *about speculation.* In what he writes something must derive from the speculation of which he speaks. But I will not content myself with this corruption by reapplication. I am alleging that speculation is not only a mode of research named by Freud, not only the oblique object of his discourse, but also the operation of his writing, the scene (of that) which he makes by writing what he writes here, that which makes him do it, and that which he makes to do, that which makes him write and that which he makes—or lets—write. To make to do, to make write, to let do, or to let write: the syntax of these operations is not given.

No *Weg* without *Umweg:* the detour does not overtake the road, but constitutes it, breaks open the path. Freud here does not seem to interrogate the graphics of this *différant* detour *for itself.* But can it be interrogated for *itself?* Itself, it is not. Nevertheless it can eventually account for the interminable detour of this text (is it itself here?), and for its speculative athesis.

Pure pleasure and pure reality are ideal limits, which is as much as to say fictions. The one is as destructive and mortal as the other. Between the two the *différant* detour therefore forms the very actuality of the process, of the "psychic" process as a "living" process. Such an "actuality," then, is never present or given. It "is" that which in the gift is never presently giving or given. There is (*es gibt*)—it gives, *différance.* Therefore one cannot even speak of effective actuality, of *Wirklichkeit,* if at least, and in the extent to which, it is coordinated with the value of presence. The detour thereby "would be" the common, which is as much as to say the *différant,* root of the two principles, the root uprooted from itself, necessarily impure, and structurally given over to compromise, to the speculative transaction. The three terms—two principles plus or minus *différance*—are but one, the same divided, since the second (reality) principle and *différance* are only the "effects" of the modifiable pleasure principle.

But from whichever *end* one takes this structure with one-two-three terms, it is death. *At the end,* and this death is not opposable, does not differ, in the sense of opposition, from the two principles and their *différance.* It is inscribed, although non-inscribable, in the process of this structure—which we will call later stricture. If death is not opposable it is, already, *life death.* This Freud does not say, does not say it presently, here, nor even elsewhere in this form. It gives (itself to be) thought without ever being given or thought. Neither here nor elsewhere. But the "hypothesis" with which I read this text and several others would go in the direction of disengaging that which is engaged here between the first principle and that which appears as *its other,* to wit, the reality principle as *its* other, the death drive as its *other:* a structure of alteration without opposition. That which seems, then, to make the belonging—a belonging without interiority—of death to pleasure more continuous, more immanent, and more natural too, also makes it more scandalous as concerns a dialectics or a logic of opposition, of position, or of thesis. There is no thesis of this *différance.* The thesis would be the death sentence (*arrêt de mort*) of *différance.* The syntax of this *arrêt de mort,* which arrests death in two *différant* senses (a sentence which condemns to death and an interruption suspending death), will be in question elsewhere.[17]

My "hypothesis," and you can see in what sense I will use this word henceforth, is that the speculative structure has its place and its necessity in this graphics.

How does death await at the end, at all the ends (the three interlaced ends which only make up one divided end) of this structure, at every step of this speculation?

Each time that one of the "terms," the pseudo-terms or pseudo-pods, sets forth [*marche*] and goes *to the end* of itself, and therefore of its other, keeping to its extreme and pure autarky, without negotiating, without speculating, without passing through the mediation of any third party, it is death, the mortal sprain which puts an end to the strain of calculation. If the reality principle autonomizes itself and functions all alone (an absurd hypothesis by defini-

17. TN. *Arrêt de mort* means "death sentence" but can also be translated as "arrest of death." Derrida is referring to Blanchot's *Arrêt de mort,* and to his analysis of it in "Living On—Borderlines," translated by James Hulbert in *Deconstruction and Criticism* (New York: Seabury Press, 1979).

tion, covering the field said to be pathological), it cuts itself off from all pleasure and all desire, from the entire auto-affective relation without which there is neither any desire nor pleasure that can appear at all. This is the sentence of death [*arrêt de mort*], of a death that is also at the two other ends: equally in the fact that the reality principle then would affirm itself without any erotic enjoyment, and in the other fact that it would be the death of its service, its delegated service of the pleasure principle. It would die itself, in its ordered service, due to the economic zeal of pleasure, of a pleasure too jealous of itself and of what it sets aside. It would already be pleasure that, by itself protecting itself too much, would come to asphyxiate itself in the economy of its own reserves.

But inversely (if it can be put thus, for this second eventuality does not invert the first one), to go to the end of the transactional compromise that is the *Umweg*—pure *différance* in a way—is also the *arrêt de mort*: no pleasure would ever present itself. But does a pleasure ever present itself? Death is inscribed, although noninscribable, "in" *différance* as much as it is in the reality principle which is but another name for it, the name of another "moment," since pleasure and reality are also exchanged within it.

Finally, inversely (if it can be put thus, for this third eventuality does not invert either of the two preceding ones), if the pleasure principle unleashes itself immediately, without protecting itself from the obstacles of the external world or from dangers in general (those of psychic reality also), or even if it follows its "own" tendential law which leads back to the lowest level of excitation, there is the "same" *arrêt de mort*. At the stage of Freud's text where we still remain, this is the only explicitly considered hypothesis: if there is a specificity of the "sexual drives," it is due to their wild, rebellious, "hard to 'educate,'" undisciplinable character. These drives have a tendency not to submit to the reality principle. But what does this mean as soon as the latter is nothing other than the pleasure principle? What does this mean if not that the sexual does not even permit itself to be bound to pleasure, to enjoyment? and that the sexual, unless it is the driven of the drive, even before any other determination, is the force that resists binding or stricture? which resists its own conservation, which resists that which protects it from itself, resists its proper, and the proper itself? resists economy?

It exposes itself to death, then, by making-letting a guard rail be jumped, a guard rail which, however, is nothing but its own production, its own modification, as the PR is the PP modified (to be pronounced as you like, this is a line to be followed in the course of the next session, everything playing itself out, as you might imagine, in the modification of such a descendance). [18] We have here a very general principle, the principle of a functioning of principles which can only differentiate itself. Freud invokes this differentiation, calling it ulterior, when he has just spoken of the *Umweg* of the PR: "The PP long persists, however, as the method of working employed by the sexual instincts, which are so hard to 'educate,' and, starting from those instincts, or in the ego itself, it often succeeds in overcoming the PR to the detriment of the organism as a whole" (10).

Until now, but we have only just begun, however complicated, the laws of this structure with one or three-in-one terms (the same in *différance*) could be exposed without having to call upon a specific agency whose name would be Repression.

Let it be said in passing, for those who already might have forgotten, that the intervention of Repression remains very enigmatic. Is it an effect that is necessary and explainable on the basis of the structure that we have just evoked? Another way of naming it? Or does Repression transform the structure affecting it in an essential way? Or does it make the structure possible in its primary constitution?

The import of these questions cannot be limited. What is going on in them, in sum, concerns the specificity in the "last analysis" of something like psychoanalysis *itself:* as a "theory," as a "practice," a "movement," a "cause," an "institution," "tradition," "inheritance," etc. If this irreducible specificity could be demonstrated, if it could be recognized rigorously, it is in that other modes of demonstration and recognition will have had to be appealed to; and this specificity should not find itself represented anywhere else, neither in what is commonly called experience, nor in science according to its traditional, i.e. philosophical, representations, nor in the philosophy of philosophy. Science as objective knowledge, for example, cannot formulate the question of the quantitative evalua-

18. TN. PR and PP stand for reality principle (*principe de réalité*) and pleasure principle. In French the pronunciation of PP is *pépé*, which is also the affectionate term for grandfather. Derrida will play upon this double meaning throughout. I will indicate in brackets the double meaning of any pronouns or possessives relating to the PP. For example, "*le PP et son principe de réalité*" will be given as "the PP and its (his) reality principle." In French the abbreviation for *principe de réalité* is PR, which also stands for *poste restante,* as when one sends a letter to be held at the post office.

tion of a qualitative—or to go quickly let us say "subjective"—affect, one in which a subject is irreducibly engaged. As for the philosophical or usual concept of experience, one finds presupposed within it a knowledge or a foreknowledge of what pleasure is, and of what "pleasure" "means"; to use this concept implies that the ultimate criterion of something like pleasure or unpleasure, as well as their distinction, is conscious or perceptual experience, experience itself: a pleasure that would not be felt as such would have no sense as pleasure; a pleasure in the experience of nonpleasure, and *a fortiori* of unpleasure, would be considered either as an absurdity not worthy of a moment's attention, or as a speculative folly that no longer would even permit discourse to be organized and communicated. The minimal contract of signification would be declared suspended. Which would make every philosophy that speaks of the subject, or of subjective affect, phenomenological in its essence. Now, it is here that the very possibility of a speculation that would be neither philosophical nor scientific in the classical sense (the devil for science and philosophy), nevertheless could open onto another science, as it does to another fiction; this speculative possibility supposes something which here is named Repression, to wit that which permits a pleasure to be lived and perceived as unpleasure, for example. Without these words losing their sense. Repression itself in its specificity is possible only on the basis of this speculative hypothesis. And one can only write about it speculatively, provided that one understand the concept of speculation according to these protocols.

As soon as it—and it alone—is principially capable of giving rise to this concept of speculation and to this concept of repression, the graphics of *différance* belongs neither to science nor to philosophy in their classical limits. But it does not suffice to *speak* of Repression—and therefore, it is believed, of psychoanalysis—in order to cross or confuse these limits.

This first itinerary will have led us to the point at which the recourse to Repression intervenes in its place in a first chapter that is entirely submitted to the hypothesis of what has been gained in psychoanalysis, as this has been recalled right from the first sentence. There will have been no doubt about the authority, in the last analysis, of the PP.

Why Repression? The substitution, or rather the replacement, of the PR explains only a small part of our experiences of unpleasure, and the least intense ones. Thus, there is another source, "another occasion of the release" of unpleasure, of its discharge, its deliverance, its delivery (*Unlustentbindung*). In the constitution of the Ego, in the synthesis of the personality, certain drive components show themselves incompatible with other ones. Freud does not open up the question of this incompatibility, he starts from it as a fact. These incompossibles find themselves split apart by the process called Repression. They do not participate in the synthesis of the Ego, remaining at an interior or archaic level of psychic organization, more or less deprived of satisfaction. And as it can happen that these drive components can obtain satisfaction by direct or substitutive routes, but always according to the *différance* of an *Umweg*, this event is felt by the organized Ego as an unpleasure: by the Ego and not, as the French translation says, by the "organism." Along with the topical differentiation and the structuration of agencies that it constructs—or rather that it informs and signifies— Repression upsets the logic implicit in all philosophy: it makes it possible for a pleasure to be experienced—by the Ego—as unpleasure. This topical differentiation is inseparable from Repression in its very possibility. It is an ineluctable consequence of *différance*, of the structure of the *1, 2, 3 in one différant from itself.* It is difficult to describe in the classical logos of philosophy, and it engages one in a new speculation. This is what I wished to emphasize in recalling these "well-known facts." What I have just called the classical logos of philosophy is the order of that which *represents* itself or *presents* itself clearly and easily in order to coordinate itself with the value of presence which governs everything that is *self-evident* in *experience*. Is this not the difficulty that Freud in his way envisages? "The details [the singularities: *Einzelheiten*] of the process by which repression turns a possibility of pleasure into a source of unpleasure are not yet clearly understood (*verstanden*), or cannot be clearly represented [not describable, representable, presentable: *darstellbar*]; but there is no doubt that all neurotic unpleasure is of that kind—pleasure that cannot be felt as such."[1] And a note not translated [in the French edition] specifies further: "No doubt the essential point is that pleasure and unpleasure, being conscious feelings, are attached to the ego" (11).

". . . pleasure that cannot be felt as such . . ." (. . . *Lust die nicht als solche empfunden werden kann.*) The German phrase seems less paradoxical and upsetting than Jankelevitch's French translation, which says: "a pleasure that is not experienced as such" [*un plaisir qui n'est pas éprouvé comme tel*]. Certainly this translation is faulty by omission, since it says "is not" in the place where the original says "cannot be." But due to this it renders to the (unconscious) "experience" of pleasure which is not felt (implied: consciously) as such an actuality or an effectiveness which seems to be as close as possible to what Freud visibly means. Unfaithful to the literality of what it translates, omitting the "non-capacity" that situates the agency of Repression, it faithfully puts the accent back on the paradox of this Repression: there is actually effective pleasure that is effectively, actually lived as unpleasure. Experience in the classical, philosophical, and usual senses (all the same), the "*as such*" given by conscious experience: these are what is no longer applicable. If, faithful to the literality of the text, one maintains the "cannot be experienced as such," the paradox is less striking. One might even be led to think, against Freud's very intention apparently, that it might be a question of a pleasure that cannot come to an end, rather than an effective, actual pleasure but that is also actually "lived" as unpleasure.

However, this second possibility conforms only to a Freudian radicalization that is not yet brought to term in this first chapter. For as long as pleasure and the *experience* of unpleasure are localized in different agencies (what is pleasure *here* is *unpleasure* there), the topical differentiation introduces an element of systematic coherence and of classical rationality. Pleasure and unpleasure remain in their place. *Obediently,* since no mélange is possible, and mélange is madness. The principle of identity is respected by the topology and by the division of sites. Although the topical distribution is an effect of *différance,* it still retains *différance* in a reassuring medium and in an oppositional logic: it is not yet pleasure *itself* that is felt *as* unpleasure. But with the problematics of narcissism and of primary masochism, we will have to go to the end of this paradox and, without reducing the topical differentiation, not content ourselves with it.

Where are we? The authority of the PP is intact. Freud even announces at the end of the chapter that other sources of unpleasure are still to be inventoried: they do not contest the legitimate authority of the PP any more than the preceding ones. It is only in chapter IV, announcing the speculation of great breadth, that Freud envisages a function of the psychic apparatus which, without being *opposed* to the PP would be no less independent from it, and more originary than the tendency (as distinct from the function) to seek pleasure and to avoid unpleasure: the first exception before which, in sum, "speculation" would never have begun.

But will it begin then? And has not everything been said or

rather engaged concerning this speculation about which nothing would have been said yet?

Thus, the speculative overflowing still awaits. And the great breadth. It will lead to another "hypothesis": drives "in the service of which" the absolute master, the PP, would work. The drives said to be of death. But were they not *already* at work in the logic we have just recognized?

To be at work already: this is what the case of the aforenamed drives later will make heard as the inaudible. It will have been written (to itself) in silence.

2

FREUD'S LEGACY

The title of this chapter is a deliberately corrupt citation, which doubtless will have been recognized. The expression "Freud's legacy" [*legs de Freud*]¹ is often encountered in the writings of Jacques Lacan and Wladimir Granoff. Naturally I leave the reader as judge of what is going on in this corruption.

This chapter was first published in the number of *Etudes freudiennes* devoted to Nicolas Abraham. I had then prefaced it with this note:

> Extract of a seminar held in 1975 at *l'Ecole normale supérieure* under the heading *Life death*. Maria Torok, who became aware of this last year, told me that she was sensitive to certain intersections, convergences, affinities with some of the still unpublished works of Nicolas Abraham, among those which soon will appear in *L'Ecorce et le noyau* (*Anasemies* II, Aubier-Flammarion, coll. "La philosophie en effet"). This is what has encouraged me to publish this fragment here. Those who wish to delimit its import can also consider it as a reading of the second chapter of *Beyond the Pleasure Principle*. At this determined stage of the seminar, the question was to examine the (problematic and textual) specificity of *Beyond. . . ,* of rebinding what is irreducible about a "speculation" with the economy of a scene of writing, which itself is inseparable from a scene of inheritance implicating both the Freuds and the psychoanalytic "movement." The session immediately preceding this one had specified the space of this investigation and the singularity of Freud's *speculative procedure* [*démarche*]. This session had proposed some abbreviations, for example PP

---

1. TN. The bilingual pun—legs, legacy—is at work throughout. It is related to Derrida's analysis of the rhetoric of *Beyond . . . ,* Freud's repeated gesture of taking another *step* forward that goes nowhere, the rhetoric of the athesis. Step in French is *pas,* which is also the most common word of negation. This fits extremely well with the idea of steps for nothing, the "legwork" of the legacy. I have indicated the play on *pas* in brackets throughout. See also the entry "*legs*" in *L Before K* above.

for pleasure principle, PR for reality principle. Other fragments of the
same seminar will appear soon in book form.

THE "SAME ROOF" OF THE AUTOBIOGRAPHY

Nothing yet has contradicted or in any way contested the authority
of a PP which always comes back [*revient*] to itself, modifies itself,
delegates itself, represents itself without ever leaving itself [*se quit-
ter*]. Doubtless, in this return to itself there may be, as we have
demonstrated, the strict implication of being haunted by something
totally other. The return never "acquits" the speculation of the PP.
Doubtless it is never quits with it because it *takes place* within the
PP it(him)self, and indebts it (him) at every *step* [*pas*]. And yet in
Freud's discourse, let us say in the discourse of a certain speculator,
on the subject of the PP which never quits itself, and therefore always speaks of it(him)self, nothing yet has contradicted the authority of the first principle. Perhaps it is that the PP cannot be contradicted. What is done without it (him), if anything is, will not
contradict: first because it will not oppose itself to the PP (it will be
done without him in him, with his own step without him), and then
because it will be done without him by not saying anything, by stifling itself, inscribing itself in silence. As soon as it speaks it submits to the authority of the absolute master, the PP which (who) as
such cannot be quiet. But which (who), by the same token, lets the
other ventriloquate it (him): in silence then.

At the end of the first chapter the PP is thus confirmed in its absolute sovereignty. Whence the necessity of new problematics, of
"fresh questions bearing upon our present problem."

Now, if one attempts to make oneself attentive to the original
modality of the "speculative," and to the singular *proceeding*
[*démarche*] of this writing, its *pas de thèse*[2] which advances without advancing, without advancing itself, without ever advancing
anything that it does not immediately take back, for the time of a
detour, without ever positing anything which remains in its position, then one must recognize that the following chapter repeats, in
place and in another place, the immobile *emplacement* of the *pas*

2. TN. To continue the last note, I have also indicated the play on *démarche*
throughout. The best English equivalent is procedure, but this loses the play on
marche, from *marcher* (to walk, to work, as in *ça marche*) and on *de-* as a prefix of
negation. To put it elliptically, the *athesis* depends upon a *dé-marche*, or as Derrida
puts it here, a *pas de thèse:* a *no*-thesis that is as formally organized as any ballet
step.

de thèse. It repeats itself, it illustrates only the repetition of that very thing (the absolute authority of the PP) which finally will not let anything be done without it (him), except repetition itself. In any event, despite the richness and novelty of the content adduced in the second chapter, despite several marching orders and steps forward, not an inch of ground is gained; not one decision, not the slightest advance in the question which occupies the speculator, the question of the PP as absolute master. This chapter nonetheless is one of the most famous in *Beyond.* . . , the one often retained in the exoteric, and occasionally the esoteric, space of psychoanalysis as one of the most important, and even decisive, chapters of the essay. Notably because of the story of the spool and of the *fort/da.* And as the repetition compulsion (*Wiederholungszwang*) is put into communication with the death drive, and since in effect a repetition compulsion seems to dominate the scene of the spool, it is believed that this story can be reattached to the exhibition, that is, the demonstration, of the so-called death drive. This is due to not having read: the speculator retains *nothing* of this story about the *fort/da,* at least in the demonstration in view of a beyond of the PP. He alleges that he can still explain it thoroughly within the space of the PP and under its authority. And, in effect, he succeeds. It is indeed the story of the PP that he is telling us, a certain episode of its fabulous reign, certainly an important moment of its (his) own genealogy, but still a moment of it(him)self.

I do not mean to say that this chapter is without interest, nor, above all, that the anecdote of the spool is without import. Quite to the contrary: it is simply that its import is perhaps not inscribed in the register of the *demonstration* whose most apparent and continuous thread is held in the question: are we correct, we psychoanalysts, to *believe* in the absolute domination of the PP? Where is this import inscribed them? And in what place that could be both under the *mouvance*[3] of the PP, the graphics we pointed out the last time, and, simultaneously, the *mouvance* of the speculative writing of this essay, that which commits the essay to the stakes of this speculative writing?

3. TN. *Mouvance* refers both to the relation of dependence between two fiefs, and to the state of being in movement. The former meaning relates to everything that Derrida has to say about the *dominance* of the PP, the prince and the satellites in the "society" of the drives. The latter meaning relates to Derrida's use of noun-verbs suspended between the active and the passive, as in *différance, restance, revenance* (cf. above, "Athesis," note 5). In fact, as a description of the relation between fiefs, *mouvance* has either an active or a passive sense also.

Let us first extract a skeleton: the argumentative framework of the chapter. We observe that something repeats itself. And (has this ever been done?) the repetitive process is to be identified not only in the content, the examples, and the material described and analyzed by Freud, but already, or again, in Freud's writing, in the *démarche* of his text, in what he does as much as in what he says, in his "acts," if you will, no less than in his "objects." (If Freud were his grandson, one would have to attend to repetition on the side of the gesture, and not only on the side of the *fort/da* of the spool, of the object. But let us not shuffle the cards; who has said that Freud was his own grandson?) What repeats itself more obviously in this chapter is the speculator's indefatigable motion in order to reject, to set aside, to make disappear, to distance (*fort*), to defer everything that appears to put the PP into question. He observes every time that something does not suffice, that something must be put off until further on, until later. Then he makes the hypothesis of the beyond come back [*revenir*] only to dismiss it again. This hypothesis comes back [*revient*] only as that which has not truly come back [*revenu*], that which has only passed by in the specter of its presence.

Keeping, at first, to the argumentative framework, to the logical course of the demonstration, we observe that after having treated the example of traumatic neurosis, Freud renounces, abandons, resigns himself. He proposes to leave this obscure theme (*Ich mache nun den Vorschlag, das dunkle und düstere Thema der traumatischen Neurose zu verlassen . . .*). *First dismissal.*

But after having treated "children's play," the anecdote of the spool and of the *fort/da,* Freud renounces, abandons, resigns himself again: "No certain decision (*keine sichere Entscheidung*) can be reached from the analysis of a single case like this" (16). *Second dismissal.* But what kind of singularity is this? Why is it important, and why does it lead to disqualification? Then, after another wave, another attempt to derive something from children's play, Freud renounces, abandons, resigns himself: "Nor shall we be helped in our hesitation between these two views by further considering children's play" (16). *Third dismissal.* Finally, the last words of the chapter. Freud has just invoked games and the imitative drives in art, an entire aesthetics oriented by the economic point of view. He concludes: "They are of no use for *our* purposes, since they presuppose the existence and dominance [*Herrschaft,* mastery] of the pleasure principle; they give no evidence of the operation [*Wirksamkeit,* being-at-work] of tendencies *beyond* the pleasure principle, that is, of tendencies more primitive (*ursprünglicher*) than it and independent of it" (17). *Fourth dismissal.* (Let us retain this code of mastery and of service or servitude; it will be less and less indifferent for us here. It can appear strange when in question are the relations between principles, and it is not *immediately* explained by the fact that a principle (*archē*) is both at the beginning and in command within language.) This is the conclusion of the chapter. We have not advanced one step, only steps for nothing on the path of the manifest investigation. It repeats itself in place. And yet, in this stamping, repetition insists, and if these determined repetitions, these contents, kinds, examples of repetition do not suffice to dethrone the PP, at least the repetitive form, the reproduction of the repetitive, reproductivity itself will have begun to work without saying anything, without saying anything other than itself silencing itself, somewhat in the way it is said on the last page that the death drives say nothing. They seem to accomplish their work without themselves being remarked, putting into their service the master himself who continues to speak out loud, the PP. In what can no longer even be called the "form" of the text, of a text without content, without thesis, without an object that is detachable from its detaching operation, in the *démarche* of *Beyond. . .* , this has come to pass in the same way, even before it is a question of the death drive in person. And even without one ever being able to speak of the death drive in person.

Such would be the de-monstration. Let us not abuse this facile play on words. The de-monstration makes its proof without showing [*montrer*], without offering any conclusion as evidence, without giving anything to carry away, without any available thesis. It proves according to another mode, but by marching to its *pas de démonstration*. It transforms, it transforms itself in its process rather than advancing the signifiable object of a discourse. It tends to fold into itself everything that it makes explicit, to bend it all to itself. The *pas de démonstration* is of that which remains in this *restance*.

Let us come back briefly to the content exhibited by this second chapter.

Among the new materials called upon at the end of the first chapter, among the questions which seem to resist the analytic explanation dominated by the PP, there are the so-called traumatic neuroses. The war has just given rise to great numbers of them. The explanation of the disorder by organic lesions has shown itself to be insufficient. The same syndrome (subjective ailments, for example melancholia or hypochondria motor symptoms, enfeeblement and disturbance of mental capacities), is seen elsewhere, without any mechanical violence. In order to define the trauma, one must then distinguish between *fear* (*Furcht*) and *anxiety*. The first is provoked by the *presence* of a *known* and *determined* dangerous object; the second is related to an *unknown, indeterminate* danger; as a preparation for danger, anxiety is more a protection against trauma; linked to repression, it appears at first to be an effect, but later, in *Inhibition, Symptom and Anxiety* Freud will say, *à propos* of Little Hans, that anxiety produces repression. Neither fear (before a *determined* and *known* danger) nor anxiety (before an *unknown* and *indeterminate* danger) causes trauma; only fright (*Schreck*)— which actually puts one face to face with an *unknown* and *determined* danger for which one was not prepared, and against which anxiety could not protect—can do so.

Now what does one observe in the case of the fright that induces the so-called traumatic neuroses? For example that dreams—the most trustworthy method of investigating deep mental processes, Freud says at this point—have the tendency to reproduce the traumatic accident, the situation of fright. Here, Freud pirouettes curiously. Since it is granted, or if it is granted, that the predominant tendency of the dream is wish-fulfillment, how is one to understand what a dream reproducing a situation of violent unpleasure might be? Except by granting that in this case the function of the dream has been subject to an alteration that turns it away from its aim, or again by evoking "mysterious masochistic trends." At this point Freud drops these two hypotheses (but why?), to pick them up later, in chapter IV, at the moment of the most unrestrained speculation. He will admit then that certain dreams are the exception to the rule of wish fulfillment, which itself can be constituted only late, when all of psychic life has submitted itself to a PP whose beyond is then envisaged. He also will admit (in chapter IV) the operation of masochism, and even, contrary to what he had held previously, of a primary masochism. But for the moment, Freud drops these hypotheses, which, from the point of view of the rhetoric of the investigation, might appear unjustified. In an arbitrary and decisive style, he proposes to leave there the obscure theme of the traumatic neurosis, and to study the way the psychic apparatus works "in one of its earliest *normal* activities—I mean in children's play" (14).

Thus, he is in a hurry to get to this point, at the risk of abandoning an unsolved problem that he will have to come back to later, and especially at the risk of having the demonstration of a beyond of the

PP not advance at all (which in effect will be the case). What is at stake in this haste, therefore, is something other, of another order. This *urgency* cannot be deciphered in the import of the demonstrative declaration, the manifest argumentation. The only justification for proceeding this way, in terms of classical logic or rhetoric, would be the following: one must first *come back* [*revenir*] to "normality" (but then why not begin with it?), and to the "earliest," most precocious normality in the child (but then why not begin with it?). When the normal and original processes will have been explored, the question of the traumatic neuroses will be taken up again. The problematic of the binding of energy then will have disengaged a more propitious space; the question of masochism also will be taken up again when the notions of topical agencies, of narcissism, and of the Ego will have been more fully elaborated.

Let us begin then with the "normal" and the "original": the child, the child in the typical and normal activity usually attributed to him, play. Apparently this is an activity entirely subject to the PP—and it will be shown that indeed it is, and entirely under the surveillance of a PP which (who) nevertheless permits it(him)self to be worked upon in silence by its (his) other—and as unaffected as possible by the second principle, the PR.

And then the argument of the spool. I am saying argument, the legendary argument, because I do not yet know what name to give it. It is neither a narrative, nor a story, nor a myth, nor a fiction. Nor is it the system of a theoretical demonstration. It is fragmentary, without conclusion, selective in that it gives something to be read, more an argument in the sense of a schema made of dotted lines, with ellipses everywhere.

And then what is given to be read here, this legend, is already too legendary, overburdened, obliterated. To give it a title is already to accredit the deposit or the consignment, that is, the investiture. As for the immense literature whose investment this legendary argument has attracted to itself, I would like to attempt a partial and naive reading, as naive and spontaneous as possible. As if I were interesting myself for the first time in the first time of the thing.

Initially, I remark this: this is the first time in this book that we have an apparently autobiographical, that is domestic, piece. The appearance is veiled, of course, but all the more significant. Of the experience Freud says he has been the witness. The motivated witness. It took place in his family, but he says nothing about this. Moreover we know this just as we know that the motivated witness was none other than the child's grandfather. ". . . I lived under the same roof as the child and his parents for some weeks . . ." (14). Even if an experiment⁴ could ever be limited to observation, the conditions as they are defined were not those of an observation. The speculator was not in a situation to observe. This can be concluded in advance from what he himself says in order to accredit the seriousness of his discourse. The protocols of experimentation, including sufficient observation ("It was more than a mere fleeting observation, for I lived under the same roof as the child and his parents for some weeks . . ."), guarantee the observation only by making of the observer a participant. But what was his part? Can he determine it himself? The question of objectivity has not the slightest pertinence here—nor does any epistemological question in canonic form—for the primary and sole reason that the experiment and its account will pretend to nothing less than a genealogy of objectivity in general. How, then, can they be subject to the authority of the tribunal whose institution they repeat? But inversely, by what right is a tribunal forbidden to judge the conditions of its establishment? and, what is more, forbidden to judge the account, by a motivated witness, a participant, of the so-called establishment? Especially if the involved witness gives all the signs of a very singular concern: for example, that of producing the institutions of his desire, of grafting his own genealogy onto it, of making the tribunal and the juridical tradition his inheritance, his delegation as a "movement," his legacy, his *own*.⁵ I will indeed refrain from insisting on the syntax of his *own*. Both so that you will not get lost right away, and because I suspect that he *himself* has a hard time recognizing *himself* among his own. Which would not be unrelated to the origin of objectivity. Or at least of this experiment, and the singular account we are given of it.

What is given is first filtered, selected, actively delimited. This discrimination is in *part* declared at the border. The speculator who does not yet say that he has truly begun to speculate (this will be on the fourth day, for there are seven chapters in this strangely composed book: we will come back to this), acknowledges this dicrimination. He has not sought "to include the whole field covered by these phenomena." He has only retained the characteristics pertinent to the economic point of view. Economic: this might already be translated, if one plays a bit (play is not yet forbidden in this

---

4. TN. Experiment in French is *expérience*, and has the cognate double meaning.
5. TN. "His own" here are *les siens*, which has the sense of one's closest relations. This is the syntax that is referred to in the next sentence.

phase of the origin of everything, of the present, the object, language, work, seriousness, etc.), but not gratuitously, as point of view of the *oikos,* law of the *oikos,* of the proper as the domestico-familial and even, by the same token, as we will verify, as the domestico-funerary. The grandfather speculator does not yet say that he has begun to speculate in broad daylight (the daylight will be for the fourth day, and yet), he will never say that he is the grandfather, but he knows that this is an open secret, *le secret de Polichinelle.* Secret for no one. The grandfather speculator justifies the accounts he is giving, and the discrimination he operates in them, in broad daylight. The justification is precisely the economic point of view. Which until now has been neglected by the "different theories of children's play," and which also constitutes the privileged point of view for *Beyond.* . . , for what he who here holds or renders the accounts is doing, to wit, writing. "These theories attempt to discover the motives which lead children to play, but they fail to bring into the foreground the *economic* motive, the consideration of the yield of pleasure (*Lustgewinn*) involved. Without wishing to include the whole field covered by these phenomena, I have been able, through a chance opportunity which presented itself, to throw some light upon the first game invented by himself (*das erste selbstgeschaffene Spiel*) that was played by a little boy of one and a half. It was more than a mere fleeting observation, for I lived under the same roof as the child and his parents for some weeks, and it was some time before I discovered the meaning of the puzzling activity which he constantly repeated" (14; sl. mod.).

He has profited from an opportunity, a chance, he says. About the possibility of this chance he says nothing. From the immense discourse which might inundate us here, but which is held back, let us retain only this: the opportune chance has as its propitious terrain neither the family (the narrow family, the small family in its nucleus of two generations: Freud would not have invoked the opportune chance if he had observed one of his nearest, son, daughter, wife, brother or sister, mother or father), nor the non-family (several weeks under the same roof is a familial experience). The field of the experiment is therefore of the type: family vacationcy.[6]

6. TN. *Vacance* in French is both vacation and the state of vacancy. Derrida is punning on the fact that Freud observed Ernst while on vacation with a grandson who is also somewhat outside the family, in that he has a different last name. And of course vacation is the time when the family is *away* (*fort*).

A supplement of generation always finds here reason to employ or deploy its desire.

From the first paragraph of the account on, a single trait to characterize the object of the observation, the action of the game: repetition, repeated repetition (*andauernd wiederholte Tun*). That is all. The other characteristic ("puzzling," *rätselhafte*) describes nothing, is void, but with a vacancy that calls out, and calls for, like every enigma, a narrative. It envelopes the narrative with its vacancy. It will be said: yes, there is another descriptive trait in this first paragraph. The game, of which the repetition of repetition consists, is a *selbstgeschaffene* game, that the child has produced or permitted to be produced by itself, spontaneously, and it is the first of this type. But none of all this (spontaneity, autoproduction, the originality of the first time) contributes any descriptive content that does not amount to the self-engendering of the repetition of itself. Hetero-tautology (definition of the Hegelian speculative) of repeated repetition, of self-repetition. In its pure form, this is what play will consist of.

It gives time. There is time.

The grandfather (who is more or less clandestinely the) speculator (although not yet) repeats the repetition of repetition. A repetition between pleasure and unpleasure, of a pleasure and an unpleasure whose (agreeable/disagreeable) content, however, is not added to repetition. It is not an additive but an internal determination, the object of an analytic predication. It is the possibility of this analytic predication which slowly will develop the hypothesis of a "drive" more original than the PP and independent of it (him). The PP will be overflowed, and is so in advance, by the speculation in which it (he) engages, and by its (his) own (intestine, proper, domestic, familial, sepulchral) repetition.

Now—fold back (reapply) what the grandfather, who still is hiding from himself that he is the grandfather, says here without hiding it from himself, reapply what he has said, by repeating it, about the repetition of the grandson, the eldest of his grandsons, Ernst. We will come back to this in detail. Fold back what he says his grandson is doing, with all the seriousness appropriate to an eldest grandson called Ernst (*the importance of being earnest*),[7] but not Ernst Freud, because the "movement" of this genealogy passes through

7. TN. In English in the original.

the daughter, the daughter wife who perpetuates the race only by risking the name, (I leave it to you to follow this factor[8] up to and including all of those women about whom it is difficult to know whether they have maintained the movement without the name or lost the movement in order to maintain, in that they have maintained, the name; I leave it to you to follow this up, suggesting only that you not forget, in the question of the analytic "movement" as the genealogy of the son-in-law, Judaic law), fold back, then, what he says his grandson is doing seriously on what he himself is doing by saying this, by writing *Beyond*. . . , by playing so seriously (by speculating) at writing *Beyond* . . . For the speculative heterotautology of the thing is that the beyond is *lodged* (more or less comfortably for this *vacance*) in the repetition of the repetition of the PP.

Fold back: *he* (the grandson *of* his grandfather, the grandfather *of* his grandson) compulsively repeats repetition without it ever advancing anywhere, not one step. He repeats an operation which consists in distancing, in pretending (*for a time,* for time: thereby writing and doing something that is not being talked about, and which must give good returns) to distance pleasure, the object or principle of pleasure, the object and/or the PP, here represented by the spool which is supposed to represent the mother (and/or, as we will see, supposed to represent the father, in the place of the son-in-law, the father as son-in-law, the other family name), in order to bring it (him) back indefatigably. It (he) pretends to distance the PP in order to bring it (him) back ceaselessly, in order to observe that itself it (himself he) brings itself (himself) back (for it (he) has in it(him)self the principial force of its (his) own economic return, to the house, his home, near it(him)self despite all the difference), and then to conclude: it (he) is still there, I am always there. *Da.* The PP maintains all its (his) authority, it (he) has never absented it(him)self.

One can see that the description to follow of the *fort/da* (on the side of the grandson of the house) and the description of the speculative game, so painstaking and so repetitive also, of the grandfather writing *Beyond* . . . overlap down to their details. They are applied to the same thing. I have just said: one can see that they overlap. Rigorously speaking, it is not an overlapping that is in question, nor a parallelism, nor an analogy, nor a coincidence. The

---

8. TN. Factor is *facteur,* which is also the mailman, as in *le facteur de la vérité.*

necessity that binds the two descriptions is of another kind: we would have difficulty naming it; but of course this is the principal stake for me in the selective and motivated reading that I am repeating here.

Who causes (himself) to come back [*revenir*], who makes who come back [*revenir*] according to this double *fort/da* which conjugates into the same genealogical (and conjugal) writing the narrated *and* the narrating of this narrative (the game of the "serious" grandson with the spool and the serious speculation of the grandfather with the PP)?

This simple question in suspense permits us to foresee: the description of Ernst's serious game, of the eldest grandson of the grandfather of psychoanalysis, *can no longer be read solely* as a theoretical argument, as a strictly theoretical speculation that tends to *conclude* with the repetition compulsion *or* the death drive *or* simply with the internal limit of the PP (for you know that Freud, no matter what has been said in order vehemently to affirm or contest it, *never concludes on this point*), but can also be read, according to the supplementary necessity of a *parergon,* as an autobiography of Freud. Not simply an autobiography confiding his life to his own more or less testamentary writing, but a more or less living description of his own writing, of his way of writing what he writes, most notably *Beyond* . . . In question is not only a folding back or a tautological reversal, as if the grandson, by offering him a mirror of his writing, were in advance dictating to him what (and where) he had to set down on paper; as if Freud were writing what his descendence prescribed that he write, in sum holding the first pen, the one that always passes from one hand to another; as if Freud were making a return to Freud through the connivance of a grandson who dictates from his spool and regularly brings it back, with all the seriousness of a grandson certain of a privileged contract with the grandfather. It is not only a question of this tautological mirror. The autobiography *of the writing* posits and deposits simultaneously, in the same movement, the psychoanalytic movement. It performs, and bets on that which gave its occasional chance. Which amounts [*revenant*] to saying in sum, (but who is speaking here?), I bet that this double *fort/da* cooperates, that this cooperation cooperates with initiating the psychoanalytic cause, with setting in motion the psychoanalytic "movement," even being it, even *being* it, in its being *itself,* in other words, in the singular structure of its tradition, I will say in the proper name of this "science," this "movement," this "theoretical practice" which maintains a relation to its history like none other. A relation to the history of its writing and the writing of its history also. If, in the unheard-of event of this cooperation, the unanalyzed remainder of an unconscious remains, if this remainder works, and from its alterity constructs the autobiography of this testamentary writing, then I wager that it will be transmitted blindly by the entire movement of the return to Freud. The remainder which in silence works upon the scene of this cooperation is doubtless illegible (now or forever, such is a *restance* in the sense in which I take it), but it defines the sole urgency of what remains to be done, is truly its only interest. Interest of a supplementary repetition? interest of a genetic transformation, of a renewal effectively displacing the essential? This alternative is lame, it is in advance made to limp by the *démarche* one can read here, in the bizarre document which concerns us.

I have never wanted to abuse the abyss, nor, above all, the *mise "en abyme."* [9] I do not believe in it very much, I am wary of the confidence that it inspires fundamentally, I believe it too representative either to go far enough or not to avoid the very thing toward which it allegedly rushes. I have attempted to explain myself on this question elsewhere. Onto what does a certain appearance of *mise "en abyme"* open—and close—here? This appearance is not immediately apparent, but it has had to play a more or less secret role in the fascination exerted on the reader by the small story of the spool, this anecdote that could have been taken as banal, impoverished, truncated, told in passing, and without the slightest import for the ongoing debate, if one is to believe the relater of the story himself. The story that is related, however, seems to put into *"abyme"* the writing of the relation (let us say the history, *Historie,* of the relation, and even the history, *Geschichte,* of the relater relating it). Therefore the related is related to the relating. The site of the legible, like the origin of writing, is carried away with itself. Nothing is any longer inscribable, and nothing is more inscribable [*rien n'est plus inscriptible*]. The notion of the repetition *"en abyme"* of Freud's writing has a relation of structural *mimesis* with the relation between the PP and "its" death drive. The latter, once again, is not opposed to the former, but hollows it out with a testamentary writing *"en abyme"* originally, at the origin of the origin.

Such will have been the "movement," in the irreducible novelty

9. TN. *En abyme* is the heraldic term for infinite reflection, e.g. the shield in the shield in the shield . . . Derrida has used this term frequently. The appearance of

of its repetition, in the absolutely singular event of its double relation.

If one wished to simplify the question, it could become, for example: how can an autobiographical writing, in the abyss of an unterminated self-analysis, give to a worldwide institution *its* birth? The birth of whom? of what? and how does the interruption or the limit of the self-analysis, cooperating with the *mise "en abyme"* rather than obstructing it, reproduce its mark in the institutional movement, the possibility of this remark from then on never ceasing to make little ones, multiplying the progeniture with its cleavages, conflicts, divisions, alliances, marriages, and regroupings?

Thus does an autobiography speculate, but instead of simplifying the question, one would have to take the process in reverse, and recharge its apparent premise: what is autobiography if everything that follows from it, and out of which we have just made a long sentence, then is possible? We do not yet know, and must not pretend to know. Even less as concerns a self-analysis. He who called himself the first, and therefore the only, one to have attempted, if not to have defined it, did not himself know, and this must be taken into account.

To go forward in my reading, I now need an essential possibility whose chance, if it can be put thus, will have been momentous: it is that every autobiographical speculation, to the extent that it constitutes a legacy and the institution of a movement without limit, must take into account, in its very performance, the mortality of the legatees. As soon as there is mortality, death can in principle overtake one at every instant. The speculator then can survive the legatee, and this possibility is inscribed in the structure of the legacy, and even within this limit of self-analysis whose system supports the writing somewhat like a grid. The precocious death, and therefore the mutism of the legatee who can do nothing about it: this is one of the possibilities of that which dictates and causes to write. Even the one who apparently will not have written, Socrates, or whose writing is supposed to double discourse, or above all listening, Freud and several others. One then gives oneself one's own movement, one inherits from oneself for all time, the provisions are sufficient so that the ghost at least can always step up to the cashier. He will only have to pronounce a name guaranteeing a signature. One thinks.

---

mise en abyme here is the overlap between what Freud says and what Freud does in *Beyond* . . . See also below, "Du Tout," n. 10.

This has happened to Freud, and to several others, but it does not suffice that the event occupy the world theater for its possibility to be illustrative of it.

And what follows is not only an example.

CONJOINT INTERPRETATIONS

There is a mute daughter. And more than another daughter who will have used the paternal credit in an abundant discourse of inheritance, it is she who will have said, perhaps, this is why it is up to your father to speak. Not only my father, but your father. This is Sophie, the daughter of Freud and mother of Ernst whose death soon will toll in the text. Very softly, in a strange note added afterward.

I am taking up my account exactly at the point at which I left it off, without skipping over anything. Freud sets the stage, and in his fashion defines the apparently principal character. He insists upon the normality of the child. This is the condition for justifiable experimentation. The child is a paradigm. He is therefore not at all precocious in his intellectual development. He is on good terms with everyone.

Particularly with his mother.

Following the schema defined above, I leave it to you to relate— to refold or to reapply—the content of the narrative to the scene of its writing, and to do so here for example, but elsewhere too, and this is only an example, by exchanging the places of the narrator and of the principal character, or principal couple, Ernst-Sophie, the third character (the father—the spouse—the son-in-law) never being far off, and occasionally even too close. In a classical narrative, the narrator, who allegedly observes, is not the author, granted. If it were not different in this case, taking into account that it does not present itself as a literary fiction, then we would have to, will have to reelaborate the distinction between the narrator's *I* and the author's *I* by adapting the distinction to a new "metapsychological" topic.

Thus he is apparently on good terms with everyone, especially his mother, since (or despite the fact that) he did not cry in her absence. She occasionally left him for hours. Why didn't he cry? Freud simultaneously seems to congratulate himself for the child's not crying and to be surprised, that is sorry, about it. Is this child fundamentally as normal as Freud himself imagines him to be? For in the very same sentence in which he attributes his grandson's excellent personality to the fact that he did not cry for his daughter (his mother) during such long absences, he adds "although" or "and yet." He was very attached to her, not only had she herself breast-fed him, she had cared for him with help from no one. But this small anomaly is quickly erased, and Freud leaves his "although" without consequences. Everything is fine, excellent child, *but.* Here is the *but:* this excellent child had a disturbing habit. One does not immediately get over Freud's imperturbable conclusion at the end of his fabulous description of the disturbing habit: "I eventually realized that it was a game." Here is the description, and I will interrupt my translation at moments.

"The child was not at all precocious in his intellectual development. At the age of one and a half he could say only a few comprehensible words; he could also make use of a number of sounds which expressed a meaning [*bedeutungsvolle Laute,* phonemes charged with meaning] intelligible to those around him. He was, however, on good terms with his parents and their one servant-girl, and tributes were paid to his being a 'good [*anständig,* easy, reasonable] boy.' He did not disturb his parents at night, he conscientiously obeyed orders not to touch certain things or go into certain rooms, and above all [*vor allem anderen,* before all else] he never cried when his mother left him for hours, although he was greatly attached to this mother, who had not only fed him herself but had also looked after him without any outside help" (p. 14).[10]

I interrupt my reading for a moment. The picture painted is apparently without a shadow, without a "but." There is indeed an "although" and a "however," but these are counterweights, internal compensations used to describe the balance: he was not at all precocious, even a bit slow, *but* he was on good terms with his parents; he did not cry when his mother left him, *but* he was attached to her, and for good reason. Am I alone in already hearing a restrained accusation? The excuse itself has left an archive within grammar; "however," "although." Freud cannot prevent himself from excusing his daughter's son. What, then, is he reproaching him for? But is he reproaching him for what he excuses him for, or for what excuses him? the secret fault for which he excuses him, or precisely

10. TN. Strachey's translation sometimes does not convey the nuances of the German original which are particularly important in this chapter. I will give a few instances of these discrepancies. All references to the German text are to the *Gesammelte Werke,* vol. 13 (London: Imago, 1940), and will be given as *GW* and a page number. Thus Strachey has translated Freud's "*wenn die Mütter es für Stunden verliess*" (*GW,* 13) as "when his mother left him for *a few* hours."

that which excuses him for his fault? and with whom would the prosecutor be identified in the mobile syntax of this trial?

The big "but" will arise immediately afterward and this time as a shadow in the picture, although the word "but" itself is not there. It is translated as "however" (*nun*): now, still it happens that, nonetheless it remains that, it must be said however, and nevertheless, fancy that, "This good little boy, however, had an occasional disturbing habit . . ."

What (despite everything) is satisfactory about this excellent child, that is, his normality, his calm, his ability to bear the absence of the beloved daughter (mother) without fear or tears—all of this makes some cost foreseeable. Everything is very constructed, very propped up, dominated by a system of rules and compensations, by an economy which in an instant will appear in the form of a disturbing habit. Which permits him to bear what his "good habits" might cost him. The child too is speculating. How does he pay (himself) for accepting the order not to touch certain things? How does the PP negotiate between good and bad habits? The grandfather, the father of the daughter and mother, actively selects the traits of the description. I see him rushing and worried, like a dramatist or director who has a part in the play. Staging it, he has to act with *dispatch:* to control everything, have everything in order, before going off to change for his part. This is translated by a peremptory authoritarianism, unexplained decisions, interrupted speeches, unanswered questions. The elements of the *mise en scène* have been put in place: an original normality in relation to the good breast, an economic principle requiring that the removal of the breast (so well dominated, so well removed from its removal) be overpaid by a supplementary pleasure, and also requiring that a bad habit reimburse, eventually with profit, good habits, for example the orders not to touch certain things . . . The *mise en scène* hastens on, the actor-dramatist-producer will have done everything himself, he also knocks the three or four times,[11] the curtain is about to rise. But we do not know if it rises on the scene or in the scene. Before the entrance of any character, there is a curtained bed. All the comings and goings, essentially, will have to pass before the curtain.

I myself will not open this curtain—I leave this to you—onto all the others, the words and things (curtains, canvases, veils, hymens, umbrellas, etc.) with which I have concerned myself for so long.

---

11. TN. Referring to the traditional knocks that precede the raising of the curtain in French theater.

One could attempt to relate all these fabrics to one another, according to the same law. I have neither the time nor the taste for this task, which can be accomplished by itself or done without. Rather, here is Freud's curtain along with the strings pulled by the grandfather.

"This good little boy, however, had an occasional disturbing habit of taking any small objects he could get hold of and throwing them away from him into a corner, under the bed, and so on, so that hunting for his toys (*Spielzeuge,* playthings) and picking them up [*zusammensuchen,* to search in order to bring together, to reassemble] was often not easy work" (p. 14).[12]

The work is for the parents, but also for the child who expects it from them. And the work consists of reassembling, of searching in order to bring together, of reuniting to order to *give back.* This is what the grandfather calls work, an often difficult work. In return, he will call play the dispersion which sends far away (the operation of distantiation), and will call playthings the collection of manipulated objects. The entire process is itself divided; there is a division which is not the division of labor, but the division between play and work: the child *plays* at throwing away his "toys," and the parents *work* at reassembling them, which is often not easy. As if in this phase of the operation the parents were not playing and the child were not working. He is completely excused from working. Who would dream of accusing him of this? But the work is not always easy, and one's breath grows heavy. Why does he disperse, why does he send far away everything he has at hand, and who and what?

The spool has not yet made its appearance. In a sense, it will be only an example of the process Freud has just described. But it will be an exemplary example, yielding a supplementary and decisive "observation" for the interpretation. In the exemplary example the child throws away and brings back to himself, disperses and reassembles, gives and takes back by himself: he reassembles the reassembling *and* the dispersion, the multiplicity of agents, work and play, into a single agent, apparently, and into a single object. This is what the grandfather will understand as "a game," at the moment when all the strings are brought back together, held in one hand, dispensing with the parents, with their work or play which consisted in straightening up the room.

---

12. TN. The last three words are "*keine leichte Arbeit*" (*GW,* 13) which Strachey has given as "quite a business."

The spool has not yet made its appearance. Until now *Spielzeug* has designated only an aggregate, the set of toys, the unity of a multiplicity that can be scattered, that the parents' work at reassembling, precisely, and that the grandfather here reassembles in one word. This collective unity is the apparatus of a game that can *dislocate* itself: can change its place and fragment or disperse itself. The word for things as a set, in this theory of the set, is *Zeug*, the instrument, the tool, the product, the "thing," and, according to the same semantic transition as in French or in English, the penis. I am not commenting on what Freud says, I am not saying that Freud is saying: by dispersing his objects or playthings into the distance the child not only separates himself from his mother (as will be said further on, and even from his father), but also, and primarily, from the supplementary complex constituted by the maternal breast and his own penis, allowing the parents, but not for long, to reassemble, to cooperate in order to reassemble, to reassemble themselves, but not for long, in order to reassemble what he wants to dissociate, send away, separate, but not for long. If he separates himself from his *Spielzeug* as if from himself and with the aim of allowing himself to be reassembled, it is that he himself is also an aggregate whose reassemblage can yield an entire combinatorial of sets. All those who play or work at reassembling are participants. I am not saying that Freud says this. But he will say, in one of the two footnotes I have mentioned, that it is indeed himself or his image that the child "plays" at making appear-disappear also. He is part of his *Spielzeug*.

The spool has not yet made its appearance. Here it is, again preceded by an interpretive anticipation: "As he did this [throwing away his entire *Spielzeug*] he gave vent to a loud, long-drawn-out 'o-o-o-o,' accompanied by an expression of interest and satisfaction, which according to the common judgment [13] of his mother and the writer of the present account [the daughter and the father, the mother and the grandfather are here conjoined in the same speculation] was not a mere interjection but represented the German word '*fort*' [gone, far away]. I eventually realized that it was a game and that the only use he made of any of his toys [*Spielsachen*] was to play 'gone' [*fortsein*] with them" (pp. 14–15).

Freud's intervention (I am not saying the grandfather's intervention, but the intervention of whoever recounts what the observer

---

13. TN. Freud's phrase (*GW*, 13) is "*übereinstimmenden Urteil*," which Strachey has given as "were agreed in thinking."

experienced, whoever finally realized that "it was a game": there are at least three instances of the same "subject," the narrator-speculator, the observer, the grandfather, the latter never being openly identified with the two others by the two others, etc.)— Freud's intervention deserves to give us pause. He recounts that as an observer he has also interpreted. And has named. Now, what does he call a game, rather than work, the work itself consisting of reassembling? Well, paradoxically, he calls a game the operation which consists in not playing with one's toys: he did not employ them, he did not use (benütze) his toys, he says, he did not make them useful, utensiles, except by playing at their being gone. The "game" thus consists in not playing with one's toys, but in making them useful for another function, to wit, being-gone. Such would be the deviation or teleological finality of this game. But a teleology, a finality of distantiation with its sights set on what, on whom? For what and for whom, this utilization of that which is usually given as gratuitous or useless, that is, play? What does this non-gratuitousness yield? And for whom? Perhaps not a single profit, nor even any profit at all, and perhaps not for a single speculative agency. There is the teleology of the interpreted operation and there is the teleology of the interpretation. And the interpreters are many: the grandfather, the so-called observer, the speculator, and the father of psychoanalysis, here the narrator, and then, and then, conjoined to each of these instances, she whose judgment would have concurred, in coinciding fashion (übereinstimmenden Urteil) to the extent of being covered by it, with the father's interpretation.

This coincidence which conjoins the father and the daughter in the interpretation of the o-o-o-o as fort is odd for more than one reason. It is difficult to imagine the scene in detail, or even to accredit its existence and everything recounted within it. But it remains that Freud reports it: the mother and the observer are somehow reassembled in order to make the same judgment on the meaning of what their son and grandson articulated before, that is, for them. Try to figure out where the induction of such an identity, such an identification of point of view, comes from. But we can be sure that wherever it does come from, it has come round, and has bound the three characters in what must more than ever be called the "same" speculation. They have secretly named the "same" thing. In what language? Freud asks himself no questions about the language into which he translates the o/a. To grant it a semantic content bound to a determined language (a given opposition of German words) and from there a semantic content which surpasses language (the interpretation of the child's behavior), is an operation impossible without multiple and complex theoretical protocols. One might suspect that the o/a is not limited to a simple formal opposition of values whose content could vary without being problematical. If this variation is *limited* (which is what must be concluded from the fact—if, at least, one is interested in it—that the father, the daughter, and the mother find themselves reunited in the same semantic reading), then one can put forward the following hypothesis: there is some proper noun beneath all this, whether one takes the proper noun in the figurative sense (any signified whose signifier cannot vary or be translated into another signifier without a loss of signification induces a proper noun effect), or in the so-called literal, "proper" sense. I leave these hypotheses open, but what seems certain to me is the necessity of formulating hypotheses on the conjoining interpretations of o-o-o-o, that is, o/a, in whatever language (be it natural, universal, or formal), the interpretations conjoining the father and the daughter, the grandfather and the mother.

And the grandson and the son: for the two preceding generations have sought to be together, have been, says one of the generations, conscious of being together in order to understand in their common verdict what their child intended to have them understand, and intended that they understand together. There is nothing hypothetical or audacious about saying this; it is an analytical reading of what Freud's text says explicitly. But we know now what a tautology can bring back by gushing over.

And what if this were what the son, I mean the grandson, were after, what if this superimposing coincidence in the judgment (*Urteil*) were what he believed without knowing it, without wanting it? The father is absent. He is far away. That is, since one must always specify, one of the two fathers, the father of a little boy so serious that his play consists in not playing with his toys but in distancing them, playing only at their distantiation. In order to make his play useful for himself. As for the father of Sophie and of psychoanalysis, he is still there. Who is speculating?

The spool still has not yet made its appearance. Here it is. To send it off, the child was not lacking in *address*.[14]

It follows immediately. "One day I made an observation which

14. TN. *GW*, 13. The pun on *address* exists in German as well (*Geschick*), and is crucial to Derrida's analysis of this passage.

confirmed my view. The child had a wooden spool[15] (*Holzspule*) with a piece of string (*Bindfaden*) tied round it. It never occurred to him to pull it along the floor behind him, for instance, and play at its being a carriage, but rather he held the spool by the string and with great address (*Geschick*) threw it over the edge of his little curtained bed (or veiled bed, *verhängten Bettchens*), so that it disappeared into it, at the same time uttering his expressive (*bedeutungsvolle*, meaningful) 'o-o-o-o.' He then pulled the spool out of the bed again by the string and hailed its appearance with a joyful '*Da*' (*there*). This, then, was the complete game (*Komplette spiel*)—disappearance and return (*Verschwinden und Wiederkommen*). As a rule one only witnessed its first act, which was repeated untiringly as a game in itself, though there is no doubt that the greater pleasure was attached to the second act."

And with this word a call for something. A call for a footnote that I will read presently.

"This, then," says Freud, "was the complete game." Which immediately implies: this, then, is the complete observation, and the complete interpretation of this game. Nothing is missing, the game is saturable and saturated. If the completion were obvious and certain, would Freud insist upon it, remark upon it as if he quickly had to close, conclude, enframe? One suspects an incompletion (in the object, or in its description) all the more in that: (1) this is the scene of an interminably repeated supplementation, as if it never finished completing itself, etc; and (2) there is something like an axiom of incompletion in the structure of the scene of writing. This is due at very least to the position of the speculator as a motivated observer. Even if completion were possible, it could neither appear for such an "observer," nor be declared as such by him.

But these are generalities. They designate only the formal conditions of a determined incompletion, the signifying absence of a particularly pertinent given trait. Which may be on the side of the scene described, or on the side of the description, or in the unconscious which binds the one to the other, their unconscious that is shared, inherited, telecommunicated according to the same teleology.

It speculates on the return, it is completed in coming back: the

---

15. TN. *GW*, 13. I have consistently modifed Strachey's "reel" to read "spool" (*Spule*). The "spool" in French is *bobine*, which has an additional slang sense of "face" or "head." This play on *bobine* will be indicated in the text.

greater pleasure, he says, although this spectacle is less directly seen, is the *Wiederkommen,* the re-turn. And yet, that which thereby again becomes a revenant must, for the game to be complete, be thrown away again, indefatigably. It speculates on the basis of the return, on the departure of that which owes it to itself to return. On what has once more just again left or just left again [*A ce qui revient de partir ou vient de repartir*].

It is complete, he says.

And yet: he regrets that it does not roll along as it should roll along. As it should have rolled along if he, himself, had been holding the string.

Or all the strings. How would he, himself, have played with the kind of yo-yo that is thrown in front of or beneath oneself, and which returns as if by itself, on its own, by rolling itself up anew? Which comes back as if by itself, if it has been sent off correctly? One must know how to throw it in order *to make* it return by itself, in other words in order *to let* it return. How would the speculator himself have played? How would he have rolled the thing, made it roll, let it roll? How would he have manipulated this lasso? Of what would his address consist?

He seems surprised, adding to this surprise a confident regret that the good little boy never seemed to have the idea of pulling the spool behind him and playing at its being a carriage: or rather at its being a wagon (*Wagen*), a train. It is as if one could wager (*wagen* again) that the speculator (whose contrary preference, that is, railway phobia, *Eisenbahn,* is well enough known to put us on the track) would himself have played choo-choo with one of these "small objects" (*kleinen Gegenstände*). Here then is the first problem, the first perplexity of the father of the object or the grandfather of the subject, of the father of the daughter (mother: Ernst's object) or the grandfather of the little boy (Ernst as the "subject" of the *fort/da*): but why doesn't he play train or carriage? Wouldn't that be more normal? And why doesn't he play carriage by pulling the thing behind him? For the thing is a vehicle in convoy.[16] If he had been playing in his grandson's place (and therefore playing with his daughter, since the spool replaces her, as he will say in the next paragraph, or at least, following its/his thread, is but a trait or train leading to her, in order to come just to depart from her again), the

16. TN. To indicate the impossibility of translating Derrida's sentence here, and the long commentary to which it could give rise, I will simply cite it: "*Car la chose est un véhicule en translation.*"

(grand)father would have played carriage [I must be pardoned all
these parentheses, the (grand)father or the daughter (mother), they
are necessary in order to mark the syntax in erasure of the genealogical scene, the occupation of all the places and the ultimate
mainspring of what I began by calling the athesis of *Beyond* . . .]:
and since the game is serious, this would have been more serious,
says he, quite seriously. Too bad that the idea never occurred to him
(for instance!) to pull the spool behind him on the floor, and thus to
play carriage with it: *Es fiel ihm nie ein, sie zum Beispiel am Boden
hinter sich herzuziehen, also Wagen mit ihr zu spielen, sondern es
warf* . . . This would have been more serious, but the idea never
occurred to Ernst. Instead of playing on the floor (*am Boden*), he
insisted on putting the bed into the game, into play, on playing with
the thing over the bed, and also in the bed. Not in the bed as the
place where the child himself would be, for contrary to what the
text and the translation have often led many to believe, (and one
would have to ask why), he is not in the bed at the moment when he
throws the spool, it appears. He throws it from outside the bed over
its edge, over the veils or curtains that surround its edge (*Rand*),
from the other side, which quite simply might be into the sheets.
And in any event, it is from "out of the bed" (*zog* . . . *aus dem Bett
heraus*) that he pulls back the vehicle in order to make it come
back: *da.* The bed, then, is *fort,* which perhaps contravenes all desire; but perhaps not *fort* enough for the (grand)father who might
have wished that Ernst had played more seriously on the floor (*am
Boden*) without bothering himself with the bed. But for both of
them, the distancing of the bed is worked upon by the *da* which
divides it: too much or not enough. For the one or for the other.

What is to play train, for the (grand)father? To speculate: it
would be never to throw the thing (but does the child ever throw it
without its being attached to a string?), that is, to keep it at a distance continuously, but always at the same distance, the length of
the string remaining constant, making (letting) the thing displace
itself at the same time, and in the same rhythm, as oneself. This
trained train does not even have to come back [*revenir*], it does not
really leave. It has barely come to leave when it is going to come
back.

It is going. This is what would go for the (grand)father-specula-
tor. Which enables him to be certain of the measure of the thing
only by depriving himself of an extra pleasure, the very pleasure
that he describes as the principal one for Ernst, to wit, the second
act, the return. He deprives himself of this pleasure in order to

spare himself the pain or the risk of the bet. And in order not to put
the desired bed into play.

To play carriage also indeed would be "to pull" the invested object "behind him" (*hinter sich herzuziehen*), to keep the locomotive
well in hand and to see the thing only by turning around. One does
not have it before one. As does Eurydice or the analyst. For the speculator (the analyst) is obviously the first analysand. The analysand-
locomotive for whom the law of listening is substituted for the law
of looking.

It is not for us to judge the normality of the child's choice, and
we know about it only according to what the ascendant reports. But
we might find the ascendant's inclination [17] strange. Everything occurs around a bed, and has never occurred except around a bed surrounded with veils or curtains: what is called a "skirted crib." If
the child were indeed outside the bed but near it, occupied with it,
which his grandfather seems to reproach him for, then these curtains, these veils, this cloth, this "skirt" that hides the bars, form
the inner chamber of the *fort/da,* the double screen which divides it
inside itself, dividing its internal and its external aspects, but dividing it only by reassembling it with itself, sticking it to itself doubly,
fort:da. I am calling this, once more, and necessarily, the *hymen* [18]
of the *fort:da.* The veil of this "skirt" is the interest of the bed and
the *fort:da* of all these generations. I will not venture saying: it is
Sophie. How could Ernst have seriously played carriage using a
veiled bed, all the while pulling the vehicle behind him? One asks
oneself. Perhaps quite simply it was his *duty* not to do anything
with the object (obstacle, screen, mediation) named bed, or edge of
the bed, or limen or hymen, his duty to stay off to one side completely, and thereby to leave the place free, or to stay inside completely (as is often believed), which would have set loose less laborious identifications. But in order to have the *Spielzeug* or "small
object" behind onself, with or without bed, in order to have the toy
represent the daughter (mother) or the father [the son-in-law, as will

17. TN. "*. . . la pente de l'ascendant.*" An elaborate play on words, since
pente also has the sense of a cloth that goes over the canopy of a bed. *Ascendant,* of
course, is the opposite of *descendant,* but has a resonance of *ascent,* again relating it
to *pente* ("inclination" in both senses).
18. TN. *Hymen* is irreducibly both virginity and consummation (marriage), related here to the *conjoined* interpretations of the father and the daughter, grandfather
and mother, of what takes place around the bed. See also "The Double Session," in
Dissemination.

be envisaged further on, and the (grand)father's syntax easily skips the parenthesis of a generation with a step to the side], one must have ideas. Follow the comings and goings of all these *fils* (strings/sons). The grandfather regrets that his grandson did not have them, these (wise or foolish) ideas of a game without a bed, unless it be the idea of a bed without a curtain, which does not mean without hymen. He regrets that his grandson has not had them, but he himself has not failed to have them. He even considers them natural ideas, and this is what would better complete the description, if not the game. By the same token, if one might say, he regrets that his grandson has indeed had the ideas that he has had for himself. For if he has had them for himself, it is indeed that his grandson has not failed to have them for him also.

(This entire syntax is made possible by the graphics of the margin or the hymen, of the border and the step, such as was remarked elsewhere. I will not exploit it here.)

For, in the end, was this bed with so necessary and so undecidable a border a couch? Not yet, despite all the Orphism of a speculation. And yet.

What the grand(father-)speculator calls the complete game, thus, would be the game in its two phases, in the duality, the redoubled duality of its phases: disappearance/re-turn, absence/re-presentation. And what binds the game to itself is the *re-* of the return, the additional turn of repetition and re-appearance. He insists upon the fact that the greatest quantity of pleasure is in the second phase, in the *re*-turn which orients the whole, and without which nothing would come. *Revenance,* that is, returning, orders the entire teleology. Which permits one to anticipate that this operation, in its so-called complete unity, will be entirely handed over to the authority of the PP. Far from being checked by repetition, the PP also seeks to recall itself in the repetition of appearing, of presence, of representation, and, as we shall see, via a repetition that is mastered, that verifies and confirms the mastery in which it consists (which is also that of the PP). The mastery of the PP would be none other than mastery in general: there is not a *Herrschaft* of the PP, there is *Herrschaft* which is distanced from itself only in order to reappropriate itself: a tauto-teleology which nevertheless makes or lets the other return in its domestic specter. Which thus can be foreseen. What will return [*reviendra*], in having already come, but not in order to contradict the PP, nor to oppose itself to the PP, but to mine the PP as its proper stranger, to hollow it into an abyss from the vantage of an origin more original than it and independent of it, older than it within it, will not be, under the name of the death drive or the repetition compulsion, an *other master* or a *counter-master,* but something other than mastery, something completely other. In order to be something completely other, it will have to not oppose itself, will have to not enter into a dialectical relation with the master (life, the PP *as* life, the living PP, the PP alive). It will have to not engage a dialectic of master and slave, for example. This nonmastery equally will have to not enter into a dialectical relation with death, for example, in order to become, as in speculative idealism, the "true master."

I am indeed saying the PP as mastery in general. At the point where we are now, the allegedly "complete game" no longer concerns any given object in its determination, for example the spool or what it supplements. In question is the *re-* in general, the returned or the returning [*le revenu ou le revenant*]—to return [*revenir*] in general. In question is the repetition of the couple disappearance/reappearance, not only reappearance as a moment of the couple, but the reappearance of the couple which must return. One must make return the repetition of that which returns, and must do so on the basis of its returning. Which, therefore, is no longer simply this or that, such and such an object which must depart/return, or which departs-in-order-to-return, but is departure-returning itself, in other words the presentation of itself of representation, the return to-itself of returning. No longer an object which would re-present itself, but re-presentation, the return of itself of the return, the return to itself of the return. This is the source of the greatest pleasure, and the accomplishment of the "complete game," he says: that is, that the re-turning re-turns, that the re-turn is not only of an object but of itself, or that it is its own object, that what causes to return itself returns to itself. This is indeed what happens, and happens without the object itself re-become the subject of the *fort/da,* the disappearance-reappearance of itself, the object reappropriated from itself: the reappearance, one can say in French, of one's own "*bobine*" [see note 15], with all the strings in hand. This is how we fall upon the first of the two footnotes. It is called for by the "second act" to which "the greater pleasure" is unquestionably attached. What does the note say? That the child plays the utility of the *fort/da* with something that is no longer an object-object, a supplementary spool supplementing something else, but with a supplementary spool of the supplementary spool, with his own "*bobine*" with himself as object-subject within the mirror/without the mirror. Thus: "A further observation subsequently confirmed this interpretation fully. One day the child's mother had been away for several hours and on her return (*Wiederkommen*) was met with the words, 'Baby o-o-o-o!' which was at first incomprehensible. It soon turned out, however (*Es ergab sich aber bald*), that during this long period of solitude (*Alleinsein*), the child had found a method of making *himself* disappear (*verschwinden zu lassen*). He had discovered his reflection in a full-length mirror which did not quite reach to the ground, so that by crouching down he could make his mirror-image '*fort*' [gone away] [11] (p. 15 n. 1).

This time, one no longer knows at what moment it came to pass, led one to think (*Es ergab sich* . . .), or for whom. For the grandfather-observer still present in the absence of his daughter (mother)? Upon the return of the latter, and conjointly again? Did the "observer" still need her to be there in order to reassure himself of this conjunction? Does he not make her return himself without needing her to be there in order to have her at his side? And what if the child knew this without needing to have his knowledge?

Therefore he is playing at giving himself the force of his disappearance, of his "*fort*" in the absence of his mother, in his own absence. A capitalized pleasure which does without what it needs, an ideal capitalization, capitalization itself: by idealization. One provides oneself (and dispenses with) the head of what one needs by doing without it in order to have it. A capitalized pleasure: the child identifies himself with the mother since he disappears as she does, and makes her return with himself, by making himself return without making anything but himself, her in himself, return. All the while remaining, as close as possible, at the side of the PP which (who) never absents itself (himself), and thus provides (for himself) the greatest pleasure. And the enjoyment is coupled. He makes himself disappear, he masters himself symbolically, he plays with the dummy, the dead man, as if with himself, and he makes himself reappear henceforth without a mirror, in his disappearance itself, maintaining himself like his mother at the other end of the line. He speaks *to himself* telephonically, he calls himself, recalls himself, "spontaneously" affects himself with his presence-absence in the presence-absence of his mother. He makes himself *re-*. Always according to the law of the PP. In the grand speculation of a PP which (who) never seems to absent itself-(himself) from itself-(himself). Or from anyone else. The telephonic or telescripted recall provides the "movement" by contracting itself, by signing a contract with itself.

Let us mark a pause after this first footnote.

For in having been played out for all ages, all of this has just begun.

''LA SÉANCE CONTINUE''

(RETURN TO SENDER, THE TELEGRAM, AND THE GENERATION OF THE SONS-IN-LAW)

The serious play of the *fort/da* couples absence and presence in the *re-* of returning [*revenir*]. It overlaps them, it institutes repetition as their relation, relating them the one and the other, the one to the other, the one over or under the other. Thereby it plays with itself *usefully,* as if with its own object. Thus is confirmed the abyssal "overlapping" that I proposed above: of the object or the content of *Beyond.* . . , of what Freud is supposedly writing, describing, analyzing, questioning, treating, etc., and, on the other hand, the system of his writing gestures, the scene of writing that he is playing or that plays itself. With him, without him, by him, or all at once. This is the same "complete game" of the *fort/da.* Freud does with (without) the object of his text exactly what Ernst does with (without) his spool. And if the game is called complete on one side and the other, we have to envisage an eminently symbolic completion which itself would be formed by these two completions, and which therefore would be incomplete in each of its pieces, and consequently would be completely incomplete when the two incompletions, related and joined the one to the other, start to multiply themselves, supplementing each other without completing each other. Let us admit that Freud is writing. He writes that he is writing, he describes what he is describing, but this is also what he is doing, he does what he is describing, to wit, what Ernst is doing: *fort/da* with his spool [*bobine*]. And each time that one says *to do,* one must specify: *to allow* to do (*lassen*). Freud does not do *fort/da,* indefatigably, with the object that the PP is. He does it with himself, he recalls himself. Following a detour of the *télé,*[19] this time an entire network. Just as Ernst, in recalling the object (mother, thing, whatever) to himself, immediately comes *himself* to recall *himself*

---

19. TN. *Télé* is the French equivalent of the American expression TV—the English "telly" is almost perfect here—as well as the prefix to "telecommunication," communication at a distance, from the Greek *tele* (distant, *loin, fort*). "Network" at the end of this sentence translates *chaîne,* which has the senses of chain and of network, as in a television or radio station, one of the télé-'s byways or detours.

in an immediately supplementary operation, so the speculating grandfather, in describing or recalling this or that, recalls *himself.* And thereby makes what is called his text, enters into a contract with himself in order to hold onto all the strings/sons [*fils*] of the descendance. No less than of the ascendance. An *incontestable* ascendance. The incontestable is also that which needs no witness. And which, nevertheless, cannot not be granted its rights: no counter-testimony appears to have any weight before this teleological auto-institution. The net [*filet*] is in place, and one pulls on a string [*fil*] only by getting one's hand, foot, or the rest, caught. It is a lasso or a lace.[20] Freud has not positioned it. Let us say that he has known how to get caught in it. But nothing has been said yet, nothing is known about this knowledge, for he himself has been caught in advance by the catching. He could not have or foresee this knowledge entirely, such was the condition for the overlapping.

Initially this is imprinted in an absolutely formal and general way. In a kind of *a priori.* The scene of the *fort/da,* whatever its exemplary content, is always in the process of describing in advance, as a deferred overlapping, the scene of its own description. The writing of a *fort/da* is always a *fort/da,* and the PP and *its* death drive are to be sought in the exhausting of this abyss. It is an abyss of more than one generation, as is also said of computers. And is so, as I said, in an absolutely formal and general way, in a kind of *a priori,* but the *a priori* of an aftereffect. In effect, once the objects can substitute for each other to the point of laying bare the substitutive structure itself, the formal structure yields itself to reading: what is going on no longer concerns a distancing rendering this or that absent, and then a rapprochement rendering this or that into presence; what is going on concerns rather the distancing of the distant and the nearness of the near, the absence of the absent or the presence of the present. But the distancing is not distant, nor the nearness near, nor the absence absent or the presence present. The *fortsein* of which Freud is speaking is not any more *fort* than *Dasein* is *da.* Whence it follows, (for this is not immediately the same thing), that by virtue of the *Entfernung* and the *pas* in question elsewhere, the *fort* is not any more distant than the *da* is here. An overlap without equivalence: *fort:da.*

Freud recalls himself. His memories and himself. As Ernst does with the glass and without the glass. But his speculative writing

20. Concerning the double stricture of the *lace* in relation to the *fort:da,* I must refer to *Glas* (Paris: Galilee, 1974), and to "*Restitutions—de la vérité en pointure*" in *La vérité en peinture* (Paris: Flammarion, 1978).

also recalls itself, something else and itself. And specularity above all is not, as is often believed, simply reappropriation. No more than the *da*.

The speculator himself recalls himself. He describes what he is doing. Without doing so *explicitly,* of course, and everything I am describing here can do without a thoroughly auto-analytic calculation, whence the interest and necessity of the thing. It speculates without the calculation itself analyzing itself, and from one generation to another.

He recalls *himself.* Who and what? Who? himself, of course. But we cannot know if this "himself" can say "myself"; and, even if it did say "myself," which me then would come to speak. The *fort:da* already would suffice to deprive us of any certainty on this subject. This is why, if a recourse, and a massive recourse, to the autobiographical is necessary here, the recourse must be of a new kind. This text is autobiographical, but in a completely different way than has been believed up to now. First of all, the autobiographical does not overlap the auto-analytical without limit. Next, it demands a reconsideration of the entire *topos* of the *autos.* Finally, far from entrusting us to our familiar knowledge of what autobiography means, it institutes, with its own strange contract, a new theoretical and practical charter for any possible autobiography.

Beyond. . . , therefore, is not an *example* of what is allegedly already known under the name of autobiography. It writes autobiography, and one cannot conclude from the fact that in it an "author" recounts a bit of his life that the document is without value as truth, science, or philosophy. A "domain" is opened in which the inscription, as it is said, of a subject in his text, (so many notions to be reelaborated), is also the condition for the pertinence and performance of a text, of what the text "is worth" beyond what is called an empirical subjectivity, supposing that such a thing exists as soon as it speaks, writes, and substitutes one object for another, substitutes and adds itself as an object to another, in a word, as soon as it *supplements.* The notion of truth is quite incapable of accounting for this performance.

Autobiography, then, is not a previously opened space within which the speculating grandfather tells a story, a given story about what has happened to him in his life. What he recounts is autobiography. The *fort:da* in question here, as a particular story, is an autobiography which instructs: every autobiography is the departure/return of a *fort/da,* for example this one. Which one? The *fort/da* of Ernst? Of his mother conjoined with his grandfather in the read-

ing of his own *fort/da?* Of *her* father, in other words of *his* grandfather? Of the great speculator? Of the father of psychoanalysis? Of
the author of *Beyond.* . . ? But what access is there to the latter
without a spectral analysis of all the others?

Elliptically, lacking more time, I will say that the graphics, the
autobiographics of *Beyond.* . . , of the word *beyond* (*jenseits* in
general, the step beyond in general), imprints a prescription upon
the *fort:da,* that of the overlapping by means of which proximity
distances itself in *abyme* (*Ent-fernung*). The death drive is *there,* in
the PP, which is a question of a *fort:da.*

Freud, it will be said, recalls himself. Who? What? Trivially,
first of all, he recalls himself, he remembers himself. He tells himself and tells us an incident which remains in his memory, in his
conscious memory. The remembrance of a scene, which is really
multiple, consisting as it does of repetitions, a scene that happened
to another, to two others (one male, one female), but who are his
daughter and his grandson. His eldest grandson, let us not forget,
but who does not bear the name of the maternal grandfather. He
says that he has been the regular, durable, trustworthy "observer"
of this scene. He will have been a particularly motivated, present,
intervening observer. Under a roof which although not necessarily
his, nor simply a roof in common, nevertheless belongs to *his own,*
almost, with an almost that perhaps prevents the economy of the
operation from closing itself, and therefore conditions the operation. Under what headings can one say that in recalling what happens (on) to the subject (of) Ernst he is recalling himself, recalling
that it happened to him? Under several interlaced, serial headings,
in the "same" chain of writing.

First, he recalls to himself that Ernst recalls (to himself) his
mother: he recalls Sophie. He recalls to himself that Ernst recalls
his daughter to himself in recalling his mother to himself. The
equivocal syntax of the possessive here is not merely an artifact of
grammar. Ernst and his grandfather are in a genealogical situation
such that the most possessive of the two can always be relayed by
the other. Whence the possibility immediately opened by this scene
of a permutation both of places and of what indeed must be understood as genitives: the mother of the one is not only the daughter of
the other, she is also his mother; the daughter of the one is not only
the mother of the other, she is also his daughter, etc. Even at the
moment when the scene, if this can be said, took place, and even
before Freud undertook to relate it, he was in a situation to identify
himself, as is all too readily said, with his grandson, and, playing

both colors, to recall his mother in recalling his daughter. This identification between the grandfather and the grandson is attested to as an ordinary privilege, but, and we will soon have more than one proof of this, it could be particularly spectacular for the forebear of psychoanalysis.

I have just said: "Already even at the moment when the scene, if this can be said, took place." And I add *a fortiori* at the moment of desiring to write about it, or of sending oneself a letter about it, so that the letter makes its return after having instituted its postal relay, which is the very thing that makes it possible for a letter *not* to arrive at its destination, and that makes this possibility-of-never-arriving divide the structure of the letter from the outset. Because (for example) there would be neither postal relay nor analytic movement if the place of the letter were not divisible and if a letter always arrived at its destination. I am adding *a fortiori*, but let it be understood that the *a fortiori* was prescribed in the supplementary graphics of the overlapped taking place of what too hastily would be called the primary scene.

The *a fortiori* of the *a priori* makes itself (a bit more) legible in the second note of which I spoke above. It was written afterward, and recalls that Sophie is dead: the daughter (mother) recalled by the child died soon after. Was in a completely different way recalled elsewhere. Before translating this supplementary note, it must be situated in the itinerary. It follows the first note only by a page, but in the interval a page has been turned. Freud has already concluded that no certain decision can be reached from the analysis of so singular a case. Such is his conclusion after a paragraph full of peripateias, a paragraph which begins by confirming the rights of the PP: this is the moment when the interpretation (*Deutung*) of the game explains how the child compensates himself, indemnifies himself, reimburses himself for his pain (the disappearance of the mother) by playing at dis-reappearance. But Freud immediately distances, sends off, this interpretation to the extent of its recourse to the PP. For if the mother's departure is necessarily disagreeable, how can it be explained according to the PP that the child reproduces it, and even *more often* in its disagreeable phase (distancing) than in its agreeable one (return)? It is here that Freud is obliged, curiously, to modify and to complete the previous description. He must, and in effect does, say that one phase of the game is more insistent and frequent than the other: the completion is unbalanced, and Freud had not mentioned it. Above all, he tells us now that the "first act," the distancing, the *Fortgehen*, was in fact independent:

it "was staged as a game in itself" (". . . *fur sich allein als Spiel inszeniert wurde*"). Distancing, departure, is therefore a complete game, a game quasi-complete unto itself in the great complete game. We were correct, even more correct than we said, not to take the allegation of completion as coin of the realm. Thus, it is because distancing is itself an independent and more insistent game that the explanation by the PP must once more *fortgehen,* go away, distance itself in speculative rhetoric. And this is why no decision can be reached from the analysis of such a case.

But after this paragraph Freud does not simply renounce the PP. He tries it twice more, after the final resigned suspension of it in this chapter. 1. He tries to see in the active assumption of a passive situation (since the child is unable to affect his mother's displacement) a satisfaction (and therefore a pleasure), but a satisfaction of a "drive for mastery" (*Bemächtigungstrieb*), which Freud curiously suggests would be "independent" of whether the memory was pleasurable or not. Thus would be announced a certain beyond of the PP. But why would such a drive, (which appears in other texts by Freud, but which plays a strangely erased role here), be foreign to the PP? Why could it not be juxtaposed with a PP that is so often designated, at least metaphorically, as mastery (*Herrschaft*)? What is the difference between a principle and a drive? Let us leave these questions for a while. 2. After this try, Freud again attempts "another interpretation," another recourse to the PP. It is a question of seeing it function *negatively.* There would be pleasure in making disappear; the sending away that distances the object would be satisfying because there would be a (secondary) interest in its disappearance. What interest? Here, the grandfather gives two curiously associated or coupled examples: the sending away of his daughter (mother) by his grandson and/or the sending away of his son-in-law (father), who here—a significant fact and context— makes his first appearance in the analysis. The son-in-law-father appears only to be sent away, and only at the moment when the grandfather attempts a negative interpretation of the PP according to which the grandson sends his father off to war in order not to be "disturbed in his exclusive possession of his mother." This is the sentence that calls for the note on Sophie's death. Before translating this paragraph on the two negative functionings of the PP, note included, I am extracting a notation from the preceding paragraph. I have extracted it only because it did appear dissociable to me, like a parasite from its immediate context. Perhaps it is best read as an epigraph for what is to follow. In the preceding paragraph it resonates like a sound come from elsewhere, that nothing in the preceding sentence calls for, and that nothing in the following sentence develops: a kind of assertive murmur that peremptorily answers an inaudible question. Here it is then, to be read without premises or consequences: "It is of course naturally indifferent (*natürlich gleichgültig*) from the point of view of judging the affective nature of the game whether the child invented it himself or made it his own on some outside suggestion (*Anregung*)." (p. 15).[21] Oh? Why? Naturally indifferent? Really! Why? What is a suggestion in this case? What are its byways? From whence would it come? That the child made his own, appropriated (*zu eigen gemacht*), the desire of someone else, man or woman, or the desire of the two others conjoined, or that inversely he gave occasion to the appropriation of his own game (since the appropriation can take place in both senses, either hypothesis being excluded)—all this is "naturally indifferent"? Really! And even if it were so for the "affective evaluation," which therefore would remain the same in both cases, would this be equivalent for the subject or subjects to whom the affect is related? What is incontestable is that all these questions have been deferred, distanced, dissociated.

I now translate the attempt at another interpretation, concerning the negative strength of the PP. In it, the successive sending away of the mother and the father is pleasurable and calls for a note: "But still another interpretation may be attempted. Throwing away (*Wegwerfen*) the object so that it was 'gone' (*fort*) might satisfy an impulse of the child's, which was suppressed in his actual life, to revenge himself on his mother for going away from him. In that case it would have a defiant meaning: 'All right, then, go away! I don't need you. I'm sending you away myself.' A year later, the same boy whom I had observed at his first game used to take a toy, if he was angry with it, and throw it on the floor, exclaiming: 'Go to the war! [*Geh in K(r)ieg!*, the *r* in parentheses taking into account the actual and reconstituted pronunciation of the child]. He had heard at that time that his absent father was 'at the war,' and was far from regretting his absence; on the contrary he gave the clearest indications that he had no desire to be disturbed in his exclusive possession of his mother[1]" (p. 16). Call for a note on Sophie's death. Before coming to it, I emphasize the certainty with which Freud differentiates

---

21. TN. *GW*, 13. Freud's phrase is "*fur die affektive Einschätzung dieses Spieles,*" which Strachey mistakenly gives as "judging the *effective* nature of the game." (Perhaps an uncorrected typographical error?)

between, if it can be put thus, the double sending away. In both cases, the daughter [mother] is desired. In the first case, the satisfaction of the sending away is secondary (vengeance, spite); in the second it is primary. "Stay where you are, as far away as possible," signifies (according to the PP) "I prefer that you come back" in the case of the mother, and "I prefer that you do not come back" in the case of the father. This, at least, is the grandfather's reading, his reading of the indications which, he says, do not deceive, "the clearest indications" (*die deutlichsten Anzeichen*). If they do not deceive, actually, one might still ask who they do not deceive, and concerning whom. In any event, concerning a daughter (mother) who should stay where she is, daughter, mother. Wife, perhaps, but not divided, or divided between *the two Freuds* [*les deux Freud*] in their "exclusive possession," divided between her father and her offspring at the moment when the latter distances the parasite of his own name, the name of the father as the name of the son-in-law.

The name which is also borne by his other brother, the rival. Who was born in the interval, shortly before the death of the daughter (mother). Here, finally, is the second note, the supplementary note written afterward. The date of its inscription will be important for us: "When this child was five and three-quarters, his mother died. Now that she was really *fort* ('o-o-o') [only three times on this single occasion], the little boy showed no signs of grief. It is true that in the interval a second child had been born and had roused him to violent jealousy" (p. 16).

This cadence might lead one to believe that a dead woman is more easily preserved: jealousy is appeased, and idealization interiorizes the object outside the rival's grasp. Sophie, then, daughter there, mother here, is dead, taken from and returned to every "exclusive possession." Freud can have the desire to recall (her) (to himself) and to undertake all the necessary work for her mourning. In order to speak of this one could mobilize the entire analysis of *Mourning and Melancholia* (published several years before, three at most) and the entire descendance of this essay. I will not do so here.

In the most crushing psychobiographical style, there has been no failure to associate the problematic of the death drive with Sophie's death. One of the aims has been to reduce the psychoanalytic significance of this so ill-received "speculation" to a more or less reactive episode. Several years later, will not Freud himself say that he had somewhat "detached" himself from *Beyond. . .* ? But he had also foreseen the suspicion, and the haste with which he counter-

acts it is not designed to dispel it. Sophie dies in 1920, the very
year in which her father publishes *Beyond* . . . On July 18, 1920,
he writes to Eitingon: "The '*Beyond*' is finally finished. You will be
able to certify that it was half finished when Sophie was alive and
flourishing."²² He actually knows, and says so to Eitingon, that
"many people will shake their heads over it [*Beyond* . . .]."²³ Jones
recalls this request to bear witness, and wonders about Freud's insistence upon his "unruffled conscience over it [*Beyond*]": is there not
here some "inner denial"?²⁴ Schur, who can hardly be suspected of
wanting to save *Beyond* . . . from such an empirico-biographical
reduction (he is among those who would seek to exclude *Beyond* . . . from the corpus), nevertheless affirms that the supposi-
tion of a link between the event and the work is "unfounded." However, he specifies that the term "death drive" appears "shortly after
the deaths of Anton von Freund and Sophie."²⁵

For us, there is no question of accrediting such an empirico-
biographical connection between the "speculation" of *Beyond* . . .
and the death of Sophie. No question of accrediting even the hypothesis of this connection. The passage we are seeking is otherwise, and more labyrinthine, of another labyrinth and another
crypt. However, one must begin by acknowledging this: for his
part, Freud admits that the hypothesis of such a connection has a
meaning in the extent to which he envisages and anticipates it, in
order to defend himself against it. It is this anticipation and this
defense which have meaning for us, and this is where we start to
seek. On 18 December 1923 Freud writes to Wittels, the author of a
Sigmund Freud, His Personality, His Teaching, and His School: "I
certainly would have stressed the connection between the death of
the daughter and the Concepts of the *Jenseits* in any analytic study
on someone else. Yet still it is wrong. The *Jenseits* was written in
1919, when my daughter was young and blooming, she died in
1920. In September 1919 I left the manuscript of the little book
with some friends in Berlin for their perusal, it lacked then only the

22. TN. Cited in Max Schur, *Freud: Living and Dying* (New York: International
Universities Press), p. 329.

23. TN. Cited in Ernest Jones, *The Life and Work of Sigmund Freud*, vol. 3
(New York: Basic Books, 1957), p. 40. Hereafter I will refer to Jones 1 and Jones 3
to distinguish between the volumes of this work.

24. TN. Jones 3, p. 40.

25. TN. Schur, pp. 328–29.

part on mortality or immortality of the protozoa. *Probability is not always the truth.*"[26]
Freud therefore admits a *probability*. But what *truth* could be in question here? Where is the truth of a *fort:da* from which everything derives/drifts away (*dérive*), including the concept of truth? I will confine myself to "overlapping" Freud's work after Sophie's definitive *Fortgehen* with the work of his grandson as *Beyond . . .* will have reported it.

1. The irreparable wound *as* a narcissistic injury. All the letters of this period speak of the feeling of an "irreparable narcissistic injury" (letter to Ferenczi, 4 February 1920, less than two weeks after Sophie's death).[27]

2. But once she is *fort,* Sophie can indeed stay where she is. It is a "loss to be forgotten" (to Jones, 8 February). She is dead "as if she had never been" (27 January, to Pfister, less than a week after Sophie's death). "As if she had never been" can be understood according to several intonations, but it must be taken into account that one intonation always traverses the other. And also that the "daughter" is not mentioned in the phrase: "snatched away from glowing health, from her busy life as a capable mother and loving wife, in four or five days, as if she had never been."[28] Therefore the work goes on, everything continues, *fort-geht* one might say. *La séance continue.*[29] This is literally, and in French in the text, what he writes to Ferenczi in order to inform him of his mourning: "My wife is quite overwhelmed. I think: *La séance continue.* But it was a little much for one week."[30] What week? Watch the numbers. We had pointed out the strange and artificial composition of *Beyond . . .* in *seven* chapters. Here, Sophie, who was called "the Sunday child" by her parents, is snatched away in "four or five days," although "we had been worried about her for two days," starting with the arrival of the alarming news, on the very day of von Freund's burial. This is the same week, then, as the death of von Freund, which we know, at least via the story of the ring [requested by the widow of the man who was to have been a member of the "Committee" of 7, where he was replaced by Eitingon, to whom Freud gave the

26. TN. Cited in Jones 3, p. 41; Freud's emphasis.
27. TN. Cited in Schur, p. 331.
28. TN. Ibid., p. 330.
29. TN. *La séance continue* means "the session proceeds, continues," in the sense of parliamentary procedure, but also the resonance of an analytic session.
30. TN. Cited in Jones 3, p. 19.

ring that he himself wore],³¹ was yet another wound in what I will call Freud's alliance. The "Sunday child" is dead in a week after seven years of marriage. Seven years—is this not enough for a son-in-law? The "inconsolable husband," as we soon will see, will have to pay for this. For the moment the "*séance*" continues: "Please don't worry about me. Apart from feeling rather more tired I am the same. The death, painful as it is, does not affect my attitude toward life. For years I was prepared for the loss of our sons; now it is our daughter . . . 'The unvaried, still returning hour of duty' [Schiller], and 'the dear lovely habit of living' [Goethe] will do their bit toward letting everything go on as before" (to Ferenczi, 4 February 1920, less than two weeks later).³² On 27 May, to Eitingon: "I am now correcting and completing 'Beyond,' that is, of the pleasure principle, and am once again in a productive phase . . . All merely [a matter of] mood, as long as it lasts." ³³

3. Third "overlapping" characteristic: ambivalence concerning the father, the father of Ernst, that is, the son-in-law of the grandfather, and the husband of Sophie. The battle for the "exclusive possession" of the daughter (mother) rages on all sides, and two days after her decease (*Fortgehen*), Freud writes to Pfister: "Sophie leaves behind two boys, one aged six and the other thirteen months [the one Ernst would have been jealous of, as of his father], and an inconsolable husband [indeed] who will have to pay dearly for the happiness of these seven years . . . I do as much work as I can, and am grateful for the distraction. The loss of a child seems to be a grave blow to one's narcissism; as for mourning, that will no doubt come later . . ." ³⁴ The work of mourning no doubt comes later, but the work on *Beyond* . . . was not interrupted for a single day. This letter is situated between Sophie's death and cremation. If the work is a "distraction," it is that he is not just working on just anything. This interval between the death and the cremation (a form of *Fortgehen* which can only have quite singular effects on a work of mourning) is marked by a *story about trains and even of children's trains,*

31. TN. Anton von Freund was a wealthy Hungarian supporter of psychoanalysis who donated several funds for analytic publications and instruction. The "Committee" was the unofficial, secret group that was formed around Freud after the break with Jung. Freud presented each member with a Greek intaglio ring. Communication was by circular letter. The original 1913 members were Jones, Ferenczi, Rank, Abraham, Sachs, and Freud.

32. TN. Cited in Schur, p. 331.

33. TN. Ibid.

34. TN. Ibid., p. 330.

FREUD'S LEGACY   331

an anecdote imprinted on all of Freud's letters of this week. No train to go to the deceased, she who is already gone (*fort*), before going up in ashes. A letter to Binswanger first alludes to von Freund's death: "We buried him on 22 January. The same night we received a disquieting telegram from our son-in-law Halberstadt in Hamburg. My daughter Sophie, aged 26, mother of two boys, was stricken with the grippe; on 25 January she died, after a four days' illness. At that time our railroads were shut down, and we could not even go there. Now my deeply distressed wife is preparing for the trip, but the new unrest in Germany makes it doubtful that this intention can be carried out. Since then a heavy oppression has been weighing on all of us, which also affects my capacity for work. Neither of us has got over the monstrous fact of children dying before their parents. Next summer—this will answer your friendly invitation—we want to be together somewhere with the two orphans and the inconsolable husband whom we have loved like a son for seven years. If this is possible!"[35] Is it possible? And in the letter to Pfister I have already cited in order to point out the allusion to the "seven years" and to the "distraction" of work, the problem of the train to the deceased is posed again, placed in a differentiated network: ". . . as if she had never been. We had been worried about her for two days, but were still hopeful [will she come back?]. From a distance it is so difficult to judge. The distance still remains. We could not, as we wished to, go to her at once when the first alarming news came, because there were no trains, not even a children's train. The undisguised brutality of our time weighs heavily on us. Our poor Sunday child is to be cremated tomorrow. Not till the day after tomorrow will our daughter Mathilde and her husband, thanks to an unexpected concatenation of circumstances, be able to set off for Hamburg in an Entente train. At least our son-in-law was not alone. Two of our sons who were in Berlin are already with him . . ." ("Children from starving Austria were sent abroad by an international children's aid association," notes Schur.)[36]

The "inconsolable husband who will have to pay dearly for the happiness of these seven years" will not have remained alone with the deceased. Freud is represented by his own, despite the suspension of the trains, by another daughter and two sons, bearers of the name (recall his *preferred* game—the train kept at a constant distance).

35. TN. Ibid., p. 329.
36. TN. Ibid.

The classical institution of a science should have been able to do without the Freuds' name. Or at least should have made of its forgetting the condition and proof of its transmission, its proper inheritance. This is what Freud believed or affected to believe, half believed, as in the classical model of science, the model which he fundamentally will have never renounced *playing* at for psychoanalysis. Two weeks after Sophie's death, he writes to Jones. Havelock Ellis has just maintained that Freud is a great artist, and not a scientist. Keeping to the same categories, the same oppositions, the very ones that we are putting to the test here, Freud makes a rejoinder. In it, the great speculator in sum declares himself ready to pay for science with his own, proper name, to pay the insurance premium with his own name. "This [what Ellis says] is all wrong. I am sure in a few decades my name will be wiped away and our results will last." [37] (January 12, 1920) To pay for (the) science (of) with his proper name. To pay, as I said, the insurance premium with his own name. And to be able to say "we" ("our discoveries") while signing by himself. It is as if he did not know, already, that in paying for science with his proper name, it is also the science of his proper name that he is paying for, that he pays himself with a postal money order sent to himself. For this operation it suffices (!) to produce the necessary postal relay. The science of his proper name: a science which for once is essentially inseparable, as a science, from something like a proper name [*nom propre*], as an effect of a proper name which the science allegedly accounts for (in return) by making its accounts *to it*. But the science of his proper name [*nom propre*] is also that which remains to be done, as the necessary return to the origin of and the condition for such a science. Now, the speculation will have consisted—perhaps—in allegedly paying in advance, paying as dearly as necessary, the charges for such a return to sender. This is a calculation without foundation, for the abyssal devaluation or surplus value ruin it, and ruin even its structure. And yet there must have been a way to bind his name, the name of his own (for this cannot be done alone), to this ruin, a way to speculate on the ruin of his name (new life, new science) which preserves what it loses. No one any longer has to be there in order to preserve, but it preserves itself in the name which for itself preserves it. Who? What? It remains to be had/seen [*Reste à s'avoir*].

4. Let us continue to analyze the "overlapping" structure of the *Fortgehen*. Freud, in his name, recalls his daughter (his "favorite"

---

37. TN. Cited in Jones 3, p. 21.

daughter, let us not forget, the one whose image preserved in a medallion around his wrist he will show to a female patient: from his hand, held by a kind of band, she will have followed, preceded, accompanied the entire movement), and recalls his grandson. Within the *fort:da,* identification in every sense passes through the relay of the structural identification with the grandson. This privileged identification once more will be paid for by an event that is exemplary for more than one reason. In itself this event implies Ernst's younger brother, the very one who exasperated, like another son-in-law, the jealousy of the older brother, a jealousy very comprehensible to and well understood by the grandfather. The "exclusive posssession" of the daughter (mother) is at stake. This exemplary event indeed confirms that in its "overlapping" the *fort:da* leads autobiographical specularity into an autothanatography that is in advance expropriated into heterography. In 1923, the year in which he warns Wittels against any probabilistic speculation on the relation between *Beyond* . . . and Sophie's death, what happens? The cancer of the mouth reveals its malign and fatal character. First of the thirty-three operations. Freud had already asked Deutsch to help him "disappear from the world with decency" when the time came. In 1918 he already thought that he was going to die (in February 1918, as you know he had always believed), but then recalled (himself to) his mother: "My mother will be eighty-three this year, and is now rather shaky. Sometimes I think I shall feel a little freer when she dies, because the idea of her having to be told of my death is something from which one shrinks back."[38] All speculation, as we said above, implies the terrifying possibility of this *usteron proteron*[39] of the generations. When the face without face, name without name, of the mother returns, in the end, one has what I called in *Glas* the logic of obsequence. The mother buries all her own. She assists whoever calls herself her mother, and follows all burials.

In 1923, then, first operation on the mouth. On the grandfather's mouth, yes, but also, almost at the same time, on Heinerle's (Heinz Rudolph) mouth, Sophie's second son, Ernst's younger brother. Tonsils. He is the preferred grandson, the preferred son of the preferred daughter. His grandfather considered him, says Jones, "the most intelligent child he had ever encountered." (He did not think as much of Ernst, the older brother.) They talk together about their

---

38. TN. Cited in Schur, pp. 314–15.

39. TN. The *usteron proteron* is the "preceding falsehood" on which a fallacious argument is based. Freud used the term in his theoretical explanation of hysteria in *The Project for a Scientific Psychology* (1895).

operation, as if it were the same, of their mouth, as if it were the same, the mouth eating itself and speaking through what it eats: " 'I can already eat crusts. Can you too?' "[40] Following the operation, and then weakened by miliary tuber-ʿculosis, less resistant than his grandfather, Heinerle dies. On 19 June 1923: Freud is seen to cry. For the only time. The following month he confides to Ferenczi that he feels depressed for the first time in his life. Several years later, in 1926, Binswanger loses his elder son, and on this occasion Freud tells Binswanger what Heinerle had been for him: he who had taken the place of children and grandchildren. Thus he lives the death of his entire filiation: "This is also the secret of my indifference—it was called courage—toward the danger to my own life."[41] The following year: "I have survived the Committee that was to have been my successor. Perhaps I shall survive the International Association. It is to be hoped that psychoanalysis will survive me. But it all gives a somber end to one's life" (to Ferenczi, 20 March 1924).[42] That he hoped for this survival of psychoanalysis is probable, but *in his name,* survival on the condition of his name: by virtue of which he says that he *survives* it as the place of the proper name.

He also confides to Marie Bonaparte, 2 November, 1925: since the death of the one who took the place of filiation for him, who was a kind of universal legatee, and bearer of the name according to the affect (the community's filiation assured by the woman, here by the "favorite" daughter; and in certain Jewish communities the second grandson must bear the first name of the maternal grandfather; everything could be settled by a Judaic law), he no longer succeeds in attaching himself to anyone.[43] Only the previous ties are maintained. No more ties, no more contracts, no more alliances, no more vows to attach him to any future, to any descendance. And when the ties are only from the past, they have passed. But Marie Bonaparte, who is part of the old alliance, receives the confidence, the act of this confidence which in a way renews the engagement by declaring it past. Of this, as of a certain effect of inheritance, she will remain the depository. If I insist upon the confession to Marie Bonaparte, it is in order to have it forwarded. By the *facteur de la vérité* (mailman/factor of truth) into the family scene on the side of the French branch, at the moment when one believes that a testa-

40. TN. Cited in Jones 3, p. 92.
41. TN. Cited in Schur, p. 360.
42. TN. Cited in Jones 3, p. 66.
43. TN. Ibid., p. 92.

ment is unsealed. Who then will not enter into "exclusive possession," as one enters into a dance or trance? One of the elements of the drama: several families bear the same name without always knowing it. And there are *other* names in the *same* family. (Here, I interrupt this development. If one is willing to read its consequences, including its appendix in *Le facteur de la vérité*, one will perceive, perhaps, a contribution to a decrypting still to come of the French analytic movement.) The condition of filiation: its mourning or, rather, as I named it elsewhere, its mid-mourning. In 1923 Heinerle, the place holder of filiation, is gone (*fort*), the pains in the mouth remain, terrible and threatening. He is more than half sure of what they hold in store for him. He writes to Felix Deutsch: "A comprehensible indifference to most of the trivialities of life shows me that the working through of the mourning is going on in the depths. Among these trivialities I count science itself." [44] As if the name, in effect, was to be forgotten, and this time along *with* science. But even if he more than half believed it, this time or the preceding one, when he linked science to the loss of the name, will we believe it? No more this time than the preceding one.

Of this *fort:da* as the work of mid-mourning and of speculation operating on itself, as the great scene of the legacy, the abyss of legitimation and delegation, there would still be, to the point of no longer being countable, other sons/strings [*fils*]. Let us limit ourselves here to the work of mid-mourning (introjection and/or incorporation, mid-mourning here being represented by the bar between *and and/or or,* which for structural reasons seems to me as necessary as it is necessarily impure),[45] to the work of mid-mourning in the relationship to oneself *as grandson and as younger brother of the grandson.* It is with the younger brother of the grandson, the place holder of all filiation, that death seems irremediable, descendance wiped out, and for the first time *cried over,* the depression insurmountable (for a time), new alliances forbidden. But in order to understand, in order to attempt to understand the closure of alliances to his future, perhaps one has to pull on other strings/sons of the past. For example, let us name Julius. Freud's younger brother, who occupied Heinerle's place in relation to Ernst. He died at the

44. TN. Cited in Jones 3, p. 91.

45. See *"Fors, les Mots anglés de Nicolas Abraham et Maria Torok,"* preface to *Cryptonomie, Le Verbier de l'homme aux loups* (Paris: Aubier-Flammarion, 1976), especially p. 17. On mid-mourning (*demi-deuil*), see *"Ja ou le faux-bond,"* *Digraphe* 11.

age of eight months. Freud at that time was two. Ernst was one and a half when the *fort:da* was observed.[46] Says Jones: "Before the newcomer's birth the infant Freud had had sole access to his mother's love and milk, and he had to learn from the experience how strong the jealousy of a young child can be. In a letter to Fliess (1897) he admits the evil wishes he had against his rival and adds that their fulfilment in his death had aroused self-reproaches, a tendency which had remained ever since. In the light of this confession it is astonishing that Freud should write twenty years later how almost impossible it is for a child to be jealous of a newcomer if he is *only fifteen months old* when the latter arrives."[47]

It repeats (itself) and overlaps. But how to separate this graphics from that of the legacy? Between the two, however, there is no relation of causality or condition of possibility. Repetition legates itself, the legacy repeats itself.

If the guilt is overlapped with the one whose death he lived as his own death, *to wit* the death of the other, of Ernst's younger brother as of his younger brother, Julius, one holds several (only) of the strings in the lace of murderous, mournful, jealous, and guilty identifications which entrap speculation, infinitely. But since the lace constrains speculation, it also constrains it with its rigorous stricture. The legacy and jealousy of a repetition (already jealous of itself) are not accidents which overtake the *fort:da,* rather they more or less strictly pull its strings. And assign it to an auto-bio-thanato-hetero-graphic scene of writing.

This scene of writing does not recount something, the content of an event which would be called the *fort:da.* This remains unrepresentable, but produces, there producing itself, the scene of writing.

We would come, if it were possible, to follow or to forward: the *steps [pas]* beyond the pleasure principle, all these steps which do not advance, the entire topics of the march which even literally [*dans la lettre et au pied de la lettre*] add one "step further" (*einen Schritt weiter*)—Freud uses this expression ten times—only to take it back in advance.

Each step lets itself be registered, a step for nothing, in the athesis of this scene of writing. I recognize in this an exemplary movement of what was elsewhere[48] named *paralysis.*

---

46. TN. The original edition of *La carte postale* read that Freud was one and a half when Julius died, i.e. the age of Ernst when the *fort:da* was observed. This was corrected in discussion with Derrida.

47. TN. Jones I, pp. 7–8.

48. "Pas" in *Gramma* 3–4, 1975 [reprinted in *Parages,* Paris: Galilée, 1986].

What goes on and what does not? Who marches or does not march, works or does not work [*marcher*], with Freud? What makes him march/work? what prevents him from marching/working? Who? And if it were *the same* which gives and suspends the "movement" that "there is" (*es gibt*), if there is? The same step [*pas*]?

(More than ten years ago, in its very last lines, "Freud and the Scene of Writing" gave a *step of Freud's* to be continued. This— coming back as a deferred supplement—is to be continued.)

3
PARALYSIS

THE ZONE, THE POSTS, NAME CARRYING THEORY

Paralysis: the step beyond the PP will have remained interdicted. Third chapter: once more the possibility of progress is announced, and finally as a kind of promise. But this progress will not belong to the order of that which one might acquire. It will yield no profit, nothing that might be consigned to a demonstration. No thesis will be posited. As will be confirmed again today, no step will authorize a progress of this type. For whatever by itself engages itself in the movement, and answers for an unpayable debt, this book will never deliver, no more for its author than for anyone else, the slightest acquittance. Why?

Nevertheless, the third chapter advances to the point of admitting a hypothesis. Not yet that of a death drive, but that of a repetition compulsion.

The repetition compulsion will be examined *as a hypothesis.* To what function, *within this hypothesis,* would it correspond? Function is not tendency, and this distinction soon will play an indispensable role.

The hypothesis is welcomed at the end of the chapter. The assumption (*Annahme*) of a repetition compulsion (*Wiederholungszwang*) is set in place: thus there would be something more "primitive," more "elementary," more "instinctual" than the PP. Thus: "But if a compulsion to repeat does operate in the mind, we should be glad to know [the (French) translation renders the connotation well by adding: we would be curious to know. In fact, and Freud insists on this more than once: this is being written for curiosity's sake—which is curious—in order to "look around a bit." But a disinterested curiosity interested in what? Curiosity about what? About whom? To look around a bit at what? Whom? He assumes this curiosity, without any excuse] we should be glad to know something about it, to learn what function it corresponds to, under what conditions it can step forward [*hervortreten:* it seems necessary to insist upon the literality of this *hervortreten,* on its metaphoric literality, and not to erase it via the "emerge" of the English translation, or the *se manifester* of the French translation, as soon as the compulsion can operate without stepping forward as such "in person"], and what its relation is to the PP—to which, after all, we have hitherto ascribed dominance (*Herrschaft*) over the course of the processes of excitation in mental life" (23).

How has such a hypothesis, under its rubric as hypothesis, I am insisting on this, been granted in this third chapter?

I am supposing it reread. And as I had stated, I am only discerning algebraically the motifs on which I would have insisted if we did not have to gain time. To gain time—or the essential form of that which interests the speculation.

Four characteristics.

1. *Failure of a purely interpretive psychoanalysis,* its time is over. Psychoanalysis is no longer what it was, "an art of interpretation" (*Die Psychoanalyse war vor allem eine Deutungskunst*), an interpretation the consciousness of which in reality had no therapeutic effect for the patient. At the moment of this practical failure another means has to be found. And a real transformation of the analytic situation. It is through the "transference" (*Übertragung*) that one will attempt to reduce the "resistances" of the patient, who cannot be reached by simply becoming conscious of a *Deutung.* Transference itself displaces, but it only displaces the resistance. It operates a resistance, *as* a resistance.

(I specify in passing: no legacy without transference. Which also gives us to understand that if every legacy is propagated in transference, it can get underway only in the form of an inheritance of transference. Legacy, legation, delegation, *différance* of transference: the analyst himself, not even his generation, does not need to be "there," in person. He can be all the stronger in not being there. He sends himself—and the postal system forwards. The post never gives or asks for any definitive acquittance to meet the balance of the money order. No receipt. Liquidation, to the extent that it sends itself, interminably follows its course.)

Transference operates as a resistance.

The "transference neurosis" supplements the previous neurosis. A tendency toward "reproduction" comes to light here, and sets Freud's analysis off again. (Reproduction, such is the title of that which we have been examining since the beginning of this seminar:

340 TO SPECULATE—ON "FREUD"

repetition as reproduction, the reproduction of life-death, determined by Freud here as *wiedererleben*.) The tendency toward reviviscence would pose no problem if, in lifting the ego's repression (which has unconscious elements), it negotiated the topical differentiation from the PP. In this case, what is relived could indeed present itself as "unpleasure" for the ego which had repressed it. The PP would maintain its (his) authority: no contradiction would threaten it (him), it suffices that whatever presents itself as unpleasure for one system gives satisfaction elsewhere, for another system. The enigma, on the contrary, is the reviviscence which appears to reproduce no pleasure for any system. This is what compels a hypothesis.

2. *The exemplary narcissistic wound,* or rather narcissistic scar, the stitches, the gash (*Narbe*), and the mid-mourning that reproduction most often causes to be relived, is, so this chapter's very Oedipo-centric analysis tells us, "jealousy over the birth of a new baby—unmistakable proof of the infidelity of the object of the child's affections," which undoes the "bind" (*Bindung*) which attaches the child to the parent of the opposite sex. Mid-mourning forms an original and irreducible category; there are no gradations here. If mid-mourning, in this gash or narcissistic defiguration, refers to the scene of writing of the *fort:da,* in other words, the scene of inverted inheritance, then what I have just called the Oedipocentrism of this chapter has to be understood cautiously. Doubtless, on the preceding page, Freud relates transferential reviviscence to the "reproduction" of a portion of infantile sexual life, "of the Oedipus complex, thus, and its derivatives" ("the Oedipus complex, *thus*. . . ," *also,* and not "notably" as the French translation says in a nonetheless interesting way). But all the interlacings of the *fort:da* (the scene of writing and of inheritance played out in it in ellipsis, the abyss of its "overlapping," the commutation of places, the skipping of generations, the dissymmetry of contracts, in sum everything that *sends itself/is sent* [*s'envoie*] in a graphics of repetition which dislocates the summary "triangle") can be called Oedipal only if, by means of some synecdoche, it is named on the basis of only one of its *strictest* effects, I mean most narrowly restricted effects, determined in its exemplarity. In its most notorious and narrow sense, the Oedipal characteristic is only a rection for the guiding thread of the spool. If one insists upon surnaming the figure of the *fort:da,* such as we saw it function the last time, Oedipus, one does so by *remarking* within it a nebulous and more than abyssal matrix of only one of its effects or, if you prefer, its

offspring. It is as if one were pulling this nebulous matrix with chain fusions or fissions, with bottomless permutations and commutations, with disseminations without return, by only one of its strings/sons [*fils*]. It is true that this temptation (only one of its strings/sons in order to form the characteristic) is not a contingent limitation that one might dispense with accounting for. For it is as if one wished to make it amount to [*revenir à*] one of its strings/sons [*fils*], in other words to the matricial mother, to a mother who would be only what she is. (On this effect of the spool, and on what it might mean *to write oedipally,* I refer to *Glas,* which concerns itself with only (strings) sons, with the gash, and with mid-mourning in the affectations of the proper surname, etc.).

If the narcissistic gash does not have a contingent relation to the birth of the other child, if it is the program of all jealousies, the paradigm for all infidelities, the model of betrayal, Freud is not just choosing this example from among others. The putting of the "legacy" to the test, the last time, will have convinced us of this. All the more in that in relation to all this, in the same paragraph, Freud speaks of his "own experiences" (*nach meinen Erfahrungen,* rather than of his own "observations" as the French translation says, or of his "opinion" as the English says), and not only of Marcinowski's investigations, which he associates to his own, like a guarantor, at the very moment when he speaks of the narcissistic scar, the root of the " 'sense of inferiority.' "

3. *The return of the demonic,* not far from the " 'perpetual recurrence of the same thing,' " is in convoy with repetition beyond the PP. This will recur regularly from now on.

Truly speaking, there is not a return *of the* demonic. The demon is that very thing which *comes back* [*revient*] without having been called by the PP. The demon is the *revenance* which repeats its entrance, coming back [*revenant*] from one knows not where ("early infantile influences," says Freud), inherited from one knows not whom, but already persecutory, by means of the simple form of its return, indefatigably repetitive, independent of every apparent desire, *automatic.* Like Socrates' demon—which will have made everyone write, beginning with him who passes for never having done so—this automaton comes back [*revient*] without coming back [*revenir à*] to anyone, it produces effects of ventriloquism without origin, without emission, and without addressee. It is only posted, the post in its "pure" state, a kind of mailman [*facteur*] without destination. Tele—without telos. Finality without end, the beauty of the devil. It no longer obeys the subject whom it persecutes with its return. It no longer obeys the master, the name of the master being given to the subject constructed according to the economy of the PP, or to the PP it(him)self. Freud insists upon the passivity, the *apparent* passivity of the persons thus visited (*die Person etwas passiv zu erleben scheint*), but also upon the fact that such a demonic visitation is not confined to neurosis.

Who are these "non-neurotic" people (*im Leben nicht neurotische Personen*) of whom he speaks? From what category does being-in-the-grip-of-the-demonic derive? No answer here. Freud speaks of "normal" subjects in this case, but does not limit himself to them.

What is interesting is the index of a power surpassing the PP. And yet, the latter has not yet been exceeded, or if it (he) is, it is by it(him)self in it(him)self. Ventriloquism is not an example or an object of *Beyond*. . . , it is the structure of the PP *as overlapping* with *Beyond*'s scene of writing or inheritance. This book is worked upon by the demonic of which it says that it speaks, and which speaks before it, just as it says itself that the demonic speaks, that the demonic arrives by making its return, *that is* by preceding its arrival (that is, that is), by preceding itself with its announcement for those who hold the place ready for its coming back [*revenue*]: like a letter, a post card, a contract, or a will that oneself sends oneself [*s'envoie*] before leaving on a long, a more or less long, voyage, with the always open risk of dying en route, on the way [*en voie*], and also with the hope that it will arrive, and that the message will become archival, or even the indestructible monument of the interrupted *en-voie*. The document is ciphered, it will remain secret if "his own" die before the "author" returns. But will be "his own" all those who will know how to decipher, and first constitute themselves in their history by means of the will of this code. Who will know how, or *will believe* they know how.

4. *"Literary fiction" is therefore already involved.* The demonic demonstrates one of the trajectories which link *Beyond* . . . to *Das Unheimliche*. Here, I cannot take up again what was set in place elsewhere,[1] (the logic of duplicity without original, the inexhaustible resistance of the "literary" to the schemas of *Das Unheimliche*, the wellspring of so-called fantastic literature, etc.). I note only this, at the greatest proximity: the recourse to the literary "example" cannot simply be illustrative in *Beyond*. . . , no matter what Freud seems to say about it. It is visibly so in Freud's inten-

---

1. For example, in "The Double Session" (in *Dissemination*, pp. 248, 268).

tional rhetoric, as it remained, even yesterday, in the entire psychoanalytic "literature" when the latter occupied itself with, or rather
let itself be occupied by, literature. But this intentional rhetoric is
dislocated by that which occurs (without it) even before it occupies
itself with what occupies it. "Literary fiction," which this rhetoric
would seek to contain in the imaginary, already watches over, like a
fairy or a demon, the structure of the *fort:da,* its scene of writing or
of inheritance in dissemination. Thus, the *Gerusalemme Liberata*
at the end of chapter III. What is "most moving" in what Freud
calls a "romantic epic," is not only the twice repeated unconscious
murder of the beloved disguised as a man (in the armor of an enemy
knight, the tree of the fantastic forest full of spirits and revenants,
"*in den unheimlichen Zauberwald*"); not only the return of Clorinda's ghostly voice; not only the *unheimlich* repetition, beyond the
PP, of the murder of the beloved. No, what is "*most* moving" (*er-
greifendste,* "seizing"), no matter what Freud states, and which is
stated here before him in order to impose itself upon him, is the
repetition (call it "literary" if you will, a kind of fiction which in
any event no longer derives from the imaginary), of these *unheimlich* repetitions of repetitions. The element of that which creates a
work (*fait-oeuvre*), in the abyss in which these repetitions operate,
takes over the aesthetics dominated by the PP, the aesthetics that
Freud again mentions at the end of the second chapter, and which
he never abandoned. The "*creates the work*" already takes over,
grasps this aesthetic anticipation without letting itself be regrasped
by it. It is more "original" than it, is "independent" of it: it can be
described in the very terms that Freud uses elsewhere to describe
the beyond of the PP. And it constitutes the element of the scene of
writing, of the "work" entitled *Beyond the Pleasure Principle,* in
what is most gripping and ungraspable about it, and first of all for
he who believed he could affix the seal of the Freuds to it while
hearing voices.

The hypothesis then is granted—as such, as a hypothesis: the
repetition compulsion can go beyond the PP. But it can also "con-
verge" with the PP, forming so "intimate" a "partnership" with it
that the problem of its "functioning" still entirely remains.

The admission of the hypothesis will have a trigger effect. Speculation now liberates its discourse. It is unleashed as such. But it unleashes *itself,* by *itself,* as such, by treating of the unleashing. Its
unobstructed discourse is a treatise on unleashing, on detaching, on
unbinding. On destricturation. The speculative hypothesis of the
repetition compulsion and of the death drive *does not work* without

unleashing, without the very principle of that which unbinds from all contracture: in this context it is named free, unleashed, unbound, paradoxically disbanded energy, the *pp,* or the primary process. Binding always will occur in the service of the PP whose mastery, thus, will tend to make an essentially rebellious *pp* submit to itself. To understand something about this, one must not only hear voices, always more than one, but also speak several languages. And count with several generations of computers. Without recoiling from the "equation with two unknowns" that Freud cannot avoid just before appealing to the *Symposium.*

A short paragraph opens chapter IV. It pronounces the new beginning, the step further, the beginning of the passage beyond, the passage finally freed. But it announces the step beyond as that which follows, gives it to follow, making it follow, forwarding it, but not yet effectively taking it: "What now follows is speculation, *Was nun folgt ist Spekulation . . .*"

What follows now is Speculation. In a word. This is why the French translation says "pure speculation" (*"Ce qui suit doit être considéré comme de la pure speculation"*). Speculation pure and simple. And Freud adds, after the comma, "often far-fetched speculation (*oft weitausholende Spekulation*), which the reader will consider or dismiss according to his individual predilection" (24).

In other words: the "author" already is no longer there, no longer responsible. He has absented himself in advance, leaving the document in your hands. At least this is what he states. He does not seek to convince you of a truth. He does not seek to detract anything from the power, the proprietary investments, that is, the associations and projections of anyone. Association is free, which holds also for the contract between the writing and the reading of this text, along with the exchanges, engagements, and gifts, along with everything whose performance is attempted. At least this is what he says. The speculative discourse would have the value of what is performed in analysis, or in the field called "literary": you make of it what you like or what you can, it no longer concerns me, it has no law, especially scientific law. It concerns you. But the "it no longer concerns me," "it concerns you," more than ever compels you to the thing. Heteronymy is almost naked in the dissymmetry of the "it concerns." Given over to yourself, you are more than ever bound to the cause, autonomy is the autonomy of a "movement" prescribed by the thing which concerns you, concerns only you. You can no longer get rid of the uncontestable inheritance. The last free-

will in person (the signer of the will) no longer has anything to do
with it or with anyone. You carry his name. In a procession. On your shoulders, until the end of time you
will formulate the theory carrying his name.
The athesis is stated, then, on the threshold of unleashed speculation. But it is also, in a certain way, the "proper" of science or of
literature. There are theses in philosophy, and every thesis is philosophical, there are no theses in either science or literature. In this
way we are as close as possible, then, to the specificity of science or
literature. If there were any, I mean any specificity.
The procedure (*démarche*), thus, is curious. It obeys the law
of curiosity. But we can see the infinite trick (more tricky than itself) that this curiosity has armed itself with, when Freud lets fall,
in the following sentence: ". . . an attempt to follow out an idea
consistently, out of curiousity (*aus Neugierde*) to see where it will
lead" (24).
We begin to see. As it does concern us, and as we do understand it.
Chapter IV sets in place a kind of topology. An indispensable
setting in place, as indispensable as the knowledge of a map, all the
places (here, the psychic apparatus) that configure *frontiers,* and
even a battlefield, one all too easily could say a *front,* the lines of a
capital front, simultaneously in the strategico-military sense and in
the physiological or physiognomic sense: the front above the eyes
(the spool that does or does not come back, always). In question is
the front on which the PP might, as Freud himself puts it, be placed
out of action (*ausser Kraft*). This is where its (his) authority, pre-
dominance, mastery might find itself routed. And routed, finally, in
a way which would be not only a turning back, a detour, or a step to
the side in order to regroup one's forces and to find oneself once
more among one's own, one's derivatives, offspring, representatives, couriers, postmen, ambassadors, and lieutenants.
Why have I called this place of defeat for the master a front?
As we did the last time, let us first disengage the rhetorical and
demonstrative skeleton of this first part, let us take reconnaissance
of that which is also, in its way, a reconnaissance of places. Once
again, according to the same procedure, *dé-marche,* the description
of this topics will not reach its end, to wit, the frontier, the line of
demarcation, the limit of the PP. One more step is again necessary.
Five pages from the beginning of the chapter, a provisional review:
"I have an impression that these last considerations have brought us

to a better understanding of the dominance of the PP; but no light has yet been thrown on the cases that contradict that dominance. *Gehen wir darum einen Schritt weiter.* Let us therefore go a step further" (29).

In what way does this topological description that is indispensable for the intelligence of the PP show itself inadequate to account for its defeat? I recall several well-known principles. In metapsychological terminology, consciousness is a system that receives the perceptions coming from the outside or the sensations of pleasure or unpleasure coming from the inside. This system (Perception-Consciousness) has "a position in space" (*räumliche Stellung*) and limits. It is itself a limit or a system of limits, a post, a frontier post between the outside and the inside. This is nothing new, says Freud, only an adoption of the views on localization of cerebral anatomy (we are not far from the front), which locates the " 'seat' " (*Sitz*) of consciousness in the peripheral layer of the central organ, the cerebral cortex.

What distinguishes this system from the others? The relation to permanent traces (*Dauerspuren*) and to remainders of memory (*Errinerungsreste*)? In all the systems the most intense and tenacious of these traces or remainders come from processes which have never reached consciousness. There cannot be permanent traces in the system Perception-Consciousness, for if there were, this system soon would be limited in its receptive capacity. Therefore, processes of excitation must leave no trace in it. If there are traces, they must be inscribed elsewhere, in another system. The schema of this description orients the entire problematic of the "Mystic Writing Pad." [2] Consciousness must be born where the "mnemic trace" stops or, more precisely, in the place of (*an Stelle*), instead of, the "mnemic trace." Differing from all the other systems, the system Perception-Consciousness is never permanently modified by what stimulates it, by virtue of its being exposed to the outer world. If one takes as a point of departure the hypothesis stated twenty years earlier in the *Project* . . . that a permanent trace supposes the breaking open of a path (*Bahnung*) and an overcome resistance, then one must conclude that there is no trace here, because no resistance is opposed to it. The reference to Breuer's distinction between bound (*gebundene*) and mobile cathectic energy intervenes here. In the system Perception-Consciousness there is

---

2. See "Freud and the Scene of Writing," in *Writing and Difference.*

neither trace nor resistance, but a free circulation of energy without obstacle or binding.

Now, Freud interrupts this argumentation abruptly. In the current state of the "speculation," he says, once more using this word, it is best to leave things as indeterminate as possible, although we have already glimpsed a certain relation between the origin of consciousness, the site of the system Perception-Consciousness, and the peculiarities of the processes of excitation.

From this point on, still in the same topological description that forms the first part of the chapter, Freud's discourse becomes more and more obscure and elliptical. He acknowledges this: "I know that these remarks must sound very obscure, but I must limit myself to these hints" (28). This obscurity is not unrelated to the metaphor of the "vesicle." We will come back to the metaphoricity of this discourse later. The "vesicle" (rather than the "*boule*" of the French translation for *Blaschen*), or the bell, the protoplasmic bulb, with its cortical layer, must protect itself against excitations coming from the outer world, must amortize them, sort out the messages, filter them, limit their quantity of energy. The "sense organs," which can be compared to retractable antennae, inform the organism about external energies by sampling only limited quantities of them, small *doses*.[3] Protected against external aggression, the vesicle is vulnerable on the other line of the front, or rather on its other side: it remains defenseless against stimuli coming from within, for example sensations of pleasure or of unpleasure. These latter predominate over stimuli from the outside. Consequently, the attitude of the organism arranges itself in order to be able to oppose the internal excitations which could increase unpleasure, the major enemy, the one against which the organism is most vulnerable.

Concerning this topic of the "vesicle" (whose metaphor can be transferred onto every corpus, every organism, every organization, for example—but what an example—the Freudian corpus, or the organization of the analytic "movement" protecting, in its tradition, the transmission of its protective vesicle, this pocket of a system sorting out the information come from the outside, protecting against internal dangers, and that the same transference would pass

3. On this point, as on the critique of Kant's transcendental aesthetics which would remain at the level of an abstract representation of time linked to the system Perception-Consciousness, while unconscious psychic processes would be "atemporal" ("*zeitlos*" says Freud, but in quotation marks), I again must refer to the "Mystic Writing Pad" and to *Freud and the Scene of Writing*.

along from one legatee to another, like the simulacrum of a secret), Freud reaffirms again that it is entirely at the orders of the PP. He even sees in this the explanation of the pathological "projections" which would consist in treating excitations of internal origin as messages or emissaries coming from the outside, in order to oppose them with a more effective technique of protection. This too is to be applied and transferred onto the "vesicle" of every corpus and every organization.

The authority of the PP is still uncontested. The PP remains the author of everything that appears to escape it (him) or oppose it (him). As author or authority it (he) is only increased by all the noisy dissidences which allegedly speak against it (him). This entire topology is constructed so that it (he) can reign over the territory of the system Perception-Consciousness. End of the first act: another step is necessary.

The topology of the vesicle at least has permitted the definition of trauma. There is trauma when, at the limit, on the frontier post, the protective barrier is broken through. In this case the entire defensive organization is defeated, its entire energetic economy routed. The great menace of the *return* makes its return. The PP is put out of action (*ausser Kraft gesetzt*). It no longer directs the operations, it loses its mastery when faced with submersion, flooding (*Überschwemmung,* the image of a sudden inundation, as at the breaking of a dike): great quantities of excitation whose inrush instantaneously overflows the psychic apparatus. Panicked, the latter apparently no longer seeks pleasure. It is occupied only with *binding* (*binden*) the quantities of excitation and with "mastering" (*bewältigen*) them. In the invaded region the psychic apparatus then proceeds to an " 'anticathexis,' " a counter-charge (*Gegenbesetzung*), but it pays for this operation with a psychic impoverishment of the other regions. Freud surrounds the word "*Gegenbesetzung*" with quotation marks. Is this a "metaphor," a strategico-military figure? A front is unmanned by displacing forces in order to send them [*envoyer*] hastily to close up another front that has been broken at an unforeseeable place and time, that is, in order to *dispatch* them. Unless the armed forces speak a *founded* language: I mean a language derived from a common necessity of which psychoanalysis would be the science—or in any event of which the theory of cathexes and counter-cathexes, along with their entire system, would be the *general theory.*

Freud calls these "metaphors" *Vorbilder,* models, prototypes, paradigms. He believes them necessary in order to support metapsychology. The metaphoric detour is singularly indispensable here. And interminable. Why? Freud states the law according to which a system's capacity to *"binden,"* to bind or band energies together, increases with the increase of its own charge in the quiescent state. Now, at the moment when he speaks of the quantity of binding, of the band and the contra-band, or the counter-investing, anti-cathectic band, he does not know *what* he is talking *about.* And he acknowledges this. We do not know *what* is bound, unbound, banded together, contrabanded, disbanded. We know nothing of the nature of the excitatory process in the psychic system. This content remains a "large unknown factor, which we are obliged to carry over into every new formula" (31). Obviously it is in the place of this *thing X* that the *"Vorbilder,"* the images, the models, the prototypes, and the paradigms, from whatever field they come, try themselves out. But it suffices that there be a field and a force for the medical and military codes to be close to carrying the day. And they always do so via a code, the rhetoric of a *code,* the code of the code, in other words an implicit theory of tele-information, of the message, the missive, the emissary, the mission or the emission: of the *envoi* and the postal network.

Thus, Freud has come back [*revenu*] to the example of trauma that he had abandoned in the first chapter. And even to an explanation which is not far, as he recognizes, from the "old, naive theory of shock" (31). It is simply that nothing can any longer be localized as a direct lesion of the molecular or histological structure: there is a rupture of the protective barrier, such as it is described in this new topology, when the apparatus is no longer prepared, notably by anxiety, to bind inflowing amounts of excitation. After trauma reaches a certain intensity and pressure becomes too unequal, the surcharge prevents the PP from functioning normally. The step beyond appears to have been taken when the threshold of this surcharge has been reached. Dreams, for example, no longer bring back the hallucinatory satisfaction of desire, they reproduce the traumatic situation. "We may assume, rather, that these dreams are helping to carry out another task, which must be accomplished [*Lösung,* solution] before the dominance of the pleasure principle can even begin . . . They thus afford us a view of a function of the mental apparatus which, though it does not contradict [*wider-*

sprechen] the pleasure principle, is nevertheless independent of it and seems to be more primitive than the purpose of gaining pleasure and avoiding unpleasure" (32; sl. mod.).

This is the first exception to the law according to which the dream fulfills a wish. But this law is not "contradicted," the exception does not speak *against* the law: it precedes the law. There is something older than the law within the law. The law could appear to govern the function of the dream only after the institution of the PP in its dominance. This latter therefore would be a relatively late effect of a history, of an original genesis, a prior victory on a field that does not belong to the PP in advance, and of which the PP is not even a native: victory and capture, binding triumphs over unbinding, the band over the contra-band, or even the contra-band over the a-band or the disband. Over absolute astricture, if some such thing could take place and shape.

This hypothesis remains a hypothesis, let us not forget. And it has just been admitted as if *from the outside,* induced by the example of the traumatic neuroses. The front thus gives way and crumbles under the pressure of *external* excitations. Chapter V extends the import of the hypothesis: in the direction of *internal* excitations, those coming from the drives and their representatives, in other words from that which constitutes "at once the most important and the most obscure element of psychological research" (34).

Here we are entering the richest and most active phase of the text. The essential characteristic of these processes of internal origin (drives and their representatives) is that they are *not bound.* In the *Traumdeutung* Freud had given these unconscious processes the name *primary process.* They correspond to a free, non-bound, non-tonic charge. The work of the higher layers of the psychic apparatus is to tie into the "secondary" process the drive excitations issuing from the *pp.* Now, and this is what is most important, the PP (or its modified form, the PR) can affirm its dominance only by binding the *pp.*

$$\frac{PP\ (+\ PR):}{pp}$$ this is the *generation of the master* and the condition for rightful pleasure.

And yet, this does not mean that before this moment, before the concatenating mastery of the PP over the pp via the PR, there is no effort to bind excitation. The psychic apparatus *also* attempts to bind its excitations "in part," without regard for the PP and before it. But still without being in opposition to it, without contradicting it or speaking against it. This "in part" (*zum Teil*) remains quite undecided. However, its stakes are considerable, and this indecision might confuse the limit of all the concepts involved here. In cases of failure, non-binding produces disturbances "analogous" (*analoge*) to the traumas of external origin. This obscurity, which Freud does not insist upon, is due to the fact that before the instituted mastery of the PP there is *already* a tendency to binding, a mastering or stricturing impulse that foreshadows the PP without being confused with it. It collaborates with the PP without being of it. A median, *differing or indifferent* zone (and it is differing only by being indifferent to the oppositional or distinctive difference of the two borders), relates the primary process in its "purity" (a "myth," says the *Traumdeutung*) to the "pure" secondary process entirely subject to the PP. A *zone*, in other words a *belt* between the pp and the PR, neither tightened nor loosened *absolutely*, everything *en différance de stricture*. The differantial stricture of a belt. Their overlap: $\frac{PP+PR}{pp}$. The apparent indecision of this belt or detached lace: such is the concept of repetition that agitates this entire text. Such a concept, the conceptuality or conceptual form of this concept, has the *allure* of this lace of differantial stricture. More or less tightened, it passes like a lace (for example, a shoe lace) through both sides of the object, which here is repetition *itself*.

But there is never repetition *itself*.

Sometimes repetition, classically, repeats something that precedes it, repetition comes after—as it is said, for example, that Plato comes after Socrates—, repetition succeeds a first thing, an original, a primary, a prior, the repeated itself which in and of itself is supposed to be foreign to what is repetitive or repeating in repetition. As it is also imagined that a narrative relates something that would be previous and foreign to itself, or in any event independent of it. This is the classical distinction, within repetition, of the repeated and the repeating; and within the narrative or the relation, the distinction between the narrated and the narrating, the repeated or narrated "side" being further divisible into the "referent" and the "signified." In the classical hypothesis, repetition in general would be secondary and derivative.

But sometimes, according to a logic that is other, and nonclassical, repetition is "original," and induces, through an unlimited propagation of itself, a general deconstruction: not only of the entire classical ontology of repetition, along with all the distinctions recalled a moment ago, but also of the entire psychic construction, of everything supporting the drives and their representatives, insuring the integrity of the organization or of the corpus (be it psychic or otherwise) under the dominance of the PP. Here, we are coming back to what was said above concerning the *Ab-bauen*. Sometimes, consequently, repetition collaborates with the PP's mastery, and sometimes, older than the PP, and even permitting itself to be repeated by the PP, repetition haunts the PP, undermining it, threatening it, persecuting it by seeking an unbound pleasure which resembles, as one vesicle resembles another, an unpleasure chosen for its very atrocity.

But there is no "sometimes . . . sometimes." As in the epilogue or rear of the shop in *Plato's Pharmacy,* "one repetition repeats the other," and this is all the *différance.*

It would take place, if it takes place, a sole place, *in the zone.*

Two logics then, with an incalculable effect, two repetitions which are no more opposed to each other than they identically reproduce each other, and which, if they do repeat each other, are the repercussions of the constitutive duplicity of all repetition: and it is only if this incalculable double bind (*double bande*) of repetition is taken into "account"—and even though it is not *presently* thematized by Freud—that there is any chance of *reading* the illegible text that immediately follows, and of reading it *as illegible.*

It seems to mean this. The repetition compulsion, in the child and in the first phases of the treatment, has a "driven" quality. When it finds itself "in opposition to the PP," it takes on a "demonic" character. Sometimes repetition "seems to strengthen mastery" (*Beherrschung*), and sometimes it does the contrary. One comes back [*revient*] to the example of children's play: its normally repetitive aspect contributes to mastery, giving the pleasure linked to the identification, recognition, and appropriation of the same (to idealizing interiorization we could say in Hegelian or Husserlian language). In this case, that of the child, repetition engenders pleasure. For the adult, on the contrary, novelty is the condition for pleasure, says Freud. Among all the examples that he gives (the joke, theatrical productions, etc.), the example of the narrative perhaps has an extra place, its (his) own place and the place of the others within which it (he) is necessarily represented. Faced with repetition, with the relation of the related of the scene, the child indefatigably asks for more, erasing the variant, while the adult flees it—at least as an adult—, becomes bored, and seeks division. And when this adult compulsively reproduces the repetitive demand (for example in analysis, and in the transference), he goes beyond the PP, and acts like a child. Henceforth, however, we must no longer say, and we know why, that he *goes beyond,* but that he *comes back within* [*revient en-deçà*] the PP. Repressed memory traces, those of primeval experiences, remain unbound, in their unleashed state, untamable by the secondary processes and their police. Certainly the repetition compulsion, in the transference neurosis, remains one of the first conditions of analysis. But it becomes an obstacle if it persists, and makes the dissolution of the transference difficult. Since this possibility is inscribed in the transferential structure, i.e. that the condition of its possibility can become the condition of its impossibility, what we said above about the scene of inheritance can help us to understand it better: an undissolved transference, like an unpaid debt, can be transmitted beyond one generation. It can construct a tradition with this possibility in its entrails. One can even begin a tradition for this purpose, giving it the forms necessary for this effect, and using all possible means to make the encysted threat endure, sleeping. When Freud speaks of the demonic as concerns the therapeutic obstacle, or even the fear of psychoanalysis (the dread of awakening something better left asleep), one can also relate (and overlap) this to (with) the relation that a tradition, for example the tradition of the psychoanalytic "movement" or "cause," maintains with itself, with the archive of its own demon. But the demonic is not more or less inherited, like one content or another. It belongs to the structure of the will. A scene of inheritance confers its ascendant upon it *a priori.*

COURIERS OF DEATH

Dead silence about death. It has not yet been mentioned. Almost half the book. The differantial stricture of repetition has not demanded a word about death. But what has been spoken about? Pleasure? Perhaps. In any event, the undecidable relation to pleasure. But what is pleasure in this case?

Nothing about death, then, until the moment when, examining the relation between drive and repetition, Freud advances a hypothesis about the nature of the drive in general, and perhaps about organic life in general. There is an "attribute" inscribed in every drive, and perhaps in all organic life. We may have been on "the track" of this program, says Freud, in everything we have followed up to this point. What is this trait, this "attribute"? The well known definition: "*It seems, then, that a drive* (Trieb) *is an urge* (Drang) *inherent in organic life to the restoration* (Wiederherstellung) *of an earlier state of things* which the living entity has been obliged to abandon under the pressure of external disturbing forces; that is, it is a kind of organic elasticity, or, to put it another way, the expression of the inertia inherent in organic life" (36, mod.; Freud's emphasis).

In this hypothesis the programmatic writing, the writing which formulates the "attribute" whose "track" we have been following, is confounded with the hypothesis of a force, an urge, a driving power. This force of the attribute is written as force. But also, and *a priori*, in opposition to another force, an external force, a counterforce. The force of inscription organizes the field in a network of differences of forces. The living is nothing other than this differential. It is transmitted and "reproduced" as such.

The "external" force which disturbs the immanent tendency, and which in a way produces the entire history of a life that does nothing other than repeat itself and regress, is what is usually called nature, the system of the earth and the sun. Here, Freud is not afraid of being reproached for the "profound," i.e. "mystical" allure of this meditation. But the results sought after are only those of a "sober" "certainty" that is totally uninebriated.

The detour is expanding immeasurably. I mean the *Umweg*. We had already encountered, starting with the first chapter, this notion of the *Umweg*. At that point, in question were the relations between PP and PR. Here, the determination of the detour in the procedure [*démarche*] would be more general. This determination overflows the one in the first chapter, and provides its basis. The *Umweg* would differ/defer not with the aim of pleasure or of conservation (the relay of the PR in the service of the PP), but with the aim of death, or of the return to the inorganic state. The *Umweg* of the first chapter would constitute only an internal, secondary, and conditional modification of the absolute and unconditional *Umweg*. It would be in the service of the general *Umweg*, of the (no) step of the detour [*pas de détour*] which always leads back to death. *Leads back*—here again it is not a question of going, but of coming back [*revenir*]. It is this double determination that I had assigned to the "word" *différance* with an *a*. It follows equally, then, that the *Umweg* is not a derivative type of path or step. It is not a passing determination, a narrower or stricter definition of the passage, it is the passage. (The) *Weg* (is) *Umweg* from the first step of the step [*pas du pas*]. And recall in passing: *weg,* the adverb, also signifies "far away." It can be understood as an order, a demand, or a desire: *fort!* go away! But all this is not self-evident: of course. More than one angle is necessary here. The end of the living, its aim and term, is the return to the inorganic state. The evolution of life is but a detour of the inorganic aiming for itself, a race to the death. It exhausts the couriers, from post to post, as well as the witnesses and the relays. This death is inscribed as an internal law, and not as an accident of life (what we had called the law of supplementarity in the margins of *The Logic of the Living*). It is life that resembles an accident of death or an excess of death, in the extent to which it "dies for internal reasons" (*aus inneren Gründen*). We had located that text of Nietzsche's which said that life is a very rare species of death.

But Freud also has to account for the conservative drives that he recognizes in all that is living, the very drives that motivate recourse to repetitive processes. If the force of death is so internal and so general, why this conservative detour? Why pass through this path, this *Weg* as *Umweg?* Why this labyrinthine (no) step of death [*pas de mort*]? Why does death intersect with itself in this (no) step [*pas*]?

Confronted with risk of contradiction, Freudian speculation on the *one-more-step* [*pas de plus*] operates in two meters. *First,* the driving detour in its conservative form, the conserver of the drive, is a *partial* process. There are "component drives" (*Partialtriebe*). *Second,* as confident in the distinction between the outside and the inside as in that between the part and the whole, Freud then determines the final sense of these conservative "component drives": their movement *tends* to insure that the path (*Weg-Umweg*) toward death, the death (no) step [*pas de mort*], corresponds to internal, "immanent" possibilities. The component drives are *destined* to *insure* that the organism dies *of its own death,* that it follows its own, proper path toward death. That it arrives by its own step at death (*eigenen Todesweg*). That are kept far from it (*weg!* we might say, *fernzuhalten* he says) all the possibilities of a return to the inorganic which would not be "immanent" to it. The step must occur within it, from it to it, between it and itself. Therefore one must send away the non-proper, reappropriate oneself, make oneself come back [*revenir*] (*da!*) until death. Send oneself [*s'envoyer*] the message of one's own death.

Such would be the function of these component drives: to help (auxiliary function) to die one's own death, to help (function of assistance: to assist in death) in death's being a return to the most proper, to the closest to oneself, as if to one's origin, according to a genealogical circle: to send oneself [s'envoyer]. The organism (or every living organization, every "corpus," every "movement") conserves itself, spares itself, maintains itself via every kind of differentiated relay, intermediary destination, correspondences of short or long term, short or long letters [courrier]. Not in order to keep oneself from death, or to maintain oneself against death, but only in order to avoid a death which would not amount to itself [ne lui reviendrait pas], in order to cut off a death that would not be its own or that of its own. In the detour of the step, in the step of the detour, the organism keeps itself from the other which might still steal its death from it. It keeps itself from the other who might give it the death that it would not have given to itself by itself (for this is a theory of suicide deferred, or by correspondence), the death that it would not have announced to itself, signified by a sentence, a letter, or a notification that is more or less telegraphic, and of which it would be simultaneously the sender, the receiver, and the transmitter, that is, from one end of the itinerary to the other, and in every sense of the word, the facteur.[4] Addressor and addressee of the news, teleguiding its (his) legacy, autoteleguiding it, it (he) wishes to toll its (his) own knell, wishes the impossible. The drive of the proper would be stronger than life *and* than death. We must, then, unfold the implications of such a statement. If, auto-teleguiding its (his) own legacy, the drive of the proper is stronger than life and stronger than death, it is because, neither living nor dead, its force does not qualify it otherwise than by its own, proper drivenness, and this drivenness would be the strange relation to oneself that is called the relation to the proper: the most driven drive is the drive of the proper, in other words the one that tends to reappropriate itself. The movement of reappropriation is the most driven drive. The proper of drivenness is the movement or the force of reappropriation. The proper is the tendency to appropriate oneself. Whatever the combinatory of these tautologies or analytic statements, never can they be reduced to the form S *is* P. Each time, concerning the drive, the force, or the movement, the tendency or the *telos,* a division must be maintained. This forbids the drive of the proper from being designated by a pleonastic expression defining the simple relation to itself of the inside. Heterology is involved, and this is why there is force, and this is why there is legacy

4. TN. That is, *facteur* as maker, creator, agent, postman, factor, etc.

and scene of writing, distancing of oneself and delegation, sending, *envoi*. The proper is not the proper, and if it appropriates itself it is that it disappropriates itself—properly, improperly. Life death are no longer opposed in it.

Correspondence, here, between two who, according to all appearances and all usual criteria, never read each other, and even less encountered each other. Freud and Heidegger, Heidegger and Freud. We are moving in the space outlined by the beacons of this historic correspondence—and at heart I am certain that the two "texts" indicated by these proper names, and of course largely overflowing them, for the reasons around which I am busying myself here, are preoccupied with each other, passing all their time in deciphering each other, in resembling each other, as one ends up by resembling that which is excluded, or, in absolute mourning, whoever has died. They could not read each other—therefore they have spent all their time and exhausted all their forces in doing so. Let us leave this, there are a thousand ways to settle affairs with Freud and Heidegger, between Freud and Heidegger. No matter, for it is done by itself, without one having to take the slightest initiative.

Everything remains to be done in order to ask the question of what *there is* in a text when one allegedly delimits its "corpus." To think on the track, about the trace [*à la trace*], should be, for a rather long time now, to reconsider the tranquil self-evidence of the "there is" and the "there is not" "in" a "corpus" by exceeding, on the track [*à la trace*], the opposition of the present and the absent, the *indivisible* simplicity of the *limes* or of the marginal trait, the simplisticness of the "this has been thought" or the "that has not been thought," its sign is present or absent, S is P. This would compel us to reelaborate, from top to bottom, all the notions, which themselves are distinct (up to a certain point), and often confused, of the *unthought*, the *non-thematized*, the *implicit*, the *excluded* in the mode of *foreclosure* or of *disavowal*, of *introjection* or *incorporation*, etc., all the silences which by so many traces work upon a corpus from which they appear "absent." Thereby one would avoid the decrees of incompatability or of heterogeneity, of untranslatableness, between "Freud" and "Heidegger"; these decrees are always accompanied by a hierarchizing judgment: they often take as their pretext the effects of *Daseinsanalyse* or, from the other side, some of the philosophical improvisations of Freud or his heirs. Inversely, one also would avoid opportunistic assimilations or passageways, and would avoid increasing the weight of an *auctoritas* by guaranteeing one procedure [*démarche*] by means of the other.

For in effect, these are two procedures [*démarches*] preoccupied by proceeding [*démarche*], each in its way, each according to its proper step, and two paths on the path of distantiation, performing distantiation (*weg!*), each distancing itself and sending itself [*s'envoyant*] by its own step. Why does "our" "era" have nothing other to suspend itself from than the treading movement of a step? Why would the step [*pas*] of a *démarcheur*[5] be the final judgment today? And why would *Dasein*, "our own," have to constitute itself as a *démarcheur*? Do all these questions and all these ways intersect at the moment when, and in the place where, the thought of the proper dominates all these distinctions and oppositions?

"What we are left with is the fact that the organism wishes to die only in its own fashion" (39). It wishes to die only in its own fashion: *nur auf* seine Weise *sterben will*. This is what is left, what remains: it remains (*es erübrigt*) that the organism wishes to die only in its own fashion, solely (*nur*) in its own way. Not slightly in its way, slightly in another: solely in its own. And if this is what remains, the only certitude to which one can return [*revenir*], then it is that at bottom we do not know what the organism itself is outside this or before this: that it is that which wishes to die only in its own fashion, and not, not even a bit, in any other. And the "component drives" assist it, they are *there*, destined, called upon to see that it, the organism, the living corpus, dies properly. It, moreover, is not *there* itself, the living corpus, it is nothing other outside this demand and this order: let me die properly, I am living so that I may die properly, and so that my death is my own, my inheritance [*me revienne*], like this mandate. To mandate is this.

Not to go right to it, but to have the right to one's own death, and to assume this death, to charge oneself with this command as if with a message or a mission. What has been translated as the "authenticity" of *Dasein* "resolutely" assuming its Being-for-death in the original (non-"vulgar") temporality of its "care," was also a certain quality of the relation to the proper: *Eigentlichkeit* assumed. Beyond the metaphysical categories of the subject, of consciousness, of the person, beyond the metapsychological categories which would be, to corrupt slightly the joke in *The Psychopathology of Everyday Life*, but the conversions of metaphysics, this movement

5. TN. See above, "Freud's Legacy," note 2 on *démarche*. Here, *démarcheur* must be understood in terms of the pun implicit in the *dé-marche* and the *pas*, as well as in its usual senses of traveling salesman, or stockbroker.

of propriation would come back [*reviendrait*] to the *Da* of *Sein* and the *Da* of *Dasein*. And the existential analytic of *Da-sein* is inseparable from an analysis of dis-tancing and proximity which would not be so foreign to the analysis of the *fort:da*, at least such as we are reading it here. And that we can also follow on the track [*à la trace*], up to the relation to one's own death as a condition of authenticity (*Eigentlichkeit*). When Freud speaks of *Todestrieb, Todesziel, Umwege zum Tode,* and even of an "*eigenen Todesweg des Organismus,*" he is indeed pronouncing the law of life-death as the law of the proper. Life *and* death are opposed only in order to serve it. Beyond all oppositions, without any possible identification or synthesis, it is indeed a question of an *economy* of death, of a law of the proper (*oikos, oikonomia*) which governs the detour and indefatigably seeks the proper event, its own, proper propriation (*Ereignis*) rather than life *and* death, life *or* death. The prolongation or abbreviation of the detour would be in the service of this properly economic or ecological law of oneself as proper, of the auto-mobile auto-affection of the *fort:da*. Does not everything that Freud ventures on the subject of time in these environs have to be related to the auto-affective structure of time (that which there gives itself to receive is no present-being) such as it is described in Husserl's *Lectures on Internal Time Consciousness* or Heidegger's *Kantbuch?* We will take on this problem for itself in another problematic context.[6] The measures of prolongation or abbreviation have no "objective" signification, they do not belong to objective time. They have value only as concerns the oneself (*soi-même*) which apostrophizes and calls (to) itself as an other in auto-affection. Before all else one must auto-affect oneself with one's proper death (and the self does not exist before all else, before this movement of auto-affection), make certain that death is the auto-affection of life or life the auto-affection of death. All the *différance* is lodged in the desire (desire is nothing but this) for this auto-tely. It auto-delegates itself and arrives only by itself differing/defering itself in (its) totally-other, in a totally-other which should no longer be its own. No more proper name, no proper name that does not call (to) itself, or call upon this law of the *oikos*. In the guarding of the proper, beyond the opposition life/death, its privilege is also its vulnerability, one can even say its essential impropriety, the exappropriation (*Enteignis*) which constitutes it. It serves "propriation" all the better in that it is proper to no one, and above all does not belong to

6. *Donner—le temps* (*To Give—Time*), in preparation, to appear later.

its "carrier." Nor to its "*facteur.*" Anymore than it does to the discourses to which we are affecting a reference here. The desire for the idiom—nothing is less idiomatic.

I have indeed spoken, I believe, of Freud and of Heidegger, of their irreplaceable signature, but the same is said, in another way, according to another proper treading, another step [*pas*], under the signature of Rilke or of Blanchot, for example. The proper name does not come to erase itself, it comes by erasing itself, to erase itself, it comes only in its erasure, or, according to the other syntax, it *amounts to, comes back to* [*revient à*] *erasing itself. It arrives only to erase itself.* In its very inscription, *fort:da.* It guards itself from and by itself, and this gives the "movement." It sends [*envoie*].

This notion of *guarding* (which Heidegger recalls to its truth as truth—*bewahren, Wahrheit,* etc.—and to the truth as un-truth, *Un-Wahrheit*) finds itself reassembled, guarded, in all its polysemia or polymetaphoricity, particularly in the strategico-military code, at the moment when Freud defines the conservative drives. They are the guardians of life, but by the same token also the sentinels or satellites of death. The sentinels of life (*Lebenswachter*) watch over life, take care of it, guarding and watching it, standing guard near it. They assist it. But these same drives are "originally" the "guardians" or "satellites" [7] (*Trabanten*) of death. They are so originally, which is as much as to say that this is what they have been (*sind ursprünglich Trabanten des Todes gewesen*), making them incapable, beneath this change of sign, of not remaining faithful to their primary *destination.* The satellites of life death. The word "satellite" is borrowed from the code of the army, the plot, or the secret service. Bodyguard or prince's escort, the *satelles* is a kind of minor accomplice (*ministre*) who is nevertheless indispensable in the shadows where he remains, generally armed. There is something suspect and unspeakable about him. The term is always one of "ill repute," Littré recalls: "Any armed man in the wages and service of another, in order to carry out his violence, in order to serve his despotism." In the wages and in the service of is indeed what we have here. These "drives" are the satellites of life-death, of the secret contract binding the one to the other. They are agents in the more or less obscure, secret, or clandestine service of an absolute power, a corps dispatched as a delegation, a detachment of frontrunners, a legated and detached body—and therefore always

7. TN. To keep the play on *satelles* I have had to modify Strachey's excellent translation of *Trabanten* as "myrmidons."

partial—sent on a mission, couriers or emissaries whose movement (*mouvance*) obeys the revolution of a greater body, another magisterial body, a star which might sometimes be dead, which is in fact the dead man, unless it is pretending to be the dead man, or woman. And only miming disaster.

That which guards life remains within the domain [*mouvance*] of that which guards death. It is as much a question of guarding death as of being exposed to it, of guarding death in order to save one's proper death, the death of the living (*except within it*) in its own fashion (*auf seine Weise*) and in its own rhythm. The very idea of rhythm, which has no "objective" meaning, is to coordinate itself with that which must be *guarded* here. For example, the organism defends its rhythm against that very thing which might prevent it from reaching its proper aim by "shortened paths" (*auf kurzem Wege*), and "by a short-circuit, so to speak" (*durch Kurzschluss sozusagen*). What counts is less the *telos* than the rhythm of *différance* and the speed of the step.

One must [*il faut*]: guard death or guard life. Such is the syntax of this vigilance in truth. The sentinel of life having to become that which it "originally" will have been, the courier of death, everything changes sign at every moment. This vacillation is set forth more obviously, more thematically in *Das Unheimliche*. Nothing surprising about this. *Heimlichkeit* is also the German name of what we have in mind here as the "economic law of the proper" or of the "house," of domesticity, along with its genealogy of the properly familial, of its "patronage" and its "parentage."

Like sexuality in general, sexual difference plays its part according to the same economy. Although a latecomer in history, it nevertheless would have been active "from the very first" (41). Hence, its "work of opposing" (*Gegenarbeit*) always already would have begun against "the activities of the 'ego-instincts' " (we had examined *The Logic of the Living* in this sense, occasionally against its manifest statements on the subject of sexuality as a latecomer, come, like death itself, "as a supplement"—Jacob's own word). Freud is preparing a map of routes and a record of *différances* of rhythm. A differantial, and not an "alternating" rhythm, as the French translation gives "*Zauderrythmus*" [English: "vacillating"]. *Zaudern* is to hesitate, certainly, but it is above all to *temporize,* to defer, to delay. One group of drives rushes forward in order to reach the final aim of life as quickly as possible. But, division of labor, another group comes back [*revient*] to the start of the same path (*dieses Weges zurück*) in order to go over the route and

"so prolong the journey" (*so die Dauer des Weges zu verlängern*).
Between the two groups, on the same map, a network coordinates,
more or less well, more or less regularly, communications, transports, "locals" and "expresses," switch points, relays, and correspondences.[8] This great computer can be described in the code of
the railway or the postal network. But the unity of the map is always
problematic, as is even the unity of the code within the computer.

Therefore the *exappropriating* structure is irreducible and un-
decomposable. It redirects repression. It always prevents reappropriation from closing on itself or from achieving itself in a circle,
the economic circle or the family circle. No progress, no progres-
siveness of man. And if Freud, to conclude, again "cites" the Poet,
it is in order to leave the last word to Mephistopheles. Whose name
is curiously omitted from the French translation, which only gives
the reference to *Faust* I. The repressed drive " '*ungebändigt immer
vorwärts dringt*' ": undisciplined, refractory, untamed, never permitting itself to be bound or banded by any master, it always pushes
forward. It is that the backward path (*Der Weg nach rückwarts
. . .*) is always both displaced and "obstructed" (*verlegt*) by a repression. The latter does not affect the *Weg* or the *step* of the outside, it is its very proceeding [*démarche*], and in advance finds itself *unterwegs, en route*. The entire book is scanned by a rhetoric
of the "*zurück.*"

We are reaching the end of chapter V. One might be led to believe
that the "hypothesis" is finally confirmed: indeed it seems that
there exists (or rather that *there is, il y a,* for it could not exist or
present itself as such) a step beyond the PP, as well as a death drive
developed within the logic of the repetition compulsion.

But such is not at all the case. Once again Freud says that he is
dissatisfied. Dissatisfied with this discourse on dissatisfaction—an
affirmation made at the beginning of the next chapter (VI). No (step
of) satisfaction [*pas de satisfaction*]. The conclusion of the last
chapter is "unsatisfactory . . . even to ourselves" (*wird uns . . .
nicht befriedigen*). At this stage the unsatisfactory is reassembled
into the following form, and again in a hypothesis: two groups of

8. TN. In French, *correspondance* means both correspondence, with all the
multiple senses it has in English, plus the connection between two means of transport, whether in the sense of connecting trains, or the connection between (e.g.) a
train and a bus.

drives, the "ego-drives" and the sexual drives. The first group, obeying a conservative, regressive, and deathly logic of repetition, seeks to return from initial animation to the inanimate. The second group, while reproducing original states, seeks, by means of the fusion of two germ cells, to legate life and to give it the appearance of immortality.

Freud then undertakes to question, from a point of view that he calls "scientific," the very thing that formed the axis of the preceding chapter, to wit, the notion of *immanence:* death as an internal necessity of life, the "proper path toward death." A critical question on the part of the scientist: and if this alleged propriety, more literally, this notion of the immanence of death in life, if this familiar domesticity of death were nothing but a consoling belief? And if it were an illusion destined to help us, as the Poet once more says, "to bear the burden of existence" (*"um die Schwere des Daseins zu ertragen"*)? To make it more bearable as *Anankē* than it would be as accident or chance? Let us translate: and if the authenticity proper to *Dasein* as *Sein zum Tode,* if its *Eigentlichkeit* were but the lure of a proximity, of a self-presence (*Da*) of the proper, even if in a form which would no longer be that of the subject, of consciousness, of the person, of man, of living substance? And if it were precisely the *poem,* the poetic itself, this death which is immanent and proper to life? A great narrative poem, the only story that one always tells oneself, that one addresses to oneself, the poetics of the proper as reconciliation, consolation, serenity? The only "belief" too, or rather counter-belief, for this belief is not original. Take, says Freud, the "primitive races." This time the index of original normality is not the child, but the "primitive": who so little believes in a *natural* death that he always attributes it to the aggression of an enemy. Every death is a murder. The logic of this argument was at work in "Thoughts for the Times on War and Death" (1915, S.E. XIV): faced with death, the unconscious is like the primitive, it does not know it, does not believe in it, overlooks it as it does negation. Anxiety about death, *Inhibitions, Symptoms, and Anxiety* will specify, has no *proper* content, precisely, it is the analogon of castration anxiety. Those who consider this argument to be incompatible with what they believe to be the thesis of the "death drive" should refer to this syntaxic articulation of the athesis, in the precise place that we are pointing out at the moment.

We are then taken along the biologistic detour via the genetics of the period. This is the only section that Freud acknowledged was

not yet edited at the death of his daughter—mother of his grandson.
These few pages are to be reread in and of themselves in relation to
both *The Logic of the Living,* and that which we had previously ac-
centuated within it: concerning death (immanent or not), sexuality
(original or late), protozoa (immortal or not), and the logic of the
"supplement," whose ineluctable program we had pointed out. In
their principial schemas the two books remain astonishingly contemporary. The new content of scientific advances and of positive
discoveries has not, since 1920, displaced the slightest conceptual
element in the position of the problems, the kinds of questions, and
of the answers or non-answers.

One genetic model particularly interests Freud. I am indeed saying "model," in order to tie up with our initial problematic, and
because Freud indeed speaks of an "unexpected analogy" (*uner-
wartete Analogie*), of a striking resemblance or relationship (*auf-
fällige Ähnlichkeit*), of a "significant correspondence" (*bedeut-
same Übereinstimmung*) (as significant, you are whispering, as the
Übereinstimmung between the grandfather and his daughter in the
interpretation of the o-o-o-o). The genetic model which fascinates
Freud is the one proposed by Weismann. In the morphology of
living substance, Weismann distinguishes the *soma,* the body apart
from the sexual and hereditary material, from the germ-plasm,
which serves the conservation and propagation of the species. The
abstract body, dissociated from any value of inheritance, is mortal.
It is condemned to death. In a way, it is the body's body. Inversely,
the germinal power of the plasm is immortal.

The limits of the analogy do not escape Freud. In effect, Weismann reserves this duality for multicellular organisms; for them
alone would death be natural, while protozoa would be "potentially
immortal." But despite these limits, the analogy seems acceptable
to Freud. Weismann's dualist framework corresponds to the distinction between death and life drives. This is the place where allusion
is made to the harbor of Schopenhauer's philosophy, according to
which death would be the " 'true [proper] result' " (*eigentliche Resultat*) of life, and the sexual drive the incorporation of the will
to live.

And yet, while he is in the process of accrediting the "scientific"
analogy, Freud still seems dissatisfied with his procedure [*démarche*]. Once again, he proposes the "bold attempt at another step
forward" (50), *"einen Schritt weiter zu gehen."* Will the steps forward permit themselves to be counted?

The biological model already invites a temptation, the temptation to transport the model into that which creates a body of work in a corpus, that which is inherited or not in a tradition. For example in the analytic "movement." What can be discerned then would be the body's body, the abstract or mortal body, the one which is not inherited, and to which nothing comes back [*à qui rien ne revient*]. And then, the other body, etc. Does not Freud help us to do this? At first he seems to turn this model toward a politico-psychoanalytic metaphor: the vital association of cells in order to preserve the life of the organism. The State, or the multicellular society, guards life beyond the death of any given subject. The primitive *socius,* the original, "natural" contract: copulation serves both reproduction and the rejuvenation of the other cells.

One *could* at this point play upon the transferential metaphor, transfer the transference, and compare, *übertragen* says Freud, the psychoanalytic theory of libido with these bio-political cells. Present in every cell, the two drives (life, death) partially neutralize the effects of the death drive in the other cells which they are keeping alive, occasionally pushing the thing to the sacrifice of themselves. This sacrifice, of course, would be coordinate with the great reckoning, the great economy of the inheritance. With the altruistic heroism of certain cells which suddenly begin to resemble the "privates" of the first world war, on the Austrian side of course (the side of Freud's two sons, the announcement of whose death he kept awaiting), and vulnerable to traumatic neuroses. To these decorated cells closest to the front are opposed the other cells, the "narcissistic" ones which keep all their libido for themselves. They refuse to transfer the slightest part of their libido onto any object. They keep it to themselves to use for an eventually constructive (for example art, science, institutions in general) and sublime activity. At this point Freud does not exclude the possibility that malignant tumors, so destructive to everything around them, also might be "narcissistic" in this sense: they increase, authorize, and multiply themselves in unleashed fashion, simultaneously more invulnerable and more exposed to "narcissistic wounds" in that they lead to proliferation. They become autonomous and free themselves without concern for the other cells or for the totality of the organism, for the rights of authors or of succession, after having withdrawn from everything, and having hidden themselves behind the front. A hypothesis to be taken from Freud's own mouth, of course.

This entire "malignant" strategy exploits and disturbs, as we know, the networks of communication or of genetic information, the switch points and ciphers of its graphic code.

A page after the "step forward" (*einen Schritt weiter*), a new step, a "next step" (*der nächste Schritt*) follows, a step prescribed by the concept of narcissism. The preceding step had left us "walking in place." This step is due to the discovery of a libido directed toward the Ego when the latter becomes a sexual object, and even the most important sexual object. Freud refers to "On Narcissism: An Introduction" (1914). Now, if such a libido exists, the opposition between the (deathly) ego drives and the (procreative) sexual drives is dissolved. In any event, this opposition no longer has a qualitative value, it corresponds only to a topographical differentiation.

The risk of this novelty is the *monistic* risk. Which at this time has to be given a proper name: Jungian dissidence. Every drive is allegedly sexual or libidinal. It must be recognized that the oppositional alternative between dualism and monism, the alternative that seems to impassion Freud in this context, belongs to a very simplistic framework (as does the concept of narcissism itself) in relation to the differantial stricture that we deciphered in the athetic reading of *Beyond* . . . The decisive firmness with which Freud reaffirms dualism within this oppositional framework, the dogmatic tone, the inability to do anything other than to assert—all this is legible in his very rhetoric, and indeed shows that his strategy is unintelligible outside a certain state of the psychoanalytic "movement" and "cause," outside the great scene of the rights of succession that is being played out. This is better known today, at least as concerns the "facts," and the duel with Jung. But since it continues, unquestionably, it cannot be deciphered without being entered into in some way. And it must indeed be said that Freudian dogmatism—no matter what one might say about the other side— has been very faithfully, often very blindly, inherited in this dark affair.

"Our views have from the very first been *dualistic,* and today they are even more definitely (*schärfer*) dualistic than before—now that we describe the opposition as being, not between ego drives and sexual drives but between life drives and death drives. Jung's libido theory is on the contrary *monistic* . . ." (53)

Now, does Freud argue against Jung? In a compromise whose theatrical and rhetorical complexity would merit a very close analysis, Freud combines a childish stubbornness with the objectivity of an impassioned man of science. The one says: I will not give in a foot or an inch, I will continue, I will start over, and above all no monism, Jung *fort! weg!* But the other acknowledges: it is true for the moment, and this is\indeed regrettable, that the dualism I will not let go of cannot be the object of any scientific demonstration, we must wait, it is only a suspicion, a hypothesis (*wir vermuten*), a presumption, a presupposition. We suspect, he says, that drives other than the libidinal, self-preservative ones are at work. This would have to be proven. "Unfortunately, however, the analysis of the ego has made so little headway (*fortgeschritten*) that it is very difficult for us to do so" (53). And is also completely useless: twice in the same paragraph the same vague and redundant rhetoric puts forward the suspicion, the necessity of supposing, and the imperative of proving, and then takes it back: unfortunately, *it is very regrettable* that until now we have only been able to demonstrate the existence of libidinal drives (*Es ist zu bedauern . . . Es bleibt misslich . . .*) In other words, it is very regrettable that being unable to demonstrate our hypotheses, the only demonstrations of which we are certain remain, on the whole, in the service of Jung, *at least for the moment:* they thereby risk making the movement go astray and seducing the succession. But since it cannot be a question of establishing the succession while betraying the ideal of scientificity, we must still work out the proof. The (institutional) inheritance must be assured (sure and certain), and therefore invulnerable. The "cause," then, must be one with the cause of science, this is its best chance of survival, the most infallible right of succession, the ultimate solidity, the best assay of the rings, links, alliances, etc.

So shall we try again, one more time, another step forward? Let's go. Freud has decided upon neglecting no "promissory" of demonstration. Now, the sadistic component of the sexual drives promises something. It had been discovered a long time ago (*Three Essays. . .* , 1905), at a time when, and in a context from which, the current enigma was absent. Everything was different, the state of theoretical development, metapsychology, the economy of the family and the movement. Today, however, the sadistic component can be of new service, once it is reinscribed in a new analysis of the Ego. In effect, do we not have the authority to hypothesize that the sadistic component would be "properly a death drive" (*eigentlich ein Todestrieb*) forced away, extorted from the Ego under the influence of narcissistic libido? Originally belonging to the Ego, sadism would come to appear as such only once it is turned around or turned onto the object. It is only then that it "enters the service" of the sexual function. In passing, but only in passing and apparently,

it would render service to monistic Jungianism by dissimulating itself in its libidinal form. Apparently it would disserve the dualist
cause, and this is why it must be restored to its essential nature, and
its authentic origin: *eigentlich ein Todestrieb.*

This is a bit much, at least as concerns the gesture and the rhetorical process. We no longer have to seek, the thesis has been demonstrated. But Freud then distances certainty, once again. He has
just evoked the ambivalence of love and hate, which bears witness,
in erotic life, to an original sadism preserved from any mitigation
or intermixture. He has just recalled that his hypothesis might attest to the existence of a death drive that is certainly deferred (*ver-
schoben*), relayed, and displaced, but nonetheless exemplary. Now,
starting with the next sentence, objection: this interpretation has to
be *distanced* precisely because it is too *distant* (*entfernt*), in this
form, from the intuitive evidence, and produces a mystical impression (. . . *diese Auffassung von jeder Anschaulichkeit weit entfernt
ist und einen geradezu mystischen Eindruck macht*). And then, an
apparent improvisation in order to get out of an "embarrassing situation." First appearance of this word (*Verlegenheit*). However, this
argument was already available at a time when we were not, he continues, in an "embarrassing situation" (second time). The proof
that the argument of sadism might be reappropriated into our service and turned toward us (implied: against Jung), is masochism.
From the outset we had conceived masochism as a component drive
complementary to sadism in its turning back against one's proper
Ego (*Rückwendung . . . gegen das eigene Ich*). This extra turn
(*Wendung*), this return onto "myself," or to "myself," is nothing
other than the turn which turns the same drive toward the object.
The only correction made since then: masochism may be primary.
As this is a major correction, and as it at once proves too much or
too little, but in any event operates otherwise than as a supplementary and derivative turn, Freud does not exploit it, sends it away or
drops it, deciding, without any other transition, to return (*Aber
kehren wir . . . zurück*) to the drives which preserve life. He drops
the matter, like the note at the bottom of the page which punctuates
the end of this act: "All these discussions [those of Sabina Spielrein
and of A. Stärcke, which he has just mentioned], like that in the
text, give evidence of the demand for a clarification of the theory of
the drives such as has not yet been achieved" (55).

PARALYSIS 369

INHERITANCE TRAFFIC: PLATO'S DEBT

Fort:da. A new effort to distance the PP again, after having made or let it come back [*revenir*], a new effort to come close to the death drive which always *comes* from *leaving*, which always *has just left.* Do not the drives which preserve life, for example in protozoa, illustrate the Nirvana principle, the tendency to the lowering, or even to the suppression of all tension, that is, Freud underlines, of all "difference"? And does this not militate (it is indeed the code of militantism that has to be employed here) in favor of the death drive that nothing yet has proven? Does not the probably late, "accidental," secondary character of sexuality deprive the drives of any originality? Unfortunately, we have to distance this argument. What we sought to distance comes back, truly has never left the place that it already occupied. Even if sexuality appeared late, secondarily, derivatively, it could not emerge and become fixed except in the extent to which some presexual drive preceded it while announcing it, virtually animating it. Teleology organizes the return of the old, the oldest, the furthest away, of the "potentially" most archaic. It always authorizes one more detour. Decidedly, the life drive is indissolubly coupled to the death drive, is as one with it. The only progress so far, if this can be said seriously: we now have a double hypothesis instead of a single one, and an "equation with two unknowns."

It is exactly *there* (where? *there*), in the paralysis of this further step that always has to be taken away, it is there (but why there? why not one more or one less step? Where, there? *there*, answers life death), when Freud's step cannot go on having to walk further for nothing, it is exactly there, by virtue of an apparently external constraint (fatigue? lack of time? rules of composition for the last or next to last chapter, etc.?), that Freud calls upon a "myth": Aristophanes' discourse in the *Symposium*. One no longer dares say anything about it. After the story of the spool, this place is the one most well trodden in the psychoanalytic literature, and how could the grass grow again in such a spot? Therefore, I will say almost nothing about this too familiar story. It is true that whatever becomes *too* familiar can always be suspected of jealously keeping a secret, of standing guard over the unexpected. This could have been the case, already, of the so familiar and so familial story of the *fort:da* and of the grandson's spool. It has in common with the recourse to the myth from the *Symposium* of also being a "story." Which is the more mythic of the two, and of a "fantastic kind" (*phantasticher Art*), as Freud says only about the second? Each time, there is the moment of the interruption of a certain type of questioning in order to recount a narrative. Pause: I am going to tell you a story. In both cases, the content of the story, narrative, or citation of the narrative, comes to us *filtered:* the most active selection is marked by ellipses in great number, and the most efficacious lacunae are not punctuated by the author. In different narrative modes, certainly, which themselves deserve a minute analysis, a tissue of lacunae tends to compose another fable. In both cases, the narrative is concerned with the theme of repetition, of relation, of the narrative as a return to a previous state. This is too evident for the *fort:da* of the spool. Here, the only characteristic that Freud says he is retaining from the *Symposium,* the only one that corresponds to the "condition whose fulfillment we desire," is the characteristic which makes the drive derive from the need to restore "an earlier state of things" (57). *Fort:da.* Rest assured, I am not going to hunt too far and too long for the analogy between the two fabulous narratives. I will not look for the androgyne in the triangle of the first scene, nor for the couple which desperately seeks to reconstitute itself. Nevertheless, these two "narrative" moments must be brought together: if they are the most famous and fabulous moments of the book, it is not only because they seem to interrupt a scientific or speculative discourse, thereby making us dream. It is also because they reveal and reconstitute the narrative necessity, or rather the structure as "narrative" at the limit of which, and with which, "speculation" constantly has to deal throughout the "book." The *fort:da* is a narrative. This is a reminder which can only be recalled, fabulously, from before memory, just as the entire book is concerned with what comes back from further away than the simple origin.

The origin is a speculation.

Whence the "myth" and the *hypothesis.* If there is no thesis in this book, it is because its proper object cannot be the object of any thesis. It will have been noticed that the concept of *hypothesis* is the most general "methodological" category of the book: all the "methodical" procedures amount to [*reviennent à*] hypotheses. And when science leaves us in the dark, providing us, for example as concerns the origin of sexuality, "not so much as a ray of a hypothesis" (*nicht der Lichtstrahl einer Hypothese*), it is again to a "hypothesis," of another order certainly, that we must recur. Aristophanes' myth is presented as a "*Hypothese*" of a "fantastic" kind. It is fantastic only in an accessory way, Freud wants to emphasize, because it seriously meets the required condition: to make the drive derive from a need to restore a previous state. In effect, this is the only service that Freud at first seems to expect from this hypothesis. In any event, this is what he begins by saying: "In quite a different region, it is true, we do meet with such a hypothesis; but it is of so fantastic a kind—a myth rather than a scientific explanation—that I should not venture to produce it here, were it not that it fulfills precisely the one condition whose fulfillment we desire. For it traces the origins of a drive to *a need to restore an earlier state of things*" (57). But already in the next paragraph, a secondary profit seems to be expected from Aristophanes. Is it secondary? Is it otherwise? In question is "the most important of [the drive's] variations in relation to its object." This myth's "theory"—and Freud indeed says "theory"—, the theory which Plato "lets Aristophanes develop" [mod.] "deals not only with the *origin* of the sexual drive but also with the most important of its variations in relation to its object" (*seiner wichtigsten Variation in Bezug auf das Objekt*). Is this another goal of the same demonstration? an accessory or a principal goal? or a supplementary one, and in what sense then? And if they were the same? If there were no origin of the sexual drive except in this variation, in the variability which conditions it, in other words in the play of vicariance and of the supplement?

Rushing to extract a fragment of it, to retain only its *discursive* content—a "hypothesis," a "theory," a "myth," all three at once, for such are his own words in the lines preceding the citations—, completely preoccupied by the consideration of this fragment, which moreover he has punctured with ellipses after lifting it out of the body of the text, Freud seems barely attentive to what the *Symposium* puts onstage or hides from view in its theater. He is interested in this theater as barely as possible. Here, I am not only speaking of what by convenience might be called the literary or fictional "form" of this theater, the form of this narrative of narratives, interlacing *diagesis* with *mimesis,* and also inscribing the one in the other, thus calling for the greatest possible circumspection in listening to the invisible quotation marks. I am also speaking of the "content" of this theater, of the stories told by the narrators or speakers, stories in which other stories are told. I am speaking of the "stories," the "affairs" between the characters of the *Symposium,* of what is placed onstage within it or is hidden from sight. Now, this is not without relation to the *origin-of-the-sexual-drive,* that is to the *variation-of-the-trait-in-relation-to-the-object*. This variation is not only the theme of the symposium, as is also the birth of Eros, it is also its performance, its condition, its milieu.

Now, in the time of this performance, Aristophanes' discourse represents only one episode. Freud is barely interested in this fact, and he retains only those shards of a fragment of this episode which appear to him pertinent to his own hypothesis, to what he *says* he means. Once again, he sets himself to relating a piece of a piece of a narrative related in the *Symposium*. This is a habitual operation. Who does not do so? And the question is not one of approving or disapproving in the name of the law. Of what law? Beyond any criteria of legitimation, we can nevertheless attempt to understand what is going on in a putting into perspective, in a reading, a writing, in citations, liftings, omissions, suspensions, etc. To do this, one must set oneself to it, in the same perspective, but one must also make the relation to the object vary. Without these two conditions, the very identity of the perspective could not appear as such. As concerns Freud and Plato, the *Symposium* and *Beyond*. . . , the variety of possible perspectives is inexhaustibly rich. Obeying a law of selective economy (the limits of what I can say here, in this context whose givens are too complex for me even to attempt to reassemble them) as much as the rightful pleasure that I can give myself tonight, I will limit myself to the following traits.

First, if Aristophanes' discourse represents only a limited episode, notably as concerns what is to occur afterward, it is to limit it even more to reduce it to ten lines; but what to say then about the gesture which consists in taking no account of the person who holds the floor, of the person whom Plato "lets develop" the "theory"? No allusion to Aristophanes, save [*fors*] his name. No allusion to Socrates, who is not even named. Now, Aristophanes is not just anyone. Not just anyone for Socrates. Or for Plato. He is the other. In *The Clouds* he had violently attacked Socrates. In the *Apology*, Plato accuses him of the worst: of having been the first accuser of Socrates, or even his betrayer. He would have lent his hand to the murder, or even the suicide. And Plato, in accusing Aristophanes, defends Socrates, is behind him. Or in *front* of him, showing him with his finger as a lawyer presents the defendant: here is the innocent man, the martyr, admire him, be pardoned by him, *he* is judging you. But what is he doing by "letting" Aristophanes "develop" what Freud calls the "theory"? Alcibiades too will be behind Socrates. Further on in the *Symposium* his praise of Socrates will be a response to the calumnies of *The Clouds*, etc.

For the moment, let us be content with the following indices. In order to suggest that an immense reconstitution around these lacunae certainly would be necessary, but above all, primarily, in order to become attentive to the abyssal structure of the lacunary phenomenon. The corpus from within which Freud operates his fragmentary and lacunary liftings will never have been a complete body whose integral reconstitution would be promised to us. Narratives of mimetico-diagetic narratives, opened by a "mimed" demand for "diagesis" ("it is from you that I expect this narrative . . ."), for diageses which relate "*logoi*" (". . . *alla diegesai tines esan oi logoi . . .*"), but *logoi* which are also performing gestures; these tales begin by stating their lacunae, if not by taking an exact account of them, since this is impossible. One cannot remember everything. Even before relating the first discourse on love, Phaedrus', the lacunae are pointed out, as well as the lapses of memory, but one insists: the essential has been maintained. Of course, and Freud too will maintain the "essential." Of what was said by each Aristodemus did not remember everything (*oute panu o Aristodemos ememneto*). And I, Apollodorus, I did not remember everything that Aristodemus had said to me (*out'au ego a ekeinos elege panta, a de malista*), but the most important things—who could doubt it?—and so on, up to Freud and beyond, right here. Each one makes himself into the *facteur,* the postman, of a narrative that he transmits by maintaining what is "essential" in it: underlined, cut out, translated, commented, edited, taught, reset in a chosen perspective. And occasionally, within the narrative, lacunae are again pointed out, which makes a piece of supplementary history. And this supplement can embed itself in *abyme* within another lacuna that is bigger or smaller. Bigger or smaller because here we are within a logic that makes possible the inscription of the bigger in the smaller, which confuses the order of all limits, and forbids the *arrangement of bodies.*

Which is indeed what is going on here—the bodies are not very well arranged—and if Aristophanes' discourse is cut out of the great lacunary body of the *Symposium,* it happens that it comes as a response, in the *mise en scène,* to a demand concerning the lacuna, precisely, and the ellipsis of memory: if I have omitted or elided something, let it be your job, Aristophanes, to supplement it and to fill in the lacuna (188e). And what is Aristophanes going to recount, in order to supplement the lacuna? A story of a lacuna and of supplementation at the origin of love, of sexual difference, and of variation in relation to the object. Etc.

Thus, Freud omits the scene of the text, including the placing in *abyme* of the memories of lacunae. In this great omission, he forgets Socrates. He leaves Plato alone with Aristophanes, he leaves it to Plato to leave it to Aristophanes to develop the theory. Why? The most banal answer certainly is not incorrect. For his purpose this little extract sufficed, and let us not make mountains of molehills. Nothing else has happened. This is true. But why did nothing else happen? Why has the relation to the object not been different? Why has it not varied? What has immobilized it?

To omit Socrates when one writes, is not to omit just anything or anyone, especially when one is writing about Plato. Especially when one is writing about a dialogue of Plato's in which Socrates, a Socrates and the Socrates, is not a simple supernumerary. This omission is not a murder, of course, let us not overdramatize. It erases a singular character written or described by Plato as a character in the *Symposium*, but also as the one who will have caused or let the *Symposium* be written without writing himself, an infinitely complex scene of the signature in which the inscription arrives only to erase itself, engraves itself in depth in proportion to its erasure. Plato remains *behind* Socrates' signature, but what is this position? What does "behind" mean in this case? What does it sign, and what does it signify?

If Freud in his turn erases Socrates, which only accentuates his profile in what remains here of a *Symposium*, is this in order to pay homage to Plato for an acknowledgment of debt? Is it in order to praise an inheritance, a genealogy, a descendance? Is it in order to trace a tradition back to Plato, and to constitute himself as its heir? Is it in order to attribute to Plato the merit of an inauguration, or even a paternity? No, on the contrary. It is in order to take the origin away from Plato, and to make him, already, an heir. Not of Socrates, who is too close and too proper to him. But of someone much further away. It would be to exaggerate—a bit—to read this passage as a destitution of Plato. It would be to exaggerate, a bit, to say that Freud is vehemently determined to secondarize, to minimize, to devalue, but in the end he does insist a great deal on the fact that Plato has invented nothing, that his lack of originality is indeed the sign of the truth of what he says, that he had to inherit an entire tradition, etc. This is the object of a note which is not only the longest in the book, but also much longer than the passage it annotates. It begins curiously with the acknowledgment of a debt: not a debt to Plato, but to the person who helped Freud to think that he owed nothing to Plato, and that Plato himself was indebted to the

Hindu tradition: "I have to thank Professor Heinrich Gomperz, of Vienna, for the following discussion on the origin (*Herkunft*) of the Platonic myth . . ." (58). The note then follows, more than twice as long as the citation from the *Symposium*. It gives the impression that Freud, in effect, is more worried about "the origin of the Platonic myth" (*Herkunft des platonischen Mythus*), than about the Platonic myth of "the origin of the sexual drive" (*Herkunft des Geschlechtstriebes*). Freud compulsively seeks, q.e.d., to displace the object and to restore an "earlier state." Which is rather laborious, we are rather uneasy about this, please rest assured that we are giving you Gomperz's own words, a tug on your sleeve: I would like to draw your attention to the fact that essentially, *wesentlich,* this same theory is already to be found in the Upanishads, etc., and that "in contradiction to the prevailing opinion" I will not purely and simply deny the possibility of Plato's "dependence" (or subjection, *Abhängigkeit*), even indirectly, upon Indian thought. The word "*Abhängigkeit*" comes back further on, in the middle of confused concessions: Plato would not have appropriated (*sich nicht zu eigen gemacht*) this story through some "oriental tradition" if he had not been in a situation to be illuminated by its tenor of truth. Etc. One's eyes widen.[9]

What exactly did he wish to prove? What primarily interests him in this story, in these narratives of narratives? What story is he telling us in his turn? about what object, what earlier state? Is this a supplementary sequence of the *Symposium?* A lacuna—among others—filled in by a Viennese Aristophanes interested in relating what another Viennese has told him about the origins—not about the origins of love—but about the origins of the Platonic myth? How to delimit these narrative corpuses? and these mythic bodies [*corps*]? Who writes what? Who lets what be developed by whom? Who writes, makes or lets what be written in the abyssal embedding of couches and transferences? Where has Socrates gone? Who keeps himself behind or in front of him finally?

In this immense chain of an inheritance that is negotiated, received and rejected, incorporated or denied, in an abyssal scene of a legacy, of delegation and denegation, in this traffic of influence,

9. This is doubtless not the only place in which I must have intersected, I am pleased to say, with several of Samuel Weber's analyses in a very recent book, analyses certainly both different and much richer than the ones I was attempting here. On all these questions it seems to me that *The Freud Legend* (Minneapolis: University of Minnesota Press, 1982) will become uncircumventable.

he who says *I* here (*Ich meine natürlich die Theorie, die Plato im Symposion . . .* or *Prof. Heinrich Gomperz (Wien) verdanke ich . . .* or *möchte ich . . . nicht unbedingt verneinen. . .* , etc.) is also a *protagonist.*

What is the protagonist doing, right here? Many things at once, of course, since he is speculating.

For example, he intervenes here, in this instance in which the speculative succeeds in failing, in which it finally gives up becoming science or philosophy, whose model haunt it. It succeeds in failing *at the limit,* at the moment when the issue indeed is to go beyond the oppositional limit. Not only a given oppositional limit, but the very notion of the limit as a front between two opposed terms, between two identifiable terms. For example, but these are the examples of that in which every term terminates, life/death.

The "poet-philosopher" has beckoned, an engaging wink, but the protagonist turns down the invitation, once again. He rejects the myth's help, which must be emphasized in order to take into account the textual procedure [*démarche*] in this passage of *Beyond . . .* It must also be recalled that this mythological help, Aristophanes' discourse, meets the *same* fate in the *Symposium*. Whence the repetition. But who will have made it be written?

Once again, Freud gives up going forward. *Ich glaube, es ist hier die Stelle, abzubrechen.* "But here, I think, is the place to break off." Make it brief, time is up, end of session.

But it is not over. *La séance continue,* and the narrative follows its course. The listener-patient has gotten up, certainly. It is difficult to be sure that in fact he did not have the floor until now. Freud also gets up. He is going to speak, for himself. He already had said "I," but the mode and the tone seem to change. Now he appears to comment. He says, opening another sequence, that he is going to permit himself a "critical reflection" (*kritische Besinnung*) on what is going on. More precisely on what has just gone on, and what has gone on in the form of a "no go" and a "nothing is going on," "it goes without a step [*pas*]." Perhaps others would say that he is treating the status of his own discourse. But is this discourse a discourse? Is it his own? Is it standing on its feet? Is it walking? Does it have a status? Is its *restance* statutary?

Let us see. In what resembles a postscript or an epilogue, the protagonist-speculator affects placing himself back onstage. He acts as if he were going to define his place, to situate the "place-from-which-he-is-speaking," and even the non-place, the *non-lieu,* which does more than "acquit" him, which absolves him from any debt, any engagement, any guilt, however "symbolic." He will answer for nothing that is going on here, and which seems to have gone on *without him*, without this discourse, these advances he has made, these retreats, *faux-pas*, false exits, this imperturbably generalized *fort:da*.

Thus, he places himself onstage as if to renounce everything. I have nothing to do with it or with anyone. What he states then is very important for us. I do not mean to say that we have to believe it or not believe it. But the very suspending of this alternative has an essential signification as concerns the "status," and actually the *non-status*, of *Beyond*. . . , of the discourse held within it without being held, the multiple and mobile place of the protagonist-signer, his variable relation to psychoanalysis as science, as practice, as mythology, as literature, as speculation, etc. What does a scene of writing like this one consist of? What is its structure, and the condition for it as an event? Where, how, when, to what, and to whom does it happen?

By all rights these questions have precedence over any possible debate on the subject of the alleged theses of this book, the theses too precipitously perceived in it, as I am attempting to demonstrate. Prior questions which, to my knowledge, have never been asked. They have never even bothered all those, especially within the analytic movement, who since 1920 have entered into a battle with (very) well-drawn lines around these "theses."

There are those who have taken them "seriously," and have constructed an entire discourse about the seriousness of *Beyond* . . . In this respect, the most interesting and spectacular case, I believe, is that of Lacan.

Others, more light- or heavy-handedly, as you will, have shrugged their shoulders and politely looked away from this attack of mysticism, speculative deviation, mythological dreaming: the master has played, he was not serious, etc.

But no one on either side has examined the testamentary singularity of this scene of writing. For itself, and for its consequences for the psychoanalytic context in general. At the most, some have contented themselves with remarking on the mythological or literary *ornaments* with which Freud's thetic prose is supposed *surrounded*.

This is why we must insist upon the textual (autobiographical, heterobiographical, thanatographical, all of this in the same framework) procedure, *dé-marche*, and particularly upon this kind of postscript to the next to last chapter.

What does Freud say at the beginning of this new paragraph?

Despite the indentation, the sentence seems to continue, as a subordinate, adjunct, the end of the preceding paragraph, which said: "But here, I think, is the place to break off." New paragraph, adding: "Not, however, without adding (*anzuschliessen*) a few words of critical reflection" (59).

Thus, he is going to add, to adjoin, almost as an accessory, several supplementary, subordinate reflections. And the subordinate adjunct announces the subordinate and adjunct, supplementary, reflections, a kind of annexation. *Anschluss* is also an added piece, but also, again, a connecting train.

Let us go on: "It may be asked whether and how far I am myself convinced of the truth of the hypotheses that have been developed here. My answer would be that . . ." (59, mod.).

Let us wait a bit. What is he going to answer? Hypotheses have been *developed*, right here (*den hier entwickelten Annahmen*). By whom? This is not very clear. Freud, above all, has related the hypotheses of the ones and the others, somewhat like a narrator, a translator, a spokesman. Of course he has not lacked initiative, which is the least one might say, but finally he has *let* the others develop their hypotheses (*entwickeln lassen* were his words to describe the relation of Plato to Aristophanes' discourse). If you prefer, the others have let him develop their hypotheses. But in both cases the delegation of the "to let develop" opens a kind of mortgage or mortgaging of irresponsibility. All the more in that one is dealing with hypotheses every time: there is no engagement, not as much as there would be for theses or conclusions.

"My answer would be that . . ." (*Meine Antwort würde lauten . . .*)

What would his answer be? Another conditional hypothesis. If I were asked, then, perhaps, I might answer that . . . But what? ". . . that I am no more convinced of them than I am engaging anyone else to believe them." He does not say that he is convinced, but he does not say the opposite, he does not say that he does not believe them. And above all he does not seek to convince anyone else, to involve, to enroll, to recruit, to enlist (*werben*). The syntax of the answer is curious, and the procedure would be strange on the part of a scientist convinced of the truth of a demonstration, a philosopher advancing a thesis, or even a poet or priest always seeking to involve or to touch the other. Here, the relation to the other is not suspended, far from it, but it is entirely other. Everything seems to occur as if one were seeking to reach the other, to join him, only through a game for oneself. He no more believes in the hypotheses developed than he seeks to make anyone else believe them. But no more does he say that he does not believe them. He does not reject them. The suspense goes even further. One might think that he knows himself, Freud, to be suspended between belief and nonbelief. No, not even. It is his own knowledge about this suspension that is suspended: "More precisely (*Richtiger*), I do not know how far I believe in them (*ich weiss nicht, wie weit ich an sie glaube*)." A question of extent on which *I* is divided. A certain *I*, the same but immediately an other, does not know to what extent *I* believes in them. It is not only belief, but the relation to belief which finds itself suspended, the relation of science or of consciousness.

An *epokhē* suspends judgment, conclusion, thesis: precisely as it does in a phenomenology, which would have to be invoked here, invoked beyond the real limits, but also beyond the prohibitions and slogans, which exclude it from psychoanalysis. Freud also determines this suspensive attitude as the exclusion of the affective factor (*affektive Moment*) which accompanies any conviction or belief. "There is no reason, as it seems to me, why the affective factor of conviction should enter into this question at all."

And yet, if the affect of conviction is suspended, this is not the case for all affect, far from it. On the contrary, affect continues all the more to enliven the investigation, even if it is pursued out of simple curiosity, just to see. Once the affect of conclusion (conviction or belief) has been suspended, it "is nevertheless possible to throw oneself [to abandon oneself, a strong word, *sich hingeben*] into a line of thought (*Gedankengang*), and to follow it wherever it leads out of simple scientific curiosity, or, if the reader prefers, as an *advocatus diaboli,* who is not on that account himself sold to the devil [via a written contract: *sich darum nicht dem Teufel selbst verschreibt*]."

The devil comes back [*revient*], once again. A strange reappearance: why compare to a diabolical operation that which is presented here as a suspensive procedure, a concern of curiosity, or even scientific curiosity? Actually, the comparison is not to the devil himself—and this is even more double, more duplicitous, more diabolical—, but to the devil's advocate. But why would scientific curiosity be on that side? on the side or at the sides of the devil? What of the devil in science or in psychoanalysis? The devil's advocate is not the devil. But this is perhaps more cunning. The advocate *represents* the devil at the bar. At the bar, he feigns, conventionally, and in order to make his profit, taking the devil's part. For a time. But what the devil, for no one demands that he believe in the devil, in the devil's guilt or innocence. One demands nothing of him, no one wants to know anything about what he thinks in his heart of hearts [*dans son for intérieur*]. Even if he believes, in the devil, he can act so as to take his part or to place the devil on his side without placing himself on the devil's side, without placing himself there fully, without giving himself, selling himself, or promising himself to the devil. No contract beyond representation, the time to plead the case. No written promise to the devil, neither in red nor in black, blood nor ink, like the double pact of Chistoph Haitzmann, the painter of *Eine Teufelsneurose* (1923, S.E. 19). All this suspense holds back the "third step."

This is the third step (*der dritte Schritt*) in the theory of the drives which does not reach the certainty of the two preceding steps, when the issue was to extend the concept of sexuality or to posit narcissism. In these last two cases, or steps, the transition from observation to theory would only have been a translation (*Übersetzung*), and Freud seems to mean by this that a translation does not unbalance equivalences. While at the third step, an advance that concerns precisely, the "regressive character" of the drives, the translation (*Übersetzung*) might comport an exaggeration, an overestimation (*Überschätzung*) of the "significance" of the facts and materials of observation. From whence would this overestimating translation come, this transgression in translation? From whence, in this third step, would the step too many come?

The question rigorously concerns the speculative threshold, the separation or interval that speculation properly crosses over. It passes over (*Über, Übersetzung* like *Überschätzung*), it is beyond measure. It goes beyond the observable and the *visible*. It has nothing to do with *intuition*. In work of this kind, says Freud "I do not think a large part is played by what is called 'intuition'" (*der sogennannten Intuition*), that is, by "intellectual impartiality." One is rarely impartial when "ultimate things," "the great problems of science and life," are concerned. This is where "speculation" enters the scene, it is proper to "each of us," its strategy is idiomatic every time, and it is "dominated" by "predilections," by "preferences" (*Vorliebe*). This is what the protagonist-speculator *believes* here, this is what he confesses of his belief, this is his credo, his "I believe": "I believe that each of us here is dominated (*beherrscht*) by predilections which have deep internal foundations" (59; mod.). Henceforth, each of us lets himself be motivated, in his "speculation," "unwittingly" (*unwissentlich*).

But what is going to permit the unconscious "predilections" to govern the work and to have the advantage over speculation? This is not the most serious question. One first has to know how to comport oneself in relation to these preferences once they act "unwittingly" on the researcher or speculator, once that they can precisely make of the researcher a speculator, once that without them the very impetus of scientific *and* speculative research could not be given.

Everything would be simpler if these preferences intervened only within the separation between intuitive observation (which, from Freud's point of view at least, is what guarantees the scientificity of an undertaking) and speculative construction. Now, it does indeed seem that Freud acknowledges this, at the end of a reasoning entangled by its comings and goings: the simple transition from descriptive intuition to language, the simple setting into discourse of an empirical given opens the field for speculation, and therefore for predilections. And this is due to the structure of scientific language, to its history and irreducible metaphoricity.

In effect, one has to link the problem of "figurative language" (*Bildersprache*), such as it comes up at the end of this chapter, with the considerations about the speculator's predilections. In this entire passage, the dominant code is that of faith, of confidence, of distrust, of belief. Freud has very little "faith" in so-called intuition, or rather he believes very little in it, just as he believes very little in intellectual impartiality. He "believes" in the effects of predilections, which leads him not to believe, and to the greatest "distrustfulness" (*Misstrauen*) as being the best grounded. The only possible solution: a cool benevolence (*ein kühles Wohlwollen*) that is indifferent to the results of our own deliberations: a self-critical attitude (*Selbstkritik*) which does not engage one in any tolerance and any pluralism, any relativism. Freud seems to wish to maintain *simultaneously*—insofar as the "first step" is concerned—the primacy of observation, which is to govern everything, and the suspensive floating of an always "provisional," and an always already speculative theory.

And the site of this provisional floating is indeed language, but, as we shall see, this provisionalness is irreducible. Of course one has to be inflexible, intransigent, intolerant as concerns theories that contradict observation from their "first steps." Of course, in order to judge our speculations, one must not let oneself be disturbed by strange processes foreign to intuition (*unanschauliche*). And the example that Freud then gives is precisely that of which he has just spoken, the repression of one drive by another or the displacement of a drive turned away from the ego toward the object. At this point, what distances us from intuition, and legitimately provokes distrust, is language, or more precisely the figurative structure of language and the necessity of borrowing these figures from already constituted sciences, here psychology, and more precisely the psychology said to be of the depths. Everything is due to the difficulty of properly *naming* the thing itself. Actually this difficulty is an impossibility, a difficulty whose limits can only be indefinitely pushed back. Let us try to name, more or less properly, this difficulty, this impossibility, their necessity. It is more difficult to situate and to reassemble than one might believe at first approach.

There is the necessity of *translating* an observation (whether it is considered as foreign to language or already caught in it) into a description (*Beschreibung*), that is into language.

There is the necessity of translating this translation into the language of *theory* (*Übersetzungen der Beobachtung in Theorie*): the observation must not only be translated into a descriptive language, it must be translated into a theoretical language.

There is the necessity of borrowing the schemas of this theoretical language from another science, an already existing science, in other words the necessity of again translating the previous translations by making them pass, by transposition, from a scientific region of departure to a scientific region of arrival. One does not only borrow ordinary language for all these translations, but also the borrowings that the constituted sciences—from which one is borrowing—make from ordinary language.

Finally, there is the necessity of working with the *Bildersprache* of this borrowed scientific language. This is the only recourse: "We are obliged to operate with the scientific terms, that is to say with the figurative language, proper to psychology (*mit der eigenen Bildersprache der Psychologie*), or, more precisely, to depth psychology" (60; mod.).

All these trajectories—transitional, transcriptive, transpositional and transgressive, transferential trajectories—open the very field of speculation. It is there that speculation finds its possibility and its interest. There, that is, in the trans—or the *Über*—of translation (*Übersetzung*), of overestimation (*Überschätzung*), of metaphor or of transference (*Übertragung*).

But this entire surplus value is itself the object of a double evaluation by Freud. On the one hand, an entire series of statements implies the primacy of intuition, of observation, of perception, all of which are to guarantee the ulterior translations as much as possible, the entire series of transpositions which *would come only after the first step.* In this case the profits and the risks would be secondary, derivative, after the fact. There would be the first and the second step, or even the third step, there would be the origin and the series of repetitions, but no repetition or translation at the origin.

But, on the other hand, other statements situate discourse at the very heart of perception, from its first step, and as its condition. All the movements in *"trans-,"* the ones that involve repetitions, displacements, and speculations, would not be after the fact in relation to a perceptive or intuitive origin, they would inhabit this origin on its very threshold. And they would habilitate it, would make it possible by giving it right of way: "We could not otherwise [without the help of this language] describe the processes in question at all, and *indeed we could not even have perceived* (wahrgenommen) *them"* (60; mod.). My emphasis. Thus, the oppositional limit between perception and its other has been erased. Nevertheless Freud appeared to hold to it as to the tribunal of science, the critical agency and source of all legitimacy. It is this limit which was to guarantee the emission of conceptual signs and to protect all the movements in *trans-* from speculative excess. Now, this safeguard has disappeared *en route: en route,* that is, as soon as one has sought to take more than one step. But it is not a question—*en route*—of a simple disappearance of the safeguard *after the first step.* For the first step to have opened the way it already will have been necessary that the safeguard be unavailable. It will have been necessary, as the very condition of what is called a perception or a description at the edge of perception, that all the movements in *trans-* be of the party. From the first intuition, from its threshold, all the speculative transferences are of the party. I am purposely regrouping all the movements in *trans-* under the word *transference,* whether in question is translation toward descriptive or theoretical language, transposition from one science to another, metaphoric transposition within language, etc. The word transference reminds one of the unity of its metaphoric network, which is precisely metaphor and transference (*Übertragung*), a network of correspondences, connections, switch points, traffic, and a semantic, postal, railway sorting without which no transferential destination would be possible, in the strictly technical sense that Freud's psychoanalysis has sought to assign to this word (see the end of chapter III).

The corresponding "concept" remains no less enigmatic, and when Freud or others attempt to define the "strict" sense of the word, they call upon an entire stock of metaphors and of metaphors of metaphors. This is not fortuitous. All these metaphors regroup themselves around the notions of repetition, of analogy, of correspondence in view of a destination, of relay, of reedition or corrected and revised edition, transcription, translation from an "original." The passage between transference (in every sense) and speculation that we are situating here perhaps becomes more salient. Speculative transference orients, *destines,* calculates the most original and most passive "first step" on the very threshold of perception. And this perception, the desire for it or its concept, belongs to the destiny of this calculation. As does every discourse on this subject. This one, of course, Freud's, of which he speaks also. Freud designates the "predilections" which orient speculative transference, shows their necessity and their effects only by speaking of himself, in the self-critical movement which at no moment alleges that it escapes from the fatalities that it defines. Once the term and the oppositional limit are erased, and replaced by an entirely other structure, the suspensive procedure [*démarche*] appears interminable. The interminable is not accidental, does not come, as if from the outside, to mark incompletion and infirmity. Speculative repetition and transference start the march.

Thus, one is less surprised to see that Freud does not expect from scientific progress a finally proper language, purified of every metaphor, and finally *surpassing* its *trans*ference: even if one could replace the terms of psychology with those of physiology or chemistry, one would dispose only of more "familiar" and "simpler" significations, but not of appropriated significations. The language of physiology or of chemistry is also a "*Bildersprache.*" Therefore, progress can be made only within metaphoric transference. *To borrow* is the law. Within every language, since a figure is always a borrowed language, but also from one discursive domain to another, or from one science to another. Without borrowing, nothing begins, there is no proper fund/foundation [*fonds*]. Everything begins with the transference of funds, and *there is interest in borrowing,* this is even its initial interest. To borrow yields, *brings back,* produces surplus value, is the prime mover of every investment. Thereby, one begins by speculating, by betting on a value to be produced as if from nothing. And all these "metaphors" confirm, as metaphors, the necessity of what they state.

It is true that Freud often describes this structural necessity as an external and provisional fatality, as if the provisional were only what it is, provisional. A very classical logic: suspense is provisional, the borrowing supposes a proper fund, the notes and the coins must be guaranteed in the final judgment. He bends the last paragraph of this chapter to this logic, the paragraph which concerns biologism or the biological model, "borrowings" (*Anleihen*) from biological science. Such borrowings increase "by degrees" "the uncertainty of our speculation": for the possibilities of biology are infinitely open and in several years the entire landscape of these questions and answers might be overturned. Thus, our construction of hypotheses can crumble in a minute. Like a *house of cards,* says the French translation: an interesting metaphor, a significant transposition or transference which translates aptly the necessarily ludic characteristic of this speculation. But there is no house of cards in the literality of the original text. There is: ". . . *unser ganzer künstlicher Bau von Hypothesen,"* another, not less interesting, not less interested, metaphor: it states art or artifice, which is not far from play; it also states the construction (of the engineer or the artist, the player, the narrator or the child) which, in its fragility as an artifact, can be "blown away" (*umgeblasen*), deconstructed according to a necessity which cannot be without relation to the "dissimilating" process of the *Ab-bauen* of which we spoke above.

Confronted by risk, by notes drawn on an uncertain future, by terminable-interminable suspense, Freud assumes both his desire and the throw of the dice. And there is never the one without the other.

These are the last words of the chapter. To every chagrined, anxious or pressing objection, to every attempt at scientistic or philosophizing intimidation, this is how I hear Freud's answer resonate, at my own risk and peril, and I translate it: "go look for yourself, as for me I like it, the beyond of the PP is my rightful pleasure. The hypothesis of the death drive: for myself I like it, and above all it interests me, I find, and thus I take my interest there." Here is the original text that I have just translated, and that I translate now in another way. If one has confidence in certain norms, one will doubtless find it more faithful. "If so, it may be asked why I have embarked upon efforts such as those consigned to this chapter, and why they are delivered for publication. Well—I cannot deny that some of the analogies, correlations and connections which it contains *seemed* to *me* to deserve consideration" (60; mod.). My emphasis: *mir der Beachtung würdig erschienen sind.* Period, the end. This is the final point, the last words of the chapter. Only a note finds itself called upon by these last words, it concerns the evolution of the terminology, the nomenclature, the names given, the *Namengebung* precisely.

The last words of the chapter could have been the last of the book. They indeed seem like it. And what else is there to say, in effect, after this signature in the form of "if I wish to"? Did it not in fact seal a kind of codicil? the supplementary postscript of an "auto-critique" without pity? What remains to be added?

Nothing perhaps, if not a seventh chapter, at the end of an exhausting week, our "Sunday"—or, if you prefer, Saturday—chapter. In certain respects, this seventh chapter adds nothing, and this is what might seal speculation on the figure.

4

SEVEN: POSTSCRIPT

INSOLVENCY—POST EFFECT

The seventh, then. The last, by far the shortest. It resembles another postscript, another codicil, the postscript or codicil to the entire book this time. Everything seems finished when it begins. Then, due to its briefness, it seems to scan a cadence. It is shorter than the shortest of the other chapters, the first one. The pace and rhythm of this composition are rather remarkable. One thinks of a series of rockets or salvos. The chapters rise, press forward, and grow increasingly longer until the smallest final repercussion: five pages, then twice seven pages, then twice a dozen, finally twenty pages—and suddenly, the last chapter, the shortest, three little pages.

This is the end: an appendix that is as reduced as possible, free, detachable too, a play appendix. This supplement of a postscript is all the more detachable in that it seems to add nothing, in its content, to the total corpus. One more *fort:da* for nothing, a repetitive, redundant review in the shape of a comet's tail. It immediately denounces its redundance, it begins by declaring, once again, that everything still remains unresolved (*noch ungelöst*). The problem remains unresolved, as well as the task (*Aufgabe*) it proposed. The problem is still, one repeats again, that of the repetition compulsion in its relation to the mastery of the PP. And the chapter closes by limping with a poetic reference to limping. A citation of Scripture cited by the script of a poet ("What we cannot reach flying we must reach limping . . . Scripture tells us it is no sin to limp" Ruckert, the *Maqamat* of al-Hariri), this allusion to limping in a way cites the chapter itself, in its brief uselessness, summons it to appear and to testify, causing it to be remarked as a kind of atrophied member or club foot.

But is all this, in the last analysis, as short and as useless as it appears? Does nothing happen with this shortened member or club foot? Does it advance nothing? One must first recall that the citation of Scripture, and the citation of this citation, like the club foot itself, like limping in general, are there in order to supplement, or more precisely, in order to "console" (*trösten*). To compensate. And they do so within a difficulty or a misfortune, the destiny or the fatality of the "advance" [*marche*]. It is because the *rate of advance* is slow in the order of "scientific knowledge" that one calls upon this assistance. The poet is to console us "*über die langsamen Fortschritte unserer wissenschaftlichen Erkenntnis.*" Next, as concerns the supplementary prosthesis, in chapter V there was an example that I did not wish to cite in passing. There, Freud spoke of the repetition compulsion and of reproduction in the biological domain, or more precisely of the prosthesis with which a living organism replaces a lost member: "So too the power of reproduction, by means of which a lost organ is replaced (*ersetzt*) by the new formation (*Neubildung*) of a precisely similar one, extends far up into the animal kingdom" (37; mod.).

Again transference, ersatz, transposition into the analogical supplement, and prosthesis. And Freud was beginning to know, or at least to foresee, what it meant to speak of the prosthesis, or to have the prosthesis at the mouth. I am not only thinking of the cigars, but also of the terribly narcissistic and supplementary cells that it will have been necessary, interminably, until death, to replace with a more and more sumptuous artificial palate, with which a PP has a hard time reckoning. But the discourse on the prosthesis had begun much earlier.

Is nothing happening then in this little prosthesis of the last chapter? After all the exhausting crises, indecisions, departures-returns, all the additional steps and no more steps [*les pas de plus et les plus de pas*], doubtless the problem remains "unresolved." But what kind of irresolution is in question? What kind of insolution and insolvency?

Irresolution and insolvency: perhaps these words do not resonate solely in the register of the theoretical problem to be resolved. Perhaps one also has to understand the lexical keyboard of speculation: an investment made by borrowing would be underwriting a speculation without any possibility of amortization. Unpayable debts would have been contracted, engagements taken on that no one could be "acquitted" of or could answer for. Thus the debtor, and first of all the theoretician who will have promised more than he can provide, knows himself to be insolvent. The speculator would be bankrupt. The death drive and the repetition compulsion would have led him, sucked him into the abyss of the PP by always adding a supplement of abyss beneath his steps. The *engagement* to treat a question then becomes a debt, that is a guilt of which he never again will be absolved. No reconciliation ever will be possible. The psychoanalyst-theoretician responsible for the Beyond of the PP will never be pardoned. There is fault, violence, crime. An unpayable debt would have been contracted. Why unpayable, at bottom? Perhaps because economy itself has been transgressed here, not economy in general, but an economy in which the principle of equivalency would have been violated. All the movements in *trans-* would have violated this principle, and along with it everything that can insure a payment, a reimbursement, an amortization, an "acquittal": coins, signs and their *telos,* the adequation of the signified to the signifier. This infraction, to wit the speculative transference, would have rendered debt both infinite or unpayable, and therefore nul. It is the economic space of the debt which finds itself overturned, immensely enlarged and by the same token neutralized. Whence the double tonality of a writing: at once grave, discouraged, sighing over the task or the inexhaustible debt, and simultaneously carefree, cavalier, affirmative.

Insolvency and irresolution—perhaps these words also call upon what might be called *bindinal* economy. Economy of the tie or the bond (*bind,* band, double band, double bind, contra-band). The German *Binden,* concept or metaphor, plays, as we know, a formidable role in this text and this problematic. Everything seems to be played out, or rather knotted, in the more or less loose stricture of energy, in the more or less dissolved, detached, resolved, absolved (*aufgelöst*) ties or bonds.

Unbinding, unknotting, detachment, resolution of a problem, acquittal of a task, a duty, a debt, withdrawal of promise or engagement kept, all these regimes of the *lösen* govern the text we are reading, and that we are reading as an interminable narrative.

At the seventh step it has not yet reached its denouement. Binding continues to dominate the scene, in the form that is essentially and par excellence dominating, that of the PP.

For the binding with which one cannot finish is not a binding among others. It is binding itself, the principle of binding which is intimately bound up with the authority "in person," if this can be said, the PP.

What is going to happen now? Are we to know the denouement?

No, of course. But will we be able to say that nothing has happened? No, of course.

First paragraph of chapter VII: the last lap is begun, it will be brief, truncated, as if interrupted, but for the moment we are only holding onto a hypothesis, one might say to a thread. What Freud calls irresolution is maintained within the dependence of this hypothesis. The argument has the following form: even with our hypothesis, even if it were confirmed as a thesis, we would not have the solution. Our problem and our task would remain what they are for the moment: *ungelöst*. Certainly the usage of this word is trivial here, and Freud indeed seems to mean something very banal: the problem is not resolved. Why seek in this word a depth or bearings that appear in neither a cursory writing nor reading? Is it not abusive to go beyond a kind of immediate semantic consciousness which has nothing to do, in the functional contract that guides it, with a great reawakening of allegedly sleeping metaphors? Certainly. But this is not what is in question. It is not a question of gaining access to the hidden metaphor, and even less to the used-up metaphor of a word. No more is it a question of tracking down the secret of Freud's writing when he has recourse to a given word. It is not the word, the word alone, or the word primarily that retains us. Nor even Freud's intention at the moment when he uses this word.

But then why come to a halt at this word, and by what right place it in relation to the binding and unbinding of energy, to the stricture of the *Binden,* which in effect forms the conceptual armature of the entire Freudian argumentation?

This placing in relation, to which in effect I am proceeding, is not an immediate one. It passes through the relay of an entire chain of questions. For example this one: what is it *to resolve* a problem? Whether a theoretical or a practical problem is in question, one is concerned with difficulties, obstacles, at least provisional blockages. To tend toward the solution is to accumulate and to bind, "to band" the maximum of energy at the greatest proximity to the obstacle, to make the tension mount until the solution unknots not only the "problem," but also the bonds of energy accumulated around the problem. The solution resolves the physical and psychical drive tensions that the problem had accrued to itself. In their great banality, these schemas are Freudian. If I am recalling them here, and if I insist upon invoking them simultaneously from the in a way "objective" side of the (theoretical or practical) problems and from the "subjective" side, it is in order to place in constant relation, as I have been doing from the beginning, what Freud says and what Freud does, what *Beyond* . . . treats (its objects, hypotheses and laws, its problems) *and* its writing procedure [*démarche*], its performances and operations. When Freud says "we find ourselves before an unresolved problem. . . ," the state he is then describing must correspond to what he says in the same book about the resolution of a problem or of a difficulty or of a tension in general. In any event, this state must be put to the test of such a correspondence and such a responsibility. But is the question of such a correspondence or such a responsibility solvable? What happens when acts or performances (discourse or writing, analysis or description, etc.) are part of the objects they designate? When they can be given as examples of precisely that of which they speak or write? Certainly, one does not gain an auto-reflective transparency, on the contrary. A reckoning is no longer possible, nor is an account, and the borders of the set are then neither closed nor open. Their trait is divided, and the interlacings can no longer be undone.[1] Perhaps this where the ultimate resistance to the solution is found, and to make it appear more clearly, or rather to infer it more accurately, for it never appears, one must place in relation the procedure of *Beyond* . . . and the structure of its objects, the irresolution of its problems (in its procedure) and what the book says about the solution of problems in general (in its objects). Its procedure [*démarche*] is one of its objects, whence its pace (*allure*), and this is why it does not advance [*aller*] very well, or work [*marcher*] by itself. One of its objects among others, but also the object for which there are other objects with which to effect *trans-* and to speculate. This object among others is not just any object. Thus it limps and is hard to close.

What has just been said, principially, about "solution," can be said, in the greatest proximity, about "analysis." The stakes appear even more clearly. But let us leave this. (*To leave, laisser:* is this another modality of *to unbind?* Let us leave this, the problem was knotted elsewhere.)

The notion of solution, in the case of the problem to be resolved, is found therefore, as we said, in the *mouvance,* in the *dépendance*[2] of the principial hypothesis. But it can be put more precisely: this hypothesis not only concerns bonds, it also touches upon dependence or independence (*Unabhängigkeit*) in relation to the PP. In

1. Other essays (to appear) analyze this figure under the heading of "double chiasmatic invagination of the borders."

2. TN. On *mouvance,* on the double, active and passive relations of dependence, and on words in *-ance,* see above, "Freud's Legacy," note 3.

other words in relation, as we will verify, to a principle which functions on the condition of *binding*.

Dependence or independence as concerns a principle of binding: here is the first sentence of the chapter, it begins with an *if:* "If it is really the case that seeking to restore an earlier state of things is such a universal characteristic of the drives, we need not be surprised that so many processes take place in mental life independently of the pleasure principle" (62).

This is the intermediary stage of an argument: if our hypothesis is the right one, if it is true that the drives tend to restore an earlier state, then we need not be surprised that so many processes are independent of the PP. This is not very clear, and the thing will rebound very soon, for why wouldn't this be surprising once pleasure has also been defined as a drop in tension and as discharge, that which tends to restore the earlier state? In any event, for the moment we are told that we need not be surprised about independence in relation to the PP.

Now, the entire difficulty resides in this notion of independence. It is rather indeterminate. Independence is a relation in the mode of the non-relation. And to say that given processes remain independent of the PP is to say nothing about their relation to the PP. Now, it is just this problem of the relation that is going to remain *ungelöst,* unresolved. *Ungelöst* also qualifies (the problem of) this non-relation or this indeterminateness of the relation between the processes of drive repetition and the PP. "But all of this," says Freud [these processes of return to the earlier state] "in this place where the PP has not yet exercised its power (*Macht*), thus has no need to stand in opposition to it (*im Gegensatz zu ihm zu stehen*), and our problem [our task, *Aufgabe*] remains unresolved (*ungelöst*), to wit, how to determine the relation of the processes of drive repetition to the dominance of the PP" (62, mod.).

Power, dominance, mastery (*Herrschaft*), the PP extends its domination over the psychic, over the *domain* of the psychic. Once it dominates all living subjectivity, the sense of such a mastery knows no regional limit: another way of saying that we are not speaking here of mastery as a simple metaphor. It is on the basis of this mastery, exercised by what is called here the PP, over every psychic subject (over every living organism, conscious or unconscious) that afterward one can determine any mastery at all, figuratively or derivatively. Thus it would be from this "psychic" mastery that mastery in its so-called current, usual or literal, to wit proper, sense would be derived, in the "domains" of technique or expertise, of politics or the struggle between consciousnesses. All these masteries call upon the subject or consciousness. Once that the mastery of the PP is what initially reigns over this subject or consciousness, one must first refer to this mastery in order to seek out some "proper" meaning, or even some meaning "of the proper." It remains to be seen whether one might not be very disarmed, upon approaching this "domain," for summoning up the proper. We will come soon to the process of exappropriation which principially structures the PP. And above all, as we had already recognized, we are in a domain without domain in which the search for the proper, law of laws and law without law, exceeds all oppositions, and *par excellence* the opposition of life and death. The death drive pushing toward autodestruction, toward dying-of-one's-proper-death—the proper is produced here as autothanatography, and sufficiently separates itself from itself in this "relation," this "report," this "narration," so that we no longer know just what we are saying when we say proper, law of the proper, economy, etc.

What holds here for the figure of mastery, with the necessary inversion of the figurative and the quasi-proper, the regional and the non-regional, also holds for all notions and all figures, whether they depend directly on mastery or not. For example, those that play a determining role in this chapter, those of *service* (processes are *in the service, im Dienste* of the PP, the PP is *in the service* of the death drives), of tendency, or of function. The idea of functioning must be submitted to a reevaluation all the more rigorous in that one might easily take it for a technological figure, a machinelike regularity transported into the psycho-biological domain. Today this functionalist vocabulary invades everything, and often in pre-critical usages.

In this context Freud distinguishes function from tendency. Starting, if you will, from the "metaphor" of the psychic apparatus, he recalls one of its most "important" "functions," and especially the most ancient, most primitive, quasi-congenital, and therefore essential functions. This "function" (*Funktion*) is the *Binden,* the operation which consists in binding, enmeshing, tying up, garroting, tightening, banding. But what? Well, that which is as original as this function of stricture, to wit, the forces and excitations of the drives, the X about which one does not know what it is before it is banded, precisely, *and* represented by representatives.

For this early and decisive function consists of binding *and* of replacing: to bind is immediately to supplement, to substitute, and therefore to represent, to replace, to put an *Ersatz* in the place of that which the stricture inhibits or forbids. To bind, therefore, is also *to detach,* to detach a representative, to send it on a mission, to liberate a missive in order to fulfill, at the destination, the destiny of what it represents. A *post* effect. *Of a postman [facteur] charged with proceeding toward delivery.*

In the same statement, describing one and the same operation, one and the same function, Freud says that it consists of binding (*Binden*) the primary process (*pp*) and of replacing (*ersetzen*) the *pp* which has mastery (*herrschenden*) over the life of the drives with the secondary process: displacement, replacement of mastery, stricture as supplementary detachment. The secondary is the supplementary *sending* (*envoi*). It transforms freely mobile cathectic energy into immobile cathectic energy, it *posits* and *posts*. Now here is a thesis. The immobilized cathexis becomes more tonic. The notion of tonicity regularly finds itself associated with the effect of binding, which thus signifies both elasticity and tension. Which consolidates the legitimacy of the translation of *binden* by *to band* [*bander*].³ And, taking into account the supplementary relays that I have just recalled, to post:to band. Postal:binding.

The function of the *Binden* is one of the most original and decisive functions of the psychic apparatus. Whether or not it is accompanied by pleasure matters little for Freud at this moment. He keeps this out of his consideration. He keeps out of his consideration the entire relation between these movements and modes of the *pose,* of the *Setzen* (*Ersetzen* of the primary by the secondary, transformation—*Umsetzung*—of free cathectic energy—*Besetzung*—into tonic cathexis, etc.) and the eventual development of an unpleasure. What is important to him is that this entire transformation (*Umsetzung*) does not undermine, affect, or contradict the PP, on the contrary, and rather occurs "in its service."

Now, since we are reading Freud with one hand, and with the other, via an analogous vocabulary, the Hegel of the dialectic of the master and the slave, let us notice the word that Freud uses in order to say that the function of the *Binden* does not come to contradict the PP, and rather keeps itself in its service: "but the PP does not thus find itself suspended (*aufgehoben, relevé.*)" ⁴ One might liter-

3. TN. It must be recalled that the usual French translation of *binden* is *lier.* Thus it is a short step from *liaison* ("binding") to *banding*. The end of this paragraph reads in the original "*bander: poster. Liaison: postale.*" Further consequences of the translation of *binden* by *bander* will be discussed in note 6, below.
4. TN. I have followed Strachey here, and have given *aufgehoben* (from *aufheben*) as "suspended," instead of following my usual practice of keeping to Der-

ally say, relieved of, suspended from its function. The displacement-replacement operated by binding is rather "in the service" of the PP (*Die Umsetzung geschieht vielmehr im Dienste des Lustprinzips*). Binding (to band, to post) works for the PP. How? Here, two moments, two predicates, two descriptive themes. *Bindung* is a preparatory act (*vorbereitender Akt*) in the exercise of the PP. As such, it is not yet the PP, it only paves the way for the mastery of the latter . . . Then, the way paved, it introduces the master and, second moment, inaugurates him, assures him, confirms and affirms him in his mastery. Therefore *Bindung* overflows mastery as the seat of its condition. There is no mastery which has not been prepared, introduced, and confirmed by *Bindung*, by the band or by the post. There is no mastery without this, and what to master means cannot be understand otherwise. ". . . binding (*Bindung*) is a preparatory act which introduces and assures (*einleitet und sichert*) the dominance of the pleasure principle" (62).

PLATO BEHIND FREUD

The *relève* (*Aufhebung*) has just been named. In the hypothesis in which the PP would come to be suspended (*aufgehoben, relevé*), would this be a *relève* in the conventionally Hegelian sense? This could mean many things, but not the PP's simple defeat or suppression. And this does not amount to a particular question of rhetoric or translation, nor even one example among others of the difficulties, at least since Hegel, of translating *Aufhebung*.[5] If the PP corresponds to an original and general function of the psychic apparatus, then what we said above about mastery holds here for the *relève*: what is going on with the PP will not be understood *on the basis of* what we understand under the heading of *Aufhebung*. In fact, the entire interpretation of the *relève* in return finds itself determined by what we might say, if we could say something, about the functioning of the PP, about (postal) binding, the supplement of stricture, the detachment of the band, etc.

---

rida's *relever*. "Suspended" conforms to Freud's sense here, and includes one of the meanings of "*relever*," i.e. to be relieved of; of course it does not have the rich, Hegelian resonances of *aufheben*, especially in relation to the question of mastery. On *Aufhebung* and *relève*, see "Différance," in *Margins of Philosophy*, p. 19 n. 23.

5. On this entire problematic, today, the reading of Jean-Luc Nancy's admirable book, *La remarque spéculative* (*un bon mot de Hegel*) (Paris: Galilée, 1973), seems imperative to me. The relation between *Aufheben* and *Auflösen* in Hegel is precisely what is analyzed there, pp. 45ff.

If, as such, binding is not yet accompanied by either pleasure or unpleasure, if at least it can be isolated from them, where is this *preparatory* act to be situated? What does to prepare signify in this case? What about this *pre?* It is simultaneously, in this *lapse* or *capsule,* indifferent to pleasure and to unpleasure *and* rather interested, inspired, called upon, by the PP, since it announces the PP in its turn and *makes room* for it. It precedes and prefigures it. Of the two modes of the *pre,* only the latter one seems teleological. The first one seems indifferent. How to adjust the *telos* to indifference, the ends of one to the ends of the other?

Freud sharpens the already mentioned distinction between *function* and *tendency.* Between the two the relation is precisely one of service (*Dienst*). The functions of binding are rather in the service of the PP. But the latter is a tendency in the service of a still more general function, the most general and most unconditioned function there is. Which one? The one destined to render the psychic apparatus unexcitable, impassive, without excitation (*erregungslos*), or at least to maintain excitation at as constant and as low a level as possible. Such a function would participate in the general tendency of living organisms to make their return to the repose of the inorganic world. This tendency, this dynamic movement which pushes backward and makes every force tend toward coming back [*revenir*], this *streben* would be *the most general* function. Freud does not prove it here, but contents himself with an appeal to shared experience: "We have all experienced . . ." What? where? In the greatest enjoyment, the enjoyment bound to the sexual act, or rather bound-unbound by the sexual act. This enjoyment is bound (*verbunden*) to the momentary extinction (*Erlöschen*) of a very intensified drive excitation. "But the binding (*Bindung*) of the drive excitation would be a preliminary function" (62; mod.). Every preliminary binding *tends, stretches*[6] (itself) toward the pleasure of discharge or of the final relaxation.

At this point the PP would not be a function but a tendency in the service of this general function. But it would have another function

6. TN. *Bander* in French also means *tendre,* to stretch. Derrida is playing on Freud's calling the PP a *tendency,* in French a *tendance.* (Note the *-ance* of *tendance,* to which the English "tendency" does not do justice.) Further, *bander,* in relation to *tendre,* also means to get an erection. The relations between tending, banding, and posting that Derrida is elaborating here make the erection into a *tendance,* a stretching without finality that always *comes back.* Further, "double bind" in French is "*double bande,*" and *bande* here can be understood either as noun or verb. The latter reading gives "the double bands" or "the double has an erection"; *la double bande* or *le double bande.* See also below, "Du Tout," note 4.

(binding) in its service. The general functioning would move from one function to the other, from the function of the *Binden* to the function in its most general form (return to the inorganic and Nirvana) via the intermediary or place of passage, the *step* [*pas*] of a *tendency,* to wit the PP. The *pas de PP* between two functions or two forms of general functioning.

If, once again, we *overlap* what Freud says with what he does, or rather with what happens (without happening) in *Beyond* . . . , we will say that the irresolution of the scene of writing that we are reading is that of a *Bindung* which tends, stretches itself and ceaselessly posts (sends, detaches, displaces, replaces) to the extreme, without conclusion, without solution, without acting, and without a final orgasm (rather a series of orgasmic tremors, of enjoyments deferred as soon as obtained, posted in their very instance), along the line of the greatest tension, at the limit of the beyond of the PP, without simply stepping over the line, the best way of stepping beyond remaining that of stepping this way, the beyond of pleasure remaining the end of pleasure. And when one insists upon pleasure without end, one is taking one's stand from the end of pleasure. One takes pleasure only to lose it—and to keep it *comes back, amounts* [*revient*] to the same. Everything must come to pass in the "solution."

"Literal" pleasure, pleasure at its proper moment: we still do not know what it is. We are still speaking, under this heading, of a tendency, served by a function, and in the service of a function. The function which orients the tendency is also the function of a trajectory, a transit. The step or the *trans-* always already have the form of the return. It begins by coming back [*revenir*], by tending toward the annulling of its own process. This is also the progress of the proper which lets itself be enmeshed by this circular ring. Pleasure is found en route, the place of passage and moment of the ring. It would be found en route, and would render service in order to return to the way of the inanimate. To fall asleep is the best example of this.

Pleasure, if it is found, the tendency to pleasure and the mastery of the PP thus would have their proper place between the two limits of the without-pleasure, stricture and discharge, preparation and end, desire, if you prefer, and its final fulfillment: banding-posting and delivering (*Erledigung,* Freud had just said). An always liminary place of passage (an undecided hymen caught in the ring). No pleasure before, no pleasure after, but during, only the passage of the step [*pas de plaisir avant, pas de plaisir après, mais pendant, c'est seulement le passage du pas*]. Over what, then, would the PP reign, the PP whose step, however, would be so difficult to take? Does not pleasure remain, between these two limits, a master whose sole indefinitely reproduced operation, whose sole compulsive reproduction, insensitive to any lesson from experience, would always amount [*reviendrait*] to producing itself only by limiting itself strictly, as strictly as possible? in arriving only to erase itself?

It is that we are not at the end of our pains. Or of our pleasures. Neither he nor they, the latter nor the former. In the place at which we presently find ourselves posted, the propriety of pleasure appears more and more enigmatic. Do we know what pleasure is? we asked at the beginning. What is confusedly called "everyday language" seems to imply a kind of implicit and precomprehensive consensus, the shared reference to an invariant meaning. This consensus itself seems to be presupposed by the least naive problematics. Philosophical aporia, *skepsis,* maieutics, etc., cannot skip over this presupposition. In this respect, no matter what Freud's reservations or dismissals in relation to philosophical questioning, *Beyond* . . . belongs to the tradition of the *Philebus.* The inheritance is assured, Plato is behind Freud. Or, if you prefer, Socrates, with all the inversions induced by the structure of a legacy. It is also the *Philebus* that we are reading via the scene of *Beyond* . . . We could verify this step by step. But the *Philebus,* multiplying its scene, its authors and actors, in turn reads *Beyond* . . . , deciphers it from afar like a teleguided reading device, is lodged in *Beyond,* takes place or part in it like a lexicon or deciphering code inserted in the volume; or inversely, but the topological structure of textual volumes does not compel one to choose between the two hypotheses, *Beyond* . . . in turn becoming a supplementary chapter of the *Philebus,* a new scene that in passing recalls other dialogues of Plato, the *Symposium* for example, etc. The two corpuses are part of each other. They write (themselves) to each other. The one to the other, they address each other a fabulous correspondence. The athesis of *Beyond* . . . sets adrift the *Philebus,* which proceeds only by "theses" and series of "*logoi,*" from Socrates' first word until the moment when, and this is his last word, he asks that he be "let go." But this setting adrift is itself programmed by the discourse on the *apeiron,* the indefiniteness of the limit and the mixture. This could be put to an exacting proof—the entire Freudian athesis at least virtually, structurally, runs through the system of the Socratic "*logoi*" concerning pleasure. The athesis follows this system like a kind of score, or at very least coordinates itself with the system's major motifs: the motif of division, first of all, and also that of limit and unlimitedness, of measure and of excess, of a "genetic" process opposed to the repose of Being in-itself, etc. Let us not forget that the singular division between *différance* and opposition is marked at the very opening of the *Philebus* (12e): this division has seemed to us to be indispensable for the interpretation of *Beyond* . . . , even if, of course, we have developed and carried further its treatment. Let us not forget that the question of the name and of the reference also opened the *Philebus*. What is called pleasure? Is there a unity of the thing called pleasure? Can one give a proper name (for example Aphrodite) to such a diverse, polymorphous, ungraspable phenomenon? (Socrates sets aside the proper name of the goddess whose testimony has just been invoked by Philebus: her "truest name" is "pleasure" (*ēdonē*), and the proper name is not proper enough.) And if pleasure were produced only by differing from itself, if it occurred only on this condition? However suspended and problematical it might be, everyday language from Socrates to Freud could not avoid presupposing: one knows, one must know what Pleasure is, even if as the strange, ungraspable limit between two limits, a within and a beyond that reduce a step to nothing.

No/step of pleasure [*pas de plaisir*], certainly, but if it is pleasure that incessantly limits itself, dealing with itself, contracting itself in order to prepare itself for itself, producing *itself,* resolving, regenerating, losing and keeping itself in the service of a general function of which it is the tendency, then, equally, there is only Pleasure.

Is this possible?

The following paragraph brings the enigma or the paradox to its limit. In it, it appears in sum that the pleasure *principle* makes war on pleasure. This hostility resembles, at least, a hostility to itself, and this schema is still not foreign to the division of the *Philebus,* or to the message, or even to the letter of Socrates. The very principle of pleasure would manifest itself as a kind of counter-pleasure, band contra band which comes to limit pleasure in order to make it possible. Everything then occurs in the differences of banding. The economy is not general. The general economy is often understood as one simply open to absolute expenditure. Here, to the point of its ultimate collapse, economy would be strictural.

What does Freud say? that the PP extends its mastery to the extent that the quantity of possible pleasure decreases. The primary processes are distinguished from the secondary ones by two characteristics. On the one hand, of course, they are absolutely original.

On the other hand, they can engender much "more intense feelings" than the secondary processes. Much more intense in both directions, pleasure or unpleasure. Now if *Bindung* is the violent replacement (banding, posting, supplementing, suspending[7]) of the original by the supplementary, and if this deposition or transposition (*Umsetzung*) alone assures the mastery of the PP, then one comes to a highly paradoxical result, what Freud delicately names "a result which at bottom is not simple" (*im Grunde nicht einfache Ergebnis*): it is by limiting the possible intensity of pleasure or unpleasure that the PP conquers its mastery. The PP takes its profits only from moderation. The problem it has to resolve, and again let one consult the *Philebus,* is indeed that of the essential *unmeasuredness* of pleasure. This unmeasure is what it shares with unpleasure, and this communication has to be interrupted: such is the mission of the PP. It can fulfill it only by moderating force or intensity, the force or intensity of pleasure as much as that of unpleasure. It cannot master (and therefore weaken) the one without mastering (and therefore weakening) the other.

If it is to assure its mastery, the principle *of* pleasure therefore first must do so *over* pleasure and at the expense *of* pleasure. Thus it becomes the prince *of* pleasure, the prince whose pleasure is the conquered, chained, bound, restricted, tired subject. The game is necessarily played on two boards. Pleasure loses in *measure* itself: in which it brings its principle to triumph. It loses on every turn, it wins on every turn *by measure* of its being there before being there, as soon as it prepares itself for its presence, by measure of its still being there when it reserves itself in order to produce itself, invading everything beyond itself. It wins on every turn, it loses on every turn *by measure:* its unleashed intensity would destroy it immediately if it did not submit itself to the moderating stricture, to measure itself. Death threat: no more principle of pleasure therefore no more *différance* that *modifies* it into a reality principle. What is called reality is nothing outside this law of *différance.* Reality is an effect of this law. Stricture produces pleasure by binding it. It plays between two infinities, betting and speculating on the surplus value that the restriction will bring it. The PP, the master, is not the master, subject or author of this speculation. It is only charged with this mission, an emissary, a *facteur,* one might almost say a courtier. Pleasure, the great speculator, calculates with the effects of aphrodisiac stricture (Socrates wanted nothing to do with the proper

7. TN. "Suspending" here for *relever* as in note 4 above.

name of Aphrodite). Binding, or letting itself be bound, it gives rise, *makes place* for the mastery of the PP, letting the PP regulate circulation from its post, limiting the quantities of pleasure, and letting them increase to the only possible measure. The quasi-proper name is the X which speculates without identity, the X (the unknown excitation concerning which Freud said that by definition nothing was known about it, making it suitable to designate it algebraically) which calculates and sets in place the proper trap of its suspension [*relève*]. It limits itself in order to increase itself. But if it limits itself, it does not increase itself. If it limits itself absolutely, it disappears. Inversely, if it can be put thus, if it liberates something as close as possible to the *pp* (a theoretical fiction), thus if *it does not limit itself*, not *at all* [*pas* du tout], it limits itself absolutely: absolute discharge, disbanding, nothingness or death.

Irresolution belongs to this impossible logic. It is the speculative stricture between the solution (non-binding, unleashing, *absolute* untightening: absolution itself) and the non-solution (absolute tightening, paralyzing banding, etc.).

This great speculative calculation has nothing theoretical about it, is not effectuated from the angle of, *on the part of* the researcher, the psychoanalyst theoretician questioning himself about the relations between the repetition compulsion and the beyond of the PP. Or at least it is effectuated from this angle only in the extent to which it is also at the angle of the "thing itself," or rather the Thing, the Other Thing.[8] As this *Causa* is tried, there is no more opposition between pleasure and unpleasure, life and death, within and beyond. The graphics of the strictural supplement are not dialectical, do not proceed by oppositions in the last analysis. If they necessarily produce dialectical *effects,* for example the entire dialectic said to be of the master and the slave, they do not know negativity, lack, opposition; in this graphics desire is without "without," is of a *without* without *without.*[9] There is only pleasure which itself limits itself, only pain which itself limits itself, with all the differences of force, intensity, and quality that a set, a corpus, a "body" can bear or give "itself," let itself be given. A "set" being *given,* which we are not limiting here to the "subject," the individual, and

8. An allusion, in the seminar on *Life death,* to other seminars organized, for three years running, under the title of *La Chose* (*The Thing*) (Heidegger/Ponge, Heidegger/Blanchot, Heidegger/Freud), at Yale University and in Paris. Perhaps they will give rise to other publications later.

9. Cf. *Pas* and *Le Parergon* in *La vérité en peinture*. [The phrase here is "un sans sans sans."]

even less to the "ego," to consciousness or the unconscious, and no more to the set as a *totality* of parts, a greater stricture can give rise to "more" pleasure and pain than, in another "set," in another non-systematic adjoining, a lesser stricture. The force of stricture, the capacity to *bind itself,* remains in relation to *what there is to bind* (what gives something and gives itself to be bound), the power binding the binding to the bindable. One consequence of this among others, and it concerns everything indicated in the figure of the "bond," from the ribbon to the obligation of the categorical imperative, from the most physical strictions and restrictions to the most sublime alliances: a very free "set," as unleashed as possible, can remain, account taken of the few forces that there are to bind, weakly erotized, weakly hedonized. And vice versa. Of course what we are saying here is already valid for what we are calling the "set" itself. If this word is to refer to a "unity" which rigorously is neither that of the subject nor that of consciousness, the unconscious, the person, the soul and/or the body, the socius or a "system" in general, then it is indeed necessary that the set as such *bind itself* to itself in order to constitute itself as such. Every being-together, even if its modality is not limited to any of those we have just placed in a series, begins by *binding-itself,* by a binding-itself in a differantial relation to itself. It thereby sends and posts itself. Destines itself. Which does not mean: it arrives.

Is it still legitimate to say of such a relation to itself of stricture that it is weakly or strongly erotized, weakly or strongly hedonized? Freud has situated *Bindung* before pleasure and before sexual pleasure. With its sights set on pleasure, doubtless, but before and without it. The within and the beyond of sexuality work silently. The PP, itself served by the presexual, also works in the service of non-sexuality. Its "mastery" is no more sexual than metasexual: a movement analogous to the one we had sketched out as concerns the "proper." There would be, bound to stricture, and by means of it, a notion of mastery which would be neither of life nor of death. It would be even less what is at stake in a struggle of consciousness or a struggle for recognition. And sexuality would no longer determine it in the last analysis.

Is there mastery in this other sense? where is it to be situated? over what, and with its sights set on what would it speculate? The issue is not to answer these questions. But for the moment to submit to this necessity: if it is necessary to follow rigorously, that is, *if it is necessary* to submit to what follows *strictly,* if it is necessary to have followed or let be followed in its consequences that which is indicated here under the heading of mastery, in the context which has just been formed, and if *consequently* it is necessary to go beyond oppositional or dialectical logic with all that it engages in its system, then the very form of our questions (where? over what? its sights set on what? in what sense? etc.) no longer suffices. And involved here is a "there is" (*is there* mastery? we had asked) whose stakes remain to be thought.[10]

In the Freudian corpus, the guiding thread of such a problematic, one of its threads [*fils*] at least, intersects with a word and a concept that we have encountered. Coming back [*revenant*] to the scene of the *fort:da*, one might attribute all the grandson's efforts, in the repetition of the game, to a "drive for mastery" (*Bemächtigungstrieb*). At least this is one of the possible interpretations that Freud ventures in passing, before trying another one (immediately after: "But still another *Deutung* may be attempted").

In question, then, is a simple allusion, but what the allusion designates calls upon the singularity of a drive that would not permit itself to be reduced to any other. And it interests us all the more in that, being irreducible to any other, it seems to take part in all the others, in the extent to which the entire economy of the PP and its beyond is governed by relations of "mastery." One can envisage, then, a quasi-transcendental privilege of this drive for mastery, drive for power, or drive for domination [*emprise*]. The latter denomination seems preferable: it marks more clearly the relation to the other, even in domination *over oneself*. And the word immediately places itself in communication with the lexicon of *giving, taking, sending,* or *destining* that is inciting us here from a distance, and that soon will concern us more directly. The drive to dominate must also be the drive's *relation to itself:* there is no drive not driven to bind itself to itself and to assure itself of mastery over itself as a drive. Whence the transcendental tautology of the drive to dominate: it is the drive as drive, the drive of the drive, the drivenness of the drive. Again, it is a question of a relation to oneself as a relation to the other, the auto-affection of a *fort:da* which gives, takes, sends and destines itself, distances and approaches itself by its own step, the other's.

Bemächtigung: the word and the concept have never been center-stage. But they appear very early: starting with the *Three Essays* and intermittently thereafter. Laplanche and Pontalis spell this out

10. The problematic of the "*Il y a*" (*Es gibt*, There is) was engaged in another seminar (*Donner—le temps*), fragments of which are to be published.

clearly in their *Language of Psychoanalysis*. *Beyond* . . . constitutes, precisely, an important reference in this itinerary, especially
in the passages relative to sadism. The sadistic component can
come to "dominate" (*beherrschen*) all of sexuality. It then becomes, in what Freud has called the "pre-genital organization," a
"dominant" component drive (*als dominierender Partialtrieb*). If it
tends to destroy the object, how is it to be deduced from Eros, asks
Freud, once the erotic function is destined to preserve life? Is this
not "properly" a question of a death drive turned away from the
Ego by narcissistic libido and redirected toward the object? One
then believes it to be in the service of the sexual function: "erotic
mastery" (*Liebesbemächtigung*) in the oral phase of libidinal organization coincides with the destruction of the object. And in the
genital phase the sadistic component becomes autonomous, and
tends to take hold of the sexual object, to master it, and to dominate
it violently, to exercise its power (*bewältigen*) over it. Which is unleashed in the ambivalence love/hate when the "original sadism"
has remained pure and without measure. *Bewältigung*, the violent
exercise of power, domination, is a concept that Laplanche and
Pontalis relate precisely to *Bemächtigung* (domination, power, possession). Now, if such a drive for power exists, if it sees itself attributed a specificity, then it indeed has to be admitted that it plays a
very original role in the most "meta-conceptual," "metalinguistic,"
precisely the most "dominant" organization of Freudian discourse.
For it is indeed within the code of power, and this is not only meta-
phorical, that the problematic is lodged. It is always a question of
knowing who is the "master," who "dominates," who has "authority," to what point the PP exercises power, how a drive can become independent of it or precede it, what are the relations of service between the PP and the rest, what we have called the prince
and his subjects, etc. The "posts" are always posts of power. And
power is exercised according to the network of posts. There is a
society of drives, whether or not they are communally possible, and
in the passage to which we have just referred (chapter VI), the dynamics of sadism are dynamics of power, dynamics of dynasty: a
component drive must come to dominate the entirety of the body
driven, and must subject this body to its regime; and if this suceeds,
it is with the aim of exercising the violence of its domination over
the object. And if this desire to dominate is exercised within as well
as without, if it defines the relation to oneself as the relation to the
other of the drives, if it has an "original" root, then the drive for
power can no longer be derived. Nor can postal power. In its auto-

heterology, the drive for postal power is more originary than the PP and independent of it. But it equally remains the only one to permit the definition of a death drive, and for example an original sadism. In other words, the motif of power is more originary and more general than the PP, is independent of it, is its beyond. But it is not to be confused with the death drive or the repetition compulsion, it gives us with what to describe them, and in respect to them, as well as to a "mastery" of the PP, it plays the role of transcendental predicate. Beyond the pleasure principle—power.[11] That is, posts. But even so, we will not say, despite the transcendental function to which we have just alluded, beyond the death drive—power—or posts. For it is equally the case that everything described under the heading of the death drive or the repetition compulsion, although proceeding from a drive for power, and borrowing all its descriptive traits from this drive, no less overflows power. This is simultaneously the reason and the failure, the origin and the limit of power. There is power only if there is a principle or a principle of the principle. The transcendental or meta-conceptual function belongs to the order of power. Thus there is only *différance* of power. Whence the posts. Beyond all conceptual oppositions, *Bemächtigung* indeed situates one of the exchangers between the drive to dominate as the drive of the drive, and the "will to power."

FORT:DA, RHYTHM

Third return of Nietzsche, third circular recourse before leaving again. This seminar will have played the *fort:da* of Nietzsche.
    Which is rhythm.
    Pleasure is a kind of rhythm, says a fragment from 1884.
    Is what we have retained from *Beyond* . . . anything other than a rhythm, the rhythm of a step which always *comes back* [*revient*], which again has just left? Which has always just left again? And if there is a theme, in the interpretation of this piece, a theme rather

11. Could what I was then attempting in a seminar, on the basis of a reading and a "monographic" exercise, in the environs of a single text by Freud, join up or intersect in some way with the project that provides the title for Laruelle's latest book *Au-delà du principe de pouvoir* (Paris: Payot, 1978)? I am not yet certain. Without directly treating the Freudian text, Laruelle's book refers to it and displaces it in depth, beyond the citational parody of its title. From *Machines textuelles* (Paris: Seuil, 1976), *Nietzsche contre Heidegger* (Paris: Payot, 1977), and *Le Déclin de l'écriture* (Paris: Aubier-Flammarion, 1977) onward, a powerful elaboration is following its course.

than a thesis, it is perhaps *rythmos,* and the rhythm of the theme no less than the theme of a rhythm.

Fort:da. The most normal step has to bear disequilibrium, within itself, in order to carry itself forward, in order to have itself followed by another one, the same again, that is a step, and so that the other comes back, amounts to [*revienne*] the same, but as other. Before all else limping has to be the very rhythm of the march, *unterwegs.* Before any accidental aggravation which could come to make limping itself falter. This is rhythm.

If speculation necessarily remains unresolved because it plays on two boards, band contra band, losing by winning and winning by losing, how can one be surprised that it advances painfully [*que ça marche mal*]? But it has to advance painfully in order to advance; if it has to, if it has to advance, it must advance hesitatingly. It limps well, no?

The allusion to limping, on the last line of the book, has an oblique, lateral, winking *relation* to Freud's very procedure [*démarche*]. It designates first, obviously, a law of scientific *progress;* to this extent it belongs to a kind of discourse on *method.* But it is also to be read in relation to the procedure [*démarche*] of Freud's *fort:da.* I would even say that it is also the relation of it, the contracted narrative. And the translation. The citation of the poet remarks everything in a scene of writing without border, without theoretical suture, disjointed according to the aspect and pace [*allure*] of a prosthetic graft.

It is suddenly immobilized over limping, at the moment of stepping across the last line of the text. But wait, it was going to start up again, it had left in order to start up one more time. He was going to begin again. On the last page, just before the great speculator decides, will we ever know why, "enough," he had almost proposed another step forward, which would have been, we cannot doubt, once again, a step forward for nothing, only rhythm.

The last page, that is, the last paragraph—one could just as well say paraph in this place—begins with the project of a new engagement, another initiative, as if it were still necessary to institute (*einzusetzen*) another problematic, to posit again, and to inaugurate. Here, now. But in the conditional: *Hier wäre die Stelle, mit weitere Studien einzusetzen.* This would be the place to open up further investigations. At the end of the paragraph, new questions, "other" questions and "other" means will be spoken of. And yet, at the moment of (provisionally) "abandoning" the game, or rather the path, at the moment of getting off the road (one must always be ready, he says, "to abandon yet another path" [*einen Weg wieder zu verlassen*] that has been followed for a time), at the moment of abandoning, a final allusion to the prosthesis, to the supplementary *Ersatz*. It is unconsolable believers who, after having "abandoned" (also, *aufgeben*) their catechism, demand that science provide them with an *Ersatz* in the form of unvarying dogma and undisturbed progress. But after having disqualified this representation of scientific progress, *Ersatz* consolation of religion, he unabashedly asks the poet to "console" (*trösten*) him. The poem of limping is to console for the too slow step via which scientific knowledge progresses (. . . *über die langsamen Fortschritte unserer wissenschaftlichen Erkenntnis trösten*).

Silence is going to descend, this is the last paragraph, and also the last page. Even though this last scene of the last act seems to mean nothing, nothing other than "one would have to begin or begin again," even though it seems to remain rather silent, at bottom, something is still to be heard in it. Something which does not have to do with silence itself (for example, Freud does not literally say, as the [French] translation makes him say, that the death drives "seem to work in silence," but rather unobtrusively, imperceptibly, without making themselves noticed, *unauffällig,* differing from the life drives which are in its service). Something which does not have to do with silence but with time, with units of time, and therefore with rhythm. The new investigations to be undertaken would bear, principially, on a question for which the "unit of time" constitutes an irreducible term. In question is the following hypothesis: do feelings of tension, whether agreeable or disagreeable, exist in order to permit us to distinguish between bound and unbound processes of energy? or do these feelings exist in relation to the absolute magnitude, eventually to the level of cathexis, while "the pleasure and unpleasure series indicates a change (*Änderung*) in the magnitude of the cathexis within a given unit of time?" (63).

The "unit of time" (*Zeiteinheit*) is not cut out from within the homogenous element of a form of the senses. This must be remarked, without engaging ourselves here in this immense problem. I have attempted to situate it elsewhere (in "Freud and the Scene of Writing"), and it demands a systematic "explication" between, shall we say, Freud and, at least, for example, Aristotle, Kant, Hegel, Husserl, Heidegger: on the question of time.

Inseparable from the phenomena of *binding* (and therefore of pleasure-unpleasure) as from the *quantities* (of cathexis), the so-called units of time cannot not also be *metrical* and *rhythmical*

notions. Beyond opposition, *différance* and rhythm. Beyond a beyond whose line would have to divide, that is to oppose entities,
beyond the beyond of opposition, beyond opposition, rhythm.[12]
Can one think pleasure?
One can think about it. Thus it cannot be a question of asking
oneself, properly, what it is. It is that which asks itself.
One can still compare, translate, transfer, traffic, sort [*trier*].
Fort:da of Nietzsche according to the rhythm. He compares pleasure, he says that it compares *itself* to a "kind of rhythm" in the
series of lesser pains, and always according to differences of degree, "more or less." He says "perhaps," and does so in a context
in which his rhetoric purposely appears more disconcerting than
ever; he says perhaps, and he says it in parentheses "(One might
perhaps characterize pleasure in general as a rhythm of small painful excitations.)" Elsewhere he speaks of pleasure, of a "kind of
pleasure" and in certain "cases," on the condition of a "certain
rhythmic series of small painful excitations." We are henceforth in
a logic of difference—which can be radical alterity—and no longer
in a logic of opposition or contradiction: "Pain is something other
than pleasure, I mean that it is *not* the opposite of pleasure."
Other aphoristic lines appear to essentialize the beyond of the
pleasure principle: pain is due to the very essence of existence, the
will to suffer would inhabit life fundamentally, constituting the very
aspiration of the will to power, the *differential* necessity which does
not go without resistance. If one follows this series of statements,
the beyond of the pleasure principle would be the affirmation of life
rather than the aspiration to return to the inorganic. But, as we have
verified, this latter motif is far from being absent in Nietzsche's
texts. Therefore it is necessary (q.e.d.) to take into account precisely, within reading itself, both serial *différance* and rhythm. For
other lines also come to deride all those, men and women, who
are worried by the question of knowing what *carries the day* in
the end, and what *commands* in this world, of pleasure or of pain.
Such a question is to be abandoned: to philosophical dilettantism,
to women, he says, and once again, why not, to the poets, to certain poets (he specifies).
All this is to be read in the *Nachlass* of the 80s, surrounding this
sentence which I no longer wish to translate: "*. . . aber in plötz-*

---

12. Cf. certain indications concerning *rythmos* in *The Double Session* (*Dissemination*, pp. 178 and 279–80), and more precisely related to Freud (*The Economic Problem of Masochism*) in *Glas* (p. 174) in which everything is regulated by a
"saccadic" rhythm, between "to limp" (*boiter*) and "to falter" (*clocher*).

*lichen Fällen kommt, wenn man genau beobachtet, die Gegen-
bewegung ersichtlich früher als die Schmerzempfindung. Es stünde
schlimm um mich, wenn ich bei einem Fehltritt zu warten hätte,
bis das Faktum an die Glöcke des Bewusstseins schlüge und ein
Wink, was zu tun ist, zurücktelegraphiert würde. Viehlmehr unter-
scheide ich so deutlich als möglich, dass erst die Gegenbewegung
des Fusses, um den Fall zu verhüten, folgt und dann . . ."* This is to
be continued.

LE FACTEUR DE LA VÉRITÉ

First published in *Poétique* 21 (1975), a special issue put together by Philippe Lacoue-Labarthe under the title *Littérature et philosophie mêlées.*

LE FACTEUR DE LA VÉRITÉ[1]

They thank him for the great truths he has just proclaimed—
for they have discovered (O verifier of that which cannot be
verified!) that everything he has uttered is absolutely true;—
although at first, the good people confess, they had had the
suspicion that it might indeed be a simple fiction. Poe answers
that, for his part, he never doubted it. —Baudelaire

DIVESTED PRETEXTS

Psychoanalysis, supposedly, is found.

When one believes one finds it, it is psychoanalysis itself, supposedly, that finds itself.

When it finds, supposedly, it finds itself/is found—something.[2]

To be satisfied, here, with deforming the generative, as it is called, grammar of these three or four statements.

Where then? Where does psychoanalysis, always, already refind itself, where is it to be refound?

That in which, finding itself, it is found, if finding itself it is found, let us call text. And let us do so not only in order to recall that the theoretical and practical inscription of psychoanalysis (in the text as "language," "writing," "culture," "mythology," "the history of religions, of philosophy, of literature, of science, of medicine," etc., in the text as a "historical," "economic," "political," "instinctual," etc., field, in the heterogeneous and conflictual weave of *différance,* which is elsewhere defined as *general text* and without border) must have effects that have to be taken into ac-

---

1. TN. The title of this essay must remain untranslated in order to capture the double meaning of *facteur:* both postman and factor. Thus, the postman/factor of truth, the question of the delivery of truth in psychoanalysis.

2. TN. *La psychanalyse, à supposer, se trouve. Quand on croit la trouver, c'est elle, à supposer, qui se trouve. Quand elle trouve, à supposer, elle se trouve—quelque chose.* The double meaning of reflexive verbs in French is being played on here. *Se trouver* can mean both to find itself and to be found. Thus, these are three or four statements, since the third sentence must be read in two ways. The passage from three to four via irreducible doubleness is a constant theme in Derrida's works. Throughout this essay, I have given *se trouver* in brackets whenever this wordplay occurs.

count. But also in order to demarcate the space of a determined question.

Unless we are concerned, here, with a singular logic: the species including the genus.

For example: what happens in the psychoanalytic deciphering of a text when the latter, the deciphered itself, already explicates itself? When it says more about itself than does the deciphering (a debt acknowledged by Freud more than once)? And especially when the deciphered text inscribes in itself *additionally* the scene of the deciphering? When the deciphered text deploys more force in placing onstage and setting adrift the analytic process itself, up to its very last word, for example, the truth?

For example, the truth. But is truth an example? What happens—and what is dispensed with—when a text, for example a so-called literary fiction—but is this still an example?—puts truth onstage? And when in doing so it delimits the analytic reading, assigns the analyst his position, shows him seeking truth, and even finding it, shows him discoursing on the truth of the text, and then in general proffering the discourse on truth, the truth on truth? What happens in a text capable of such a scene? A text confident, in its program, of situating analytic activity grappling with the truth?

This surplus does not convey the mastery of an author, and even less the meaning of fiction. Rather, it would be the regular effect of an energetic squaring-off. Within which truth would play a piece: lifted, by the philosopher or the analyst, from within a more powerful functioning.

As an apologue or parabolic pretext, and in order first to rehearse the question of a certain multiplicative coefficient of the truth, I am opening the *Traumdeutung* approximately in its middle.

Examining the history of repression between *Oedipus Rex* and *Hamlet,* demolishing all the differences between (1) the "Oedipus complex," (2) the legend, and (3) Sophocles' tragedy, Freud establishes a rule: everything in a text that does not constitute the semantic core of the two "typical dreams" he has just defined (incest with mother and murder of father), everything that is foreign to the absolute *nudity* of this oneiric content, belongs to the "secondary revision of the material" (*sekundären Bearbeitung des Stoffes*). The formal (textual, in the usual sense) differences that come, as if from the outside, to affect the semantic structure, here the "Oedipus complex," thus constitute secondary revisions. For example, when one views *Oedipus Rex* as a tragedy of destiny, as a conflict between men and the gods, a theological drama, etc., one has taken as essential what actually remains an after-the-fact construction, a garment, a disguise, a material added to the literal *Stoff* precisely in order to mask its nudity.

The denuding of this *Stoff,* the discovery of the semantic material—such would be the end of analytic deciphering. By denuding the meaning behind the formal disguises, by undoing the work, analytic deciphering exhibits the primary content beneath the secondary revisions.

Is the nudity of the meaning hidden beneath the veiling forms of secondary revision a metaphor? Or already a metaphor of metaphor? A metaphor in order to say metaphoricity? Bouhours, as cited by Condillac in *On the Art of Writing:* "Metaphors are transparent veils which allow to be seen that which they cover, or costumes beneath which one recognizes the costumed person."

After having opposed the (primary) semantic content to the (secondary) formal revision, Freud, in parentheses, refers to what he said above about dreams of exhibiting: "Its [the Oedipus legend's] further modification originates once again in a misconceived secondary revision of the material, which has sought to exploit it for theological purposes. (Cf. the dream-material in dreams of exhibiting, pp. 243 f.)" (IV, 264.)

Exhibiting, denuding, undressing, unveiling: the familiar acrobatics of the metaphor *of* the truth. And one just as well could say the metaphor of metaphor, the truth of truth, the truth of metaphor. When Freud intends to denude the original *Stoff* beneath the disguises of secondary fabrication, he is anticipating the truth of the text. The latter, starting from its original content, is to be coordinated with its naked truth, but also with truth as nakedness.

The subchapter to which Freud refers us is very short: six pages. It deals with certain dreams of shame or embarrassment (*Verlegensheitstraum*). The dreamer is embarrassed about his nakedness (*Nacktheit*). These six pages contain two to four literary references. Two to four because in question each time is an "initial" text taken up and transformed by a "second" text: Homer by Keller, Andersen by Fulda, which, no more than the *illustrative* recourse to literary material, also provokes no question on Freud's part.

Dreams of nakedness, then, provoking a feeling of modesty or shame (*Scham*). They are "typical," precisely, only by virtue of their association with distress, embarrassment, discomfort. This "gist of [their] subject-matter" can then lend itself to all kinds of transformations, elaborations, changes. Nakedness gives rise to substitutes. The lack of clothing, or undress (*Entkleidung, Un-*

bekleidung), is displaced onto other attributes. The same typical core organizes the dream of the former officer pushed into the street without his saber, without his necktie, or wearing civilian check trousers. All the examples proposed by Freud concern men, and men who exhibit the lack of a phallic attribute, or rather who adopt this exhibitionistic activity. Or, more precisely still: nakedness does not exhibit the penis or the absence of the penis, but the absence of the phallus as an attribute supplementing a possible fault, the absence of the colossal double. Already a certain chain is indicated: truth-unveiled-woman-castration-shame. Schreber: "Besides, we know in our hearts that men's lust is aroused much less, if at all, by the sight of male nudes; yet female nudes arouse *both* sexes to the same degree."

Another typical invariant: the contrast between the unbearable shame of the dreamer and the apparent indifference of the onlookers. The dreamer alone sees himself naked. And in seeing himself naked he is alone. Here, Freud says, "is a suggestive point." Everything transpires as if two parts, two "pieces" (*Stücke*) were "out of harmony with each other" in the dream. The onlookers *should* look, should mock or become indignant, but they do not. There is here a force or a motion that the dreamer's desire must have set aside. Only the other motion, the exhibitionistic one, remains and maintains its power (*macht*). What is typical in such a dream is precisely this "contradiction." In order to describe this contradiction, and also in order to explain it, Freud needs an example, a literary illustration, what he calls "an interesting piece of evidence" which we happen to "possess" (*Wir besitzen ein interessantes Zeugnis dafür*). We possess an interesting piece of evidence: this is Benveniste's gesture and very word in referring to Aristotle's categories, which seem to crop up at just the right moment in order to illustrate his own demonstration.[3] We see here another example of the illustrative jubilation which treats the very element of its "scientific" discourse as a marvelous paradigm *there to be found* [*se trouve là*], happily available for the instructing discourse. And most often in the form of a fable, a story, a tale. "For it [the content of the typical dream] has become the basis (*Grundlage*) of a fairy tale (*Märchen*) which is familiar to us all in Hans Andersen's version, *The Emperor's New Clothes*, and which has quite recently been put into verse by Ludwig Fulda in his *Der Talisman*. Hans Andersen's fairy

3. I have attempted to analyze the framework and implications of this procedure in "The Supplement of Copula," in *Margins*.

tale tells us how two impostors weave the Emperor a costly garment which, they say, will be visible only to persons of virtue and loyalty. The Emperor walks out in this invisible garment, and all the spectators, intimidated by the fabric's power to act as a touchstone, pretend not to notice the Emperor's nakedness.

"This is just the situation in our dream. It is hardly rash to assume that the unintelligibility of the dream's content (*der unverständliche Trauminhalt*) as it exists in the memory has led to its being recast in an *Einkleidung* [the word is more important here than ever: the translation reads "form designed," thereby reducing the metaphoric fold, the very one that I wish to emphasize here, and that Freud too had begun by erasing: thus, a garment that disguises and falsifies] designed to make sense (*sinnreich*) of the situation. That situation, however, is in the process deprived (*beraubt*) of its original meaning (*ursprünglichen Bedeutung*) and put to extraneous uses. But, as we shall see later, it is a common thing for the conscious thought-activity of a second psychical system to misunderstand the content of a dream in this way, and this misunderstanding must be regarded as one of the factors (*Faktor*) in determining the final form assumed by dreams" (IV, 243).

Freud then gives the key to the "transcription" (*Umdeutung*): "The impostor is the dream and the Emperor is the dreamer himself; the moralizing purpose [the modesty of those good subjects who cannot or will not see the king's nakedness] of the dream reveals an obscure knowledge of the fact that the latent dream-content is concerned with forbidden wishes that have fallen victim to repression. For the context in which dreams of this sort appear during my analyses of neurotics leaves no doubt that they are based upon memories from earliest childhood. It is only in our childhood that we are seen in inadequate clothing (*in mangelhafter Bekleidung*) both by members of our family and by strangers—nurses, maidservants, and visitors; and it is only then that we feel no shame at our nakedness.* [Freud's note.] * A child plays a part in the fairy tale as well; for it was a small child who suddenly exclaimed: 'but he has nothing on!'" (IV, 244).

Freud pays no attention to a fold in the text, to a structural complication which envelops his discourse. Which is ineluctably to be found there (*s'y trouver*).

What does he state first of all? that the literary narrative is a secondary elaboration, and thus an *Einkleidung*—this is Freud's word—, a formal garment, a covering, the disguising of a typical dream, of its original and infantile content. The fairy tale dissimulates or disguises the nudity of the *Stoff*. Like all narratives, like all secondary elaborations, the tale veils a nudity.

Now, what is the nature of the nudity that it covers up in this way? It is the nature of nudity: the dream of nakedness itself and its essential affect, shame. For the nature of the nudity thus veiled/unveiled is that nudity does not belong to nature, and that its truth is in shame.

The hidden theme of *The Emperor's New Clothes* is the hidden theme. What the formal, literary, secondary *Einkleidung* veils and unveils is the dream of veiling/unveiling, the unity of the veil (veiling/unveiling), the disguise, and the denuding. Such a unity finds itself [*se trouve*] in a seamless structure, placed onstage in the form of a nudity *and* a garment that are both invisible, in the form of a cloth visible for some and invisible for others, a nudity both inapparent and exhibited. The same material hides and shows the oneiric *Stoff*, which is to say it hides and shows the truth of what is present without a veil. If one takes into account the more than metaphoric equation between veil, text, and textile, Andersen's text has the text as its theme. Or more precisely the determination of the text as a veil within the space of the truth, the reduction of the text to a movement of *aleitheia*. The fairy tale puts Freud's text onstage when the latter explains that the text, for example the text of the tale, is an *Einkleidung* of the nakedness of the dream of nakedness. What Freud states about secondary elaboration (Freud's explicating text) already finds itself placed onstage and represented in advance in the explicated text (Andersen's fairy tale). The latter *also* described the analytic scene, the position of the analyst, the forms of his discourse, the metaphorico-conceptual structures of what he seeks and what he finds. One text finds itself, is found [*se trouve*] in the other.

Does that mean, then, that there is no difference between the two texts? Yes, of course, many and many a difference. But their co-implication is more contorted than one might believe. It will be said that Freud's text has a scientific value, or pretensions to such: it is not a literary fiction. But what is the criterion of the last analysis for such a distinction? Its self-evidence appears no more certain from a formal point of view than from a semantic point of view. One might say that their content is equivalent, that they mean the same thing. As for the "form" of Freud's text, it derives no more from traditional scientific discourse than from any classified fictional genre. Is the *Traumdeutung* related to the *New Clothes* as the statement of a law to the narration of an instance? But the instance here is one of language, where the event disappears into the veils in which the discourse of science is implied (the king, the law, the truth, nakedness, etc.).

In attempting to distinguish science from fiction, one finally will resort to the criterion of truth. And in asking oneself "What is truth?" one will come back very quickly, beyond the waystations of adequation or of *homoiosis*, to the notion of unveiling, of revelation, of laying bare what is, such as it is, in its Being. Who will allege then that the *Clothes* do not put the truth itself onstage? that is, the possibility of the true as a denuding? and as a denuding of the king, the master, the father, the subjects? And if the shame of the denuding had something to do with woman or with castration, the figure of the king would play all the roles here.

A "literature," then, can produce, can place onstage, and put forth something like the truth. Therefore it is more powerful than the truth of which it is capable. Does such a "literature" permit itself to be read, to be questioned, or even deciphered according to the psychoanalytic schemas that have emerged from what this literature itself produces? The denuding of denuding, such as Freud proposes it, the denuding of the motif of nudity such as it would be secondarily elaborated or disguised (*eingekleidet*) by Andersen's tale, will have been exhibited/dissimulated in advance by the tale, which therefore no longer belongs to the space of decidable truth. According to an abyssal structure to be determined, this space is overflowed by powers of simulacrum. The analytic scene, the denuding, and the deconstitution of the *Einkleidung* are all produced by *The Emperor's New Clothes* in a scene of writing that unclothes, without seeming to, the master meaning, the master of meaning, the king of the truth and the truth of the king. Psychoanalysis finds itself/is found [*se trouve*]—everything that it finds—in the text that it deciphers. More than itself. What are the consequences of this, as concerns the truth and as concerns the text? Where are we led to?

THE SURPLUS OF EVIDENCE
OR THE LACK IN ITS PLACE
a little too *self evident*

What is at stake in this question can be measured in very diverse ways. Within the limits of the cultural field to which I can refer, and taking into account an analysis begun elsewhere,[4] I believe that one of the stages of the elaboration of this problematic, today, must be the reading of Freud proposed by Jacques Lacan. And, more narrowly, within the space at my disposal here, the "Seminar on *The Purloined Letter.*"[5]

In France, the "literary criticism" marked by psychoanalysis had not asked the question of the text. Its interest was elsewhere, as was its wealth. This can be said without injustice, apparently, of Marie Bonaparte's psychobiography, of the psychoanalyses of material imagination, of existential psychoanalysis, of psychocriticism, of the thematist phenomenology tinted with psychoanalysis, etc.

It is entirely otherwise in the "Seminar on *The Purloined Letter.*" Or so it appears. Although Lacan has never directly and systematically been interested in the so-called "literary" text, and although the problematic of *Das Unheimliche* ["The Uncanny"] does not intervene in his discourse to my knowledge, the *general* question of the text is at work unceasingly in his writings, where the logic of the signifier disrupts naive semanticism. And Lacan's "style" was constructed so as to check almost permanently any access to an isolatable content, to an unequivocal, determinable meaning beyond writing.

Three other claims on our interest. They derive more precisely from the "Seminar on *The Purloined Letter.*"

1. The "Seminar" deals with Poe, with an example of the so-

4. *Passim.,* and more punctually, according to the basted effect of certain footnotes, all of them active in their program of ferreting out small texts of Freud's, prudently left in corners, animal-machines camouflaged in shadows, threatening the security of a space and a logic. Here, in particular, I must presuppose "Freud and the Scene of Writing" (as concerns "The Note on the Mystic Writing Pad," 1925), in *Writing and Difference* (1966–67); "The Double Session" (as concerns *Das Unheimliche,* 1919, see especially notes 32, 52, and 67), in *Dissemination* (1969–72); "Outwork" (as concerns *Das Medusenhaupt,* 1922, see note 38), also in *Dissemination.* A note in *Positions* (1971–72, p. 107 n.44) announced this reading of the "Seminar on *The Purloined Letter,*" which was first the object of a lecture at the Johns Hopkins University in November 1971.

As concerns Freud, I refer throughout to the works of Sarah Kofman (*L'Enfance de l'art,* Paris: Payot, 1970; *Camera obscura—de l'idéologie,* Paris: Galilée, 1973; *Quatre Romans analytiques,* Paris: Galilée, 1974) and to Jean-Michel Rey, *Parcours de Freud* (Paris: Galilée, 1974). And, for a rigorous reading of Lacan, to the fundamental and indispensable book by Jean-Luc Nancy and Philippe Lacoue-Labarthe, *Le Titre de la lettre* (Paris: Galilée, 1973).

5. TN. Throughout, I will refer to the English version of the Seminar, translated by Jeffrey Mehlman, in *French Freud, Yale French Studies,* no. 48, 1972. All references will be given in the text by the letter S and a page number.

called fantastic literature which mobilizes and overflows *Das Unheimliche*.

2. Although it is not chronologically the first of Lacan's *Ecrits*, the "Seminar" is placed at the head of the collection, prefaced by an opening that grants it a determining strategic place.[6] And, right from the opening, the analysis of *The Purloined Letter* is anticipated by a horizon: the question of the truth in its relation to fiction. After having granted the "Seminar" "the privilege of opening the progression [of the *Ecrits*] despite its diachrony," Lacan names that which "is no more feigned than the truth when it inhabits fiction." To inhabit fiction: is this, for the truth, to make fiction true or truth fictive? Is this an alternative? a true or fictive one?

3. Finally, the "Seminar" belongs to an investigation of the "repetition compulsion" (*Wiederholungszwang*) which, in the group of texts from 1919 to 1920 (*Beyond the Pleasure Principle, Das Unheimliche*) transforms, at least in principle (see *The Double Session*, notes 52 and 67), the relation of psychoanalysis to literary fiction. All of Lacan's work supposes that one should take seriously the problematic of *Jenseits* (*Beyond . . .*), the very problematic that for so many psychoanalysts appears mythological, poetic, speculative. The issue, then, is to take the *Wiederholungszwang* back in

6. Given in 1955, written in 1956, published in 1957, it is in 1966 that the Seminar receives its place *at the head* of the *Ecrits*, following an order which, although no longer chronological, perhaps is not simply derived from the theoretico-didactic system. This order could organize, perhaps, a certain scene of the *Ecrits*. In any event, the necessity of this priority finds itself confirmed, recalled, and underlined by the presentation of the *Ecrits* in the "*Points*" collection (1970): ". . . the text which maintains the gateway post that it has elsewhere will be essayed . . ." For whoever might wish to limit the import of the questions asked here, nothing prevents their being contained in the *place* which its "author" gives the Seminar: gateway post. "*Le poste* [in the sense of position] differs from *la poste* [in the sense of mail] only by gender," says Littré. [An explanation of the various editions and translations of Lacan: Derrida refers throughout to the two French editions of Lacan's *Ecrits*, the complete one-volume edition (Paris: Seuil, 1966), and the two-volume selection, with a new preface by Lacan, published in the "*Points*" collection (Paris: Editions de Minuit, 1970). I will refer to the former throughout as *Ecrits* (F), and to the latter as *Points*. The English version, a selection, also called *Ecrits*, translated by Alan Sheridan (New York: Norton, 1977), will be referred to as *Ecrits* (E). The latter volume does *not* contain the "Seminar," which is why I refer to the Mehlman translation here. In his translator's note, Alan Sheridan states that the selection of essays for the English *Ecrits* is "Lacan's own" (p. vii). Thus, for reasons to be determined, something has changed: the "Seminar" no longer has the gateway post that Lacan previously had emphasized, and, as just stated, does not appear in the volume at all.]

hand, and to pursue its consequences in a logic of the signifier: "Our inquiry has led us to the point of recognizing that the repetition automatism[7] (*Wiederholungszwang*) finds its basis in what we have called the *insistence* of the signifying chain. We have elaborated that notion itself as a correlate of the *ex-sistence* (or: eccentric place) in which we must necessarily locate the subject of the unconscious if we are to take Freud's discovery seriously." (*S.*, p. 39) These are the opening lines of the "Seminar."

Which will demonstrate, in effect, "the pre-eminence of the signifier over the subject," "the supremacy of the signifier in the subject." The subject is no more the master or author of the signifier than meaning is. The subject does not command, emit, or orient, give rise to place, meaning, or origin. If there is a subject *of the* signifier, it is in being subject to the law of the signifier. The subject's place is assigned by the signifier's recourse, by the signifier's literal topology and by the rule of its displacements. First consequence: this analysis of a "literary" text does without[8] any reference to the author (Freud never believed this had to be given up), that is, to Poe, whose psychobiography organizes Bonaparte's entire analysis. So much for the reference to the author of the text. But the latter is not "the author of the letter" whose *circulation* (my italics) Lacan examines. Thus, second consequence, "the author of the letter" too, "remains out of play." "From then on, the responsibility of the author of the letter takes second place to that of its holder" (*S.*, p. 58). There is a holding, but not an appropriation, of the letter. The latter is never possessed, either by its sender or by its addressee. "We say: the *holder* and not the *possesser*. For it becomes clear that the addressee's proprietorship of the letter may be no less debatable than that of anyone else into whose hands it comes . . ." (*S.*, p. 58).

This letter, apparently, has no proprietor. It is apparently the

7. TN. Lacan consistently renders *Wiederholungszwang* as "repetition automatism," for reasons that Mehlman explains (S, p. 39, n. 1). The more familiar English term is "repetition compulsion."

8. Let us specify immediately, for more clarity: does without any reference to the author almost totally, does without reference to the author apparently, as we will see further on.

On several occasions the *Ecrits* denounce the "resistance" the analyst betrays via the psychobiographical reference to the writer. While subscribing to this suspicion, one can extend it to a certain formalist neutralization of the effects of the signature. Which supposes the opening of another (theoretical and more than theoretical) space for the elaboration of these questions. The very opening in which we are engaged here.

property of no one. It has no proper meaning, no proper content, apparently, that bears on its itinerary. Structurally, then, it is *volante* and *volée*.[9] And this theft/flight would not occur if the letter had a meaning, or at least if it were constituted by the content of its meaning, if it limited itself to being meaningful and to being determined by the legibility of this meaning: "And the mobilization of the elegant society whose frolics we are following would as well have no meaning if the letter itself were content with having one" (S., p. 56).

Lacan does not say that the letter has no meaning: it is not content with having one. This can be understood: with having, meaning, and there is something else, more or less, than meaning in this letter which displaces itself and mobilizes. This can also be understood: with having one, one meaning, and the possible multiplicity would provide the impetus. In any event, as concerns meaning, according to Lacan, the letter itself is not content with having one. What would happen if one could demonstrate that as concerns meaning, according to Lacan, the letter itself were content with having one, and one alone? We are not there yet.

That the signifier apparently cannot permit itself to be taken back to its emitting origin, that it depends neither on the signified, nor on the subject, which on the contrary it determines via its own movements ("the displacement of the signifier determines the subjects in their acts," S. p. 60)—all this *would have* as its consequence that the signifier, in its letter, as a sealed text and as a locality, remains and falls in the end. Thus, we *would have* two remainders. 1. A remainder that can be destroyed precisely because it is a surplus. The minister has left behind a letter in order to replace the one he has stolen: "A *remainder* that no analyst will neglect, trained as he is to retain whatever is significant, without always knowing what to do with it: the letter, left in exchange by the Minister, and which the Queen's hand is now free to roll into a ball" (S., p. 42, mod.). 2. A remainder that is indestructible precisely because it is elusive, the "unforgettable" insistence of the purloined letter which determines repetition and the "persistence of conduct": "The Minister then is not *altogether* mad in his insane stagnation, and that is why he will behave according to the mode of neurosis. Like the man who withdrew to an island to forget, what? he has forgotten—so the Minis-

9. TN. *The Purloined Letter* in French is *La lettre volée. Voler* has the double sense of to steal and to fly: thus the meaning of the stolen letter always flies off, it is structurally *volante* (flying, stealing) and *volée* (flown, stolen).

ter, through not making use of the letter, comes to forget it. As is expressed by the persistence of his conduct. But the letter, no more than the neurotic's unconscious, does not forget him. It forgets him so little that it transforms him more and more in the image of her who offered it to his capture, so that he now will surrender it, following her example, to a similar capture.

"The features of that transformation are noted, and in a form so characteristic in their apparent gratuitousness that they might validly be compared to the return of the repressed" (S., p. 65).

If the critique of a certain semanticism constitutes an indispensable phase in the elaboration of a theory of the text, then one may discern in the "Seminar" a very distinct advance in relation to an entire kind of post-Freudian psychoanalytic criticism. Without precipitation toward the semantic, that is, thematic, content of a text, the organization of the signifier is taken into account. In its materiality as well as its formality.

In its materiality: not the empirical materiality of the sensory signifier (*scripta manent*), but the materiality due, on the one hand, to a certain *indivisibility* (this "materiality is *odd* [*singulière*] in many ways, the first of which is not to admit partition. Cut a letter in small pieces, and it remains the letter it is—and this in a completely different sense than *Gestalttheorie* could account for with the dormant vitalism which informs its notion of the whole." S., p. 53, mod.), and on the other hand, to a certain *locality.* A locality which itself is non-empirical and *non-real* since it gives rise to that which is not where it is, that which is "missing from its place," is not found where it is found or (but is this the same thing?) *is found* [*se trouve*] where it *is* not *found.* The notions of indivisibility (protection from partition) and of locality are themselves indissociable; they condition each other, and later we will have to examine them simultaneously. Somewhere, perhaps, their function could be to rivet us, to make us arrive, once more, at that which properly links the signature to the singular. Which the unity of the signifier would guarantee, in exchange for an assurance that it receives in return. But we are not there yet. Here, first of all, is what solders, beneath the conceptual heading of the *letter* or of the *materiality of the signifier,* the indivisible to the local: "But if it is first of all on the materiality of the signifier that we have insisted, that materiality is *odd* [*singulière*] in many ways, the first of which is not to admit partition . . . For the signifier is a unit in its very uniqueness, being by nature symbol only of an absence. Which is why we cannot say of the purloined letter that, like other objects, it must be *or* not be in a particular place but that unlike them it will be *and* not be where it is, wherever it goes . . . For it can *literally* be said that something is missing from its place only of what can change it: the symbolic. For the real, whatever upheaval we subject it to, is always in its place; the real carries its place glued to its heel, ignorant of what might exile it from it." (S, pp. 54–55; mod.)

Question of the letter, question of the materiality of the signifier: perhaps it will suffice to change a letter, perhaps even less than a letter, in the expression *manque à sa place* [lack in its place, missing from its place], perhaps it will suffice to introduce into this expression a written *a,* that is, an *a* without accent mark, in order to make apparent that if the lack has its place [*manque a sa place*] [10] in this atomistic topology of the signifier, if it occupies a determined place with defined contours, then the existing order will not have been upset: the letter will always refind its proper place, a circumvented lack (certainly not an empirical, but a transcendental one, which is better yet, and more certain), the letter will be where it always will have been, always should have been, intangible and indestructible via the detour of a *proper,* and properly *circular,* itinerary. But we are not there yet.

Lacan, then, is attentive to the letter, that is, to the materiality of the signifier. To its formality also, which determines the subject as much as does the site of the literal atom: "Subjectivity originally is of no relation to the real, but of a syntax which engenders in the real the signifying mark." [11]

A break with naive semanticism and psycho-biographism, an elaboration of a logic of the signifier (in its literal materiality and syntactic formality), an assumption of the problematic of *Beyond the Pleasure Principle:* such are the most general forms of an advance legible in the "Seminar" at first glance. But the excess of evidence always demands the supplement of inquiry.

Now we must come closer, reread, question.

From the outset, we recognize the classical landscape of applied psychoanalysis. Here applied to literature. Poe's text, whose status is never examined—Lacan simply calls it "fiction"—, finds itself invoked as an "example." An example destined to "illustrate," in a

10. TN. Derrida is playing on the fact that Lacan's conception of the phallus as signifier, *le manque à sa place,* the lack in its place, sounds the same as *le manque a sa place,* the lack has its place. This reading should be extended to the subtitle of this section, which can be read in many ways, e.g. "or the lack in its place," "where the lack has its place," etc.

11. TN. *Ecrits* (F), p. 50.

didactic procedure, a law and a truth forming the proper object of a seminar. Literary writing, here, is brought into an *illustrative* position: "to illustrate" here meaning to read the general law in the example, to make clear the meaning of a law or of a truth, to bring them to light in striking or exemplary fashion. The text is in the service of the truth, and of a truth that is taught, moreover: "Which is why we have decided to illustrate for you today the truth which may be drawn from that moment in Freud's thought under study—namely, that it is the symbolic order which is constitutive for the subject—by demonstrating in a story the decisive orientation which the subject receives from the itinerary of a signifier.

"It is that truth, let us note, which makes the very existence of fiction possible" (S, p. 40).

Again, illustration, and the illustration of instruction, Freud's instruction: "What Freud teaches us in the text that we are commenting on is that the subject must pass through the channels of the symbolic, but what is illustrated here is more gripping still: it is not only the subject, but the subjects, grasped in their intersubjectivity, who line up . . ." (S, p. 60).

The "truth which may be drawn from that moment in Freud's thought under study," the truth with which the most decorative and pedagogical literary illustration is coordinated, is not, as we will see, this or that truth, but is the truth itself, the truth of the truth. It provides the "Seminar" with its rigorously philosophical import.

One can identify, then, the most classical practice. Not only the practice of philosophical "literary criticism," but also Freud's practice each time he demands of literature examples, illustrations, testimony, and confirmation in relation to knowledge, truth, and laws that he treats elsewhere in another mode. Moreover, if Lacan's statements on the relation between fiction and truth are less clear and less unequivocal elsewhere, here there is no doubt about the order. "Truth inhabits fiction" cannot be understood in the somewhat perverse sense of a fiction more powerful than the truth which inhabits it, the truth that fiction inscribes within itself. In truth, the truth inhabits fiction as the master of the house, as the law of the house, as the economy of fiction. The truth executes the economy of fiction, directs, organizes, and makes possible fiction: "It is that truth, let us note, which makes the very existence of fiction possible" (S, p. 40).

The issue then is to ground fiction in truth, to guarantee fiction its conditions of possibility in truth, and to do so without even indicating, as does *Das Unheimliche*, literary fiction's eternally renewed resistance to the general law of psychoanalytic knowledge. Additionally, Lacan never asks what distinguishes one literary fiction from another. Even if every fiction were founded in or made possible by the truth, perhaps one would have to ask from what kind of fiction something like literature, here *The Purloined Letter,* derives, and what effects this might have on that very thing which appears to make it possible.

This first limit contains the entire "Seminar," and it reprints its marks indefinitely on it: what the literary example yields is a *message.* Which will have to be deciphered on the basis of Freud's teaching. Reprint: "The Opening of This Collection" (October 1966, ten years after the "Seminar") speaks of "Poe's message deciphered and coming back from him, the reader, in that to read it, it says itself to be no more feigned than the truth when it inhabits fiction" (*Ecrits,* p. 16).

What Lacan analyzes, decomposing it into its elements, its origin, and its destination, uncovering it in its truth, is a *story* [*histoire*].

The word *story* [*histoire*] appears at least four times from the second page. What serves as an example is a "story":

a) "Which is why we have decided to illustrate for you today the truth which may be drawn from that moment in Freud's thought under study—namely, that it is the symbolic order which is constitutive for the subject—by demonstrating in a *story* [*histoire*] the decisive orientation which the subject receives from the itinerary of a signifier" (S, p. 40).

b) "It is that truth, let us note, which makes the very existence of fiction possible. And in that case, a fable is as appropriate as any other *story* [*histoire*] for bringing it to light . . ." (S, p. 40; mod.).

c) "Which is why, without seeking any further, we have chosen our example from the very *story* [*histoire*] in which the dialectic of the game of even or odd—from whose study we have but recently profited—occurs" (S, p. 40).

d) "It is, no doubt, no accident that this *story* [*histoire*] revealed itself propitious to pursuing a course of inquiry which had already found support in it" (S, pp. 40–41; mod.).

This story is certainly that of a letter, of the theft and displacement of a signifier. But what the "Seminar" treats is only the content of this story, what is justifiably called its history, what is recounted in the account, the internal and narrated face of the narration. Not the narration itself. The "Seminar's" interest in the agency of the signifier in its letter seizes upon this agency to the extent that it constitutes, precisely, on the first approach, the exemplary content, the meaning, the written of Poe's fiction, as opposed to its writing, its signifier, and its narrating form. The displacement of the signifier, therefore, is analyzed as a signified, as the recounted object of a short story.

One might be led to believe, at a given moment, that Lacan is preparing to take into account the (narrating) narration, the complex structure of the scene of writing played out within it, the very curious place of the narrator. But once it is glimpsed, the analytic deciphering excludes this place, neutralizes it, or, more precisely, along lines we will follow, allows the narrator to dictate an effect of neutralizing exclusion (the "narration" as "commentary") that transforms the entire "Seminar" into an analysis fascinated by a content. Which makes it miss a scene. When it sees two ("There are two scenes." S, p. 41), there are three. At least. And when it sees one or two "triads," there is always the supplement of a square whose opening complicates the calculations.

How is this neutralization operated, and what are its effects, if not its aims?

There is a first moment, then, when it seems that the position of the narrator and the narrating operation are going to intervene in the deciphering of "Poe's message." Certain distinctions made at the moment when the "tale" is presented lead in this direction: "As you know, we are talking about the tale which Baudelaire translated under the title: *La lettre volée*. At first reading, we may distinguish a drama, its narration, and the conditions of that narration" (S, p. 41). The "drama" is the recounted action, the (narrated) *history* which forms the "Seminar's" proper object. As for the narration, at the very moment when it is invoked, we find it reduced to a "commentary" that "doubles" the drama, something that stages and makes visible, with no specific intervention of its own, like a transparent element, a general diaphanousness. Later on, the issue will be one of the "general narrator." "The narration, in fact, doubles the drama with a commentary without which no *mise en scène* would be possible. Let us say that the action would remain, properly speaking, invisible in the theater—aside from the fact that the dialogue would be expressly and by dramatic necessity devoid of whatever meaning it might have for an audience:—in other words, nothing of the drama could be grasped, neither seen nor heard, without, dare we say, the indirect lighting which the narration, in each scene, casts on the point of view that one of the actors had while performing it.

"There are two scenes . . ." (S, p. 41; mod.). There follows the analysis of the two triangles, the content of the "tale," the object of the analytic deciphering.

After which, the narrator, the narration, and the operation of the *mise en scène,* the staging, are dropped. The original place of the narrator on both sides of the narration, the specific status of his discourse—which is not neutral, or whose effect of neutrality is not neutral—, his interventions, and even his psychoanalytic position will never be questioned in the rest of the "Seminar," which will remain the analysis of the so-called "intersubjective triads," the triads which constitute that which is inside the recounted story, what Lacan calls the "history" or the "drama," the "real drama" ("each of the two scenes of the real drama is narrated in the course of a different dialogue" S, p. 47). All the allusions to the narrator and to the act of narration are made in order to exclude them from the "real drama" (the two triangular scenes), which is thus to be delivered to the analytic deciphering of the message in clearly demarcated fashion. This is accomplished in two moments, following the two *dialogues* which divide *The Purloined Letter.*

First moment. The exclusion is quite clear, facilitated by Poe's text, which seems to do everything it can to favor it. This is the moment of what Lacan calls *exactitude.* The narrator is named the "general narrator"; he is like the neutral, homogeneous, transparent element of the narration. He "adds nothing," says Lacan (S, p. 48). As if one had to add something to a relation in order to intervene in a scene. Especially in a scene of narration. And as if his questions and remarks and exclamations—these are the forms of the so-called general narrator's interventions in what Lacan demarcates as the "first dialogue"—added nothing. Further, even before this "first dialogue" gets underway, the "general narrator" says things to which we will have to turn later. Finally, the narrator who is onstage in what he places onstage is in turn placed onstage in a text more ample than the so-called general narration. A supplementary reason not to consider him as a neutral place of passage. The "Seminar" gives no specific attention to this overflowing text: rather, it isolates, as its essential object, the two "narrated" triangular scenes, the two "real dramas," neutralizing simultaneously the fourth character who is the general narrator, his narrating operation, and the text which puts onstage the narration and the narrator. For *The Purloined Letter,* as a text and as fiction, begins neither with the triangular dramas, nor with the narration which puts them onstage by implicating itself in these dramas in a way whose analysis we are delaying here. And no more does Poe's text end with these dramas. *The Purloined Letter* places onstage a narrator and a director who— feigned by *The Purloined Letter*—feign by *The Purloined Letter* recounting the "real drama" of the purloined letter, etc. So many supplements which undermine the narrated triangle. So many reasons to think that the so-called general narrator always adds something, and from before the first dialogue; that he is not the general condition of possibility for the narrative, but an actor with a highly unusual status. So many reasons not to be satisfied with what Lacan says about him in what I have called the first moment of the exclusion. If the filter of the general narrator is not "a fortuitous arrangement," if it reminds us that the "message" "indeed belongs to the dimension of language," then one cannot exclude this fourth position, under the rubric of its being a general medium, from the triangular scenes which would form the object contained under the rubric of the "real drama."

Second moment. In question is what Lacan demarcates or frames as a "second dialogue," again overlooking, this time between the two dialogues, a long paragraph not in dialogue form in which the narrator says things to which we will have to turn later. In the course of this "second dialogue" we would pass from the register of "exactitude" to the register of "truth," "strictly speaking . . . the very foundation of intersubjectivity" (S, p. 49). This time one expects an analysis of the specific position of the narrator. Lacan writes in effect:

"Thus the indirect telling sifts out the linguistic dimension, and the general narrator, by duplicating it, 'hypothetically' adds nothing to it. But his role in the second dialogue is entirely different" (S, p. 48).

No: for his role already was entirely different in the first dialogue, and Lacan does not treat things in an entirely different way in the second one. He describes the narrator as the receptacle or the mediator or the purely formal assistant whose only function would consist in permitting Dupin to delude, to delude us by deluding the passive narrator, to play his tricks "in still purer form" at the very moment when he feigns exhibiting how they work, at this point tricking us (the narrator and ourselves) "truly."

"What could be more convincing, moreover, than the gesture of laying one's cards face up on the table? So much so that we are momentarily persuaded that the magician has in fact demonstrated, as he promised, how his trick was performed, whereas he has only renewed it in still purer form: at which point we fathom the measure of the supremacy of the signifier in the subject.

"Such is Dupin's maneuver . . ." (S, pp. 49–50).

But from whence does it come that the narrator was content to listen passively and to let himself be tricked truly? Who can be tricked truly as soon as the narrator is narrated by himself? Etc.

To what does this neutralization of the narrator commit the "Seminar"?

1. The narrator (himself doubled into a narrating narrator and a narrated narrator, not limiting himself to reporting the two dialogues) is evidently neither the author himself (to be called Poe) nor, less evidently, the inscriber of a text which recounts something for us, or rather which makes a narrator speak, who himself, in all kinds of ways, makes many people speak. The inscriber and the inscribing are original functions that are not to be confused with either the author and his actions, or with the narrator and his narration, and even less with the particular object, the narrated content, the so-called "real drama," which the psychoanalyst hastens to recognize as "Poe's message deciphered." That the inscribing in its entirety—the fiction named *The Purloined Letter*—is covered, over its entire surface, by a narration whose narrator says "I" does not permit us to confuse the fiction with a narration. And even less, of course, with any given narrated section, however lengthy and apparent. There is here a problem of framing, of bordering and delimitation, whose analysis must be very finely detailed if it wishes to ascertain the effects of fiction. Without ever saying a word about it, Lacan excludes the textual fiction from within which he has extracted the so-called general narration. An operation made that much easier, and all too self-evidently easier, by the fact that the narration does not surpass by a word the fiction entitled *The Purloined Letter*. But that is the fiction. There is an invisible, but structurally irreducible, frame around the narration. Where does it begin? With the first letter of the title? With the epigraph from Seneca? With "At Paris, just after dark . . ."? The question is even more complicated than that—we will come back to it—and this complication even now suffices to indicate everything about the structure of the text that is misconstrued in overlooking the frame. Within this neutralized or naturalized frame, Lacan takes up the narration without border and operates another extraction, again by dropping the frame. From within the narration he lifts out two dialogues which form the narrated history, that is, the content of a rep-

resentation, the internal meaning of a story, the all-enframed, which demands all the attention, mobilizes all the psychoanalytic schemas (Oedipal ones here), and pulls toward its center the entire deciphering enterprise. There is missing here an elaboration of the problem of the frame, the signature, and the *parergon*. This lack permits the scene of the signifier to be reconstructed into a signified (a process always inevitable in the logic of the sign), permits writing to be reconstructed into the written, the text into discourse, and more precisely into an "intersubjective" dialogue (and it is not fortuitous that the "Seminar's" commentary concerns only the two dialogued parts of *The Purloined Letter*).

2. There is here, first of all, a *formal* limit of the analysis. The formal structure of the text is overlooked, in very classical fashion, at the very moment when, and perhaps in the extent to which, its "truth," its exemplary message, allegedly is "deciphered." The structure of fiction is reduced at the very moment when it is related to its condition of truth. This leads to poor formalism. Formalism is practiced because one is not interested in the subject-author, something which might, in certain theoretical stiuations, constitute progress, or even a legitimate demand. But this formalism is rigidly illogical once that, on the pretext of excluding the author, one no longer takes into account either the "scription-fiction" and the "scriptor-fictor," or the narrating narration and the narrator. This formalism guarantees, as always, the surreptitious extraction of a semantic content, within which psychoanalysis applies its entire interpretive work. Formalism and hermeneutic semanticism always support one another: question of the frame.

3. The limit, then, is not only a formal one, and for the moment it does not concern a science of poetic fiction or of narrative structure. The issue here is not—quite to the contrary—one of rescuing something like literature or literary form from the grasp of psychoanalysis. There is a deep historical and theoretical complicity between psychoanalysis *applied* to literature and the formalist withdrawal which would pretend to escape this application. We have just seen how this works in principle. What is important here is that the formal deficiency implies a semantic and psychoanalytic decision. Once the narrator is distinguished from the author and then the "scriptor," he is no longer the formal condition of the narration that might symmetrically be opposed to the content, as the narrating to the narrated, for example. He intervenes in a specific fashion, is simultaneously *too self evident* and invisible in a triangle, and therefore in a triangle that touches the other triangle at one of

its "angles," touching both "intersubjective" triangles. Which singularly complicates the "intersubjective" structure, and this time from within the framed, the twice-framed, scenes, from within the represented content. Not to take into account this complication is not a failure of "formalist" literary criticism; it is an operation of the semanticist psychoanalyst. The narrator is not effaced as the "general narrator," or rather, in effacing himself within the homogeneous generality, he puts himself forward as a very singular character within the narrated narration, within the enframed. He constitutes an agency, a "position" with which the triangle, through the intermediary of Dupin (who in turn himself represents all the positions), maintains a very determined, very invested relation. By framing in this violent way, by cutting the narrated figure itself from a fourth side in order to see only triangles, one evades perhaps a certain complication, perhaps of the Oedipal structure, which is announced in the scene of writing.

Before demonstrating this more concretely, let us follow Lacan within the framed content, in his analysis of the two triangles: this constitutes the specific contribution of the Seminar. Let us start with his own premises and his own framing. Let us act as if the frame could be neutralized, both as a de-limitation and as a precarious construction, an artifact with four sides, at least.

The expressions "trio," "triangles," and "intersubjective triangle" arise very frequently in the description of the two scenes of the "real drama" thus deciphered. A long citation first, in order to recall and place in evidence this logic of the excluded fourth. Of the Oedipus complex:

> There are two scenes, the first of which we shall straightway designate the primal scene, and by no means inadvertently, since the second may be considered its repetition in the very sense we are considering today.
> The primal scene is thus performed, we are told ['told' neither by Poe, nor by the "scriptor," nor by the narrator, but by G., the Prefect of Police who is put into this dialoguing scene by all the latter—J.D.], in the royal *boudoir,* so that we suspect that the person of the highest rank, called the "exalted personage," who is alone there when she receives a letter, is the Queen. This feeling is confirmed by the embarrassment into which she is plunged by the entry of the other exalted personage, of whom we have already been told [again by G.] prior to this account that the knowledge he might have of the letter in question would jeopardize for the lady nothing less than her honor and safety. Any doubt that he is in fact the King is promptly dissipated in the

course of the scene which begins with the entry of the Minister D . . .
At that moment, in fact, the Queen can do no better than to play on the
King's inattentiveness by leaving the letter on the table "face down,
address uppermost." It does not, however, escape the Minister's lynx
eye, nor does he fail to notice the Queen's distress and thus to fathom
her secret. From then on everything transpires like clockwork. After
dealing in his customary manner with the business of the day, the
Minister draws from his pocket a letter similar in appearance to the
one in his view, and, having pretended to read it, he places it next to
the other. A bit more conversation to amuse the royal company, whereupon, without flinching once, he seizes the embarrassing letter, making
off with it, as the Queen, on whom none of his maneuver has been
lost, remains unable to intervene for fear of attracting the attention of
her royal spouse, close at her side at that very moment.

Everything might then have transpired unseen by a hypothetical
spectator of an operation in which nobody falters, and whose *quotient*
is that the Minister has filched from the Queen her letter and that—an
even more important result than the first—the Queen knows that he
now has it, and by no means innocently.

A *remainder* that no analyst will neglect, trained as he is to retain
whatever is significant, without always knowing what to do with it: the
letter, left in exchange by the Minister, and which the Queen's hand is
now free to roll into a ball.

Second scene: in the Minister's office. It is in his hotel, and we
know—from the account the Prefect of Police has given Dupin,
whose specific genius for solving enigmas Poe introduces here for the
second time—that the police, returning there as soon as the Minister's
habitual, nightly absences allow them to, have searched the hotel and
its surroundings from top to bottom for the last eighteen months. In
vain,—although everyone can deduce from the situation that the Minister keeps the letter within reach.

Dupin calls on the Minister. The latter receives him with studied
nonchalance, affecting in his conversation romantic *ennui*. Meanwhile Dupin, whom this pretense does not deceive, his eyes protected
by green glasses, proceeds to inspect the premises. When his glance
catches a rather crumpled piece of paper—apparently thrust care-
lessly in a division of an ugly pasteboard card-rack, hanging gaudily
from the middle of the mantelpiece—he already knows that he has
found what he is looking for. His conviction is re-enforced by the very
details which seem to contradict the description he has of the stolen
letter, with the exception of the format, which remains the same.

Whereupon he has but to withdraw, after "forgetting" his snuff-box
on the table, in order to return the following day to reclaim it—armed
with a facsimile of the letter in its present state. As an incident in the
street, prepared for the proper moment, draws the Minister to the window, Dupin in turn seizes the opportunity to snatch the letter while

substituting the imitation, and has only to maintain the appearances of a normal exit.

Here as well all has transpired, if not without noise, at least without commotion. The quotient of the operation is that the Minister no longer has the letter, but far from suspecting that Dupin is the culprit who has ravished it from him, knows nothing of it. Moreover, what he is left with is far from insignificant for what follows. We shall return to what brought Dupin to inscribe a message on his counterfeit letter. Whatever the case, the Minister, when he tries to make use of it, will be able to read these words, written so that he may recognize Dupin's hand: ". . . *Un dessein si funeste / S'il n'est digne d'Atrée est digne de Thyeste,"* ("So infamous a scheme, / If not worthy of Atreus, is worthy of Thyestes"), whose source, Dupin tells us, is Crébillon's *Atrée.*

Need we emphasize the similarity of these two sequences? Yes, for the resemblance we have in mind is not a simple collection of traits chosen only in order to supply their difference. And it would not be enough to retain those common traits at the expense of the others for the slightest truth to result. It is rather the intersubjectivity in which the two actions are motivated that we wish to bring into relief, as well as the three terms through which it structures them.

The special status of these terms results from their corresponding simultaneously to the three logical moments through which the decision is precipitated and the three places its assigns to the subjects among whom it constitutes a choice.

That decision is reached in a glance's time. For the maneuvers which follow, however stealthily they prolong it, add nothing to that glance, nor does the deferring of the deed in the second scene break the unity of that moment.

This glance presupposes two others, which it embraces in its vision of the breach left in their fallacious complementarity, anticipating in it the occasion for larceny afforded by that exposure. Thus three moments, structuring three glances, borne by three subjects, incarnated each time by different characters.

The first is a glance that sees nothing: the King and the police.

The second, a glance which sees that the first sees nothing and deludes itself as to the secrecy of what it hides: the Queen, then the Minister.

The third sees that the first two glances leave what should be hidden exposed to whomever would seize it: the Minister, and finally Dupin.

In order to grasp in its unity the intersubjective complex thus described, we would willingly seek a model in the technique legendarily attributed to the ostrich attempting to shield itself from danger; for that technique might ultimately be qualified as political, divided as it here is among three partners: the second believing itself invisible because the first has its head stuck in the ground, and all the while letting the third calmly pluck its rear; we need only enrich its proverbial denomination by a letter, producing *la politique de l'autruiche* [the politics of the ostrich, *autruche, of the* Other, *autrui,* and of Austria, l'*Autriche*], for the ostrich itself to take on forever a new meaning. Given the intersubjective modulus of the repetitive action, it remains to recognize in it a *repetition automatism* in the sense that interests us in Freud's text (S, 41–44).

We will analyze later the singular relation between the "subject" (the narrated narrator) of the narration and Dupin, to the extent that this relation from the outset definitively complicates the triangular structure. For the moment, let us consider what this exclusion of the fourth, or of the third-plus-or-minus-one, implies in the precipitation toward the truth. And how the demand for truth leads to putting aside the scene of writing, to putting aside that which almost always in and of itself permits itself (feigns) to be put aside, apart, as the fourth.[12] One must take into account the remainder, that which can fall, and one must do so not only in the narrated content of the writing (the signifier, the written, the letter), but in the operation of writing.

Lacan leads us back to the truth, to a truth which itself cannot be lost. He brings back the letter, shows that the letter brings itself back toward its *proper* place via a *proper* itinerary, and, as he overtly notes, it is this destination that interests him, destiny as destination. The signifier has its place in the letter, and the letter refinds its proper meaning in its proper place. A certain reappropriation and a certain readequation will reconstitute the proper, the place, meaning, and truth that have become distant from themselves for the time of a detour or of a non-delivery. The time of an algorithm. Once more a hole will be stopped: and to do so one does not have to fill it, but only to see and to delimit its contour.

We have read: the signifier (in the letter, in the note) has no place identical to itself, it *is missing from its place.* Its meaning counts for little, it cannot be reduced to its meaning. But what the Seminar insists upon showing, finally, is that there is a single *proper* itinerary of the letter which returns to a determinable place that is always the same and that is *its own;* and that if its meaning (what is written in the note in circulation) is indifferent or unknown for our purposes (according to the hypothesis whose fragility nevertheless sup-

---

12. TN. An untranslatable play on words: ". . . *ce qui se laisse toujours presque (feint) de soi-même (se) mettre de côté, à l'écart, comme le quart."* The fourth, *le quart,* entails division, *l'écart,* which the demand for truth cannot tolerate.

ports the entire logic of the Seminar), the meaning of the letter and the sense of its itinerary are necessary, unique, and determinable in truth, that is, as truth.

Certainly the place and meaning of the letter are not at the disposition of the subjects. Certainly the latter are subjected to the movement of the signifier. But when Lacan says that the letter has no proper place, this must be understood henceforth as objective place, a place determinable in an empirical and naive topology. When he says that it has no proper meaning, this must henceforth be understood as the exhaustible content of what is written in the note. For the signifier-letter, in the topology and psychoanalytico-transcendental semantics with which we are dealing, has a proper place and meaning which form the condition, origin, and destination of the entire circulation, as of the entire logic of the signifier.

The proper place, first of all. The letter has a place of emission and of destination. This is not a subject, but a hole, the lack on the basis of which the subject is constituted. The contour of this hole is determinable, and it magnetizes the entire itinerary of the detour which leads from hole to hole, from the hole to itself, and which therefore has a *circular* form. In question is indeed a regulated *circulation* which organizes a return from the detour toward the hole. A transcendental reappropriation and a transcendental readequation fulfilling an authentic contract. That the itinerary is proper and circular is what Lacan literally says: "Thus we are confirmed in our detour by the very object which draws us on into it: for we are quite simply dealing with a letter which has been diverted from its path; one whose course has been *prolonged* (etymologically, the word of the title), or to revert to the language of the post office, a letter that has not been delivered (*lettre en souffrance*).

"Here then, *simple and odd,* as we are told on the very first page, reduced to its simplest expression, is the singularity of the letter, which as the title indicates, is the *true subject* of the tale: since it can be diverted, it must have a course *which is proper to it:* the trait by which its incidence as signifier is affirmed. For we have learned to conceive of the signifier as sustaining itself only in a displacement comparable to that found in electric news strips or in the rotating memories of our machines-that-think-like-men, this because of the alternating operation which is its principle, requiring it to leave its place, even though it returns to it by a circular path" (S, pp. 59–60; Lacan's italics).

Quitte: "leave [*quitte*] its place, even though [*quitte à*] it returns to it by a circular path." Circulation, the acquitting of a debt, comes to repair the dehiscence which, in opening the debt and the contract for a time (the time of the signifier), has expulsed the signified from its proper origin. Circulation permits the signified to return to its origin. This readequation (the truth) therefore indeed implies a theory of the proper place, and the latter implies a theory of the letter as an indivisible locality: the signifier must never risk being lost, destroyed, divided, or fragmented without return.

The proper meaning, next. The letter having a (single) place of origin and destination, and remaining what it is *en route* (what guarantees this?), it has a proper meaning: the law of its itinerary first of all, if not its content, although the latter gains from the deciphering a minimal determination which says enough about it. The letter must have a relation to whatever constitutes the contract or the "pact," that is, a relation with the subjection of the subject, and therefore somewhere with the hole as the proper place of the letter. Its place has an essential relation with its meaning, and the latter must be such that it makes the letter come back to its place. In fact, we know what is in the note. Lacan indeed is obliged to speak of and hold onto its meaning, at very least as that which threatens the pact which constitutes the letter's meaning: the phallic law represented by the King and guarded by the Queen, the law that she should share with him according to the pact, and that she threatens to divide, to dissociate, and to betray. "But all this tells us nothing of the message it conveys.

"Love letter or conspiratorial letter, letter of betrayal or letter of mission, letter of summons or letter of distress, *we are assured of but one thing:* the Queen must not bring it to the knowledge of her lord and master.

"Now these terms, far from bearing on the nuance of discredit they have in *bourgeois* comedy, take on a certain prominence through allusion to her sovereign, to whom she is bound by pledge of faith, and doubly so, since her role as spouse does not relieve her of her duties as subject, but rather elevates her to the guardianship of what royalty according to law incarnates of power: and which is called legitimacy.

"From then on, to whatever vicissitudes the Queen may choose to subject the letter, it remains that the letter is the symbol of a pact, and that, even should the recipient not assume the pact, the existence of the letter situates her in a symbolic chain foreign to the one which constitutes her faith . . . Our fable is so constructed as to show that it is the letter and its detour which governs their entries and roles. If it is not delivered [*en souffrance*], they shall endure the pain. Should they pass beneath its shadow, they become its reflection. Falling in possession of the letter—admirable ambiguity of language—its meaning possesses them" (S, 57–58, 60; my italics).

A formulation that is Heideggerian in its type, as is most often the case in these decisive pauses.

Therefore the letter has a proper meaning, its own proper itinerary and location. What are they? In the triangle, only Dupin seems to know. For the moment, let us set aside the question of this knowing, and let us concern ourselves first with what is known. What does Dupin know? He knows that finally the letter *is found,* and knows where it must *be found* in order to return circularly, adequately to its proper place. This proper place, known to Dupin, and to the psychoanalyst, who in oscillating fashion, as we shall see, occupies Dupin's position, is the place of castration: woman as the unveiled site of the lack of a penis, as the truth of the phallus, that is of castration. The truth of the purloined letter is the truth, its meaning is meaning, its law is the law, the contract of truth with itself in logos. Beneath this notion of the pact (and therefore of adequation), the notion of veiling/unveiling attunes the entire Seminar to the Heideggerian discourse on the truth. Veiling/unveiling here concerns a hole, a non-being: the truth of Being as non-being. The truth is "woman" as veiled/unveiled castration. This is where the signifier (its inadequation with the signified) gets underway, this is the site of the signifier, the letter. But this is also where the trial begins, the promise of reappropriation, of return, of readequation: "the search for and restitution of the object" (S, p. 45). The singular *unity* of the letter is the site of the contract of the truth with itself. This is why the letter *comes back to, amounts to* [*revient à*] woman (at least in the extent to which she wishes to save the pact and, therefore, that which is the King's, the phallus that is in her guardianship); this is why, as Lacan says elsewhere, the letter amounts to, comes back to Being [*la lettre revient à l'être*], that is to the nothing that would be opening itself as the hole between woman's legs. Such is the proper place in which the letter is found, where its meaning is found, where the minister believes it to be in the shadows and where it is, in its very hiding place, the most exposed. Possessing the letter in the shadows, the minister begins to identify himself with the Queen (but must not Dupin, and the psychoanalyst within him, do so in turn? We are not there yet).

Thus ". . . everything seems intended for a character [*the minister*], all of whose utterances have revealed the most virile traits, to exude the oddest *odor di femina* when he appears.

"Dupin does not fail to stress that this is an artifice, describing behind the bogus finery the vigilance of a beast of prey ready to spring. But that this is the very effect of the unconscious in the precise sense that we teach that the unconscious means that man is inhabited by the signifier: could we find a more beautiful image of it than the one Poe himself forges to help us appreciate Dupin's exploit? For with this aim in mind, he refers to those toponymical inscriptions which a geographical map, lest it remain mute, superimposes on its design, and which may become the object of a guessing game: who can find the name chosen by a partner?—noting immediately that the name most likely to foil a beginner will be one which, in large letters spaced out widely across the map, discloses, often without an eye pausing to notice it, the name of an entire country . . .

"Just so does the purloined letter, like an immense female body, stretch out across the Minister's office when Dupin enters. But just so does he already *expect to find it* [my italics—J.D.], and has only, with his eyes veiled by green lenses, to undress that huge body.

"And that is why without needing any more than being able to listen in at the door of Professor Freud, he will go straight to the spot in which lies and lives what that body is designed to hide, in a gorgeous center caught in a glimpse, nay, to the very place seducers name the Castle Sant'Angelo in their innocent illusion of being certain that they can hold the city from there. Look! between the jambs of the fireplace there is the object already within reach of the hand the ravisher has but to extend . . ." (S, p. 66; mod.).

The letter—place of the signifier—is found in the place where Dupin and the psychoanalyst expect to find it: on the immense body of a woman, between the "legs" of the fireplace. Such is its proper place, the terminus of its circular itinerary. It is returned to the sender, who is not the signer of the note, but the place where it began to *detach* itself from its possessor or feminine legatee. The Queen, seeking to reappropriate for herself that which, by virtue of the pact which subjects her to the King, i.e. by virtue of the Law, guaranteed her the disposition of a phallus of which she would otherwise be deprived, of which she has taken the risk of depriving herself, that she has taken the risk of dividing, that is, of multiplying—the Queen, then, undertakes to reform, to reclose the circle of the restricted economy, the circulatory pact. She wants the letter-fetish brought back to her, and therefore begins by replacing, by exchanging one fetish for another: she emits—without really spending it, since there is an equivalence here—a quantity of money which is exchanged for the letter and assures its circular return. Dupin, as (the) analyst, is found [*se trouve*] on the circuit, in the circle of the restricted economy, in what I call elsewhere the stricture of the ring, which the Seminar analyzes as the truth of fiction. We will come back to this problem of economics.

This determination of the proper, of the law of the proper, of *economy,* therefore leads back to castration as truth, to the figure of woman as the figure of castration *and* of truth. Of castration as truth. Which above all does not mean, as one might tend to believe, to truth as essential dislocation and irreducible fragmentation. Castration-truth, on the contrary, is that which contracts itself (stricture of the ring) in order to bring the phallus, the signifier, the letter, or the fetish back into their *oikos,*[13] their familiar dwelling, their proper place. In this sense castration-truth is the opposite of fragmentation, the very antidote for fragmentation: that which is missing from its place has in castration a fixed, central place, freed from all substitution. Something is missing from its place, but the lack is never missing from it [*Quelque chose manque à sa place, mais le manque n'y manque jamais*]. The phallus, thanks to castration, always remains in its place, in the transcendental topology of which we were speaking above. In castration, the phallus is indivisible, and therefore indestructible, like the letter which *takes its place.* And this is why the motivated, never demonstrated presupposition of the materiality of the letter as *indivisibility* is indispensable for this restricted economy, this circulation of the proper.

The difference which interests me here is that—a formula to be understood as one will—the lack does not have its place in dissemination.

By determining the place of the lack, the topos of that which is lacking from its place, and in constituting it as a fixed center, Lacan is indeed proposing, at the same time as a truth-discourse, a discourse on the truth of the purloined letter as the truth of *The Purloined Letter.* In question is a hermeneutic deciphering, despite any appearances or denegation. The link of Femininity and Truth is the ultimate signified of this deciphering. Fourteen years later, reintroducing the Seminar at the head of the *Ecrits* with an *Unpublished Presentation,* Lacan insists above all on this link and this meaning. He gives to Woman or to Femininity a capital letter that elsewhere he often reserves for Truth: "What Poe's tale demon-

13. TN. The Greek *oikos* means the house, the dwelling, and is also the root from which the word *economy* is derived.

strates through my efforts is that the signifier's effect of subjection, in this instance the purloined letter's, bears above all on whoever wields it after the theft, and that along its itinerary what it conveys is the very Femininity that it has taken into its shadows . . ."[14] Femininity is the Truth (of) castration, is the best figure of castration, because in the logic of the signifier it has always already been castrated; and Femininity "leaves" something in circulation (here the letter), something detached from itself in order to have it brought back to itself, because she has "never had it: whence truth comes out of the well, but only half-way."

This first castration (pre-castration) afterward affects with castration, and with femininity therefore, whoever holds the letter that signifies the phallus and castration: "This is why the Minister comes to be castrated, castrated, the very word of that which he still believes he has: the letter that Dupin was able to pick out between the legs of his very smooth fireplace.

"Here is but completed that which initially feminizes him [the minister] as in a dream (. . .) To which extent our Dupin shows himself equal in his success to the success of the psychoanalyst."[15]

POINT DE VUE[16]
TRUTH IN (THE) PLACE OF FEMALE SEXUALITY

What about this success? In order to answer, let us await reconsideration, in all its complexity, of the relation between Dupin's position and the analyst's positon, and then the relation between the analyst and him who says Freud and myself in the Seminar and in the introductions to the Seminar. This requires a long detour.

Until now, our questions have led us to suspect that if there is something like a purloined letter, perhaps it has a supplementary trap: it may have no fixed location, not even that of a definable hole or assignable lack. The letter might not be found, or could always possibly not be found, or would be found less in the sealed writing whose "story" is recounted by the narrator and deciphered by the Seminar, less in the content of the story, than "in" the text which escapes, from a fourth side, the eyes both of Dupin and of the psychoanalyst. The remainder, what is left unclaimed, would be *The Purloined Letter*, i.e. the text bearing this title whose location,

14. TN. *Points*, p. 1.

15. TN. Ibid., pp. 7–8.

16. TN. *Point de* means both "point of" and "no, none at all." Thus, point of view/no view, blindness.

like the large letters once more become invisible, is not where one would expect to find it, in the framed content of the "real drama" or in the hidden and sealed interior of Poe's tale, but rather in and as the open, the very open, letter that is fiction. The latter, because it is written, at the very least implies a self-divesting fourth agency, which at the same time divests the letter of the text from whoever deciphers it, from the *facteur* of truth who puts the letter back into the circle of its own, proper itinerary: which is what the Seminar does in repeating Dupin's operation, for he, in accord with the circularity of the "proper itinerary," "has succeeded in returning the letter to its proper course" (S, p. 69), according to the desire *of* the Queen. To return the letter to its proper course, assuming that its trajectory is a line, is to correct a deviation, to rectify a departure, to recall, for the sake of the rule, i.e., the norm, an orientation, an authentic line. Dupin is adroit, knows his address, and knows the law. At the very moment one believes that by drawing triangles and circles, and by wielding the oppostion imaginary/symbolic one grasps *The Purloined Letter,* at the very moment one reconstitutes the truth, the proper adequation, *The Purloined Letter* escapes through a too self-evident opening. As Baudelaire bluntly reminds us. The purloined letter is in the text: not only as an object whose proper itinerary is described, contained in the text, a signifier become the theme or signified of the text, but also as the text producing the effects of the frame. At the very moment when Dupin and the Seminar find it, when they determine its proper location and itinerary, when they believe that it is here or there as on a map, a place on a map as on the body of a woman, they no longer see the map itself: not the map that the text describes at one moment or another, but the map [*carte*] that the text "is," that it describes, "itself," as the deviation of the four [*l'écart du quatre*] with no promise of topos or truth. The remaining[17] structure of the letter is that—contrary to what the Seminar says in its last words ("what the 'purloined letter,' that is, the not delivered letter [*lettre en souffrance*] means is that a letter always arrives at its destination." S,

17. TN. "*La structure* restante *de la lettre* . . ." For Derrida, writing is always that which is an excess remainder, *un reste.* Further, in French, mail delivered to a post office box is called *poste restante,* making the dead letter office the ultimate *poste restante,* literally "remaining mail." Thus, Derrida is saying that Lacan's notion that the non-delivered letter, *la lettre en souffrance,* always arrives at its destination overlooks the structural possibility that a letter can always *remain* in the dead letter office, and that without this possibility of deviation and remaining—the entire postal system—there would be no delivery of letters to any address at all.

p. 72)—a letter can always not arrive at its destination. Its "materiality" and "topology" are due to its divisibility, its always possible partition. It can always be fragmented without return, and the system of the symbolic, of castration, of the signifier, of the truth, of the contract, etc., always attempt to protect the letter from this fragmentation: this is the point of view of the King or the Queen, which are the same here; they are bound by contract to reappropriate the bit. Not that the letter never arrives at its destination, but it belongs to the structure of the letter to be capable, always, of not arriving. And without this threat (breach of contract, division or multiplication, the separation without return from the phallus which was begun for a moment by the Queen, i.e. by every "subject"), the circuit of the letter would not even have begun. But with this threat, the circuit can always not finish. Here dissemination threatens the law of the signifier and of castration as the contract of truth. It broaches, breaches [*entame*] the unity of the signifier, that is, of the phallus.

At the moment when the Seminar, like Dupin, finds the letter where it is found [*se trouve*], between the legs of woman, the deciphering of the enigma is anchored in truth. The sense of the tale, the meaning of the purloined letter ("what the 'purloined letter,' that is, the not delivered letter [*lettre en souffrance*], means is that a letter always arrives at its destination") is uncovered. The deciphering (Dupin's, the Seminar's), uncovered via a meaning (the truth), as a hermeneutic process, itself arrives at its destination.

Why then does the Seminar refind, along with the truth, the same meaning and the same topos as did Marie Bonaparte when, skipping over the text, she proposed a psycho-biographical analysis of *The Purloined Letter* in 1933.[18] Is this a coincidence?

Is it a coincidence if, in allegedly breaking with psychobiographical criticism (see *Ecrits,* p. 860), one rejoins it in its ultimate semantic anchorage? And after a perhaps more simplifying textual analysis?

For Bonaparte too, the castration of the woman (of the mother) is the final sense, what *The Purloined Letter* means. And truth means readequation or reappropriation as the desire to stop up the hole. But Bonaparte does what Lacan does not: she relates *The Purloined Letter* to other texts by Poe. And she analyzes the gesture

18. *Edgar Poe, sa vie, son œuvre: Etude analytique* (Paris: Presses Universitaires de France, 1933). [References to Bonaparte will be given in the text, and will refer to *The Life and Works of Edgar Allan Poe,* trans. John Rodker, London, 1949.]

of doing so. Further on we will comprehend the *internal* necessity of this operation.

For example, *The Black Cat,* in which "the castration fear, embodied in the woman as the castrated being, lies at the core of the tale" (Bonaparte, p. 481). "Nevertheless, all the primitive anxieties of the child, which often remain those of the adult, seem to be gathered here as if by appointment, in this story of extreme anxiety, as if at a crossroads" (Bonaparte, p. 481). Within this quadrifurcum, named absentmindedly, omitted like a frame, there is the representation of a circle or a triangle. The Seminar: "Here we are, in fact, yet again at the crossroads at which we had left our drama and its round with the question of the way in which the subjects replace each other in it" (S, p. 60). Bonaparte continues with a page of generalizations about castration anxiety that could be summarized by a statement of Freud's that she does not cite here: the assertion that the mother's lack of a penis is "the greatest trauma"; or of Lacan's: "Division of the subject? This point is a knot.

"Let us recall where Freud spells it out: on the mother's lack of a penis in which the nature of the phallus is revealed" (*Ecrits,* p. 877).

After treating the Law and fetishism as a process of rephallicizing the mother (what has been stolen or detached from her is to be returned to her), Bonaparte writes the following, in which the knot of the Lacanian interpretation is to be found, along with several other things:

> Finally, with the gallows theme, we see death-anxiety, or fear of death.
>
> All these fears, however, remain subordinate to the main theme of fear of castration, with which all are closely interwoven. The cat with the white breast has also a missing eye; hanging represents not only death, but rephallization; the urge to confess leads to the discovery of a corpse surmounted by an effigy of castration; even the cellar and tomb, and the gaping aperture of the chimney, recall the dread cloaca of the mother.
>
> Other tales by Poe also express, though in different and in less aggressive fashion, regret for the missing maternal penis, with reproach for its loss. First among these, strange though it seem, is "The Purloined Letter."
>
> The reader will remember that, in this story the Queen of France, like Elizabeth Arnold, is in possession of a dangerous and secret correspondence, whose writer is unknown. A wicked minister, planning political blackmail and to strengthen his power, steals one of these letters under the Queen's eyes, which she is unable to prevent owing to the King's presence. This letter must at all costs be recovered. Every

attempt by the Police fails. Fortunately Dupin is at hand. Wearing dark spectacles with which he can look about him, while his own eyes are concelaed, he makes an excuse to call on the Minister, and discovers the letter openly displayed in a card-rack, hung 'from a little brass knob just beneath the middle of the mantelpiece.'' [1]

Here, then, is Bonaparte's note:

1. ". . . that hung . . . from a little brass nob just beneath the middle of the mantelpiece." Baudelaire's translation: "*suspendu . . . à un petit bouton de cuivre au-dessus du manteau de la cheminée.*" The imprecision of Baudelaire's translation, as far as this sentence is concerned, is obvious: in particular, "beneath" is translated by "*au-dessus*" [above], which is completely wrong. (Bonaparte, p. 483)

This note is not without importance. First, it shows that Lacan had read Bonaparte, although the Seminar never names her. As an author so scrupulous about debts and priorities, he could have acknowledged an exploration which orients his entire interpretation, to wit the process of rephallization as the proper itinerary of the letter, the "return of the letter" to its "destination" after having been refound between the legs of the fireplace. Or could have silenced it. But since footnotes are, if not the truth, the appendix in which is shown that which must not be said, or that which, as Schelling cited in *Das Unheimliche* says, "should remain hidden," the Seminar lets fall a footnote in response: "Look! between the jambs of the fireplace, there is the object already within reach of the hand the ravisher has but to extend . . . The question of deciding whether he seizes it above the mantelpiece, as Baudelaire translates, or beneath it as in the original text, may be abandoned without harm to the inferences of cooking.[38]" Here, then, is Lacan's note: "38. And even to the cook herself" (S, p. 67).[19]

Without harm? On the contrary, the damage would be irreparable, within the Seminar itself: *on* the mantelpiece of the fireplace, the letter could not have been "between the jambs of the fireplace," "between the legs of the fireplace." What is at stake, then, is something major, even if one sets aside, imagining it not relevant, the

19. TN. I have modified Mehlman's clever translation of Lacan's phrase (". . . *peut être abandonnée sans dommage aux inférences de la cuisine*"). Mehlman gives it as ". . . the inferences of those whose profession is grilling," which captures the sense of *cuisiner* as interrogation. Thus, Lacan is mocking Bonaparte as a member of the "psychoanalytic police," perhaps comparing her to the police in *The Purloined Letter,* and perhaps also referring to his own expulsion from the International Psychoanalytic Association.

Seminar's disdainful nervousness as concerns a psychoanalyst and her legacy.[20] Why relegate the question to the kitchen, as if to an outbuilding, and the woman who answers it to the status of cook? Certain "masters of the truth" in Greece knew how to keep the kitchen a place for thinking.

Just before this note, it will be recalled, the Seminar had invoked the "toponymical inscriptions," the "geographical map" of the "immense body," and the location of that which Dupin "expects to find," since he is repeating the gesture of the minister, who himself is identified with the Queen whose letter still, properly, occupies the same place: the place of detachment and reattachment.

After her note, Bonaparte continues:

> By a further subterfuge, he possesses himself of the compromising letter and leaves a similar one in its place. The Queen, who will have the original restored to her, is saved.
>
> Let us first note that this letter, the very symbol of the maternal penis also 'hangs' over the fireplace, in the same manner as the female penis, if it existed, would be hung over the cloaca which is here represented—as in the foregoing tales—by the frequent symbol of the fireplace. We have here, in fact, what is almost an anatomical chart, from which not even the clitoris (or brass knob) is omitted. Something very different, however, should be hanging from that body. (Bonaparte, p. 483)

20. Legacy [*legs*] and rephallization: 1. "Could it be the letter which brings Woman to be that subject, simultaneously all-powerful and enslaved, such that every hand to which Woman leaves the letter, takes back along with it, that which in receiving it, she herself has legated (*fait lais*)? 'Legacy' [*lais*] means that which Woman bequeaths in never having had it: whence truth emerges from the well, but only halfway" (Presentation of the *Ecrits, Points* 7–8). 2. "To the grim irony of rephallicizing the castrated mother, by hanging, we must now add the irony that relactifies her dry breasts by the broad spattering of the splotch of milk . . . even though the main resentment comes from the absence of the penis on the woman's body" (Bonaparte, p. 475). Further on we will come back to the question of the "part object" that is implied here. As for the well, in *The Murders in the Rue Morgue,* Dupin, after the discovery of the "fearfully mutilated" "body of the mother," recalls: "He (Vidocq) impaired his vision by holding the object too close. He might see, perhaps, one or two points with unusual clearness, but in so doing he, necessarily, lost sight of the matter as a whole. Thus there is such a thing as being too profound. Truth is not always in a well." *Selected Writings of Edgar Allan Poe,* ed. Edward Davidson (Boston: Houghton Mifflin, 1956), p. 153. All further references to Poe will be to this edition. Also note that the French for "legacy" is *legs;* Derrida constantly plays on the *leg* in *leg*acy. Moreover, the older form of *legs* is *lais,* which is the homonym of *lait,* milk. Thus the question of legacy, rephallization, and re*lact*ification.

After this brief allusion to the knob (which the Seminar does not pick up), Bonaparte reattaches her interpretation to an Oedipal typology and clinical practice. Her interest in "the-author's-life" no more simplifies her reading of the text than the Seminar's lack of interest suffices to guarantee a reading. The accent is placed on a "pre-genital, phallic and archaic" Oedipal struggle for the possession of the maternal penis, which is here determined as a part object. Bonaparte is never tempted to grant Dupin the position of the analyst, not even in order to watch over him with an other kind of mastery. Dupin's lucidity comes to him from the war in which he is engaged, as he himself states at the end, ("'You know my political prepossessions. In this matter, I act as a partisan of the lady concerned. For eighteen months the Minister has had her in his power. She has him now in hers; since, being unaware that the letter is not in his possession, he will proceed with his exactions as if it was. (. . .) D—, at Vienna once, did me an evil turn, which I told him, quite good-humoredly, that I should remember'"),[21] and this has motivated him throughout. As it has situated him on the circuit of the debt, of the phallus, of the signifier in its letter, and of the money which, unlike Lacan, Bonaparte does not consider as neutralizing or as "destructive of" "all signification." She writes: "Small wonder that Dupin, the embodiment of the son, when speaking of his 'political prepossessions,' should declare himself 'a partisan of the lady concerned.' Finally, in return for a cheque of 50,000 francs, leaving to the Prefect of Police the fabulous reward, Dupin restores to the woman her symbolic letter or missing phallus. Thus, once more, we meet the equation gold = penis. The mother gives her son gold in exchange for the penis he restores. So, too, in 'The Gold Bug'" (Bonaparte, p. 484).

The circle of this restitution indeed forms the "proper course" of the Seminar. What, then, of the Seminar's attempted thrust to identify Dupin's position with the analyst's position? This idea never tempts Bonaparte. And it is strangely divided or suspended in the Seminar. The signs of the identification first:

1. The third glance, which is not ensnared, sees the triangle. Certainly Dupin occupies within the triangle a position identical to the minister's, but to the minister's in the first scene and not in the second, where the minister occupies the place of the powerless Queen. Dupin, thus, would be the only one not to let himself be

21. TN. Poe, pp. 224–25.

plucked like an ostrich. ("The third sees that the first two glances leave what should be hidden exposed to whoever would seize it: the Minister, and finally Dupin . . . Three partners: the second believing itself invisible because the first has its head stuck in the ground, and all the while letting the third calmly pluck its rear." S, p. 44). Dupin finally: at the end Dupin breaks off his provisional identification with the minister, and remains alone in seeing all, thereby withdrawing from the circuit.

2. This is confirmed by an initial interpretation of the money demanded by Dupin in exchange for the letter, by "the business of Dupin's remuneration." The process of debt that this story raises finds itself examined by Lacan soon after the note on the cook. And a supplementary space of several lines. The "we" is that of the community of analysts, among whom the author of the Seminar at first seems to count himself. "Do we not in fact feel concerned with good reason when for Dupin what is perhaps [this "perhaps" will be forever suspended—J.D.] at stake is his withdrawal from the symbolic circuit of the letter—we who become the emissaries of all the purloined letters which at least for a time remain not delivered [en souffrance] with us in the transference. And is it not the responsibility their transference entails that we neutralize by equating it with the signifier most destructive of all signification, namely: money" (S, p. 68).

As the "perhaps" indicates, as these questions without question marks also announce (along with the "But that is not all" that opens the next paragraph), the question will remain without a clear answer. The very position of the question, in its form, in its terms, is constructed to forbid the answer: in effect, how is one to determine the conceptual rigor of the expression "equating it with the signifier most destructive of all signification"? The question, we know, is not a formal one, nor is it simply one of knowing who is being the ostrich in wielding a greater or lesser quantity of destruction. If money is not totally destructive of all signification, if it is only what is "most destructive," then it cannot "be equivalent" to a "neutralization." And it does not provide for a "withdrawal" from the "symbolic circuit of the letter."

3. This is confirmed again in the new introduction to the *Ecrits* (in the *Points* edition) already cited above: "This is why the Minister comes to be castrated, castrated, the very word of that which he still believes he has: the letter that Dupin was able to pick out between the jambs of his very smooth fireplace. (. . .) To which ex-

tent our Dupin shows himself equal in his success to the success of the psychoanalyst." [22]

With the help of the indetermination that we have just noted ("perhaps," "the most destructive"), these signs of an identification between Dupin and us-psychoanalysts will become more complicated. Not simply in order to refuse Dupin admission into the analytic institution which would neutralize "the responsibility" that the "transference entails," but in order to divide "us-psychoanalysts" into two Dupins: the fool, the Dupin who remains an integral part of the triangle while believing himself the master of it, and the other Dupin, the Dupin who sees all from the place whence are apostrophized all the psychoanalysts who understand nothing about Dupin, about his "true strategy," that is, about the author of the Seminar who knows how to return to the letter of Freud, how to refind it where it is found [se trouve] for purposes of restitution, and by whose efforts both Freud's teaching and Poe's demonstration are dispensed: the entire Seminar is opened by the project, repeated elsewhere a hundred times, of "taking Freud's discovery seriously" and of basing "the instruction of this Seminar" on this discovery, and to do so against the corruption which the letter of Freud has suffered in his colleagues' institution; and "what Poe's tale demonstrates through my efforts" collaborates with the return of Freud's text to its proper place. From this position the Seminar ridicules the too rapid identification of (all) the other analysts with Dupin, with a Dupin about whom they do not see that in possessing the letter he still resembles the minister, and thus finds himself in the latter's place and begins like the minister to become feminized, to become identified with the Queen. The author of the Seminar excludes himself from the analytic community. We, henceforth, are Freud, Poe, one of the two Dupins, and I: "To which extent our Dupin shows himself equal in his success to the success of the psychoanalyst, whose action can be brought to bear only on some unexpected blunder by the other. Usually, his message is the only effective failure of his treatment: as is Dupin's message, which is to remain unrevealed, although it closes the affair.

"But, would I explain, just as the text, which here maintains the post at the entryway that it has elsewhere, will be judged, these terms always the more, the less will they be understood.

"The less understood by psychoanalysts, for whom these terms

22. TN. *Points*, pp. 7–8.

are as clearly in sight as the purloined letter, and who even see the letter in these terms, but on the basis of this believe themselves, like Dupin, the masters of it. "In fact they are only masters of using my terms without rhyme or reason. At which enterprise several have made themselves ridiculous. And these are the very same ones who tell me that what the others are suspicious of is a rigor to which they feel themselves unequal." [23] The ridiculous heirs or disciples thus corrupt, without rhyme or reason, the master's proper terms; and the master reminds them that they must not take themselves for masters by identifying with the naive Dupin. And to use the master's terms properly, to bring them back to him, is to remind oneself also of the right direction, and to remind oneself that the master, like Dupin (which one?), is master of the return to Freud of his proper letter. [24] (To be continued.) In beginning by identifying Dupin with the psychoanalyst, a

23. TN. *Points*, p. 8.
24. Also not delivered [*en souffrance*], Freud's letter awaited restitution. The analytic community is organized like a *poste restante*, keeping sealed the threatening power of an inheritance. The literal return to/of Freud's literality (*le retour à la lettre de la lettre de Freud*) motivates, as we know, the entire itinerary of the *Ecrits*. This is stated everywhere, particularly under the heading *D'un dessein*, (further on we will read this word between quotation marks within quotation marks), in an introduction proposed afterward (1966) to the *Introduction to Jean Hyppolite's Commentary on Freud's Negation*. This note concerning denegation begins by insisting: above all do not go off thinking about a "consecration" of the letter of Freud, nor about some "rendez-vous" given in advance for a meeting there: "The two samples, which follow, of our seminar impel us to communicate to the reader some idea of the design [*dessein*] of our instruction . . . For to let oneself be guided in this way by the letter of Freud even up to the illumination that it necessitates, without giving it any rendez-vous in advance, not to recoil before the residue, found again at the end, of its departure from an enigma, and even not to consider oneself at the end absolved from the proceeding via astonishment which provided the entry into it—this is what an experienced logician brought us the guarantee of as that which composed our quest, when, three years ago already, we set out to depend upon a *literal commentary* of Freud.
"This *demand for reading* has none of the vagueness of culture that one might think was in question.
"For us, the privilege granted to the letter of Freud has nothing superstitious about it. It is when one is most comfortable with it that one brings to it a kind of consecration highly compatible with its degradation to a routine usage.
"That every text, whether proposed as sacred or profane, sees its literality increase in prevalence to the extent that it properly implies a confrontation with the truth, is that for which the Freudian discovery shows the structural reason.
"Precisely in that the truth which it brings us, that of the unconscious, owes to

double profit is prepared: 1. The lucidity of the one who is able to see what no one else has seen: the place of the thing, between the legs (and the author of the Seminar says then: we-psychoanalysts, we withdraw ourselves from the symbolic circuit and we neutralize the scene in which we are not participants); 2. The possibility—by emphasizing that Dupin remains a participant (and how), by maintaining the identification Dupin-psychoanalyst—of denouncing the naïveté of the analytic community, of saying: you-psychoanalysts, you are deluding yourselves at precisely the moment when like Dupin you believe yourselves to be masters.

In effect. After the paragraph whose indecision we have delineated ("perhaps," "the signifier the most destructive," etc.), a very clever game is played, but in order to demonstrate how Dupin's ruse—the biggest of all in the Oedipal scene—bears within its own trap a *motivation*, the game will go to the point of getting carried away with itself.

In question are the last pages of the Seminar, pages punctuated by a "But that's not all" (S, p. 68) and an "Is that all . . ." (S, p. 72). As soon as one interprets the retribution demanded by Dupin as an analytic procedure in order to withdraw from the circuit thanks to "the signifier most destructive of all signification, namely: money," it is difficult to account for all the signs of non-neutrality multiplied at the end of *The Purloined Letter.* Is this not a shocking paradox? "But that's not all. The profit Dupin so nimbly extracts from his exploit, if its purpose is to allow him to withdraw his stakes from the game, makes all the more paradoxical, even shocking, the partisan attack, the underhanded blow, he suddenly permits himself to launch against the minister, whose insolent prestige, after all, would seem to have been sufficiently deflated by the trick Dupin has just played on him" (S, p. 68). Thus, that was not all. And Dupin's "explosion of feeling at the end of the story" (S, p. 68), his "rage of manifestly feminine nature" (S, p. 71) when he claims to be settling his account with the minister by signing his own maneuver, must be pointed out. Dupin, then, reproduces the process called feminization: he subjects himself to the (desire of the) minister, whose place he occupies as soon as he possesses the letter—the place of the signifier—and conforms to the Queen's desire. Here, by virtue of the pact, one can no longer distinguish between the place of the King (which is marked by blindness) and the place of the

---

the letter of language, to what we call the signifier." *Ecrits* (F), pp. 363–64. See also, for example, p. 381.

Queen, the place to which the letter, in its "right course" and following its "proper itinerary," must return in circular fashion. As the signifier has but one proper place, fundamentally there is but one place for the letter, and this place is occupied successively by all those who possess it. It must be recognized, then, that Dupin, once he has entered into the circuit, having identified with the minister in order to take the letter back from him and to put it back on its "proper course," can no longer depart from this course. He must go through it in its entirety. The Seminar asks a strange question on this topic: "He is thus, in fact, fully participant in the intersubjective triad, and, as such, in the median position previously occupied by the Queen and the Minister. Will he, in showing himself to be above it, reveal to us at the same time the author's intentions?

"If he has succeeded in returning the letter to its proper course, it remains for him to make it arrive at its address. And that address is in the place previously occupied by the King, since it is there that it would re-enter the order of the Law.

"As we have seen, neither the King nor the Police who replaced him in that position were able to read the letter because that *place entailed blindness*" (S, p. 69).

If Dupin now occupies the "median position," has he not always done so? And is there any other position in the circuit? Is it only at this moment of the narrative, when he has the letter in hand, that he once more finds himself in this position? We cannot stop here: from the outset Dupin acts with his sights set on the letter, on possessing it in order to return it to its rightful owner (neither the King, nor the Queen, but the Law which binds them), and thus finds himself preferable to his (brother) enemy, his younger or twin brother (Atreus/ Thyestes), to the minister who fundamentally pursues the same aims, with the same gestures. Therefore, if he is in a "median position," the differentiation of the three glances given above is no longer pertinent. There are only ostriches, no one can avoid being plucked, and the more one is the master, the more one presents one's rear. Which will be the case for whoever identifies with Dupin.

Concerning Dupin, a strange question, as we said: "Will he, in showing himself to be above it, reveal to us at the same time the author's intentions?"

This is not the only allusion to "the author's intentions" (see also S, p. 41). Its form implies that the author, in his intention, is in a situation of general mastery, his *superiority* as concerns the triangles placed on stage (supposing that he is staging only triangles) being representable only by the superiority of an actor, to wit Dupin. Let us abandon this implication here: an entire conception of "literature."

Will Dupin have shown himself superior? The Seminar, because it proceeds from what Dupin sees where he expects to find it, because it repeats the operation of the restitution of the letter, cannot answer no. Or yes, since Dupin too is an ostrich. Thus Dupin's "true" position will be left in the obscurity of something unrevealed or in the suspension of a hypothesis, nonetheless without giving up (and here there is no more obscurity, nor is there a hypothesis) the idea of having "deciphered Dupin's true strategy." Here is the unrevealed: "To which extent our Dupin shows himself equal in his success to the success of the psychoanalyst, whose action can be brought to bear only on some unexpected blunder by the other. Usually, his [?] message is the only effective failure of his [?] treatment: as is Dupin's message, which is to remain unrevealed, although it closes the affair." [25]

Here is the suspended hypothesis: "But if he is truly the gambler we are told he is, he will consult his cards a final time before laying them down and, upon reading his hand, will leave the table in time to avoid disgrace" (S, p. 72). Will he have done so? Nothing in the Seminar states this, although it has dwelt on the spot long enough to be certain, despite what is unrevealed, or despite the hypothesis, of possessing the cipher of the letter, Dupin's true strategy, and the true meaning of the purloined letter. The "yes" here is a "no doubt." Just as Dupin, whom the narrator lets speak at the end of the story, appears certain of having succeeded in his maneuver. The Seminar's conclusion: he "will leave the table in time to avoid disgrace.

"Is that all, and shall we believe we have deciphered Dupin's real strategy above and beyond the imaginary tricks with which he was obliged to deceive us? No doubt, yes, for if 'any point requiring reflection,' as Dupin states at the start, is 'examined to best purpose in the dark,' we may now easily read its solution in broad daylight. It was already implicit and easy to derive from the title of our tale, according to the very formula of intersubjective communication we have long submitted to your discretion: in which the sender, we tell you, receives from the receiver his own message in reverse form. Thus it is that what the 'purloined letter,' nay the 'undelivered letter' (*lettre en souffrance*) means is that a letter always arrives at its destination" (S, p. 72. These are the final words of the Seminar).

---

25. TN. *Points*, p. 8.

FIRST SECOND
THE TRUTH OF THE LETTER FROM FREUD'S HAND

In seeing what Dupin sees (not seen by the others), and even what Dupin himself does not see, or sees only, double that he is (on and off the circuit, "participant" and out of play), halfway (like all the others, finally), the Seminar is proffered from the place in which everything is seen "easily," "in broad daylight."

Like Dupin, in sum, at the moment when, without taking into account his blindness as a "participant," he is called "the third (who) sees that the first two glances . . . , etc." And like Dupin, the Seminar returns the letter to its destination after having recognized its place and its trajectory, its law and its destiny, to wit, destination *itself:* arrival at destination.

But Dupin-the-lucid can be so only by entering into the circuit to the point of successively occupying all its places, including, although unwittingly, those of the King and the Police. Like all the others he has perfectly doubled, he is set in motion by the desire of the Queen and by the pact which contracts itself in this desire. And "to show himself superior," even if in relation to all the other masters, his rivals, twins, brothers or confreres, is to repeat the trick without being able to look behind. Which does not necessarily deprive him of pleasure at the moment when another holds the plume in hand.

Repetition of Dupin then. In that he may "now easily read its solution in broad daylight," the author of the Seminar, let us not forget, is making a scene for his confreres, the bad, and unfaithful, guardians of the legacy of Freud. With the "explosion of feeling," whose signs we have pointed out, he is seeking, at least, to get back on course: to rectify, to redress, to put back onto the right path that which is not delivered [*en souffrance*], and, "armed" with the "return to Freud," "to correct a deviation too manifest not to have been avowed as such at every turn." He reproaches his brother, but also his sister, confreres for having corrupted, because they believe themselves masters of them ("like Dupin," see above), his "terms," his very own, those of the author of the Seminar. He reappropriates his terms for himself, then, but he too does so in order to give them back, to return them to Freud, for the issue here is to restore the true instruction, the correct doctrine.[26] Just as Dupin, by calling

26. More literally "the Freudian experience along its authentic lines." *Ecrits* (E), p. 171.

himself a "partisan of the lady," both obliges the Queen and mimes the contract which links her to the King, so there would be something like a pact between Freud—who, dead too soon, and like the King, then, will never have known anything of the consequences—and the author (the place of the author) of the Seminar. But is a King bound by a pact? Or are the dead? The question must wait.

The most remarkable disputation, shall we say the most insidious "under-handed blow," the "rage of manifestly feminine nature," is unleashed concerning the brother or sister confrere, Bonaparte, who in France long believed (him)herself the most authorized depository, the legatee of Freud's authority, maintaining a correspondence with him, personal ties of confidence, and even representing him in our country like a kind of minister whose simultaneous betrayal and blindness is known to the author of the Seminar. This minister even sought, in her book, to place her hand[27] on *The Purloined Letter.* And first of all on the letter diverted from Freud. And she has at her disposition, placed at the head of her book on Poe, an attestation signed by Freud, a kind of letter which seals both the pact and the betrayal (depending on the place), which places the father of psychoanalysis *simultaneously* in the place of the King, the Queen (to whom "her" letter must be restored in order to reconstitute the pact, erase the betrayal, and "correct the deviation"), and the mysterious signer of the purloined letter, the Queen's friend or fellow plotter. As will be said further on about the truth (*causa sui* in being both cause and effect), Freud is the only

27. The question of the hand: as the so-called detainer of the Freudian message, Bonaparte was destined for assault. Insistently, repetitively, automatically. The footnote attacking the cook, which confined itself to a discreet disdain for cooking, was added to the *Ecrits* almost ten years after the first publication of the Seminar in *La Psychanalyse*. But actually from the time of Rome, in the discourse of the same name, five years before, the major accusation against Bonaparte already had been launched: secondhand! Her texts do not at first hand hold the letter of Freud. A given author is "hardly aware" of Freudian theory, "since he tackles the theory through the work of Marie Bonaparte, which he repeatedly cites as an equivalent of the text of Freud—without the reader being in any way advised of the fact—relying no doubt on the good taste of the reader, not without reason, not to confuse the two, but proving no less that he has not the remotest understanding of the true level of the secondary text (*seconde main*)" *Ecrits* (E), p. 39. And since one must simultaneously keep the first hand for oneself and not generalize too much about the second, there are therefore two "levels," a good and a bad second hand. The "good" one, as we will see, takes the letter of the Freudian text as a "text which is the vehicle of speech, in that it constitutes a new emergence of the truth," knows how "to treat it as a true speech," "to experience it in its authenticity" as "full speech," *Ecrits* (F), p. 381; it is a question of Freud's text. And the zealous setting aside of Bonaparte's "second hand" can be read several lines before the chapter to the glory of "full speech."

one (and by virtue of his decease, since he also occupies the place of the dead (king)) to contract only with himself. This signed attestation, from Freud's hand, must be read here. For amusement, but also in order to appreciate how the King, in effect, will have seen that in carrying off the last plume at first hand, he finds himself having mobilized many since his death, while awaiting restitution, that is, restoration. In the position of being dead too soon, *a priori,* he will have never prefaced the Seminar, which took this task on itself, and on several occasions. But one can dream of the figure a foreword by Freud would have made. In order to encourage the reverie, here is the one he did sign, with his own hand and at very first hand, and for Bonaparte alone (from the *pretexts* on, the theory of the *facteurs* is there only to be forwarded):

> In this book my friend and pupil, Marie Bonaparte, has shone the light of psycho-analysis on the life and work of a great writer with pathological trends.
> Thanks to her interpretative effort, we now realize how many of the characteristics of Poe's works were conditioned by his personality, and can see how that personality derived from intense emotional fixations and painful infantile experiences. Investigations such as this do not claim to explain creative genius, but they do reveal the factors (*facteurs*) which awaken it and the sort of subject matter it is destined to choose. Few tasks are as appealing as enquiry into the laws that govern the psyche of exceptionally endowed individuals. Sigm. Freud.
> (Bonaparte, p. xi)

Without suspecting its exactitude, but rather in order to concede that it does not appear in an authenticity of absolutely first hand, let it be said that this seal arrives initially in Bonaparte's translation.

At the very moment when he cuts off the identification with Dupin the "participant" in order to maintain only the other identification; when he deciphers Dupin's "real strategy" at the moment of leaving the table; when "no doubt, yes" he exhibits in broad daylight the true meaning of "the purloined letter," it is at this very moment, then, that the analyst (which one? the other) most resembles Dupin (which one? the other), when the chain of identifications makes him run through, in the opposite direction, the entire circus, automatically, compulsively repeating the minister, the Queen, the King (the Police). Each one, at one moment or another, occupying the place of the King, there are at least four kings (to be continued) in this game.

The Purloined Letter indeed demonstrates, without one's having to attend to this, the crushing repetition compulsion. It is even on this point that Freud's inheritors, cook or master of truth,[28] repeat each other most faithfully. Like Lacan, Bonaparte inscribes her entire analysis under the heading of the *Wiederholungszwang*. She explains this in order to justify the monotony of a monosemic truth. Freud also excuses himself for this in his analysis of Schreber: "The sun, therefore, is nothing but another sublimated symbol for the father; and in pointing this out I must disclaim all responsibility for the monotony of the solutions provided by psycho-analysis" (XII, 54). Bonaparte: "Before going on with this macabre review of Poe's heroines, I must excuse myself for the monotony of the theme . . . For five or six consecutive tales, not much else will be found here. Doubtless the reader will be overcome by some fatigue in reading these pages. Nevertheless, I cannot spare him this lassitude (. . .) this monotony of the theme as of its expression permits one to feel the crushing *repetition compulsion* . . ." (Bonaparte, p. 283).

Here, the insistent monotony has at least led to the construction of a textual network, the demonstration of the recurrence of certain motifs (for example the chain castration-hanging-mantelpiece) outside *The Purloined Letter*. Thus the letter hanging *under* the mantel of the fireplace has its equivalent in *The Murders in the Rue Morgue*.[29] For us, the interest of this recurrence, and of pointing it out, is not that of an empirical enrichment, an experimental verification, the illustration of a repetitive insistence. It is structural. It inscribes *The Purloined Letter* in a texture that overflows it, to which it belongs, and within which the Seminar had effected a cur-

28. "We play a recording role by assuming the function, fundamental in any symbolic exchange, of gathering what *do kamo,* man in his authenticity, calls 'the lasting word' (*parole qui dure*).

"As a witness called to account for the sincerity of the subject, depositary of the minutes of his discourse, reference as to his exactitude, guarantor of his uprightness, custodian of his testament, scrivener of his codicils, the analyst has something of the scribe about him.

"But above all he remains the master of the truth of which this discourse is the progress. As I have said, it is he above all who punctuates its dialectic. And here he is apprehended as the judge of the value of this discourse." *Ecrits* (E), p. 98.

29. "Now, Rosalie is found here, her 'body quite warm,' stuffed head downward in the fireplace of the bedroom, just like the infant in the maternal genitals before birth, by the powerful arm of the anthropoid. The bedroom was the body of the mother, the fireplace, according to an equally common symbolism, is her vagina—or rather her cloaca, the cloaca alone corresponding to the infantile sexual theories which survive in the unconscious." Bonaparte, pp. 548–49. [TN. A curious mistake here. The daughter in "The Murders in the Rue Morgue" is named Camille, not Rosalie.]

sory framing or cross-section. We know that *The Purloined Letter* belongs to what Baudelaire called a "kind of trilogy," along with *The Murders in the Rue Morgue* and *The Mystery of Marie Roget.* The "Seminar" does not breathe a word about this Dupin trilogy; not only does it lift out the narrated triangles (the "real drama") in order to center the narration in them and to make them bear the burden of the interpretation (the destination of the letter), but it also lifts one-third of the Dupin cycle from an ensemble that it omits like a naturalized frame.

As for the equivalence of hanging and the phallus, Bonaparte places more than one text in the network, and suggests that here the man's point of view is not the same as the woman's, thus leading one to think that veiled/unveiled/castrated Femininity is the figure of the Truth only for the man. Who would be master of the truth only from this *point de vue*.[30]

When Bonaparte, following Freud, recalls that "the castration of the woman" is one "of the little boy's central fantasies," she is certainly articulating this proposition, via an immediate symbolic system and a very spontaneous semanticism, with Poe's biography, and in fact with a real observation of the primal scene. But it happens that her laborious psycho-biographical concern, her very applied psychoanalysis, (if one is to do it, let one apply oneself to the application), opens up textual structures that remain closed to Lacan. So, to retain just this one index, in examining Poe's unconscious (and not the author's intentions), in identifying him with a given position of his characters, Bonaparte herself is quite attentive to the position of the narrator, not only in *The Purloined Letter,* but also "before" it, from the moment when his relation to Dupin is constituted.[31] Quite attentive also, and consequently, to all the phenomena of the double: the very phenomena which orient, and then disorient and fictionalize, *Das Unheimliche* (which Bonaparte speaks of no more than Lacan, apparently). Bonaparte, interested in Poe's division into two characters who represent him equally, the narrator and Dupin, thereby finds herself moved to remark upon the

30. Cf. what is said about "fiction" in which everything is organized "from the male point of view (*point de vue*)": from which Bonaparte, however, does not simply escape, especially in these two pages. She refers with gratitude to the letter in which Freud provided her with certain clarifications "concerning 'The Black Cat,' which I discussed with him" (Bonaparte, pp. 566–68). [TN. On *point de vue* see note 16 above.]

31. Bonaparte, pp. 518ff. "The Purloined Letter" is the *third* appearance of Dupin.

in fact remarkable fact—omitted by the Seminar—that the narrator, who is himself double (narrating-narrated, which Bonaparte
does not pick up), insists a great deal on the double nature of Dupin: Dupin is double, doubles himself, and splits himself in two by
himself. If Dupin is a double by himself alone, and if he is the
double of a double (the narrator), etc., this risks creating some disturbance in the delimitation of triangles in the "drama" called
"real," as well as in the identification of positions and glances
within the "drama." All the more so in that, as we have seen, in the
"real drama" itself, Dupin successively identifies with all the characters, as do all those who find the letter in its proper place and
evident meaning. The Seminar forecloses this problematic of the
double and of *Unheimlichkeit* without mercy. And does so, doubtless, in order to deem it contained in the imaginary, in the dual relation which must be kept rigorously apart from the symbolic and the
triangular. Of course it is this division between the symbolic and
the imaginary which, in problematical fashion, appears to support,
along with the theory of the letter (place of the lack in its place and
indivisibility of the signifier), the entire discourse of the Seminar in
its recourse to the truth. All the "*unheimlich*" relations of duplicity, which unfold without limit in a dual structure, find themselves
omitted or marginalized in the Seminar. They are of interest only at
the moment when they appear neutralized, dominated, mastered in
the constitution of the triangular symbolic system, when the intersubjectivity called "veritable," which forms the object of the instruction and of the return to Freud, appears. "It is thus that in
order to demonstrate for our listeners what distinguishes the dual
relation implied in the notion of projection from a veritable intersubjectivity, we had already used the reasoning reported favorably
by Poe himself in the story which will be the subject of the present
seminar, as that which guided an alleged child prodigy in order to
have him win more often than he should have in the game of odd or
even." [32] What thus finds itself controlled is *Unheimlichkeit,* and the
anguishing disarray which can be provoked—without any hope of
reappropriation, of closure, or of truth—by references from simulacrum to simulacrum, from double to double. If one wished to
make it the example of a law at any price, the Dupin trilogy, and we
will come back to this, exemplifies this uncontrollability, disrupting
every verification of an identity. By neutralizing the double in the
trilogy, the Seminar does everything necessary in order to avoid

32. TN. *Ecrits* (F), p. 57.

what "Aggressivity in Psychoanalysis" calls "uncontrollable anxi-ety." The analysand's anxiety, of course: "But let us imagine what would take place in a patient who saw in his analyst an exact replica of himself. Everyone feels that the excess of aggressive tension would set up such an obstacle to the manifestation of the trans-ference that its useful effect could only be brought about extremely slowly, and this is what sometimes happens in the analysis of pro-spective analysts. To take an extreme case, if experienced in the form of strangeness proper to the apprehensions of the *double,* this situation would set up an uncontrollable anxiety on the part of the analysand." [33]

Perhaps now it is more understandable why, since they both op-erate on the basis of Freud and from within a certain functioning of the purloined letter, Bonaparte and Lacan both interpret it accord-ing to the same meaning: the castration of the mother as the ulti-mate meaning and proper site of the letter. But the two of them do not jump over the text in the same way. Differences of style and of proportion are not negligible here. Thus, the one always falls back, with all the well-known risks and habitual dogmatic imprudence, onto the author's unconscious. The other, with a philosophical vigi-lance incomparable in this field, onto Truth. Not only the truth of the text, but Truth. Itself, precisely. The "truth which may be drawn from that moment in Freud's thought under study" (S, p. 40), "that truth, let us note, which makes the very existence of fiction pos-sible" (ibid.), the "register of truth" which "is situated entirely elsewhere, strictly speaking at the foundation of intersubjectivity" (S, p. 49), "real intersubjectivity" (elsewhere called "authentic"), "real subject of the tale," "course which is proper to it," "Dupin's real strategy," "solution in broad daylight," etc.—the value of truth mobilizes the entire Seminar. It articulates all the Seminar's con-cepts as soon as it is found at the proper site of the signifier. At the place of the lack which finally has but one—to be distributed—and always comes back to itself in it, properly, the proper having be-come the relation of the lack to itself, in a proper place of the proper body. "Proper," "real," and "authentic" relay the value of truth according to a necessity that we will analyze.

What about the truth according to Lacan then? Is there *a* doc-trine, a Lacanian *doctrine* of the truth? We might doubt this for two reasons. The first is a general one, and has to do with the terms of the question. That a purely homogenous system is structurally impossible we have seen elsewhere. The second reason has to do with the mobility of the discourse which concerns us here. In the publications subsequent to the *Ecrits,* in their indications of a continuing oral instruction, one perceives a certain withdrawal [*retrait*] that muffles the incantations on *aletheia, logos,* speech, the word, etc. And one perceives an even more palpable erasure of the postwar existentialist connotations, if not concepts. It remains that a certain type of statement on the truth has been made, and enlarged, at a specific moment, in the form of a system. And these statements bore all the characteristics necessary for this effect. Since the Seminar belongs to this system (such, at least, is my hypothesis), as do a certain number of other essays to which I will refer (in order not, in turn, to enclose the *Ecrits* in the Seminar), it must be demarcated if one wishes to understand the reading of *The Purloined Letter.* One can and must do this, even if after 1966, in a transformed theoretical field, the Lacanian discourse on the truth, the text, and literature lent itself to a certain number of major rearrangements or decisive reworkings, although this is not certain.[34] The chronological and theoretical outline of this system would always be subject to caution, moreover, given the distant aftereffects of publication.

Whatever may have happened after 1965–66, all the texts situated, or more precisely published, between 1953 (the Discourse said to be of Rome) and 1960 appear to belong to the same system of the truth. Or, quantitatively, almost the entirety of the *Ecrits,* including, therefore, the Seminar (1955–57): works of the young Lacan, as will perhaps be said one day, and once more, by the academics who are always in a hurry to cut to the quick that which does not bear partition.

We are not going to give an exposition of this system of the truth, which is the condition for a logic of the signifier. Moreover, it consists of what is *non-exposable* in the exposition. We will only attempt to recognize those characteristics of it which are pertinent to the Seminar, to its possibility and its limits.

First of all, what is at issue is an *emphasis* [*emphase*], as could

---

34. The doctrine of the truth as cause (*Ursache*), as well as the expression "effects of truth," can be aligned with the system we are about to examine. The effects of truth are the effects of the truth, as "The Direction of the Treatment" (in which it is a question of "directing the subject towards 'full' speech," or in any event of leaving him "free to try it," *Ecrits* (E), p. 275), had already said: "it is a question of truth, of the only truth, of the truth about the effects of truth" (ibid.). Circulation will always be circulation of the truth: toward the truth. Cause and effect of the circle, *causa sui,* proper course and destiny of the letter.

equally be said in English, on the authentic excellence of the spoken, of speech, and of the word: of *logos* as *phonē*. This emphasis must be explained, and its necessary link to the theory of the signifier, the letter, and the truth must be accounted for. It must be explained why the author of *The Agency of the Letter in the Unconscious* and of the Seminar on *The Purloined Letter* ceaselessly subordinates the letter, writing, and the text. For even when he repeats Freud on rebuses, hieroglyphics, engravings, etc., in the last analysis his re-course is always to a writing spiritualized (*relevé*) by the voice. This would be easy to show. One example, among many others: "A writing, like the dream itself, may be figurative, it is like language always articulated symbolically, that is, it is like language *pho-nematic,* and in fact phonetic, as soon as it may be read." [35] This *fact* has the stature of a *fact* only within the limits of the so-called phonetic systems of writing. At the very most, for there are non-phonetic elements in such systems. As for the non-phonetic field of writing, its factual enormity no longer has to be demonstrated. But small matter. What does count here, and even more than the rela-tion of the *de facto* to the *de jure,* is the implied equivalence ("that is") between symbolic articulation and phonematicity. The sym-bolic occurs through the voice, and the law of the signifier takes place only within vocalizable letters. Why? And what relation does this phonematism (which cannot be attributed to Freud, and thus is lost in the unfolding of the return to Freud) maintain with a certain value of truth?

Both imports of the value of truth are represented in the Semi-nar, as we have seen. 1. *Adequation,* in the circular return and proper course, from the origin to the end, from the signifier's place of detachment to its place of reattachment. This circuit of adequa-tion guards and regards [*garde et regarde*] the circuit of the pact, of the contract, of sworn faith. It restores the pact in the face of what threatens it, as the symbolic order. And it is constituted at the mo-ment when the *guardianship* [*la garde*] of the phallus is confided as guardianship *of the* lack. Confided by the King to the Queen, but thereby in an endless play of alternations. 2. *Veiling-unveiling* as the structure of the lack: castration, the *proper* site of the signifier, origin and destination of its letter, shows nothing in unveiling itself. Therefore, it veils itself in its unveiling. But this operation of the truth has a proper place: its contours *being* [*étant*] the place of the lack of Being [*manque à être*] on the basis of which the signifier

35. "*Situation de la psychanalyse en 1956.*" *Ecrits* (F), p. 470.

detaches itself for its literal circuit. These two values of truth lean on and support each other (*s'étaient*). They are indissociable. They need speech or the phonetization of the letter as soon as the phallus has to be *kept* [*gardé*], has to return to its point of departure, has not to be disseminated en route. Now, for the signifier to be kept [*pour que le signifiant se garde*] in its letter and thus to make its return, it is necessary that in its letter it does not admit "partition," that one cannot say *some* letter [*de la lettre*], but only a letter, letters, the letter (S, pp. 53–54). If it were divisible, it could always be lost en route. To protect against this possible loss the statement about the "materiality of the signifier," that is, about the signifier's indivisible singularity, is constructed. *This "materiality," deduced from an indivisibility found nowhere, in fact corresponds to an idealization.* Only the ideality of a letter resists destructive division. "Cut a letter in small pieces, and it remains the letter it is" (S, p. 53): since this cannot be said of empirical materiality, it must imply an ideality (the intangibility of a self-identity displacing itself without alteration). This alone permits the singularity of the letter to be maintained [*se garder*]. If this ideality is not the content of meaning, it must be either a certain ideality of the signifier (what is identifiable in its form to the extent that it can be distinguished from its empirical events and re-editions), or the "*point de capiton*"[36] which staples the signifier to the signified. The latter hypothesis conforms more closely to the system. This system is in fact the system of the ideality of the signifier. The idealism lodged within it is not a theoretical position of the analyst; it is a structural effect of *signification* in general, to whatever transformations or adjustments one subjects the space of *semiosis*. One can understand that Lacan finds this "materiality" "odd" [*"singulière"*]: he retains only its ideality. He considers the letter only at the point at which it is determined (no matter what he says) by its content of meaning, by the ideality of the message that it "vehiculates," by the speech whose meaning remains out of the reach of partition, so that it can circulate, intact, from its place of detachment to its place of reattachment, that is, to the same place. In fact, this letter does not only escape partition, it escapes movement, it does not change its place.

Aside from a phonematic limitation of the letter, this supposes an interpretation of *phonē* which also spares it divisibility. The

36. TN. *Capitonner* means to quilt; *point de capiton* is Lacan's term for the "quilted stitch" that links signifier to signified.

voice occasions such an interpretation in and of itself: it has the phenomenal characteristics of spontaneity, of self-presence, of the circular return to itself. And the voice retains [*garde*] all the more in that one believes one can retain [*garder*] it without external accessory, without paper and without envelope: it finds itself [*se trouve*], it tells us, always available wherever it is found [*se trouve*]. This is why it is believed that the voice remains more than do writings: "May it but please heaven that writings remain, as is rather the case with spoken words" (S, p. 56). Things would be quite otherwise if one were attentive to the writing within the voice, that is, before the letter. For the same problem is reproduced concerning the voice, concerning what one might still call its "letter," if one wished to conserve the Lacanian definition of this concept (indivisible locality or materiality of the signifier). This vocal "letter" therefore also would be indivisible, always identical to itself, whatever the fragmentations of its body. It can be assured of this integrity only by virtue of its link to the ideality of a meaning, in the unity of a speech. We are always led back, from stage to stage, to the contract of contracts which guarantees the unity of the signifier with the signified through all the "*points de capiton,*" thanks to the "presence" (see below) of the *same* signifier (the phallus), of the "signifier of signifiers" beneath all the effects of the signified. This transcendental signifier is therefore also the signified of all signifieds, and this is what finds itself sheltered within the indivisibility of the (graphic or oral) letter. Sheltered from this threat, but also from the disseminating power that in *Of Grammatology* I proposed to call *Writing Before the Letter* (title of the first part): the privilege of "full speech" is examined there. The agency of the Lacanian letter is the *relève* of writing in the system of speech.

"The drama" of the purloined letter begins at the moment—which is not a moment—when the letter *is retained* [*se garde*]. With the movement of the minister who acts in order to conserve it (for he could have torn it up, and this is indeed an ideality which then would have remained available and effective for a time),[37] certainly, but well before this, when the Queen wishes to retain it or refind it [*la garder ou la retrouver*]: as a double of the pact which binds her to the King, a threatening double, but one which in her

37. For a time only: until the moment when, unable to return a "material," divisible letter, a letter subject to partition, an effectively "odd" letter, he would have to release the hold over the Queen that only a destructible document could have assured him.

guardianship [*sous sa garde*] cannot betray the "sworn faith." The Queen wishes to be able to play on two contracts. We cannot develop this analysis here; it is to be read elsewhere.

What counts here is that the indestructibility of the letter has to do with its elevation toward the ideality of a meaning. However little we know of its content, the content must be in relation to the original contract that it simultaneously signifies and subverts. And it is this knowledge, this memory, this (conscious or unconscious) retention which form its properness [*propriété*], and ensure its proper course toward the proper place. Since its ultimate content is that of a pact binding two "singularities," it implies an irreplaceability, and excludes, as uncontrollable threat and anxiety, all double simulacra. It is the effect of living and present speech which in the last analysis guarantees the indestructible and unforgettable singularity of the letter, the taking-place of a signifier which never is lost, goes astray, or is divided. The subject is very divided, but the phallus is not to be cut. Fragmentation is an accident which does not concern it. At least according to the certainty constructed by the symbolic. And by a discourse on the assumption of castration which edifies an ideal philosophy against fragmentation.[38]

In principle this is how the logic of the signifier is articulated with a phonocentric interpretation of the letter. The two values of the truth (adequation and movement of the veil) henceforth cannot be dissociated from the word, from present, living, authentic speech. The final word is that, when all is said and done, there is, at the origin or the end (proper course, circular destination), a word which is not feigned, a meaning which, through all imaginable fictional complications, does not trick, or which at that point tricks *truly,* again teaching us the truth of the lure. At this point, the truth

38. What we are analyzing here is the most rigorous philosophy of psychoanalysis today, more precisely the most rigorous Freudian philosophy, doubtless more rigorous than Freud's philosophy, and more scrupulous in its exchanges with the history of philosophy.

It would be impossible to exaggerate the import of the proposition about the indivisibility of the letter, or rather about the letter's self-identity that is inaccessible to fragmentation ("Cut a letter in small pieces, it remains the letter it is"), or of the proposition about the so-called "materiality of the signifier" (the letter) which does not bear partition. Where does this come from? A fragmented letter can purely and simply be destroyed, this happens (and if one considers that the unconscious effect here named letter is never lost, that repression maintains everything and never permits any degradation of insistence, this hypothesis—nothing is ever lost or goes astray—must still be aligned with *Beyond the Pleasure Principle,* or other letters must be produced, whether characters or messages).

permits the analyst to treat fictional characters as real, and to resolve, at the depth of the Heideggerian meditation on truth, the
problem of the literary text which sometimes led Freud (more naively, but more surely than Heidegger and Lacan) to confess his
confusion. And we are still only dealing with a literature with characters! Let us cite the Seminar first. The suspicion that perhaps the
author's purpose was not, as Baudelaire said, to state the true has just
been awakened. Which, however, does not always amount to having
a good time. Thus: "No doubt Poe is having a good time . . .

"But a suspicion occurs to us: might not this parade of erudition
be destined to reveal to us the key words of our drama? Is not the
magician repeating his trick before our eyes, without deceiving us
this time about divulging his secret, but pressing his wager to the
point of really explaining it to us without our seeing a thing? *That*
would be the summit of the illusionist's art: through one of his fictive creations *truly to delude* us. And is it not such effects which
justify our referring, without malice, to a number of imaginary he-
roes as real characters?

"As well, when we are open to hearing the way in which Martin
Heidegger discloses to us in the word *aletheia* the play of truth, we
rediscover a secret to which truth has always initiated her lovers,
and through which they learn that it is in hiding that she offers herself to them *most truly*" (S, pp. 50–51).

Abyss effects are severely controlled here, a scientifically irreproachable precaution: this is science itself, or at least ideal science, and even the truth of the science of truth. From the statements
I have just cited it does not follow that truth is a fiction, but that
through fiction truth properly declares itself. Fiction manifests the
truth: the manifestation that illustrates itself through evasion. *Dichtung* (poetic saying or fiction, this is both Goethe's and Freud's expression: just as for Heidegger, the issue is one of literary fiction as
Dichtung) is the manifestation of the truth, its being-declared:
"There is so little opposition between this *Dichtung* and *Wahrheit*
in its nudity that the fact of the poetic operation rather should give
us pause before the characteristic which is forgotten in all truth,
that it declares itself in a structure of fiction." [39] Truth governs the
fictional element of its manifestation, which permits it to be or to
become what it is, to declare itself. Truth governs this element from
its origin or its telos, which finally coordinates this concept of literary fiction with a highly classical interpretation of *mimesis:* a de-

39. *Ecrits* (F), p. 742.

tour toward the truth, more truth in the fictive representation than in reality, increased fidelity, "superior realism." The preceding citation called for a note: "The suitability of this reminder for our subject would be sufficiently confirmed, if need be, by one of the numerous unpublished texts that Delay's opus provides us, enlightening them in the most appropriate way. Here from the *Unpublished Journal,* said to be from la Brevine where Gide dwelled in October 1894 (note on page 667 of his volume 2).

"'The novel will prove that it can paint something other than reality—emotion and thought directly; it will show to what extent it can be deduced, *before the experience of things*—to what extent, that is, it can be composed—that it is a work of art. It will show that it can be a work of art, composed entirely out of its own elements, not out of a realism of petty and contingent facts, but a superior realism.'" There follows a reference to the mathematical triangle, and then: "'It is necessary that in their relation itself each part of a work prove the truth of each other part, there is no need for any other proof. Nothing is more irritating than the testimony that M. de Goncourt gives for everything he asserts—he has seen! he has heard! as if proof via the real were necessary.'" Lacan concludes: "It has to be said that no poet has ever thought otherwise . . . , but that no one follows through on this thought." And in the same article it is confirmed that it is a "person" who "bears" the "truth of fiction." This person is the "seductress" of the "young boy." [40]

Once one has distinguished, as does the entire philosophical tradition, between truth and reality, it immediately follows that the truth "declares itself in a structure of fiction." [41] Lacan insists a great deal on the opposition truth/reality, which he advances as a paradox. This opposition, which is as orthodox as can be, facilitates the passage of the truth through fiction: common sense always will have made the division between reality and fiction.

But once again, why would speech be the privileged element of this truth declared *as* fiction, in the mode or structure of fiction, of verified fiction, of what Gide calls "superior realism"?

As soon as the truth is determined as adequation (with an original contract: the acquitting of a debt) and as unveiling (of the lack

40. *Ecrits* (F), p. 753.

41. For example: "Thus it is from elsewhere than the Reality with which it is concerned that the Truth takes its guarantee: it is from Speech (*la Parole*). Just as it is from Speech that it receives the mark which institutes it in a structure of fiction.

"The primal word (*le dit premier*) decrees, legislates, aphorizes, is oracle, it confers upon the real other its obscure authority." *Ecrits* (F), p. 808.

on the basis of which the contract is contracted in order to reappropriate symbolically what has been detached), the guiding value is indeed that of propriation, and therefore of proximity, of presence, and of maintaining [garde]: the very value procured by the idealizing effect of speech. If one grants this demonstration, it will not be surprising to find it confirmed. If one does not, then how is one to explain the massive co-implication, in Lacanian discourse, of truth and speech, "present," "full," and "authentic" speech? And if it is taken into account, one better understands: 1. That fiction for Lacan is permeated by truth as something spoken, and therefore as something non-real. 2. That this leads to no longer reckoning, in the text, with everything that remains irreducible to speech, to the spoken word [le dit], and meaning [vouloir-dire]: that is, irreducible dis-regard, theft without return, destructibility, divisibility, the failure to reach a destination (le manque à destination) (which definitively rebels against the destination of the lack [la destination du manque]: an unverifiable non-truth).

When Lacan recalls "the passion for unveiling which has one object: the truth"[42] and recalls that the analyst "above all remains the master of the truth," it is always in order to link the truth to the power of speech. And to the power of communication as a contract (sworn faith) between two present things. Even if communication communicates nothing, it communicates to itself: and in this case better yet as communication, that is, truth. For example: "Even if it communicates nothing, the discourse represents the existence of communication; even if it denies the evidence, it affirms that speech constitutes truth; even if it is intended to deceive, the discourse speculates on faith in testimony."[43]

What is neither true nor false is reality. But as soon as speech is

<hr />

42. "You have heard me, in order to situate its place in the investigation, refer with brotherly love to Descartes and to Hegel. These days, it is rather fashionable to 'surpass' the classical philosophers. I equally could have taken the admirable dialogue with Parmenides as my point of departure. For neither Socrates, nor Descartes, nor Marx, nor Freud can be 'surpassed' to the extent that they have conducted their investigations with that passion for unveiling which has a single object: the truth.

"As one of those, princes of the verb, and through whose fingers the strings of the mask of the Ego seem to slip by themselves, has written—I have named Max Jacob, poet, saint, and novelist—yes, as he has written in his Dice Cup, if I am not mistaken: the true is always new." Ecrits (F), p. 193. This is true, always. How not to subscribe to it?

43. TN. "Empty and full speech in the psychoanalytic realization of the subject" in the Rome Report (Function and Field of Speech . . .), Ecrits (E), p. 43.

inaugurated, one is in the register of the unveiling of the truth as of
its contract of properness [*propriété*]: presence, speech, testimony:
"The ambiguity of the hysterical revelation of the past is due not so
much to the vacillation of its content between the imaginary and the
real, for it is situated in both. Nor is it because it is made up of lies.
The reason is that it presents us with the birth of truth in speech,
and thereby brings us up against the reality of what is neither true
nor false. At any rate, that is the most disquieting aspect of the
problem.

"For it is present speech that bears witness to the truth of this
revelation in present reality, and which grounds it in the name of
that reality. Yet in that reality, only speech bears witness to that portion of the powers of the past that has been thrust aside at each
crossroads where the event has made its choice." [44] Just before this
passage there is a reference to Heidegger, which is not surprising;
the reference resituates *Dasein* in the subject, which is more so.

As soon as "present speech" "bears witness" to the "truth of
this revelation" beyond the true or the false, beyond what is truthful
or lying in a given statement or symptom in their relation to a given
content, the values of adequation or unveiling no longer even have
to await their verification or achievement from the exterior of some
object. They guarantee each other intrinsically. What counts is not
whatever (true or false) is communicated, but "the existence of
communication," the present revelation made within communication of the speech that bears witness to the truth. Whence the necessary relaying by the values of authenticity, plenitude, properness,
etc. The truth, which is what must be refound [*retrouvé*], therefore
is not an object beyond the subject, is not the adequation of speech
to an object, [45] but the adequation of full speech to itself, its proper

44. TN. *Ecrits* (E), p. 47.
45. "True speech" is the speech authenticated by the other in faith sworn or
given. The other makes speech adequate to itself—and no longer to the object—by
sending back the message in inverted form, by making it true, by henceforth identifying the subject with itself, by "stating that it is the same." Adequation—as authen-
tification—must pass through intersubjectivity. Speech "is therefore an act, and as
such supposes a subject. But it is not enough to say that in this act the subject supposes another subject, for it is much rather that the subject is founded in this act as
being the other, but in that paradoxical unity of the one and the other, by whose
means, as has been shown above, the one depends upon the other in order to become
identical to itself.

"Thus one can say that speech manifests itself not only as a communication in
which the subject, in order to await that the other make his message true, is going to
project the message in inverted form, but also as a communication in which this

authenticity, the conformity of its act to its original essence. And
the telos of this *Eigentlichkeit,* the proper aiming at this authenticity shows the "authentic way" of analysis, of the training analysis in particular. "But what in fact was this appeal from the subject
beyond the void of his speech? It was an appeal to the very principle of truth, through which other appeals resulting from humbler

---

message transforms the subject by stating that it is the same. As is apparent in every
given pledge, in which declarations like 'you are my wife,' or 'you are my master,'
signify 'I am your husband,' 'I am your disciple.'

"Speech therefore appears all the more truly speech in that its truth is less
founded in what is called adequation to the thing: true speech, thereby, is opposed
paradoxically to true discourse, their truth being distinguished by the fact that the
former constitutes the subjects' acknowledgment of their Beings in that they have an
inter-est in them, while the latter is constituted by the knowledge of the real, to the
extent that the subject aims for it in objects. But each of the truths distinguished here
is changed by intersecting with the other in its path." *Ecrits* (F), p. 351 (*Variantes
de la cure-type*). In this intersecting, "true speech" always appears as more true than
"true discourse," which always presupposes the order of true speech, the order of
the intersubjective contract, of symbolic exchange, and therefore of the debt. "But
true speech, in questioning true discourse about what it signifies, will find that signification always refers to signification, there being no thing that can be shown
otherwise than with a sign, and henceforth will show true discourse to be doomed to
error." *Ecrits* (F), p. 352. The ultimate adequation of the truth as true speech therefore has the form of making quits (*l'acquittement*), the "strange adequation . . .
which finds its response in the symbolic debt for which the subject as subject of
speech is responsible." *Ecrits* (E), p. 144. These are the final words of "The Freudian Thing." Adequation to the thing (true discourse) therefore has its foundation in
the adequation of speech to itself (true speech), that is to the thing itself: in other
words of *the Freudian thing to itself:* "The thing speaks of itself" (*Ecrits* (E),
p. 121), and it says: "I, the truth, speak." The thing is the truth: as cause, both of
itself and of the things of which true discourse speaks. These propositions are less
new, particularly in relation to the Rome Report, to *Variantes de la cure-type,* and to
the texts of the same period, than their author says: "This is to introduce the effects
of truth as cause at a quite different point, and to impose a revision of the process of
causality—the first stage of which would seem to be to recognize the inherent nature
of the heterogeneity of these effects.[5]" *Ecrits* (E), p. 127. (The footnote: "5. This
rewritten paragraph antedates a line of thought that I have since explored further
(1966)." *Ecrits* (E), p. 145.)

"True speech" (adequate to itself, conforming to its essence, destined to be quits
of a debt which in the last analysis binds it only to itself) therefore permits the contract which permits the subject "to become identical to itself." Therefore it reconstitutes the ground of Cartesian certainty: the transformation of the truth into certainty, subjectification (the determination of the Being of beings as subject), and
intersubjectification (the chain Descartes-Hegel-Husserl). This chain ceaselessly
captures, in the *Ecrits,* Heideggerian motions which would appear, rigorously
speaking, to be allergic to it, and would appear to have "destructive" effects on it.
For the moment, let us abandon these kinds of questions—the most decisive ones—
that Lacan's discourse never articulates.

needs will vacillate. But first and foremost it was the proper appeal of the void [*appel propre du vide*] . . ." [46]

From the proper appeal of the void to the achieving of full speech, the "realization" of full speech through the assumption of desire (of castration)—such, then, is the ideal process of analysis: "I have tackled the function of speech in analysis from its least rewarding angle, that of empty speech, where the subject seems to be talking in vain about someone who, even if he were his spitting image, can never become one with the assumption of his desire . . . If we now turn to the other extreme of the psychoanalytic experience—its history, its argumentation, the process of the treatment—we shall find that to the analysis of the here and now is to be opposed the value of anamnesis as the index and source of therapeutic progress; that to obsessional intrasubjectivity is to be opposed hysterical intersubjectivity; and that to the analysis of resistance is to be opposed symbolic interpretation. The realization of full speech beings here." [47]

Speech, here, is not full of something beyond itself which would be its object: but this is why all the more and all the better, it is full of itself, of its presence, its essence. This presence, as in the contract and the sworn faith, requires irreplaceable properness [*propriété*], inalienable singularity, living authenticity—so many values whose system we have recognized elsewhere. The double, repetition, recording, and the mimeme in general are excluded from this system, along with the entire graphematic structure they imply; and they are excluded both in the name of direct interlocution and as inauthentic alienation. For example: "But precisely because it comes to him through an alienated form, even a retransmission of his own recorded discourse, be it from the mouth of his own doctor, cannot have the same effects as psychoanalytic interlocution." [48]

The disqualification of recording or repetition in the name of the act of living and present speech conforms to a well-known program. And is indispensable to the system. The system of "true speech," of "speech in act," cannot do without the condemnation, which stretches from Plato to a certain Freud, of the simulacrum of hypomnesis, hypomnesis condemned in the name of the truth, in the name of that which links *mnēmē, anamnesis, aletheia,* etc.

Materiality, the sensory and repetitive side of the recording,

46. TN. *Ecrits* (E), p. 40.
47. TN. *Ecrits* (E), pp. 45–46.
48. TN. *Ecrits* (E), p. 49.

the paper letter, drawings in ink, can be divided or multiplied, destroyed or set adrift (since authentic originality is always already lost in them). The letter itself, in the Lacanian sense, as the site of the signifier and symbol of a sworn faith, and therefore of a true full and present speech, has as its property, its "singular," "odd" property in effect, "not to admit partition."

"Present speech," then, as "full speech": "I might as well be categorical: in psychoanalytic anamnesis, it is not a question of reality, but of truth, because the effect of full speech is to reorder past contingencies by conferring on them the sense of necessities to come, such as they are constituted by the little freedom through which the subject makes them present." [49]

Henceforth, a text, if it is living and animated, full and authentic, will be of value only by virtue of the speech it will have as its mission to transport. Therefore, there also will be full texts and empty texts. The former only "vehiculate" a full speech, that is, an authentically present truth which simultaneously unveils and is adequate to or identical with that which it speaks about. Which is itself, therefore ("the thing speaks of itself"), at the moment when it makes its return to the encircled hole and to the contract which constitute it. For example, as concerns Freud's text, which must be returned to, and be returned to itself as well (see above): "Not one of those two-dimensional, infinitely flat (as the mathematicians say) texts, which are only of fiduciary value in a constituted discourse, but a text that is the vehicle of a speech, in that speech constitutes a new emergence of the truth." Such a text, as present, inaugural, and constitutive speech, itself answers for itself if we question it, as is said in the *Phaedrus* of the logos which is its own father. It simultaneously gives the questions and the answers. Our activity of mobilizing "all the resources of our exegesis" is only in order "to make it [Freud's text] answer the questions that it puts to us, to treat it as a real speech, we should say, if we knew our own terms, in its transference value." Our "own terms": let us take this as the terms of the discourse which questions and answers, Freud's discourse. "Of course, this supposes that we interpret it. In effect, is there a better critical method than the one which applies to the comprehension of a message the very principles of comprehension of which it is the vehicle? This is the most rational mode in which to experience its authenticity.

49. TN. *Ecrits* (E), p. 48.

"Full speech, in effect, is defined by its identity with that which it speaks about."[50]

The exegete's full speech fills itself when it assumes and takes upon itself the "principles of comprehension" of the other's—here Freud's—message, to the extent that this message itself "vehiculates" a "full speech." The latter, since it is inaugural and "constitutes a new emergence of the truth," contracts only with itself: it speaks of itself by itself. This is what we are calling the *system* of speech, or the *system* of truth.

One cannot define the "hermeneutical circle," along with all the conceptual parts of its system, more rigorously or more faithfully. It includes all the circles that we are pointing out here, in their Platonic, Hegelian, and Heideggerian tradition, and in the most philosophical sense of responsibility:[51] to acquit oneself adequately of that which one owes (duty and debt).

Authenticity—the pole of adequation and of circular reappropriation for the ideal process of analysis. Certainly it is not a question of the crude readjustment which would come back to us from America. One must above all keep oneself [*se garder*] from such a mistake. No one here, of course, makes this mistake, we must insist. And this authenticity, which is a very rare thing, reserved for exceptional moments, does not qualify the speech of an "ego," but the speech of the other, and a certain relation to the speech of the other. In order to gain access to it, the psychoanalyst must pass through the screen of narcissism, returning it to a state of pure transparency: at this point, with "the authentic speech of the other," he

50. TN. *Ecrits* (F), p. 381.

51. This responsibility is defined immediately after, and on the basis of, the exchange of "full speech" with Freud, in its "true formative value": "For in question is nothing less than its adequation at the level of man at which he takes hold of it, no matter what he thinks—at which he is called upon to answer it, no matter what he wants—and for which he assumes responsibility, no matter what his opinion." *Ecrits* (F), p. 382. As concerns the "level of man," we do not have enough space to verify the essential link between metaphysics (several typical characteristics of which we are pointing out here) and humanism in this system. This link is more visible, if not looked upon more highly, in the conglomeration of statements about "animality," about the distinction between animal and human language, etc. This discourse on the animal (in general) is no doubt consistent with all the categories and oppositions, all the bi- or tri-partitions of the system. And it condenses no less the system's greatest obscurity. The treatment of animality, as of everything that finds itself in *submission* by virtue of a hierarchical opposition, has always, in the history of (humanist and phallogocentric) metaphysics, revealed obscurantist resistance. It is obviously of capital interest.

has the chance to grasp again the origin of speech and truth in the "sworn faith." He can engage his "revealing interpretation" in the circular and reappropriating chain of the "true speeches," even if these are not true words. But these moments of authenticity, like those of Heideggerian *Eigentlichkeit,* are rare in existence. For example, concerning the "subject's bad faith," through which is to be refound "the speech in which truth has its foundation," the truth to which bad faith still bears witness:

> If, then, the ideal condition for the analyst occurs, that the mirages of narcissism have become transparent for him, it is so that he may be permeable to the authentic speech of the other, and the question now is to understand how he can recognize it through its discourse.
>
> Certainly this intermediary discourse [that of "the subject's bad faith"], even as the discourse of deception and error, does not fail to bear witness to the existence of the speech in which truth has its foundation, in that it maintains itself only by proposing itself as such, and that, even in yielding itself openly as the discourse of the lie, it only more forcefully affirms the existence of this speech. And if one again finds, via this phenomenological approach to the truth, the key whose loss leads positivist logicism to search for the "meaning of meaning," does not this approach also recognize in it the concept of the concept, in that it reveals itself in speech in action?

This speech, which constitutes the subject in his truth, is, however, forever forbidden to him, outside the rare moments of his existence when he attempts, however confusedly, to grasp it in sworn faith, and forbidden in that the intermediary discourse condemns him to misconstrue it. Nevertheless, it speaks everywhere that it can be read in his Being, that is at all the levels at which it has formed him. This antinomy is the very antinomy of the meaning that Freud gave to the notion of the unconscious.

But if this speech is nonetheless accessible, it is because no true speech is only the subject's speech, since it is always toward grounding it in the mediation of another subject that it operates, and that thereby it is open to the chain without end—certainly not indefinite, since it closes itself again—of the speeches in which the dialectic of recognition is concretely realized in the human community.

It is in the extent to which the analyst can stifle within himself the intermediary discourse [bad faith] in order to open himself to the chain of true speeches, that he can place his revealing interpretation.

Since he sees himself each time that one considers in its concrete
form an authentic interpretation . . .[52]

In sum: there is an authentic and revealing interpretation, and it
supposes that one stifle bad faith in order to gain access to "speech
in act" and to the (good) sworn faith[53] without intermediary discourse, in the transparency of intersubjective dialectics. Only the
unconscious in Freud's sense, therefore, can open our ears to this
speech which speaks if one knows how to read it.[54]

52. TN. *Ecrits* (F), pp. 352–53 (*Variantes de la cure-type*).

53. On the "relation to the Other who is the guarantor of Good Faith," on the
"manifested presence of intersubjectivity," and on "the paths along which analysis
proceeds not only in order to restore an order, but in order to set in place the conditions for the possibility of restoring it," see *The Agency of the Letter in the Unconscious* (*Ecrits* (E), pp. 172–73), in which it had just been recalled: "The end that
Freud's discovery proposes for man was defined by him at the apex of his thought in
these moving terms: *Wo es war, soll Ich werden*. I must come to the place where that
was (*Là ou fut ça, il me faut advenir*).

"This end is one of reintegration and harmony, I could even say of reconciliation
(*Versohnung*)" (p. 171).

54. The values of presence (in person), of proximity, plenitude, and consistency
form the system of authenticity in the analytic dialogue, in opposition to the "discourse of the *one*." For example: "What does Freud tell us here in effect? He un-
covers for us a phenomenon that structures every revelation of the truth in dialogue.
There is the fundamental difficulty that the subject encounters in what he has to say;
the most common one being what Freud demonstrated in repression, to wit, the kind
of discordance between the signified and the signifier, determined by every censorship of social origin."

This discordance due to repression perhaps will necessitate a correction of Saussurian semiology, but somewhere this is not irreducible, therefore essential. For the
time of a detour or of a turning away: a provision. The development that immediately follows: "In this case the truth can always be communicated between the
lines. Which is to say that whoever wishes to make it understood can always recur to
the technique indicated by the identity of the truth with the symbols that reveal it,
that is, to achieve one's ends by deliberately introducing into a text the discordances
that correspond cryptographically to those imposed by censorship.

"The true subject, that is, the subject of the unconscious, does not proceed
otherwise than through the language of its symptoms, which is not sufficiently deciphered by the analyst if he does not come to address himself to it in more and more
consistent fashion, for the always renewed satisfaction of our experience. In effect,
this is what has been recognized in the phenomenon of the transference."

"What the subject who speaks says, however empty his discourse, takes its effect
from the approximation that is realized in his discourse from the speech into which
he could fully convert the truth that his symptoms express . . . we have used the
image that the speech of the subject fluctuates toward the presence of the auditor.

(Footnote: "Here will be recognized the formula which we have used to introduce what is in question since the beginnings of our instruction. The subject, as we
said, begins analysis by speaking of himself without really speaking to you, or by

Only a speech, with its effects of presence in act and of authentic life can maintain [*garder*] the "sworn faith" which links it to the desire of the other. If the "phallus is the privileged signifier of that mark in which the role of the logos is joined with the advent of desire," [55] the privileged site of this privileged signifier, then its letter is the voice: the letter as spokesman, the letter-carrying-speech. The letter alone—as soon as the *point de capiton* of the signified ensures its repeatable identity—carries the necessary ideality or power of idealization that can safeguard (in any event this is what it means) the indivisible, singular, living, non-fragmentable integrity of the phallus, of the privileged signifier to which it gives rise. The *transcendental* position of the phallus (in the chain of signifiers to which it belongs, while simultaneously making it possible) [56] thus

---

speaking to you without speaking to you about himself. When he is able to speak to you about himself, the analysis is over.")

"This presence, which is the purest relation of which the subject is capable in regard to a Being, and which is all the more vividly felt as such in that this Being is less qualified for the subject, this presence which is for an instant rendered to the extremity of the veils which cover and elide it in common discourse to that extent that it is constituted as the discourse of the *one* precisely to this end, this presence is marked in discourse by a suspensive scansion often connoted by a moment of anxiety, as I have shown you in an example from my own experience." *Ecrits* (F), pp. 372–73 (*Introduction au commentaire de Jean Hyppolite sur la "Verneinung" de Freud*).

Of course, this is what "Freud tells us": "The purest relation," "presence," is in relation to a "Being," and it is felt all the more "vividly" in that this "Being" (this subject-being) is "less qualified," that is, obviously, more indeterminate. The presence of Being is all the more pure in that the ontic determination is less. This takes place only for a privileged "instant," beyond the "one," and in a state of "anxiety." The indeterminateness of Being (here of the subject-being-psychoanalyst), unveils nothingness, (non-being in totality), as the truth of presence. What "Freud tells us" very literally would be *What Is Metaphysics?*

55. TN. *Ecrits* (E), p. 287 ("The Signification of the Phallus").

56. This is the strict definition of the *transcendental position:* the privilege of one term within a series of terms that it makes possible and which presupposes it. Thus a category is called transcendental (transcategorial) when it "transcends every genus" (*transcendit omne genus*), i.e. the list of categories of which it is nevertheless a part while accounting for it. This is the role of the phallus in the logic of the signifier. Therefore this is also the role of the hole and the lack in their determinable contours: ". . . for the phallus of his mother, that is to say, for that eminent *manque-à-être,* for that want-to-be, whose privileged signifier Freud revealed to us . . ." *Ecrits* (E), p. 170 ("The Agency of the Letter in the Unconscious"). The transcendental eminence of this privilege is therefore placed in perspective, at its height, from the point of view of the horrified perception of the child—or more precisely of the little boy and his sexual theory.

This omnipresence of a condition of possibility, this permanent implication, in every signifier, of the "signifier of signifiers" ("The Direction of the Treatment,"

would have its proper place—in Lacanian terms, its letter exempt from all partition—in the phonematic structure of language. No protest against metalanguage is opposed to this phallogocentric transcendentalism. Especially if within *metalanguage*, language is centered on the voice, that is, on the ideal site of the phallus. If by some misfortune the phallus were divisible or reduced to the status of a part object,[57] the entire edifice would collapse, and this must be

---

Ecrits (E), p. 265), of the "unparalleled signifier" (ibid., p. 277), can have as its element of presence only a milieu of ideality: hence the eminence of the transcendental eminence whose *effect* is to maintain presence, to wit *phonē*. This is what made necessary and possible, in exchange for certain corrections, the integration of Freudian phallocentrism with a fundamentally phonocentric Saussurian semio-linguistics. The "algorithmic" transformation does not appear to me to undo this tie. Here is the best definition of the transcendental phallus, in relation to which all the protestations of anti-transcendentalism (see *Ecrits* (F), p. 365) have the value of a denegation: "For the phallus is a signifier, a signifier whose function, in the intra-subjective economy of the analysis, lifts the veil, perhaps, from the function it per-formed in the mysteries. For it is the signifier intended to designate as a whole the effects of the signified, in that the signifier conditions them by its presence as a sig-nifier." *Ecrits* (E), p. 285 ("The Signification of the Phallus").

57. We have seen that the signifier (and first of all the "privileged," "unparal-leled" signifier, the phallus) is not, in its place, in its letter, "to admit partition." And no more is it (a separate, but convergent demand) to be treated as part object, subject like any other to the chain of substitutes. This is the axial demand, the most insistent plea, if not the most apparent criterion in Lacan's sexual theory. It is very significant that this is what motivates the objection to Jones in the "quarrel" over phallocentrism and female sexuality. One of the "deviations" from psychoanalysis has consisted of "reducing" the phallus "to the role of part object." This "profound mystification" (*Ecrits* (E), p. 198) sent Jones over to the side of the "feminists" only to the extent that he could not separate himself from another suspect legatee, Klein this time, and her "hesitant" work (*Ecrits* (E), p. 197), her "lack of precision" (*Ecrits* (F), p. 728). All of this ("but . . . but . . .") in order to exclude the "ana-lytically unthinkable," the analytically thinkable being limited to Freud's good faith which could not be mistaken, given that "he was better *guided* than anyone in his recognition of the order of unconscious phenomena, of which he was the inventor" (*Ecrits* (E), p. 284). Thus: "In effect, this schema [schema R] enables us to show the relations that refer not to pre-Oedipal stages, which are not of course non-existent, but which are analytically unthinkable (as is sufficiently apparent in the hesitant, but *guided* work of Melanie Klein), but to the pregenital stages in so far as they are ordered in the retroaction of the Oedipus complex." "On the Possible Treatment of Psychosis," *Ecrits* (E), p. 197; trans. mod. "In fact, what has he gained in normal-izing the function of the phallus as a part-object if he has to invoke its presence in the mother's body as an internal object, which term is a function of the phantasies revealed by Melanie Klein, and if he cannot separate himself from Klein's view that these phantasies originate as far back as in early childhood, during Oedipal formation?

avoided at all cost. This can always happen [*arriver*] if its occurrence, its taking-place, does not have the ideality of a phonematic letter (what the Seminar so bizarrely calls the "materiality of the signifier," on the precedent that it survives the burnt or torn paper, and that it endures in not permitting itself to be divided). This always does *happen* [*arrive*], but the voice is there to deceive us about this strange event, and to leave to us the ideal guardianship [*garde*] of that which falls to the rank of partial or divisible object: a disseminable bit.

The lure—but the word no longer suffices—would not come from the imaginary, but from the alleged limit between the imaginary and the symbolic. The consequence: remains to be followed.

The systematic and historical link between idealization, the *relève* (*Aufhebung*), and the voice—if one now takes it as demonstrated—is insistent, therefore, in "The Signification of the Phallus." Elevation to the function of signifier is an *Aufhebung* of the "signifiable" (p. 288): which is therefore true in a privileged way of the "privileged signifier" (the phallus) and of its literal locality *par excellence* (the voice). Whence the structural complicity between the motifs of the veil and the voice, between the truth and phonocentrism, phallocentrism and logocentrism, which is exposed thus: "All these propositions merely veil the fact that it can play its role only when veiled, that is to say, as itself a sign of the latency with

---

"It might be a good idea to re-examine the question by asking what could have necessitated for Freud the evident paradox of his position. For one has to admit that he was better *guided* than anyone in his recognition of the order of unconscious phenomena, of which he was the inventor, and that, failing an adequate articulation of the nature of these phenomena, his followers were doomed to lose their way to a greater or lesser degree.

"It is on the basis of the following bet—which I lay down as the principle of a commentary of Freud's work that I have pursued during the past seven years—that I have been led to certain results: essentially, to promulgate as necessary to any articulation of analytic phenomena the notion of the signifier, as opposed to that of the signified, in modern linguistic analysis." "The Signification of the Phallus," in *Ecrits* (E), pp. 284–285. My italics; follow what is *guided*.

"We must retain the fact that Jones, in his address to the Vienna Society, which seems to have scorched the earth for any contributions since, already found nothing more to produce than his pure and simple solidarity with Kleinian concepts in the perfect brutality in which their author presents them: that is, the lack of precision in which Melanie Klein keeps herself,—including the more original Oedipal fantasies in the maternal body—, from their provenance in the reality supposed by the Name-of-the-Father." *Propos directifs pour un Congrès sur la sexualité féminine*, in *Ecrits* (F), pp. 728–729.

which any signifiable is struck, when it is raised (*aufgehoben*) to the function of signifier.

"The phallus is the signifier of this *Aufhebung* itself, which it inaugurates (initiates) by its disappearance." [58]

It appears that the Hegelian movement of the *Aufhebung* is reversed here, since the Hegelian *Aufhebung* lifts [*relève*] the sensory signifier into the ideal signified. But since Lacan has granted to *verbal* language (the preconscious, that is, consciousness for Freud) the best local guardianship [*garde*] of the phallus (the privileged signifier), the preeminence of the voice annuls the reversal. The preeminence of the voice is common to the two dialectics and idealizes the signifier.

The same thing always takes (the same) place. Again, the issue is one of not abandoning the proper place in question.

Phallogocentrism is one thing. And what is called man and what is called woman might be subject to it. All the more in that, as we are reminded, the phallus is neither a fantasy ("an imaginary effect"), nor an object ("part-, internal, good, bad, etc."), and "even less the organ, penis or clitoris, that it symbolizes." [59] Androcentrism, therefore, could be another thing.

But what happens? All of phallogocentrism is articulated on the basis of a determined *situation* (let us give this word all its imports) in which the phallus *is* the mother's desire to the extent that she does not have it.[60] An (individual, perceptual, local, cultural, historical,

58. TN. *Ecrits* (E), p. 288.

59. TN. *Ecrits* (E), p. 285.

60. ". . . the signification of castration in fact takes on its (*clinically manifest*) full weight as far as the formation of symptoms is concerned, only on the basis of its discovery as castration of the mother" (*Ecrits* (E), p. 282), that is, her lack of a penis and not of a clitoris. "The fact that the phallus is a signifier means that it is in the place of the Other that the subject has access to it. But since this signifier is only veiled, as the ratio of the Other's desire, it is this desire of the Other as such that the subject must recognize . . . If the desire of the mother *is* the phallus, the child wishes to be the phallus in order to satisfy that desire . . . *Clinical experience has shown* us that this test of the desire of the Other is decisive not in the sense that the subject learns by it whether or not he has a real phallus, but in the sense that he learns that the mother does not have it . . . in effect, the man finds satisfaction for his demand for love in the relation with the woman, in as much as the signifier of the phallus constitutes her as giving in love what she does not have . . ." *Ecrits* (E), pp. 282–90 *passim*.

I have italicized "*clinically manifest*" and "*clinical experience has shown*" without having the slightest suspicion concerning the truth of these statements. Rather, in order to examine all the bearings of a *situation* of psychoanalysis in XXXX.

"What she does not have" . . . "bequeaths in that she has never had it": recall etc.) situation on the basis of which what is called a "sexual theory" is elaborated: the phallus is not the organ, penis or clitoris, that it symbolizes, but it mostly and primarily symbolizes the penis. What follows is obvious: phallogocentrism as androcentrism, along with the entire paradoxical logic and reversals this engenders: for example, that in "phallocentric dialectics, she [woman] represents

that "Woman" and the Queen are in question here: the proper place orienting the *proper* course of the letter, its "destination," what it "means," which is deciphered on the basis of a situation that theorizes what "clinical experience shows us."

This *situation* (a theoretical discourse and an institution built upon a *phase* of the male child's experience and the corresponding sexual theory) supports, for both Bonaparte and Lacan, the interpretation of "The Purloined Letter." This interpretation corresponds rigorously, and here there is no infidelity of the legatees to the description given by Freud in the propositions that were debated during the "quarrel" just mentioned. As a reminder: ". . . the main characteristic of this 'infantile genital organization' is its *difference* from the final genital organization of the adult. The fact is that, for both sexes, only one genital, namely the male one, comes into account. What is present, therefore, is not a primacy of the genitals, but a primacy of the *phallus.*

"Unfortunately we can describe this state of things only as it affects the male child; the corresponding processes in the little girl are not known to us . . . [Little boys] disavow the fact [of the absence of a penis] and believe that they *do* see a penis, all the same. They gloss over the contradiction between observation and preconception by telling themselves that the penis is still small and will grow bigger presently; and they then slowly come to the emotionally significant conclusion that after all the penis had at least been there before and been taken away afterwards. The lack of a penis is regarded as a result of castration, and so now the child is faced with the task of coming to terms with castration in relation to himself. The further developments are too well known generally to make it necessary to recapitulate them here. But it seems to me that *the significance of the castration complex can only be rightly appreciated if its origin in the phase of phallic primacy is also taken into account . . .* At the . . . stage of infantile genital organization . . . *maleness* exists, but not femaleness. The antithesis here is between having a *male genital* and being *castrated.*" "The Infantile Genital Organization" (1923), SE 19, pp. 142–45.

One might be tempted to say: Freud, like those who follow him here, is only *describing* the necessity of phallogocentrism, only explaining its effects, which are as obvious as they are massive. Phallocentrism is neither an accident nor a speculative error that can be imputed to any given theoretician. It is an old and enormous root that must also be accounted for. Thus, one can describe it, as one describes an object or an itinerary, without having the description participate in that whose recognition it operates. Certainly. But this hypothesis, which then would have to be extended to cover all the texts of tradition, encounters in these texts, as it does in Freud, and as it does in those of his heirs who on this question wish to transform no part of his legacy, a strictly determinable limit: the description is a "participant" when it induces a practice, an ethics, and an institution, and therefore a politics that insure the truth of the tradition. Then, it is no longer only a question of knowing, showing, and explaining, but of remaining. And of reproducing. Lacan declares his ethico-institutional discourse: the motifs of authenticity, of full speech, of sworn

the absolute Other." [61] This consequence had to be marked in order
to recognize the meaning of the purloined letter in the "course
which is proper to it." From the end of "The Signification of the
Phallus," a twice repeated assertion of depth, profundity: "Cor-
relatively, one can glimpse the reason for a characteristic that had
never before been elucidated, and which shows once again the
depth of Freud's intuition: namely, why he advances the view that
there is only one *libido,* his text showing that he conceives it as
masculine in nature. The function of the phallic signifier touches
here on its most profound relation: that in which the Ancients embodied the *Nous* and the *Logos.*" [62] Depth is height. It flows out
[*débouche*] toward the high, precisely the mouth [*bouche*] in which
is "incarnated" the *Nous,* the *Logos,* and which profoundly says:
there is only *one* libido, and therefore no difference, and even less
an opposition within libido between the masculine and the feminine, and moreover it is masculine by nature. The "reason for this
never elucidated characteristic" can, in effect, only be "glimpsed":
because there is no reason for it, it is reason. Before, during, and
after Freud. The characteristic [*trait*] drawn from reason. By it, for
it, beneath it. In the logic said to be "of the kettle" [63] (a check

---

faith, and of the "signifying convention" show this adequately. "Analysis can have
for its goal only the advent of a true speech and the realization by the subject of his
history in his relation to a future" (*Ecrits* (E), p. 88). "Just before the summits of the
path on which I will place its reading [that of the work of Freud], before considering
transference, then identification, then anxiety, it is not by accident, and no one
would think of this, that this year, the fourth before my seminar at Sainte-Anne is to
end, I have thought it necessary to assure ourselves of the ethics of psychoanalysis.

"It seems in effect that we risked forgetting in the field in which we function that
an ethics is its very principle, and that henceforth, no matter what he might say to
himself, and equally well without my own statements, about the end of man, it is
with a formation that can be qualified as human that our principle torment is
concerned.

"Every human formation has as its essence, and not for accidental purposes,
the restraining of pleasure" (*Discours de clôture des Journées sur les psychoses
chez l'enfant,* in *Recherches,* special issue *Enfance aliénée,* December 11, 1968,
pp. 145–46).

61. TN. *Ecrits* (F), p. 732.

62. *Ecrits* (E), p. 291. As for the systemic link between the logic of the signifier
and phallocentrism, everything in Lacanian discourse here answers the question he
asks in the *Propos directifs pour un Congrès sur la sexualité féminine*—and answers
yes: "Is it then the privilege of the signifier that Freud has in mind in suggesting that
perhaps there is only one libido and that it is marked by the male sign?" *Ecrits* (F),
p. 735.

63. TN. The "logic of the kettle" is used by Freud to illustrate how the dream-
work accumulates contradictory arguments so that the dreamer is always right. The

[*traite*] drawn from reason), reason will always be right [*aura raison*]. By itself. It hears itself, agrees with itself [*s'entend*]. "The thing speaks of itself." It hears itself say what it cannot hear or understand.

MEETING PLACE:
THE DOUBLE SQUARE OF KINGS

But it cannot *read* the story it tells itself. Or the scene of writing—before the letter—in which the narrative is inscribed. Let us return to *The Purloined Letter* in order "to glimpse" its disseminal structure, that is, the without-possible-return of the letter, the other scene of its remaining [*restance*].

Because there is a narrator onstage, the "general" scene is not exhausted in a narration, a "tale" or a "story." We have already recognized the effects of invisible framing, of the frame within the frame, *from within which* the psychoanalytic interpretations (semantico-biographical or triado-formalist) lifted out their triangles. In missing the position of the narrator, his engagement in the content of what he seems to recount, one omits everything in the scene of writing that overflows the two triangles.

For the issue, first of all, and with no possible approach or bordering, is one of a scene of writing with ruined (*abîmé*) limits. Right from the simulacrum of an opening, from the "first word," the narrator advances by narrating to himself several propositions which engage the unity of the "tale" in an interminable drift: a textual drift of which the Seminar takes not the slightest account. But in taking this drift into account here, above all the question is not one of making of it the "*real true subject*" of the tale." Which therefore would not have one.

---

man accused of returning the kettle he borrowed from his neighbor in damaged condition retorts (1.) that the kettle he is returning is new, (2.) that the holes were already in it when he borrowed it, and (3.) that he had never borrowed a kettle in the first place. What Derrida is saying is that there is no philosophical argument to be made against Freud's position that there is only *one, male* libido: this is the essence of philosophy itself, which, like the man who borrows the kettle, will accumulate all and any arguments to support this position, all of which will be *true* in the traditional sense, and blind to their mutual contradictions. Thus Derrida's reference earlier in this paragraph to the equivalence of "depth" and "height." This is an allusion to the double meaning of *altus*—both lowest and highest—as the definition of truth: the singular *origin* at the *bottom* of things raised to the level of the *highest truth*. What reason never recognizes is that it depends upon "unreason," double meanings, in order to conceptualize itself.

I. Everything begins "in" a library: in books, writings, references. Therefore nothing begins. Only a drifting or disorientation from which one does not emerge.
  II. Additionally, an explicit reference is made in the direction of two other narratives onto which "this one" is grafted. The "analogy" between the three accounts is the milieu of *The Purloined Letter*. The independence of this tale, as presumed by the Seminar, is therefore the effect of an ablation, even if one takes the tale in its totality, with its narrator and his narration. This ablation is all the more absent-minded in that the "analogy" is recalled from the very first paragraph. It is true that the word "analogy," "coincidence" more precisely, authorizes the ablation, invites it, and therefore acts as a trap. The work of the Seminar begins only after the entry of the Prefect of the Parisian police. But before this, the title, the epigraph, the first paragraph gave us to read (silence in silence):

THE PURLOINED LETTER

Nil sapientiae odiosius acumine nimio.

Seneca

At Paris, just after dark one gusty evening in the autumn of 18—, I was enjoying the twofold luxury of meditation and a meerschaum, in company with my friend C. Auguste Dupin, in his little back library, or book-closet, *au troisième, No. 33 Rue Dunôt, Faubourg St. Germain*. For one hour at least we had maintained a profound silence; while each, to any casual observer, might have seemed intently and exclusively occupied with the curling eddies of smoke that oppressed the atmosphere of the chamber. For myself, however, I was mentally discussing certain topics which had formed matter for conversation between us at an earlier period of the evening; I mean the affair of the Rue Morgue, and the mystery attending the murder of Marie Roget. I looked upon it, therefore, as something of a coincidence, when the door of our apartment was thrown open and admitted our old acquaintance, Monsieur G—, the Prefect of the Parisian police . . . We had been sitting in the dark, and Dupin now arose for the purpose of lighting a lamp, but sat down again without doing so . . . (P. 208)

Everything "begins," then, by obscuring this beginning in the "silence," "smoke," and "dark" of this library. The casual observer sees only the smoking meerschaum: a literary decor in sum, the ornamental frame of a narrative. On this border, which is negligible for the hermeneut interested in the center of the picture and in what is within the representation, one could already read that all of this was an affair of writing, and of writing adrift, in a place of writing open without end to its grafting onto other writings, and that this affair of writing (the third of a series in which the "coincidence" with the two preceding ones already caused itself to be remarked upon), suddenly breaks into its first word "*au troisième, No. 33 Rue Dunôt, Faubourg St. Germain.*" In French in the text. Fortuitous notations, curling eddies of smoke, contingencies of framing? That they go beyond the "author's intention," about which the Seminar is tempted to question Dupin, that they are even pure accidental "coincidence," an event of fortune, can only recommend them all the more to the reading of a text which makes of chance as writing what we will indeed refrain from calling "the *real subject* of the tale."

Its remarkable ellipsis, rather. In effect, if we do as we are invited, and go back from the internal bordering of the frame to what is before *The Purloined Letter,* the remarkable insists: scene of writing, library, events of chance, coincidences. At the beginning of *The Murders in the Rue Morgue* what might be called the meeting place between the (narrating-narrated) narrator and Dupin is already an "obscure library," the "accident" (which Baudelaire this time translates as "*coincidence,*" and not as "*analogie*")[64] "of

64. Kitchen questions: in translating "coincidence" by "*analogie*" at the beginning of the tale, at the very moment of the reference to the two other "affairs" (the *Rue Morgue* and *Marie Rogêt*), Baudelaire misses not only the insistence of this word but also the fact that *The Purloined Letter* itself is presented in a series of these coincidences, as one of them, the coincidences whose network is elaborated before this third fiction. One detail from among all of those that now can be analyzed in an open reading of the trilogy: the epigraph to the *Mystery of Marie Rogêt*, a citation from Novalis both in German and in English translation, which begins: "There are ideal series of events which run parallel with the real ones. They rarely coincide . . ." Baudelaire purely and simply omits the last three words. The word *coincidences* then appears three times in two pages, always underlined. And the last time it has to do with the intersection of the three affairs: "The extraordinary details which I am now called upon to make public, will be found to form, as regards sequence of time, the primary branch of a series of scarcely intelligible *coincidences,* whose secondary or concluding branch will be recognized by all readers in the late murder of MARY CECELIA ROGERS at New York." The subtitle of the *Mystery of Marie Rogêt: "A Sequel to The Murders in the Rue Morgue."*

    These reminders, which could be multiplied endlessly, are to make us attentive to the effects of the frame and to the paradoxes of parergonal logic. The point is not to show that "The Purloined Letter" functions within a frame (a frame that is omitted by the Seminar, which thereby can assure itself of the tale's triangular interior by means of an active and subreptitious limitation on the basis of a metalinguistic overlay), but that the structure of the effects of framing is such that no totalization of the bordering can even occur. The frames are always enframed: and therefore enframed by a given piece of what they contain. Parts without a whole, "partitions" without unification: this is what checks the dream of a letter without partition, a letter al-our both being in search of the same very rare and remarkable volume." And the least one might say about the relationship formed in this meeting place is that it will never leave the so-called general narrator in the position of a neutral and transparent reporter who does not intervene in the narration in progress. For example (but this time the example read on the frame is not at the beginning of the text. The frame describing the "meeting" cuts through the narration, if you will. Before the appearance of Dupin in the narrative, the frame is preceded by a feint in the guise of an abandoned preface, a false short treatise on analysis: "I am not now writing a treatise, but simply prefacing a somewhat peculiar narrative by observations very much at random." Not a treatise, a preface (to be dropped[65] as usual), and random observations. At the end of the preface the narrator feigns the Seminar):

---

lergic to partition. On the basis of which the linguistic unit "phallus" [*le sème "phallus"*] wanders, begins by disseminating, and not even by disseminating *itself*.

The naturalizing neutralization of the frame permits the Seminar, by virtue of its imposition or importation of an Oedipal contour, finding (itself within) this contour in truth—and, in effect, it is there, but as one part, even if a precisely central part, within the letter—to constitute a metalanguage and to exclude the text in general in all the dimensions that we began here by recalling (return to the "first page"). Without even going further into details, the trap of metalanguage—which in the last analysis is used by no one, is at the disposition of no one, involves no one in the consequences of an error or a weakness—is a trap belonging to writing before the letter, and shows and hides itself in the shown-hidden of the feigned title: "The Purloined Letter" is the title of the text and not only of its object. But a text never entitles itself, never writes: I, the text, write, or write myself. It causes to be said, it lets be said, or rather it leads to being said, "I, the truth, speak." I am always (I am still following) [*Je suis toujours*] the letter that never arrives at itself [*s'arrive*]. And right up to its destination.

65. Before dropping them, as everyone drops a preface, or before exalting them as the properly instructive theoretical concepts, the truth of the story, I will lift out, somewhat at random, several propositions. Which are not necessarily the best ones. One also would have to recall each word of the title, and again the epigraph on the name of Achilles when he hid himself among women. "The mental features discoursed of as the analytical, are, in themselves, but little susceptible of analysis . . . the analyst glories in that moral activity which *disentangles* [*dont la fonction est de débrouiller*]. He derives pleasure from even the most trivial occupations bringing his talents into play. He is fond of enigmas, of conundrums, of hieroglyphics . . . Yet to calculate is not in itself to analyze. A chess-player, for example, does the one without effort at the other . . . I will, therefore, take occasion to assert that the higher powers of the reflective intellect are more decidedly and more usefully tasked by the unostentatious game of draughts than by all the elaborate frivolity of chess [*la laborieuse futilité des échecs*] . . . To be less abstract—Let us suppose a game of draughts where the pieces are reduced to four kings ["draughts" in French is *le jeu de dames,* and Baudelaire's translation here speaks of four *dames,* not kings], and

The narrative which follows will appear to the reader somewhat in the light of a commentary upon the propositions just advanced.

Residing in Paris during the spring and part of the summer of 18—, I there become acquainted with a Monsieur C. Auguste Dupin. This young gentleman was of an excellent—indeed of an illustrious family, but, by a variety of untoward events, had been reduced to such poverty that the energy of his character succumbed beneath it, and he ceased to bestir himself in the world, or to care for the retrieval of his fortunes. By courtesy of his creditors, there still remained in his possession a small remnant of his patrimony; and, upon the income arising from this, he managed, by means of a rigorous economy, to procure the necessaries of life, without troubling himself about its superfluities. Books, indeed, were his sole luxuries, and in Paris these are easily obtained. (P. 142)

By means of a *remnant* of the paternal inheritance, apparently left out of account for the debtor, who by calculating (*rigorous economy*) can draw an *income,* a revenue from it, the surplus-value of a capital which works by itself, Dupin permits himself to pay for a single superfluity, a sole luxury in which the initial remnant is relocated [*se retrouve*] therefore, and which cuts across the space of the restricted economy like a gift without return. This sole luxury (*sole luxuries:* the very word found for the second time on the second line of *The Purloined Letter,* but this time as a singular *double luxury,* the *twofold luxury of meditation and a meerschaum*)

---

where, of course, no oversight is to be expected. It is obvious that here the victory can be decided (the players being at all equal) only by some *recherché* movement [*tactique habile*], the result of some strong exertion of the intellect. Deprived of ordinary resources, the analyst throws himself into the spirit of his opponent, identifies himself therewith, and not unfrequently sees thus, at a glance, the sole methods (sometimes indeed absurdly simple ones) by which he may seduce into error or hurry into miscalculation . . . But it is in matters beyond the limits of mere rule [*les cas situés au-delà de la règle*] that the skill of the analyst is evinced [*se manifeste*] . . . Our player confines himself not at all; nor, because the game is the object, does he reject deductions from things external to the game . . ." (Poe, pp. 139–41 *passim*). Etc. the entire passage must be read, and in both languages. I have allowed myself to do some cooking based on Baudelaire's translation, which I do not always respect.

Meryon had asked Baudelaire if he believed "in the reality of this Edgar Poe," and had attributed his stories "to a society of very adept, very powerful litterateurs, up to date on everything." This society does not specify, therefore, if the "things external to the game" border a game recounted in the text or constituted by the text, nor whether *the game* which is *the object* is or is not (in) the story. Nor whether seduction seeks its prey among the characters or the readers. The question of the "narratee," and then of the addressee, which is not the same thing, never arrives at itself [*ne s'arrive jamais*].

is writing: the books which will organize the meeting place and the ruination [*mise en abîme*] of the entire so-called general narration. The meeting place of the meeting between the narrator and Dupin is due to the meeting of their interest in the same book; it is never said whether they find it. Such is the literal accident:

> Our first meeting was at an obscure library in the Rue Montmartre, where the accident of our both being in search of the same very rare and very remarkable volume, brought us into closer communion. We saw each other again and again. I was deeply interested in the little family history which he detailed to me with all that candor which a Frenchman indulges whenever mere self is the theme. (P. 142)

Thus the narrator permits himself to narrate: that he is interested in Dupin's family history ("I was deeply interested in the little family history . . ."), the very history which leaves a remnant of income with which to pay for the luxury of books; and then, as we shall see, that Dupin's capacity for reading astonishes him above all, and that the society of such a man is without a price for him, beyond all evaluation ("a treasure beyond price"). The narrator, therefore, will permit himself to pay for the priceless Dupin, who permits himself to pay for priceless writing, which is without a price for this very reason. For the narrator, in confiding—in yielding [*se livrant*] as Baudelaire says—frankly to Dupin must pay for doing so. He must rent the analyst's office. And provide the economic equivalent of the priceless. The analyst—or his own fortune, more or less equivalent to Dupin's, simply "somewhat less embarrassed"—authorizes him to do so: "I was permitted to be at the expense of renting . . ." The narrator is therefore the first to pay Dupin in order to be certain of the availability of letters. Let us then follow the movement of this chain. But what he pays for is also the place of the narration, the writing within which the entire story will be recounted and offered to interpretations. And if he is paying in order to write or to speak, he is also making Dupin speak, making him return his letters, and leaving him the last word in the form of a confession. In the economy of this office, as soon as the narrator is placed on stage by a function which is indeed that of a public corporation [*société anonyme*] of capital and desire, no neutralization is possible, nor is any general point of view, any view from above, any "destruction" of signification by money. It is not only Dupin but the narrator who is a "participant." As soon as the narrator makes Dupin return his letters, and not only to the Queen (the other Queen), the letter divides itself, is no longer atomistic (atomism,

Epicurus's atomism is also one of Dupin's propositions in *The Murders in the Rue Morgue*), and therefore loses any certain destination. The divisibility of the letter—this is why we have insisted on this key or theoretical safety lock of the Seminar—is what chances and sets off course, without guarantee of return, the remaining [*restance*] of anything whatsoever: a letter does *not always* arrive at its destination, and from the moment that this possibility belongs to its structure one can say that it never truly arrives, that when it does arrive its capacity not to arrive torments it with an internal drifting.

The divisibility of the letter is also the divisibility of the signifier to which it gives rise, and therefore also of the "subjects," "characters," or "positions" which are subjected to it and which "represent" them. Before showing this in the text, a citation as reminder:

> I was astonished, too, at the vast extent of his reading; and above all, I felt my soul enkindled within me by the wild fervor, and the vivid freshness of his imagination. Seeking in Paris the objects I then sought, I felt that the society of such a man would be to me a treasure beyond price; and this feeling I frankly confided to him. It was at length arranged that we should live together during my stay in the city; and as my worldly circumstances were somewhat less embarrassed than his own, I was permitted to be at the expense of renting, and furnishing in a style which suited the rather fantastic gloom of our common temper, a time-eaten and grotesque mansion, long deserted through superstitions into which we did not inquire, and tottering to its fall in a retired and desolate portion of the Faubourg St. Germain. (Pp. 142–43)

Thus we have two gloomy (melancholic) fantastics, one of whom does not tell us what objects he previously was seeking in Paris, or who the "former associates" are, from whom he now is going to hide the secret of the locality. The entire space is now one of the speculation of these two "madmen":

> Had the routine of our life at this place been known to the world, we should have been regarded as madmen—although, perhaps, as madmen of a harmless nature. Our seclusion was perfect. We admitted no visitors. Indeed the locality of our retirement had been carefully kept a secret from my own former associates; and it had been many years since Dupin had ceased to know or be known in Paris. We existed within ourselves alone. (P. 143)

From here on, the narrator permits himself to narrate his progressive identification with Dupin. And first of all with the love of night, the "sable divinity" whose "presence" they "counterfeit" when she is not there:

> It was a freak of fancy in my friend (for what else shall I call it?) to be enamored of the Night for her own sake; and into this *bizarrerie*, as into all his others, I quietly fell; giving myself up to his wild whims with a perfect *abandon*. The sable divinity would not herself dwell with us always; but we could counterfeit her presence. (P. 143)

Himself doubled in his position, the narrator thus *identifies* with Dupin, whose "peculiar analytic ability" he cannot help "remarking and admiring"; and Dupin gives him multiple proofs of his "intimate knowledge" of his own, the narrator's, personality. But Dupin himself, precisely at these moments, appears double. And this time it is a "fancy" of the narrator, who sees Dupin as double: "his manner at these moments was frigid and abstract; his eyes were vacant in expression; while his voice, usually a rich tenor, rose into a treble which would have sounded petulantly but for the deliberateness and entire distinctness of the enunciation. Observing him in these moods, I often dwelt meditatively upon the old philosophy of the Bi-Part Soul, and amused myself with the fancy of a double Dupin—the creative and the resolvent" (p. 144).

The fancy of an identification between two doubled doubles, the major investment in a relationship which engages Dupin *outside* of the "intersubjective triads" of the "real drama" and the narrator *inside* what he narrates;[66] the circulation of desires and capital, of

66. The Seminar never takes into account the very determined involvement of the narrator in the narration. Ten years later, in a 1966 addition, Lacan writes the following:

"An effect (of the signifier) so manifest as to be grasped here as it is in the fiction of the purloined letter.

"Whose essence is that the letter could import its effects within: on the actors of the tale, including the narrator, as well as without: on us, readers, and equally on its author, without anyone ever having to be concerned with what it meant. Which of everything that is written is the ordinary fate" (*Ecrits* (F), pp. 56–57).

Although we subscribe to this up to a certain point, we again must specify that the Seminar said nothing about the effects on the narrator, *neither in fact nor in principle*. The structure of the interpretation would exclude it. And as for the nature of these effects, the structure of the narrator's involvement, the repentance still says nothing, limiting itself to the framing operated by the Seminar. As for the allegation that in this affair everything occurs "without anyone ever having to be concerned with what it [the letter] meant," *it is false* for several reasons.

1st: Everyone, as the Prefect of Police reminds us, knows that the letter contains enough to "bring in question the honor of a personage of most exalted station," and therefore also that person's "peace": a solid semantic bond.

signifiers and letters, before and beyond the "two triangles," the "primal" and secondary ones, the consecutive fissioning of the positions, starting with the position of Dupin, who like *all* the characters, inside and outside the narration, successively occupies *all* the places—all of this makes of triangular logic a very limited play within the play. And if the dual relation between two doubles (which

---

2d. This knowledge is repeated by the Seminar, and supports the Seminar, at two levels:

a) As concerns the minimal and active meaning of the letter, the Seminar reports or transcribes the Prefect's information: "But all this tells us nothing of the message it conveys.

"Love letter or conspiratorial letter, letter of betrayal or letter of mission, letter of summons or letter of distress, we are assured of but one thing: the Queen must not bring it to the knowledge of her lord and master" (S, p. 57). This tells us the essentials of the message that the letter vehiculates: and the variations just proposed are not indifferent to this message, no matter what they would have us believe. In each of the possible hypotheses, the letter's message (not only its being-sent, its emission, but the content of what is emitted within it) necessarily implies the betrayal of a pact of a "sworn faith." It was not forbidden for just anyone to send just any kind of letter to the Queen, nor for her to receive it. The Seminar contradicts itself when, several lines later, it radicalizes the logic of the signifier and of its literal place by allegedly neutralizing the "message," and then brings to rest or anchors this logic in its meaning or symbolic truth: ". . . it remains that the letter is the symbol of a pact" (S, p. 58). Contrary to what the Seminar says (an enormous proposition, by virtue of the blindness it could induce, but indispensable to the demonstration), everyone had "to be concerned with what it [the letter] meant." On the subject of this meaning, ignorance or indifference remains minimal and provisional. Everyone is aware of it, everyone is preoccupied with it, starting with the author of the Seminar. And if it did not have a very determined meaning, no one would be so worried about having another one palmed off on him, which happens to the Queen, and then to the minister. At least. All of them assure themselves, starting with the minister and including Lacan, passing through Dupin, that it is indeed a question of the letter which indeed says what it says: the betrayal of the pact, and what it says, "the symbol of a pact." Otherwise there would be no "abandoned" letter: whether by the minister first of all, or then by Dupin, or finally by Lacan. They all verify the contents of the letter, of the "right" letter, and they all do what the Prefect of Police does at the moment when, in exchange for a retribution, he takes the letter from Dupin's hands, and checks its tenor: "This functionary grasped it in a perfect agony of joy, opened it with a trembling hand, cast a rapid glance at its contents, and then, scrambling and struggling to the door, rushed at length unceremoniously from the room . . ." (Poe, p. 216). The exchange of the check and the letter takes place across an *escritoire* (in French in the text) where Dupin had the document locked up.

b) As for the law of the meaning of the purloined letter in its exemplary generality, such, once again, are the last words of the Seminar. ("Thus it is that what the 'purloined letter,' nay the 'non-delivered letter' means is that a letter always arrives at its destination," S, p. 72)

Lacan would reduce to the imaginary) includes and envelops the entire space said to be of the symbolic, overflows and simulates it, ceaselessly ruining and disorganizing it, then the opposition of the imaginary and the symbolic, and above all its implicit hierarchy, appears to be of very limited pertinence: that is, if one measures it against the squaring of such a scene of writing.

We have seen that *all* the characters of *The Purloined Letter,* and those of the "real drama" in particular, Dupin included, successively and structurally occupied *all* the positions, the position of the dead-blind king (and of the Prefect of Police thereby), then the positions of the Queen and of the minister. Each position identifies itself with the other and divides itself, even the position of the dummy and of a supplementary fourth. This compromises the distinction of the three glances proposed by the Seminar in order to determine the proper course of the circulation. And above all the (duplicitous and identificatory) opening set off to the side, in the direction of the (narrating-narrated) narrator, brings back one letter only to set another adrift.

And the phenomena of the double, and therefore of *Unheimlichkeit,* do not belong only to the trilogic "context" of *The Purloined Letter.* In effect, the question arises, between the narrator and Dupin, of knowing whether the minister is himself or his brother ("There are two brothers . . . both have attained reputation"; where? "in letters," p. 219). Dupin affirms that the minister is both "poet and mathematician." The two brothers are almost indistinguishable in him. In rivalry within him, the one playing and checking the other. " 'You are mistaken,' " says Dupin, " 'I know him well; he is both. As poet *and* mathematician, he would reason well; as mere mathematician, he could not have reasoned at all, and thus would have been at the mercy of the Prefect' " (p. 219).

But Dupin strikes a blow against the minister, who is " 'well acquainted with my MS.,' " a blow signed by a brother or confrere, a twin, younger, or elder brother (Atreus/Thyestes). This rivalrous and duplicitous identification of the two brothers, far from entering into the symbolic space of the familial triangle (the first, second, or next triangle), endlessly carries off the triangle into a labyrinth of doubles without originals, of *fac-similes* without an authentic and indivisible letter, of forgeries without something forged, thereby imprinting on the purloined letter an incorrigible indirection.

The text entitled *The Purloined Letter* imprints (itself in) these effects of indirection. I have indicated only the most salient ones in order to begin to unlock a reading: the play of doubles, divisibility without end, textual references from *fac-simile* to *fac-simile*, the framing of the frames, the interminable supplementarity of the quotation marks, the insertion of *The Purloined Letter* into a purloined letter beginning before it, through the narratives of narratives in *The Murders in the Rue Morgue,* and the newspaper clippings in *The Mystery of Marie Rogêt* (A Sequel to *The Murders in the Rue Morgue*). The *mise en abîme* of the title above all: *The Purloined Letter* is the text, the text in a text (the purloined letter as a trilogy). The title is the title of the text, it names the text, it names itself, and thus includes itself by pretending to name an object described in the text. *The Purloined Letter* operates as a text which evades every assignable destination, and produces, or rather induces by deducing itself, this unassignableness at the precise moment when it narrates the arrival of a letter. It feigns meaning to say something, and letting one think that "a letter always arrives at its destination," authentic, intact, and undivided, at the moment when and in the place where the feint, written before the letter, by itself separates from itself. In order to take another jump to the side.

Who signs? Dupin absolutely wants to sign. And in fact the narrator, after having made or let him speak, leaves him the last word,[67] the last word of the last of the three stories. It seems. I am not remarking this in order to place the narrator in turn, and even less the author, in the position of the analyst who knows how to keep silent. Measured against the squaring of this scene of writing, perhaps

67. One might even consider that he is the only one "to speak" in the tale. His is the dominant discourse which, with a loquacious and didactic braggadocio that is magisterial in truth, dispenses directives, controls directions, redresses wrongs, and gives lessons to everyone. He spends his time, and everyone else's, inflicting punishments and recalling the rules. He posts himself and addresses himself. Only the address counts, the right and authentic one. Which comes back, according to the law, to its rightful owner. Thanks to the man of law, the guide and rector of the proper way. The entire "Purloined Letter" is written in order for him to bring it back, finally, while giving a lecture. And since he shows himself more clever than all the others, the letter plays one more trick on him at the moment when he recognizes its place and true destination. It escapes and entraps him (literature stage-left) at the moment when, at his most authoritatively arrogant, he hears himself say that he entraps while explaining the trap, at the moment when he strikes his blow and returns the letter. Unwittingly he gives in to all the demands, and doubles, that is replaces, the minister and the police; if there were only one, a hypothesis to be dismissed, he would be the greatest dupe of the "story." It remains to be seen—what about the lady. He addresses-her-the-Queen-the-address-dupes-her. [. . . *s'il n'y en avait qu'une, hypothèse en congé, ce serait la plus belle dupe de l' "histoire." Reste à savoir—quoi de la belle. Il-l'adresse-la-Reine-l'adresse-la-dupe.*]

there is here no possible enclosure for an analytic situation. Perhaps there is no possible analyst here, at least in the situation of psychoanalysis in X . . . Only four kings, and therefore four queens, four prefects of police, four ministers, four analysts-Dupins, four narrators, four readers, four kings, etc., each of them more lucid and more stupid than the others, more powerful and more disarmed.

Yes, without a doubt, Dupin wants to sign the last word of the last message of the purloined letter. First by not being able to prevent himself from leaving his own imprimatur—or at least the seal with which he will have to be identified—beneath the *fac-simile* which he leaves for the minister. He is afraid of the *fac-simile,* and insisting upon his very confraternal vengeance, he absolutely wants the minister to know where it is coming from. Thus he limits the *fac-simile,* the counterfeit, to the outside of the letter. The inside is authentic and properly identifiable. In effect: at the moment when the madman (who is a false madman paid by him: " 'the pretended lunatic was a man in own pay' ") distracts everyone with his "frantic behavior," what does Dupin do? He adds a note. He sets in place the false letter, that is the one concerning his own interests, the *true one,* which is an *ersatz only on its outside.* If there were a man of truth in all this, a lover of the authentic, Dupin would indeed be his model: " 'In the meantime I stepped to the card-rack, took the letter, put it in my pocket, and replaced it by a *fac-simile,* (so far as regards externals) which I had carefully prepared at my lodgings; imitating the D— cipher, very readily, by means of a seal formed of bread' " (p. 224)

Thus will D. have to decipher, internally, what the decipherer will have meant and from whence and why he has deciphered, with what aim, in the name of whom and of what. The initial—which is the same, D, for the minister and for Dupin—is a *fac-simile* on the outside, *but a proper on the inside.*

But what is this proper on the inside? This signature? This "last word" in a doubly confraternal war?

Again, a citation by means of which the signer is dispossessed, no matter what he says ". . . I just copied into the middle of the blank sheet the words—

—Un dessein si funeste,
S'il n'est digne d'Atrée, est digne de Thyeste." (P. 225)

Play of quotation marks. In the French translation, there are no quotation marks—Crébillon's text is in small type. The sentence that follows ("They are to be found in Crébillon's 'Atrée' ") thus can equally be attributed to the author of *The Purloined Letter,* to the narrator, to the author of the avenging letter (Dupin). But the American edition[68] that I am using leaves no doubt:

" '. . . He is well acquainted with my MS., and I just copied into the middle of the blank sheet the words—

—Un dessein si funeste,
S'il n'est digne d'Atrée, est digne de Thyeste.

They are to be found in Crébillon's 'Atrée.' ' "

Thus it is clear that the last sentence is Dupin's, Dupin saying to the minister: I the undersigned, Dupin, inform you of the fate of the letter, of what it means, with what aim I am filching one from you in order to return it to its addressee, and why I am replacing it with this one, remember.

But this last word, aside from the invisible quotation marks that border the entire story, Dupin is obliged to cite between quotation marks, to recount his signature: this is what I wrote to him and this is how I signed. What is a signature between quotation marks? And then, within these quotation marks, the imprimatur itself is a citation between quotation marks. This remainder is (again) still (from) literature.

Two out of three times, the author of the Seminar will have forced *dessein* [design] into *destin* [destiny], perhaps, thereby, bringing a meaning to its destination: expressly, no doubt, for in any case nothing permits one to exclude a design [*dessein*] somewhere. (This coda dedicates itself to Abbé D. Coppieters de Gibson. The thing in truth—an alteration subtracting one letter and substituting another, in order to achieve its destiny while *en route*—did not escape him.)

"Whatever the case, the Minister, when he tries to make use of it, will be able to read these words, written so that he may recognize Dupin's hand: '. . . *Un dessein si funeste/S'il n'est digne d'Atrée est digne de Thyeste,*' whose source, Dupin tells us, is Crébillon's *Atrée*" (S, p. 43). Then, after a lapse of time: "The commonplace of the quotation is fitting for the oracle that this face

68. In the first publication of this text, the following remark concerning the quotation marks could be read: "It is incorrect, however, in presenting itself thus, and in leaving the internal quotation marks, the so-called 'English' quotation marks, suspended." I was wrong: the last quotation marks signal the end of Dupin's discourse, which is what was important to me, and there is no error in the edition to which I am referring. The deletion of this phrase (which is inconsequential) is the only modification of this essay since its first publication.

bears in its grimace, as is also its source in tragedy: '. . . *Un destin si funeste,/S'il n'est digne d'Atrée, est digne de Thyeste*'" (S, p. 71). And finally (*Points*, p. 8): ". . . and I add (p. 52) that the song with which this Lecoq, in the love note that he destines for him, would like to awaken him ('*un destin si funeste* . . .'), has no chance of being heard by him."

DU TOUT

First published in *Confrontation* I (1978), preceded by this editorial note:

"On 21 November 1977, a session of 'Confrontation' with Jacques Derrida was organized around *Glas* (Galilée, 1974), and other texts in thematic relation to the theory, movement and institution of psychoanalysis, notably "Freud and the Scene of Writing" (in *Writing and Difference*); *Le facteur de la vérité; Fors* (in *Le verbier de l'homme aux loups* by Nicholas Abraham and Maria Torok; English version in *The Georgia Review*); and *Spurs*. In response to René Major's initial questions, Jacques Derrida advanced several introductory propositions. We are reproducing them here in the literality of their recording. Only the title is an exception to this rule."

René MAJOR: Jacques Derrida, I first of all would like to convey to you the profound malaise that I experienced reading *Glas*. To employ the figure suggested to me by a word close to *glas* [funeral bell], but feminine, the word *glène,* and in its double usage [the shallow cavity in which one bone is joined to another; a coiled portion of rope], I would say that you make Knowledge and the Body (yours, mine) submit to a treatment which makes them cave in on themselves, coil themselves, box themselves into a cavity in which they grind themselves, fragment themselves, dislocate themselves. Caught in a *"dessein si funeste"* [1] one does not emerge, if one ever does emerge, intact.

I am not the only one to have experienced such a malaise. From the pen of a critic I have been able to read: "This book is detestable, of an immense vulgarity, a diabolical book." But it is true that this critic adds that "coming from the person who is doubtless the greatest mind of contemporary French thought"—and, for my part, I would say the best armed and the best disarmed—(this book) "at least shows us at what level the true challenges are placed today."

For whosoever tolls the bell (*glas*) of the SA, of *savoir absolu,* absolute knowledge, and is now without knowing that the power of the evasive letter comes from the until then vacant place that it occupies—in Poe's tale this place is situated between the jambs of the

1. TN. Major is referring to Derrida's discussion of Lacan's misquotation of Poe's quotation of Crébillon on the last page of "Le facteur de la vérité" (see above). The reader is reminded that *dessein* means scheme, design, while *destin* means destiny, fate. (*Destin* is Lacan's misquotation of *dessein.*)

fireplace—, one question cannot not be asked. You bear witness to this question, moreover, in the commentary on the "Seminar on *The Purloined Letter*," that is in "Le facteur de la vérité," by interrogating *analytically* what could have made the author of the seminar write *destin* in the place of *dessein* two out of three times in the citation of Crébillon (. . . *Un dessein si funeste, s'il n'est digne d'Atrée, est digne de Thyeste*). That within this separation, whoever wants to put the cross of the *destin* on the SE or the ES (le *ÇA*)[2] of the *dessein*, is engulfed in a "remains to be seen" [*"reste à savoir"*][3] is indeed what was left in suspense at our last Confrontation with François Roustang.

This question, then, asked and held back—you hold it back and it holds you back—is to be understood as a deconstruction of another SA, *le savoir analytique*, analytic knowledge, and of the limits or confines of the psychoanalytic field. I even ask myself if there subsists for you an inside and an outside of the place in which the knowledge is enveloped, the place which is conventionally called *la Situation Analytique*, the analytic situation.

Jacques DERRIDA: I should try to answer or perhaps to carry on.

But I will tell you that I indeed feel disarmed. This evening I have come as disarmed as *possible*. And disarrayed. I did not want to prepare for this session, I did not want to prepare myself. As deliberately as possible, I have chosen—which I think has never happened to me before—to expose myself to the course of a debate, and it must also be said of a show, without any defensive or offensive anticipation (which always somewhat amounts to the same). In any event with as little anticipation as *possible*. I thought that if something was to occur tonight, by hypothesis the event would be on this condition, to wit, that I come without preparation,

---

2. TN. Major is utilizing an elaborate set of allusions here. The spelling difference between *destin* and *dessein* is the difference between *t* and *se*. The aural difference is that of *t* and *s;* in French, as in English, the name of the letter is "es." *Es* in German means "it," and is the psychoanalytic term that is rendered "id" in English, and *ça* in French. *Ça* is pronounced *sa*, which brings us back to the acronym SA, which in this interview alludes first to the Hegelian concept of absolute knowledge (*savoir absolu*), and then to analytic knowledge (*savoir analytique*) and the analytic situation (*situation analytique*).

3. TN. *Reste à savoir* is the usual expression for "it remains to be seen," but Major is playing on Derrida's concept of the *reste*, the remainder. To cross the *t* of *destin* as a way of eliminating the "es" of *dessein*, Major is saying, inevitably engenders a remainder that envelops the entire operation.

neither on display or on parade, as without ammunition as *possible,* and if it is possible.

I will not say "my hands in my pockets." Who could I hope to convince or to reassure, in such a saloon, by stating so loudly that I have come with my hands in my pockets?

This is on tonight's program, even if said in passing: in *Glas* and in *Fors,* precisely, I recalled everything that can be put in one's pocket, and under one's hand, from the matchbox to one's own coffin in the shape of a matchbox. This coffin is not the least redoubtable of arms.

Nor the least bankable at such a banquet.

Therefore I have not come—if, at least, I have come—with my hands in my pockets in this saloon overflowing with all kinds of bands that are more or less bankable, more or less ready for détente, that are looking out of the corners of their eyes from the bar. Certain of them pretend to be playing poker, peacefully, in a corner. They feign pretending: I am sure that at this very moment all kinds of games are being played *within* each band, and no less ferociously than from one band to another. And since you, René Major, question me about *Glas,* you know that this book, among other things and designedly, is on bands, in bands, the word "*bande*" (noun or verb) and the thing, in every sense, gender and quantity.[4]

Therefore I have come, if, at least, I have come, saying to myself: something will happen tonight only on the condition of your disarmament.

But you might suspect me of exaggerating with this agonistic language: he says that he is disarmed in order to disarm, a well-

4. TN. *Bande* as noun has the same senses in French as in English, band as gang and band as strip. On *bander* as noun *and* verb, see above, "To Speculate—On "Freud," part 4 ("Seven: Post-Script"), notes 3 and 6. That *Glas* is on bands and in bands refers to both its formal construction (each page is in two columns) and its content (bands, groups in Hegel and Genet). Derrida is also alluding to the structure of *Confrontation* itself, as a forum that assembled analysts from the four French analytic "bands" that existed at the time. These were the Association Psychanalytique de Paris (the first French psychoanalytic group), the Association Psychanalytique de France (the first major group to split from the latter, originally including such members as Lacan and Granoff), l'Ecole freudienne (the institute founded by Lacan), and le Quatrième groupe (one of the first "splits" from the Ecole freudienne). In the year before his death (September 1981) Lacan attempted to dissolve the Ecole freudienne, leading to further changes in the analytic "bands."

known device. Certainly. Therefore, I immediately add: I have not come, I did not want to, I still do not want to, I have not come naked.

I have not come naked, not come without anything.

I have come accompanied by a small—how to put it, a small phrase, if it is one, only one, very small.

Further, I am not sure that I assume this small phrase. Nothing yet guarantees that I hold myself accountable for it.

Let us say that I will pronounce this small phrase between quotation marks, as if what is invisible here could take a reading into account. I will pronounce it, let us say, between quotation marks, although I formulated it myself or it formulated itself within me following another small phrase heard at the end of the last session, the only one of the "Confrontation" sessions that I have attended, outside the one that assembled us more than two years ago around my friends Nicolas Abraham and Maria Torok.

Let us say that I will hold this small phrase between quotation marks despite the fact that I formulated it myself or that it induced itself in me after the last session and the allusive discourse of a given analyst friend, a woman.

This discourse must have immediately found itself plugged into, within me, a system of anticipations, of interests, of hypotheses on the work of an entire logic which since then has formalized itself in the most economical, and also the most elliptical fashion in the following small phrase that, once again, I do not assume, I cite it. *Speech act* theoreticians would say that I mention it rather than *utilize* it, supposing a distinction made in this state is acceptable to analysts' ears. I have made several objections to it in a somewhat polemical text that appeared in the United States under the title *Limited inc.*

Here then is this small phrase, it is made to disappoint, I say it slowly, without any punctuation for the moment—its punctuation is in fact mobile, multiple, and essentially labile—I read it then without any punctuation for the moment as if there were a dash of equal length between each word, here it is:

CE-N'EST-PAS-DU-TOUT-UNE-TRANCHE.[5]

There.

I do not yet know—will I know one day?—if I did well to come here this evening.

I doubtless have come, if I have come, because—it must have been stronger than me.

Not that it simply must have been stronger than me, but because I must have been fascinated, irresistibly grabbed, harpooned by something that gave itself as stronger-than-me.

If it is stronger than me, I have got to go see what it is, which is all that interests me. "Stronger than me" is a locution that torments me, it imposes itself upon me indiscreetly, at least since the last session when I began to ask myself if I was wise to accept coming here.

In general, until now, until this evening, I have rather easily checked the solicitations or temptations of the "spectacle," the ingenuousness or political effects of the scenic codes that are available today—the channels, studios, and platforms offered to the intellectuals of our time who believe they are able to make use of them.

This time, apparently, it was stronger than me. But I must say to you now: up to the last moment, just now at the corner café, I asked myself if I would come (this too is happening to me for the first time, think of it what you will), I asked myself if I would not be, as is said, a "no-show" [*"faux-bond"*].

Some who are here know that in a recently published exchange I took a great interest in the *"faux-bond,"* in the word, in all the

5. TN. This sentence plays on lexical and syntactic undecidability. *Une tranche* is the usual French word for a slice, as in a slice of cake, from the verb *trancher,* to slice. In French psychoanalytic slang, *une tranche* is also the period of time one spends with a given analyst. There is no equivalent English expression. Further, the expression *du tout* can mean either "of the whole" or "at all." Thus, the sentence can mean "This is not a 'slice' [a piece, in the analytic sense or not] of the whole," or "This is not at all a 'slice' [in any sense]." The verb *trancher* can also mean to decide on a question or to resolve it in a clear-*cut* way; the English "trenchant" has a similar sense. Throughout this interview, the senses of *tranche* and "trench" beckon toward each other, finally coming together in the concluding discussion of schisms and seisms (earthquakes, cracking ground).

words engaged in this untranslatable locution, and in the strange
"thing" that a "*faux-bond*" is, if at least there is any.[6]

Although I am not, as you all know, and according to the canonic
criteria in effect in your four groups of limited responsibility,[7] either
analyst or analysand, I am sure that "*faux-bond*" is a word, and a
thing, which must interest you.

Among the thousand and one *faux-bonds* that one might cite as
examples, there is the one made by an analyst in relation to his own
"group" by going to do a "*tranche*" in another group. And I wager
that what I will call the "*confrontation*" *effect* has an essential relation to all *faux-bonds,* and to the *faux-bond* in the form of a *tranche,*
transferring or trancheferring from one group to another.

I am even tempted to believe, in the actual and doubtless limited
state of my information, that this problem of the *tranche,* and more
precisely of the one that you can go do in another group, this problem which does not with any certainty lead back to the problem of
unterminated or interminable analysis, although perhaps touching
it to the quick, this problem remains struck by a theoretical and
practical, as is said, interdiction. By an interdiction and an en-
trediction that perhaps organizes the entire suburban network of
psychoanalysis in your societies. It is what goes on, but must not be
talked of, or can be talked of without being made into a "critical"
problem. And I will soon try to say, if I am left the floor, why the
"*confrontation*" *effect* has an essential relation to a certain lifting—this evening perhaps—, only glimpsed, as always, of such an
interdiction.

Thus, I almost committed a *faux-bond.* Let us suppose, and this
is still only a hypothesis, that I am here and that I have *not* committed a *faux-bond.* Why would I not have done so?

6. TN. As indicated in the text, a *faux-bond* is a "no-show," but Derrida consistently plays not only on the "literal" meaning of the expression ("false bound"), but
also on the similarity, more striking in English, between "bond" and "band." At
Confrontation, whatever is not (at all/of the whole) a *tranche* must come from the
"false band." The recently published exchange Derrida refers to is "Ja, ou le faux
bond" in *Digraphe* 11.

7. TN. "Groups of limited responsibility": Derrida is alluding to the common
French acronym S.A.R.L., for *société à responsabilité limitée,* meaning a company
in which each associate is responsible only to the extent of his investment. This relates to the bond and the band. The question of what bonds an analytic band is put
elsewhere by Derrida as, "is the association ever free?"

I did not want to abuse it, which perhaps amounts to saying that I did not have the strength, but the strength to do what? In that case, if you had waited for me and if this place had remained empty for an indefinite amount of time, ten minutes one band would say, forty-five to fifty another, then in that case, if you had waited for me, I am sure that something would have occurred.

From myself, from yourselves to myself, there would have been some event, inevitably. And on both sides. I did not have the strength to abuse it, this strange facility. This is why I have said that it will have been stronger than me.

And then I was caught in the trap, in the trap of all traps, the desire still to attend one's own *faux-bond:* to commit a *faux-bond* in relation to oneself and to toll one's own bell (*glas*). It fails every time, and whatever the chance might be.

Unless, unless the *faux-bond* still has all its chances, this evening. I believe that this hypothesis is still open, I believe it intact.

René MAJOR.—The possible, and probable, *faux-bond* to which is opposed that which is stronger than you—and which therefore comes from *elsewhere*—is it not linked to something inevitable and to its denuding, which your coming to Confrontation implies? This does not make a wave, but waves, and what is disarming is that this is stronger than us.

Jacques DERRIDA.—If what has been stronger than me has been stronger than me, it is so at the moment when I could say to myself: the psychoanalysts must say the same thing to themselves, the psychoanalysts could not avoid inviting me into this place reserved, until this evening, for the alleged inside of the analytic fold to which I am supposed to be a stranger—neither analyst nor analysand according to the criteria in effect in the code which is the minimal consensus of their four listed groups.

I do not form by myself alone, according to certain regulated appearances, a group 5 or a group 0. Therefore, something must have occurred, according to the effect of a program at work, let us say for a good ten years, so that an entity in formation, and which entitles itself or itself calls upon the existence of the name *Confrontation,* cannot avoid inviting me, can no longer avoid me, and so that I myself can no longer avoid appearing at its invitation.

Here we are inevitable for each other. What is going on?

All of this still leaving us to suppose that we are not still avoiding each other this evening, and that the *faux-bond* did not take
place in spite of everything.

For we are not foolish enough, yourselves and myself, not to exclude the hypothesis that such a rendez-vous might be premeditated
precisely according to the most infallible of apotropaic logics so
that nothing occurs, so that the most efficacious avoidance takes the
form, as it often does, of the face-to-face. You know as well as I do,
and more so today than ever, that one can multiply signs of busyness around the very thing one wants to circumvent as a measure
of protection. One can feverishly multiply acts of presence in order
better to hide oneself or in order not to meet on the same sidewalk.
One can, on the subject of dark affairs of exclusion or extradition,
compulsively publish voluminous dossiers, juridico-constabulary
organization charts, formal and allegedly exhaustive correspondences, all in order to turn around that which is in question (I am
thinking of the recent extradition of Croissant),[8] in order to turn
away that which then acts up, which one has always avoided, and
that the finally published "official" dossier perpetuates, archive and
consolidation of the avoidance. The latter then leaves within the archive the borders of a crypt. One must know how to deal with it on
the basis of this logic of avoidance.

Let us change examples. To take another one which interests me
more at present: What proves that we have not met this evening, and
by appointment, in order to be more certain of avoiding each other?
or of avoiding the texts inscribed on the session's program, of acting
as if they had been read because one has kept in one's gaze for two
hours, in person, their presumed author, or because one will have
spoken of them, of the said texts, so spectacularly? Now, these are
texts about which the least that one might say is that they are not
made for that, for being spoken of, and in this way.

But that which checks all the police forces of avoidance is, if I
can put it thus, avoidance itself. There are, for example, what are
called "publications": one can fail to know them, this is always
possible in a given context; but one can arrange things, in a certain

8. TN. Croissant was the lawyer for the Baader-Meinhof "gang." He was extra-
dited from France to Germany in connection with his defense of Baader and Mein-
hof. Many thought that the extradition was illegal.

milieu, in order to avoid knowing that they exist; one can also, knowing of their existence, avoid reading them; one can read while avoiding "understanding"; one can, understanding, avoid being affected by them or using them; one can also, using them, avoid referring to them; but one can further, referring to them, enclose them, contain them, exclude them, and therefore avoid them better than ever, etc. But what is to be thought of the fact that one cannot avoid avoiding, of inevitable avoidance in all its forms—rejection, foreclusion, denegation, incorporation, and even the introjective and idealizing assimilation of the other at the limit of incorporation—?

In a somewhat algebraic and elliptical fashion, I could say that it is this program that interests me and that is calculated, up to a certain point, in *Glas*. It is calculated along with all the programs of rejection, of vomiting that expels outside or inside, along with all the forces of avoidance active within a "field of production" (to borrow this code, it is not my own), with all the conditions of non-receivability, of illegitimacy, with the greatest possible number that might be, for example according to *Glas* and for me, payable.

It is not a question of not being received in order not to be received (although there I am certain of nothing and I like to go (to write) at the point where the greatest calculation is lost) but of making appear (disgorge) what solders all the forces of exclusion or of non-reception to each other: there is a fundamental pact between all the apparently antagonistic forces which compose the unity of a politico-cultural field, of a field in general; and it seals what they understand each other to exclude.

Now, among these forces one finds a certain state of the psychoanalytic apparatus, of that which creates an alloy between its theoretical apparatus, its institutional pragmatics, and other apparatuses.

So then, what relation would all this have with *Confrontation?* And with *"Ce n'est pas du tout une tranche"?* What would have been stronger than us?

The "confrontation" effect: this effect bears an admirable title, admirably chosen. There could not be a worse one, and therefore a better one, to say by antiphrase what is going on here. This is the definition of the antiphrase: a counter-truth in a word. *Confrontation* says by antiphrase what could not possibly take place either here or, I suppose, in analysis, to wit, the frontal face-to-face, conversational affronting. The structure of this title corresponds to a classical type, the title that does not present the thing or the act but announces that one is going to treat it: of confrontation. "*Confrontation*" not in order to give rise to confrontations, to organize or present them, but in order to treat in a way that is oblique, on the bias, divergent, profiled, the lure or the impossibility which have as their name "confrontation." "Confrontation" is here our object rather than the scene or the event which occupies us.

The "confrontation" effect therefore deals with the ends and confines [*les fins et les confins*] of psychoanalysis, the impossible ends and confines of psychoanalysis.

Let us set aside for the moment the fact that this evening someone from the alleged outside of your institution has been invited (or avoided, as you will, let us say for the moment inavoided). Let us set aside the fact that the inavoided person in question is someone who does not show himself often, a kind of beast who emerges from his hole only at the moment when he hears or feels coming toward him the vibrations of cracked walls, of collapsing partitions, of trembling supports, of threatened impermeability, etc., in a word all the signs of what I have formerly called a deconstruction; and deconstruction, as I have often had to insist, is not a discursive or theoretical affair, but a practico-political one, and it is always produced within the structures (somewhat quickly and summarily) said to be institutional. Let us set aside this beast who does not emerge from his hole in order to set things straight.

The "confrontation" effect has to do with the deconstruction of the so-called psychoanalytic institution. It is signaled—and this is even its most manifest characteristic—by the fact that the partition of allegiances within the four French groups is no longer, no longer totally, the rule. It is no longer completely [*Ce n'est plus du tout*] impermeable, impermeable and airless, as previously.

Now—and this is why I speak of the *"confrontation" effect,* without taking away anything from what is due to the extraordinary initiative of its founders, to those who have so lucidly made of this "effect" their cause—even before occurring on the public scene in effects of surface, of discourse, and of spectacles, the "confrontation" effect is not disengaged by producing transparencies. It is *already* the effect of movements of destructuration and of restructuration which are *already* at work between the groups and at the interior of each group. I suppose this, of course, but the fact that there are indices of it on "the exterior" is something that appears very significant of this new distribution of the borders, the confines, the interests, as it is of the relations between the so-called outside and the so-called inside.

Now, what you name, without making a concept or a problem of it, the "*tranche*," I ask myself whether it does not decide the most pertinent perspective of the "*confrontation*" *effect*.

I suppose, without the slightest certain information, do not doubt, that one does, that one can do "*tranches*" from one group to another. Let us call this a scholastic hypothesis, and let us see what might follow from it.

What is a *tranche?*

Is it—a *tranche?*

Perhaps it is not at all [*pas du tout*]. *Pas du tout du tout.*[9]

First of all, a *tranche* of analysis, whatever its name indicates, is not a partial process. It is not the part of a whole. It is not a "slice" of the whole at all, it is not at all of the whole a slice [*Ce n'est pas une tranche du tout, ce n'est pas du tout une tranche*]. A new transferential and counter-transferential process is engaged within it on the basis of a limit (incomplete rather than unfinished analysis, says Freud in what still remains to be read under the title of *Die endliche und die unendliche Analyse*). The concept of the *tranche* could be formulated only subsequent to the concept of transference, unless it makes the latter even more problematical, which leads one to think that a transmittable theorization on this subject will not take place tomorrow.

The new process is engaged in completely other conditions, I suppose, than at the time of the "first" analysis: one is conscious, I suppose, of "choosing" more deliberately, more knowledgably, if this is possible, both the group and the analyst, whose sex can be varied, for example, I mean from one analysis to another; one can also leave one's own group somewhat in order to go look elsewhere, according to all kinds of motivations; one can do all this at once, etc., and nevertheless one has analysands.

And the end of a *tranche* is not the end at all of (the whole) analysis [*n'est pas la fin du tout de l'analyse*].

So then, for the moment I retain only this possibility of going to do a *tranche*—which is not of the whole [*qui n'est pas du tout*]—in another group, this possibility of going to do that *tranche* which, being neither a part nor a whole, is not, is not at all of the whole [*n'est pas du tout*] (neither a part of the whole nor at all of the whole a whole), I retain then only the possibility of going to do this disturbing *tranche* in another group.

Well then, I allege that the "*confrontation*" *effect* has an essential relation to this possibility and probably, a pure hypothesis on my part, to the increasing permeability, for several years now, of such a *tranche*-ference.

Now, what is a "group" among you?

It too is not the part of a whole.

In France there is not an analytic institution cut into four slices that it would suffice to adjoin in order to complete a whole and to recompose the harmonious unity of a community. If it were a cake, it would not be a *quatre-quarts* [four fourths, i.e. pound cake].

Each group—this implication is inscribed in its juridical structure and in its constitutive project—allegedly forms the only authentic analytic institution, the only one legitimately wielding the Freudian heritage, the only one that develops this heritage authentically in its practice, its didactics, its modes of formation and of reproduction.

This implies that, *de jure* at least, the three + n other groups are for each group, and this consequence has to be assumed, THE outside of psychoanalysis ITSELF when it refers to itself and calls itself by this name.

Consequence: to go do a *tranche* (which is not at all of the whole [*qui n'est pas du tout*]) in another group (which is not of the whole [*qui n'est pas du tout*]), is to *tranche*-fer onto the non-analyst, who then can counter-*tranche*-fer onto the analyst. One can make all kinds of factual compromises with this juridical consequence, one can treat it empirically in the vaguest or haziest way, which is also the most inconsequent way, but its juridical rigor is intransigent.

This minimal *tranche*-ference can be augmented or multiplied *en abyme:*[10] imagine that a given male or female analyst A of group A' does a *tranche* with analyst B of group B' who for his own part will not have been without doing more than one *tranche* (every five years, Freud recommends) with C of group C' who has been in analysis with A[2] of group A' and who comes back to it regularly. This situation, I imagine, can be infinitely more complicated in its intersections, as well as in the putting into *abyme* of its couches and chairs, its passages "from the chair to the couch," to come back to René Major's magisterially calculated joke from last time,[11] and in everything that makes the *tranche,* every time, eat into another *tranche,* according to the punctuation of the mobile "*ce n'est pas du tout une tranche,*" this is what interests me.

Henceforth, if one *tranche* does not eat up the whole at all but eats into a *tranche* already, it is the limits or the borders of the psychoanalytic which find themselves marked, practically and in the actual state of the theoretico-practical apparatus, by indecision.

For it is equally so that if the confines of interminability open the *tranche* onto the "outside" of the psychoanalytic (of the theory or of the practice or of the "movement"), but onto an outside such that the *tranche*-ference, far from being impossible or forbidden, today finds itself overactivated, intensified, jammed up, then the consequences of this are massive and implacable. Political and more than political.

Everything is to be redefined, the transference, for example, and the so-called "analytic situation," that is to say, not a few other things.

And all the articulations of the psychoanalytic to its "outside" (for example what is summarily called *the* political, *the* philosophical, *the* literary, etc.), all these articulations appear to me to require

10. TN. *En abyme* is Derrida's usual expression for the infinite regress of a reflection within a reflection, etc. The term originally comes from the heraldic notion of an escutcheon within an escutcheon; Derrida plays on *abyme* and *abîme,* abyss. See also above, "Freud's Legacy," note 9, and the passage following this note in the text.

11. TN. In the previous session Major had made a "slip" about the end of analytic training involving the passage from "the chair to the couch," instead of vice versa. The *tranche* that the analyst does with someone not from his "band" is also a passage from the chair to the couch.

reelaboration at the point of their most rigorous internal pertinence, at the point where the internal no longer suffices, precisely,
and the pertinent no longer touches only on the limit, to wit, those
disturbing *tranches* which are not at all of the whole from one
group to another which is not at all of the whole [*qui ne sont pas du
tout d'un groupe à l'autre qui n'est pas du tout*].

Therefore, the concept of the *tranche*-ference has to be reelaborated from top to bottom.

If it is operable, *de jure,* onto the non-analyst, or between non-
analysts, what is a non-analyst?

The consequence is not only that the psychoanalytic milieu is
notched by its outside. Inversely, if the inside is no longer strictly
delimitable, neither is the outside. No more outside.

And the *tranche* itself no longer permits itself to be dominated,
determined in its unity according to criteria that are rigorously interior to psychoanalysis, in the traditional sense of the term, by reference to the rules of analytic technique. Such is the consequence of
the fact that one *tranche* eats into another.

Ce n'est pas du tout une tranche also means that the internal
multiplicity, and the *divisibility* of the *tranche* do not permit the
arrest of its limit.

René MAJOR.—If I am following you, the question of the *tranche* and of its divisibility permits, at the greatest proximity to the
insertion of analytic knowledge [*savoir analytique*] into its practice, to pursue the putting into question of that which is given in the
"Seminar on *The Purloined Letter*" as the indivisibility of the letter
and the materiality of the signifier. It is the fundamental argument
of "Le facteur de la vérité" that you are deploying. Is it not this
argument that designedly made you point out that an always acting
lapsus calami transformed a "*dessein si funeste*" into a "*destin,*"
giving over the addressee to his implacable destiny?

Jacques DERRIDA.—Yes. A few words in parentheses, first of all,
on this question of divisibility. The motif of divisibility is perhaps
the argument of last resort in "Le facteur de la vérité," about which
you question me. It is formally, in the chain of consequences, that
on which everything depends. The affirmation of the indivisibility
of the letter (which does not support, says Lacan, "partition"), in
other words the affirmation of the place and of the materiality of the

signifier, and of the phallus as the signifier of signifiers, this affirmation of indivisibility, in order to describe the *faktum* of idealization, is no less gratuitous and dogmatic, even if it is necessary to the entire architectonics of the "Seminar on *The Purloined Letter*" and to the entire logic of the signifier. It is a philosopheme, an undemonstrable theorem or matheme, although it remains analyzable in its unanalyzed interest, as I have tried to give it to be read in "Le facteur de la vérité." There are numerous and powerful consequences for analytic theory and practice at stake here. *Mutatis mutandis,* and according to an analogous formal schema, I would say the same about the divisibility of the *tranche*-ference.

I will not close this short parenthesis without responding to your allusion, I mean the one that, picking up on the previous session [François Roustang], recalled that in 1975 in effect (and even earlier, this essay first having been given as a very public lecture in the United States and in Brussels), I had mentioned, not without relation to the ensemble of my own designs, the fate to which the citation of Crébillon and of Poe was subjected in the different places, that is the different editions of the "Seminar on *The Purloined Letter*. Sometimes *"dessein"*—a faithful citation of Crébillon and of Poe citing Crébillon—, sometimes *"destin,"* an altering citation, an alteration about which "Le facteur de la vérité" did not say all that I think, but that in any event carefully refrained from qualifying as "typographical error" or as "slip," even supposing, you are going to see why I am saying this, that a somewhat enlightened analytic reading could lightheartedly content itself with such a distinction, I mean between "typo" and "slip." So carefully refrained from doing so that one can read the following, which I permit myself to cite, having it at hand: "Two out of three times, the author of the Seminar will have forced *dessein* into *destin,* perhaps thereby bringing a meaning to its destination: no doubt expressly [I leave this *expressly* to be heard in the sense of the—conscious or unconscious—design and of the postal metaphor of the "express" *envoi,* of the letter that one hastens to write, of the dispatch that one dispatches oneself in order not to entangle oneself, of the missive that one wishes at any cost and at greatest speed to see arrive "at its destination"—the best means, to do this, is to *send it* to oneself], in any event nothing permits one to exclude the design somewhere."

I do not want to retain you too long by analyzing here the complication of this gesture, legible elsewhere moreover, and that which makes it communicate with the entire logic of the "Facteur." Therefore, I will pass on to what followed [*la suite*], since it is always a question of following or forwarding [*faire suivre*].

François Roustang, himself, ignores everything, or acts as if he were ignoring the whole thing: he tranquilly inscribes the word "*destin*" on the cover of his book,[12] without concerning himself for a single moment, apparently, either with the fact that the so-called "typo" was on the way to correction, or with the fact that "Le facteur de la vérité" already treated, in an entirely different style, it is true, certain problems that he had just inscribed in the table of contents of his work.

There then occurs the most ludicrous episode. But the most infallibly programmed one, I am certain.

This year, there appears, in effect, in the illustrated organizational sheet of one of your four groups, a letter or a study, as you will. Commissioned or certified [*commandé ou recommandé*], it directs its attack in the direction of Roustang's book, and here is its conclusion, that I have brought you, not excluding that we might have to speak of it this evening: "We will simply remain with the *typographical error, coquille* (my italics—J.D.) whose reprise in the title is a *slip* (my italics again—J.D.). Crébillon and Poe, and then Lacan, in at least one of the two citations of the couplet in the *Ecrits,* do indeed print '*un* dessein *si funeste*' and not '*un destin.*'" End of citation.

Truly, you will agree, Chicago in the thirties, or rather the saloon during the period of the postal wagon.

A so-called analyst believes that he knows, with tranquil knowledge, what a typographical error is; and that a "typo," especially this one, is only a typo [*coquille*], that it sleeps peacefully in its shell [*coquille*], without the risk of becoming something somewhat different.

In the event, it must indeed be said, that it falls from the hand of the master, a *coquille* is only a *coquille,* and for whoever listens to the voice of the master, one must call a *coquille* a *coquille.*

Now here is the most ingenious finding: what remains a typographical error two out of three times in given *Ecrits* becomes

12. TN. François Roustang's book, a psychoanalytic examination of the master-disciple relationship, is entitled *Un destin si funeste.*

Roustang's "slip," Roustang having contented himself, somewhat quickly it is true, with reproducing the ur-typo, everyone, including its author, turning all around that which must not be read. What perhaps created the greatest impression on me, is yet another effect of this implacable programming.

Who, in effect, is the author who illustrated himself with the short immortal paragraph that I have just read to you? Who has known how to metamorphose a "typo" proper to protect the one with a slip into which the other can fall?

Well then, it is expressly, and dispatching himself again, the *facteur* himself who, perhaps imagining himself targeted by name in "Le facteur de la vérité," shows himself prompt, more or less, to react. In the English language, which, since Poe's tale, orders all these trajectories not without itself being overtaken in them, *facteur* is *mailman*.[13] An ear alert to the word that I have just pronounced will not translate it as *homme mâle*, male man, an insistent tautology, nor in all confusion of languages as *homme qui mêle tout*, man who mixes up everything, or as *courrier qui ment*, lying mail, *à la française*, but indeed as *facteur: mailman* is the usual word for *facteur*, it is a compound word, a divisible signifier, as in *air mail*, when the dispatched makes itself hurry, or as in *mail box*, in which the demonstrations sometimes make themselves waited for. One more reason to think that contrary to the conclusion of the "Seminar on *The Purloined Letter*," letters can always not arrive at their destination, and that the mail, in all languages, does not always tell the truth, even the most certain one.

Here I close this parenthesis.

You have questioned me about what one believes is known under the heading of text or of writing, and whose relation to psychoanalysis is no longer today very clear or very dominable.

I will say in too economical a fashion, and in order to plug my answer into "that which is not at all of the whole a *tranche*," that

---

13. TN. The analyst on whose name Derrida is about to make a series of bilingual puns is Charles Melman, one of those closest to Lacan in the Ecole freudienne. The French pronunciation of Melman sounds almost the same as the French pronunciation of the English "mailman." Thus, in the next sentence Derrida exploits the puns implicit in the name: "male man," a tautology; "*mêle* man," from the verb *mêler*, to mix; and "mail *ment*," literally "mail lies," from the verb *mentir*, to lie.

Glas, for example, describes in all its states the *gl* (what I have called the +*l* effect) in its relation to a graphics of the stricture, of the double bind of the double stricture, of the whole in the part, and of the remainder that follows, unthinkable in a *logic,* in a philosophical logic of the remainder. It is another thought of the remainder which works upon the writing of *Glas* and of the remainder as the unanalyzed. A *tranche* which is not of the whole disconcerts assurance on the subject of any possible subject. For example, it takes the form of a graphics of the *mors* (*m.o.r.s,* bit) or of the *mort* (m.o.r.t, dead man) [14] that one has in the mouth as a command, and that one cannot, as *other,* either keep or reject, either take into oneself or leave outside, either vomit or assimilate, either incorporate or introject, either realize or idealize. Elsewhere, a bit later, I called this mid-mourning.

Mors means morsel, piece—on which one bites (*mord*)—and it is said in *Glas* that this book plays (on) the morsel that in a certain way one has in the gullet, blocking the gullet or slashing the throat. It is indeed a question of a *tranche.* And which eats into [*mord sur*] the other. The truth plays a piece, says "Le facteur de la vérité," more or less, somewhere. One also reads in *Glas* that this book is written on the *transe* [trance, fear] (which in Walloon is the bell that one tolls) or on *tranches. Glas* is therefore a false book, a *fauxbond*-book written on "*tranche,*" on all the operative and inoperative, possible or impossible operations of *tranch*ing. Somewhere (p. 30) the *transe,* the limit of the *transe* literally amounts to the impossibility of *tranch*ing between the more and the less, the whole and the part.

Perhaps one could say then, still economically, that the *gl* or the +*l* effect is plugged into the *tr* effect (*tranche,* trait, trace, traction, contraction, contract, etc.) and what I entitled elsewhere, in a work with Valerio Adami, the +*r* effect (for example *fr* in the *Benjamin Front*).

So then. Within the hypothesis which says that one might *tranche*fer or counter*tranche*fer—and this transference could have only an altered relation with transference as understood within the strict

14. TN. From now until the end of the interview Derrida will play on the homonyms *mors, mort,* and *mord. Mors* means bit, piece, morsel, and thus is related to the *tranche. Un mort* is a dead man, or the "dummy" in bridge. That one has a *mors* or a *mort* in the mouth is due to the fact that *mord* is either the first or third person present of the verb *mordre,* to bite.

limits of Freudian technique—*tranche*fer or counter*tranche*fer onto or on the basis of what I call a "text," and which is no more a simple theoretical writing than it simply implies a subject supposed to know or to write,[15] the relations with the said "subject" being treated entirely otherwise, particularly in *Glas,* what then is a non-analyst? Where is there any non-analyst?

Why pose the question in this form? At least because in this first intervention, this evening, I wish not to leave in the shadows the question of what I am doing here, supposing that I am doing anything whatsoever, the question of what I am here, if I am here, of whether I am wanted or not wanted. Of what is not wanted from me—and reciprocally.

When I said just now that I was citing or "mentioning" "*ce n'est pas du tout une tranche,*" rather than making use of it for my own account, you are clever enough to have immediately noticed the trap. You and I were caught in it as soon as the little phrase was uttered, without yet knowing where it was coming from, who was emitting it and who was assuming it. If I had not surrounded it with quotation marks, you would have said: denegation. You would have thought: he is in the course of denying that this is a *tranche,* nothing but a *tranche,* a simple session, a *tranche* of the *tranche.* The question itself remaining, as a third party, of whose with whom. Now, if I pick it up with the pincers of these quotation marks, thereby feigning to get rid of it in all haste, the denegation redoubles itself and even amplifies itself beyond the double, but no longer simply my own double. Perhaps yours . . .

René MAJOR.—What then of the "non-analyst"? And could you prove that there are any or that there are not any? Does not the transference just as much occasion the *non-analyst* of the said analyst as the *analyst* of the said non-analyst?

Jacques DERRIDA.—The non-analyst, yes, what is it? Is there any?

If there are any, it is doubtless something—someone, male or female—that is completely, let us say, there it is: IM-PROBABLE.

Improbable. It would call for a singular demonstration. While waiting for it, instead of a demonstration, and before giving up the

15. TN. The reference is to the Lacanian concept of *le sujet supposé savoir.*

floor, I prefer to tell you a brief story. Rather strange. Quite recent.
This just happened to me.

Someone, very well informed as is said, comes and says to me
in a tone of friendship: "I know now that so and so, a very famous
analyst, of national and international renown, an analyst occupying
a position not without mastery and magisteriality, right here where
we have welcomed him or her [the scene is taking place in the
United States], I know now that so and so has been in analysis with
you for more than ten years . . ." (For a double *tranche*, therefore,
twice five years, nothing less than that.)

This declaration, made quite calmly and assuredly, naturally
leaves me speechless. My interlocutor, a woman, knew that I was
not an analyst, and for my own part I knew, to refer to the same
shared criteria, that what she was saying with so much assurance
was false, quite simply false.

After several seconds, I get over my astonishment, and find
nothing better to say to her, hoping at least to confuse her, than:
"*prove it*" (this was occurring in an American university).

Answer: "oh, I could give all kinds of proofs (of *evidence,* she
says in English). For example the following (and she gives several,
more or less abstract or convincing, indices rather than proofs) . . ."
and then she immediately added, "But that doesn't matter, you
prove to me, if you can, the opposite."

Of course, for essential reasons, the ones that interest me here, I
could not prove, strictly prove the opposite for her. The classical
criteria for such a proof are lacking, and the trenchant standard that
would permit one to "trench" between the *tranche* and the non-
tranche, this trenchancy is improbable within the actual state of the
theory and the practice. This improbability, which concerns the
analytic situation itself, is not without consequences. And these
consequences still remain incalculable, which does not mean that
one day they must cease to be so.

René MAJOR.—Given the point we have reached, what prevents
you from saying who is in question? To state his name now seems
inevitable to me.

Jacques DERRIDA.—René Major asks me the name of the analyst
in question. Is this really necessary? Moreover, my interlocutor did
not name him. She contented herself with characteristics that in her

eyes sufficed to recompose an identity. No name was pronounced. It was only after the fact, reflecting on the composite that she had sketched, that I attempted an induction. I thought, the trip to the United States pointed me toward this hypothesis, that she probably had in mind someone whose name I can say because I believe that he is now dead. It is, would be, in my hypothesis (what is his name? the misfortune is that I regularly forget this name), there it is: Loewenstein.

So then. If today someone can say, without any fear that the contrary might be proven, that his Loewenstein, whom I have never met, from near or far, and who is dead, has been in analysis with me for a double *tranche,* you see where this can lead, from consequence to consequence, for whoever forwards, and from implication to implication.

What must be thought then, is this remainder of a *tranche,* this supplementary *tranche* which works at the confines of the psychoanalytic, at the limit of its intermination, at the origin and at the end of what is summarily called its institution, its movement or its community. This limit, which relates it to its outside, is not a limit like any other.

To say it in a word, or with a name (and then I will have finished), suppose that there were a founder, male or female, of psychoanalysis, a first analyst. Let us take the name of Freud as the index, for the sake of purely provisional convenience, of such a function. Let us act as if, another provisional convenience, Freud had not had an analyst. This is even what is often said with much ingenuousness. Let us admit this for a moment in order to support our ideal and unfliessured hypothesis.

Suppose now that this founder, this so-called institutor of the analytic movement, had need of a supplementary *tranche.*

Then this unanalyzed remainder which in the last analysis relates it to the absolute outside of the analytic milieu will not play the role of a border, will not have the form of a limit *around* the psychoanalytic, that to which the psychoanalytic as theory and as practice would not, alas, have had access, as if there still remained some ground for it to gain. Not at all [*pas du tout*]. This unanalyzed will be, will have been that upon which and around which the analytic movement will have been constructed and mobilized: everything will have been constructed and calculated so that this unanalyzed might be inherited, protected, transmitted intact, suitably bequeathed, consolidated, enkysted, encrypted. It is what gives its structure to the movement and to its architecture.

The decrypting, in these conditions, can no longer come from the simple and alleged interior of what is still called, provisionally, psychoanalysis. And it will not have a partial effect of rearrangement or reform.

I believe that the schisms, the seisms whose cracking is heard everywhere today (amplified in proportion to the extension without border of the psychoanalytic field), these movements of dividing ground, crossing and multiplying *tranches* in every sense, in an accelerated, accumulating, abyssal fashion, make it heard via their cracking that a *mort(s)* can do a *tranche*.

A *mort(s)* can do a *tranche*. A remainder of a supplementary *tranche*. And as for Freud's, for that which is indicated and inherited under this name, the work has been broached.

The *"confrontation" effect* should have, according to me, an essential relation with that which works upon this work whose repercussions could not be localizable. They can change everything everywhere and from top to bottom [*tout à tout et du tout au tout*].

Which means that this *tranche* is not at all of the whole a *tranche* [*n'est pas du tout une tranche*]. I mean parceled out.

So then who pays?

One never provides oneself with, pays for, anything at all [*On ne se paie jamais quoi que* ce *soit*].

No matter what the wish for it, no one will ever provide himself [*ne* se *paiera*] with a *tranche* of Freud's. No one will ever provide himself with the remainder, the rest, the supplementary *tranche* of Freud's which, less than ever today, he could not provide himself with [*se payer lui-même*].

The question then becomes—and it is not only political, although it is also political, it is the question of a general deconstruction and it is the question that I pose *to Confrontation, to,* that is, *in* this place, but also to the address of *Confrontation*—the question then becomes:

Who will pay whom for Freud's *tranche?*

Or, if you prefer, the thing already having been broached, who has it paid to whom?

The bidding has been opened—for some time.

Let us say that what I write or what makes me write (for example, since there are not only the texts, this time I mean the publications) would represent in this respect only one offer.

An offer on the scene in which the attempts to occupy the place of the *Sa* (that is, of the *Savoir absolu* stenographed in *Glas*) are multiplying, that is, simultaneously all the places, those of the seller, the buyer, and the auctioneer.